SNOWMOBILE HANDBOOK

CHILTON'S

CEO	Rick Van Dalen
President	Dean F. Morgantini, S.A.E.
Vice President–Finance	Barry L. Beck
Vice President–Sales	Glenn D. Potere
Executive Editor	Kevin M. G. Maher, A.S.E.
Manager–Marine/Recreation	James R. Marotta, A.S.E.
Manager–Consumer Automotive	Richard Schwartz, A.S.E.
Manager–Professional Automotive	Richard J. Rivele
Manager–Electronic Fulfillment	Will Kessler, A.S.E., S.A.E.
Production Specialists	Brian Hollingsworth, Melinda Possinger
Project Managers	Thomas A. Mellon, A.S.E., S.A.E., Christine L. Sheeky, S.A.E., Todd W. Stidham, A.S.E.; Ron Webb
Schematics Editors	Christopher G. Ritchie, A.S.E., S.A.E., S.T.S., Stephanie A. Spunt
Editor	Christopher Bishop, A.S.E. and James R. Marotta, A.S.E.

PUBLISHED BY **W. G. NICHOLS, INC.**

Manufactured in USA
© 1999 W. G. Nichols, Inc.
1020 Andrew Drive
West Chester, PA 19380
ISBN 0-8019-9124-2
Library of Congress Catalog Card No. 99-072322
2345678901 9876543210

Contents

Contents

ACCESSORIZING YOUR
SNOWMOBILE **7**

CLEANING YOUR
SNOWMOBILE **8**

BASIC TROUBLESHOOTING
(HOW YOUR SNOWMOBILE
WORKS) **9**

LONG-TERM STORAGE **10**

GLOSSARY

MASTER INDEX

See last page for information on additional titles

SAFETY NOTICE

Proper service and repair procedures are vital to the safe, reliable operation of all vehicles, as well as the personal safety of those performing repairs. This manual outlines procedures for servicing and repairing snowmobiles using safe, effective methods. The procedures contain many NOTES, CAUTIONS and WARNINGS which should be followed, along with standard procedures, to eliminate the possibility of personal injury or improper service which could damage the vehicle or compromise its safety.

It is important to note that repair procedures and techniques, tools and parts for servicing these vehicles, as well as the skill and experience of the individual performing the work, vary widely. It is not possible to anticipate all of the conceivable ways or conditions under which vehicles may be serviced, or to provide cautions as to all possible hazards that may result. Standard and accepted safety precautions and equipment should be used during cutting, grinding, chiseling, prying, or any other process that can cause material removal or projectiles.

Some procedures require the use of tools specially designed for a specific task. Before substituting another tool or procedure, you must be completely satisfied that neither your personal safety, nor the performance of the vehicle, will be endangered.

Although information in this manual is based on industry sources and is complete as possible at the time of publication, the possibility exists that some manufacturers made later changes which could not be included here. While striving for total accuracy, Nichols Publishing cannot assume responsibility for any errors, changes or omissions that may occur in the compilation of this data.

PART NUMBERS

Part numbers listed in this reference are not recommendations by Nichols Publishing for any product brand name. They are references that can be used with interchange manuals and aftermarket supplier catalogs to locate each brand supplier's discrete part number.

SPECIAL TOOLS

Special tools are recommended by the manufacturers to perform their specific job. Use has been kept to a minimum, but, where absolutely necessary, they are referred to in the text by the part number of the tool manufacturer. These tools can be purchased, under the appropriate part number, from your local dealer or regional distributor, or an equivalent tool can be purchased locally from a tool supplier or parts outlet. Before substituting any tool for the one recommended, read the SAFETY NOTICE at the top of this page.

ACKNOWLEDGMENTS

Nichols Publishing expresses appreciation to the following companies for their generous assistance in the production of this manual:
- Arctic Cat Sales Inc.—Thief River Falls, MN
- Bell Helmets—Irvine, CA
- Blue Ribbon Coalition—Pocatello, ID
- Joe Rocket—Windsor, Ontario
- Deltran Corporation—Cypress, CA
- Load Rite Trailers Inc.—Fairless Hills, PA
- M&S Sales and Service—New Holland, PA
- Polaris Industries Inc.—Minneapolis, MN
- Saber Traction Products—Lannon, WI
- Ski-Doo/Bombardier Recreational Vehicles—Valcourt, Quebec
- Smith Marine—New Brittan, PA
- Yamaha Motor Corporation—Cypress, CA
- YUASA/Exide—Reading, PA

Nichols Publishing expresses sincere appreciation to Chuck, Jack and Harold Smith at Smith Marine for their generous contributions to the content of this manual. Smith Marine also provided the screaming yellow Ski-Doo which brightens the pages of this manual.

We can not forget the guys at M&S Sales and Service who spent an entire day with us explaining the intricacies of snowmobile mechanics. Thanks guys!

Last, but certainly not least, we would like to thank Mike Molloy for getting us started on this project by donating his ancient Suzuki snowmobile to the cause.

ALL RIGHTS RESERVED

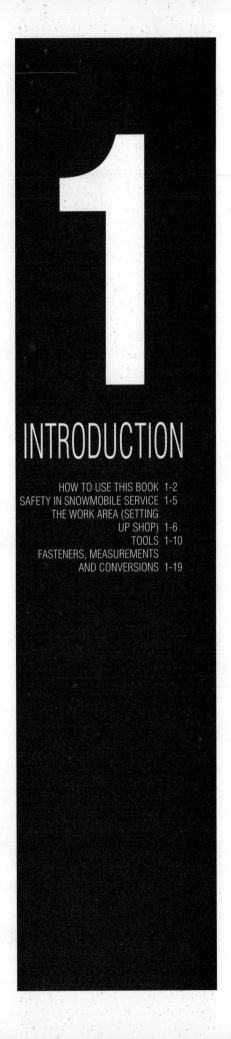

1

INTRODUCTION

HOW TO USE THIS BOOK

This book is designed to be a handy reference guide to choosing, buying and maintaining your snowmobile, riding gear and accessories. We strongly believe that regardless of how many or how few years of riding or wrenching experience you may have, there is something new in this book for you. And, probably more importantly, we feel that the information contained in this book should be available to all snowmobile enthusiasts before they sit on a snowmobile, or spend money on it.

This book IS NOT a complete repair manual and no attempt has been made to supplant the need for one if you desire to fully rebuild or repair a snowmobile. Instead, this manual covers all of the topics that a factory service manual (designed for factory trained technicians) and a manufacturer owner's manual (designed more by lawyers these days) will not. This manual will take you through the basics of maintaining a snowmobile, step-by-step, in detail, to help you understand what the factory trained technicians already know by heart. By using the information in this manual, any snowmobile owner should be able to make better informed decisions about what he or she needs to do to maintain and enjoy his/her snowmobile.

Keeping all of that in mind, we have divided the book into the following topics:

- HOW TO USE THIS BOOK
- CHOOSING THE RIGHT SNOWMOBILE
- RIDING GEAR
- ENGINE & DRIVETRAIN MAINTENANCE
- CHASSIS MAINTENANCE
- BEFORE YOU RIDE
- ACCESSORIZING YOUR SNOWMOBILE
- CLEANING YOUR SNOWMOBILE
- TROUBLESHOOTING YOUR SNOWMOBILE
- SNOWMOBILE STORAGE

Even if you never plan on touching a wrench (and if so, we hope that you will change your mind), this book will still help you understand what a technician needs to do in order to maintain your snowmobile. And, even if you don't perform the maintenance services, we will provide you with information on everything from accessorizing to cleaning, from pre-ride checks to pre-storage preparation.

Can You Do It? (and Should You?)

▶ See Figures 1, 2, 3 and 4

If you are not the type of person who feels comfortable taking a wrench to something, NEVER FEAR. The procedures in this book cover basic topics at a level virtually anyone will be able to handle, with some guidance. Besides, the fact that you purchased this book shows your interest in better understanding the mechanics of your snowmobile. Yes, you can do it.

You may find that maintaining your snowmobile yourself is preferable in most cases. From a monetary standpoint, it's actually quite beneficial. The money spent on hauling your snowmobile to a shop and paying a technician to change a drive belt or align your track could practically buy you gas and oil for a whole weekend's riding. If you don't trust your own mechanical abilities, at the very least you should fully understand what a service technician does for your sled. You may decide that anything other than changing coolant and adjusting cables be performed by a technician (and that's your call), but every time you throw a leg over your snowmobile, you are placing faith in the technician's work, and trusting him or her with your well-being, and maybe your life. Understanding what that technician has done for your snowmobile will allow you to keep an eye on its condition and its adjustments.

Where to Begin

Before spending any money on parts or accessories, and before removing any nuts or bolts, read through the entire procedure or topic. This will give you

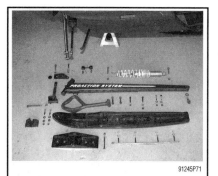

Fig. 1 Although it may look complicated, things like suspension maintenance are actually fairly simple

91245P71

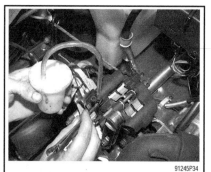

Fig. 2 Some maintenance tasks may seem difficult, but can be made easy with the proper tools

91245P34

Fig. 3 A meter makes diagnosing electrical problems easier

91249P20

Fig. 4 Some maintenance tasks are as simple as occasional lubrication to keep things operating smoothly

91245P31

the overall view of what tools and supplies will be required for work or what questions need to be answered before purchasing gear. So read ahead and plan ahead. Each operation should be approached logically and all procedures thoroughly understood before attempting any work.

Avoiding Trouble

▶ See Figure 5

Some procedures in this book may require you to "label and disconnect . . ." a group of lines, hoses or wires. Don't be lulled into thinking you can remember where everything goes — you won't. If you reconnect or install a part incorrectly, things may operate poorly, if at all. If you hook up electrical wiring incorrectly, you may instantly learn a very, very expensive lesson.

A piece of masking tape, for example, placed on a hose and another on its fitting will allow you to assign your own label such as the letter A, or a short name. As long as you remember your own code, the lines can be reconnected

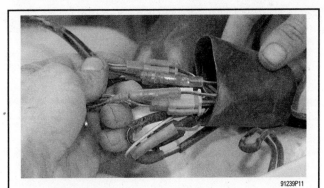

Fig. 5 Disconnecting wires without marking them is a sure way to get yourself in trouble

by matching letters or names. Do remember that tape will dissolve in parts cleaner or other fluids. If a component is to be washed or cleaned, use another method of identification, such as marking with a small punch or a scratch awl. A permanent felt-tipped marker can be very handy for marking metal parts; but remember that fluids such as degreaser or brake cleaner will remove permanent marker. Also, be sure to remove any tape or paper labels after assembly.

SAFETY is the most important thing to remember when performing maintenance or repairs. Be sure to read the information on safety in this book. Your personal well-being depends on it.

Maintenance or Repair?

▶ See Figures 6, 7 and 8

Proper maintenance is the key to long and trouble-free snowmobile life, and the work can yield its own rewards. A properly maintained snowmobile will

inspection guidelines with the information in this book. But, remember that manufacturer guidelines do vary. Don't take a chance on missing an odd item or replacement interval that is unique to your year or model. Refer to the manufacturer's recommended maintenance charts whenever possible.

It's necessary to mention the difference between maintenance and repair. Maintenance includes routine inspections, adjustments, and replacement of parts that show signs of normal wear. Maintenance compensates for wear or deterioration. Repair implies that something has broken or is not working. A need for repair is often caused by lack of maintenance. While no maintenance program can prevent items on your snowmobile from breaking or wearing out, a general rule can be stated: MAINTENANCE IS CHEAPER THAN REPAIR.

Two basic rules should be mentioned here. First, whenever the left side of the snowmobile is referred to, it is meant to specify your left while sitting in the riding position (this assumes you are not sitting on the handle bars . . .). Conversely, the right side means your right side while seated. Second, screws and bolts are removed by turning counterclockwise, and tightened by turning clockwise (unless it is specifically noted that they use "left hand threads" in which case they are removed backwards). An easy way to remember this is: "righty, tighty; lefty, loosey". Corny, but effective. And if you are really dense (and we have all been so at one time or another), buy a ratchet that is marked ON and OFF, or mark your own. Even the best s get confused once in a while, especially when working on something from an odd angle.

Professional Help

▶ See Figure 9

Occasionally, we all need professional help. . . . Well, let me put that a different way. When working on your sled there may be some procedures that are beyond your comfort level or the tools you have in your garage. This shouldn't include most of the topics of this book, but you will have to be the judge. Some snowmobiles require special tools or a selection of special parts, even for basic maintenance.

Talk to other riders of the same model or speak with a trusted dealer or repair

Fig. 6 Maintenance includes tasks like drive belt replacement . . .

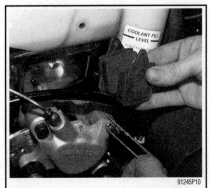

Fig. 7 . . . and brake pad replacement, but . . .

Fig. 8 . . . NOT replacement of the entire suspension! (note missing suspension and ski on left sled)

always perform better than one that is neglected. As a conscientious owner and rider, set aside a little time to perform a thorough check of items which could cause problems. Keep your own personal log to jot down which services you performed, parts that were purchased and installed, and the date (or hour reading) the service was performed.

Since snowmobiles are seasonal machines, keeping track of maintenance is critical. At the start of the season, you most likely will forget what maintenance you performed on your snowmobile when you put it in storage for the summer—unless you wrote everything down and/or kept track of receipts.

Also, as a do-it-yourselfer, these receipts are the only proof you have that the required maintenance was performed. In the event of a warranty problem, these receipts will be invaluable.

The literature provided with your snowmobile when it was originally delivered includes the factory recommended maintenance schedule. If you no longer have this literature, replacement copies are usually available from the dealer. Also, you can purchase a repair manual through the dealer parts department. For the most part, we will provide average recommended replacement and

Fig. 9 The experienced technicians at your local snowmobile dealer will gladly take on any repairs you don't feel comfortable handling yourself

shop to find if there is a particular system or component on your snowmobile that is difficult to maintain. Some sleds are more complex than others, and experienced technicians and owners can give you the "in's and out's" of your particular sled.

You will have to decide for yourself where basic maintenance ends and where professional service should begin. Take your time and do your research first (starting with the information in this book) and then make your own decision. If you really don't feel comfortable with attempting a procedure, DON'T do it. If you've gotten into something that may be over your head, don't panic. Tuck your tail between your legs and call your local dealer service department or independent shop. They should be willing to finish the job for you. Your ego may be damaged, but your sled will be properly be restored to its full running order. So, as long as you approach jobs slowly and carefully, you really have nothing to lose and everything to gain by doing it yourself.

Avoiding the Most Common Mistakes

♦ See Figures 10, 11, 12 and 13

Pay attention to the instructions provided. There are 3 common mistakes in mechanical work:

1. Incorrect order of assembly, disassembly or adjustment. When taking something apart or putting it together, performing steps in the wrong order usually just costs you extra time; however, it CAN break something. Read the entire procedure before beginning disassembly. Perform everything in the order in which the instructions say you should, even if you can't immediately see a reason for it. When you're taking apart something that is very intricate, you might want to draw a picture of how it looks when assembled at one point in order to make sure you get everything back in its proper position. When making adjustments, perform them in the proper order; often, one adjustment affects another, and you cannot expect satisfactory results unless each adjustment is made only when it cannot be changed by any other.

2. Overtorquing (or undertorquing). While it is more common for overtorquing to cause damage, undertorquing may allow a fastener to vibrate loose causing serious damage. Especially when dealing with aluminum parts, pay attention to torque specifications and utilize a torque wrench in assembly. If a torque figure is not available, remember that if you are using the right tool to perform the job, you will probably not have to strain yourself to get a fastener tight enough. The pitch of most threads is so slight that the tension you put on the wrench will be multiplied many times in actual force on what you are tightening.

A good example of how critical torque is can be seen in the cylinder head bolts on engines. The cylinder heads found on snowmobile engines today can be damaged if the bolts are not tightened evenly. Failure to use a torque wrench may allow the head to warp, causing the head gasket to fail.

There are many commercial products available for ensuring that fasteners won't come loose, even if they are not torqued just right (a very common brand is Loctite®). If you're worried about getting something together tight enough to hold, but loose enough to avoid mechanical damage during assembly, one of these products might offer substantial insurance. Before choosing a threadlocking compound, read the label on the package and make sure the product is compatible with the materials, fluids, etc. involved, and make sure to clean any grease or oil from the threads.

91245P79

Fig. 10 Threadlocking compound can provide you with peace-of-mind when assembling critical suspension parts

91239P04

Fig. 11 Overtightening fasteners may result in breakage, requiring drilling and tapping

91235P92

Fig. 12 ALWAYS replace cotter pins after they have been used once

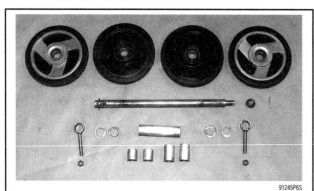

91245P6S

Fig. 13 When disassembling components, keep the individual items in proper order for correct assembly

3. Crossthreading. This occurs when a part such as a bolt is screwed into a nut or casting at the wrong angle and forced. Crossthreading is more likely to occur if access is difficult. It helps to clean and lubricate fasteners, then to start threading with the part to be installed positioned straight in. Always, start a fastener with your fingers if possible. If you encounter resistance, unscrew the part and start over again at a different angle until it can be inserted and turned several times without much effort. Keep in mind that some parts may have tapered threads, so that gentle turning will automatically bring the part you're threading to the proper angle, but only if you don't force it or resist a change in angle. Don't put a wrench on the part until it has been tightened a few turns by hand. If you suddenly encounter resistance, and the part has not seated fully, don't force it. Pull it back out to make sure it's clean and threading properly.

Always take your time and be patient; once you have some experience, working on your snowmobile may well become as enjoyable as riding!

Storing Parts

▶ **See Figure 14**

Above all, we can't emphasize too strongly the necessity of a neat and orderly disassembly. Even if you are an experienced , parts can get misplaced, misidentified and just plain lost.

Start with an indelible marker, lots of cans and/or boxes and tags. Each time a part is removed, label it and store it safely. "Parts" includes all fasteners (bolts, nuts, screws, and washers). Bolts and nuts may look the same and not be alike. Similar looking bolts may be different lengths or thread pitch. Lock-washers may be required in some places and not in others. Everything should go back exactly from where it came.

Fig. 14 Don't laugh, but that old muffin baking tray can be very helpful in the garage once its life is over in the kitchen

SAFETY IN SNOWMOBILE SERVICE

It is virtually impossible to anticipate all of the hazards involved with maintenance and service, but care and common sense will prevent most accidents.

The rules of safety for s range from "don't smoke around gasoline," to "use the proper tool(s) for the job." The trick to avoiding injuries is to develop safe work habits and to take every possible precaution. Whenever you are working on your snowmobile, pay ATTENTION to what you are doing. The more you pay attention to details and what is going on around you, the less likely you will be to hurt yourself or damage your sled.

Do's

▶ **See Figures 15 and 16**

• Do keep a fire extinguisher and first aid kit handy.
• Do wear safety glasses or goggles when cutting, drilling, grinding or prying, even if you have 20–20 vision. If you wear glasses for the sake of vision, wear safety goggles over your regular glasses.
• Do shield your eyes whenever you work around the battery. Batteries contain sulfuric acid. In case of contact with the eyes or skin, flush the area with water or a mixture of water and baking soda, then seek immediate medical attention.
• Do use adequate ventilation when working with any chemicals or hazardous materials. Like carbon monoxide, the asbestos dust resulting from some brake lining wear can be hazardous in sufficient quantities.
• Do disconnect the negative battery cable when working on the electrical system. The secondary ignition system contains EXTREMELY HIGH VOLTAGE. In some cases it can even exceed 50,000 volts.
• Do follow manufacturer's directions whenever working with potentially hazardous materials. Most chemicals and fluids are poisonous if taken internally.
• Do properly maintain your tools. Loose hammerheads, mushroomed punches and chisels, frayed or poorly grounded electrical cords, excessively worn screwdrivers, spread wrenches (open end), cracked sockets, slipping ratchets, or faulty droplight sockets can cause accidents.
• Likewise, keep your tools clean; a greasy wrench can slip off a bolt head, ruining the bolt and often harming your knuckles in the process.
• Do use the proper size and type of tool for the job at hand. Do select a wrench or socket that fits the nut or bolt. The wrench or socket should sit straight, not cocked.
• Do, when possible, pull on a wrench handle rather than push on it, and adjust your stance to prevent a fall.
• Do be sure that adjustable wrenches are tightly closed on the nut or bolt and pulled so that the force is on the side of the fixed jaw. Better yet, avoid the use of an adjustable if you have a fixed wrench that will fit.
• Do strike squarely with a hammer; avoid glancing blows. But, we REALLY hope you won't be using a hammer much in basic maintenance.

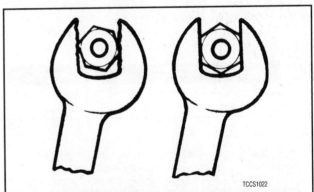

Fig. 16 Using the correct size wrench will help prevent the possibility of rounding off a nut

Fig. 15 A clean, well lit work area is essential for preventing accidents

Don'ts

• Don't run the engine in a garage or anywhere else without proper ventilation—EVER! Carbon monoxide is poisonous; it takes a long time to leave the human body and you can build up a deadly supply of it in your system by simply breathing in a little every day. You may not realize you are slowly poisoning yourself. Always use power vents, windows, fans and/or open the garage door.
• Don't work around moving parts while wearing loose clothing. Short sleeves are much safer than long, loose sleeves. Hard-toed shoes with neoprene soles protect your toes and give a better grip on slippery surfaces. Jewelry, watches, large belt buckles, mufflers or scarves, or body adornment of any kind is not safe working around any vehicle. Long hair should be tied back under a hat or cap.
• Don't use pockets for toolboxes. A fall or bump can drive a screwdriver deep into your body. Even a rag hanging from your back pocket can wrap around a spinning shaft or rotor.

• Don't smoke when working around gasoline, cleaning solvent or other flammable material.

• Don't smoke when working around the battery. When the battery is being charged, it gives off explosive hydrogen gas. Actually, you shouldn't smoke anyway. Save that cigarette money and trick out your sled!

• Don't use gasoline to wash your hands; there are excellent soaps avail-

able. Gasoline contains dangerous additives which can enter the body through a cut or through your pores. Gasoline also removes all the natural oils from the skin so that bone dry hands will suck up oil and grease.

• Don't use screwdrivers for anything other than driving screws! A screwdriver used as an prying tool can snap when you least expect it, causing injuries. At the very least, you'll ruin a good screwdriver.

THE WORK AREA (SETTING UP SHOP)

The size and complexity of your work area will vary with the amount of work you plan to do on your snowmobile. It is easy (and fun) to get carried away when setting up a shop, but the more time you spend in it, the more you will appreciate the preparation work. What we have described here is all that most people would ever need to maintain a snowmobile. That doesn't mean you can't maintain your snowmobile if you don't have a garage, it just means that you might not be as comfortable.

So, if you are lucky enough to set up a shop just to work on your sled, here are some things you'll want to consider.

Floor Space

The average one car garage will give you more than enough workspace, but a decent sized tool shed will also do the trick. A floor plan of 16 X 12 feet (4.8 X 3.6 meters) is more than sufficient for shelving, workbenches, tool shelves or boxes and parts storage areas. 12 X 16 (4.8 X 3.6) works out to 192 square feet (or about 17 square meters). You may think that this sounds like a lot of room, but when you start building shelves, and constructing work benches almost half of that can be eaten up!

Also, you may wonder why a lot of floor space is needed. There are several reasons, not the least of which is the safety factor. You'll be working around a large, heavy object — your snowmobile. You don't want to be tripping, falling, crashing into things or hurting yourself, because your snowmobile takes up a surprising amount of your work space. Accidents can happen! You can easily trip over a misplaced tool.

Most garages have concrete floors. Portable lifts or work stools roll best on a smooth surface. If your garage floor has cracks with raised sections or blocks with deep grooves, you may have a problem if you plan on using either of these. If the wheels hang up on these cracks or grooves while moving a snowmobile on a workstand, you might be in for an unpleasant surprise.

Storage Areas

SHELVES

▶ See Figures 17, 18 and 19

You can't have enough shelf space. Adequate shelf space means that you don't have to stack anything on the floor, where it would be in the way.

Making shelves isn't tough. You can make your own, buy modular or buy prefab units. The best modular units are those made of interlocking shelves and uprights of ABS plastic. They're lightweight and easy to assemble, and their

load-bearing capacity is more than sufficient. Also, they are not subject rust or rot as are metal and wood shelves.

Probably the cheapest and best shelves are ones that you make yourself from one inch shelving with 2 X 4 uprights. You can make them as long, wide and high as you want. For at least the uprights, use pressure treated wood. Its resistance to rot is more than worth the additional cost.

TOOL CHESTS

▶ See Figures 20 and 21

There are many types and sizes of tool chests. Their greatest advantage is that they can hold a lot of tools, securely, in a relatively small area. If you decide that you need one, make sure that you buy one that's big enough and mobile enough for the work area. Remember, you get what you pay for, so purchase a good brand name, and it should last a lifetime.

There are several things to look for in a tool chest, depending on how much you plan on using it, and just how many tools you plan to stuff in it. Check the overall construction. In general, bolted-together chests are stronger than riveted or tabbed, because they are sturdier. Drawers that ride on ball bearings are better than compound slide drawers, because they can hold more and are easier to open/close. Heavy-duty, ball bearing casters are better than bushing type wheels, because they will roll better and last longer. Steel wheels are better than plastic, as they are less prone to damage. Compare different boxes, you'll have to make up your own mind exactly what style is best for you.

WORK BENCHES

▶ See Figure 22

As with the shelving, work benches can be either store-bought or homemade. The store-bought workbenches can be steel, precut wood, or even plastic kits. They all work (though heavy duty benches are obviously better suited to heavy parts and related work), and most types should be available at your local building supply stores or through tool catalogs.

Homemade benches, as with the shelves have the advantage of being made-to-fit your workshop. A freestanding workbench is best, as opposed to one attached to an outside wall. The freestanding bench can take more abuse since it doesn't transfer the shock or vibration to wall supports.

A good free-standing workbench should be constructed using 4 x 4 pressure treated wood as legs, 2 x 6 planking as header boards and ¾ inch plywood sheathing as a deck. Diagonal supports can be 2 x 4 studs and it's always helpful to construct a full size ¾ inch plywood shelf under the bench. Not only can

Fig. 17 Typical homemade wood shelves, crammed with stuff. These shelves are made from spare ⁵⁄₄ x 6 in. pressure treated decking

Fig. 18 Modular plastic shelves, such as these are inexpensive, weatherproof and easy to assemble

Fig. 19 These shelves were made from the frame of old kitchen cabinets

Fig. 20 Different types of mobile, steel tool chests

Fig. 21 A good tool chest has several drawers, each designed to hold a different type tool

Fig. 22 Homemade workbenches

you use the shelf for storage but also it gives great rigidity to the whole bench structure. Assembling the bench with screws rather than nails takes longer but adds strength and gives you the ability to take the whole thing apart if you ever want to move it.

Lighting

♦ See Figures 23 and 24

The importance of adequate lighting can't be over emphasized. Good lighting is not only a convenience but also a safety feature. If you can see what you're working on you're less likely to make mistakes, have a wrench slip or trip over an obstacle. A lot of frustration can be avoided when you can see all the fasteners on which you are working (some of which may be hidden or obscured).

For overhead lighting, at least 2 twin tube fluorescent shop lights should be in place. Most garages are wired with standard light bulbs attached to the wall studs at intervals. Four or five of these lights, at about a 6 foot height combined with the overhead lighting should suffice. However, no matter where the lights are, your body is going to block some of it so a droplight or clip-on type work light is a great idea.

Ventilation

At one time or another, you'll be working with chemicals that may require adequate ventilation. Now, just about all garages have a big car-sized door and all sheds or workshops have a door. In bad weather the door will have to be closed so at least one window that opens is a necessity. An exhaust fan or regular ventilation fan is a great help, especially in hot weather.

Heaters

Since you live in an area where the winters are cold (obviously, or you wouldn't own a snowmobile!) it's nice to have some sort of heat where we work. If your workshop or garage is attached to the house, you'll probably be okay. If your garage or shop is detached, then a space heater of some sort — electric, propane or kerosene — will be necessary. NEVER run a space heater in the presence of flammable vapors! When running a non-electric space heater, always allow for some means of venting the carbon monoxide!

Electrical Requirements

Obviously, your workshop should be wired according to all local codes. As to what type of service you need, that depends on your electrical load. If you have a lot of power equipment and maybe a refrigerator, TV, stereo or whatever, not only do you have a great shop, but your amperage requirements may exceed the capacity of your wiring. If you are tripping the circuit breakers on a regular basis, that's a clue that you're overloading the wiring. If at all in doubt, consult your local electrical contractor.

Safety Equipment

♦ See Figure 25

FIRE EXTINGUISHERS

♦ See Figure 26

There are many types of safety equipment. The most important of these is the fire extinguisher. You'll be well off with two 5 lbs. extinguishers rated for oil, chemical and wood.

FIRST AID KITS

Next you'll need a good first aid kit. Any good kit that can be purchased from the local drug store will be fine. It's a good idea, in addition, to have something easily accessible in the event of a minor injury, such as hydrogen peroxide or other antiseptic that can be poured onto or applied to a wound immediately.

Fig. 23 At least two of this type of twin tube fluorescent lights are essential

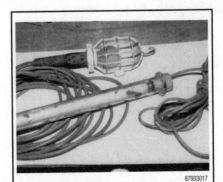

Fig. 24 Two types of droplights—Incandescent and fluorescent

Fig. 25 Three essential pieces of safety equipment. Left to right: ear protectors, safety goggles and respirator

Fig. 26 A good, all-purpose fire extinguisher

Remember, your hands will be dirty. Just as you wouldn't want dirt entering your engine when you open the oil filler plug, you certainly don't want bacteria entering a blood stream that has just been opened!

WORK GLOVES

▶ **See Figure 27**

Unless you think scars on your hands are cool, enjoy pain and like wearing bandages, get a good pair of work gloves. Canvas or leather are the best. And yes, we realize that there are some jobs involving small parts that can't be done while wearing work gloves. These jobs are not the ones usually associated with hand injuries.

A good pair of rubber gloves (such as those usually associated with dish washing) or vinyl gloves is also a great idea. There are some liquids such as solvents and penetrants that don't belong on your skin. Avoid burns and rashes. Wear these gloves.

And lastly, an option. If you're tired of being greasy and dirty all the time, go to the drug store and buy a box of disposable latex gloves like medical professionals wear. You can handle greasy parts, perform small tasks, wash parts, etc. all without getting dirty! These gloves take a surprising amount of abuse without tearing and aren't expensive. Note however, that it has been reported that some people are allergic to the latex or the powder used inside some gloves, so pay attention to what you buy.

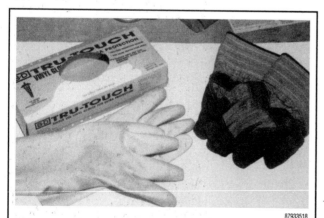

Fig. 27 Three different types of work gloves. The box contains latex gloves

WORK BOOTS

It's up to you, but a good, comfortable pair of steel-toed work boots is a sensible idea. Primarily because heavy parts or tools get dropped sooner or later. A heavy piece of metal can do significant damage to a sneaker-clad foot.

Good work boots also provide better support (you're going to be on your feet a lot), are oil-resistant, and they keep your feet warm and dry.

To keep the boots protected, get a spray can of silicone-based water repellent and spray the boots when new, and then periodically thereafter.

EYE PROTECTION

Don't begin any job without a good pair of work goggles or impact resistant glasses! When doing any kind of work, it's all too easy to avoid eye injury through this simple precaution. And don't just buy eye protection and leave it on the shelf. Wear it all the time! Things have a habit of breaking, chipping, splashing, spraying, splintering and flying around. And, for some reason, your eye is always in the way!

If you wear vision correcting glasses as a matter of routine, get a pair made with polycarbonate lenses. These lenses are impact resistant and are available at any optometrist.

EAR PROTECTION

Often overlooked is hearing protection. Power equipment is noisy! Loud noises damage your ears. It's as simple as that!

The simplest and cheapest form of ear protection is a pair of noise-reducing ear plugs. Cheap insurance for your ears. And, they may even come with their own, cute little carrying case.

More substantial, more protection and more money is a good pair of noise reducing earmuffs. They protect from all but the loudest sounds. Hopefully those are sounds that you'll never encounter since they're usually associated with disasters.

WORK CLOTHES

Everyone has "work clothes." Usually they consist of old jeans and a shirt that have seen better days. That's fine. In addition, a denim work apron is a nice accessory. It's rugged, and you don't feel bad wiping your hands or tools on it. That's what it's for.

If you're so inclined, shop aprons are a cheap and easy way to protect your clothes. They're rugged and can be put on quickly for quick tasks.

When working in cold weather, a one-piece, thermal work outfit is invaluable. Most are rated to below zero (Fahrenheit) temperatures and are ruggedly constructed.

Chemicals

There is a whole range of chemicals that you'll find handy for maintenance work. The most common types are, lubricants, penetrants and sealers. Keep these handy, on some convenient shelf. There are also many chemicals that are used for detailing or cleaning, but these are covered elsewhere.

When a particular chemical is not being used, keep it capped, upright and in a safe place. These substances may be flammable, may be irritants or might even be caustic and should always be stored properly, used properly and handled with care. Always read and follow all label directions and be sure to wear hand and eye protection!

LUBRICANTS & PENETRANTS

▶ **See Figure 28**

In this category, a well-prepared shop should have:
• A full complement of fluids for your snowmobile (coolant, chain case oil, brake fluid, etc.)
• Anti-seize
• Lithium grease
• Chassis lube
• Assembly lube
• Silicone grease
• Silicone spray
• Penetrating oil

Anti-seize is used to coat certain fasteners prior to installation. This can be especially helpful when two dissimilar metals are in contact (to help prevent corrosion that might lock the fastener in place). This is a good practice on a lot of different fasteners, BUT, NOT on any fastener which might vibrate loose caus-

Fig. 28 A variety of penetrants and lubricants is a staple of any DIYer's garage

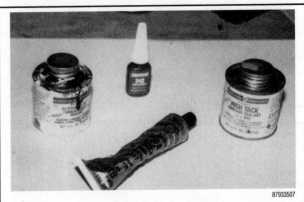

Fig. 29 Sealants are essential for preventing leaks

ing a problem. If anti-seize is used on a fastener, it should be checked periodically for proper tightness.

Lithium grease, chassis lube, silicone grease or a synthetic brake caliper grease can all be used pretty much interchangeably. All can be used for coating rust-prone fasteners and for facilitating the assembly of parts that are a tight fit. Silicone and synthetic greases are the most versatile.

➡**Silicone dielectric grease is a non-conductor that is often used to coat the terminals of wiring connectors before fastening them. It may sound odd to coat metal portions of a terminal with something that won't conduct electricity, but here is it how it works. When the connector is fastened the metal-to-metal contact between the terminals will displace the grease (allowing the circuit to be completed). The grease that is displaced will then coat the non-contacted surface and the cavity around the terminals, SEALING them from atmospheric moisture that could cause corrosion.**

Silicone spray is a good lubricant for hard-to-reach places and parts that shouldn't be gooped up with grease.

Penetrating oil may turn out to be one of your best friends when taking something apart that has corroded fasteners. Not only can they make a job easier, they can really help to avoid broken and stripped fasteners. The most familiar penetrating oils are Liquid Wrench® and WD-40®. A newer penetrant, PB Blaster® also works well. These products have hundreds of uses. For your purposes, they are vital!

Before disassembling any part (especially on an exhaust system), check the fasteners. If any appear rusted, soak them thoroughly with the penetrant and let them stand while you do something else. This simple act can save you hours of tedious work trying to extract a broken bolt or stud.

SEALANTS

▶ **See Figure 29**

Sealants are an indispensable part for certain tasks on snowmobile's, especially if you are trying to avoid leaks. The purpose of sealants is to establish a leak-proof bond between or around assembled parts. Most sealers are used in

conjunction with gaskets, but some are used instead of conventional gasket material.

The most common sealers are the non-hardening types such as Permatex® No.2 or its equivalents. These sealers are applied to the mating surfaces of each part to be joined, then a gasket is put in place and the parts are assembled.

➡**A sometimes overlooked use for sealants like RTV is on the threads of vibration prone fasteners.**

One very helpful type of non-hardening sealer is the "high tack" type. This type is a very sticky material that holds the gasket in place while the parts are being assembled. This stuff is really a good idea when you don't have enough hands or fingers to keep everything where it should be.

The stand-alone sealers are the Room Temperature Vulcanizing (RTV) silicone gasket makers. On some engines, this material is used instead of a gasket. In those instances, a gasket may not be available or, because of the shape of the mating surfaces, a gasket shouldn't be used. This stuff, when used in conjunction with a conventional gasket, produces the surest bonds.

RTV does have its limitations though. When using this material, you will have a time limit. It starts to set-up within 15 minutes or so, so you have to assemble the parts without delay. In addition, when squeezing the material out of the tube, don't drop any globs into the engine. The stuff will form and set and travel around the oil gallery, possibly plugging up a passage. Also, most types are not fuel-proof. Check the tube for all cautions.

CLEANERS

▶ **See Figures 30, 31 and 32**

You'll have two types of cleaners to deal with: parts cleaners and hand cleaners. The parts cleaners are for the parts; the hand cleaners are for you.

There are many good, non-flammable, biodegradable parts cleaners on the market. These cleaning agents are safe for you, the parts and the environment. Therefore, there is no reason to use flammable, caustic or toxic substances to clean your parts or tools.

Fig. 30 Three types of cleaners. Some are caustic; some are not. Always read and follow label instructions

Fig. 31 This is one type of hand cleaner that not only works well but smells pretty good too

Fig. 32 One of the best things to clean up all types of spills is kitty litter

As far as hand cleaners go, the waterless types are the best. They have always been efficient at cleaning, but leave a pretty smelly odor. Recently though, just about all of them have eliminated the odor and added stuff that actually smells good. Make sure that you pick one that contains lanolin or some other moisture-replenishing additive. Cleaners not only remove grease and oil but also skin oil.

One other note: most women know this already but most men don't. Use a hand lotion when you're all cleaned up. It's okay. Real men DO use hand lotion! Believe it or not, using hand lotion **before** your hands are dirty will actually make them easier to clean when you're finished with a dirty job. Lotion seals your hands, and keeps dirt and grease from sticking to your skin.

SHOP TOWELS

◗ See Figure 33

One of the most important elements in doing shop work is a good supply of shop towels. Standard household paper towels just don't cut it! Most auto parts stores sell packs of shop towels, usually 50–100 in a pack. They are relatively cheap and can be washed over and over. Some manufacturers now produce a heavy paper towel, just for shop use, and these are often just as good as the cloth types (although they are obviously disposable and might not be considered as environmentally friendly. Not that washing oil soaked rags would be

considered "environmentally sound" either . . .). Ideally, you may want to keep both types handy.

One of the best shop towels known to science, is the old-fashioned cloth diaper. They're highly absorbent and rugged, but, in these days of disposable diapers, are hard to find.

Fig. 33 A pack of shop towels

TOOLS

◗ See Figures 34, 35 and 36

Tools; this subject could require a completely separate book. Again, the first thing you will need to ask yourself, is just HOW involved do you plan to get. Most snowmobiles come with a small tool kit for unexpected trailside repairs. And, with some kits, you could reasonably perform all required maintenance using only the kit. But, that is probably more the exception than the rule and if you are serious about your snowmobile maintenance you will want to gather a quality set of tools to make the job easier, and more enjoyable. BESIDES, TOOLS ARE FUN!!!

Almost every do-it-yourselfer loves to accumulate tools. Though most find a way to perform jobs with only a few common tools, they tend to buy more over time, as money allows. So gathering the tools necessary for maintenance does not have to be an expensive, overnight proposition.

When buying tools, the saying "You get what you pay for" is absolutely true! Don't go cheap! Any hand tool that you buy should be drop forged and/or chrome vanadium. These two qualities tell you that the tool is strong enough for the job. With any tool, power or not, go with a name that you've heard of before, or, that is recommended buy your local professional retailer. Let's go over a list of tools that you'll need.

Most of the world uses the metric system. However, some American-built snowmobiles and aftermarket accessories use standard fasteners. So, accumulate your tools accordingly. Any good DIYer should have a decent set of both U.S. and metric measure tools.

Don't be confused by terminology. Most advertising refers to "SAE and metric", or "standard and metric." Both are misnomers. The Society of Automotive

Engineers (SAE) did not invent the English system of measurement; the English did. The SAE likes metrics just fine. Both English (U.S.) and metric measurements are SAE approved. Also, the current "standard" measurement IS metric. So, if it's not metric, it's U.S. measurement.

Hand Tools

SOCKET SETS

◗ See Figures 37, 38, 39 and 40

Socket sets are the most basic, necessary hand tools for snowmobile repair and maintenance work. For our purposes, socket sets basically come in three drive sizes: ¼ inch, ⅜ inch and ½ inch. Drive size refers to the size of the drive lug on the ratchet, breaker bar or speed handle.

You'll need a good ½ inch set since this size drive lug assures that you won't break a ratchet or socket on large or heavy fasteners. Also, torque wrenches with a torque scale high enough for larger fasteners (such as axle nuts) are usually ½ inch drive. The socket set that you'll need should range in sizes from ⁷⁄₁₆ inch through 1 inch for standard fasteners, and a 6mm through 19mm for metric fasteners.

A ⅜ inch set is very handy to have since it allows you to get into tight places that the larger drive ratchets can't. Also, this size set gives you a range of smaller sockets that are still strong enough for heavy duty work.

¼ inch drive sets can be VERY handy in tight places, though they usually duplicate functions of the ⅜ inch set.

Fig. 34 The well-stocked garage pegboard. Pegboards can store most tools and other equipment for ease of access. Besides, they're cool looking

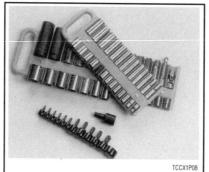
Fig. 35 Socket holders, especially the magnetic type, are handy items to keep tools in order

Fig. 36 A good set of handy storage cabinets for fasteners and small parts makes any job easier

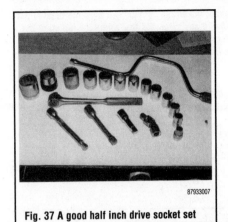

Fig. 37 A good half inch drive socket set

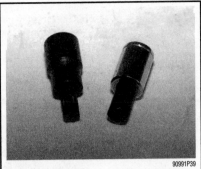

Fig. 38 Two common drivers for snowmobile service: Left, a Torx® drive socket; right, a hex drive socket

Fig. 39 A swivel (U-joint) adapter, and two types of drive adapters

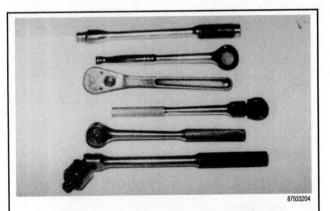

Fig. 40 Ratchets come in all sizes from rigid to swivel-headed

As for the sockets themselves, they come in standard and deep lengths as well as standard and thin walled, in either 6 or 12 point.

Standard length sockets are good for just about all jobs, however, some stud-head bolts, hard-to-reach bolts, nuts on long studs, etc., require the deep sockets.

Thin-walled sockets are not too common and aren't usually needed in most work. They are exactly what you think, sockets made with a thinner wall to fit into tighter places. They don't have the wall strength of a standard socket, of course, but their usefulness in a tight spot can make them worth it.

6 and 12 points. This refers to how many sides are in the socket itself. Each has advantages. The 6 point socket is stronger and less prone to slipping which would strip a bolt head or nut. 12 point sockets are more common, usually less expensive and can operate better in tight places where the ratchet handle can't swing far.

Most manufacturers use recessed hex-head fasteners to retain many of the engine and chassis parts from engine covers to caliper pins. These fasteners require a socket with a hex shaped driver or a large sturdy hex key. To help prevent torn knuckles, we would recommend that you stick to the sockets on any tight fastener and leave the hex keys for lighter applications. Hex driver sockets are available individually or in sets just like conventional sockets. Any complete tool set should include hex driver sockets.

More and more, manufacturers are using Torx® head fasteners, which were once known as tamper resistant fasteners (because many people did not have tools with the necessary odd driver shape). They are still used where the manufacturer would prefer only knowledgeable technicians or advanced Do-It-Yourselfers (DIYers) be working.

There are currently three different types of Torx® fasteners; internal, external and a new tamper resistant. The internal fasteners require a star-shaped driver. The external fasteners require a star-shaped socket. And, the new tamper resistant fasteners use a star-shaped driver with a small hole drilled through the center. The most common are the internal Torx® fasteners, but you might find any of them on your particular snowmobile.

Torque Wrenches

▸ See Figure 41

In most applications, a torque wrench can be used to assure proper installation of a fastener. Torque wrenches come in various designs and most supply stores will carry a variety to suit your needs. A torque wrench should be used any time you have a specific torque value for a fastener, such as cylinder head bolts. A torque wrench can also be used if you are following the general guidelines in the charts accompanying the fastener information in this section. Keep in mind that because there is no worldwide standardization of fasteners, the charts are a general guideline and should be used with caution. Again, the general rule of "if you are using the right tool for the job, you should not have to strain to tighten a fastener" applies here.

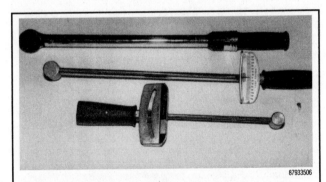

Fig. 41 Three types of torque wrenches. Top to bottom: a ½ inch drive clicker type, a ½ inch drive beam type and a ⅜ inch drive beam type that reads in inch lbs.

BEAM TYPE

▸ See Figure 42

The beam type torque wrench is one of the most popular types. It consists of a pointer attached to the head that runs the length of the flexible beam (shaft) to a scale located near the handle. As the wrench is pulled, the beam bends and the pointer indicates the torque using the scale.

CLICK (BREAKAWAY) TYPE

▸ See Figure 43

Another popular torque wrench design is the click type. To use the click type wrench you pre-adjust it to a torque setting. Once the torque is reached, the wrench has a reflex signaling feature that causes a momentary breakaway of the torque wrench body, sending an impulse to the operator's hand.

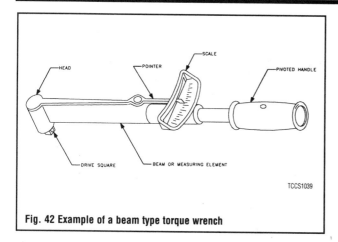

Fig. 42 Example of a beam type torque wrench

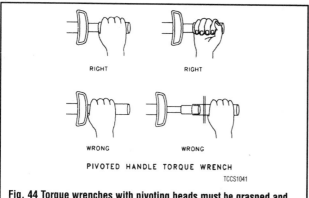

Fig. 43 A click type or breakaway torque wrench—note this one has a pivoting head

PIVOT HEAD TYPE

▶ See Figure 44

Some torque wrenches (usually of the click type) may be equipped with a pivot head that can allow it to be used in areas of limited access. BUT, it must be used properly. To hold a pivot head wrench, grasp the handle lightly, and as you pull on the handle, it should be floated on the pivot point. If the handle comes in contact with the yoke extension during the process of pulling, there is a very good chance the torque readings will be inaccurate because this could alter the wrench loading point. The design of the handle is usually such as to make it inconvenient to deliberately misuse the wrench.

→ It should be mentioned that the use of any U-joint, wobble or extension would have an effect on the torque readings, no matter what type of wrench you are using. For the most accurate readings, install the socket directly on the wrench driver. If necessary, straight extensions (which

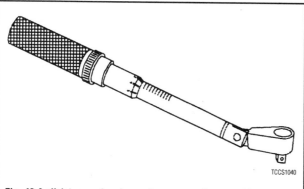

Fig. 44 Torque wrenches with pivoting heads must be grasped and used properly to prevent an incorrect reading

hold a socket directly under the wrench driver) will have the least effect on the torque reading. Avoid any extension that alters the length of the wrench from the handle to the head/driving point (such as a crow's foot). U-joint or wobble extensions can greatly affect the readings; avoid their use at all times.

RIGID CASE (DIRECT READING)

▶ See Figure 45

A rigid case or direct reading torque wrench is equipped with a dial indicator to show torque values. One advantage of these wrenches is that they can be held at any position on the wrench without affecting accuracy. These wrenches are often preferred because they tend to be compact, easy to read and have a great degree of accuracy.

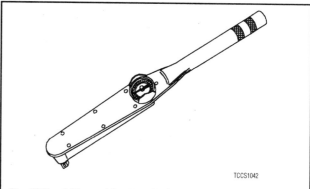

Fig. 45 The rigid case (direct reading) torque wrench uses a dial indicator to show torque

Torque Angle Meters

▶ See Figure 46

Because the frictional characteristics of each fastener or threaded hole will vary, clamp loads which are based strictly on torque will vary as well. In most applications, this variance is not significant enough to cause worry. But, in certain applications, a manufacturer's engineers may determine that more precise clamp loads are necessary (such is the case with many aluminum cylinder heads). In these cases, a torque angle method of installation would be specified. When installing fasteners that are torque angle tightened, a predetermined seating torque and standard torque wrench are usually used first to remove any compliance from the joint. The fastener is then tightened the specified additional portion of a turn measured in degrees. A torque angle gauge (mechanical protractor) is used for these applications. You will probably never have the use for a torque angle meter for most normal maintenance.

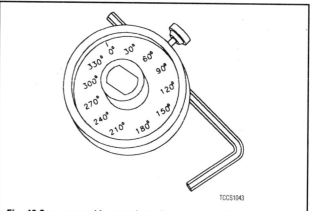

Fig. 46 Some assembly procedures (mostly on machined aluminum parts such as cylinder heads) require the use of a torque angle meter (mechanical protractor)

Breaker Bars

♦ See Figure 47

Breaker bars are long handles with a drive lug. Their main purpose is to provide extra turning force when breaking loose tight bolts or nuts. They come in all drive sizes and lengths. Always wear gloves when using a breaker bar.

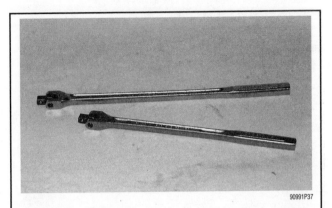

Fig. 47 Breaker bars are great for loosening large or stuck fasteners

Speed Handles

♦ See Figure 48

Speed handles are tools with a drive lug and angled turning handle that allow you to quickly remove or install a bolt or nut. They don't, however have much torque ability. You might consider one when installing a number of similar fasteners such as an engine cover.

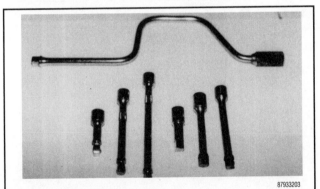

Fig. 48 A speed driver and extensions. The 3 on the left are called "wobbles" since they allow some lateral movement

WRENCHES

♦ See Figures 49, 50, 51 and 52

Basically, there are 3 kinds of fixed wrenches: open end, box end, and combination.

Open end wrenches have 2-jawed openings at each end of the wrench. These wrenches are able to fit onto just about any nut or bolt. They are extremely versatile but have one major drawback. They can slip on a worn or rounded bolt head or nut, causing bleeding knuckles and a useless fastener.

Box-end wrenches have a 360° circular jaw at each end of the wrench. They come in both 6 and 12 point versions just like sockets and each type has the same advantages and disadvantages as sockets.

Combination wrenches have the best of both. They have a 2-jawed open end and a box end. These wrenches are probably the most versatile.

As for sizes, you'll probably need a range similar to that of the sockets, about ¼ inch through 1 inch for standard fasteners, or 6mm through 19mm for metric fasteners. As for numbers, you'll need 2 of each size, since, in many instances, one wrench holds the nut while the other turns the bolt. On most fasteners, the nut and bolt are the same size.

➡**Although you will typically just need the sizes we specified, there are some exceptions. Occasionally you will find a nut which is larger. For these, you will need to buy ONE expensive wrench or a very large adjustable. Or you can always just convince the spouse that we are talking about safety here and buy a whole, expensive, large wrench set.**

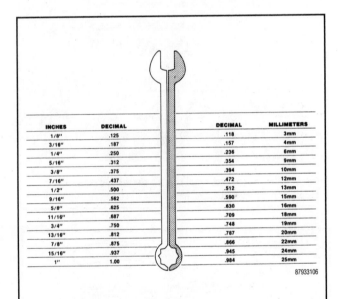

Fig. 49 Comparison of U.S. measure and metric wrench sizes

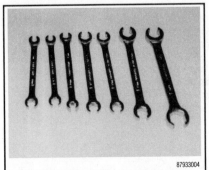

Fig. 50 Flarenut wrenches are critical for brake lines or tubing, to make sure the fittings do not become rounded

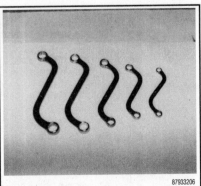

Fig. 51 These S-shaped wrenches are called obstruction wrenches

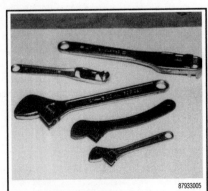

Fig. 52 Several types and sizes of adjustable wrenches

One extremely valuable type of wrench is the adjustable wrench. An adjustable wrench has a fixed upper jaw and a moveable lower jaw. The lower jaw is moved by turning a threaded drum. The advantage of an adjustable wrench is its ability to be adjusted to just about any size fastener. The main drawback of an adjustable wrench is the lower jaw's tendency to move slightly under heavy pressure. This can cause the wrench to slip if the wrench is not facing the right way. Pulling on an adjustable wrench in the proper direction will cause the jaws to lock in place. Adjustable wrenches come in a large range of sizes, measured by the wrench length.

PLIERS

♦ See Figures 53 and 54

At least 2 pair of standard pliers is an absolute necessity. Pliers are simply mechanical fingers. They are, more than anything, an extension of your hand.

In addition to standard pliers there are the slip-joint, multi-position pliers such as ChannelLock® pliers and locking pliers, such as Vise Grips®.

Slip joint pliers are extremely valuable in grasping oddly sized parts and fasteners. Just make sure that you don't use them instead of a wrench too often since they can easily round off a bolt head or nut.

Locking pliers are usually used for gripping bolts or studs that can't be removed conventionally. You can get locking pliers in square jawed, needle-nosed and pipe-jawed. Pipe jawed have slightly curved jaws for gripping more than just pipes. Locking pliers can rank right up behind duct tape as the handy-man's best friend.

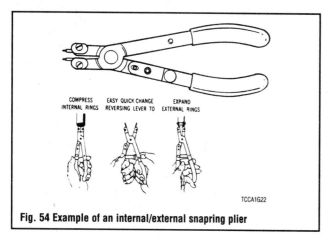

Fig. 53 Pliers and cutters come in many shapes and sizes. You should have an assortment on hand

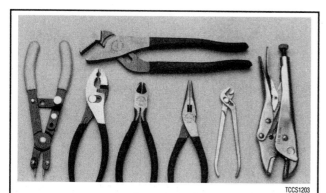

Fig. 54 Example of an internal/external snapring plier

SCREWDRIVERS

You can't have too many screwdrivers. They come in 2 basic flavors, either standard or Phillips. Standard blades come in various sizes and thicknesses for all types of slotted fasteners. Phillips screwdrivers come in sizes with number

designations from #1 on up, with the lower number designating the smaller size. Screwdrivers can be purchased separately or in sets.

HAMMERS

♦ See Figure 55

You always need a hammer—for just about any kind of work. For most metal work, you need a ball-peen hammer for using drivers and other like tools, a plastic hammer for hitting things safely, and a soft-faced dead-blow hammer for hitting things safely and hard. Hammers are also VERY useful with impact drivers (if you are not fortunate enough to have an air compressor).

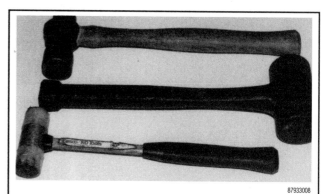

Fig. 55 Three types of hammers. Top to bottom: ball peen, rubber dead-blow, and plastic

OTHER COMMON TOOLS

♦ See Figures 56 thru 65

There are a lot of other tools that every workshop will eventually need (though not all for basic maintenance). They include:
- Funnels (for adding fluid)
- Chisels
- Punches
- Files
- Hacksaw
- Bench Vise
- Tap and Die Set
- Flashlight
- Magnetic Bolt Retriever
- Gasket scraper
- Putty Knife
- Screw/Bolt Extractors
- Prybar

Chisels, punches and files are repair tools.

Chisel, punches and files are repair tools. Their uses will come up periodically.

Hacksaws have just one use—cutting things off. You may wonder why you'd need one for something as simple as maintenance, but you never know. Among other things, guide studs for parts installation can be made from old bolts with their heads cut off.

A large bench vise, of at least 4 inch capacity, is essential. A vise is needed to hold anything being worked on.

A tap and die set might be something you've never needed, but you will eventually. It's a good rule, when everything is apart, to clean-up all threads, on bolts, screws and threaded holes. Also, you'll likely run across a situation in which stripped threads will be encountered. The tap and die set will handle that for you.

Gasket scrapers are just what you'd think, tools made for scraping old gasket material off of parts. You don't absolutely need one. Old gasket material can be removed with a putty knife or single edge razor blade. However, putty knives may not be sharp enough for some really stubborn gaskets and razor blades

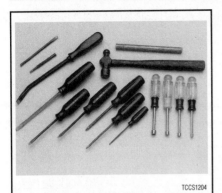

Fig. 56 Various drivers, chisels and pry-bars are great tools to have in your box

Fig. 57 Punches, chisels and drivers can be purchased separately or in sets

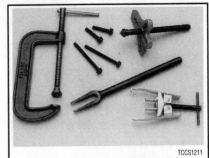

Fig. 58 An assortment of pullers, clamps and separator tools are also needed for many larger repairs (especially engine and suspension work)

Fig. 59 A good quality, heavy-duty bench vise, like this 5½ in. type, with reversible jaws, is ideal for shop work

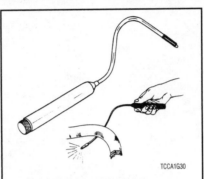

Fig. 60 A flexible flashlight can become invaluable in tight places

Fig. 61 A telescoping mirror is also great for tight places

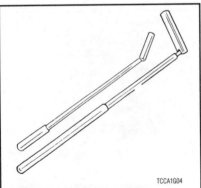

Fig. 62 A magnetic pick-up tool pays for itself the first time you need it

Fig. 63 Two good tap and die sets; US measure (left) and metric

Fig. 64 A set of drill bits and a set of screw extractors

have a knack of breaking just when you don't want them to, inevitably slicing the nearest body part! As the old saying goes, "always use the proper tool for the job". If you're going to use a razor to scrape a gasket, be sure to always use a blade holder.

Putty knives really do have a use in a snowmobile repair shop. Just because you remove all the bolts from a component sealed with a gasket doesn't mean it's going to come off. Most of the time, the gasket and sealer will hold it tightly. Lightly driving a putty knife at various points between the two parts will break the seal without damage to the parts.

A small—8–10 inches (20–25 centimeters) long—prybar is extremely useful for removing stuck parts. NEVER, NEVER, use a screwdriver as a prybar! Screwdrivers are NOT meant for prying. Screwdrivers, used for prying, can break, sending the broken shaft flying!

Screw/bolt extractors are used for removing broken bolts or studs that have broke off flush with the surface of the part.

Fig. 65 A really handy tool is the nut splitter. When a frozen nut simply won't budge, use one of these

SPECIALTY TOOLS

♦ See Figures 66 and 67

Almost every snowmobile (or motor vehicle) around today requires AT LEAST one special tool to perform certain tasks. In most cases, these tools are specially designed to overcome some unique problem or to fit on some oddly sized component.

When manufacturers go through the trouble of making a special tool, it is usually necessary to use it to assure that the job will be done right. A special tool might be designed to make a job easier, or it might be used to keep you from damaging or breaking a part.

Don't worry, MOST basic maintenance procedures can either be performed without any special tools OR, because the tools must be used for such basic things, they are commonly available for a reasonable price. It is usually just the low production, highly specialized tools (like a super thin 7-point star-shaped socket capable of 150 ft. lbs. [203 Nm] of torque that is used only on the crankshaft nut of the limited production what-dya-callit snowmobile) that tend to be outrageously expensive and hard to find. Luckily, you will probably never need such a tool.

Special tools can be as inexpensive and simple as an adjustable spanner wrench (which are used on some snowmobiles to adjust preload on the shocks) or as complicated as an adjustable axle measurement tool. A few common specialty tools are listed here, but check with your dealer or with other riders of your type of snowmobile for help in determining if there are any special tools for YOUR particular model. There is an added advantage is seeking advice from other riders, chances are they may have already found not only what special tool you will need, but how to get it cheaper.

Battery Testers

The best way to test a non-sealed battery is using a hydrometer to check the specific gravity of the acid. Luckily, these are usually very inexpensive and are available at most part stores. Just be careful because the larger ones available at many automotive stores are usually designed for larger, automotive batteries and may require more acid than you will be able to draw from the battery cell. Smaller testers (usually a short, squeeze bulb type) will require less acid and should work on most snowmobile batteries.

Electronic testers are available (and are often necessary to tell if a sealed battery is usable) but these are usually more than most DIYer's are willing to spend. Luckily, many auto part stores have them on hand and are willing to test your battery for you.

Battery Chargers

♦ See Figure 68

There are many types of battery chargers available, from low amperage trickle chargers to electronically controlled battery maintenance tools which monitor the battery voltage to prevent over or undercharging. This last type is the most useful, since most everyone has to store their snowmobile for the summer (unless you're one of the brave few who drag races on the grass!).

Even if you use your snowmobile on a regular basis, you will eventually need a battery charger. Remember that most batteries are shipped dry and in a partial charged state. Before a new battery can be put into service it must be filled AND properly charged. Failure to properly charge a battery (which was shipped dry) before it is put into service will prevent it from ever reaching a fully charged state.

Carburetor Synchronization Tool

♦ See Figure 69

Most all snowmobiles have more than one carburetor. You'll eventually find the need for a carburetor synchronization tool. Most carburetor sync tools take the form of vacuum gauges (either mercury tube types or the traditional calibrated dial-type). They are connected to vacuum ports on the individual carburetors or intake manifolds in order to measure the amount of vacuum present at each. By adjusting the carburetor balance screw(s) while watching the sync tool, you can make sure each carburetor runs its cylinder(s) at the same speed as the others.

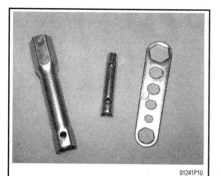

Fig. 66 Sometimes the tools supplied with the snowmobile are required for certain adjustments

91241P10

91244P9S

Fig. 67 Some models require special tools for tasks like pulley alignment

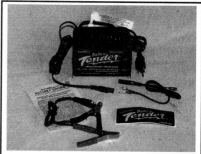

90991P34

Fig. 68 The Battery Tender® is more than just a battery charger, when left connected, it keeps your battery fully charged

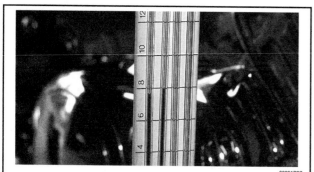

90991P27

Fig. 69 This carburetor synchronization tool (the mercury tube-type) can be used on snowmobiles to equalize the carburetors for better performance

Snowmobile Dollies/Rollers

♦ See Figures 70, 71, 72 and 73

Moving a snowmobile around in the garage/shop can be a PAIN without these useful little tools. If space in your garage is tight, or you just want to preserve the surface of the garage floor, a set of dollies are HIGHLY recommended. The dollies pictured here are medium duty, all-metal construction, and have special grooves to fit the profile of the skis.

The cost of a decent set of dollies is nominal compared to the amount of effort it takes to drag a snowmobile around in your garage or driveway. There are several companies that make dollies of this type, as well as larger, heavier dollies with handles available to make maneuvering even easier. No matter what your budget is, you can't afford **not** to have a set of dollies.

Fig. 70 There are dollies with handles to make maneuvering easier

Fig. 71 The dollies for the front skis should positioned directly underneath the ski pivots

Fig. 72 These dollies have grooves to fit the profile of the bottom of the skis for better stability

Fig. 73 The rear dolly is positioned underneath the rear track. Combined with the dollies under the skis, the snowmobile is easily movable

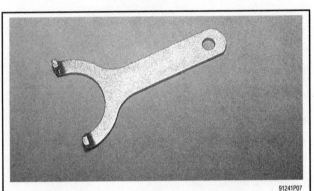

Fig. 74 A spanner wrench is required to adjust the preload on some snowmobile shocks

Spanner Wrench

♦ See Figure 74

A spanner is different than a normal wrench in that it typically uses two or more tabs that are placed within a slot and used to turn the shock sleeve. As mentioned earlier, a spanner wrench is required to adjust the shock pre-load on many snowmobiles. There are various types and sizes of spanners available, so make sure the one you are about to buy fits your shocks. Check the tool kit before purchasing one, because they are often (but not always) included in the tool kit that comes with your sled.

Measuring Tools

Eventually, you are going to have to measure something whether it is the thickness of a brake pad/rotor or the amount of play in a chain or drive belt. To do this, you will need at least a few precision tools in addition to the special tools mentioned earlier.

MICROMETERS & CALIPERS

Micrometers and calipers are devices used to make extremely precise measurements. The simple truth is that you really won't have the need for many of these items just for simple maintenance. You will probably want to have at least one precision tool such as an outside caliper to measure rotors or brake pads, but that should be sufficient to most basic maintenance procedures.

Should you decide on becoming more involved in snowmobile mechanics, such as with repair or engine rebuilding, then these tools will become very important. The success of any rebuild is dependent, to a great extent on the ability to check the size and fit of components as specified by the manufacturer. These measurements are made in thousandths and ten-thousandths of an inch.

Outside Micrometers

♦ See Figure 75

Outside micrometers can be used to check the thickness parts such as the brake rotors. They are also used during many rebuild and repair procedures to measure the diameter of components such as the pistons from a caliper or wheel cylinder. The most common type of micrometer reads in 1/1000 of an inch. Micrometers that use a vernier scale can estimate to 1/10 of an inch.

A micrometer is an instrument made up of a precisely machined spindle which is rotated in a fixed nut, opening and closing the distance between the end of the spindle and a fixed anvil.

To make a measurement, you back off the spindle until you can place the piece to be measured between the spindle and anvil. You then rotate the spindle until the part is contacted by both the spindle and anvil. The measurement is then found by reading the gradations in the handle of the micrometer.

Here's the hard part. we'll try to explain how to read a micrometer. The spindle is threaded. Most micrometers use a thread pitch of 40 threads per inch. One complete revolution of the spindle moves the spindle toward or away from the anvil 0.025 in. ($\frac{1}{40}$ in.).

The fixed part of the handle (called, the sleeve) is marked with 40 gradations per inch of handle length, so each line is 0.025 in. apart. Okay so far?

Every 4th line is marked with a number. The first long line marked 1 represents 0.100 in., the second is 0.200 in., and so on.

The part of the handle that turns is called the thimble. The beveled end of the thimble is marked with gradations, each of which corresponds to 0.001 in. and, usually, every 5th line is numbered.

Turn the thimble until the 0 lines up with the 0 on the sleeve. Now, rotate the thimble one complete revolution and look at the sleeve. You'll see that one complete thimble revolution moved the thimble 0.025 in. down the sleeve.

To read the micrometer, multiply the number of gradations exposed on the sleeve by 0.025 and add that to the number of thousandths indicated by the thimble line that is lined up with the horizontal line on the sleeve. So, if you've

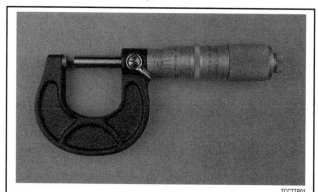

Fig. 75 Outside micrometers can be used to measure bake components including rotors, pads and pistons

measured a part and there are 6 vertical gradations exposed on the sleeve and the 7th gradation on the thimble is lined up with the horizontal line on the sleeve, the thickness of the part is 0.157 in. (6 x 0.025 = 0.150 . Add to that 0.007 representing the 7 lines on the thimble and you get 0.157). See?

If you didn't understand that, try the instructions that come with the micrometer or ask someone that knows, to show you how to work it. Also, if you didn't understand . . . don't worry. We said you probably won't ever need this for basic maintenance.

Inside Micrometers

Inside micrometers are used to measure the distance between two parallel surfaces. For example, in engine rebuilding work, the inside mike measures cylinder bore wear and taper. Inside mikes are graduated the same way as outside mikes and are read the same way as well.

Remember that an inside mike must be absolutely perpendicular to the work being measured. When you measure with an inside mike, rock the mike gently from side to side and tip it back and forth slightly so that you span the widest part of the bore. Just to be on the safe side, take several readings. It takes a certain amount of experience to work any mike with confidence.

Metric Micrometers

Metric micrometers are read in the same way as inch micrometers, except that the measurements are in millimeters. Each line on the main scale equals 1 mm. Each fifth line is stamped 5, 10, 15, and so on. Each line on the thimble scale equals 0.01 mm. It will take a little practice, but if you can read an inch mike, you can read a metric mike.

Inside and Outside Calipers

♦ See Figure 76

Inside and outside calipers are useful devices to have if you need to measure something quickly and precise measurement is not necessary. Simply take the reading and then hold the calipers on an accurate steel rule.

DIAL INDICATORS

A dial indicator is a gauge that utilizes a dial face and a needle to register measurements. There is a movable contact arm on the dial indicator. When the arms moves, the needle rotates on the dial. Dial indicators are calibrated to show readings in thousandths of an inch and typically, are used to measure end-play and runout on various parts of a snowmobile.

Dial indicators are quite easy to use, although they are relatively expensive. A variety of mounting devices are available so that the indicator can be used in a number of situations. Make certain that the contact arm is always parallel to the movement of the work being measured.

TELESCOPING GAUGES

A telescope gauge is used during rebuilding procedures (NOT usually basic maintenance) to measure the inside of bores. It can take the place of an inside mike for some of these jobs. Simply insert the gauge in the hole to be measured and lock the plungers after they have contacted the walls. Remove the tool and measure across the plungers with an outside micrometer.

DEPTH GAUGES

♦ See Figure 77

A depth gauge can be inserted into a bore or other small hole to determine exactly how deep it is. The most common use on maintenance items would be to check the depth of a rivet head (on riveted style brake pads). Some outside calipers contain a built-in depth gauge so money can be saved by just buying one tool.

Electric Power Tools

♦ See Figures 78 and 79

Power tools are most often associated with woodworking. However, there are a few which are very helpful in maintenance and repair.

The most common and most useful power tool is the bench grinder. If you get serious about maintenance and repair, then you will eventually want a grinder with a grinding stone on one side and a wire brush wheel on the other. The brush wheel is indispensable for cleaning parts and the stone can be used to remove rough surfaces and for reshaping, where necessary.

Almost as useful as the bench grinder is the drill. Drills can come in very handy when a stripped or broken fastener is encountered.

Power ratchets and impact wrenches can come in very handy. Power ratchets can save a lot of time and muscle when removing and installing long bolts or nuts on long studs, especially where there is little room to swing a manual ratchet. Impact wrenches can be invaluable especially with frozen bolts, screws with partially damaged heads or on spinning shafts, when it is difficult or impossible to hold the shaft. Let's be real for a second: will you actually need them for maintenance? probably not. But, when you finally do need them one day, BOY WILL YOU BE GLAD YOU HAD 'EM.

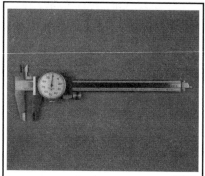

Fig. 76 Outside calipers are fast and easy ways to measure pads or rotors

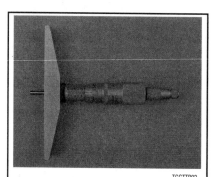

Fig. 77 Depth gauges, like this micrometer, can be used to measure the amount of pad remaining above a rivet

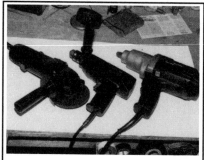

Fig. 78 Three types of common power tools. Left to right: a hand-held grinder, drill and impact wrench

Fig. 79 The bench grinder can be used to clean just about everything

➡One last thought before you buy any electric tools. If you plan on buying an air compressor (and there are many reasons why you should at least think about it), then you might save money on tools by purchasing air tools instead of electric. Shop around and compare prices to your needs, then make your decision.

Air Tools and Compressors

♦ See Figures 80 and 81

Air-powered tools are usually not necessary for simple maintenance procedures. They are, however, useful for speeding up many jobs and for general clean-up of parts. If you don't have air tools, and you want them, be prepared for an initial outlay of money.

The first thing you need is a compressor. Compressors are available in electrically driven and gas engine driven models. As long as you have electricity, you don't need a gas engine driven type.

The common shop-type air compressor is a pump mounted on a tank. The pump compresses air and forces it into the tank where it is stored until you need it. The compressor automatically turns the pump on when the air pressure in the tank falls below a certain preset level.

There are all kinds of air powered tools, including ratchets, impact wrenches, saws, drills, sprayers, nailers, scrapers, riveters, grinders and sanders. In general, air powered tools are usually cheaper than their electric counterparts (but be careful, there are some cheap electric tools available that might not last as long as comparably priced air tools).

When deciding what size compressor unit you need, you'll be driven by two factors: the Pounds per Square Inch (PSI) capacity of the unit and the deliver rate in Cubic Feet per Minute (CFM). For example, most air powered ratchets require 90 psi at 4 to 5 cfm to operate at peak efficiency. Grinders and saws may require up to 7 cfm at 90 psi. So, before buying the compressor unit, decide what types of tools you'll want so that you don't short-change yourself on the compressor purchase.

If you decide that a compressor and air tools isn't for you, you can have the benefit of air pressure rather cheaply. Purchase an air storage tank, available in sizes up to 20 gallons at most retail stores that sell auto products. These storage tanks can safely store air pressure up to 125 psi and come with a high pressure nozzle for cleaning things and an air chuck for filling car tires if necessary. The tank can be filled using the common tire-type air compressor, or even at the corner gas station (with their tire pressure hose).

Fig. 80 This compressor operates off ordinary house current and provides all the air pressure you'll need

Fig. 81 An air storage tank

FASTENERS, MEASUREMENTS AND CONVERSIONS

Bolts, Nuts and Other Threaded Retainers

♦ See Figures 82, 83, 84 and 85

Although there are a great variety of fasteners found in the modern snowmobile, the most commonly used retainer is the threaded fastener (nuts, bolts, screws, studs, etc). Most threaded retainers may be reused, provided that they are not damaged in use or during the repair. Some retainers (such as stretch bolts or torque prevailing nuts) are designed to deform when tightened or in use and should not be reinstalled.

Whenever possible, we will note any special retainers which should be replaced during a procedure. But you should always inspect the condition of a retainer when it is removed and you should replace any that show signs of damage. Check all threads for rust or corrosion which can increase the torque necessary to achieve the desired clamp load for which that fastener was originally selected. Additionally, be sure that the driver surface of the fastener has not been compromised by rounding or other damage. In some cases a driver surface may become only partially rounded, allowing the driver to catch in only one direction. In many of these occurrences, a fastener may be installed and tightened, but the driver would not be able to grip and loosen the fastener again. (This could lead to frustration down the line should that component ever need to be disassembled again).

If you must replace a fastener, whether due to design or damage, you must ALWAYS be sure to use the proper replacement. In all cases, a retainer of the same design, material and strength should be used. Markings on the heads of most bolts will help determine the proper strength of the fastener. The same material, thread and pitch must be selected to assure proper installation and safe operation of the vehicle afterwards.

Thread gauges are available to help measure a bolt or stud's thread. Most part or hardware stores keep gauges available to help you select the proper size. In a pinch, you can use another nut or bolt for a thread gauge. If the bolt you are replacing is not too badly damaged, you can select a match by finding another

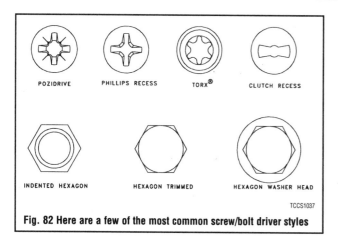

Fig. 82 Here are a few of the most common screw/bolt driver styles

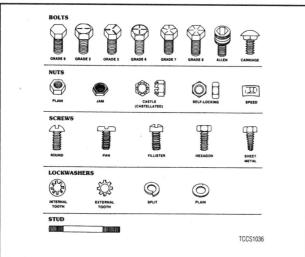

Fig. 83 There are many different types of threaded retainers found on snowmobiles

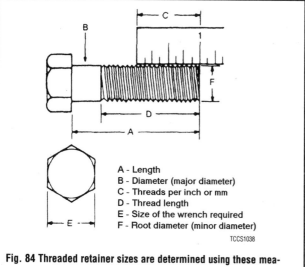

A - Length
B - Diameter (major diameter)
C - Threads per inch or mm
D - Thread length
E - Size of the wrench required
F - Root diameter (minor diameter)

Fig. 84 Threaded retainer sizes are determined using these measurements

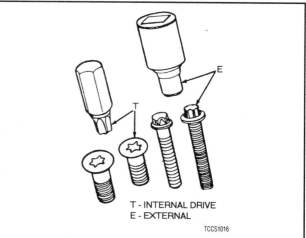

T - INTERNAL DRIVE
E - EXTERNAL

Fig. 85 Special fasteners such as these Torx® head bolts are used by manufacturers to discourage people from working on vehicles without the proper tools (and knowledge)

bolt which will thread in its place. If you find a nut which threads properly onto the damaged bolt, then use that nut to help select the replacement bolt. If however, the bolt you are replacing is so badly damaged (broken or drilled out) that its threads cannot be used as a gauge, you might start by looking for another bolt (from the same assembly or a similar location on your snowmobile) which will thread into the damaged bolt's mounting. If so, the other bolt can be used to select a nut; the nut can then be used to select the replacement bolt.

In all cases, be absolutely sure you have selected the proper replacement. Don't be shy, you can always ask the store clerk for help.

❋❋ WARNING

Be aware that when you find a bolt with damaged threads, you may also find the nut or drilled hole it was threaded into has also been damaged. If this is the case, you may have to drill and tap the hole, replace the nut or otherwise repair the threads. NEVER try to force a replacement bolt to fit into the damaged threads.

Torque

♦ See Figures 86 and 87

Torque is defined as the measurement of resistance to turning or rotating. It tends to twist a body about an axis of rotation. A common example of this would be tightening a threaded retainer such as a nut, bolt or screw. Measuring torque is one of the most common ways to help assure that a threaded retainer has been properly fastened.

When tightening a threaded fastener, torque is applied in three distinct areas, the head, the bearing surface and the clamp load. About 50 percent of the measured torque is used in overcoming bearing friction. This is the friction between the bearing surface of the bolt head, screw head or nut face and the base material or washer (the surface on which the fastener is rotating). Approximately 40 percent of the applied torque is used in overcoming thread friction. This leaves only about 10 percent of the applied torque to develop a useful clamp load (the force which holds a joint together). This means that friction can account for as much as 90 percent of the applied torque on a fastener.

Standard and Metric Measurements

♦ See Figure 88

Specifications are often used to help you determine the condition of various components on your snowmobile, or to assist you in their installation. Some of the most common measurements include length (in. or cm/mm), torque (ft. lbs., inch lbs. or Nm) and pressure (psi, in. Hg, kPa or mm Hg).

In some cases, that value may not be conveniently measured with what is available in your toolbox. Luckily, many of the measuring devices which are available today will have two scales so Standard or Metric measurements may easily be taken. If any of the various measuring tools which are available to you do not contain the same scale as listed in your snowmobile's specifications, use the accompanying conversion factors to determine the proper value.

The conversion factor chart is used by taking the given specification and multiplying it by the necessary conversion factor. For instance, looking at the first line, if you have a measurement in inches such as "free-play should be 2 in." but your ruler reads only in millimeters, multiply 2 in. by the conversion factor of 25.4 to get the metric equivalent of 50.8mm. Likewise, if the specification was given only in a Metric measurement, for example in Newton Meters (Nm), then look at the center column first. If the measurement is 100 Nm, multiply it by the conversion factor of 0.738 to get 73.8 ft. lbs.

	Mark	Class		Mark	Class
Hexagon head bolt	Bolt head No. 4 — 5 — 6 — 7 — 8 — 9 — 10 — 11 —	4T 5T 6T 7T 8T 9T 10T 11T	Stud bolt	No mark 	4T
	No mark	4T			
Hexagon flange bolt w/ washer hexagon bolt	No mark	4T		Grooved	6T
Hexagon head bolt	Two protruding lines	5T			
Hexagon flange bolt w/ washer hexagon bolt	Two protruding lines	6T	Welded bolt	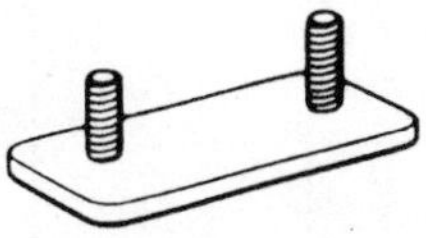	4T
Hexagon head bolt	Three protruding lines	7T			
Hexagon head bolt	Four protruding lines	8T			

TCCS1240

Fig. 86 Determining bolt strength of metric fasteners—NOTE: this is a typical bolt marking system, but there is no worldwide standard

Class	Diameter mm	Pitch mm	Specified torque					
			Hexagon head bolt			Hexagon flange bolt		
			N·m	kgf·cm	ft·lbf	N·m	kgf·cm	ft·lbf
4T	6	1	5	55	48 in.·lbf	6	60	52 in.·lbf
	8	1.25	12.5	130	9	14	145	10
	10	1.25	26	260	19	29	290	21
	12	1.25	47	480	35	53	540	39
	14	1.5	74	760	55	84	850	61
	16	1.5	115	1,150	83	—	—	—
5T	6	1	6.5	65	56 in.·lbf	7.5	75	65 in.·lbf
	8	1.25	15.5	160	12	17.5	175	13
	10	1.25	32	330	24	36	360	26
	12	1.25	59	600	43	65	670	48
	14	1.5	91	930	67	100	1,050	76
	16	1.5	140	1,400	101	—	—	—
6T	6	1	8	80	69 in.·lbf	9	90	78 in.·lbf
	8	1.25	19	195	14	21	210	15
	10	1.25	39	400	29	44	440	32
	12	1.25	71	730	53	80	810	59
	14	1.5	110	1,100	80	125	1,250	90
	16	1.5	170	1,750	127	—	—	—
7T	6	1	10.5	110	8	12	120	9
	8	1.25	25	260	19	28	290	21
	10	1.25	52	530	38	58	590	43
	12	1.25	95	970	70	105	1,050	76
	14	1.5	145	1,500	108	165	1,700	123
	16	1.5	230	2,300	166	—	—	—
8T	8	1.25	29	300	22	33	330	24
	10	1.25	61	620	45	68	690	50
	12	1.25	110	1,100	80	120	1,250	90
9T	8	1.25	34	340	25	37	380	27
	10	1.25	70	710	51	78	790	57
	12	1.25	125	1,300	94	140	1,450	105
10T	8	1.25	38	390	28	42	430	31
	10	1.25	78	800	58	88	890	64
	12	1.25	140	1,450	105	155	1,600	116
11T	8	1.25	42	430	31	47	480	35
	10	1.25	87	890	64	97	990	72
	12	1.25	155	1,600	116	175	1,800	130

TCCS1241

Fig. 87 Typical bolt torques for metric fasteners—WARNING: use only as a guide

CONVERSION FACTORS

LENGTH–DISTANCE

Inches (in.)	x 25.4	= Millimeters (mm)	x .0394	= Inches
Feet (ft.)	x .305	= Meters (m)	x 3.281	= Feet
Miles	x 1.609	= Kilometers (km)	x .0621	= Miles

VOLUME

Cubic Inches (in3)	x 16.387	= Cubic Centimeters	x .061	= in3
IMP Pints (IMP pt.)	x .568	= Liters (L)	x 1.76	= IMP pt.
IMP Quarts (IMP qt.)	x 1.137	= Liters (L)	x .88	= IMP qt.
IMP Gallons (IMP gal.)	x 4.546	= Liters (L)	x .22	= IMP gal.
IMP Quarts (IMP qt.)	x 1.201	= US Quarts (US qt.)	x .833	= IMP qt.
IMP Gallons (IMP gal.)	x 1.201	= US Gallons (US gal.)	x .833	= IMP gal.
Fl. Ounces	x 29.573	= Milliliters	x .034	= Ounces
US Pints (US pt.)	x .473	= Liters (L)	x 2.113	= Pints
US Quarts (US qt.)	x .946	= Liters (L)	x 1.057	= Quarts
US Gallons (US gal.)	x 3.785	= Liters (L)	x .264	= Gallons

MASS–WEIGHT

Ounces (oz.)	x 28.35	= Grams (g)	x .035	= Ounces
Pounds (lb.)	x .454	= Kilograms (kg)	x 2.205	= Pounds

PRESSURE

Pounds Per Sq. In. (psi)	x 6.895	= Kilopascals (kPa)	x .145	= psi
Inches of Mercury (Hg)	x .4912	= psi	x 2.036	= Hg
Inches of Mercury (Hg)	x 3.377	= Kilopascals (kPa)	x .2961	= Hg
Inches of Water (H_2O)	x .07355	= Inches of Mercury	x 13.783	= H_2O
Inches of Water (H_2O)	x .03613	= psi	x 27.684	= H_2O
Inches of Water (H_2O)	x .248	= Kilopascals (kPa)	x 4.026	= H_2O

TORQUE

Pounds–Force Inches (in–lb)	x .113	= Newton Meters (N·m)	x 8.85	= in–lb
Pounds–Force Feet (ft–lb)	x 1.356	= Newton Meters (N·m)	x .738	= ft–lb

VELOCITY

Miles Per Hour (MPH)	x 1.609	= Kilometers Per Hour (KPH)	x .621	= MPH

POWER

Horsepower (Hp)	x .745	= Kilowatts	x 1.34	= Horsepower

FUEL CONSUMPTION*

Miles Per Gallon IMP (MPG)	x .354	= Kilometers Per Liter (Km/L)
Kilometers Per Liter (Km/L)	x 2.352	= IMP MPG
Miles Per Gallon US (MPG)	x .425	= Kilometers Per Liter (Km/L)
Kilometers Per Liter (Km/L)	x 2.352	= US MPG

*It is common to covert from miles per gallon (mpg) to liters/100 kilometers (1/100 km), where mpg (IMP) x 1/100 km = 282 and mpg (US) x 1/100 km = 235.

TEMPERATURE

Degree Fahrenheit (°F)	= (°C x 1.8) + 32
Degree Celsius (°C)	= (°F – 32) x .56

TCCS1044

Fig. 88 Standard and metric conversion factors chart

Service Record

Date/Mileage	Service	Next Due

90991G01

Service Record

Date/Mileage	Service	Next Due

90991G01

Service Record

Date/Mileage	Service	Next Due

90991G01

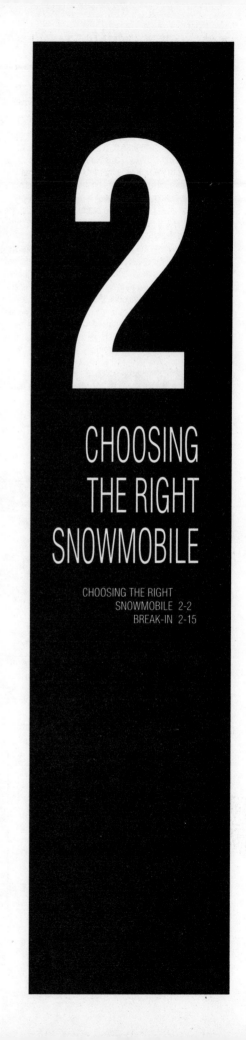

2

CHOOSING THE RIGHT SNOWMOBILE

CHOOSING THE RIGHT SNOWMOBILE

When it comes to buying a car or a house, there are literally volumes of material written about the best way make an educated, practical purchase. But for the potential snowmobile buyer, much less is available.

Dropping a big chunk of hard-earned money for a snowmobile can be a bit scary, especially if you hit the trail for the first time and find it performs nothing like you expected. Hopefully, this book will help you avoid this problem by discussing your options as a potential snowmobile owner.

Try to look ahead to the future before making a purchase. Will your snowmobile be the one that you wanted a couple of years from now? Is the overall design and /or features of your snowmobile going to benefit you, or leave you disappointed with its performance? It's important to consider all the possibilities. Weigh out your options very carefully. You might have to look around a little more than you want to, but you'll be glad to have the snowmobile of your dreams when everything is over. Otherwise, you may spend all of our hard earned money on a snowmobile that some salesman convinced you into buying, and find out later that it's not even close to what you wanted. NEVER let someone tell you what YOU want or need. Gather as much information as possible about a snowmobile that interests you, so you can make an educated decision and decide if its really the snowmobile that you really want.

Purpose

Over the years, snowmobiles have grown tremendously in popularity, and manufacturers have begun producing snowmobiles for specific purposes. As a potential buyer, this increases your options, and will allow you to find a snowmobile that suits your specific needs.

91242P23

Comparing the sled on the right with the dinosaur on the left gives a clear indication of how much snowmobiles have evolved in recent years

The diversity of today's snowmobiles have allowed them to become more specialized, allowing superior performance for their designed use. Usually, you'll have to make a compromise somewhere on a potential snowmobile to get the features that you desire.

The most important question you have to ask before buying a snowmobile is simple—What do you intend to use it for? snowmobiles can be anything from weekend toys to work horses or even search and rescue vehicles. The non-riding public often doesn't realize the variety of snowmobiles that are available. Manufacturers have been responding to customer demands and providing "crossover" models that provide elements from both camps.

Snowmobiles can be roughly grouped into four categories: Trail/Sport, Luxury/Touring, Powder/Mountain, and Utility. But, there is a degree of crossover within these categories. It is not important to decide whether a snowmobile's use defines its style or if its style defines its use. Just recognize that some snowmobiles are designed to do a particular job better than others, and one or more types may best suit your needs.

Once you've decided on how you'll be spending most of your time with your snowmobile, your choices may dwindle to a few particular models. The main thing to consider when deciding on a particular model or type is its PRIMARY use. Let's take a look at the different types of sleds to give you some ideas.

TRAIL/SPORT

▶ **See Figures 1 thru 56**

The vast majority of snowmobiles fall under this category. The average snowmobile enthusiast owns a sled of the trail/sport variety, whether it's a race-bred snowcross rocket or an all-around trail performer. Manufacturers offer sport-oriented trail sleds of different performance levels to suit your particular interest.

If you live in the northeastern states, a trail/sport snowmobile might be best suited to the climate. Most snowmobile riding areas in the northeastern states and eastern Canada have groomed, marked trails, which take the risk out of riding in unknown areas, where you have no idea what lies beneath the snow.

As with the "boy racer" set of any type of motorsports, the power and speed-hungry thrill-seekers will undoubtedly seek the biggest, fastest sled they can afford. As with motorcycles and ATVs, high-performance snowmobiles don't usually make a good first-time sled; the huge amount of power available can be dangerous to a novice rider. If you are interested in a high-performance model, you should seriously consider a smaller-displacement sled that will allow you to get acquainted with snowmobiles and their general handling characteristics before you jump onto a fire-breathing lake racer. You can always upgrade or trade in your sled when you feel the need for more power.

91242PPA

Fig. 1 With its three cylinder engine and triple exhaust, the Indy 800 XCR is a serious trail performer

91242PYV

Fig. 2 Yamaha's economical entry-level sled, the Ovation LE

91242PTD

Fig. 3 Get the whole family in on the fun with the Ski-Doo Mini Z, a great sled for the little folks

91242PPZ

Fig. 4 An excellent entry-level sled, the Polaris Indy 340 Deluxe

91242PBB

Fig. 5 When it comes to sleds in the trail sport category, the ZL 600 from Arctic Cat is a serious contender

91242PYJ

Fig. 6 The Yamaha Phazer 500 combines the economy and simplicity of an air-cooled engine with Vmax handling and style

91242PPY

Fig. 7 The simple yet sporty Indy Super Sport from Polaris features a 544cc air-cooled twin and 15" wide track

91242PBH

Fig. 8 With 115 track-churning horsepower and long-travel suspension, the ZR 700 from Arctic Cat will leave the others behind

91242PPT

Fig. 9 The Polaris Indy 700 XC Deluxe 45th Anniversary Edition

91242PSP

Fig. 10 Push-button reverse and electric start make the Ski-Doo Formula Deluxe an excellent all-around sled

91242PPW

Fig. 11 The Polaris Indy Triumph features a 600cc liquid-cooled engine and flat-slide carburetors, making it a true trail performance model

91242PPX

Fig. 12 Polaris' long-running sport trail sled, the Indy 500

91242PBG

Fig. 13 The Arctic Cat ZR 600 EFI was named Snowmobile of the Year by Snow-Goer Magazine

91242PYK

Fig. 14 The Yamaha Vmax 700 features liquid-heated flat-slide carburetors for excellent throttle response

91242PPU

Fig. 15 Polaris' Indy 600 XC Deluxe 45th Anniversary Edition features electric start and extra-large fuel tank for long days on the trail

91242PST

Fig. 16 The Ski-Doo Formula S is a fun, entry level model that will provide plenty of good times at a low price

91242PBD

Fig. 17 The ZR 500 from Arctic Cat offers serious trail performance

91242PPE

Fig. 18 The Polaris Indy 500 XC is an excellent trail performance sled 500 XC

91242PYM

Fig. 19 With a hydraulic brake, 42" ski stance, and 11.5" of rear suspension travel, the Yamaha Vmax 600 is ready for action

91242PAE

Fig. 20 Arctic Cat's Jag 340 offers styling and features of high-performance sleds at an entry-level price

91242PPV

Fig. 21 The Indy 500 Classic from Polaris features composite skis and reverse

91242PSN

Fig. 22 For those who love performance as much as comfort, Ski-Doo offers the Formula Deluxe 670

91242PAZ

Fig. 23 The ZL 500 is one of Arctic Cat's most versatile trail sport models

91242PPD

Fig. 24 Polaris' Indy 500 XC SP 45th Anniversary Edition

91242PSA

Fig. 25 Ski-Doo's Mach Z is designed for the ultimate in straight-line performance

91242PYE

Fig. 26 Like its bigger brothers, the Yamaha Vmax 500 SX is equipped with a ventilated hydraulic disc and Pro Action Plus suspension

91242PPC

Fig. 27 The Polaris Indy 600 XC SP

91242PSS

Fig. 28 When it comes to value, the Formula SL from Ski-Doo is hard to beat with its SC-10 rear suspension and 497cc air-cooled engine

91242PBE

Fig. 29 Arctic Cat also offers fuel injection on its trail-carving ZR 500

91242PSR

Fig. 30 The Formula Z 670 from Ski-Doo provides comfort for long days on the trails, yet still provides plenty of performance

91242PYF

Fig. 31 The Yamaha Vmax 700 Deluxe offers standard features such as electric start and reverse, while still providing sporty performance

91242PAY

Fig. 32 The Arctic Cat ZL 440 has features of larger ZL series sleds, only with a reliable 436cc liquid-cooled engine

91242PSE

Fig. 33 The Formula III 700 from Ski-Doo puts 699cc of pure power to the snow with its SC-10 high-performance suspension package

91242PYH

Fig. 34 Yamaha's versatile Vmax 500 Deluxe

91242PSK

Fig. 35 If you're seeking racy looks and razor-sharp handling on a tight budget, check out Ski-Doo's MXZ 440

91242PAG

Fig. 36 Arctic Cat doesn't want the little folks to miss out on the fun, so they offer the junior-sized Kitty Kat

91242PYB

Fig. 37 The Yamaha SRX 600 has plenty of power with its 598cc liquid-cooled triple cylinder engine

91242PPB

Fig. 38 SnoGoer's 1999 Sled of the year, the Polaris Indy 700 XC SP

91242PSG

Fig. 39 The MXZ 670 from Ski-Doo sets the standard for performance with a 669cc High-Output engine

91242PAF

Fig. 40 Like the Jag 340, the Jag 440 from Arctic Cat features 13.5'' of rear suspension travel and sleek styling, but with a larger engine

91242PYA

Fig. 41 Yamaha's flagship of the performance lineup, the SRX 700

91242PAX

Fig. 42 The Z 440 from Arctic Cat comes equipped with dual carbs and race-bred suspension for tearing up the trails

91242PSC

Fig. 43 Equipped with lightweight plastic skis and high-performance suspension, the Mach 1 from Ski-Doo is ready for action

91242PSF

Fig. 44 Ski Doo's Formula 600 is equipped with triple expansion chambers and variable exhaust ports for heavy-duty performance

91242PBF

Fig. 45 Arctic Cat's ZR 600 features a hydraulic disc brake and 13.5'' of rear suspension travel for heavy-duty trail action

91242PYG

Fig. 46 Yamaha combines convenience and performance with their Vmax 600 Deluxe

91242PAT

Fig. 47 Arctic Cat's Thundercat is the heavyweight contender of the high-performance lineup with its triple-cylinder 1000cc engine

91242PSH

Fig. 48 The Ski-Doo MXZ 600 was named "Best Rendition of a New Model" by Snowtech Magazine

91242PAW

Fig. 49 The Arctic Cat Z 370 offers racy styling and competition suspension at a budget-minded price

91242PBA

Fig. 50 For those who prefer fuel injection, Arctic Cat also offers the ZL 500 EFI

91242PYC

Fig. 51 The Yamaha Vmax 700 SX combines excellent trail manners with race-bred performance

91242PBJ

Fig. 52 The Arctic Cat ZRT 600 is equipped with a triple-cylinder 594cc engine and triple expansion chambers

91242PSJ

Fig. 53 The MXZ 500 from Ski-Doo sports a torque-boosting Rotax Adjustable Variable Exhaust (RAVE) system

91242PBK

Fig. 54 Producing 150 horsepower from its 794cc triple-cylinder engine, the Arctic Cat ZRT 800 is practically unbeatable on the trail

91242PYD

Fig. 55 The Vmax 600 SX is an excellent trail performance sled from Yamaha

91242PBC

Fig. 56 The ZL 600 EFI offers the same features of Arctic Cat's sporty ZR lineup, but with a smoother suspension

LUXURY/TOURING

♦ **See Figures 57 thru 73**

If your interested in long-distance riding, a luxury or touring sled might be up your alley. With plush suspension systems, two-up seating, and creature comforts like heated handgrips and passenger footrests, these type of sleds are great for a relaxing, scenic ride with a partner.

Touring sleds typically come equipped with such features as electric start, reverse, heated grips, and extra-large windshields, to make the snowmobiling experience relaxing and convenient. Keep in mind that touring sleds loaded down with all kinds of options and accessories will be considerably heavier than a nimble, sport-oriented trail-blazer.

Even if you don't plan to do a lot of two-up riding, a touring sled might still be a good choice if you're looking for a comfortable, plush ride. Sport-oriented trail sleds are designed for riders looking for maximum handling and performance; comfort is a low priority on the list. When it comes to touring sleds, the opposite holds true; rider comfort is most important. While a touring sled might not be able to "slice and dice" like a sport sled, it will offer a relaxing, smooth ride, allowing you to focus on the breathtaking scenery along the trails.

91242PPF

Fig. 57 The Polaris Indy 600 Touring features variable exhaust ports

91242PYP

Fig. 58 The Yamaha Venture XL offers long-distance convenience and comfort for two at an affordable price

91242PTE

Fig. 59 The Touring E is Ski-Doo's entry-level two-up model

91242PAH

Fig. 60 For two-up riding comfort, the Pantera 580 from Arctic Cat is an excellent choice for long-distance touring

91242PPG

Fig. 61 The Indy Classic Touring is a long-running two-up sled from Polaris

91242PYQ

Fig. 62 The father of the Yamaha touring series, the Venture 700

91242PAN

Fig. 63 The Panther 550 touring sled from Arctic Cat comes standard with a fully adjustable backrest, and passenger hand warmers

91242PYR

Fig. 64 Equipped with extra-large fuel and oil tanks, the Yamaha Venture 500 is ready for cross-country cruising for two

91242PSU

Fig. 65 The flagship of the touring lineup from Ski-Doo, the Grand Touring SE

91242PAK

Fig. 66 Arctic Cat's Panther 340 is an excellent contender in the entry level touring sled market

91242PSV

Fig. 67 The Touring SLE from Ski-Doo offers a dependable air-cooled twin cylinder engine, electric start, and passenger footrests

91242PAJ

Fig. 68 The big daddy of Arctic Cat's touring sled lineup, the Pantera 800, can hold its own against high-performance sleds, while still offering comfort and luxury

91242PSW

Fig. 69 Ski-Doo's economical Touring LE offers two-up features for an affordable price

91242PAM

Fig. 70 Convenience items like electric start and reverse make the Panther 440 from Arctic Cat a great choice for trouble-free touring

Fig. 71 Polaris also offers air-cooled engines in their touring sleds, like this Indy Trail Touring 550 model

Fig. 72 Arctic Cat's Triple Touring 600 features the sporty engine of the ZRT series, with a two-up touring chassis

Fig. 73 Polaris' Sport Touring 550

POWDER/MOUNTAIN

▶ See Figures 74 thru 88

The thrill and of riding a snowmobile in deep powder high upon a mountain top is something that snowmobile enthusiasts of the northwestern states and western Canada experience on a regular basis. Even if you live or plan to ride in a remote area where marked, groomed trails are few and far between, a mountain sled might be a logical choice.

The technique of riding in deep powder is much different than riding on groomed trails, and subsequently requires a different type of sled to cope with the demands of riding in deep snow.

Another feature of mountain snowmobiles is a narrow ski stance. The main reason for the need for a narrow ski stance is the ability to "sidehill" or travel across the side of a mountain at an angle. With a trail sled, the wider ski stance makes sidehilling more difficult. Also, the skis are a bit wider for better flotation on the snow.

A mountain snowmobile has several features to allow for deep-snow riding. One of the most distinguishable features of a mountain sled is the extra-long, extra-wide, deep-lug track. The reason why the track is so much longer and wider than the average trail sled is to allow for floatation in deep snow. Since powder is loose, the extra-deep lugs are needed to propel the sled. A trail sled with a shallow track will have a hard time with traction, since the lugs are not as deep.

Fig. 74 The Indy 800 RMK from Polaris is the ultimate in mountain performance

Fig. 75 The Yamaha Phazer Mountain Lite

Fig. 76 With its altitude-compensating fuel injection and 105 horsepower engine, the Powder Special 600 EFI from Arctic Cat effortlessly tackles the tallest mountains

Fig. 77 The Polaris Indy 700 RMK features extra bars on the handlebars for mountain riding

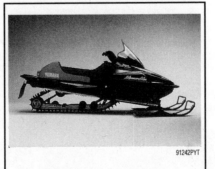

Fig. 78 The Yamaha Mountain Max 700 is sure to set the highmark with its 698cc triple cylinder liquid-cooled engine

Fig. 79 The mountain-conquering Summit X 670 from Ski-Doo

91242PAP

Fig. 80 The Powder Special 500 EFI from Arctic Cat is well-suited for mountain riding with its deep-lug track and fuel injection

91242PYU

Fig. 81 The Yamaha Mountain Max 600 boasts a heady power-to-weight ratio for serious powder-carving action

91242PPP

Fig. 82 SnoWest magazine named the Polaris Indy 600 RMK Mountain Sled of the Year in 1999

91242PAQ

Fig. 83 Arctic Cat's 600cc Powder Special is ready to carve up the side of a mountain with its 37" ski stance and extra deep-lug track

91242PAS

Fig. 84 The Powder Special 700 from Arctic Cat has plenty of muscle to climb the mountain tops with ease

91242PPQ

Fig. 85 The Polaris Indy 500 RMK is ready to tackle the mountains with its offset skis and 1.5" deep-lug track

91242PPR

Fig. 86 The Polaris Indy Trail RMK features an air-cooled engine for reliable operation in remote areas

91242PAU

Fig. 87 With a whopping 172 horsepower, the Thundercat Mountain Cat will make mincemeat of the tallest mountains

91242PPS

Fig. 88 The Indy 700 SKS from Polaris

UTILITY

▶ See Figures 89 thru 101

Utility sleds are the perfect winter companion for accessing that remote winter cabin, hauling a load of firewood on a trailer, or even carrying that prize-winning buck back to your vehicle.

Typically, utility snowmobiles are equipped with towing hitches and dual-range chaincases for hauling purposes. Also, since utility sleds tend to be used in remote locations, they are equipped with large capacity fuel tanks, and wide, long tracks to cope with varying degrees of snow conditions.

In the far north, snowmobiles actually can become the main source for transportation in the heavy winter months, when cars and trucks are rendered useless from deep snow and ice.

91242PPK

Fig. 89 The Widetrak LX is the only utility model from Polaris' lineup

91242PSX

Fig. 90 The Skandic WT LC from Ski-Doo is a hard worker with room for two

91242PYN

Fig. 91 Yamaha's workhorse sled, the VK 540 III, is equipped with a wide 20" track and dual-range chaincase

91242PSZ

Fig. 92 The Skandic WT is an excellent example from Ski-Doo's utility lineup

91242PAA

Fig. 93 Arctic Cat's Bearcat 340, with its air-cooled twin engine, and heavy-duty 136" track is a solid choice for a utility sled

91242PAC

Fig. 94 The Bearcat 440 II from Arctic Cat is equipped with dual carburetors and a 15" x 136" track for extra pulling power

91242PTA

Fig. 95 The Ski-Doo Skandic 500 plays as hard as it works

91242PSY

Fig. 96 With its huge 24 x 156" track, the Skandic SWT from Ski-Doo offers the widest track in the industry

91242PYW

Fig. 97 Yamaha's bare-bones utility model sled, the Bravo LT

91242PTB

Fig. 98 Working hard and keeping costs down is what the Skandic 380 from Ski-Doo does best

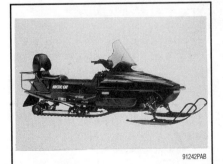

91242PAB

Fig. 99 Equipped with a trailer hitch and cargo rack, the Bearcat 440 I from Arctic Cat is ready to work

91242PTC

Fig. 100 The long-running Tundra Model from Ski-Doo is an excellent low-cost utility model

91242PAD

Fig. 101 With its monstrous 20" x 156" track, 550cc engine, and 15 gallon fuel tank, the Arctic Cat Bearcat WT is one serious workhorse

Engines

When it comes to snowmobiles, 99.9 percent use two-stroke engines. A two-stroke engine can produce substantial power for its size and weight, (and everyone who is interested in speed knows about weight, right?) which makes it perfectly suited for a snowmobile. A two-stroke engine is similar to a four-stroke (most all cars and trucks use four-stroke engines) with the exception of a valve train. A two-stroke engine doesn't use valves to control the air and fuel mixture entering and exiting the engine. There are holes, called ports, cut into the cylinder which allow for entry and exit of the fuel mixture. A two-stroke engine also fires on every second stroke of the piston, which is the primary reason why so much more power is produced than a four-stroke (given equal displacement).

Because of the design of the two-stroke engine, lubrication of the piston and cylinder walls must be delivered by the fuel passing through the engine. Since gasoline doesn't make a good lubricant, oil must be added to the fuel and air mixture. The trick here is to add just enough oil to the fuel to provide lubrication. If too much oil is added to the fuel, the spark plugs can become "fouled" because of the excessive oil within the combustion chambers. If there is not enough oil present with the air/fuel mixture, the pistons can "seize" within the cylinders. When seizure occurs, the piston rings will weld themselves to the cylinder (from extreme heat), or the piston will turn to liquid and eventually disintegrate within the cylinder.

Most snowmobiles built today utilize an oil injection system that automatically mixes the proper amount of oil with the fuel as it enters the engine, although some snowmobiles might require that the fuel and oil be mixed before being poured into the fuel tank. This is known as "pre-mixing" the fuel. For the ease of refueling, oil injection is the way to go.

DISPLACEMENT

▶ **See Figure 102**

Depending on what type of sled you plan to purchase, engine displacement, number of cylinders, and horsepower ratings can vary a great degree.

For the performance-minded, the choice seems obvious: Bigger Is Better. "The bigger the engine, the faster I'll go, right?" Well, to a point. The most important aspect of a vehicle's performance is not horsepower, but the power-to-weight ratio. For example, If you have a 170 horsepower 1000cc triple cylinder engine stuffed into a sled with a hefty weight of 650 pounds, it might not be as quick and nimble as a lightweight aluminum and plastic snowcross race sled with a 500cc twin cylinder engine. If you're not concerned with handling, and going for maximum horsepower, a large-displacement triple is probably your best choice. Performance riders seeking "tossability" and quick handling will

probably want to look toward a 500-700cc twin that offers a large amount of power for its weight.

If you're looking into a two-up sled for you and a partner, an engine of a fairly large displacement will probably be best suited for the rigors of cross-country touring. Since there's twice as many riders aboard, the engine will have to work harder to propel the weight of the snowmobile, and the weight of two people. Touring sleds with smaller displacement engines might not have the "get-up-and-go" of the heavyweights, but they will provide adequate performance, along with good fuel economy.

When it comes to utility sleds, a large displacement engine is nice, but not necessary. Since the majority of utility snowmobiles have dual-range chain-cases, the ability to pull a heavy load is increased through the lower gearing, making big engines like a fuel-sucking 1000cc triple unnecessary. In addition to load-hauling ability, utility snowmobiles need to be fuel-efficient. Most utility snowmobiles are equipped with medium-sized engines designed for low-range grunt and maximum fuel efficiency.

FORCED AIR-COOLING

▶ **See Figure 103**

If you are seeking reliability and simplicity, a forced air-cooled (also known as fan-cooled) engine is worthy of consideration. The only moving component of a forced air-cooled system is the fan, which is typically driven from the crankshaft with a belt.

Because of the simplicity and ease-of-maintenance, forced air-cooled engines are a good choice for utility and touring sleds. Even some sport-oriented sleds come equipped with forced air-cooled engines to help cut down on weight. Since forced air-cooled sleds do not need to be equipped with heat exchangers, plumbing, a pump, and coolant like liquid-cooled models, they are much lighter in weight, making the sled lighter and easier to maneuver, not to mention less complicated and easier to maintain.

Typically, the only maintenance required for a forced air-cooled engine is adjustment (and periodic replacement) of the fan belt. This can be a benefit when riding in remote locations, since the need for coolant is unnecessary, and the possibility of a hose bursting or damaging a heat exchanger are eliminated. As with any piece of machinery, the fewer moving parts, the less likely a problem will occur (in most cases).

One drawback of a forced air-cooled engine is that they are typically louder than their liquid-cooled counterparts. The combustion process in the cylinders cause the cooling fins on the cylinder(s) and cylinder head(s) to vibrate, (similar to the action of a tuning fork, or a vibrating rubber band) which magnifies the noise level of the engine.

91244P09

Fig. 102 A 1000cc liquid-cooled triple cylinder engine may be quite powerful, but it's also heavier, which affects handling

91242P08

Fig. 103 Air-cooled engines are simple and reliable

LIQUID COOLING

▶ **See Figure 104**

Years ago, a liquid-cooled snowmobile was considered a novelty, and viewed as unnecessary and overly complex. Over the years, though, manufacturers began to realize the benefits of liquid cooling and began to offer snowmobiles with liquid-cooled engines. Today, the majority of snowmobiles (performance and otherwise) are liquid-cooled.

If you are a seeking a snowmobile with a powerful, high-performance engine, consider one with liquid cooling. The power output of a liquid-cooled engine of given displacement is typically higher than that of an air-cooled unit. This is because of the superior cooling capabilities of liquid cooling. Since a liquid-cooled engine operates at a lower temperature, its power output can be increased without the fear of overheating. Because of this efficiency, and the ability to produce more power, liquid cooling is typically found on high-performance snowmobiles, but also can be found on many touring and utility sleds as well.

Even though liquid cooling requires a sizable list of components, it is fairly reliable and trouble-free. Periodic checking and changing of the coolant is necessary, along with water pump belt maintenance (some models) and the need to replace the coolant hoses every few years.

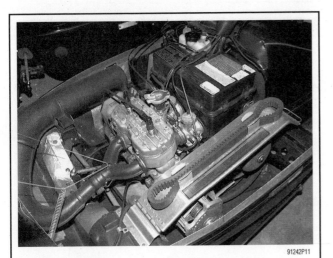

Fig. 104 Liquid cooling provides even cylinder temperatures and quieter operation

FUEL INJECTION

Since two-stroke engines discharge approximately one fourth of their fuel unburned, they have come under close scrutiny by environmentalists. Personal watercraft and small outboard two-stroke engines are the current whipping post, and snowmobiles are not far behind. The State of California has tightened its grip on two-stroke boat engines and motorcycles, and has banned the sale of certain models. Other states are quickly adopting these laws.

Most of today's snowmobiles are equipped with carburetors. But, because of the increased focus and concern for the environment, some snowmobile manufacturers are offering electronically fuel-injected engines as an option on some models. Overall, fuel injection is much more efficient (providing cleaner exhaust emissions) than carburetion, but is more complex, and is not easily serviced without special tools. Fuel injection is however, typically reliable and trouble free, and (in most cases) automatically compensates for changes in altitude and weather conditions. If you are in the market for a mountain or powder sled, or plan to ride in altitude-changing terrain, fuel injection might be worth consideration. Long-distance riders can also benefit from fuel injection, because of increased fuel efficiency.

Features

▶ **See Figures 105, 106, 107, 108 and 109**

The features of a potential snowmobile, as with purpose, will have to do mostly with its intend to use. For example, a snowcross racer has little use for a reverse gear or passenger backrest. And on the opposite side of the spectrum, someone interested in cross-country touring has little interest in a high-performance trail shredder (unless you are fortunate enough to afford both!).

Typically, the features found on most sleds compliment their intended use. For instance, a two-up touring sled will come "loaded" with features like electric start, reverse, ultra-plush suspension, and adjustable passenger backrests. A high-zoot trail-performance model might come with individual expansion chambers for each cylinder, long-travel suspension, and a low-cut windshield. Mountain sleds usually are equipped with deep-lug tracks and extra wide skis to cope with riding in deep powder. For the most part, these type of features usually "come with the territory" when you buy a particular sled, since it is built for a specialized purpose.

There are some cases, though, where a particular feature of one snowmobile might not be available might not be available on another. In this case, always find out if the manufacturer offers these features separately; you might find out that just because a manufacturer does not sell a snowmobile with a particular feature, doesn't mean it is not available as an option. A large percentage of trail sleds have optional electric start, reverse, plastic skis, or even rear view mirrors. The snowmobile manufacturers also offer extensive catalogs of optional equipment and accessories that can be added onto your potential snowmobile before or after you make the purchase.

If there's a particular sled that has been catching your eye in the showroom, but it's financially out of your reach, consider buying the "next model down" that doesn't come equipped with everything you want. Items like plastic skis, heated hand grips, electric fuel gauges, and low-oil lights are common factory and aftermarket accessories that can be added to your snowmobile later when your financial situation settles down. Your sled can ALWAYS be upgraded later on if you can't afford it now.

Fig. 105 Suspension systems, both front . . .

Fig. 106 . . . and rear, have improved dramatically in recent years on all types of snowmobiles

Fig. 109 . . . or even trailers are add-on features and accessories that are available for most snowmobiles

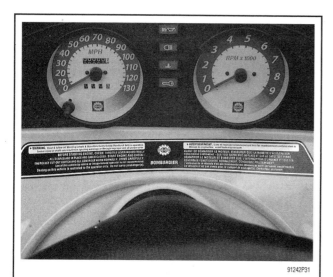

Fig. 107 Items like tachometers . . .

Other Options

Manufacturers are constantly meeting the consumer demands within the snowmobile market and offering more models and options. This ultimately will allow you find a snowmobile to specifically suit YOUR purpose. Various little features and gadgets can be useful, and even fun, but can complicate and weigh down your snowmobile, as well as jack up the price tag. Items like passenger backrests, reverse, and heated grips may or may not be of interest to you, depending on what kind of riding you intend to do. Decide if it's worth your money to have these features, and if you really need them for your purpose. Investigate these features for yourself and decide on their usefulness and practicality.

Keep referring back to that primary question: "how am I going to use this snowmobile?" You'll easily be able to eliminate a lot of choices and features with this question. Weigh out everything carefully, and make an educated decision. By now, you probably noticed that snowmobiles are not exactly cheap, either. Whatever you do, don't let a salesman talk you into a model that doesn't interest you.

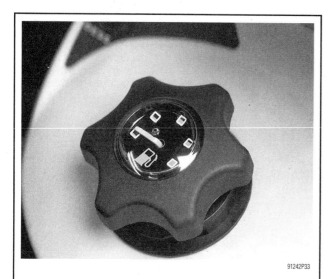

Fig. 108 . . . fuel gauges . . .

New snowmobiles, still in their shipping crates waiting for somebody to take them home

BREAK-IN

The biggest problem with breaking in a new snowmobile, (or any internal combustion engine) is that, well, everyone has his or her own opinion. And everyone claims to back it up. Maybe some people even have some data to back it up. This is another one of those items that you are really going to have to decide for yourself.

Warranty

The first, and most important thing to consider when deciding how to break-in a snowmobile is the manufacturer's warranty. The bottom line is that the manufacturer has spent a lot of money on engineering and it was probably those engineers who recommended the break-in conditions for their snowmobile. Also, a manufacturer has a lot in stake in the way of reputation, so they would never steer you wrong, would they?

We would also have to assume that a manufacturer is also driven by factors including costs. They would typically recommend something that will not affect their bottom line (meaning will not cost them anything). But most manufacturers only offer a base warranty of 12 months. Consider the fact that the vast majority of snowmobile riders do NOT place mileage on their machines that would be anywhere close to the 10,000–15,000 mile (16,000–24,000 km) per year average of the automobile driver. That would mean that by the time a machine has 10,000 miles on it, it is usually out of warranty. Many reputable engine builders would tell you that an engine really isn't broken-in until is has at least 10k miles (16k km) on the clock.

So what are you to do? You don't really think that we are going to recommend you ignore your manufacturer's recommendations for break-in, DO YOU? Of course not, you might void the warranty. If you plan on utilizing that warranty, it is extremely important that you follow the recommendations, ESPECIALLY when it comes fluid changes.

The same would be true for an engine rebuild. If the rebuilder provides as warranty, then you should follow their instructions. At least most rebuilders have a much more personal stake in the performance of your PARTICULAR sled than a major manufacturer.

Popular Theories

When asked about engine break-in, most people (including manufacturers) will probably fall in one of two camps. Most will caution you to "baby" the machine. Don't go too fast. Don't turn too sharp. Don't jam on the brakes. Don't race the engine. The minority camp is to "beat the living daylight out of it" or break it in the way you plan to use it.

Our experience is that most people fall somewhere in between. The people who want to beat the sled in tend to ease up and come in somewhere this side of actual abuse. The people who want to baby it usually break down and get on the throttle a little. It's really hard to resist nailing it just once and find out what your new baby can really do.

We tend to fall in the "realistic use" category. Remember that both extremes can have detrimental affects. Recently, a European motorcycle magazine performed an experiment involving the break-in of new motorcycles. They took multiple models of the same manufacturer and broke them into 2 groups. One group had the living daylight run out of them, while the other followed the manufacturer's recommended babying period almost to a "t". Well, after some significant miles they put them all to the dyno, and guess what . . . the hard used and thoroughly abused models scored a few percent higher in horsepower on a dynamometer than the babied machines. Of course, we never saw a LONG term test and we don't know how reliable the machines were 20 or 50 thousand miles later.

Now, this applies to four-stroke motorcycles, and not snowmobiles, but the basic mechanics still apply to most any internal combustion engine.

So what should you do? We feel you should follow the manufacturer's instructions, within reason. Don't beat the machine, but don't over baby it either.

Most manufacturers say that you should VARY the engine speed and this is probably the single most important point. Also, make sure the engine is fully warmed before taking any liberties with the throttle. Even after break-in, goosing the throttle on a cold engine is just plain a BAD idea (even though that triple-expansion chamber three cylinder sounds so cool).

Typical Recommendations

One recommendation that is quite popular with breaking in a new sled is pre-mixing the first tank of fuel. There are several advantages (and a couple drawbacks) to this concept. The main reason for this seemingly redundant procedure is to ensure proper lubrication to the engine, especially for the first few hours of operation. Having oil mixed with the fuel provides lubrication to the engine in the event that the oil injection system does not function properly. During operation with first tank of pre-mixed fuel, check that the level of the injection oil in the reservoir diminishes; this signifies that the oil injection system is working properly.

Because of the increased oil flow that the engine ingests during this period, the spark plugs may prematurely foul, so make sure to keep a couple of extra sets with you on your first few rides. Once the pre-mixed fuel in the tank is burned, and fresh gasoline is added to the tank, the spark plugs will have a normal service life.

Other guidelines or the first 50–100 miles (80–160 km):
- Keep the engine speed below ½ of total rpm before redline
- NO hard starts
- NO hard stops

For at least the first 500 miles (805 km):
- Keep the engine speed well below redline for MOST riding, but vary the speed. Do not hold at any one speed for more than a few minutes. Varying the engine speed is an important aspect of proper engine break-in.
- AVOID hard starts
- Allow the engine to warm-up fully every time you ride
- Continue to avoid hard stops or turns, but increase your intensity as the mileage accumulates.

Then at whatever interval the manufacturer recommends, begin regular service and maintenance with a complete fluid change, inspection and adjustment routine. Be aware than many manufacturers will recommend that a complete break-in inspection be performed at a short interval after delivery. This is because that is the amount of time and distance necessary for all of the new parts to wear in and seat, meaning that adjustments should be performed to make certain everything is operating properly. Keeping your snowmobile serviced at the dealership will avoid any problems with warranty claims if any problems arise.

Break-In of Other Components

TRACK

Since a track is essentially a long, wide chain, it will require frequent adjustment on a new sled until it settles in. After the first ride, check the track tension and alignment to make sure everything is working properly. For the first few hours of operation, keep the necessary tools handy to adjust and align the track as necessary. The track can typically be considered settled in when it holds its tension and alignment after a few rides.

As with engines, every track is different and made from slightly different materials. Some tracks may not require any type of break-in period, and others may require an entire day of riding before they settle in. Don't let the track become damaged from improper tension and alignment; tracks can be fairly expensive, and added with the labor cost of having a new one installed can be substantial.

SUSPENSION

Typically, the shock absorbers on a new sled will require a short break-in period before they "loosen up". Don't be alarmed if the suspension feels stiff or sticky for the first couple rides. Once the shock absorbers have been cycled for a while, they will loosen up and provide proper dampening characteristics. Then, if it becomes necessary, adjust the suspension as needed to achieve the ride and handling that you prefer.

BRAKE

New brake pads require a short break-in period to provide optimal service. Any time your brake pads are replaced, the pads need to "seat" themselves on the rotor. Hard stops should be avoided; light to medium braking force for the first couple rides should seat the pads to the rotor. Obviously, if you need the brake in an emergency during the break-in period, USE IT! Just remember that before the pads are fully seated, it is possible that they might not stop you as well, so ride accordingly, using extra caution.

9124XP99

Choosing the correct snowmobile insures your new sled will take you just where you want to go

3
RIDING GEAR

RIDING GEAR

♦ See Figure 1

Keeping your body warm while riding will only increase your enjoyment of the whole snowmobile experience. There are many types of clothes on the market to keep you warm, so here are some general guidelines. First, dress in warm layers, much like you would if you were going skiing or hiking on a winter day.

Once you get used to your sled you will realize that snowmobiling is a very physical sport which will make you sweat. You want to have several warm layers which you can add or remove depending on the conditions and your level of activity.

A good pair of warm gloves is a must. Most of the newer sleds have hand warmers or have them available as an option. Always remember that hand warmers can malfunction so be prepared with a good pair of gloves.

Also a good pair of boots which allow your feet to have room will help to keep you more comfortable. Again, basic winter outdoor smarts come in here. Keep your feet warm by layering in a couple of pairs of socks inside you boots.

Snowmobiles can travel at a pretty good speed and even though your surrounded by fluffy snow there are still plenty of hard objects from your head to come into contact with. Wear an approved helmet. If you ever wreck your sled, your family will thank you for it afterwards. There are lots of different types of helmets out there from ones made for sledding to motocross styles.

This section is designed to help you choose the proper riding gear for riding your snowmobile. The goal here is familiarize you with what options are available when it comes to buying protective gear and with what features you should look for in that gear. We have chosen examples of gear from some of the industries known leaders (and in some cases from lesser known, but just as high quality manufacturers), and we would like to thank the manufacturers again for their help with the production of this section. That is not to say the brands pictured here are your only options. However, it is to say that they are VERY GOOD examples of high quality gear that is available and, as such, are excellent standards for comparison with the gear you look at when deciding on a purchase.

When it comes to riding snowmobiles, there is one inescapable fact regarding protective gear (and other forms of clothing)— What you are wearing when you get on your snowmobile is what you will be wearing when you get off! There's just no way around it, this is going to be true regardless of whether you PLANNED on getting off at a particular time or not.

When it comes to selecting riding gear, the type of gear you choose should depend as much on your feelings of risk assessment as it will on what type of riding you intend to do (trail riding, racing . . .). Some people would NEVER consider getting on a snowmobile without full protective gear from helmet to boot, while others think nothing of climbing onto their snowmobile wearing nothing more than jeans and jackets. And time after time, a whole lot of people ride without protective clothing and nothing bad happens.

So why the big deal? Well, it is a lot like playing the lottery. If you don't play that number the day your number comes up, then you lose. If you don't wear your pro-

tective gear the day you have a mishap, then you lose. The difference being losing the lottery and losing on a sled is that you probably won't need two ER attendants to hold you down while a nurse scrubs debris out of your open wounds. (It would also probably be interesting to hear the statistics on winning the lottery versus the possibility of having some sort of snowmobile-related accident). Don't play the lottery on your sled. Whenever you ride, wear appropriate safety gear.

Buying The Right Gear

CHOOSE SOMETHING THAT YOU LIKE

♦ See Figures 2 and 3

Probably the single MOST important factor in buying the right gear is to pick items that you like. If you buy a high quality item that is comfortable and versatile, then you are far more likely to WEAR IT. If you hate the look or the fit (or if you think that you look like a complete dork in a piece of gear), then you are probably going to want to leave it at home. And as we already said, the gear doesn't do you ANY GOOD if you are not wearing it when you need it.

Fig. 2 From mild to wild . . .

Fig. 1 Regardless of your type of riding, protective gear should always be worn to prevent injury

Fig. 3 . . . and everything in between, clothing manufacturers have snow suits to fit every taste

CHOOSE GEAR TO MATCH YOUR RIDING

▶ **See Figures 4, 5, 6 and 7**

The second consideration when buying gear is to ask yourself "how do you ride?" If your snowmobile NEVER leaves the garage unless it is a perfect winter day with moderate temperatures, then you probably don't need gear that is designed for a sub-zero climate. But, if you plan on using your snowmobile during blizzards, then chances are good that you will have to deal with at least some severe weather.

The gear you choose for more varied or extreme riding conditions is going to have to do a whole lot more than gear purchased only for nice weather. This is not to say that gear can't be versatile enough to use for both. Most protective clothing used today is designed using a series of layers. This helps protect the rider in three specific ways. The first layer next to your skin is designed to wick away moisture. The second layer traps body heat to keep you warm. The third or outer layer shields against the elements. This three layer system allows plenty of area to trap air and keeps your skin dry and comfortable.

The theory behind this system is you can peel off (or add on) layers as the temperature and conditions vary. If your wallet doesn't allow for separate moderate and severe weather riding gear, then you would be wise to select items which can be used in different conditions. Besides, even if you plan on NEVER going riding unless the weather is perfect, there is one thing you can count

Fig. 6 Clothing manufacturers have gear to suit nearly every riding situation

Fig. 4 This group is ready for some serious trail action

Fig. 5 This weekend racer is ready for some serious action in specialized racing gear

Fig. 7 The lining of this Arctic Cat parka can be worn as a separate jacket for warmer days

on—the weather will always change. In most locations, it gets cool as the sun sets and if your riding takes you up in very high altitude, the temperature can drop quickly when the sunlight fades.

CHOOSE QUALITY GEAR

The last and probably most difficult part of choosing the right gear is making sure that what you have selected is high quality. There are a couple of ways to do this, but they all come down to gathering information about the product. You can never have too much information about something before you buy it.

Look At Name Brands

▶ **See Figures 8, 9 and 10**

Now, we are not going to say that a certain piece of riding gear is high quality just because a company puts its name brand on it. But, a company that has been around for a long time and that has a good reputation must be doing something right. And you probably want to buy something from a company that has a reputation SPECIFICALLY in the snowmobiling or snowmobile industry, not just that has a good reputation for clothing. A boot maker that makes a lot of outdoor gear might make excellent products, but if they don't have the experience in what makes a riding boot different from their other products, they might not make a boot that is any good for riding snowmobiles.

Talk to other snowmobile enthusiasts and see what brands they have come to trust. If everyone has something good to say about a company, they have probably done something to deserve the praise. Read magazine articles and reviews of gear before deciding to buy something. If you can't find a review on that particular item, look for similar items by the same company and look at how the reviewers feel about that company's products. Often, if someone writes a review for a product that is out of line (good or bad) with what they have come to expect from a manufacturer, they will often tell you that in the review. " . . . although much of the gear we have tested from this company has left us less than dazzled, their new blab blab blab helmet was a real departure from the past and seems to represent a great value . . ."

Look At Attention To Detail

◗ **See Figures 11, 12 and 13**

A company that has taken great care on the finish of their product has probably put that quality throughout the gear. A helmet with a poor paint finish or a jacket with seams that are tearing is usually not made of the best materials or workmanship and you would be wise to steer clear of it.

On the other side of the coin, a jacket that has many different features such as a removable lining, vents for cooling, handy pockets with large zipper pulls, etc. obviously has had a lot of thought put into its design and will likely be well made using durable materials.

Fig. 8 Names like Joe Rocket and SnoRider . . .

Fig. 9 . . . along with clothing manufactured for the factories like Yamaha . . .

Fig. 10 . . . and Arctic Cat, all make excellent choices when looking for quality riding gear

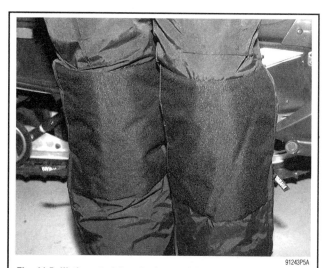
Fig. 11 Ballistic material on the knees of these riding bibs shows the manufacturer knows where riders need protection the most

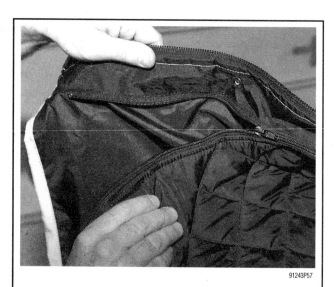
Fig. 12 Features like a removable lining and . . .

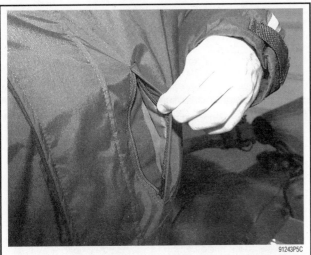

Fig. 13 . . . handy pockets show a manufacturer's attention to detail

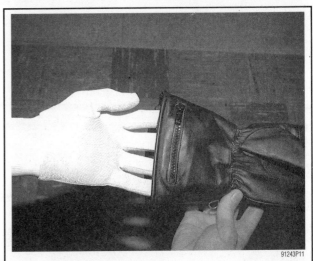

Fig. 14 The fit of snowmobiling gloves is important for a proper feel from the controls

Look At The Price

We are not going to say that an inexpensive item is no good. Nor are we going to tell you that by spending a whole wad of cash that you are guaranteed to get a high quality item. But it is hard to get away from the old fact that you tend to get what you pay for. Most high quality gear will carry a price tag that is higher than their lower quality equivalents.

Remember that many companies (even those with very good reputations) have high and low line items. If you are working on a budget, one of their low line items might offer you a chance to get a relatively high quality piece of gear, but that is probably missing some of the more convenient or versatile features of their more expensive counterparts.

When deciding on how many features are appropriate, ask snowmobiling enthusiasts which features they feel are necessary. It may be nice to have twenty pockets in your riding jacket but if you never use them, they are a waste of money.

A few other things to consider here. One, that good quality gear is normally going to last a long time (especially if it is cared for properly) so that a few dollars invested now may last a LONG TIME. Two, that because gear can be very durable you may be able to find it cheaper used (if you don't mind used clothing). People change and might grow out of a decent piece of gear (especially items like riding pants or other snug fitting clothing).

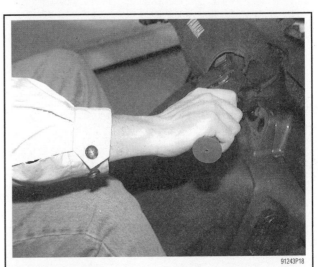

Fig. 15 The sleeves of a riding jacket tend to be a little longer than most other jackets . . .

⁂ WARNING

One warning here. Some types of gear designed as crash protection use impact absorbent materials (usually some form of foam or hard plastic). These materials lose some of their effectiveness as they age and they are usually designed to do their job only ONCE. If a piece of gear that relies upon this material (such as a helmet) is exceptionally old or appears to have been dropped or to have been down (meaning it has kissed the ground in use) before, then steer clear of it. When it comes to helmets, a good drop from the seat of your snowmobile or from your kitchen counter may significantly reduce its ability to absorb an impact in the future.

Money is a tough issue when it comes to safety. We really can't tell you what to do here, but remember that gear is designed to PROTECT the user. It's your **butt**, it's your **head**, they're your **fingers** . . . . well you probably get the picture here. There are a lot of things we would consider saving money on, but don't save money if it is going to cost you protection. Think hard about this. A new exhaust system, or a new helmet? (if you're smart, you'll buy a helmet first).

CHOOSE SOMETHING THAT FITS PROPERLY

▶ **See Figures 14, 15 and 16**

Fit is important in snowmobiling gear for two reasons. The first is simply comfort. If a helmet is too tight, if a jacket restricts movement, or a pair of

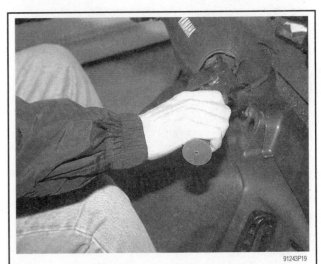

Fig. 16 . . . you don't want them to ride up when your arms are bent in a proper riding position

gloves are so big that they don't allow for proper control of the snowmobile, you will be unhappy at best or unsafe at worst. The second reason comes back to safety, which is the basis for protective gear in the first place. A helmet that is too loose may fly right off of your head during an accident. A jacket that is too big might ride up and expose skin to the elements.

Another thing you should keep in mind with snowmobile gear is that it is designed to fit a certain way and this may not agree with what you have been taught is proper fitting for fashion or other applications. For instance, the sleeves of a riding jacket tend to be a little longer than most other jackets. The reason is that you don't want them to ride up when your arms are bent in a proper riding position. Also, the jacket itself is longer to prevent it from riding up and exposing your back. Bibs/pants are made extra long to fit properly in a seated position. Gloves are designed to give proper feel from the controls. To an inexperienced rider, it may seem as if the gloves fit too snugly. In the end, make sure you consider the unique way riding gear is used before you decide for sure if it fits or not.

Helmets

▶ See Figure 17

The human brain is arguably the most important part of the body. The human brain is also the only organ almost completely encased in bone. Is this a coincidence? Definitely not. If the brain is damaged, the rest of the body cannot function properly. Even with this built-in protection, a moderate impact to the head can cause major brain damage. Brain damage can cause memory loss, mental retardation, paralysis, even death.

With that said, if you're not wearing a helmet when you fall off your snowmobile and you smack your head on a gigantic boulder or a tree, you're gonna get hurt. There's no way around it. I know, I know, "I'm a really good rider, and I never crash. Besides, helmets don't do any good anyway." BULL! Even the best race car drivers in the world occasionally crash. You can never predict when an accident will happen. Being well-prepared for mishaps is essential when riding a snowmobile, and wearing a helmet will significantly reduce your chances of sustaining a dangerous blow to the head. The old saying "Be prepared for the worst, and expect the best" is well applied in this situation.

Wearing a helmet while riding a snowmobile can be compared to an automobile carrying a spare tire. A motorist never plans on having to change a flat tire, but always carries a spare tire and jack if a flat were to occur. A foolish driver might remove his spare, feeling that he has good tires, and carrying a spare is just hauling around extra weight and taking up space. But, WHEN he gets a flat tire, he's out of luck. The same can be said for wearing a helmet. A

91243P9P

Fig. 17 The point here is simple—buy a good helmet and wear it whenever you ride

smart rider will always wear a helmet, never planning on crashing, but protecting his head just in case something does happen. Now, here is where things become more extreme. Instead of just being stranded on the side of the trail, the bare-headed rider who never planned on crashing but suddenly lost control of his snowmobile, may get hauled off in a life flight helicopter due to major head trauma.

Most people with the means to buy a snowmobile are big boys and girls, and are simply going to have to make decisions for themselves. It's a fact that if you are wearing a helmet during an accident and you hit your head on something (a rock, a tree, etc.) the chances are strong that the helmet will significantly reduce the trauma of that impact on your head.

Now seriously, do you really think riding your snowmobile without a helmet on is worth risking brain damage or death? Buy a good helmet and wear it whenever you ride.

WHAT IS A HELMET?

▶ See Figures 18 and 19

The primary purpose and function of a helmet is to reduce the shock of an impact from your head. It is NOT a panacea for all mishaps, but a simple tool that, if used effectively, may REDUCE (not eliminate) the risk to your head during an accident. Helmet technology has advanced significantly in the last 15 years, and engineers have developed excellent ways of isolating impacts to the head with helmets. Not to mention that helmets are significantly more light weight and more comfortable than ever before.

Generally speaking, a helmet consists of a rigid head covering and a retention system of flexible straps. The rigid covering portion of the helmet has 2 parts, the stiff outer shell and the crushable liner. The job of the outer shell is to protect by spreading a concentrated impact on its surface across a larger area of the liner (and eventually the user's head). The liner does its job by absorbing impact energy as it compresses. In this way less of the impact energy is conducted directly to your skull.

The helmet retention system is vitally important because the helmet isn't going to do as much good if it comes off of your head or moves out of place during an accident. So the job of the retention system is exactly as it sounds, to keep the helmet in place during a fall or an accident.

HOW TO SELECT A HELMET

So how do you select a helmet? Remember the 4 basics mentioned at the beginning of this section:
1. Choose something you like.
2. Choose something that fits your riding.
3. Choose something that is high quality.
4. Choose something that fits you properly.

But, in order for a helmet to do its job properly there is one additional VERY IMPORTANT requirement:
5. Choose something that has never been damaged or mistreated (READ THIS: Don't buy it used).

Choose a Helmet You Like

▶ See Figures 20 and 21

Ok, this one's easy. Choose something that is styled to your tastes. If you think of yourself as boy racer, then you are probably going to be happier with a helmet that contains replica graphics of your favorite race team. On the other hand, if you are more conservative, you might be happier with a simple single color helmet.

If you are really worried about style, then you may also want to take into consideration what type (and color) of jacket or snowmobile you will be buying. A neutral color helmet will coordinate with a lot more snowmobiles than a replica racer model. Heaven knows you wouldn't want to CLASH, would you? Seriously though, if you are always buying and selling snowmobiles, it is a good idea to find a helmet that matches just about anything. A white or black helmet would fit this description perfectly.

But like we keep saying, it is just as important that you feel comfortable with how your helmet looks, because you are FAR more likely to wear it if you like it. Don't buy a pink helmet just because it's cheaper than other colors. You'll never want to wear it around your friends. Unless of course, you're comfortable wearing pink on a regular basis. Certain helmets leave you looking like Darth Vader, and others like Dale Earnhardt. If you like Darth Vader or Earnhardt, then you're in luck. The bottom line here is choose something that has a style that you prefer.

When you are choosing a style and color of helmet, remember to answer the important need for visibility. Bright colors help to provide extra visibility during the day. And, when riding on sunny days, a bright color is going to reflect more of the sun's rays then a dark colored helmet to keep your head a little cooler.

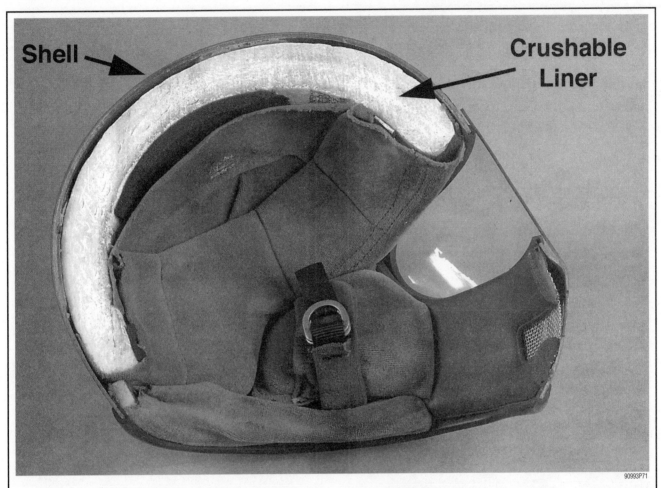

Fig. 18 This helmet has been cut away to reveal the crushable liner found under the hard shell

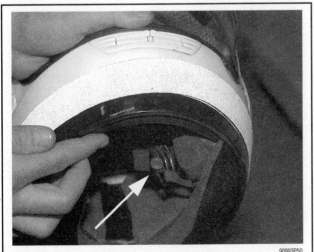

Fig. 19 The helmet chin strap is VERY important, since the helmet won't do any good if it comes off in an accident

Fig. 20 Whether open or full face, mild or wild paint scheme, if you don't wear it, it won't protect you. Choose a helmet you will wear regularly

Fig. 21 Notice that the light colored helmets in this picture stand out the most

Choose a Helmet To Match Your Riding (Types of Helmets)

▶ See Figure 22

Different riders have different needs. For example, if you primarily use your snowmobile for hunting, a full face helmet might not be the best choice. An open face helmet might be better suited for hunting purposes, since the additional visibility of an open face might be an advantage (of course your field of vision can change from one helmet to another, regardless of helmet style). On the other side of things, a serious sport rider would most definitely opt for the full face helmet. Pick out something that best suits your primary type of riding.

There are essentially 2 types of helmets commonly available to snowmobile riders. Their names give you some idea of the area and degrees of protection they offer your head (and in some cases face):

- Full face
- Open face (or ¾ helmet)

Fig. 22 Most snowmobilers opt for a full face helmet

FULL FACE HELMETS

▶ See Figures 23 thru 28

A full face helmet offers you the most protection in the form of headgear. It is usually defined as a helmet which covers your entire head and that ALSO contains a chin bar. The purpose of the chin bar is to support your face off the

ground in the event of a mishap. It should be obvious that in an accident there is a chance your face will slide along (or slam into) the ground, so a chin bar could save some of those precious features you are so proud of (your nose, your chin . . .). One of the wonderful advantages of a full face helmet is its ability to protect your whole head (face included) from not only accidents, but from the elements. These helmets provide good protection from wind noise, from cold and even (if the helmet is well ventilated) decent protection from the sun's rays.

All of this protection does not come without a cost (like some other forms of protection, the full face helmet sometimes brings the complaint, "it just doesn't feel the same when I wear one." But that isn't necessarily a good excuse to not wear one). The costs of all this safety may include restricted air flow, and a reduction in the sounds you'll be able to hear. Some full face helmets tend to give a feeling of being closed in, with the chin bar in the bottom most portion of one's peripheral vision. If your a claustrophobic type, a full face helmet might give you the creeps.

Now, most modern full face helmets have made significant improvements in minimizing their drawbacks. One feature that MUST be included in a full face helmet is adequate ventilation. A good helmet is going to contain a few air inlets and outlets to help keep a flow of forced air through the lining and help cool your head by evaporating sweat.

Ventilation in a snowmobile helmet is particularly important because all that hot breath you will be breathing when your are hot dogging it on the trial needs

Fig. 23 This snowmobile style helmet, from Bell Helmets, contains several features to protect a rider in extreme weather

Fig. 24 Full face off-road style helmets offer the most protection for your head during an accident, and still allow a clear field of vision

Fig. 25 Helmets with adjustable visors allow you to position the visor to your liking

Fig. 26 This helmet has vents in the visor to cut down on turbulence (or lift) at high speed

Fig. 27 Snowmobile helmets have unique features to deal with cold weather riding. A flap of fabric over the nose prevents fogging

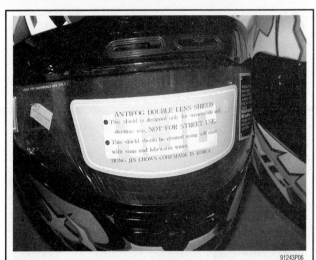

Fig. 28 Another feature of a snowmobile helmet is a double-paned lens with vents, which also helps cut down on fogging

to be ventilated. Hot breath inside and cold air outside can cause a heavy fog condition on your shield.

Most manufacturers have resolved this problem by offering breath deflectors or heated shields to cut down on the fogging problem. Others have developed double thickness shields which insulate the inside and outside layers with a pocket of air (much like the thermally efficient windows on your house). Just remember that if you can't see where you are going, you are much more likely to run into something and hurt yourself. So choose wisely!

From these descriptions it should obvious that a full face helmet with the appropriate ventilation and anti-fog shield features is probably the gear of choice for riders who are concerned with maximum protection. This should include any riders with a higher risk of going down (sport riders and racer-types) or any rider who feels the need for the best protection they can get. A full face helmet will offer the most complete protection of any type of helmet.

OPEN FACE (¾) HELMETS

▶ **See Figures 29, 30 and 31**

An open face or ¾ helmet might be considered a compromise. It provides a large area of protection for your head, but because it does not have a chin bar, it does not provide the same protection for your face that a full face helmet can. Open face helmets therefore also do not provide as much protection from wind noise or the elements. So with that said you might ask, "why do people wear them?" It is simple, an open face helmet provides much of the head impact pro-

Fig. 29 This versatile open face Bell helmet can be used when riding a snomobile, ATV or motorcycle

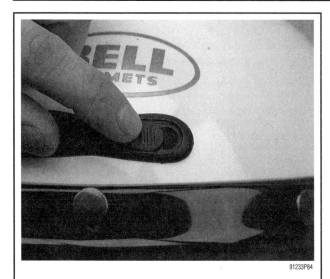

Fig. 30 These closeable vents are nice for keeping a cool head

Fig. 31 With goggles in place, an open face helmet covers most of your head, with the exception of your mouth and chin

tection of a full face helmet while providing something the full face cannot—protection of your face.

People choose to wear open face helmets for a variety of reasons, all of them having something to do with the lack of a face shield and/or a chin bar. They can provide an enhanced line of vision for non-riding applications (this is not to say that a full face helmet restricts your field of vision for riding, but that the chin bar can make looking at trail maps, looking down at something, looking into your pockets or even your jacket zipper a bit awkward). This enhanced line of vision is probably most significant in simply adding to the experience of being outside, on a snowmobile. Some people feel that full face helmets make you feel like you are in a cage, and like the less confining freedom that an open face helmet.

There are also open face helmets that have removable/adjustable chin guards. They appear to be a full face helmet, but don't be deceived. These of helmets don't really offer much more protection than a standard open face in the event of a moderate fall. They do however, provide protection from debris kicked up from the tracks of other riders, and keep you from eating flying objects. The other main advantage of this type of helmet is that the chin guard can be removed quickly if desired. This type of helmet might be appealing to some of you, but please be aware that these are not to be considered a full face helmet and do not provide as much protection as a full face. However, they do provide more protection than a regular open face helmet, and the option of the removable chin guard might be a good compromise.

Open face helmets allow you to more easily converse with other riders, because they do not muffle your voice. Since they provide less protection from noise, they allow you to hear different sounds that would be muffled by a full face, like other riders approaching on a trail. Again, this is not to say that full face helmets provide a dangerous restriction of sound. In fact, most experts agree that the noise protection of a full face helmet filters out many of the inconsequential engine noises from your snowmobile, allowing you to hear other things better.

Because open face helmets do not provide as much facial protection from the elements, riding in snow or extreme cold might be a little painful. But again, this is the sacrifice one must make when choosing an open face helmet. So if you plan to ride a lot a full face helmet might be better suited than an open face.

Like full face helmets, a quality open face helmet is going to have features that make it more useful. These features often include things like vents and snap on face shields or sun visors to make them more adaptable to varied weather conditions.

After reading our descriptions of helmets, you might be curious what our choices are when it comes to this important issue of personal protection. The best recommendation is to wear as much safety gear as possible at all times. Some people might think you're paranoid, but it is always better to play it safe and be fully prepared at all times. When it comes to helmets, a full face helmet is always recommended. A full face helmet will almost always offer more protection than an open face. Open face helmets are basic protection, and aren't going to keep you from smashing your face against a tree. If you decide to wear an open face helmet, be aware of the lesser degree of protection that you have.

Choose a Quality Helmet

▶ See Figures 32, 33, 34 and 35

As we stated at the beginning of the section, determining the quality of riding gear is not always a black and white issue, especially when it comes to helmets. Deciding if it is high quality has a lot to do with the materials used in construction and the helmet's design. A good starting point is to avoid anything that is $9.99 and is displayed under a sign saying "For novelty purposes only."

In the U.S., the Department of Transportation (DOT) helps us choose a quality helmet by setting standards of impact protection that helmets must meet in order to be legal for use in areas where a mandatory helmet law is in effect. Helmets which meet these standards are equipped with a DOT sticker showing that they meet the requirements and are legal for use. Unfortunately, DOT does not test helmets and publish lists of which ones meet the standards. Instead it is up to the each individual helmet's manufacturer to "certify" that their helmets are in compliance (not very reassuring if you are a suspicious type).

There is a non-profit group that tests helmets and certifies them (and whose standards differ from DOT, because they look at different factors). The Snell Memorial Foundation, Inc. was incorporated under California law as a nonprofit organization in 1957 and exists solely for the purpose of engaging in scientific and educational activities in order to promote safety, well-being and

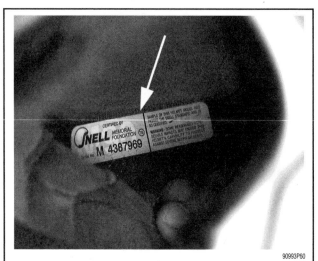

Fig. 32 Check under the helmet lining for certification labels and build dates . . .

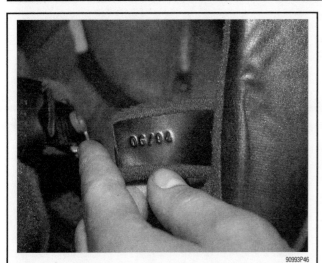

Fig. 33 . . . this helmet has a build date stamped on its chin strap—Remember it should be replaced after 5 years

90993P46

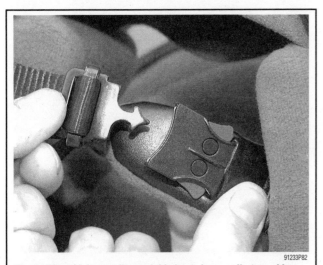

Fig. 34 Many higher-quality model helmets have a clip-type chin strap

91233P82

Fig. 35 A SNELL rating is a sign of a quality helmet

91233P86

comfort to people engaged in any type of travel or vehicular transportation. The foundation (formed by friends of William "Pete" Snell, a race car driver who died of massive head injuries received during a racing accident) conducts tests on helmets for various factors. What is comforting about the Snell standard is that the helmet manufacturers participate voluntarily by submitting samples for testing (and the foundation also performs random sample testing from stocks intended for retail sales).

The Snell tests are designed to examine a particular helmet's properties which are most critical in providing protection:

• **Impact management** or how well the helmet protects against collisions with large objects.

• **Positional stability** or how well a helmet remains in place on a head when it is properly secured.

• **Retention system strength** or the ability of the helmet chin straps to hold the helmet during an entire accident.

• **Level of protection** or the area of the head that is protected by the helmet.

Snell tests vary depending on which properties they are checking. One test includes dropping helmets (with a headform installed in the helmet) in a specified manner onto any of three unyielding anvils and then measuring the amount of shock delivered to the headform. Another test involves dropping a metal cone of specified weight, from a specified height onto the helmet and making sure that there is no penetration. Other tests include applying a solvent mix to check resistance to chemical attack from solvents or petrochemicals, testing the permanently attached chin bars of full face helmets, testing the face shields with lead pellets, checking the diameter of ventilation holes, and even checking the peripheral vision allowed by the opening.

This is a lot of testing, and the results are probably a market full of helmets which are significantly safer than if there were no such testing or certifications. But, unfortunately we cannot say that these tests will ASSURE you of a quality helmet every time or that even if you get a quality helmet, that it will protect you from all unforeseen accidents. Remember that we are talking about plastic and Styrofoam here. If you slam your helmeted head into a sharp enough object or even a dull (but immovable) object at a great enough velocity you are not going to have to worry about helmets ever again (unless you believe in reincarnation). Remember that helmets are great tools, but they have their limits. And, although quality control by most modern helmet manufacturers is exemplary, there does exist the possibility of a bad helmet slipping through.

Also remember that a helmet may be damaged on display or just from aging. The protective capabilities of a helmet diminish over time and many experts recommend a limited shelf life for helmets. At time of publication, the Snell foundation recommends that all helmets be replaced after a maximum of 5 years (or less if the helmet manufacturer has tighter standards).

So how do you try to assure yourself of a quality helmet. Buy a helmet that has BOTH DOT and SNELL stickers showing compliance with both standards. Check the manufacturer helmet labels which should include a production date to be sure it is not excessively old (remember though that you probably won't find a helmet that was produced last week or last month, but keep that 5 year life span in mind). Examine the helmet thoroughly for signs of having been dropped or of other abuse. Look at the helmet shell for evidence of cracks. Check the lining for unusual or irregular depressions showing where it may have been compacted from misuse.

Choose a Helmet That Fits Properly

♦ See Figures 36, 37, 38 and 39

A helmet does not do any good if it comes off during an accident. Therefore, the proper fit of a helmet is just as important as the quality of its construction. A helmet should fit snug, but not tight, since a tight helmet will likely place uncomfortable pressure on your head and may give you a headache. But a helmet should not be too loose, because if it is, it would be much more likely to come off or slip out of place during an accident.

➡ **It can not be stressed enough that buying a helmet should be done in person. Helmet sizing is different for each manufacturer and each style of helmet. A large in one style may fit you fine, but you may need a medium in a different style. Take your time and select the helmet that fits the best.**

Any helmet should be snug enough to prevent you from inserting a finger between your forehead and the helmet lining (we are not talking about prying your finger into place, just lightly inserting it). Similarly the padding of a full face helmet should press lightly against your cheeks, but here you are much more likely to be able to insert a finger or two. With the helmet in place, try to rotate it without turning your head. If the helmet turns significantly on your head (especially if it turns enough to interfere with your vision), it is too loose and you should try the next smaller size. Without tightening the chin straps, shake your head briskly from left-to-right a few times. The helmet should follow your head and not come out of place.

➡Remember that the crash protective portion of the helmet lining is made of a compactable material and will give slightly during use, which may make a slightly tight helmet just right or a borderline helmet slightly too loose. Take your time when trying on and selecting the right helmet.

Try out the chin strap retention system. When it has been snugged (in such a way that you can still breath or swallow), make sure it is still comfortable. An awkward retention system is going to discourage you from using it properly and then we are right back to the why bother wearing a helmet thing again because if it is not snugged properly, it may come off during an accident.

The Snell foundation recommends a simple method for checking helmet fit and making sure that you have properly secured it on your head EACH TIME you put it on:

"Position the helmet on your head so that it sits low on your forehead; if you can't see the edge of the brim at the extreme upper range of your vision, the helmet is probably out of place. Adjust the chinstraps so that, when in use, it will

Fig. 38 Next, move your head back and forth. Your head should not move inside the helmet. If things are snug fitting . . .

Fig. 36 To check if a helmet is sized properly, fit it over your head . . .

Fig. 39 . . . try moving your head up and down. The helmet should move with your head. It should be snug, but not tight

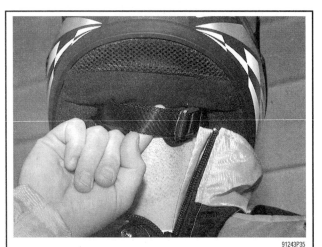

Fig. 37 . . . and tighten the chinstrap snugly. If you can fit more than one finger through the helmet and your chin, it may be too loose

hold the helmet firmly in place. This positioning and adjusting should be repeated to obtain the very best result possible. The procedure initially may be time consuming. TAKE THE TIME."

"Try to remove the helmet without undoing the retention system closures. If the helmet comes off or shifts over your eyes, readjust and try again. If no adjustment seems to work, this helmet is not for you; try another."

One more thing to consider when it comes to proper helmet fit. If you wear eyeglasses, even part of the time, be sure to try on a helmet with the eyeglasses that you plan to wear with it. Some helmets are better suited than others for glasses and if you have the wrong combination of eyewear and helmet it may place uncomfortable pressure on your temples (causing a headache) or on the bridge of your nose.

Don't Buy A Used Helmet

Now we are probably going to take some heat over this one too, but we don't care how honest the guy looks. "I never wore it, I just bought it and it didn't fit and I've never dropped it . . . ever . . . really." Look, it is your HEAD, so why take the risk? Remember that a helmet's ability to protect your head is, generally speaking, a one-time thing and it diminishes over time or with any mistreatment of the helmet. Repeated bumps into doorways and an occasional drop from the tailgate of your truck may be enough to significantly reduce its ability to absorb an impact when you really need it.

If you do decide to buy a used helmet, examine it just like you would a new one. ANY evidence of damage should make you extremely suspicious and cautious.

If you have the luxury of examining a used helmet before purchasing it (or if the price was sooooo low that you decided to risk the money), then return the helmet to the original manufacturer for examination before use. This is true of a helmet you have owned for a while and dropped as well. It is too easy to say, "ohhhhh that drop didn't hurt it" when you really don't know.

HOW TO CARE FOR YOUR HELMET

▶ **See Figures 40 and 41**

Don't Drop/Bang It

Well, if you read the part on NOT buying a used helmet, you are already aware of the most important form of care for your helmet—DON'T DROP IT. Don't bang it into things, don't let it bounce around in the bed of the truck on the way to go riding. Don't pile things on it in the garage . . . etc.

Don't Leave It Baking In The Sun

But there are other things you should be aware of when it comes to helmet care. Don't let it sit and bake in the sun every day. This is going to have an effect on the shell and the lining. Occasionally leaving it on the seat of your snowmobile may do no real harm, but doing it every day, all day is going to have a cumulative effect and weaken its ability to protect you.

Don't Place It On The Handlebars

Placing a helmet over something, so that it is supported by the impact lining, and not on the edges of the hard shell will compact the foam causing a hard spot which will not crush during an accident. This spot will not only NOT do its job in an accident, but it can directly transmit the shock from the shell to your skull, which is EXACTLY what it was supposed to prevent. Don't leave your helmet on the ends of the handlebars where the liner can get crushed.

91233PA3

Fig. 40 Placing your helmet on the handlebars will crush and distort the foam liner, lessening the helmet's ability to protect your head

Don't Expose It To Solvents

Have you ever poured gasoline in a Styrofoam cup and watched the cup disappear? Well, the impact resistant material under your helmet's shell is remarkably similar to that Styrofoam cup. Read the ingredients of any cleaner or chemical that you plan to use on your helmet and steer clear of those that may damage the shell or lining.

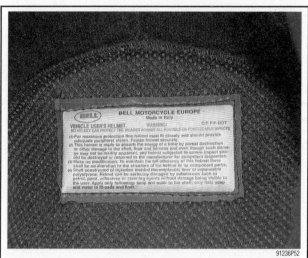

91236P52

Fig. 41 Follow the manufacturer's instructions (usually inside the helmet) regarding cleaning and examination

Do Clean And Examine It Regularly

Do yourself a favor and clean the lining with a very mild solution of water and ammonia (your friends will thank you). This solution will rid the helmet of any odors. Also, give the hard shell the same quality treatment you provide to your sled. Remove bugs and debris so that you will easily notice any damage that may occur through use. A potentially dangerous crack could be hidden by debris. If you are really vain (and aren't we all sometimes) polish it with some high quality wax once in a while, it will make it easier to keep clean.

➡**Be sure to check with the helmet manufacturer before using any chemicals or detergents on your helmet. Be certain that whatever you use will not harm the shell or protective lining.**

HOW TO PREVENT LENS FOGGING

▶ **See Figures 42 thru 48**

Fogging of your glasses or your helmet lens is a rather annoying problem which can be potentially dangerous. The cure to fogging is simple: keep the lens warmer than the dew point of the air surrounding it.

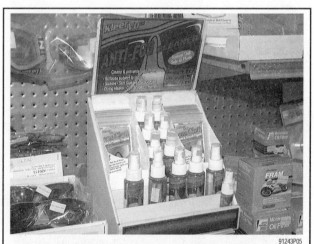

91243P05

Fig. 42 Anti-fog fluids are a thin layer of insulation applied to the lens. The coating stays the same temperature as the surrounding air which is higher than the dew point

Fig. 43 Most quality snowmobiling helmets use double lens construction to prevent fogging

Fig. 46 . . . while forehead vents evaporate the humidity caused by sweat

Fig. 44 Breath deflectors, such as this removable insulator on an Arctic Cat helmet, are designed to keep the humid breath of the rider off the lens

Fig. 47 Most importantly, good ventilation prevents the helmet from getting that "funky smell" inside after a few hours of hard riding

Fig. 45 Chin vents rid the helmet of the moist air around your mouth . . .

Several methods are currently used to accomplish this task. Double lens are a help. By using a double lens, the inside lens is never warmer than the outside lens due to the insulating air space in between thus the inside lens "may" be warmer than the dew point of the air.

Defogging fluids are a thin layer of insulation applied to the lens. The intent is that the coating will be the same temperature as the surrounding air (which is higher than the dew point). Anti-fog fluids may work in some conditions but in general are not the ultimate solution.

A breath deflector may help. Some deflectors come in nose cone form, some as a simple small air dam, and some as a complete isolator. The latter can be very effective in many conditions. The object here is to keep your humid breath off the lens. The one problem is that most deflectors can't account for humidity increases caused by sweat from your face and head.

Another solution is ventilation. The theory is to keep the humid air flowing out of the helmet and away from the lens. This method helps cure the humidity caused by sweat. It also prevents the helmet from getting that "funky smell" inside after a few hours of hard riding.

Last but not least is the heated visor. A heated visor increases the temp of the shield to above the dew point of the air. This works flawlessly for keeping frost off your visor but attaches you to your sled with an electrical tether, causes every snowflake to hit the visor to melt and run down your visor, and slightly impairs your vision because of the heating elements in the lens.

Fig. 48 This helmet from Joe Rocket just happens to have all the features we just mentioned. If you are in the market for a helmet, give them a call

Fig. 50 Riding a snowmobile with just a helmet is okay for your head, but doesn't do much for your eyes . . .

Fig. 51 . . . but with goggles, you are fully protected

Here are some features to look for in your helmet that will help to prevent or maybe eliminate the fogging problem.

• A double lens with adjustable vents at the bottom and top of the lens to keep the area behind the lens ventilated as required by the wearer

• A breath deflector that is more of a breath/face isolator. It should fit comfortably from one side of the helmet to the other and fit up against the checks and bridge of the nose. This effectively isolates the breath from the lens, not just deflecting it. It also helps the sweat problem by reducing the exposed skin area in the lens area.

• Padding on the forehead should be right down to the eyebrow which reduces the exposed skin in the lens area helping the sweat isolation problem

Goggles

▶ **See Figures 49 thru 54**

Most snowmobile goggles are of basically the same design, looking very similar to modern ski goggles. They are usually constructed out of flexible plastic, with soft foam around the perimeter of the area that fits to your face. Most all snowmobile goggles are vented, using thin foam to filter out airborne dust and allergens that can irritate your eyes. Snowmobile goggles also have adjustable thick elastic straps to compensate for different helmet sizes.

Most goggles also have lenses that can be easily changed, which can be a real advantage. If you're riding on a really sunny day, a tinted lens can be

Fig. 49 Goggles provide protection for your eyes from flying objects

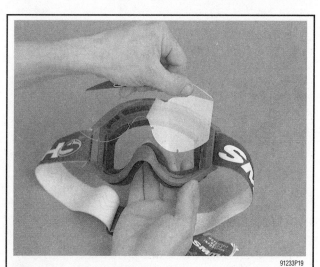

Fig. 52 To change a lens, simply separate the frame from the lens . . .

Fig. 53 . . . and snap a new one in place

Fig. 54 If you wear glasses, goggles are not a problem. Most brands are large enough to fit over glasses

quickly snapped in to cut down on glare. Or if your lens is becoming severely scratched up, a new one can be popped in, saving the cost of buying new goggles. If you ride in a lot of mud, then you know what it's like to scratch up your goggles after just a couple of rides.

➡**A good tip is to use a smoked lens to cut glare on days where the sun is shining bright and use an amber lens to increase visibility on a hazy day.**

❄❄ CAUTION

Using sunglasses in place of goggles is really DANGEROUS. Sunglasses do not provide the complete protection that goggles give. A piece of debris can easily knock sunglasses right off your face. Sunglasses also will not shield your eyes from airborne allergens as goggles do. Protecting your eyes from debris is extremely important when riding a snowmobile.

HOW TO SELECT GOGGLES

▶ **See Figure 55**

So how do you select suitable eye wear? Remember the 4 basics mentioned at the beginning of this section:

1. Choose something you like.
2. Choose something that fits your riding.
3. Choose something that is high quality.
4. Choose something that fits properly.

Choose Something You Like

Finding goggles that you like will most likely be pretty easy. The big thing here is finding goggles that fit your face. Finding the right color is important too, just like picking out a helmet. Be sure to find goggles that match your helmet. The main thing here is don't buy goggles that you think look DUMB. You are more likely to leave dumb looking goggles in your gear bag and take unnecessary chances if you hate them. Make sure to get what you really want, not just what is on sale at the local dealer.

Fig. 55 Snowmobile goggles are available in many different sizes and styles

Choose Gear To Match Your Riding

No matter what type of lens your goggles have, you should remember that although you may plan to ride only during the day, light conditions will vary. You could get caught in a storm, you might ride through a dark forest. Even on bright sunny days, you may find that tinted eye wear suddenly has become more of a danger than a benefit, so make sure you always keep some clear eye wear handy too.

Also, remember that your needs will vary based on your type of riding. If you are riding in the forest, a yellow tinted lens might be useful, since they help define the terrain in low-light conditions. Be careful to familiarize yourself with the tint before using it when riding. Some types of tint will actually hide variations in the terrain on particular surfaces. This could lead to some unexpected problems if you are unaware of the tint's ability of hiding or exaggerating terrain variations. The same can be said for polarized lenses. During really bright, sunny days a polarized lens could be really helpful to reduce snow glare. But, if the trail suddenly takes a turn into the low-light conditions of the forest canopy, vision might suddenly become impaired.

Choose Quality Gear

▶ **See Figures 56 and 57**

This one is easy. Look, if you buy cheesy goggles from a discount store, don't expect them to protect your eyes, because they probably won't do a darn thing for you when you really need them. This is the same issue as wearing a helmet: How much is your vision worth? "If you have a five dollar set of eyes, then buy yourself some five dollar goggles."

Seriously, spend the money and buy yourself a quality set of goggles. Not only will they do a better job of protecting your eyes, they will last a lot longer. If you can't see when you're riding, you're liable to really hurt yourself, as well as other riders. So the bottom line is this: Don't buy cheap gear! The only thing worse than having an emergency room doctor dig debris out of your eye would

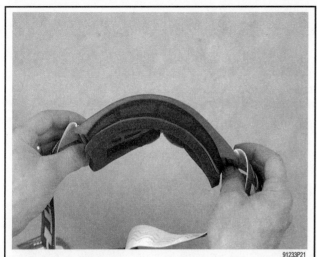

Fig. 56 Look for quality foam that surrounds the frame; it protects your eyes from dust and provides a cushion for your face

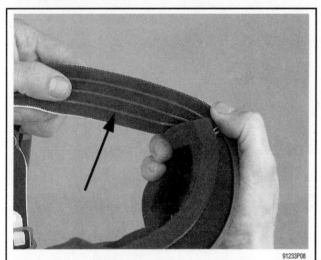

Fig. 57 A nice feature of some goggles is a silicone strip on the strap to prevent slippage

be to have the same person out dig a piece of plastic from your broken cheap goggles, because you skimped out on buying quality equipment.

Choose Something That Fits Properly

Most goggles made today are available in a ton of different sizes, so you can almost always find something that custom fits to your face. Make sure to try them on BEFORE you buy them, so you can verify a proper fit. When trying them on, check that there aren't any gaps between your face and the foam on the goggles. Debris can (and will) come up through the gaps and irritate your eyes. If you wear contact lenses, you are already aware of how much of a problem this can be. Also make sure the goggles don't press down on the bridge of your nose. If things feel kind of tight, the goggles may be too small for you. It may not seem that bad when you're trying them on, but after a couple of hours of riding, your nose might be in serious pain, or you might get a headache. Good fitting goggles should almost become unnoticed after some time spent riding. However, make sure the fit is correct BEFORE you buy them. The retailer is not going to let you return your funky, sweaty goggles after you find out they are too big for your face.

After you have found something that fits your face, look at the elastic strap. Does it look like it will last for a while? Is it adjustable? Nothing is worse than a saggy, limp strap that won't even hold your goggles to your face. Make sure that the strap is adjustable so you can position the goggles so they're not too tight

on your face. Just like goggles that don't fit right, goggles that are too tight will definitely give you a headache. Adjustability is an important feature when buying a pair of goggles.

Also, be sure to examine the frame. Does it appear to be well constructed, or does it look cheap? Is the foam around the perimeter of high quality? As the old saying goes, "You get what you pay for", really comes into play here. Do yourself a favor, and buy some high quality goggles. Let your friends buy the cheap stuff, and watch how long it lasts. You will most definitely have the last laugh here.

HOW TO CARE FOR YOUR GOGGLES

The first rule is ALWAYS clean your goggles with a soft, damp cloth. You may be able to get away with glass cleaner and paper towels on some surfaces, but a soft damp cloth will never harm your eye wear. If your goggles are really dirty, immersing them in water to get off the big stuff will help avoid scratching them up. Let them air dry, and then gently wipe them clean with a damp cloth. It may be easier to pop the lens out to clean the inside portion. Just remember, lenses are made of PLASTIC, and plastic always scratches easier than glass.

Products like Rain-X® can be FANTASTIC on some lenses, but some lenses are completely destroyed by it. SO, never use a product on your goggles without first testing it on an inconspicuous area. Try it on a small patch of the corner of your goggles. Or better yet, try it out on an old, scratched up lens. This can save your weekend. If you just grab whatever cleaner you have in the back of your seat in your truck and spray down your goggles, you could be in for a really big shock. Certain cleaners attack plastics, so watch out. Play it safe and stick with good old fashioned water if you don't feel comfortable with a particular cleaner you have laying around.

Here's a tip to keeping your goggles in good shape over years of use. Don't keep them stretched out over your helmet as if you are wearing them. Eventually, all of the straps on goggles will lose their "snap" from constant use. Keeping your goggles stored on your helmet will only shorten the life of `em. It is always best to keep your goggles in your gear bag, safe from being scratched up.

Boots

▶ **See Figures 58, 59 and 60**

Most people have lots of specialized footwear for different purposes. We all have a pair of shoes for work, some have another for hiking, a different pair for sports, running or working out.

A good pair of riding boots will address the specific needs of a snowmobile rider, including comfort, functionality and protection. Although you can easily ride a snowmobile in a pair of regular work boots, the fact is, they won't serve the purpose as well as a pair of boots designed specifically for snowmobile riding. Motocross boots will provide plenty of protection, but the smooth sole will cause you problems if you try to walk with them in the snow.

Fig. 58 Motocross boots may provide plenty of protection, but the smooth sole will cause you problems if you try to walk with them in the snow

91233P04

Fig. 59 Although you can easily ride a snowmobile in a pair of regular work boots, the fact is, they won't serve the purpose as well as a pair of boots designed specifically for snowmobile riding

91243P70

Fig. 60 Gear manufacturers have addressed the special needs of snowmobile riders and make specialized boots for riding snowmobiles

Most gear manufacturers have addressed the needs of snowmobile riders and make specialized boots for riding snowmobiles. Some are similar to a motocross boot, with the exception of a cleated sole, while others closely resemble snow boots.

An important function of your boots is to provide warmth for your feet. It is particularly important that the boots prevent frostbite by keeping your feet warm and dry. Unlike some gear whose major purpose is crash protection, you will use the most important features of your boots EVERY time you ride.

Past the key features of a good sole and protection against cold and water, riding boots can offer a list of additional features similar to that of other riding equipment. Quality boots should offer you walking and riding comfort.

HOW TO SELECT A PAIR OF BOOTS

So how do you select a pair of riding boots? Remember the 4 basics mentioned at the beginning of this section:
1. Choose something you like.
2. Choose something that fits your riding.
3. Choose something that is high quality.
4. Choose something that fits properly.

Choose Something You Like

▶ See Figure 61

As usual, the easiest of the qualifications for deciding on a good snowmobile boot is to chose something that you like. It would be safe to say that most snowmobile boots look basically the same. So, pick out a color that matches the rest of your gear. But, before you go making compromises on style or functionality, look for both in one package.

If you really can't find a boot that genuinely matches both the styling and functionality you want, then you can start thinking about compromises. Think about your personality when making the decision. Some people are simply more concerned about style while some are more concerned about function. If buying a pair of really good boots means that the color isn't exactly what you want, then consider making a compromise. Again, if you really don't like the boots, just don't buy them.

91243P08

Fig. 61 The easiest of the qualifications for deciding on a good snowmobile boot is to chose something that you like

Choose Gear To Match Your Riding

▶ See Figures 62 and 63

Special boots designed specifically for riding snowmobiles should be on the top of your gear list. Snowmobile boots typically have a cleated sole, which is a real benefit to most riders. Say you're on a long trail ride, and you find a cool

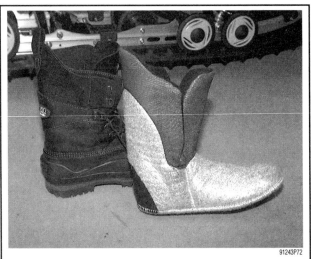

91243P72

Fig. 62 Boot manufacturers use a fleece lining to provide warmth and protection from the elements

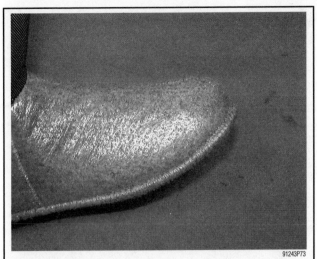

Fig. 63 This shiny fabric is actually woven with metal foil. The foil retains heated radiated by your body in your boots

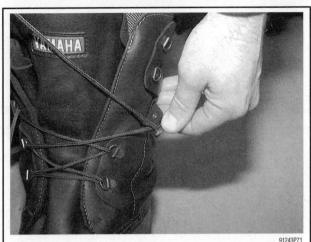

Fig. 64 Remember to buy boots made of high quality materials with workmanship which will provide support and protection in the event of a mishap

landmark a short hike away. Your cleated soles will enable you to hike the short distance in the snow. If you were wearing smooth soled boots, you would be slipping and sliding all over the place.

Waterproofing is the next consideration in a snowmobile boot. Most boot manufacturer's use a rubber sole sewn to a leather or synthetic upper. The rubber soles should be completely waterproof, however the joint between the sole and the leather upper may allow water to enter. Quality boots will have double or triple stitching at this point.

If you have purchased a pair of boots with leather uppers, then consider treating them with leather waterproofing treatment. The leather portion of the boot will never be waterproof, but they will be water resistant and should work just fine for all but the most severe conditions.

Another consideration is to find a boot that will keep your feet warm. Many manufacturers rate their boots by the lowest temperature at which the boots will protect your feet from freezing. This is especially important when you remember that your feet are especially susceptible to frostbite.

Most manufacturers will use a fleece lining inside their boots to provide warmth and protection from the boot's outer sole. This lining may be covered with a metallic looking fabric. This fabric is actually woven with metal foil. The whole idea behind this foil is that it is heated by your body heat and then retains the heat in your boots. Kind of trick, huh?

The last consideration is whether you like laces or latches. Before you make your decision, take into consideration that you will be wearing bulky gloves and that you will likely need to remove the gloves to tie your laces. Latches can be operated with gloves on.

Choose Quality Gear

▶ **See Figure 64**

Like so many things, good riding gear is specially designed for snowmobile riders. Your first place to look for a decent pair of boots is going to be a snowmobile gear supplier. Look at name brands from companies that make SNOWMOBILE gear. It doesn't matter how good a work, hiking or cowboy boot a company produces, if it doesn't understand your specific needs, then the boot will not do as good a job as one which was well thought out for snowmobile use.

Remember to buy boots made of high quality materials with workmanship which will provide support and protection in the event of a mishap. Check out the boot's method of "lacing up". If the outer flap is made of hook-and-loop, make sure it is of high quality. How do you know if it is high quality? If you have to pull really hard to separate the halves, its the good stuff. Some boots have cam-type buckles, inspect them closely and make sure they're of good quality. They're your feet, dude.

The best snowmobile boots will have a combination of these features:
• Large pull loops to help you pull the boots on easier
• Full grain leather upper to make the boot strong, durable and water resistant

• Comfortable inner liners to protect your feet from the cold
• Felt insole to trap heat and wick away moisture from your feet
• Thermal foil layer to reflect heat and deflect the cold
• Triple stitching on all seams for strength and durability
• Rubber soles that are flexible, yet durable to give you excellent traction
• A steel shank to strengthen the boot and provide extra support for your instep

Choose Something That Fits Properly

▶ **See Figures 65 and 66**

Anyone who has broken-in a new pair of boots at some point in their life knows the pain which can be caused by an ill fitting boot. Luckily, when most boots break-in, the materials stretch and the padding settles so the pain goes away. BUT, if the boot is improperly sized, that the pain will probably stay with you as long as you wear the boots.

A boot which is too small at the time of purchase may not stretch enough to alleviate the pressure (and subsequent pain) in the months of wear that follows. A boot which is too large will move around the foot when walking and will likely cause blisters. Ideally, you want a boot which is SNUG (not tight) when you try it on the first time. If you wear special socks (such as thick, sweat-wicking sport socks), then you should be wearing those socks when you try on the boot.

Any snowmobile rider will eventually spend some time walking in their boots. So it is imperative that you buy a pair of boots which will be comfortable

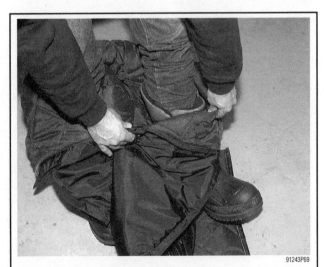

Fig. 65 Most snowmobile bibs are designed to allow you to put your boots on first, then slip them into your bibs

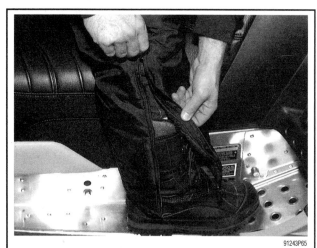

Fig. 66 You will eventually spend some time walking in your boots; buy a pair of boots which will be comfortable for more than just sitting on a snowmobile

for more than just sitting on a snowmobile. Make sure your toes are not scrunched up inside your boots when you're standing up straight.

The best riding boots will offer cam-type buckles, laces or hook and loop adjustments to assure proper fit. Remember that a slip-on boot must be loose enough to pull it on and off, and it usually cannot provide the comfort, protection or snug fit that is obtained by adjusting a boot after it is on your foot. This is why it is so important to have buckles and laces.

HOW TO CARE FOR YOUR BOOTS

▶ See Figure 67

Almost all snowmobile riding boots are a rubber and nylon/leather combination construction. The soles of the boots are made of rubber for waterproofing and the uppers are either leather, nylon or some other fabric. The same rules of care apply to your boots as to any other garment. Keep them clean and keep them in proper working order.

Whenever the leather portion of boots is exposed to water, it should be treated with a high quality leather treatment. The water will remove the natural oils which are so important to the leather's well being, allowing the leather to dryout and crack. Although some cracks in the surface of the leather will happen no matter what, deep cracking will weaken the material and eventually lead to splits (and ruining a good pair of boots).

Fig. 67 Be sure to clean and treat your boots regularly using a quality product made for leather like Lexol®

Gloves

▶ See Figures 68 and 69

Everyone owns a pair of gloves, right? And all gloves have one thing in common, whether they are ski gloves, work gloves, or driving gloves—they are all designed to protect your hands. Snowmobile gloves are no different, they are designed to protect your hands from everything you might encounter while riding a snowmobile. And like most types of snowmobile gear, they should be specially designed to live up to all of the varied tasks a snowmobiler will put to them.

A good pair of riding gloves will first and foremost provide warmth for your hands and protection against wind and cold. But your gloves will likely do a lot more than that. They will protect your hands from the heat of the engine when you fumble for the reserve petcock, or when you reach around the cylinder head to adjust the idle speed on your carburetor. Your gloves will likely be called upon to help lessen the stinging of debris which your hands come into contact with while holding the grips cruising down the trail. They will be asked to keep your dry during banzai blasts though the fresh snow. In many ways, a good pair of gloves will become another one of your best friends on the trail.

Fig. 68 Utility gloves are great for all-around use but should never be used for snowmobile riding

Fig. 69 Specialized riding gloves offer excellent protection and good looks

HOW TO SELECT A PAIR OF GLOVES

So how do you select a pair of riding gloves? (here we go again . . .) Remember the 4 basics mentioned at the beginning of this section:

1. Choose something you like.
2. Choose something that fits your riding.
3. Choose something that is high quality.
4. Choose something that fits properly.

Choose Something You Like

▶ **See Figure 70**

If you've read the rest of this section then you already should have the hang of this category, but just in case you've missed the other gear we've been describing we'll summarize it again. Don't buy gloves which you think LOOK STUPID, you won't wear them. Seems like common sense right? Well, sometime we need to state the obvious.

The rule is still simple, buy what you like, just make sure it will work for your type of riding. A pair of fingerless, chrome-studded black biker gloves might be something that you like, but let's face it; they won't do squat for protection in a crash and your fingers will most likely have to be cut off due to frostbite. Look at the other topics (make sure the glove also fits your needs, is high quality and just plain FITS).

➡ **If much of your riding will be taking place in severely cold weather, then a pair of mittens may keep your hands a little more comfortable. Mittens allow your fingers to radiate heat to each other and tend to hold the heat in better. However, remember they come with the price of decreased dexterity and should only be called upon for the most extreme of conditions.**

Fig. 70 The rule is still simple, buy what you like. We chose these leather Yamaha gloves for their looks and functionality

Choose Gear To Match Your Riding

▶ **See Figures 71, 72 and 73**

The neat thing about gloves is that compared to other snowmobile riding gear, they are inexpensive (meaning you may be able to justify owning more than one pair) and they are relatively compact (meaning you should even be able to carry more than one pair with you on the ride). We all like to save money and it is really convenient to own just one all purpose pair, so you will probably want to look for that first. But remember that most all purpose garments make compromises and when it comes to gloves you have a real option here to get more than one pair which does one particular thing VERY WELL. The case could be made for a medium weight insulated glove may be useful for milder days or for a pair of mittens for use when not operating the controls of the snowmobile.

The first and foremost job of a snowmobile glove is to keep your hands warm. The best gloves will have a good layer of insulating material underneath a

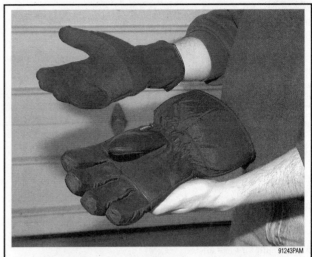

Fig. 71 These snowmobile gloves from Arctic Cat have removable liners that can also be used separately

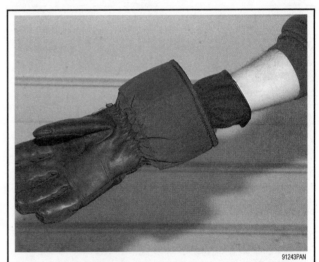

Fig. 72 The inner liner provides a good layer of insulating material, while the outer glove acts as a windproof shell

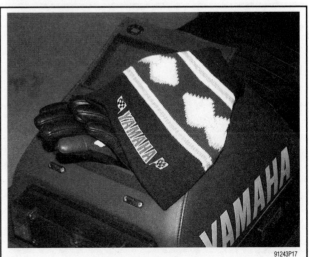

Fig. 73 It's a good idea to carry a spare pair of gloves and maybe a hat every time you go out for a ride. Better to be safe than sorry

windproof shell. The shell on many gloves is NOT leather, but the better ones will have some sort of leather or ballistic material for the fingers and for the palms (again providing abrasion protection for mishaps).

Many gloves will also contain a waterproofing layer (such as Gore-Tex®). Remember that moisture and wind combine to mean really, really cold hands.

✳✳ WARNING

Be careful about oversized or overstuffed winter gloves. If you can't safely operate the controls of the snowmobile, then who cares how warm the glove is, it is useless for riding.

Another thing to consider is whether or not the glove is a gauntlet style. A gauntlet-styled glove can be worn over the ends of your jacket sleeves (effectively blocking all air flow). A glove which fits over the sleeves of your jacket is preferred because it helps seal out the cold air.

Choose Quality Gear

▶ **See Figures 74, 75 and 76**

Can you ride with a pair of cloth work gloves? Sure, but don't expect them to protect your hands from frostbite. Like most snowmobile gear, the majority of

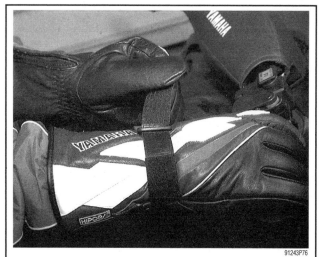

Fig. 76 . . . and Velcro®adjustments help to seal the glove to your jacket, helping to keep your whole body warm

the best stuff is specially designed for snowmobile riding. You are going to find the best quality gear from shops or catalogs that cater to serious snowmobilers.

Look for products from companies that specialize in snowmobile riding apparel. Light weight insulated materials are good signs that a company is serious about its gear. Fingers which are constructed of multiple sections, allowing the hand to curl around the grip without stretching the material will allow for the best fit. Reinforced areas on the palm and the fingers are also good hints that the glove is designed for function and not just fashion.

Choose Something That Fits Properly

▶ **See Figures 77, 78, 79, 80 and 81**

Have you ever tried to pull a zipper or work a throttle in a glove that doesn't fit? If you have too much fabric in the fingers, then you will not be able to grip anything. With gloves that are too big, your hands will be stumbling over the levers, grips and controls of your snowmobile. On the other side of the coin, a glove that is too small will pull back on your fingers, fighting your grip. A small glove will make it hard and uncomfortable to maintain your grip of the handlebars and other controls.

When trying on a pair of gloves, the tips of the fingers should just touch when you interlock your hands and push down at the base of the fingers. This is a good way to tell if the gloves are the proper size. Another test is to put on a glove, and make a fist, as tight as you can. If the glove feels really tight over the

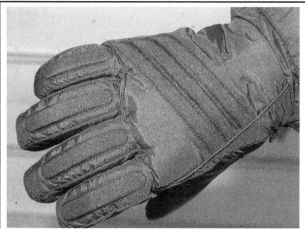

Fig. 74 Light weight insulated materials, like those used by Joe Rocket in the manufacturer of these gloves, are good signs that a company is serious about its gear

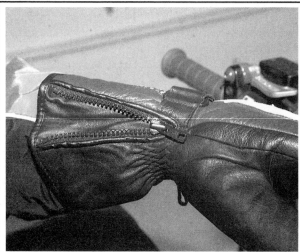

Fig. 75 Zippers . . .

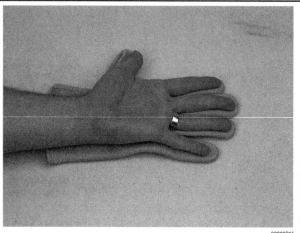

Fig. 77 A glove should be JUST barely larger than your hand, if it is too tight or too loose it will probably make it difficult to work the controls

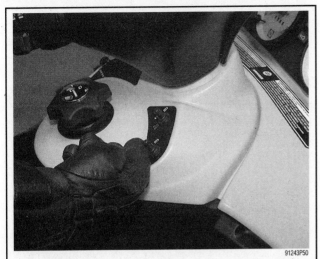

Fig. 78 When trying on a pair of gloves, make sure you can operate all the controls on your sled while wearing the gloves

Fig. 79 A proper fitting glove will allow you to operate the throttle smoothly . . .

Fig. 80 . . . but more importantly, it will allow you to operate a very important safety feature; the sled's kill switch

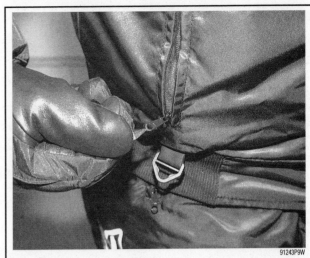

Fig. 81 Have you ever tried to pull a zipper with a glove that doesn't fit? It can be a trying experience

knuckles, it may be too small. Or if the tips of your fingers feel tight, the glove may also be too small for your hand. Try on a few different sizes, and perform these tests on each pair until you find a pair that fits your hands.

HOW TO CARE FOR YOUR GLOVES

Most gloves are made of either leather or some synthetic material. As usual, the routine is to keep the gloves clean and in the case of leather to treat the gloves to replenish their natural oils. There are some gloves which use ballistic materials and these should be cared for according to their manufacturer's instructions.

Jackets

When most people think of a jacket, they think of something to protect them from the elements, and that is certainly true of a snowmobiling jacket. But riding a snowmobile places certain demands on your gear that would not be applicable to most other activities.

SNOWMOBILE JACKET FEATURES

▶ See Figures 82 thru 88

Riding a snowmobile places certain demands on your gear that would not be applicable to most other activities. And unfortunately, many people either don't

Fig. 82 A jacket that is designed for riding will have a variety of useful features like storm flaps . . .

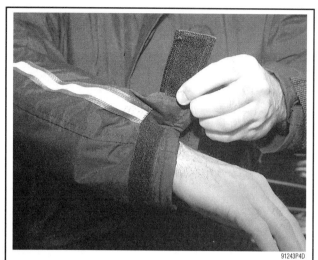

Fig. 83 . . . closures to keep the wind and water out of your sleeves . . .

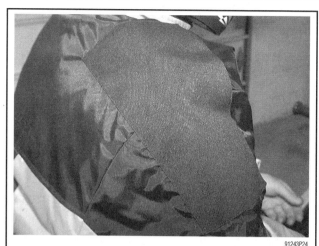

Fig. 86 Another feature of most quality jackets is some type of ballistic material in key areas like the shoulders. Cordura® is one type of this material

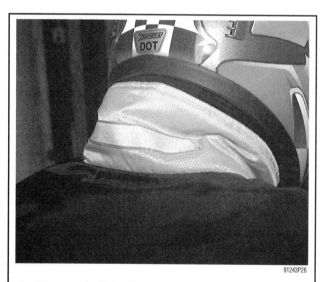

Fig. 84 . . . and a high collar to keep the elements off your neck

Fig. 87 This jacket features Joe Rocket's ballistic material

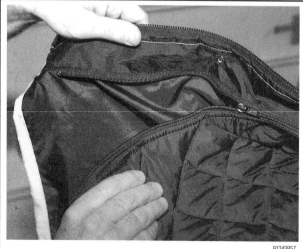

Fig. 85 Other features should include a zip out liner for those warm riding days

Fig. 88 And you thought frost free was only a feature for refrigerators

realize or don't believe the need for a jacket to do something more. A real snow-mobiling jacket will protect you from the elements, be comfortable and allow maneuverability while riding, be waterproof yet allow the jacket to breathe, will provide plenty of storage and have easy to open zippers.

A Cut To Fit Your Body When Riding

▶ See Figures 89, 90, 91, and 92

Take your favorite dress or casual jacket, put it on and then sit on your snow-mobile. Chances are you will notice a few things that make this jacket comfort-able the rest of the time, may not make it suitable for riding. For one thing, when you lean forward, even slightly, and grasp the handle bars, the sleeves will probably pull back exposing your arms, and the hem may pull upward, expos-ing your back. Depending on the material and the collar, it may flap or even whip you in the wind. And there probably aren't any other retention points, such as a cinching system at the waist to seal cold air out and keep it in place in the case of a crash.

The sleeves of most will be a little long when you are standing around before a ride, but when you climb in the saddle they should fit just right. Sleeves should have a hook and loop tab for adjustment and/or a zipper so it can be sealed to keep the air out. Waists should also have some sort of belt or adjust-ment to seal air.

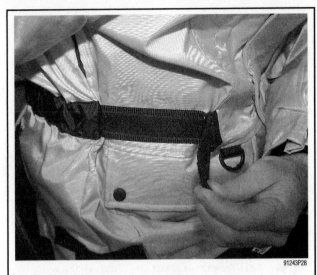

Fig. 91 Velcro® closures around the waist . . .

Fig. 89 A snowmobiling suit may seem a little big when standing . . .

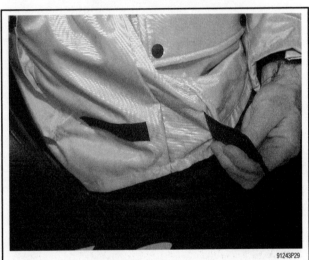

Fig. 92 . . . and the thighs are important to tailor the fit of your jacket

Ventilation

▶ See Figures 93, 94 and 95

Any riding jacket will keep you out of direct contact with the elements, and if there is sufficient airflow to allow your sweat to evaporate, it can keep you cool as well. The most popular way to do this is with a series of zippered vents and a mesh or removable liner which will allow air to circulate. Air can enter from unzipped sleeves, or through intake vents (under the arms or on either side of the lapel) and can exit one or more vents across the back.

Linings

▶ See Figures 96, 97, 98 and 99

A lining of insulating material is necessary to keep you warm. A removable lining is even better since it means the jacket can probably also be used in warmer weather. And if you are really going for the gusto, some companies offer detachable sleeves so the jacket can be turned into a vest.

A quality riding jacket will offer protection against the cold using a material such as Thinsulate®. This material is a thermal insulation that is light weight, warm, extremely moisture resistant and breathable. It is designed to resist com-pression during use. By resisting compression, it provides a quilted air pocket that insulates your body from the cold. This is much the same principle as a dual-pane insulated window.

Fig. 90 . . . but a quality suit will fit perfectly when seated in the riding position

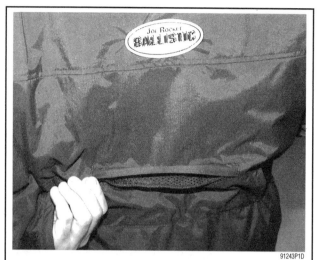

Fig. 93 Riding a snowmobile is hard work. Proper ventilation for your back . . .

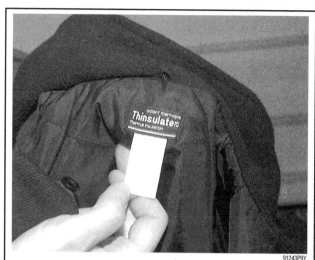

Fig. 96 A quality riding jacket will offer protection against the cold using a material such as Thinsulate®

Fig. 94 . . . and under your arms allows for air circulation through the jacket to keep you cool

Fig. 97 Serious riders want a jacket with a lining that can be removed (making the jacket suitable for all weather)—Some jackets include a lining which can be worn separately, as a windbreaker

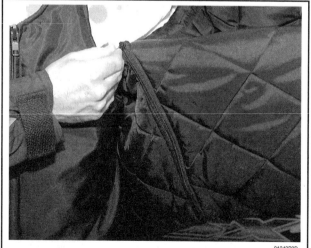

Fig. 95 Zip out linings allow you to adjust the warmth of your jacket for different climates

Fig. 98 If your jacket is not equipped with a liner, wearing multiple layers of clothing provides the same advantages

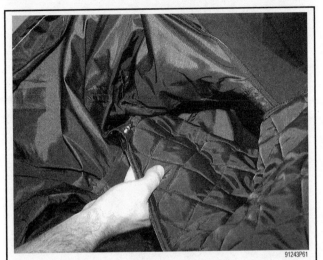

Fig. 99 Liners should fit properly without being bulky and be easily removable using zippers

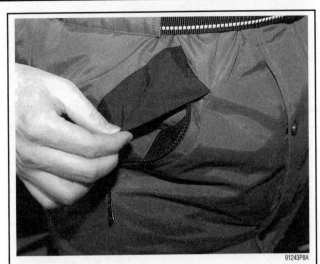

Fig. 101 This pocket uses a hood and a zipper to retain the contents and make it waterproof

Pockets

♦ See Figures 100 thru 106

When you travel on a snowmobile, you learn to pack light. But there are a lot of little things you like to keep handy, like wallets or lip balm, an oil rag or a trail map. A jacket with a lot of pockets is going to become a convenient trail companion. Of course, the pockets should have zippers or snaps to close them and prevent these precious items from falling out. Put on a glove, and see how easy it is to access the pockets. This is important, since you don't want to have to keep taking off your gloves every time you need something from a pocket on your jacket.

⁂ CAUTION

Be careful what you decide to put in your pockets. Hard and sharp objects are probably not good ideas in the case of a get-off. Remember that a key, a pair of eyeglasses or that little screwdriver you like to keep handy could be driven into your body in a crash. If you wouldn't like to fall on a particular object, DON'T KEEP IT in one of your jacket pockets.

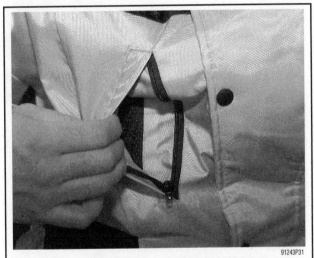

Fig. 102 Even though this pocket is positioned on the right side of this jacket, it is designed to be accessed using the left hand

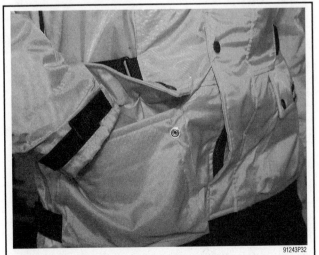

Fig. 100 If you can fit your hands in your pockets this far while wearing gloves, the pockets are big enough

Fig. 103 Inside pockets are designed to keep your important items dry and warm

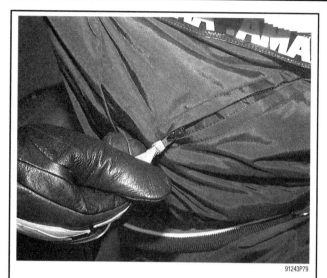

Fig. 104 Pocket zippers should be easy to operate with gloves on

Fig. 105 The most common type of pocket is the zippered patch pocket

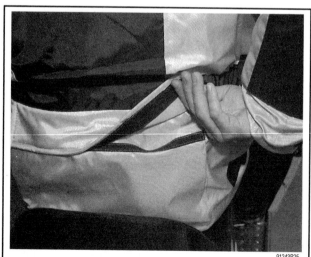

Fig. 106 This rear pocket comes in handy for larger items like maps or extra clothing

Waterproof Or Water-Resistant

◆ See Figures 107 and 108

Any decent jacket will protect you from getting wet, especially if you keep it well treated. But, there are options today with materials like Gore-Tex® which allow a very high degree of resistance to moisture and still provide plenty of ventilation. For one thing, if your jacket is already waterproof, you will never have to face the question, "Should I turn around and head back to the truck because I am soaked and freezing?" You can just keep on riding.

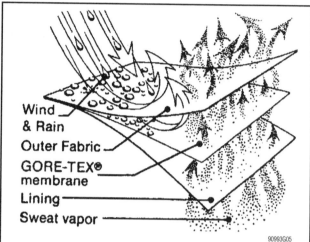

Fig. 107 Fabrics like Gore-Tex® are breathable, yet waterproof materials that allow you to stay cool and dry when the weather is warm and wet

Fig. 108 Always check the manufacturer's tag to see what materials are used to improve the performance of your jacket

HOW TO SELECT A JACKET

So how do you select a jacket? Remember the 4 basics mentioned at the beginning of this section:
1. Choose something you like.
2. Choose something that fits your riding.
3. Choose something that is high quality.
4. Choose something that fits properly.

Choose Something You Like

▸ **See Figure 109**

First things first, you've got to like the look of the jacket you pick so we are not going to tell you to buy a bright purple jacket just to be more visible if you think you look really stupid in it. Go out and try on some jackets to get a feel for what you want.

BUT, here are some things to keep in mind. Remember that a lighter color will help to reflect the sun's rays and will keep you cooler in direct sunlight. We've already said a couple of times that a brighter color helps to keep you visible to other riders, so it helps there too.

➡ **Keep in mind that in direct sunlight, taking the jacket off will not keep you as cool as you would be under the right jacket. The direct sun will heat your skin, rather than allowing a jacket to reflect some of that heat. The direct sunlight will further warm your skin which will prevent you from fully realizing the benefit of sweat evaporation (and there is that whole sunburn thing to worry about as well). Look at Arabs in the desert—they cover themselves completely with loose fitting, light colored robes. This reflects the sun's rays (and therefore some of its heat) allowing their sweat to evaporate and take body heat with it.**

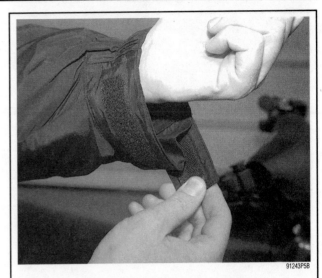

Fig. 110 Features such as this closure around the wrist . . .

Fig. 109 So you want to be noticed on the trail? This jacket features styling made of reflective material

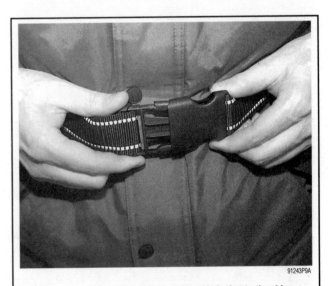

Fig. 111 . . . and this belt, custom tailor this jacket to the rider

Choose Gear To Match Your Riding

Hard-core snowcrossers are probably going to place more emphasis on crash protection (impact resistance) than they would on number of pockets. Someone who does a lot of hauling stuff around the farm during the winter is going to want a jacket that protects them from the elements and keeps them warm.

Obviously, if you live in Antarctica your needs are going to be a little different than if you live in Maine right? But that still doesn't mean the Maine resident does not have to worry about extreme weather. You'll have to make an assessment of what your needs and desires are in a jacket, but remember that the more versatile the jacket is, the more likely you are to keep it on all of the time.

Look at the various features we listed in this section and decide which ones are most important to you. Look for a jacket that fills all your needs.

Most snowmobile riding jackets are manufactured using a breathable, waterproof material. There are a few major advantages here. The light, breathable materials can be more comfortable to wear than a regular jacket, and will help to keep you comfortable, while still offering protection. And, unlike many sealed, nylon or plastic rain suits, a breathable water-resistant jacket allows your sweat to escape keeping you significantly drier. These jackets are often easy to clean, as they can often be thrown in the washing machine.

Choose Something That Fits Properly

▸ **See Figures 110 and 111**

When you try a jacket on, the best thing to do is to climb on your snowmobile (or a similar model in the showroom) and see how it fits your riding position. Do the sleeves pull back or does the waist ride up excessively? If a sample snowmobile like yours is not handy, try lifting your hands over your head, the sleeves should not expose too much of your wrists. Make sure that the jacket does not bind in the shoulders, but that it is also snug enough to stay in place in the even of the mishap (again, adjustment tabs or belts are handy for this).

If there is a lining, ask yourself if it will be sufficient for all of your riding needs. And if it won't, make sure there is some room under the jacket for one or more additional layers (might we suggest polar fleece and/or electric garments). Just make sure the jacket isn't TOO BIG, since it may balloon and be impossible to seal the wind out when riding at speed.

Choose Quality Gear

▸ **See Figures 112, 113 and 114**

If the gear is produced or sold by a company that makes its living from snowmobile riders, and has many of the features that we've described, then the chances are it is high quality. Again, there are no guarantees here, so you should do some sleuthing before you decide to buy. Look at snowmobile brand name merchandise. Look at the quality and construction (especially the seams). Even a heavyweight riding jacket won't do you much good if the seams are not reinforced to keep it from coming apart in a fall.

The best snowmobile riding jackets will have a combination of these features:

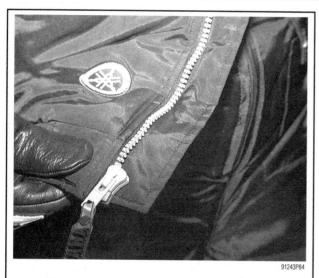

Fig. 112 Sturdy zippers . . .

Fig. 113 . . . with long pulls that can be handled easily with gloves are the hallmark of a quality jacket

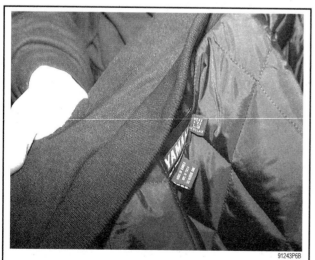

Fig. 114 Items like this elastic collar that fits tight to your neck to keep out drafts show attention to detail

- A specialized lining to help retain body heat and keep you warm
- A lightweight comfortable material that allows excellent maneuverability
- Waterproof or water-resistant outer shell to help keep you dry
- A cut to fit your body when riding (and various adjustments or retention systems to keep them in place in the case of a mishap)
- Large, easy to access pockets with easy opening zippers or snaps
- Bright colors and/or reflective material to help keep you visible

HOW TO CARE FOR YOUR JACKET

◢ See Figure 115

How you will need to care for your jacket will vary depending on the materials from which it is made. The first thing to do is read the labels or any literature that came with the jacket. The manufacturer will probably give you the best information for the particular materials used in your jacket. The materials that modern riding jackets are made from might have specific cleaning instructions. Be sure to follow the instructions provided to ensure a long life for your jacket.

Fig. 115 Special materials require special cleaning. Always follow the manufacturer's instructions for cleaning high tech materials

Kidney Belt

◢ See Figures 116, 117, 118 and 119

A kidney belt, or support belt, is basically a large elastic band that is worn around the waist to help support your back and internal organs. Motocross riders have worn them for many years, and snowmobile riders are quickly discovering their advantages. It is a good idea for all snowmobile riders to wear a kidney belt to avoid bruising internal organs. If you have ridden a snowmobile for any length of time, chances are that you are quite familiar with the "kicked in the stomach" feeling. A kidney belt will help eliminate bruising, and support your lower back.

Choose Something You Like

When you wear a kidney belt, most of it will be covered by your pants, so colors and styles won't matter too much. There are a large variety of belts available, all made from different materials. Some belts use hard foam for support, and others are made with plastic rods woven inside the fabric. Look for something that suits your taste.

Choose Gear To Match Your Riding

When it comes to kidney belts, **every** snowmobile rider can benefit from wearing one. All types of riding can really shake up your internals, and a kidney belt can help alleviate the symptoms. Riders that spend a lot of time riding on rough surfaces are going to benefit the most from a kidney belt. Utility riders

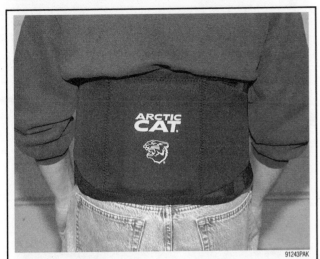

Fig. 116 An example of a kidney belt. Kidney belts can be worn inside or outside of your riding clothes

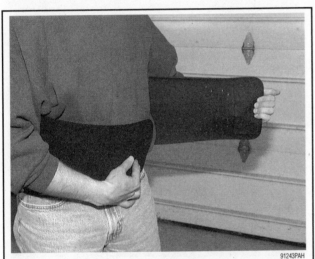

Fig. 117 To install the belt, stretch it tightly around your back and fasten the Velcro® closure in the front . . .

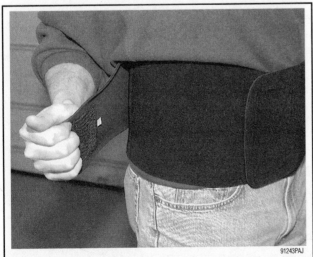

Fig. 118 . . . next, take the side pulls and adjust them to gain the best support

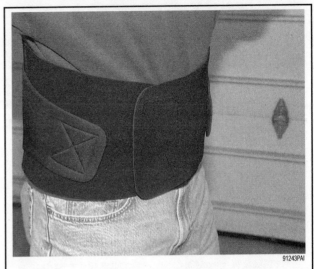

Fig. 119 This is an example of a properly adjusted kidney belt

might have less need for a kidney belt but will still realize the benefits by wearing one.

Choose Quality Gear

When looking for a quality kidney belt, the main thing to look for is high quality hook and loop fasteners. Check the strength when you separate the halves; if it takes considerable effort to pull them apart, then you can be assured of high quality. Anything less will lose its grip after a short time.

Choose Something That Fits Properly

Finding a kidney belt that fits properly shouldn't be a problem, since they are elastic and have hook and loop for adjustment. Most kidney belts are the same width; though some are available in Junior sizes. Also, keep in mind the width of the belt. A thick belt will provide good support, but may feel constrictive in anything but the most upright sitting position. Narrow belts will allow a little more freedom, but may not be as supportive. If you have never worn a kidney belt, ask to try one on and sit on a snowmobile in the showroom. If the belt feels too restrictive, try a narrower belt until you find one that fits to your liking.

Bibs/Pants

SNOWMOBILE BIBS/PANTS FEATURES

♦ **See Figure 120**

Specialized snowmobile riding bibs/pants will protect you from the elements, be comfortable and allow maneuverability while riding, be waterproof yet allow the breathability, will provide plenty of storage and have easy to open pockets.

As with jackets, the position of a rider is taken into consideration, so the possible problems of binding and tightness that you might experience from regular pants are eliminated. Another feature of bibs/pants is that they offer knee pads to provide protection that pants do not offer.

HOW TO SELECT A PAIR OF BIBS/PANTS

So how do you select a pair of riding bibs? Remember the 4 basics mentioned at the beginning of this section:
1. Choose something you like.
2. Choose something that fits your riding.
3. Choose something that is high quality.
4. Choose something that fits properly.

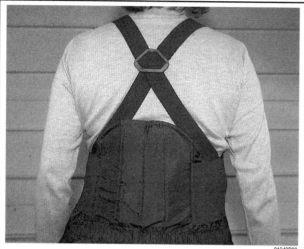

Fig. 120 These bibs/pants have sewn-in padding around the back for additional protection and support

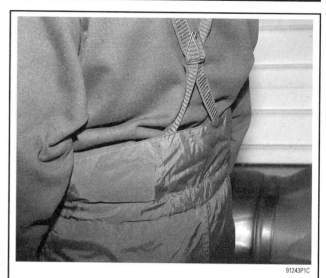

Fig. 122 These bibs have thin suspenders with a low rise back . . .

Choose Something You Like

▶ See Figures 121, 122 and 123

As with all of your other gear, find a pair of bibs/pants that appeal to you. Plain and subtle, or loud and colorful, there is something out there for you.

Female riders can choose from any number of bibs designed especially for them. These bibs have special features to custom fit the bibs to a woman's shape. Some even have the old fashioned drop bottom (like the long red flannel union suit) for when nature calls in the middle of a ride.

Choose Gear To Match Your Riding

▶ See Figures 124, 125, 126, 127 and 128

The majority of weekend riders usually wear nylon bibs that match their jackets. If you are considering a pair of specialized leather bibs, chances are you're a sport-type rider. The bibs/pants featured here are designed for normal riding; just about any snowmobile rider can benefit from the extra protection and convenience that they provide. Knee pads sewn into riding bibs/pants strengthen this much used area and can greatly reduce the chances of tearing the nylon shell.

Most riding bibs/pants are made from breathable, water-resistant materials. Another feature to consider in a pair of riding bibs/pants is ease of cleaning. If the riding bibs/pants are machine washable, they can be tossed into the laundry with your regular clothes.

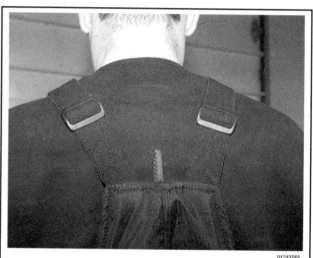

Fig. 123 . . . while these bibs offer a high rise back and more supportive suspenders

Fig. 121 These bibs from Arctic Cat are basic black and will color coordinate with anything

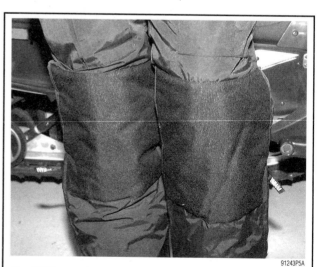

Fig. 124 Knee pads sewn into the bibs offer protection from flying objects and strengthen this area of the bib

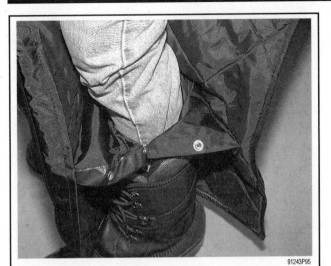

Fig. 125 If you ride in deep powder, make sure you bibs are equipped with some sort of gaiter

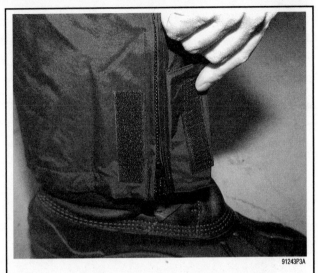

Fig. 128 . . . and close the storm flap to waterproof the zipper

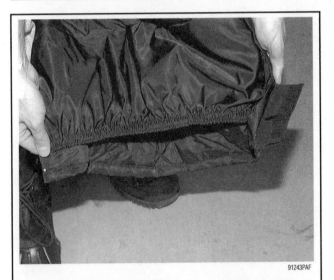

Fig. 126 This elastic bottom keeps the gaiter snug to your boots

A new innovation in bibs/pants is the Drop Seat feature. This is something like the old one piece underwear where the bottom opens to allow you to. . . well . . . you get the idea. Lets just say this feature is especially important to lady riders, although the gents will find it equally as nice on occasion.

Choose Quality Gear

◆ See Figures 129, 130, 131 and 132

Buying a quality pair of riding bibs/pants is just like any other garment. You'll want to look for durable material, heavy-duty stitching, etc. Also, looking for unique features such as a drop seat will tell you if the particular manufacturer is keeping up with modern snowmobiling trends.

Choose Something That Fits Properly

◆ See Figures 133 thru 139

Snowmobile bibs/pants are sized just like regular pants—according to waist size. However, the length of riding bibs/pants is usually standard. Riding bibs/pants are supposed to be worn over your boots, (to prevent moisture from getting under your clothing) so the length should be a little long on you when you try them on.

Fig. 127 Once the gaitors are tucked into your boots, zip the bib legs closed . . .

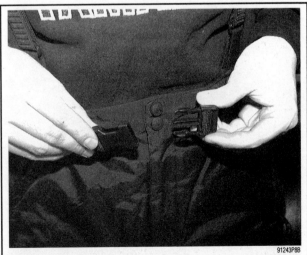

Fig. 129 These bibs feature a heavy-duty plastic buckle to provide extra security

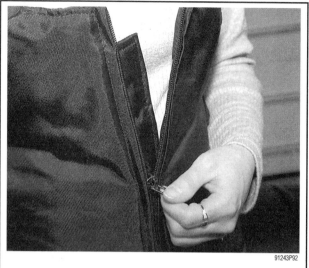

Fig. 130 Strong zippers are a must

91243P92

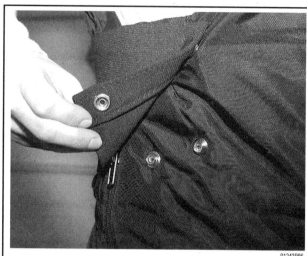

Fig. 133 High mobility areas, such as the waist, should be reinforced . . .

91243P86

Fig. 131 Bibs provide a convenient place for additional quick access storage pockets

91243P7A

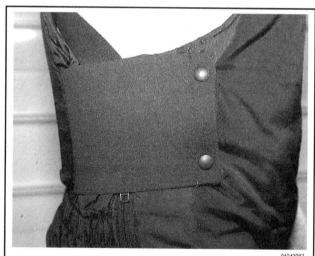

Fig. 134 . . . like this pair of bibs from Joe Rocket. This provides extra support and also tailors the fit to the rider

91243P87

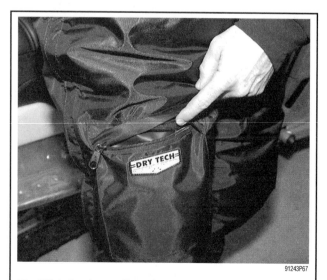

Fig. 132 Just make sure the pockets are zippered and waterproof

91243P67

Fig. 135 Properly sized bibs should slip on easily, even when wearing boots

91243PAG

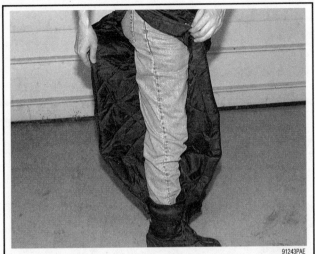

Fig. 136 Bib legs should fully unzip to ease the task of putting the bibs on

Fig. 137 Gaitors should tuck nicely into your boots to provide a waterproof fit

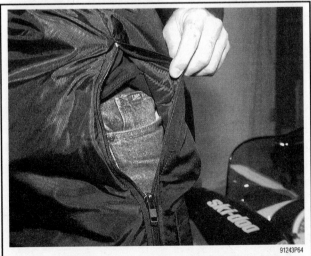

Fig. 138 Full length side zippers allow access to inside pockets without removing the bibs

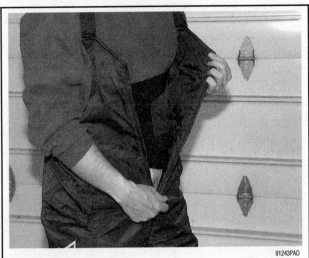

Fig. 139 Full length front zippers allow the bibs to be put on easily, yet when zipped up provide a nice fit

When trying on a pair of bibs, consider the extra space needed for wearing extra layers of clothing. If possible, it is best to trial fit bibs/pants while wearing several layers of clothes; this will provide a more accurate fit.

Now try on your boots and make sure the bibs/pants will cover them. If not, choose a longer pair of bibs/pants.

HOW TO CARE FOR YOUR BIBS/PANTS

How you will need to care for your bibs/pants will vary depending on the materials from which they are made. The first thing to do is read the labels or garment owner's manual. The manufacturer will probably give you the best information for the particular materials used in your gear, and the required method for safe washing.

Chest Protectors

A chest protector is worn over or under a jacket to provide extra crash protection to your chest, shoulders and back. They are usually made from flexible plastic, and use suspended mesh or foam padding. If you are into snowcross, or just looking for additional protection, you should seriously consider a chest protector.

HOW TO SELECT A CHEST PROTECTOR

▶ See Figure 140

Chest protectors are offered in many different styles, each for a specific use. A basic chest protector, which is usually a foam or plastic pad worn over the chest, offers minimal protection from flying debris from other riders. A more elaborate chest protectors may include shoulder pads, elbow pads and back pads, providing the ultimate in upper body protection. Some manufacturers offer modular chest protectors, so you can add (or remove) pads to customize a chest protector to your liking.

As with most of the gear within this section, there are four basic guidelines to follow:
- Choose something you like.
- Choose something that fits your riding.
- Choose something that is high quality.
- Choose something that fits properly.

Choose Something You Like

Some chest protectors can make you feel like a Storm Trooper from a Star Wars movie set. You might feel strange trying one on, but keep in mind that chest protectors are for protection, not looks. As with most snowmobile gear, a variety of colors are available, so you can match your chest protector with your other gear. You can also wear your chest protector under your riding jacket

Fig. 140 Chest protectors come in different styles and types to fit your needs

91233P02

(make sure it fits under your jacket before you buy it) if you don't care for the color or style. Remember, you're going for maximum protection here, so looks shouldn't be a top priority.

Choose Gear To Match Your Riding

Obviously, if you only use your snowmobile for work or pleasure riding, a chest protector is a bit excessive. Snowcross racers or riders who are into extreme riding are going to benefit the most from a chest protector. In the event of a crash, a chest protector will greatly reduce the chance of injury, especially one equipped with shoulder and elbow pads.

Choose Quality Gear

▶ See Figures 141 and 142

When looking at a chest protector, check where the straps attach to the plastic. Higher quality chest protectors will actually rivet or sew the nylon straps right on to the plastic. Look for a well-made connection. Also, look at the padding; how is it attached to the plastic? Is the plastic flexible, but strong, or does it seem to be brittle? As with other apparel, thoroughly inspect the quality of the construction.

91233P49

Fig. 141 The shoulder pads on this chest protector use mesh to suspend the outer shell above the shoulder

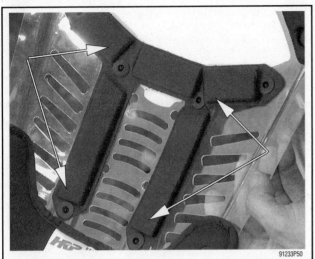

Fig. 142 The foam padding that protects the spine is held in place by plastic clips on this chest protector

Choose Something That Fits Properly

Chest protectors usually don't come in shirt sizes. Typically, there are two sizes—small and large. When trying on a chest protector, sit on a snowmobile in the showroom and see if the way things fit changes. Move your arms back and forth—does anything bind or constrict your movement? Different brands of chest protectors offer different features, and some might fit you better than others. If possible, try on a few chest protectors; hopefully one will fit you properly and won't constrict your movement.

HOW TO CARE FOR YOUR CHEST PROTECTOR

Most chest protectors are made from plastic, foam, and fabric webbing. Cleaning your chest protectors in most cases is simply a matter of wiping them clean with a soft cloth. If they are covered in muck, hosing them off with fresh water will help to loosen any heavily soiled areas, to avoid scratching. Be very careful with chemicals; the plastic or foam can easily be damaged. Mild soap and water is always a safe way to clean your chest protectors.

In addition to keeping your chest protector clean, regular inspection of any rivets, webbing, or glued joints is essential. If a worn piece of webbing or broken rivet is found, fix it (or have it fixed) immediately. Your chest protector won't do you any good if it is falling apart. If your chest protector develops any cracks in the plastic, it should be replaced, since it's ability to safeguard you in an accident is greatly diminished.

Electric Garments

 **See Figures 143 and 144**

The key to extreme weather riding is proper riding gear. A good full face helmet, a high quality jacket, bibs/pants and boots which also cut the wind and insulate you will make a tremendous difference. But even when all of this is combined, you may still find that a weekend ride is tough even with the sun shining. The answer then becomes electric garments.

By using electric garments, you are set for just about any weather. The electric vest pictured here provides the all important warming of your central core which actually makes the rest of your gear feel like it is doing a better job from your jacket to your boots. One very cool (uhhh, make that warm) feature of the vest we tested was a heated collar that brought heat right up to the base of your neck, just below the helmet.

✳✳ CAUTION

One VERY IMPORTANT POINT to make here is that electric components can fail (whether it is the accessory jack, the wiring or the garment itself). Although we have had NO problems with the

Fig. 143 Nothing matches the warmth or comfort of an electric vest and a pair of electric gloves on a cold day. This combination from Widder® shows the gloves, wiring harness with thermostat and vest with heated collar

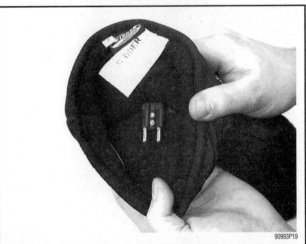

Fig. 144 Most electric gloves are attached to your snowmobile's battery using easy to connect plugs such as these banana plugs

test gear, the fact is that they COULD stop working with little notice, so DO NOT attempt a long distance ride without enough layers or other gear to keep you warm, JUST IN CASE. You'd probably survive a short trip if the harness shorted out one day or the fuse blew. But, wouldn't it suck to freeze to death deep in the woods or on a mountainside because you accidentally cut the wiring.

HOW TO SELECT ELECTRIC GARMENTS

So how do you select an electric garment? Remember the 4 basics mentioned at the beginning of this section:
1. Choose something you like.
2. Choose something that fits your riding.
3. Choose something that is high quality.
4. Choose something that fits properly.

Choose Something You Like

Let's face it, most electric garments are worn under your other riding gear so style is not particularly important here. Unless of course someone is dumb enough to make an electric vest in only one color (hot pink), in which case you probably would think twice about buying it anyway.

Of course electric gloves are a little different since they will probably be seen. Then again, most types that we have seen were not radically styled and would look decent with most riding gear. And it is really hard to escape the fact that even if someone does decide to poke fun at you for how your gear looks, chances are they are freezing their obnoxious butts off anyway, while you are riding along toasty. Ohhhhh, what was that? You want to stop to warm up for a minute?. Nahh let's keep going, I could easily do another couple hours. . . .

Choose Gear To Match Your Riding

There are two things to keep in mind when selecting electric garments, match your needs AND your snowmobile's alternator output.

ASSESS YOUR NEEDS

▶ **See Figures 145 and 146**

When it comes to your needs, we suggest a conservative approach. Start by riding with your best non-electric gear and see what gets cold.

Fig. 145 Although not a piece of electric gear, wind triangles, like this one from Aerostitch® can seal your helmet to your jacket, keeping you warm

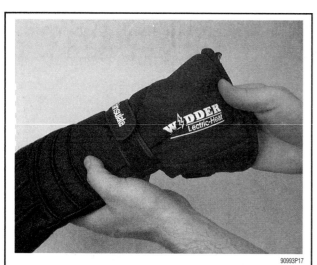

Fig. 146 An electric vest or jacket may be enough, but if not, consider a pair of gloves to keep your hands warm too

Make sure that you have blocked the wind as effectively as you can. A helmet lining or balaclava will help a lot, and make sure you seal the helmet to your jacket.

Then, once you have decided that electric garments are the way to go, start with a vest or jacket lining. The act of warming your core will help to keep the rest of your body warmer as blood carries that heat out towards your extremities. If the vest alone does not do the trick, you might want to consider gloves and/or boot warmers. We have found that the vest should be sufficient for most situations, but only if you have high quality gear in the form of bibs, boots and gloves (as we described in earlier sections). If your hands are not behind some form of brush guard, these are the next likely to get cold (even with a good pair of gloves). The combination of an electric vest, gloves and boot warmers can make you feel right at home even in sub-freezing temperatures.

ASSESS YOUR SNOWMOBILE'S ABILITY

Your snowmobile has one, important limiting factor when it comes to electric apparel; the alternator output. The simple fact is that if you add enough accessories, you will eventually start consuming more electricity than your alternator can produce (you may notice the result if your headlight starts to fade once you have turned on all of your toys). The good news is that virtually all modern snowmobiles have alternators with sufficient capacity to run one or two pieces of electric clothing.

➡**Some older snowmobiles might have underpowered charging systems. They might have difficulty keeping up with the demand of electric clothing, once the engine RPM drops below a certain point. With these older models, you've got two options; Upgrade the alternator (or lighting coil) with a higher output kit, or, you can just keep the revs up (and watch the headlight, if it goes from dim to bright at a certain point, you know where the revs should be).**

Choose Quality Gear

There aren't that many makers of electric garments. But with that said, even fewer of them have a reputation. Ask around, and look at any articles or reviews you can get your hands on. The company who supplied samples for our testing has an EXCELLENT reputation. We have even had some dealing with their customer service groups (a few years ago, Widder® was kind enough to repair a glove at no charge which was out of their warranty period, but had developed an open in the heater grid . . . impressive).

Like with most gear, if the company has a name it has earned in the snowmobile industry, that is a good indication of the quality merchandise they sell.

Choose Something That Fits Properly

When it comes to proper fit, most electric garments should fit like their non-heated counterparts. Gloves should not be too big or too small. The difference is with vests or with jacket linings. Most manufacturer's recommend that the garment be comfortable but snug (to prevent cold air from finding its way between you and the garment). You probably want to leave additional room between the garment and the jacket for other insulation layers, especially if you want to be prepared for the worst, should you unexpectedly be unable to use the electric heater one day.

HOW TO CARE FOR YOUR ELECTRIC GARMENTS

▶ **See Figure 147**

Because electric apparel has a few features most of your other riding gear lacks (like wires and heating elements) it is important that you follow the manufacturer's instructions closely. Most garments however can be washed. You should periodically inspect the wiring for breaks in the insulation and take care with when connecting or disconnecting it. Never pull directly on a wire, ALWAYS grasp and pull the wiring connector. A little dielectric grease on the connectors won't do any harm and may help make the connections easier to fasten and unfasten.

Any electric gloves which contain leather shells should be treated, just like normal leather. Clean it carefully and treat it with Lexol® or another appropriate leather treatment to restore the material's natural oils.

Fig. 147 Heated leather gloves can be treated with Lexol®

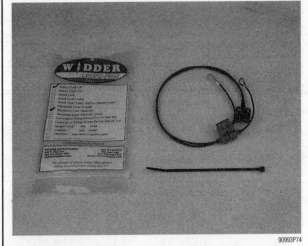

Fig. 148 Most electric garments will come with an adapter that is wired to the battery and becomes your accessory outlet

INSTALLING AN ACCESSORY OUTLET

♦ **See Figures 148 and 149**

Some of the later model snowmobiles already have built in accessory outlets, and for the rest of you, most manufacturers sell accessory outlet kits that are easy to install. One neat feature about installing an accessory jack is that it instantly gives you an easy way to check your battery (using a voltmeter) or to attach a Battery Tender® or other battery maintaining device when you are not riding.

Before installing the outlet, figure out where it should go in relation to the apparel. Start by putting on all of your riding gear and climbing onto your snowmobile. Look at where the wiring harness hangs and where it would be most convenient to locate the outlet. It is really nice to be able to plug and unplug the jack from the seated position, but this is not possible on all models and on some you will have to plug in before climbing on board.

Once you have a good idea where you would like the outlet to go, you will have to access your battery for installation. Check your owners manual, as it usually gives you some idea how to get at the battery.

1. Make sure the ignition switch is OFF and remove the key.
2. Locate your snowmobile's battery and remove any components necessary to access it.
3. Once the battery is accessible, loosen the negative battery cable by turning the retaining bolt counterclockwise. Usually this can be done with a screwdriver, wrench or a socket. The wrench or socket is really the best method to make sure you don't strip the terminal bolt, but it really depends on the amount of access you have.
4. Once the negative cable is disconnected it is always a good idea to wrap some electrical tape around it or put a small plastic baggie over the end to prevent it from touching the battery again and accidentally completing a circuit.
5. Loosen the bolt and remove the positive battery cable from the battery. Be careful never to short the battery by allowing the wrench or other tool to bridge the gap between the terminals.
6. Place the accessory outlet wiring over the battery terminal bolts, then insert the bolts back through the cables and into the battery. Start with the positive cable. If there is an inline fuse in the accessory outlet wiring, be sure to connect it to the positive battery cable.
7. Secure the positive battery cable to the battery, then secure the negative cable.
8. Use a voltmeter to check for battery voltage across the terminals of the

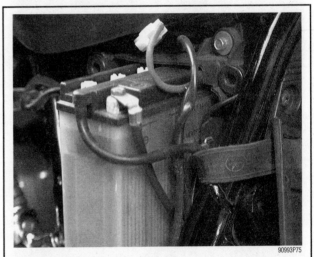

Fig. 149 To install the outlet, start by accessing the battery and disconnecting the wiring

accessory jack. Then use the voltmeter to check voltage directly across the battery terminals. The voltage should be identical or VERY, VERY close. If not, there is likely a problem with one of the two connections and you should double-check them before proceeding. If there is a significant difference in the voltages, your accessory jack may not work.

9. Once you are sure the connections are good, route the accessory outlet wiring the way you have planned to position the jack. Be sure to keep the wiring away from any moving parts (running it along frame rails and along other chassis wiring is a good idea).
10. Use a few wiring ties to make sure the accessory outlet wiring and jack remain in position.
11. Double-check battery voltage across the jack terminals one last time, then install the seat, as necessary. When installing any remaining plastic pieces, pay close attention that none of the pieces will interfere with or damage the wiring once they are in position.
12. Ride warm.

9124XP1F

Gear manufacturers have created functional and attractive clothing for the whole family

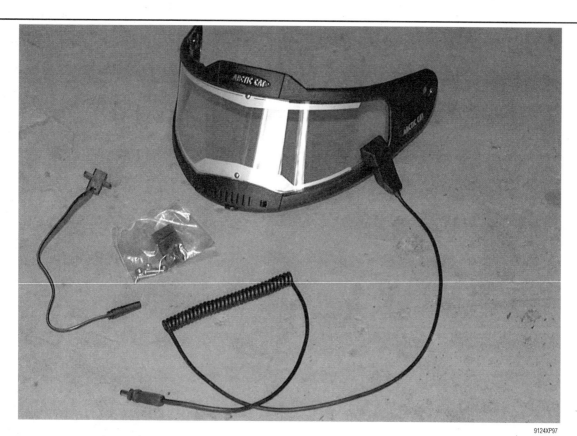

9124XP97

One of the most important electric garments is the heated windshield

4

ENGINE AND DRIVETRAIN MAINTENANCE

ENGINE MAINTENANCE

♦ **See Figures 1, 2 and 3**

In this world of throw away appliances and "drive it till it breaks" attitudes, it is easy to see why people often ignore maintenance on things from household oil burners to lawnmowers. But, ignoring to properly maintain your snowmobile could cost you (or others) greatly.

If you are serious about safety, then you should take a serious interest in the maintenance of your snowmobile. Learn from the examples of those involved with other machines that are unpleasant to be around when mechanical failures occur. Aircraft mechanics and racing pit crews are two examples of people who take their jobs VERY, VERY seriously. They use checklists and keep log books to be certain that maintenance procedures are not overlooked and that no critical part is used beyond its normal working life. To these people, maintenance is PREVENTATIVE, not corrective.

Don't wait until a part stops working to give your snowmobile attention. Periodic maintenance to the engine, drivetrain and chassis will help to make for a safer riding experience. It doesn't matter if you are trail riding, racing, or using your sled to haul logs; knowing that your snowmobile is in top shape and that it will get the job done safely will put you at ease.

Before reading any further, be sure that you have a copy of the owner's manual for your particular snowmobile. Although we will provide information

Fig. 1 Changing spark plugs . . .

Fig. 2 . . . chaincase oil . . .

Fig. 3 . . . and belts all are necessary to keep your snowmobile in top condition

regarding what is common to snowmobile maintenance, you should always check your owner's manual first. Remember that every snowmobile is built different, and a manufacturer may have a unique maintenance requirement that is very important on your particular model.

The topics in this chapter cover most of the powertrain maintenance procedures common to snowmobiles built today. But, not all snowmobiles will contain all systems. For instance, if you have an air cooled engine, then you do not have Glycol coolant to check or replace periodically (your engine uses air cooling purposes, NOT coolant).

Make sure that you have a complete checklist of maintenance items for your model, then follow the techniques provided to help assure a long and healthy life for you and your snowmobile.

A Word About Warranties

If you have a new snowmobile with a manufacturer's warranty, then it is critically important that you follow ALL OF THE MANUFACTURER'S recommendations regarding care and maintenance. It is also very important that you document everything that you do (or that a mechanic does, if you choose). Keep a log book with receipts, time and dates of services and notes of anything in particular that was noticed during your service. For instance:

"June 12th, I performed a 600 mile service. Changed all fluids (receipt attached). I noticed that the track was slightly out of alignment. So I adjusted it, and now its perfectly set up. I'll make a note to keep a close eye on that . . ."

If you perform your own maintenance on a snowmobile that is under warranty, this will be the only proof that the required procedures were performed (just in case something goes wrong that the manufacturer is reluctant about fixing for free).

MANUFACTURER FLUIDS

♦ **See Figure 4**

This is a tough one. Ask anyone involved with snowmobile maintenance and they will probably have an opinion on which fluids are best for your snowmobile. Some will say to use only specially made oils only for snowmobiles and motorcycles, while others will swear that normal automotive fluids are fine for items like the chaincase. Each will probably have a story to back up their position like, "I once knew a guy who used synthetic car oil in his snowmobile and BAMMM! It blew up! Just like that, I mean he poured it in an' both he and the snowmobile, well they was vaporized in an instant, like one o' `em thar ray-guns on TV."

Ok, maybe we are exaggerating a little here. Well, we are going to give you some recommendations. We may even suggest that there are alternatives to the special products sold by snowmobile and motorcycle manufacturers (in some

Fig. 4 Snowmobile manufacturers provide just about every type of chemical needed for snowmobile maintenance

cases). BUT, again, remember that if your precious baby is under warranty, you have another source of motivation to buy manufacturer oil from the dealer.

Manufacturers will have less to complain about if they want to dispute a warranty claim and you can prove that you have used ONLY their recommended fluids in your snowmobile. ALSO, the more often you go in and buy oil from your local dealer (the same guy/gal who would be responsible for convincing the manufacturer's rep to go ahead and pay for a warranty repair), the more likely it is that they are going to know you. And they are going to remember you as one of their valued customers, who is always in their shop every couple of months buying oil, a fuel filter, some gaskets and a new T-shirt (hey you didn't think they made ALL their money from snowmobile sales and oil did you?).

Once the warranty expires on your snowmobile, well, then you have a lot more freedom to make your OWN decision on what fluids to use and where to buy them.

MANUFACTURER PARTS

♦ See Figure 5

Using manufacturer parts while your snowmobile is under warranty is just like using manufacturer lubricants. It is always a good idea to stick with what the manufacturer recommends in the owner's manual, should any problems arise with your snowmobile. Using a factory thermostat would be a much better choice than an aftermarket one, although it may cost you a few extra bucks. The

Fig. 5 In some cases, factory parts are your best option

manufacturer will have little to dispute if you've shown that factory parts and fluids have been used for maintaining your snowmobile.

Fuel Requirements

SELECTING THE PROPER FUEL

Gasoline is a mixture of hydrocarbons (composed of hydrogen and carbon), produced by refining crude oil. When gasoline burns, these compounds separate into hydrogen and carbon atoms and unite with oxygen atoms. The results obtained from burning gasoline are dependent upon its most important characteristics: octane rating, volatility and density.

Gasoline mixtures and additives will vary slightly from brand-to-brand, but it could also vary from station-to-station too (if a particular station has a problem with moisture or contamination in one or more of its tanks). When deciding on a gasoline, start with the manufacturer's recommended octane rating and try tank fulls from various local stations. Run a few tank fulls of each and settle on the one that gives you the best gas mileage and anti-knock protection. If you get similar results from various brands and stations, then you can likely count of those results from most fill-ups. If one particular gas station or brand seems to give your snowmobile trouble, look for a new station to buy fuel from.

➡**DON'T WASTE YOUR MONEY buying gasoline with super-high octane. If your manufacturer doesn't require it, and your snowmobile runs fine on a lower octane, then go ahead and use the lower octane. For the most part, the quality of the gasoline and the use of additives will be reasonably comparable from one octane to another with a single brand of gas. Always filling-up with Super-Elite-Mega-Premium 115 octane probably will not have any appreciable benefits over the same brand's regular gasoline, unless your engine has a seriously high compression ratio (read as extreme aftermarket engine work) or seriously clogged with carbon.**

Octane Rating

Simply put, the octane rating of a gasoline is its ability to resist knock, a detonation or uncontrolled combustion in the cylinder that sounds like a sharp metallic noise. Knock can occur for a variety of reasons, one of which is the incorrect octane rating for the engine in your snowmobile. To understand why knock occurs, you must understand why knock doesn't occur.

Under normal operating conditions, the firing of the spark plug initiates the burning of the fuel/air mixture in the combustion chamber. Once the plug fires, a wall of flame starts outward from the plug in all directions at once. This flame front moves evenly and rapidly throughout the entire combustion chamber until the entire fuel/air mixture is burned. This even, rapid progress of the burning fuel/air mixture is highly dependent on the octane rating of the gasoline. If the octane rating is too low, the last part of the compressed fuel/air mixture may ignite before the flame front reaches it, in effect creating two areas of combustion within the cylinder. The problem occurs because, while the original combustion is proceeding at a carefully controlled rate, this new combustion is simply a sudden sharp explosion. This abrupt increase in pressure is what creates the knocking sound in the combustion chamber. As far as the piston is concerned, the damage it inflicts is exactly like striking the piston top with a heavy hammer. Knock is very damaging to the engine, since it causes extraordinary wear to bearings, piston crowns, and other vital engine parts. Engines can actually be destroyed through excessive engine knock.

Engine knock can be controlled by using a gas with the proper octane rating. Octane measurements made under laboratory conditions have led to "Research" and "Motor" octane ratings. In general, the research octane number tends to be about 6 to 10 points higher than the motor octane rating (for what is essentially the same gasoline). Since the early seventies, most octane ratings on gas pumps in the U.S. have been the average of the research and motor octane numbers. For instance, if the gasoline had a research octane rating of 100, and a motor octane rating of 90, the octane rating found on the pump would be 95.

Your owner's manual will probably indicate the type and octane of gasoline recommended for use in your snowmobile. However, octane requirements can vary according to the manufacturer and the conditions under which the sled is operating. If you encounter sustained engine knock, wait until your tank is nearly empty, then try a gasoline with a slightly higher octane rating. If the manufacturer doesn't require it, buying gasoline of a higher octane than your engine is a waste of money.

As a new snowmobile is driven, combustion deposits build up and the octane requirement increases until an equilibrium level is reached. Other factors which can increase the octane an engine requires are higher air or engine temperatures, lower altitudes, lower humidity, a more advanced ignition spark timing, a leaner carburetor setting, sudden acceleration, and frequent stop-and-go riding which increases the build-up of combustion chamber deposits.

Volatility

The volatility of any liquid is its ability to vaporize. A highly volatile gasoline will help a cold engine start easily and run smoothly while it is warming up. However, the use of a highly volatile gasoline in warm weather tends to cause vapor lock, a condition not uncommon for older, carbureted automobiles, but almost never seen in snowmobiles. The condition occurs when gasoline actually vaporizes before it arrives at the carburetor jet where atomization is supposed to take place. This premature vaporization used to occur in the fuel lines or in a section of the carburetor on automobiles. When use of too highly volatile fuel leads to vapor lock, the engine becomes starved for fuel and will either lose power or stall. Although refiners used to vary the percentage of volatile components in their gasoline according to season and locality, in order to help prevent this, vapor lock was more likely to occur in the early spring, when some stations may not have received supplies of lower-volatility gasoline.

Luckily, the design of most carbureted snowmobiles makes vapor lock unlikely. Whereas carbureted automobiles used long fuel lines to travel from the fuel tank to the engine (and a large carburetor fuel bowl which sat right on TOP of the engine), the gasoline in most snowmobiles has a short trip to take from the tank to the float bowl (which is smaller than car's) and to the intake manifold. The gasoline spends less time in the lines and float bowls and they are both likely to be cooler than their counterparts on an automobile.

Density

Density is another property of gasoline that can affect your fuel economy. It indicates how much chemical energy the gasoline contains. Density is generally measured in BTU's per gallon (the BTU, or British Thermal Unit, is a standard unit of energy), and usually varies less than 2% among most gasolines but can vary as much as 4–8%. This indicates that gas mileage could vary by as much as 4–8%, depending on the density of the gasoline you happen to choose.

Oxygenated gasoline has become popular (or necessary) in many areas in order to help reduce emissions. Oxygenated gasoline contains less combustible material than a non-oxygenated counterpart. The result is fewer hydrocarbons per gallon. Oxygenated fuels do not harm your snowmobile, they do however rob it of some power and some gas mileage.

Additives

Practically as important as octane rating and volatility are the additives that refiners put into their gasolines. The "fuel injector cleaners" found in nearly every major brand of gasoline today include detergent additives which help clean the tiny passages in the carburetor or fuel injector systems. This helps to ensure consistent fuel/air mixtures necessary for smooth running and good gas mileage. Winter additives include fuel line de-icers to reduce carburetor icing. Other additives are used to help control combustion chamber deposits, gum formation, rust, and wear.

Engine Lubrication

▶ See Figures 6, 7 and 8

There are probably more myths, misunderstandings and urban legends regarding two-stroke engine oil, than any other mechanical "thing." What we would like to do here is help demystify the facts about two-stroke engine oil and help you make the best decision for what type of oil is best suited to your snowmobile.

A two-stroke engine is a completely different animal than a car or truck. Unlike four-stroke engines, two-strokes do not use valves and camshafts to control the entry and exit of the fuel and air mixture. In order for the air and fuel to enter and exit the combustion chamber, two-stroke engines use ports, or holes, that are on the sides of the cylinder wall. Because of the unique design of the two-stroke engine, the oil needed for lubrication of internal parts cannot be separated from the fuel. If there were engine oil in the crankcase, (as on a four-stroke engine) the oil would escape through the ports (and make quite a mess!).

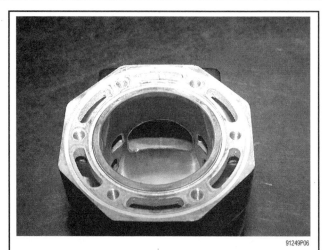

91249P06

Fig. 6 Since two-stroke engines use ports in the cylinders to control the entry and exit of the fuel/air mixture, oil must be added to the fuel for lubrication

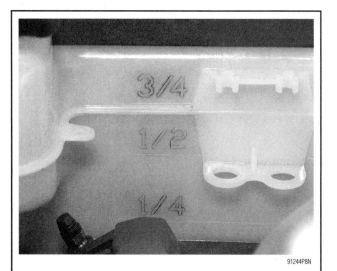

91244P8N

Fig. 7 Check the level in the oil tank before every ride, . . .

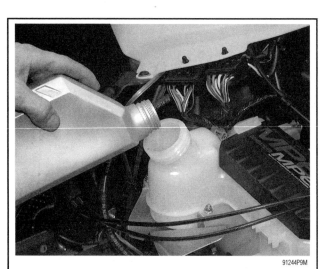

91244P9M

Fig. 8 . . . and add oil as necessary to keep the oil tank full to avoid problems on the trail

To provide lubrication to a two-stroke engine's internal components, the oil must be carried into the engine with the air and fuel mixture, or injected into the crankcase. Different manufacturers employ various methods to provide lubrication, but they all have the same effect: supplying the internal components of the engine with enough oil to provide adequate lubrication.

So, since two-strokes have this unique design, there is no "engine oil" to check or change. The oil you change in a snowmobile engine is actually the chaincase oil (More on this later).

Now that we have discussed the unique method of lubricating a two-stroke engine, lets discuss the different types of two-stroke engine oil.

TYPES OF ENGINE OIL

▶ See Figure 9

Since two-stroke engine oils can be vegetable-based, petroleum-based or synthetic, you have quite a large selection of oils to choose from. If you don't know a lot about different types and brands of two-stroke oils, talk to other snowmobile owners and see what they use. You might get a lot of different opinions, but you'll at least get some ideas on what types and brands of oil are popular. Let's discuss the different types of two-stroke engine oils, and their advantages and drawbacks.

Fig. 9 There are a lot of choices when it comes to selecting two-stroke engine oil

Petroleum-Based Oil

Of all types of engine oil, petroleum-based oil is the most common. Derived from crude oil through a refining process, this type of oil is typically blended with additives to perform properly. These additives include pour point depressants, oxidation inhibitors, and detergents and dispersants. All of these additives work together to allow oil to flow properly and maintain viscosity, regardless of temperature. In colder temperatures (when a snowmobile is in its element), these additives help keep the oil from becoming too thick to flow through the injection pump.

Petroleum-based two-stroke oil is very similar to four-stroke engine oil, but includes additives to promote cleaner burning, better lubrication, and less carbon build-up in the combustion chambers.

Overall, petroleum-based oil is an excellent lubricant for internal combustion engines, and has been the "standard" within the industry for quite a while.

Synthetic Oil

▶ See Figure 10

Synthetic oils are another of those topics that can raise the blood pressure of many who are just "certain" that they have the answer to the world's problems. When synthetics were first marketed, like with so many innovations, people reacted as if this mysterious oil was evil and would surely lead to the downfall of the person who used it (and the engine in which it was used), if not to the complete downfall of our entire civilization.

Fig. 10 Many aftermarket companies offer high-quality synthetic oil

BUT, take a look around you. Synthetic oils are the first choice of many people who are HARD on their engines. Many racing teams, in all forms of motorsports, rely upon synthetic oil of all types to protect their high dollar, high rpm and high-visibility investments. So what is the big deal?

Conventional oils are based on hydrocarbons, but because they are refined, the sizes and shapes of these molecules are highly irregular. Synthetic oils are assembled from different compounds into specifically sized and shaped hydrocarbons. They are completely compatible with conventional oils, but they benefit from having more predictable reactions to severe conditions. In high heat conditions (such as that which can be found in many snowmobile engines), synthetics will resist breaking down better than conventional oils.

Synthetic oils are often more expensive than conventional oils, but if the extra protection they offer is worth it to you (sorta like an insurance policy without the hassle of an agent), then you may want to give them a try.

Vegetable-Based Oil

Vegetable based two-stroke engine oil (castor oil) actually has excellent lubrication properties, despite one's vision of pouring salad oil into their snowmobile's oil tank (please don't try this!). Castor oil is actually derived from the bean of the castor plant (Ricinus communis). The oil that is extracted from the plant is an almost scentless, viscous oil with excellent anti-friction properties.

Castor oil has been in use by many cultures for thousands of years as a folk medicine as medicinal oil. In addition to being a health aid, castor oil is used in the manufacture of industrial products such as nylon fibers, hydraulic fluids, jet engine lubricants, plastic, and soap.

➡**Castor oil is not compatible with other oils. It should not be mixed with mineral or synthetic oils and engines that have previously run on castor oil must be disassembled and thoroughly cleaned before petroleum or synthetic oils are used in the engine.**

Despite the excellent lubrication properties of castor oil, it is highly impractical for use on most snowmobiles. Castor oil can quickly build up sludge and varnish on the pistons and rings, causing the rings to stick, and variable exhaust ports to clog. Because of this drawback, castor oil is typically only used in competition situations, where racers are regularly disassembling their engines for cleaning and service. For most snowmobile riding situations, castor oil is not recommended.

ENGINE OIL RECOMMENDATIONS & TIPS

▶ See Figures 11, 12, 13 and 14

• Using the manufacturer recommended two-stroke oil while the snowmobile is under warranty is advisable, just in case problems arise. If engine damage occurs, having proof that factory lubricants were used (and properly mixed into the fuel) will help to avoid any battles with the manufacturer, should you make a warranty claim. Once your snowmobile is "out of warranty" you can use whatever oil you choose.

Fig. 11 It's a good idea to use factory oil while your sled is under warranty

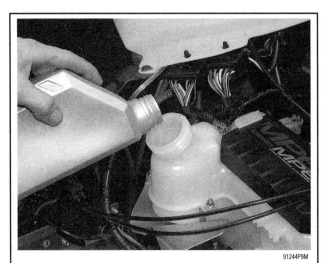

Fig. 12 ALWAYS keep the oil tank full; if the level is low, air can be drawn into the injection pump while riding

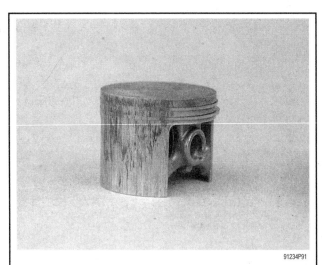

Fig. 13 This piston is from a two-stroke engine that ran out of oil; note the heavy damage on the skirt and rings

Fig. 14 In addition to destroyed pistons and cylinders, VERY expensive components like this connecting rod can be ruined by oil starvation

• DON'T let the oil tank run dry! If your sled is equipped with a "low oil" light, stop your sled IMMEDIATELY and pour a standby container of oil into the tank to prevent air from being sucked into the pump. (You DO have an extra bottle of oil in your seat compartment, don't you?) Keeping your oil tank full is VERY important, because air can enter the lines when the level is low (especially when riding on rough trails).

✳✳ WARNING

If air is drawn into the oil injection pump, there will be no indication from the engine that this has occurred. Your engine will be seriously damaged due to lack of lubrication.

• When the level in the oil tank becomes low, air can be drawn into the oil pump, (even if your warning light is not illuminated) and the engine will be starved of oil. By the time you have figured out that there is something wrong with your oil pump, the motor will most likely be seriously damaged, leaving you stranded on a cold trail.

✳✳ WARNING

If your snowmobile's oil tank is run dry, and it is not equipped with a warning light, your engine can be destroyed.

• If the filler neck on your snowmobile's oil tank is small, don't be afraid to use a funnel when filling up. On most snowmobiles, the oil tank filler is near the disc brake. If you happen to spill oil on your brake caliper, the pads can be PERMANENTLY damaged. Brake pads are porous, and will soak up oil like a sponge. Brake pads aren't exactly cheap either! Oil contaminated brake pads will not provide adequate stopping power, which put you and other sled riders at risk. So even if it takes an extra minute or two to scrounge up a funnel, its well worth the hassle, from a monetary standpoint, as well as a safety standpoint.

OIL INJECTION FILTER

The majority of snowmobiles use a filter in the oil injection system to prevent dirt and debris from entering the oil pump (and fuel pump and carburetors, depending on the method of oil injection used).

The oil injection filter is typically an in-line type, located between the injection oil reservoir (or tank) and the oil pump. In some cases, the filter may be inside the tank, or attached to the bottom of the tank.

➡**If you're looking around furiously in your engine compartment for an oil tank filter, and can't seem to find one, don't be alarmed; some snowmobiles do not use a filter in the oil injection system. In this case, extreme care must be taken when adding engine oil to the tank. Additionally, the oil tank should be periodically removed, inspected, and cleaned of build-up and dirt.**

Replacement

▶ **See Figures 15, 16, 17 and 18**

1. Locate the oil filter in the engine compartment.
2. If necessary, remove any components necessary to allow access to the filter and oil injection pump. On some models, it may be necessary to disconnect the carburetor(s) from the inlets if necessary to allow access to the oil pump. When removing the carburetors, do not disconnect the lines and cables, but remove them from the inlets and set them aside.
3. Disconnect the two hoses that attach to the oil filter. Use a rag to contain any excess oil. Pinch the oil line with your fingers to keep oil from draining from the line until the new filter is attached.
4. Connect the hoses to the new filter, making sure it is installed in the proper direction. Typically, there is an arrow on the filter to indicate flow direction; the arrow should point to the hose that attaches to the oil injection pump.
5. Once the hoses are connected and the clamps installed, (if equipped) loosen the air bleed screw on the oil pump.
6. When oil begins to flow from the screw, tighten it securely. It may take a couple minutes to allow gravity to push the air bubbles out of the line.

➡️If your snowmobile's oil filter lines are transparent, it will be much easier to bleed the air from the lines, since the air bubbles can be viewed. When bleeding the air from the line, allow the oil to flow from the bleed screw until the line is free of bubbles.

⁑⁑ **WARNING**

If the air is not properly bled from the oil line, the engine may be severely damaged from lack of lubrication.

7. An additional method which can be employed to bleed excess air from the oil pump involves holding the oil pump lever fully open when the engine is at idle. This should be done only after the steps described above are performed.
   a. Siphon the fuel tank of raw fuel and add a small amount (1 gallon) of 50:1 **pre-mixed** two-stroke oil and fuel to the fuel tank. This will ensure proper lubrication to the engine while the air is being bled from the pump.
   b. Using a rubber band or other means, hold the lever on the oil pump to the full-throttle position. If the oil pump cannot be accessed with the carburetors installed, disconnect the oil pump cable from the throttle lever to hold the oil pump at its full-throttle position.
   c. Start the engine and let it idle for approximately 2-3 minutes, with the oil pump still in the full-throttle position. By running the oil pump at its full position when the engine is idling, any air trapped in the system will be expelled.
   d. Once it is verified that the air is bled from the system, the fuel tank can be filled with straight gasoline. Keep in mind the additional oil mixed with the fuel for the oil pump bleeding process may cause the spark plugs to prematurely foul. Keep an eye on the condition of the spark plugs until the pre-mixed fuel is burned through the engine.

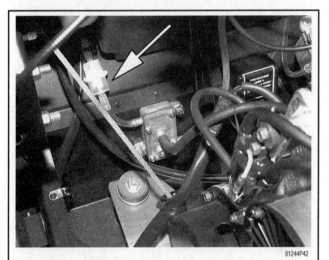
Fig. 15 Oil filters typically look like inline-type fuel filters (arrow); make sure to replace the right one!

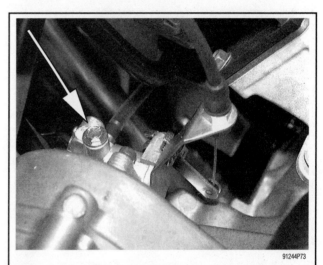
Fig. 17 The bleed screw on this injection pump (arrow) is easily accessed

Fig. 16 On some models, it may be necessary to remove the airbox and carburetors to access the bleed screw on the oil injection pump (Middle arrow is pointing to pump, and left arrow to one injector)

Fig. 18 Loosening the bleed screw on the injection pump after the filter is changed to bleed the air from the line

Airbox & Filter

▶ See Figures 19 and 20

In the early days of snowmobiling, carburetors on sleds were equipped with nothing more than an air horn and a coarse-mesh screen to keep debris from entering the engine. Since there is very little dust in the snow (makes sense doesn't it?) on which a snowmobile operates, an "air filter" wasn't really necessary.

Over time though, manufacturers discovered the drawback to this design was excessive air induction noise emitted from the carburetor(s) under medium to heavy acceleration. Combined with the inherently loud exhaust note from a typical two-stroke, snowmobiling was a borderline ear-splitting experience.

With the recently magnified focus on the environment in recent years, activist groups and government agencies have "cracked down" on the noise levels and exhaust emissions from snowmobiles.

To combat the excessive induction noise from the carburetor(s), manufacturers started producing snowmobiles with "airboxes." A typical airbox consists of an enclosed container equipped with baffles to reduce noise. The effect of an airbox is similar to a muffler on an engine, only air is being drawn through the muffler instead of being expelled.

Some airboxes are equipped with a coarse-mesh air filter over the airbox inlet, and others may simply have an open inlet. Regardless of the design of the airbox, it should be inspected and cleaned periodically.

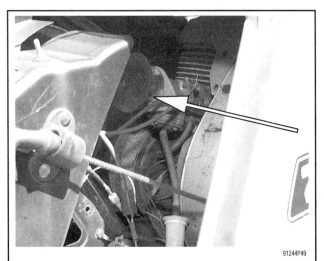

91244P49

Fig. 19 Years ago, snowmobiles were not equipped with air filters, but a coarse-mesh screen over the intake

The air filter is used to remove fine particles of dirt or debris present in the air that is drawn into the air induction system of an engine. By removing these particles **before** the inducted air flows through the carburetor, the engine and carburetor are protected from unnecessary wear and damage.

A clogged air filter will decrease the efficiency and life of the engine. A clogged air filter starves the engine of air, which will richen the air/fuel mixture. If the filter becomes damaged or torn, it could allow fine particles to enter the engine allowing for rapid wear of delicate parts such as the piston rings, cylinder walls and bearings. Dirt could also clog the tiny passages found in carburetors, causing lean or rich air/fuel mixtures and idle problems.

INSPECTION & CLEANING

Most manufacturers recommend "cleaning or replacing the air filter and airbox when it becomes dirty." Duh . . . ! That's about as obvious as telling someone not to breathe water, or they'll die. Well, in order to find out if your air filter is dirty, you'll need to inspect it regularly.

Airbox

▶ See Figures 21, 22, 23 and 24

The airbox on most modern snowmobiles is nothing more than a plastic baffle fitted to the carburetors to reduce induction noise. Over time, the airbox may become dirty, and accumulate dirt and debris.

1. To remove your airbox for cleaning and inspection, unscrew any components that may be attached, like cable ties, or ignition coils. If you have to disconnect any electrical components, make sure to mark them so they can be connected properly during assembly.

2. Once any components are removed from the airbox, loosen the clamps around the carburetor inlets. This may require the use of an extra long Phillips head screwdriver.

3. Once the airbox inlets have been loosened, carefully wiggle them free of the carburetor inlets (or throttle bodies) and draw the airbox away from the engine compartment. It may look and sound complicated to remove the airbox, but it is actually a simple procedure.

4. Once the airbox is removed, it can be inspected for any cracks, splits, or loose debris. If the airbox has loose debris inside, use compressed air to blow it clean. If compressed air is unavailable, use a rag sprayed with a light coating of WD-40 to wipe down the inside of the airbox. If the rubber boots that attach to the carburetors are torn, excessively hard, or cracked, they should be replaced.

✳✳ WARNING

Never run a snowmobile engine without the airbox. Dirt and debris can easily be sucked into an unprotected carburetor, possibly causing serious engine damage.

91244P8A

Fig. 21 To remove the airbox, carefully remove any attached components and set them aside . . .

Fig. 20 Today's sleds use enclosed airboxes to reduce noise and protect the engine from snow and debris inhalation

Fig. 22 . . . then, if necessary, separate the halves . . .

Fig. 23 . . . and remove the airbox from the carburetor inlets

Fig. 24 With the airbox removed, other components can be better accessed for maintenance and adjustments

5. After the airbox is inspected and cleaned, take the opportunity to inspect other parts and components that may be blocked from view when the airbox is installed.

6. If everything seems to be in proper order, install the airbox, and attach any components that were removed. Make sure the rubber airbox boots are properly positioned on the carburetors (or throttle bodies) before tightening the clamps. Also, be careful not to overtighten the clamps; the rubber boots can be torn if excessive clamping force is used.

Air Filter

♦ **See Figures 25 and 26**

The majority of all airboxes on snowmobiles have a filter that consists of a coarse-mesh foam element. Some foam elements are simply pressed in position, and others are supported with a plastic frame or a metal screen. Filters with a screen are usually held in place with clips, or in some cases, a couple of screws.

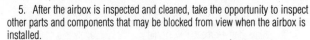
❄❄ WARNING

Be careful when installing removing and installing the airbox filter. Many of the filters use frames that are made of plastic and are easily broken (requiring a special order part and some downtime).

Fig. 25 The filters on airboxes may have a frame . . .

Fig. 26 . . . or just a piece of removable foam

Foam filter elements have the advantage of being cleaned using a mild solvent and reused.

1. To clean a foam element, you should wash it thoroughly in a heavy detergent, letting the filter soak like a sponge. Then, rinse the element is fresh water, and squeeze the element dry. Allow the filter to **completely** dry before installing it on your sled.

⁜ WARNING

Be sure that you SQUEEZE the element and do not wring it out. Twisting the element in a wringing fashion will risk tearing and will likely damage the close-knit pores of the element.

2. If the foam filter element on your snowmobile is attached to a plastic or metal screen, simply soak in a warm soapy water solution, and flush it with clean water. Make sure the element is fully dry before putting it to use.

⁜ CAUTION

DO NOT USE GASOLINE TO CLEAN YOUR AIR FILTER! Gasoline is extremely volatile, and can ignite without warning, causing severe personal injury.

3. If you choose, the foam element can be oiled for additional protection. A light motor oil or spray oil can be used on the element to enhance the dirt-trapping abilities of the foam mesh.

4. An easy way to distribute the oil onto the foam element is with the use of a plastic bag. Place the foam element in the bag, followed by pouring a little oil into the bag. Close off the end of the bag, then squeeze the element to allow for the oil to soak in until it is completely saturated. Once you are done oiling the element in the bag, take it out of the bag, squeeze off the excess and return it to service. You don't need a bag to oil your filter element, it just keeps your hands from getting soaked with oil.

REPLACEMENT

Like any other air cleaner, even the reusable foam element will have a limited life span. Be sure to check it carefully for damage, deterioration or tears and replace it when it has become unserviceable.

The only time it should be necessary to replace your airbox and/or filter is if they become damaged. In most cases, a factory replacement will be necessary, since the air filters are usually mounted onto the airbox.

⁜ WARNING

It is not recommended that the airbox be removed and be replaced with aftermarket air filters; the excessive induction noise from the carburetors can make your snowmobile illegal for use in many riding areas.

Replacing your airbox with sock-type air filters, air inlet horns, or removing it completely will seriously increase the induction noise from the carburetors. Many snowmobile riding areas have strict rules regarding noise, and removing your factory airbox may make your snowmobile too loud for legal operation.

Cooling System

Since the internal combustion engine produces heat, a means of regulating the temperature must be used to prevent overheating. The two most popular ways of removing excess heat from an engine are with air and water. Both methods have their advantages, depending on the specific application. Let's discuss in detail the three main types of engine cooling systems, and the maintenance required for optimum efficiency.

OPEN AIR COOLING

Open air-cooling is popular with small, single cylinder engines because of the simplicity and almost non-existent need for maintenance of any kind. The reason for this is the fact that there are no moving parts to the open air cooling system. The **cooling fins** cast onto the cylinder and cylinder head are responsible for cooling the engine. The purpose for the fins is to increase the surface area of the cylinder and head, which allows the heat to dissipate into the air faster. A cylinder and head without fins will still be cooled by the air passing around them, but not as much as if they were equipped with fins.

In order for the cooling fins to operate properly, ambient air needs to travel over the fins at a moderate speed. This is where one of the drawbacks of open air-cooling comes into play. If air is not traveling over the fins and transferring heat fast enough, the efficiency is lost, and the operating temperature of the engine rises. To put this in a practical perspective, if your not moving fast enough on your snowmobile, it may overheat.

From a maintenance angle, open air-cooling is a no-brainer. The only two things to keep in mind are to keep the cooling fins free of dirt and mud, and most of all, **don't break them off!** If a cooling fin breaks off of the cylinder or cylinder head, a "hot spot" will develop, possibly causing engine damage. If you do break off a cooling fin, welding may be possible, depending on the type of metal that the cylinder (or cylinder head) is made from.

FORCED AIR (FAN) COOLING

♦ See Figure 27

Forced air-cooling operates in the same manner as open air cooling, with the addition of a few extra components designed to increase the efficiency of the cooling fins. A blower motor and ductwork enclosing the cylinder head are employed to force air over the fins at a higher rate than open air-cooling can provide. This becomes a real advantage while traveling at low speeds, when airflow would normally be low on an open air-cooled engine.

One disadvantage of forced air-cooling however, is that one cylinder of the engine will always run at a slightly hotter temperature. This is because of the orientation of the fan in relationship to the cylinders. To compensate for this difference in temperature, one carburetor is adjusted to provide a slightly richer mixture.

Since forced air-cooling uses moving parts (a blower), some occasional maintenance may be required to keep things in top running order. Since the blower is essentially an air pump, it sucks air from one area (usually from within the airbox) and blows it out of another. Occasionally, debris can get sucked into the blower, and get caught between the cooling fins. It is important to occasionally remove the ductwork and clean the cooling fins and blower impeller (especially at the beginning of the season) of any accumulated dirt and debris.

The major drawback of forced air-cooling is the power required from the engine to spin the blower impeller. On a large displacement engine, this is hardly a problem and the horsepower required to spin the blower impeller is minimal. With that said, small displacement two-stroke engines (which make good horsepower, but little torque) may have to sacrifice a small amount of power to keep things cool. Overall, forced air-cooling is a relatively inexpensive and reasonably efficient way to cool a snowmobile engine.

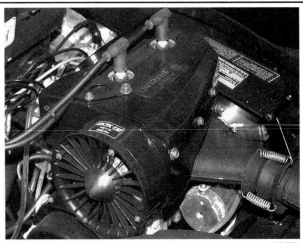

91242P08

Fig. 27 Example of a typical forced air cooled engine (note jet engine-like air intake)

Inspection

▶ See Figure 28

Engines with forced air-cooling may need to be occasionally inspected for excessive debris buildup within the ductwork, rodent nesting, and cooling fin condition. This usually involves removing the sheetmetal that covers the cylinder head. Depending on the model, this may be a straightforward process, or may be a little complicated.

1. Remove the spark plug wires from the cylinder head. Make sure you mark the wires so they do not get crossed when they are installed.

2. Other components that may need to be removed may be the ignition coil, cable brackets, and/or exhaust brackets.

➡Removal of the entire cooling shrouding metal may not be necessary for inspection. The important thing here is to check for any debris or damage to the cooling fins. During storage, rodents can make nests inside the cooling ductwork. (You won't BELIEVE the smell of burning rodents and nests when you start your engine at the beginning of the season!)

3. If everything looks in order, install the ductwork onto the cylinder head. It might not be a bad idea to use some medium-strength locking compound on the bolts and screws to keep everything secure.

4. Install any components that were removed from the ductwork to allow for removal.

5. Finally, install the spark plug wires, in the proper order. Make sure the boots are situated properly within the ductwork to ensure peak efficiency from the blower.

Fig. 28 Make sure the cooling fins are not clogged with debris

Fan Belt

▶ See Figures 29 and 30

For forced-air cooled snowmobile engines, keeping an eye on the condition of the fan belt is essential. If the belt were to break, or excessively slip, the engine may overheat. Also, keeping the belt tensioned properly will help keep the belt from deteriorating prematurely.

INSPECTION

The fan belt on forced-air cooled engines should be inspected at least every 20 hours of operation, or every 250 miles (400 km). Look for signs of excessive deterioration, such as cracking, separating, and glazing. If the belt is in question, **replace** it immediately to avoid problems with the cooling of the engine.

It should be noted there are three main causes of drive belt failure. The most common is fatigue of the load-bearing, tensile cords leading to belt failure from the inside out. Tensile cord failure is due to a gradual weakening of the tensile cords that results from a combination of side stress, bending stress, and cen-

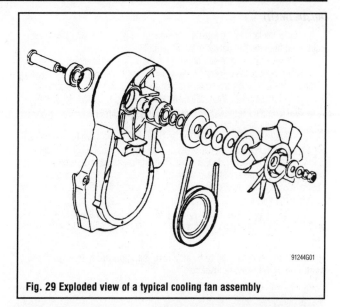

Fig. 29 Exploded view of a typical cooling fan assembly

Fig. 30 In most cases, removal of the fan cover screws (arrows) are required to inspect and adjust the fan belt

trifugal force imposed on the belt as it travels around the pulleys. Because this type of failure takes place inside the belt, there is no easy way to determine when the belt is about to break.

The other major cause of drive belt failure is improper tension. This causes the belt to slip as it travels around the pulleys, generating heat build-up. Excessive heat eventually causes the rubber compounds in the belt to break down, and crack, leading to belt failure.

Additionally, the close proximity of the fan belt to the engine makes belts more susceptible to heat. High temperatures can cause belts to dry, harden and crack.

Also, any damage to the pulley surfaces can contribute to premature failure of a belt. Any knicks, heavy scratches, or bending can wreak havoc on a drive belt. If your sled has been stored in a humid area during the off-season, rust may form on the pulleys (if they are made of steel), also causing problems with the belt.

❋❋ WARNING

DO NOT use belt dressings in an attempt to extend belt life. Belt dressing will soften the belt, causing accelerated deterioration. Oil or grease contamination on the belt or pulleys will have the same effect. Keep the drive belt system clear of oil, grease, or other contaminants.

ADJUSTMENT

To adjust the fan belt on most forced-air cooled engines, shims are added or subtracted from the two halves of the upper pulley.

1. Remove the fan protector or grill from the fan shroud to access the fan belt. If necessary, remove the exhaust system to allow access. Keep track of the locations of the springs that secure the exhaust; they may be of slightly different lengths.

2. On most models, the belt tension should be set to allow a ¼ inch of deflection between the pulleys when using a finger. As always, follow the guidelines and specifications recommended by the manufacturer.

3. If the tension is too loose, (or too tight) Shims will have to be removed (or added) from between the upper pulley halves to correct the belt tension.

4. Remove the nut on the fan shaft. The primary clutch may need to be held stationary by an assistant to allow the nut to be removed. There are also special tools that are available that hold the fan shaft stationary while loosening or tightening the nut.

5. Making sure to keep everything in order, remove the spacers, washers, shims, and fan (if required) to allow for adjustment of the shims between the pulley halves.

➥**When removing the fan belt, also take the opportunity to inspect the condition of the shaft bearings.**

6. To adjust the belt tension, shims are added or subtracted from between the fan pulley halves.

To increase belt tension, **remove** shims from between the pulleys; decreasing the belt tension (belt too tight) requires **adding** shims.

7. After the adjusting shims have been added or subtracted from between the pulleys, slip the belt onto the fan shaft, with the inner pulley half in position. With the adjusting shims against the inner pulley half, place the outer pulley into position onto the shaft.

8. Install any spacers, or extra shims that were not used between the two pulley halves onto the fan shaft.

➥**When adding or subtracting shims from between the pulley halves, they should be relocated on the outer pulley to keep the overall spacing on the shaft equal, regardless of adjustment.**

9. Tighten the nut on the fan shaft securely. Be sure not to pinch the belt between the pulley halves when tightening the nut.

10. Use the recoil starter and rotate the engine a few times to allow the belt to properly position itself on the pulleys; then check the belt tension.

11. If the belt tension is correct, tighten the fan shaft nut to the torque specified by the manufacturer.

12. If the tension is incorrect, add or subtract shims from between the two pulley halves until the tension is correct. Make sure to torque the shaft nut properly as specified by the manufacturer.

13. Install the fan protector, if equipped.

14. Install the exhaust system if it was removed.

REMOVAL AND INSTALLATION

1. Remove the fan protector from the fan shroud to access the fan belt.

2. Remove the recoil starter, if necessary.

3. Remove the cover on the engine that houses the flywheel, ignition system, and lower belt pulley. If necessary, remove the exhaust system to allow access. Keep track of the locations of the springs that secure the exhaust; they may be of slightly different lengths.

4. Remove the nut on the fan shaft. The primary clutch may need to be held stationary by an assistant to allow the nut to be removed. There are also special tools that are available that hold the fan shaft stationary while loosening or tightening the nut.

5. Making sure to keep everything in order, remove the spacers, washers, shims, and fan (if required) to allow removal of the belt.

➥**When removing the fan belt, also take the opportunity to inspect the condition of the bearings. Depending on the model, the bearings may be pressed into the fan housing, or on the shaft itself.**

6. Remove the belt from the engine. It may be necessary to wiggle the belt from the lower pulley and engine case, depending on which side of the flywheel the pulley is mounted.

7. Visually inspect each of the pulleys for chips, nicks, cracks, tool marks, bent sidewalls, severe corrosion or other damage. Replace any pulley showing these signs as they will eventually lead to belt failure.

To install:

8. Compare the two belts, and make sure that the belts are of the same size.

➥**Always make sure the new fan belt is of the same length and width as the old unit. It is normal for the old belt to be slightly longer than the new belt; keep this in mind when installing the new belt, since shims may need to be added between the pulleys.**

9. Install the belt on the lower pulley.

10. Slip the belt onto the fan shaft, with the inner pulley half in position. With the adjusting shims against the inner pulley half, place the outer pulley into position.

11. Install any spacers, or extra shims that were not used between the two pulley halves onto the fan shaft.

12. Tighten the nut on the fan shaft securely. Be sure not to pinch the belt between the pulley halves when tightening the nut.

➥**When adding or subtracting shims from between the pulley halves, they should be relocated on the outer pulley to keep the overall spacing on the shaft the same.**

13. Use primary pulley and rotate the engine a few times to allow the belt to position itself on the pulleys; then check the tension. If the belt is too tight (or too loose) the whole assembly will have to be removed to allow for repositioning of the shims.

14. On most models, the belt tension should be set to allow a ¼ inch of deflection between the pulleys when using a finger.

➥**When installing a new belt, keep in mind that it may take a couple of tries to properly set the tension. It can become somewhat time-consuming having to remove and install the fan and assembly, reposition the shims, and check the tension.**

15. If the belt tension is correct, tighten the fan shaft nut to the torque specified by the manufacturer.

16. Install the ignition cover on the engine case.

17. Install the fan protector, if equipped.

18. Install the exhaust system if it was removed for access to the ignition cover.

LIQUID COOLING

♦ See Figures 31 thru 36

Using water to cool an engine is nothing new, since water-cooling has been around since the turn of the century, used mainly for automobile engines. Within the last ten years, water cooling snowmobile engines has become quite popular, and has become the standard within the industry.

➥**The term "water-cooled" is slightly misleading because the liquid coolant should never be more than 50 percent water. The balance of the solution should usually be a high-quality ethylene glycol (or propylene glycol) solution otherwise known as antifreeze, or coolant.**

Using water, mixed with ethylene glycol, is the most effective way to cool an internal combustion engine. (unless you want to talk to the guys at NASA, who have probably come up with something better.)

The water is circulated through the engine with a water pump (which is usually operated from the crankshaft) to the heat exchangers underneath the sled. Heat from within the engine is transferred to the coolant mixture, which travels through "jackets" or passages surrounding the cylinder heads. The heat exchangers (similar to radiators on automobiles) then cool the coolant mixture with the air and snow powder kicked up from the track. Once the heat is removed from the mixture, it flows back to the engine to pick up another load of heat generated by the engine.

The major components of a water cooling system are:

- **Heat Exchanger(s)**
- **Water Pump**

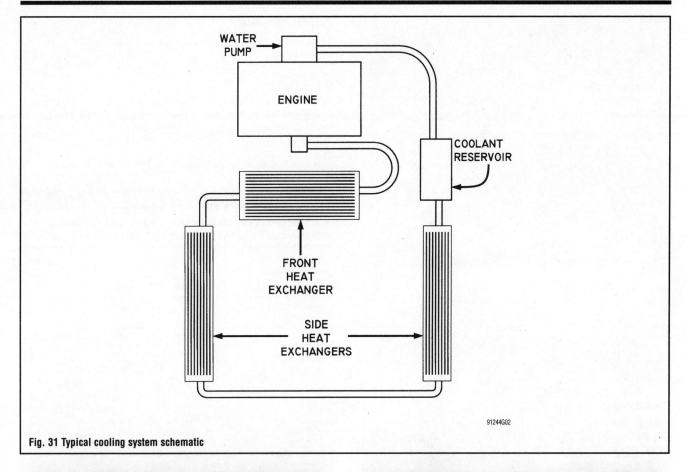

Fig. 31 Typical cooling system schematic

Fig. 32 Liquid-cooled engines are much more compact than their air-cooled counterparts

Fig. 33 Heat exchangers are the heart of the cooling system. They are typically found in the rear tunnel, but sometimes located . . .

- **Thermostat**
- **Hoses**
- **Coolant**
- **Coolant Tank**

Water cooling an engine may add performance and reliability, but it also adds complexity, as shown by the list of additional components. It is another system that must be properly maintained in order to keep the engine working properly.

One of the most common misunderstandings about cooling systems is that the coolant can be ignored and considered maintenance free. Although liquid cooling systems are typically considered low-maintenance, coolant ages over time, losing its ability to resist boiling and conduct heat. But, more importantly, it also loses its anti-corrosion properties, and will allow the build-up of scale and residue in the cooling system. This build-up will reduce the cooling system's ability to do its job and could eventually render the system useless. Regular inspection of the condition of the coolant will prevent any problems on the trail.

Fig. 34 . . . in front of the track . . .

Fig. 35 . . . and the sides of the tunnel as well

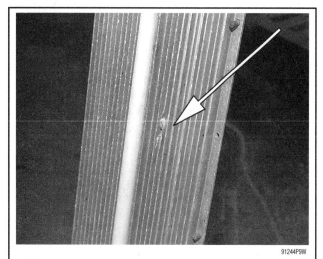

Fig. 36 Here's an example of a damaged heat exchanger. Damage like this can cause "hot spots" as well as leakage

Checking Your Coolant

▶ **See Figures 37, 38, 39 and 40**

You should check the coolant level in your snowmobile as frequently as you check the level of your engine oil tank. It can be just as important to the life of your engine. If the level begins to drop suddenly (and you don't see any leaks), then IMMEDIATELY check for leaks, and your expansion chamber(s) for signs of coolant residue. Coolant residue has a sweet "maple syrup" type smell. If you detect coolant in your expansion chamber(s) or muffler, your engine may be experiencing head gasket problems.

But, (on a lighter note) most of the time you will probably notice that the coolant level remains the same.

> ✳✳ **CAUTION**

Never open, service or drain cooling system when hot; serious burns can occur from the steam and hot coolant.

Most water-cooled snowmobiles use a coolant reservoir so the level can be checked without removing the pressure cap. The reservoirs are typically marked with LOW and FULL or COLD and HOT markings. Manufacturers typically suggest that the coolant level should be checked with the snowmobile on a level

Fig. 37 The coolant reservoir should be maintained at the FULL mark

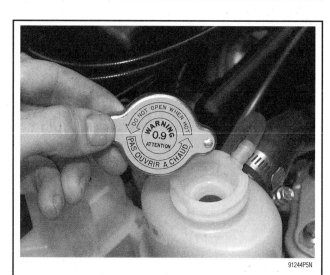

Fig. 38 Pay attention to the warnings on the reservoir and cap; you can be severely burned by hot coolant

Fig. 39 Some systems locate the pressure cap on one of the coolant hoses instead of the reservoir/expansion tank

Fig. 40 It's a good idea to use a funnel when adding coolant to prevent spillage onto the brake assembly

surface and with the engine at normal operating temperature. BUT, there are always some exceptions, so check your owner's manual to be sure.

✲✲ CAUTION

Ethylene-glycol antifreeze is highly toxic. It is also cool and green. Some children might think it looks a lot like a soft drink so KEEP IT AWAY FROM THEM. Also, it has a sweet taste and smell that can attract animals, and in sufficient quantity it could kill them, so protect your kids AND your pets from coolant.

If you experience a coolant-related problem, like boiling over and pouring out the overflow tube, for example, check the specific gravity of the coolant using a hydrometer. These should be readily available at most automotive stores. Make sure that the hydrometer is small enough to obtain a sufficient cooling sample; some of the larger ones found in automotive stores may require more coolant than you can obtain from your snowmobile's cooling system. The hydrometer can help you determine if the mixture of coolant and water is incorrect, or if the coolant is old and has lost its heat transferring abilities.

➡You should always use distilled water in the cooling system since the minerals and chemicals that are usually present in tap or drinking water may contribute to cooling system corrosion. And that is exactly what you are trying to avoid by changing the coolant in the first place.

Whenever you check your coolant, take a few minutes to inspect the condition of your coolant hoses as well. With the engine cool, run your hands along the hoses looking for damp or soft spots which indicate a weakening hose that could be getting ready to burst. Excessively hard or cracking hoses should also be replaced. Check the clamps at the ends to be sure the hoses are secure on the fittings. Clamps should be snug, but not over-tight (which might cause the ends of the hose to crack and split). Hoses that are suspect should be replaced; you wouldn't want it to burst on the trail and leave you stranded.

Draining & Filling The Cooling System

If you have determined that the coolant in your snowmobile is losing its heat-transferring ability (by checking it with a hydrometer) or if it is excessively dirty, it should be replaced with a fresh mixture of coolant/antifreeze and water.

DRAINING THE SYSTEM—THE MESSY WAY

Unlike cars and trucks, modern snowmobiles do not lend themselves to easy, quick coolant draining procedures. Most of today's sleds do not have a "drain plug" underneath the engine to allow the coolant to be drained into a receptacle. Because of this, there is really no easy way to completely drain the cooling system on a modern sled.

Draining the cooling system becomes a huge mess, with coolant all over the bottom of the engine compartment, and all over the garage floor. If you've ever spilled a significant amount of coolant, then you already know how difficult it can be to clean. Ethylene glycol-based coolant leaves a slippery, greasy residue that is difficult to remove from most surfaces.

One way to combat the mess of coolant emitting from underneath your sled is with the use of extra large drain pans. Typically available at auto parts stores, these can contain most (if not all of) the coolant and keep it from spilling all over the garage floor. In addition, large absorbent pads, kitty litter, and old towels can be used to help contain coolant. When removing a hose, a towel wrapped around the connection will help soak up most of the coolant.

✲✲ CAUTION

Ethylene-glycol antifreeze is highly toxic. It is also cool and green. Some children might think it looks a lot like a soft drink so KEEP IT AWAY FROM THEM. Also, it has a sweet taste and smell that can attract animals, and in sufficient quantity it could kill them, so protect your kids AND your pets from coolant.

1. Place the snowmobile on a level surface, with the engine **cold**.
2. Remove the system pressure cap to de-pressurize the system.
3. Disconnect the overflow hose from the reservoir tank and siphon the fluid from the tank. If necessary, the tank can be completely removed, rinsed and re-installed.
4. Remove the expansion chamber and muffler if necessary to allow better access of the cooling system hoses on the engine.

➡On some models, (depending on the quantity of heat exchangers and their locations) the seat may need to be removed to allow for access to the heat exchanger air bleed screw(s).

5. Remove the drain screw on the water pump housing on the front of the engine. For models with side-mounted water pumps, look for drain screws on the front of the cylinders to allow draining of the coolant. Allow the coolant to drain from the engine.
6. Remove the reservoir tank (or expansion tank, depending on the type of system) and drain any remaining coolant from the system.
7. Attach any coolant hoses that were removed to facilitate coolant drainage. Install the drain screws/bolts to the water pump and/or cylinders.

DRAINING THE SYSTEM—THE CLEAN WAY

◆ See Figures 41 and 42

There is alternate method to removing coolant that can be used on most snowmobiles to remove most of the coolant/water mixture from the engine, to allow a thermostat or coolant hose to be changed.

A siphon (like the kind used to fill kerosene heaters) can be used to empty out a large amount of coolant from the engine, without spilling it all over the place. This procedure requires a little bit of engineering, with the use of a hose (like a long piece of fuel line) that is attached to the end of the siphon.

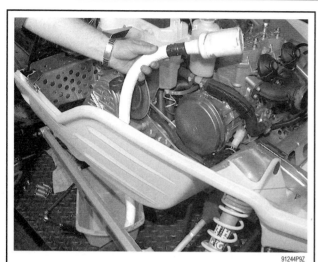

Fig. 41 Here's one method to draining the cooling system without making a mess. The hose runs through the muffler hole into a drain pan

Fig. 42 Note how the cutout oil bottle fits underneath the coolant reservoir hose

The ability to perform this procedure depends on the design of the engine, the location of the water pump, and the type of coolant tank that is used.

Some sleds have an "expansion tank" that has a small hose attached to it that fills with coolant when the system is warm (and the coolant expands). Others have a tank that is basically a reservoir for the coolant. With these type of cooling systems, placing the siphon hose as far as possible into the hose which runs to the lowest point of the engine will yield the best results.

✻✻ CAUTION

Ethylene-glycol antifreeze is highly toxic. It is also cool and green. Some children might think it looks a lot like a soft drink so KEEP IT AWAY FROM THEM. Also, it has a sweet taste and smell that can attract animals, and in sufficient quantity it could kill them, so protect your kids AND your pets from coolant.

1. Using the siphon, remove the coolant from the expansion tank/reservoir.

➡If you do not have a siphon, a drain hose can be fabricated with an old oil bottle and a length of hose, which can be placed underneath the

coolant reservoir to keep spillage to a minimum. Use your own ingenuity to create your own removal system to fit your particular sled.

2. Remove the hoses that attach to the coolant tank, and set it aside. Keep a supply of old towels handy, and use them to soak up any remaining coolant by wrapping the towel around the ends of the hoses when they are removed from the tank.

3. Place the siphon hose as far as possible into the front coolant hose, continuing to remove coolant. On models with an expansion tank, insert the siphon hose into the pressure cap opening and route it to whichever hose attaches to the lowest point of the cooling system.

➡The further the siphon hose reaches inside of the engine, the more coolant will be drained from the system.

4. Once the coolant has been siphoned from the engine as much as possible, remove the thermostat housing on the top of the cylinder head, and lift out the thermostat. Again, with the siphon hose, remove as much coolant as possible from the engine.

➡The idea is to use the siphon and keep removing coolant from the system as each hose is removed.

5. Once you've removed as much coolant as possible from the system, install any hoses that were removed, and install the coolant expansion tank/reservoir.

FILLING THE SYSTEM

♦ See Figures 43, 44, 45 and 46

Regardless of how you chose to remove the old coolant from your snowmobile's cooling system, the method in which it is filled is universal. One might think that filling the cooling system involves nothing more than pouring fresh coolant into the system until the level is correct. Well, for the most part, that is correct; however, the air must be bled from the cooling system to prevent air pockets that can cause "hot spots" which can lead to engine damage.

Since every snowmobile's cooling system is configured differently, make sure to check with the owner's manual or manufacturer about refilling the system. Although a generic procedure is given here, it is virtually impossible to give a specific method of filling the cooling system of every snowmobile, since they are all configured differently. The air bleed screws (located in different areas) are usually what dictates a specific method of filling the cooling system; check your owner's manual for further details.

1. Using a clean five gallon bucket or other suitable container, mix the appropriate amount of coolant with water as recommended by the manufacturer. This should be done in a clean bucket or other container. In most cases, the ratio is 50:50, but some manufacturers call for 60:40 and higher mixtures.

Fig. 43 Most cooling systems have an air bleed screw (arrow) to release air pockets when fresh coolant is added to the system

Fig. 44 Sometimes the hoses connecting the rear heat exchangers may need to be temporarily disconnected when filling the system to allow air to escape

Fig. 45 With the seat removed, the coolant hoses for the main heat exchanger (arrows) can be easily accessed

Fig. 46 Once the bleed screw(s) are loosened, slowly add coolant to the system

2. Add the properly mixed ratio of coolant and water to the cooling system. Use a funnel to prevent spilling coolant onto the disc brake caliper. If your sled has an air bleed screw on the rear heat exchanger, remove the screw when adding the coolant; when solid coolant (free of air bubbles) flows from the bleed screw, install the screw and tighten it securely. Lifting up the rear of the sled with the bleed screw open will also help free any air bubbles trapped in the system.

3. Remove the air bleed screw on the cylinder head(s), and continue to add coolant. When solid coolant (free of air bubbles) flows from the bleed screw, install the screw.

4. Add coolant to the expansion tank until the level is correct.

5. Start the engine and allow the water pump to circulate the coolant throughout the system.

6. Before the engine warms the coolant, shut the engine **off** and loosen the bleed screws and let out any trapped air within the system. Use a rag or towel to contain any excess coolant.

7. Finally, top off the coolant level to the proper mark on the expansion tank/reservoir. Make sure not to overfill the system, or the sled will "puke" coolant from the overflow hose when the engine is warm.

8. When you're done with your coolant change, do your part to help clean up the environment; dispose of used coolant properly by taking it to a local recycling facility.

Flushing The Cooling System

New EPA regulations state that coolant is considered a toxic waste, and draining of coolant onto the ground (driveway, grass, etc) is illegal. Because of this, the old method of "flushing" out your cooling system with a garden hose and tap water can be hard to do without breaking the law.

Unless you have a way to contain all of the water that is flushed through the cooling system, flushing is not recommended.

Because of these EPA regulations, we at Chilton recommend this procedure to be left to a dealer or qualified service facility. Dealers are properly equipped to flush a cooling system, and properly (read: legally) dispose of the old ethylene glycol-based coolant from your sled.

Thermostat

▶ See Figures 47 and 48

The majority of liquid-cooled snowmobiles use a thermostat as part of the cooling system. The thermostat helps regulate the temperature of the engine's cooling system, keeping it within a certain temperature range. If the coolant is too cold, the engine will not reach full operating temperature, causing accelerated wear on the internal components of the engine, and poor performance. If the engine temperature is too hot, the engine will overheat, and damage will also occur. The thermostat helps regulate how much coolant is passed through the heat exchangers, which in turn keeps the engine temperature constant.

TESTING

Testing the thermostat can be done by suspending the unit in a pot of boiling water and noting at what temperature it opens. Obviously, you must also suspend a thermometer in the boiling water to indicate the temperature. If the temperature the thermostat opens does not correspond to temperature stamped on top of the unit, the thermostat is defective.

In reality, it's much easier to simply replace the thermostat with a new one instead of going through the hassle of testing. The small cost of a new thermostat is more than off set by the time it takes to remove, clean and test the unit.

Water Pump Belt

A large percentage of snowmobile engines use a water pump driven directly from the crankshaft by a gear, but on some liquid-cooled snowmobiles, a belt is used to drive the water pump. This belt is typically driven from a pulley on the crankshaft, and turns the water pump pulley (and sometimes the oil injection pump too) mounted on the side of the engine. As with the fan belt on liquid cooled engines, the water pump belt is of utmost importance for proper cooling of the engine.

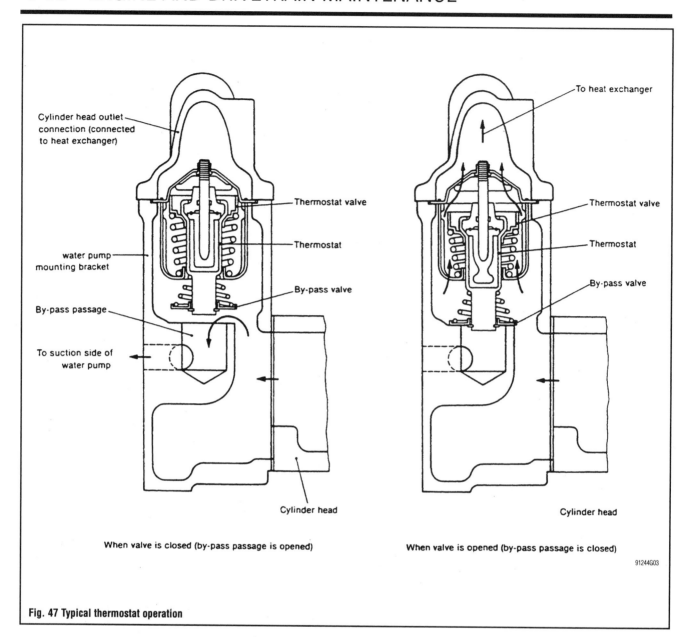

When valve is closed (by-pass passage is opened)

When valve is opened (by-pass passage is closed)

Fig. 47 Typical thermostat operation

Fig. 48 The thermostat can be removed on most engines by removing the bolts that attach the outlet pipe to the cylinder head

INSPECTION

▶ See Figures 49, 50, 51, 52 and 53

The water pump belt on liquid-cooled engines should be inspected at least every 20 hours of operation, or every 250 miles (400 km). When inspecting the belt, look for signs of excessive deterioration, such as cracking, separating, and glazing. If the belt is in question, **replace** it immediately to avoid problems with the cooling of the engine. On models that use the water pump belt to drive the oil injection pump, this becomes even more critical.

It should be noted there are three main causes of drive belt failure. The most common is fatigue of the load-bearing, tensile cords leading to belt failure from the inside out. Tensile cord failure is due to a gradual weakening of the tensile cords that results from a combination of side stress, bending stress, and centrifugal force imposed on the belt as it travels around the pulleys. Because this type of failure takes place inside the belt, there is no easy way to determine when the belt is about to break.

The other major cause of drive belt failure is improper tension. This causes the belt to slip as it travels around the pulleys, generating heat build-up. Excessive heat eventually causes the rubber compounds in the belt to break down, and crack, leading to belt failure. It should be noted that some engines with belt-driven water pumps do not have any provision for tightening the belt.

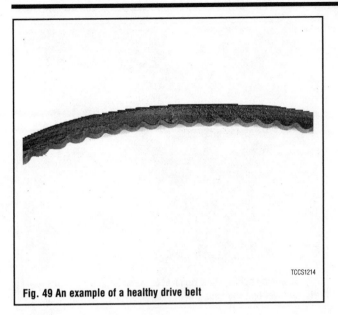

Fig. 49 An example of a healthy drive belt

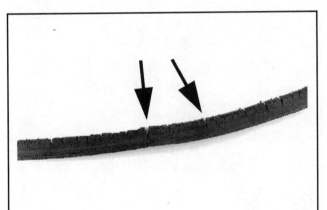

Fig. 50 Deep cracks in this belt will cause flex, building up heat that will eventually lead to belt failure

Fig. 51 Some engines have an opening in the case for viewing of the water pump belt

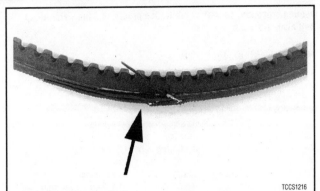

Fig. 52 The cover of this belt is worn, exposing the critical reinforcing cords to excessive wear

Fig. 53 Installing too wide a belt can result in serious belt wear and/or breakage

Since the water pump belt is in the close proximity of the rest of the engine, it is susceptible to heat damage over time. High temperatures can cause belts to dry, harden and crack.

Also, any damage to the pulley surfaces can contribute to premature failure of a belt. Any knicks, heavy scratches, or bending can wreak havoc on a drive belt. If your sled has been stored in a humid area during the off-season, rust may form on the pulleys (if they are made of steel), also causing problems with the belt.

✴✴ WARNING

DO NOT use belt dressings in an attempt to extend belt life. Belt dressing will soften the belt, causing accelerated deterioration. Oil or grease contamination on the belt or pulleys will have the same effect. Keep the drive belt system clear of oil, grease, or other contaminants.

ADJUSTMENT

1. Remove the expansion chamber(s) and muffler as necessary to allow access to the water pump belt.
2. If equipped, remove the water pump pulley cover.
3. Loosen the water pump pivot bolt, followed by the adjustment bolt.
4. While pushing or pulling on the pump, tighten the bolts temporarily.
5. Check the tension of the belt. On most models, the belt tension should be set to allow a ¼ inch of deflection between the pulleys when using a finger. As always, follow the guidelines and specifications recommended by the manufacturer.
6. If the tension is correct, tighten the bolts securely.
7. If equipped, install the water pump cover.
8. Install the expansion chamber(s) and muffler if they were removed for access to the belt.

➥As previously mentioned, some snowmobile engines belt-driven water pumps do not have a means of adjustment. If the tension becomes too loose, the belt must be replaced. A slipping water pump belt can cause cooling problems, as well as lubrication problems if the water pump belt also drives the oil injection pump.

REMOVAL AND INSTALLATION

▶ See Figures 54 thru 59

1. Remove the expansion chamber(s) and muffler.
2. Remove the recoil starter from the side of the engine as necessary.
3. Loosen the pivot bolt and adjuster bolt on the pump and slacken the belt. On models without a means of adjustment, either remove the pulley from the pump shaft, or remove the **mounting** bolts for the water pump housing. Make sure not to remove the bolts that secure the water pump to the housing, or the gasket will be broken, and coolant will leak from the pump.
4. Slip the belt from the pump pulley, followed by removing it from the lower pulley.

To install:

5. Using a new belt, (make sure it is the same size) slip it over the lower pulley.

➡Always make sure the new fan belt is of the same length and width as the old unit. It is normal for the old belt to be slightly longer than the new belt; keep this in mind when installing the new belt, since it may be slightly more difficult to install.

Fig. 56 Some engines allow removal of the water pump housing assembly for belt changing without disconnecting the coolant lines

Fig. 54 On some models, it may be necessary to remove brackets or supports to allow access to the pump

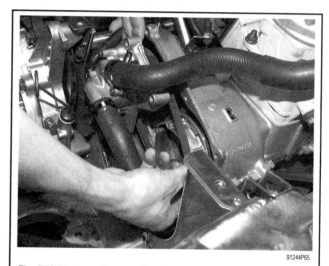

Fig. 57 With the water pump housing removed, the belt can be slipped from the pulleys

Fig. 55 Most engines require removal of the recoil starter assembly to access the belt

Fig. 58 After the new belt is installed, position the belt shaft with the bearing in the case (note notch in shaft for oil injection pump)

Fig. 59 Once the shaft is in line with the bearing, turn the engine slowly until the notch in the shaft aligns with the oil injection pump

6. Place the belt over the pump pulley, and carefully place the pump assembly into (or into) the engine case, or place the pump pulley onto the pump shaft.

➡ On models with a belt-driven injection pump, The pulley may need to be rotated to allow the slot on the water pump driveshaft to align in the pump. This can easily be achieved by rotating the lower pulley slowly until the pump housing "sets" in position.

7. On models that have a provision for adjustment, adjust the belt to the proper tension specified by the manufacturer. Typically, the belt tension should be set to allow a ¼ inch of deflection between the pulleys when using a finger.

8. On non-adjustable models, install the water pump housing bolts and/or pulley bolts and tighten them securely. Then turn the engine by hand for a few revolutions and check for proper belt tension. The belt tension MUST be correct, since there is no means for adjustment.

9. Once the belt tension is verified to be correct, install the recoil starter onto the side of the engine.

10. Remove any covers or other components that were removed to access the water pump belt.

11. Install the expansion chamber(s) and muffler.

Fuel Filter

The fuel filter is designed to do for your carburetor what the air filter does for your engine; keep out particles of dirt and debris. If however, the screen becomes clogged, the flow of gasoline will be impeded. This could cause lean fuel mixtures, hesitation and stumbling, and idle problems.

Snowmobiles almost always come equipped with a screen type filter, which is attached to the outlet hose, either inside or outside the fuel tank. These screens provide the most basic form of filtration for the fuel that enters the carburetor(s).

As long as you keep from pouring dirty fuel into your tank, the screen should be clean. But, over time, dirt and lint can get into your tank and clog the screen. It should be inspected periodically to prevent clogging, and also to check the screen itself for tears and deterioration.

In addition to the filter screen, most snowmobiles also come equipped with one or more in-line fuel filters. These are usually similar to the old carbureted automotive style filters, consisting of a filter element in a plastic housing with nipples on either end to attach the fuel lines. If your snowmobile does not come equipped with an in-line filter, you may wish to install one, just outside of the tank. These filters are readily available at most automotive supply stores. If you do this, you can usually leave the screen in the tank alone until you notice a reduction in the fuel flow (meaning that the screen is clogged). One of the additional advantages of adding an in-line filter is that most of them are clear plastic and you can actually see if fuel is filling the filter housing. This is helpful in determining if your in-tank screen is clogged.

REPLACEMENT

✳✳ CAUTION

For those of you who have led a sheltered life: YOU ARE DEALING WITH A HIGHLY FLAMMABLE SUBSTANCE HERE! Do not allow any open flames, sparks or other sources of combustion anywhere near the work area. Make sure you are working in a well-ventilated area. Protect your skin from gasoline by wearing vinyl gloves. AND DON'T SMOKE!

Inline Type

▶ See Figures 60, 61 and 62

On most carbureted sleds, replacement of the inline filter is a very simple matter or disconnecting the fuel lines from both ends removing the filter. Just remember to clamp the fuel line from the fuel tank first.

✳✳ CAUTION

Observe all applicable safety precautions when working around fuel. Whenever servicing the fuel system, always work in a well-ventilated area. Do not allow fuel spray or vapors to come in contact with a spark or open flame. Keep a dry chemical fire extinguisher near the work area. Always keep fuel in a container specifically designed for fuel storage; also, always properly seal fuel containers to avoid the possibility of fire or explosion.

1. If your snowmobile is equipped with a battery, disconnect the negative battery cable.

✳✳ CAUTION

Because the fuel lines will be opened, it is important that the engine be COLD when performing this procedure. A warm engine can easily ignite raw fuel.

2. Locate the fuel filter in the engine compartment.

3. If necessary, remove any components necessary to allow access to the filter. On some models, it may be necessary to disconnect the airbox or carburetor(s) from the inlets if necessary to allow access to the filter. When removing the carburetors, do not disconnect the lines and cables, just remove them from the inlets and set them aside.

4. Disconnect the two hoses that attach to the filter. When removing the fil-

Fig. 60 Inline fuel filters can be located before the fuel pump . . .

Fig. 61 . . . or after, directly before the carburetors

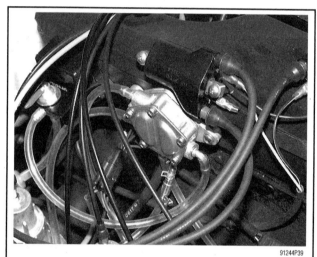

Fig. 62 While changing the filter, check the condition of the fuel pump lines too

ter, pinch the fuel line from the fuel tank with your fingers until the new filter is attached to keep gasoline from draining.

➡Use a rag to contain any excess fuel when disconnecting the fuel lines from the filter.

5. Connect the hoses to the new filter, making sure it is installed in the proper direction. Typically, there is an arrow on the filter to indicate flow direction; the arrow should point to the hose that attaches to the fuel pump or carburetors.

6. Once the hoses are connected and the clamps installed, (if equipped) install any components that were removed to access the fuel filter.

7. Connect the negative battery cable if the snowmobile is equipped with a battery.

In-tank Type

◆ See Figures 63 thru 68

❋❋ **CAUTION**

Observe all applicable safety precautions when working around fuel. Whenever servicing the fuel system, always work in a well-ventilated area. Do not allow fuel spray or vapors to come in contact with a spark or open flame. Keep a dry chemical fire

extinguisher near the work area. Always keep fuel in a container specifically designed for fuel storage; also, always properly seal fuel containers to avoid the possibility of fire or explosion.

1. If your snowmobile is equipped with a battery, disconnect the negative battery cable.

❋❋ **CAUTION**

Because the fuel lines will be opened, it is important that the engine be COLD when performing this procedure. A warm engine can easily ignite raw fuel.

2. Using a kerosene heater type fuel siphon, remove as much fuel as possible from the fuel tank.

3. Remove any components if necessary (usually the airbox) to allow access to the fuel tank outlet line.

4. Remove the outlet line from the tank. Some models use a metal fitting that is bolted to the tank, and others use a rubber grommet that is press fit in position.

❋❋ **CAUTION**

Make sure that any remaining fuel in the tank is below the level of the outlet hose fitting, or fuel will leak when the fitting is removed. Use rags as necessary to contain any fuel.

5. Once the fitting is removed from the tank, disconnect the in-tank filter hose from the fitting, and attach a long (about three feet) piece of string to the filter hose. Make sure the knot is small enough to fit through the opening in the tank.

6. Using a clean piece of welding wire, or other means, fish the filter out of the tank from the filler neck. Be careful not to pull on the filter too hard or the knot may slip on the hose.

7. Disconnect the clamp on the end of the hose, and remove the filter or screen.

8. If the filter is a metal mesh screen, clean it with a mild solvent and blow it dry with **low** level compressed air (if available).

9. Install the filter onto πthe outlet hose.

10. Drop the filter back into the gas tank.

11. Using the piece of string that is attached to the outlet hose, carefully draw it through the opening in the fuel tank.

12. Attach the outlet hose to the fitting that mounts to the fuel tank. Tighten the line securely.

13. Mount the fitting to the fuel tank. If the fitting is a press fit grommet type, smear a light coating of grease on the fitting to allow easier installation.

14. Fill the fuel tank until the level is just above the fitting; check for leaks. Replace any parts as necessary.

Fig. 63 Unbolt the outlet from the fuel tank, . . .

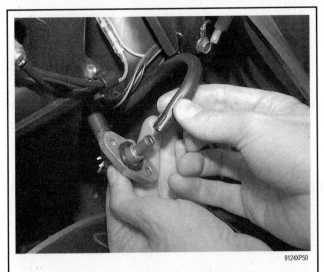

Fig. 64 . . . disconnect the pick-up line from the outlet . . .

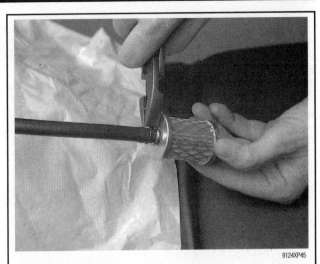

Fig. 67 Most spring-type clamps can be easily disconnected with standard pliers

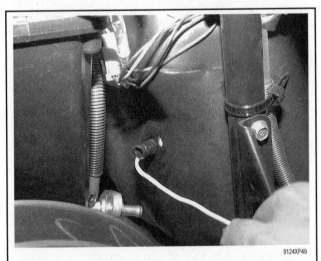

Fig. 65 . . . and tie a piece of string or wire to the end of the line. Make sure the knot fits through the opening in the fuel tank

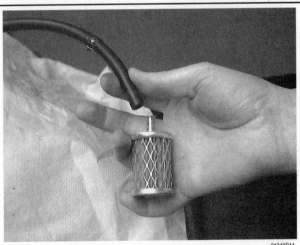

Fig. 68 The fuel filter can finally be changed. Don't let the line drop into the tank without attaching a new filter!

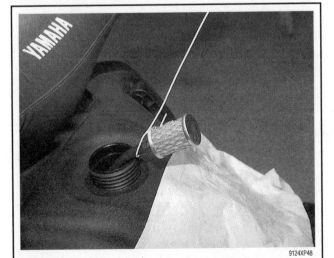

Fig. 66 Using a piece of wire, "fish" the filter out of the fuel tank

15. Install any components that were removed to allow access to the outlet hose fitting.

16. If your snowmobile is equipped with a battery, connect the negative battery cable.

Fuel Injected Type

Fuel injected snowmobiles use a high-pressure metal case type fuel filter. As with the fuel filter on carbureted models, it should be changed regularly to prevent the system from being starved of fuel.

In addition to the high-pressure filter, a primary filter located in the fuel tank may also be used on fuel injected models. Refer to the In-tank Type filter heading in this section for information on replacement.

❉❉ CAUTION

Observe all applicable safety precautions when working around fuel. Whenever servicing the fuel system, always work in a well-ventilated area. Do not allow fuel spray or vapors to come in contact with a spark or open flame. Keep a dry chemical fire extinguisher near the work area. Always keep fuel in a container specifically designed for fuel storage; also, always properly seal fuel containers to avoid the possibility of fire or explosion.

1. If your snowmobile is equipped with a battery, disconnect the negative battery cable.
2. Locate the fuel filter in the engine compartment.
3. If necessary, remove any necessary components (like the airbox) to allow access to the filter.

> ※※ **CAUTION**
>
> **Because the fuel lines will be opened, it is important that the engine be COLD when performing this procedure. A warm engine can easily ignite raw fuel.**

4. Place an appropriately sized wrench on one of the line fittings, along with a back-up wrench on the filter. Wrap the filter and the ends of the wrenches with a heavy-duty rag to prevent fuel from spraying.
5. CAREFULLY loosen the fitting on the filter. Use EXTREME caution when loosening the line; the fuel in under high pressure can spray into your eyes. Once the fuel pressure is relieved, remove the fittings from both sides of the fuel filter. Use a rag to contain any excess fuel.
6. Connect the lines to the new filter, making sure it is installed in the proper direction. New copper gaskets should be used on both sides of each fitting to prevent leakage.
7. Install any components that were removed to access the fuel filter.
8. Connect the negative battery cable if the snowmobile is equipped.

ENGINE TUNE-UP

Years ago, snowmobile riders would have to perform lengthy and sometimes complicated rituals every few thousand miles in order to keep their sleds running properly. Snowmobiles of yesterday used components that wore out quickly like ignition points, which would have to be replaced, and carburetors which would require adjustment often. In those days of yore, machines could get temperamental if ignition and carburetor adjustments were not performed regularly (and properly).

A tune-up is a sequence of component replacement and adjustment which is designed to restore engine performance which is lost to normal use and wear. Just like the preventive maintenance described earlier, a tune-up should be performed based on time, mileage and your particular pattern of usage. A snowmobile used in competition will require a tune-up before each race, while a weekend warrior's mount might only need one every few months.

To properly perform a tune-up, you must follow a set order of events. For instance, ignition timing should always precede carburetor adjustment, since they can both affect engine rpm (which is one of the items you would adjust while working on the carburetors). A typical tune-up could consist of the following items (as applicable):

- A compression test
- Spark plug inspection and replacement
- Ignition timing inspection
- Carburetor idle speed and mixture adjustments
- Vehicle test

But, you should note that the tune-up of yesterday is completely gone from the automotive world, and it is slowly, but surely, disappearing from the world of snowmobiles. Advances in engine management technology (like electronic ignition systems), and low maintenance mechanical components leaves today's rider with not too much to tweak.

The one thing that you CAN count on is that you will have to periodically check and replace your spark plugs. As a matter of fact, on some snowmobiles, that is the sum total of your tune-up, since timing and carburetor adjustments may not be possible or necessary. On other snowmobiles spark plug replacement is just the beginning. Once again, grab your owner's manual and check for the following items, then perform each of them in the proper sequence.

➡ **The steps of a tune-up ASSUME that all engine maintenance from fluid to filter changes has been properly performed. If you are performing carburetor or timing adjustments, BE CERTAIN that there are no air or fuel filter problems before proceeding.**

Engine Compression

A compression check is a great way to keep an eye on engine condition. But, if you have a new snowmobile, then you probably won't NEED to do this. Of course, performing a compression check on a new snowmobile (one that has been broken-in already) is a great way to set the baseline for years to come. You will know what the compression was when new and how to compare that with wear on future readings.

STATIC COMPRESSION TESTS

♦ **See Figure 69**

An engine compression test is performed by cranking the motor (using the recoil starter, or if equipped, an electric starter) while a pressure gauge is threaded into (or held into) the spark plug port of each cylinder. The gauge will

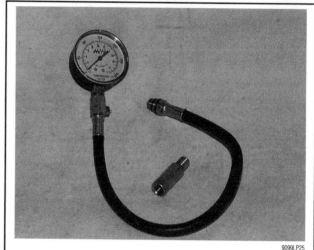

Fig. 69 A compression gauge is a relatively inexpensive tool that can help you determine the condition of the pistons and cylinders

measure the amount of pressure (read as psi or kPa depending on your gauge) which the piston, rings and are capable of building.

Compression readings are a fast and effective way to determine engine condition. Although specifications vary greatly from one motor to another, the important thing to watch for in a compression test are changes. Keep track of the readings, noting if they are significantly lower than the previous tune-up. Typically speaking, compression readings should be above 100 psi and no cylinder should be more than 15% lower than the highest reading you have taken (multi-cylinder models).

To obtain a proper reading you should be sure that the engine has been warmed to normal operating temperature (so all components are properly seated).

If possible, a threaded compression gauge should be used. Threaded gauges are more accurate, since they eliminate the possibility of compression leaking out the spark plug threads. This is a common cause for low readings when using a non-threaded, hold-in-place type gauge. Threaded gauges are also easier to use, since they leave both your hands free to do other things, like hitting the starter button.

1. Warm the engine to normal operating temperature.
2. Disable the ignition system.

➡ **Disabling the ignition system can be done in a variety of ways. Check a service manual to find the preferred method for your snowmobile. It may involve disconnecting the ignition coil primary wiring, removing a relay or fuse, or it may be as simple as using the engine kill switch on the handlebar (since some models will allow the starter to work, but will disable the ignition system when the switch is thrown). Some types of CDI ignition systems may be damaged if the spark plug wires are not grounded when checking compression.**

3. Carefully clean the area around the spark plug bores, then remove the spark plugs and set them aside.

➡**Be sure to label the spark plug wires before removing them.**

4. Install the gauge to the cylinder. When using a threaded gauge, be sure the proper sized adapter is attached, then thread it carefully into the bore.

5. Hold the throttle wide open and crank the motor a few times. If you have a snowmobile without an electric starter, you will have to give the starter a good, strong pull to be sure that you get the highest reading of which the cylinder is capable.

➡**Remember that it is assumed that all maintenance has been performed, meaning that the throttle cable is properly adjusted. If you are in doubt, visually check that the carburetor venturis are fully open before cranking the motor.**

6. Note the compression reading, release the pressure and repeat for that cylinder 1–2 more times to be certain that you have the highest possible reading.

7. Although not all manufacturers provide specifications, most two-stroke engines should have compression readings somewhere above 100 psi. Figures in the 150–160 psi range are not uncommon on high performance machines.

8. Repeat the compression check for each of the cylinders. Compare the highest readings for each cylinder. Ideally all readings should be within 10% of each other, but a variance of 15% between the lowest and the highest is usually considered the outer limit.

9. If one or more cylinders of the engine read lower than specification, or lower than the recommended percentage of the highest cylinder's reading, you should repeat the test. But, this time, add a tablespoon of fresh, clean engine oil to the cylinder (through the spark plug hole) before taking the readings. If the compression readings come up with the oil added, then it is likely that the piston rings and cylinder walls for that cylinder are worn. If the compression remains low your problem is likely broken rings, or a hole in the piston, or scoring of the cylinder from a broken wrist pin clip.

10. Keep track of the readings over a series of tune-ups. If the compression increases dramatically, the piston crown and chamber has carbon deposits, and should be decarbonized. This involves removing the cylinder head and cylinder (something that you may want to consider having done at a dealer).

LEAK-DOWN TESTS

An even better (and easier) way to check cylinder condition is with the use of a leak-down tester. The only problem to the home mechanic is expense. A leak-down tester is an expensive and specialized tool which is used along with an air compressor. Instead of using the engine to build compression, a leak-down tester pressurizes a cylinder with compressed air and then monitors how much leaks out.

To use a leak-down tester you start by warming the motor and then removing the spark plugs (just like a compression check). But, then you find TDC of the compression stroke the cylinder which is about to be tested. At this point the tester pressurizes the cylinder and you watch the gauge to see if it is leaking.

If leaks are found, listen at muffler, and the carburetor(s). Hissing sounds coming from these places will tell you which components are worn. If you have a water-cooled snowmobile, bubbles in the radiator are an indication of head gasket problems.

If you become serious about playing with and/or rebuilding motors, then a leak-down tester may be worth the investment. If not, check your local tool rental shops, they may have one available for a reasonable fee.

Spark Plugs

Unlike automobiles, whose spark plug life has increased dramatically over the years with the use of high voltage, electronic ignition systems (as opposed to points which were used in days gone by), most snowmobiles still seem to be hard on their spark plugs. During normal use, the plug gap increases and the sharp edge of the center electrode tends to dull. As the gap increases and the electrode's edge rounds off, the plug's voltage requirement increases. It requires a greater voltage to jump the wider gap and about two to three times as much voltage to fire the plug at high speeds than at idle. The improved air/fuel ratio control of modern carburetors combined with the higher voltage output of modern electronic ignition systems will often allow an engine to run significantly longer on a standard spark plug, but keep in mind that efficiency will drop as the gap widens. As the plugs wear, gas mileage and performance will drop over time. You will know if the plugs have been ignored for too long, as the engine may very well start to sputter or miss under load.

CONSTRUCTION

♦ **See Figure 70**

A typical spark plug consists of a metal shell surrounding a ceramic insulator. A metal electrode extends downward through the center of the insulator and protrudes a small distance. Located at the end of the plug and attached to the side of the outer metal shell is the side electrode. The side electrode bends in at a 90° angle so that its tip is just past and parallel to the tip of the center electrode. The distance between these two electrodes (measured in thousandths of an inch or hundredths of a millimeter) is called the spark plug gap.

The spark plug does not produce a "spark" but instead provides a gap across which the current can arc, which is considered a spark. The ignition coil produces anywhere from 20,000 to 50,000 volts (depending on the type and application) which travels through the wire to the spark plug. The current passes along the center electrode and jumps the gap to the side electrode, and in doing so, ignites the air/fuel mixture in the combustion chamber.

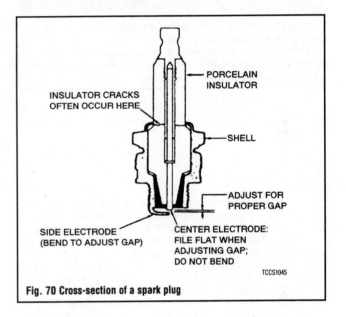

Fig. 70 Cross-section of a spark plug

HEAT RANGE

♦ **See Figure 71**

Spark plug heat range is the ability of the plug to dissipate heat. The longer the insulator (or the farther it extends into the engine), the hotter the plug will

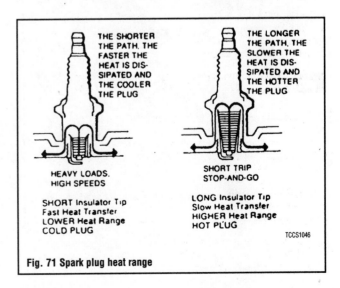

Fig. 71 Spark plug heat range

operate; the shorter the insulator (the closer the electrode is to the block's cooling passages) the cooler it will operate. A plug that absorbs little heat and remains too cool will quickly accumulate deposits of oil and carbon since it is not hot enough to burn them off. This leads to plug fouling and consequently to misfiring (quite common with two-stroke engines). A plug that absorbs too much heat will have no deposits but, due to the excessive heat, the electrodes will burn away quickly and might possibly lead to preignition or other ignition problems. Preignition takes place when plug tips get so hot that they glow sufficiently to ignite the air/fuel mixture before the actual spark occurs. This early ignition will usually cause pinging (preignition) during low speeds and heavy loads.

The general rule of thumb for choosing the correct heat range when picking a spark plug is: if most of your riding is long distance, high speed travel, use a colder plug; if most of your riding is stop and go, or tight, twisty trails, use a hotter plug. Original equipment plugs are generally a good compromise between the two styles, and most riders never have the need to change their plugs from the factory-recommended heat range.

✳✳ WARNING

Using a spark plug that is not within the proper heat range may cause serious engine damage. Just because the spark plug LOOKS the same and threads into the cylinder head doesn't mean that it can be used in your snowmobile engine. Always use a spark plug within the correct heat range to avoid engine problems.

REMOVAL & INSTALLATION

♦ See Figures 72 thru 77

1. If your sled is equipped with a battery, disconnect the negative battery cable, and allow the engine to cool if the engine has been run recently.

➡**If you are trying to take a compression reading then you obviously don't want the engine too cool off. BUT, be careful because removing spark plugs from a hot aluminum cylinder head can cause damage to the threads. If plug removal is difficult, forget the test for now (save your CYLINDER HEAD!!!) and allow the cylinder to cool. Once the cylinder head(s) has cooled sufficiently, remove the spark plugs, clean the threads on the plug and give them a good coating of anti-seize paste. Then install the plugs, warm-up the engine and start again. The anti-seize paste should allow you to safely remove the plugs from a hot head (but BE CAREFUL and DON'T FORCE THEM).**

Fig. 72 A variety of tools and gauges are needed for spark plug service

2. Carefully twist the spark plug wire boot to loosen it, then pull upward and remove the boot from the plug. Be sure to pull on the boot and not on the wire, otherwise the connector located inside the boot may become separated.

3. Use a rag or a brush to clean the area around each of the plugs.

4. Using a spark plug socket that is equipped with a rubber insert to properly hold the plug, turn the spark plug counterclockwise to loosen and remove the spark plug from the bore.

➡**Remove the spark plug when the engine is cold, if possible, to prevent damage to the threads. If removal of the plug is difficult, apply a few drops of penetrating oil or silicone spray to the area around the base of the plug, then give it a few minutes to work.**

✳✳ WARNING

Be sure not to use a flexible extension on the socket when removing or installing a spark plug. Use of a flexible extension may allow a shear force to be applied to the plug. A shear force could break the plug off in the cylinder head, leading to costly and frustrating repairs.

Fig. 73 Only pull on the spark plug boot when removing the wires

Fig. 74 Make sure to use a socket specifically designed for spark plugs to avoid damage to the plug

Fig. 75 You can also use the tools supplied with your sled for removal and installation

Fig. 77 Threading the spark plugs in by hand is advisable to prevent crossthreading

Fig. 76 Make sure to use anti-seize compound on each of the plugs to prevent damage to the threads in the cylinder head

To install:

5. Inspect the spark plug boot for tears or damage. If a damaged boot is found, the spark plug boot or boot and wire must be replaced.

6. Using a wire feeler gauge, check and adjust the spark plug gap. When using a gauge, the proper size should pass between the electrodes with a slight drag. The next larger size should not be able to pass while the next smaller size should pass freely.

7. Place a thin coating of anti-seize on the plug threads to make sure they will be easy to remove next time. DON'T FLAKE OUT HERE! If you don't have any anti-seize paste, buy some! It is way too easy to strip out a spark plug hole. Don't overdue it with the paste, a small dab is more than enough.

8. Carefully thread the plug into the bore by hand. If resistance is felt before the plug is almost completely threaded, back the plug out and begin threading again.

❋❋ WARNING

Always carefully thread the plug by hand to prevent the possibility of crossthreading and damaging the cylinder head threads.

9. Carefully tighten the spark plug. If the plug you are installing is equipped with a crush washer, seat the plug, then tighten about ¼ turn to crush the washer. If you are installing a tapered seat plug, tighten the plug to specifications provided by the snowmobile or plug manufacturer.

10. Apply a small amount of silicone dielectric compound to the end of the spark plug lead or inside the spark plug boot to prevent sticking, then install the boot to the spark plug and push until it clicks into place. The click may be felt or heard, then gently pull back on the boot to assure proper contact.

11. Unless further checks or adjustments need to be made, install the gas tank or any body plastic if it was removed to access the spark plug easier.

12. Connect the negative battery cable, if it was disconnected.

INSPECTION

▶ **See Figure 78**

Whenever the spark plugs are removed from the engine they should be examined for deposits and wear. Your used spark plugs can lend important clues to engine mechanical and operating conditions.

1. Remove the spark plug and examine the deposits to help determine the condition of each cylinder. Compare the plugs to the illustrations and descriptions we have provided.

2. If the plug insulator has turned white or is burned, the plug is too hot and should be replaced with the next colder one available for your engine.

3. If the plugs you are using are too cold, then you will notice sooty or oily deposits. These deposits could be black or only a dark brown. If found, you should try the next hotter plug. If a hotter plug does not remedy the situation, then suspect an overly rich fuel system, or an excessive amount of oil in the fuel. A compression or leak-down test would be the next step.

4. There is an additional point to be noted regarding spark plug condition. An improper ratio of oil and fuel (whether your engine has oil injection or premixed fuel) can have an effect on the spark plugs. One indication of too rich of a fuel/oil mixture is excessive oil deposits on the spark plug tip, otherwise known as fouling. Too little oil mixed with the fuel may cause a lean condition, resulting in a burned plug tip. A lean condition can destroy the piston and cylinder in a two-stroke engine if not corrected. Make absolutely certain that the fuel/oil ratio is correct before making any adjustments.

5. If the plugs have a damp or oil film over the firing end, a black tip, and a carbon layer over the entire face of the plug, it has been oil fouled. Although you can clean and reuse the plug, it should be replaced. You should also perform a compression or leak-down test to determine the cause of oil fouling.

6. If the plugs exhibit light tan or gray deposits, along with no excessive gap or electrode wear, the engine is running properly and you are using the correct spark plugs.

A normally worn spark plug should have light tan or gray deposits on the firing tip.

A carbon fouled plug, identified by soft, sooty, black deposits, may indicate an improperly tuned vehicle. Check the air cleaner, ignition components and engine control system.

This spark plug has been **left in the engine too long,** as evidenced by the extreme gap- Plugs with such an extreme gap can cause misfiring and stumbling accompanied by a noticeable lack of power.

An oil fouled spark plug indicates an engine with worn poston rings and/or bad valve seals allowing excessive oil to enter the chamber.

A physically damaged spark plug may be evidence of severe detonation in that cylinder. Watch that cylinder carefully between services, as a continued detonation will not only damage the plug, but could also damage the engine.

A bridged or almost bridged spark plug, identified by a build-up between the electrodes caused by excessive carbon or oil build-up on the plug.

TCCA1P40

Fig. 78 By reading your spark plugs you can learn a lot about what is going on inside your engine

GAPPING

▶ **See Figures 79, 80, 81 and 82**

If the spark plugs are not going to be replaced, clean the plugs thoroughly. Remember that any kind of deposit will decrease the efficiency of the plug. Plugs can be cleaned on a spark plug cleaning machine, which can sometimes be found in service stations, or you can do an acceptable job of cleaning with a stiff brush. If the plugs are cleaned, the electrodes must be filed flat. Use an ignition points file, not an emery board or the like, which will leave deposits.

The electrodes must be filed perfectly flat with sharp edges; rounded edges reduce the spark plug voltage by as much as 50%.

Check spark plug gap before installation. The ground electrode (the L-shaped one connected to the body of the plug) must be parallel to the center electrode and the specified size wire gauge must pass between the electrodes with a slight drag.

➡ **NEVER adjust the gap on a used platinum type spark plug.**

Always check the gap on new plugs as they are not always set correctly at the factory. Do not use a flat feeler gauge when measuring the gap on a used plug,

Fig. 79 Checking the spark plug gap with a feeler gauge

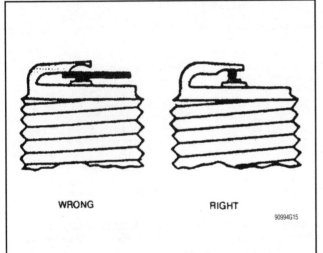

WRONG   RIGHT

90994G15

Fig. 80 This illustration shows why you must use a wire-type gauge to check the gap on a used spark plug, a flat-type feeler gauge can give an incorrect reading

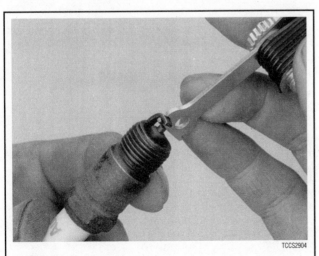

Fig. 81 Adjusting the spark plug gap

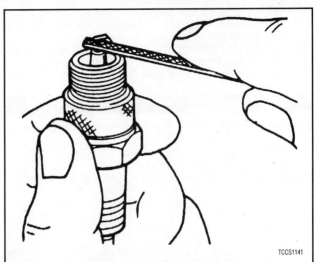

TCCS1141

Fig. 82 If the standard plug is in good condition, the electrode may be filed flat—WARNING: do not file platinum plugs

because the reading may be inaccurate. A round-wire type gapping tool is the best way to check the gap. The correct gauge should pass through the electrode gap with a slight drag. If you're in doubt, try one size smaller and one larger. The smaller gauge should go through easily, while the larger one shouldn't go through at all. Wire gapping tools usually have a bending tool attached. Use that to adjust the side electrode until the proper distance is obtained. Never attempt to bend the center electrode. Also, be careful not to bend the side electrode too far or too often as it may weaken and break off within the engine, requiring removal of the cylinder head to retrieve it.

CHECKING AND REPLACING SPARK PLUG WIRES

▶ See Figure 83

At every tune-up, visually check the spark plug cables for burns cuts, or breaks in the insulation. Check the boot and the nipple on the coil. Replace any damaged wiring.

As wires age, internal strands will break, the connectors on either end may corrode or become physically damaged, and the insulation will break down, allowing for further corrosion and arcing of the spark during use. All of these items add up to a loss of power for your snowmobile, harder starts, and sometimes to a total loss of spark in damp, misty conditions.

Every two years the resistance of the spark plug wires should be checked with an ohmmeter. If a wire is shown to have excessive resistance, it should be

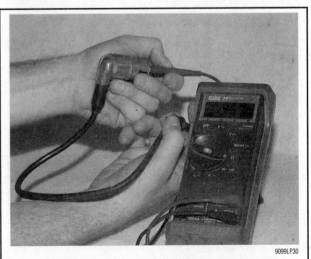

9099LP30

Fig. 83 An ohmmeter can be used to check spark plug wire resistance

replaced. Typically speaking, wire resistance for an electronic ignition system should be below 10,000 ohms. Check a shop manual to see if resistance specifications are available for your model.

To check resistance, disconnect the wire at both ends. Connect the probes of a multi-meter (such as a digital volt ohmmeter or DVOM) set to the 10K or 20K ohm scale to the ends of the spark plug wire. Read the resistance on the meter.

Ignition Timing

♦ **See Figure 84**

Ignition timing is the measurement, in degrees of crankshaft rotation, of the point at which the spark plugs fire in each of the cylinders. It is measured in degrees before or after Top Dead Center (TDC) of the compression stroke.

Because it takes a fraction of a second for the spark plugs to ignite the mixture in the cylinders, the spark plugs must fire a little before the piston reaches TDC. Otherwise, the mixture will not be completely ignited as the piston passes TDC and the full power of the explosion of the fuel will not be used by the engine.

The timing measurement is given in degrees of crankshaft rotation before the piston reaches TDC (BTDC). If the setting for the ignition timing is 5° BTDC, the spark plugs must fire 5° before the piston in each cylinder reaches TDC. This only holds true, however, when the engine is at idle speed.

As the engine speed increases, the piston goes faster. The spark plug has to ignite the fuel even sooner if it is to be completely ignited when the piston reaches TDC. To do this, ignition systems have various means of advancing the spark timing as the engine speed increases. On older snowmobiles, this was accomplished by centrifugal weights on a breaker point rotor. But on modern snowmobiles with electronic ignition systems, the ignition timing is usually advanced electronically by the control module.

If the ignition spark were too far advanced (BTDC), the ignition and expansion of the fuel in the cylinder would occur too soon and tend to force the piston down while it is still traveling up. This would cause engine ping (preignition). If the ignition spark is too far retarded, after TDC (ATDC), the piston will have already passed TDC and started on its way down when the fuel is ignited. This would cause the piston to be forced down for only a portion of its travel, resulting in poor engine performance and lack of power.

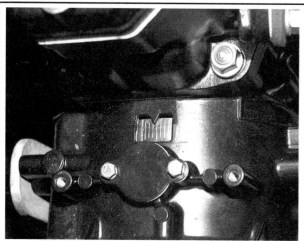

Fig. 84 Although most of today's engines do not have adjustable timing, their reference marks are helpful for diagnostic purposes

INSPECTION & ADJUSTMENT

Before transistorized ignitions took over in the late 70's and very early 80's, motorcycle and snowmobile riders would have to check, adjust and replace their breaker points very frequently. Failure to do so would lead to hard starts and eventually, no starts as the point gap widened or the points eventually became worn or burned beyond service. If you are riding an older snowmobile with points, then God bless you. But, if it is not a show-able antique, you are crazy.

There are many retrofit kits available to convert a points machine over to electronic ignition. Don't listen to those people who are afraid of electronic ignition because "if it breaks I can't just fix it on the trail." Electronic ignition works better and breaks down much less often than mechanical breaker points. As a matter of fact, it is a good thing that those die-hards who insist on keeping points CAN fix them on the trail, because eventually THEY ARE GOING TO HAVE TO.

Every modern snowmobile is equipped with an electronic ignition system, usually known as transistorized ignition, breakerless discharge or capacitor discharge ignition (CDI). On these systems, the mechanical breaker points have been replaced with an ignition module and a signal rotor of some sort. Where the mechanical breaker points were once used to physically break the primary ignition circuit, causing the ignition coil to discharge and fire the secondary circuit, an ignition module now performs that function. The module knows WHEN to perform that function based on a signal received from a signal rotor (usually a magnetized pick-up coil of some sort, which sends signals to the ignition module). The pick-up coil normally sends signals to the module based on changes to a magnetic field caused by notches machined into a part of the crankshaft, or a part turned by the crankshaft. The advantages of electronic ignition include long life (because no mechanical contacts are used to break the primary circuit which could wear like points), along with a significantly higher voltage capacity. The higher voltage is an advantage when it comes to firing plugs with larger gaps or under adverse conditions, like oil soaked plugs.

If your snowmobile is equipped with timing marks they will usually consist of a notches, dots, or letters that are either machined directly on a part of the crankshaft, or a part which the crankshaft turns such as the alternator rotor. There is usually a cover or plug that can be easily removed to view the timing mark. In some cases, the timing marks are easily viewed through an opening on the engine case.

Timing procedures vary from one manufacturer to another. In the days of points, the procedures ranged from using a dial gauge or degree wheel to using a test light or continuity checker to set "static timing." This meant timing was often set WITHOUT the engine running. "Dynamic timing" checks were made on some models, using an automotive style stroboscopic timing light (which makes the timing marks appear to stand still due to the effect of the strobe light).

On most modern snowmobiles, timing checks are designed to use a stroboscopic timing light with an inductive pick-up to perform a "dynamic timing" inspection. The timing light's pick-up is clamped to the spark plug wire and will trigger the timing light each time a pulse is detected in the wire. By pointing the timing light at the timing mark, you can see if it lines up with the appropriate marker or if it centers in the access hole, as required by your particular engine's specifications.

➡**Never pierce a spark plug wire in order to attach a timing light or perform tests. The pierced insulation will eventually lead to an electrical arc and related ignition troubles.**

The newer your snowmobile, the lesser the chance that the ignition timing can or should be adjusted. Although many modern snowmobiles still have the ability to adjust their ignition timing, it is no longer recommended as a periodic procedure. Timing marks are usually provided ONLY to be used as a check to make sure all ignition components are installed correctly and functioning properly.

Carburetor Adjustments

♦ **See Figure 85**

Carburetor tune-up procedures will largely depend upon the type of engine, the quantity of carburetors, and the method of oil injection.

Carburetor adjustments generally fall into three major categories:
- **Synchronization**
- **Idle Speed**
- **Mixture**

Periodic carburetor adjustments have become another victim of increasing technology. But this can also be attributed to increasing emissions laws that recently have affected the snowmobiling community. Some carburetors on certain snowmobiles have been fit with sealed and tamper-resistant screws to prevent adjustment to the air/fuel mixtures. Manufacturers tell us that the mixtures are set at the factory and should NOT be touched in the field. So, if you are riding one of these snowmobiles, and it has not been modified, then chances are that you only need to worry about occasionally adjusting the idle speed.

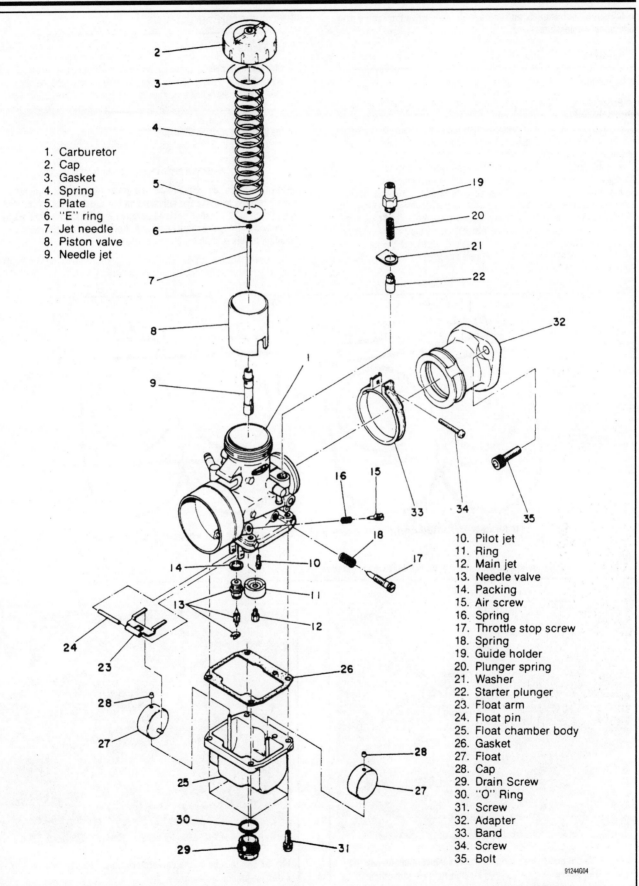

1. Carburetor
2. Cap
3. Gasket
4. Spring
5. Plate
6. "E" ring
7. Jet needle
8. Piston valve
9. Needle jet

10. Pilot jet
11. Ring
12. Main jet
13. Needle valve
14. Packing
15. Air screw
16. Spring
17. Throttle stop screw
18. Spring
19. Guide holder
20. Plunger spring
21. Washer
22. Starter plunger
23. Float arm
24. Float pin
25. Float chamber body
26. Gasket
27. Float
28. Cap
29. Drain Screw
30. "O" Ring
31. Screw
32. Adapter
33. Band
34. Screw
35. Bolt

91244G04

Fig. 85 The typical carburetor is composed of dozens of intricate parts which work together to produce proper air/fuel ratios—they do not respond well to inexperienced and unnecessary tampering

➥Carburetor adjustments must always be made when the engine is at operating temperature.

PRE-ADJUSTMENT CHECKS

▶ **See Figures 86, 87 and 88**

Before attempting to make carburetor adjustments, all of the following points should be checked:

• Carburetor alignment. On flexible mounted units, ensure that the carburetors are vertically oriented, and not tilted sideways. This may effect fuel level and high-speed operation.

• Cable condition. Check throttle operation, ensuring that the cable(s) and linkage are not kinked or binding, and that they are well lubricated.

• Ancillary systems. Carburetor adjustments should be made last after all other systems have been attended to in order to prevent misleading symptoms. Check that the air cleaner is not dirty, the spark plugs are in good condition, and the ignition is operating correctly. Also ensure that the gasoline is reasonably fresh, of the correct octane, and that foreign material, such as water or dirt, has been purged from the fuel system. Check fuel filters to make sure that the carburetors are not being starved of fuel.

THROTTLE CABLE ADJUSTMENT

▶ **See Figure 89**

On most snowmobiles, provision is made for adjusting the throttle cable to compensate for stretching. The adjuster is usually found on the top of the carburetor(s), or on the handlebars. The throttle cables should be adjusted so that the thumb lever has a small amount of noticeable free-play. In general, this free-play should amount to about $1/16$–$1/8$ in. (1.6–3.2 mm) of play at the lever tip before the slides begin to lift or butterflies begin to turn on the carburetor(s). As always, check with your owner's manual for the specification for your particular snowmobile.

1. Locate the adjustment mechanism(s) on the throttle cable(s).

➥In some cases, the only means of adjusting the free-play on the thumb lever is by using the adjusters on the carburetors. If your sled is configured in this manner, it is imperative that the carburetors are synchronized for proper engine operation. Refer to the Synchronization heading in this section for more information.

2. Using two appropriately sized wrenches, loosen the locknut on the cable adjuster(s) while holding the adjusters stationary.

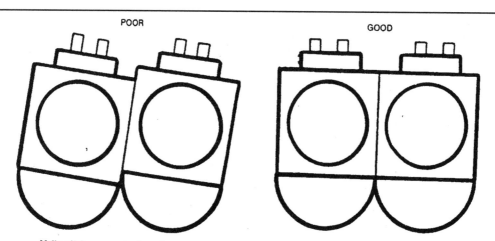

POOR   GOOD

If flexibly-mounted carburetors are fitted, be sure they are vertically aligned

90994G29

Fig. 86 The carburetors should be vertically aligned for proper operation

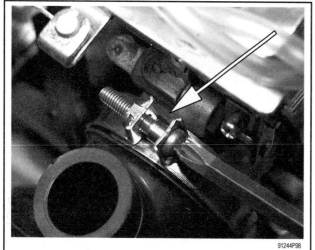

91244P98

Fig. 87 Do not overtighten the inlet clamps when repositioning the carbs. The clamp on this inlet has a collar to prevent overtightening

91244P91

Fig. 88 The linkage on the carburetors should be periodically lubricated for proper operation

Fig. 89 Using a mirror to view the throttle slides, the cables can be adjusted so both slides operate in unison

Fig. 90 With the throttle slides in the idle position, they should be exactly the same height

3. Loosen the locknut(s) on the cable adjuster(s) enough to twist the adjusters by hand. Loosen or tighten the adjuster(s) as necessary to achieve proper free-play on the throttle lever.

➡ If your sled has more than one cable that operates the carburetors, synchronizing the carburetors may be necessary after the throttle free-play is adjusted.

4. While holding the cable adjuster(s) stationary with a back-up wrench, tighten the locknut(s) on the adjuster(s).

5. Check the free-play again, with everything properly tightened. Also, turn the handlebars from side-to-side and check that the amount of free-play does not change. If the amount of free-play disappears when the handlebars are turned, the cable is binding. Check for proper cable routing, and adjust as necessary.

➡ After the throttle cable(s) have been adjusted, the oil injection pump must be checked for proper synchronization. It is essential that the oil injection pump be synchronized with the carburetors so the proper amount of oil is injected into the engine. Refer to the Oil Injection Pump heading in this section for more information.

CARBURETOR SYNCHRONIZATION

For optimum engine performance, all the cylinders of the engine must work equally. To allow all of the cylinders to produce equal power, the carburetors must be synchronized, or function together in perfect unison. If the carburetors are not synchronized, one cylinder will be forced to work harder than the other(s), causing poor acceleration, hesitation, and overheating.

Synchronizing By Sighting Throttle Plates/Slides

▶ See Figures 89, 90, 91, 92 and 93

On engines equipped with slide type carburetors, the throttle plates/slides can be synchronized by sighting or feeling the height of the slides/plates and adjusting them using the cables or linkage until they are at the same height. It should be noted that this procedure only synchronizes the slides/plates when the engine is **not** at idle.

✳✳ CAUTION

REMEMBER that running internal combustion gasoline engines produces CARBON MONOXIDE that can kill you. NEVER, EVER run an engine (even for a short time) in an enclosed area like a shed or a garage. ALWAYS make sure there is plenty of ventilation (meaning that all garage doors and windows are open and, if at all possible, the exhaust pipes are sticking out through them). Better yet, do it on a nice, sunny day, and perform all adjustments outside.

Fig. 91 To adjust the height of the throttle slides when they are at the idle position, the idle speed adjustment should be used

Fig. 92 On most multi-carburetor models, each throttle slide has its own idle speed adjustment screw (arrows)

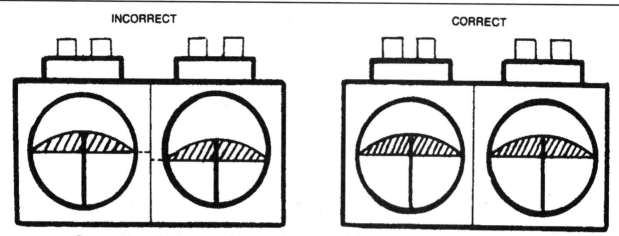

INCORRECT   CORRECT

On multi-cylinder machines, throttle slides must be synchronized

90994G30

Fig. 93 The throttle slides are synchronized when they operate together regardless of throttle position

➡Some carburetor assemblies use a unified linkage that operates the carburetors simultaneously. Depending on the type of carburetor system, the linkage may be somewhat complex, making synchronization difficult. If you are unsure about the type of linkage your carburetor assembly uses, or how it is adjusted, leave this procedure to a qualified service facility.

1. Remove the airbox from the carburetors.
2. Using a mirror, note the position of each of the slides/plates when the throttle level is fully open. The slides/plates should all be equal.
3. If the slides/plates are not equal, use the adjusters on the carburetors (whether they are individual cables, or a unified linkage) to equalize the slides/plates.

➡When synchronizing the slides/plates, keep an eye on the amount of free-play at the throttle lever, since the adjustment can be affected.

4. Operate the throttle a few times by "snapping" the throttle lever on the handlebars; then recheck the position of the slides/plates. Using a finger to "feel" the adjustment may also be employed.
5. Once the slides/plates are synchronized, install the airbox onto the carburetors.

➡After the slides/plates have been synchronized, the oil injection pump must be checked for proper synchronization. It is essential that the oil injection pump be synchronized with the carburetors so the proper amount of oil is injected into the engine. Refer to the Oil Injection Pump heading in this section for more information.

Synchronizing With Vacuum Gauge

♦ **See Figures 91, and 94 thru 98**

The best way to synchronize carburetors is by using vacuum gauges on the intake vacuum for each carburetor. By using a vacuum gauge to synchronize the slides/plates, the idle speed can be accurately adjusted. In addition, the throttle slides/plates can be adjusted when the engine is above idle.

➡If your snowmobile engine is equipped with cable operated carburetors, a vacuum gauge is the only accurate way of adjusting the idle speed.

Most carburetor synchronization tools are equipped with up to four tubes, which is more than adequate for the majority of all snowmobiles (unless your sled has an Audi 5-cylinder turbo engine in it!). One tube is attached to a vacuum port on each carburetor or intake manifold, depending on the design. When the engine is running, the mercury in each of the tubes rises, depending on the amount of vacuum in each cylinder. By viewing the level of mercury in each of the tubes, the throttle slides/plates can be accurately adjusted.

91244P6J

Fig. 94 Once the sled is situated with the track safely off the ground, remove the plugs from each vacuum port . . .

91244P4J

Fig. 95 . . . and connect the gauge lines to each port

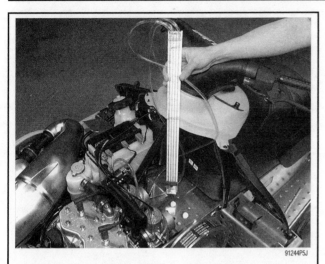

Fig. 96 With the engine at normal temperature, at idle, the levels for each carburetor should be equal

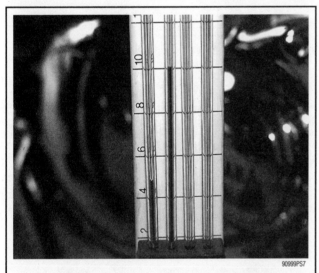

Fig. 97 This gauge indicates misadjustment of the carburetors

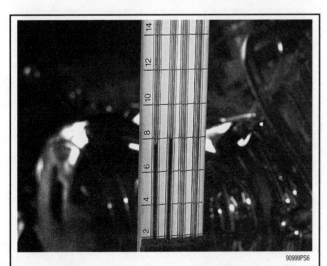

Fig. 98 Synchronization is achieved when the vacuum levels of the carburetors are equal

✳✳ CAUTION

REMEMBER that running internal combustion gasoline engines produces CARBON MONOXIDE that can kill you. NEVER, EVER run an engine (even for a short time) in an enclosed area like a shed or a garage. ALWAYS make sure there is plenty of ventilation (meaning that all garage doors and windows are open and, if at all possible, the exhaust pipes are sticking out through them). Better yet, do it on a nice, sunny day, and perform all adjustments outside.

1. To synchronize the carburetors, start by adjusting the idle speed (and mixture, if appropriate) until the engine is idling at specification.
2. Remove the airbox if necessary to gain access to the carburetors.

✳✳ WARNING

If the airbox is removed to allow access to the carburetors, be VERY careful not to allow any debris to be sucked into the carburetors, or the engine may be damaged.

3. Position the snowmobile so the tips of the skis sit against a wall, and safely raise the track from the ground so it can rotate while the engine is running. This way, if the sled were to accidentally fall from the jackstands, it cannot travel on its own.

✳✳ CAUTION

Failure to raise the track from the ground can cause the sled to move when the throttle is operated. Do NOT attempt to perform any carburetor adjustments with the engine running without safely elevating the track from the ground. Also, make sure the snowmobile skis are positioned against a wall to prevent the snowmobile from traveling if it were to accidentally fall from the jackstands.

4. Connect the synchronization tool to the intake vacuum ports for each cylinder. On most sleds, a vacuum port will be provided on the carburetor or intake manifold and covered with a small plastic or rubber cap which can easily be removed from the port nipple.
5. Start the engine and allow it to idle at normal operating temperature.
6. With the engine warm and running at or near normal idle, adjust the carburetors using the balance screws on the mechanical linkage or the individual idle screws on each carburetor until all cylinders are showing approximate equal vacuum. A variance of about 0.4–1.6 in. Hg (10–40 mm Hg) is normally allowed between the cylinders, but anything more should be adjusted to bring the cylinder vacuum closer together.
7. Using a block of wood between the throttle lever and the handle grip, hold the throttle with a piece of tape, and adjust the engine to a high idle.
8. With the engine at a high idle, check the level of the mercury in each of the tubes. If the level is off, use the linkage or cables to adjust the slides/plates as necessary to synchronize the carburetors.
9. Remove the wood block from the throttle lever, and check the vacuum level again at idle.
10. When you are finished, remove the sync tool and carefully replug all of the vacuum lines. Remember that a vacuum leak lean your air/fuel mixture, possibly causing engine damage.
11. Install the airbox, if it was removed to access the carburetors.
12. Remove the jackstand(s) from the rear of the snowmobile.

➡After the slides/plates have been synchronized, the oil injection pump must be checked for proper synchronization. It is essential that the oil injection pump be synchronized with the carburetors so the proper amount of oil is injected into the engine. Refer to the Oil Injection Pump heading in this section for more information.

IDLE SPEED ADJUSTMENTS

♦ See Figures 91, 92 and 199

Idle speeds which are recommended by the manufacturer should be adhered to in most cases. The idle running of a snowmobile engine is usually the most unsatisfactory carburetor range. There are many reasons for this. For one, the quantities of fuel and air which are going into the engine are relatively small,

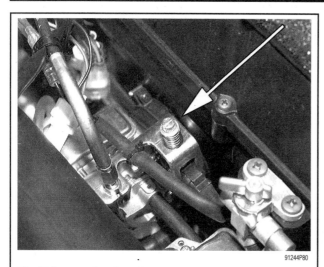

Fig. 99 Some engines have linkage that allows the use of a single idle speed screw

and are controlled by equally small passages. These are more likely to become clogged with dirt or varnish than the much larger jets, (used for off-idle operation) and the mixture will then be upset. Further, the relative quantities of gas and air are more critical at idle. Finally, since the engine is turning slowly, and is not under load, any irregularities in the mixture flow cause an erratic idle which may be irritating.

On most snowmobiles, a satisfactory idle can be obtained by carefully setting the carburetor(s) idle stop screw to the recommended specifications. As noted above, idle speed should be set to the recommended specification. An idle speed that is too low may cause trouble by making smooth transition to the slow or mid-range circuit impossible. On some snowmobiles, too low an idle may cause damage to bearings and other moving parts due to the great lapse between power pulses or to oil pressures which drop too low below specified idle.

On the other hand, too high an idle speed may cause the rpm to hang up for a moment or so when the throttle is closed. It also may cause increased drive belt wear, since the primary clutch may drag on the belt.

Because idle speed and mixture adjustments can vary so greatly with model, year and engine design, no attempt can be made to give them all here. If you need to adjust the mixture, either because your snowmobile is that old or it is that modified (exhaust systems especially), you should start with a shop manual.

It should be noted that if your snowmobile engine uses individual cables to operate the carburetors, the best way to adjust the idle speed is with a carburetor synchronization tool. Even if the idle adjusters on each of the carburetors are turned the same amount, they can be misadjusted.

✳✳ CAUTION

REMEMBER that running internal combustion gasoline engines produces CARBON MONOXIDE that can kill you. NEVER, EVER run an engine (even for a short time) in an enclosed area like a shed or a garage. ALWAYS make sure there is plenty of ventilation (meaning that all garage doors and windows are open and, if at all possible, the exhaust pipes are sticking out through them). Better yet, do it on a nice, sunny day, and perform all adjustments outside.

To check and set idle speed on most snowmobiles:
1. Position the snowmobile so the tips of the skis against a wall, and safely raise the track from the ground so it can rotate while the engine is running. This way, if the sled were to accidentally fall from the jackstands, it cannot travel on its own.

✳✳ CAUTION

Failure to raise the track from the ground can cause the sled to move when the throttle is operated. Do NOT attempt to perform any carburetor adjustments with the engine running without safely ele-

vating the track from the ground. Also, make sure the snowmobile skis are positioned against a wall to prevent the snowmobile from traveling if it were to accidentally fall from the jackstands.

2. Attach a tachometer to the engine according to the tool manufacturer's instructions. The easiest type to use are the modern tachometers which have an inductive pick-up which you clamp to the spark plug wire. If you don't have a tachometer, you can "guesstimate" the proper idle speed, although it is not nearly as accurate.
3. Start and run the engine until it reaches normal operating temperature.
4. Locate the idle speed stop screw or idle speed adjusting knob. The adjusting knob is usually found on the carburetor itself. On models with unified linkage, there is usually either a single screw attached to a mechanical linkage which actuates the throttle plates of both carburetors or there may be a knurled knob on the end of a cable which is attached to the linkage.

➡️If your snowmobile engine uses individual cables to operate the carburetors, a synchronization tool should be used to set the idle speed. Even if the idle adjusters on each of the carburetors are turned the same, they can be misadjusted.

5. With the engine running and the throttle fully closed, turn the idle speed screw until the proper specified idle has been reached.
6. Open and close the throttle a few times, and watch to see that the idle speed returns to specification. Repeat this once or twice to be certain the idle speed remains within specifications.
7. Turn the engine **off**, remove the jackstands holding the rear track from the ground, and move the sled away from the wall just enough to turn the skis.
8. Start the engine. With the engine still running at idle speed, slowly turn the handlebars from lock-to-lock. If the idle speed increases, even slightly, the throttle cable should be checked for kinks or binding. If none are found, the throttle cable should be adjusted until normal idle speed can be maintained while the bars are turned through their full range of motion.

➡️After the idle speed has been adjusted, the oil injection pump must be checked for proper synchronization. It is essential that the oil injection pump be synchronized with the carburetors so the proper amount of oil is injected into the engine. Refer to the Oil Injection Pump heading in this section for more information.

MIXTURE ADJUSTMENTS

◆ See Figures 100 thru 107

On most carburetors, the idle mixture is determined largely by the pilot air screw which controls the amount of air mixing with the idle circuit jets, or the pilot fuel screw, which controls the amount of gasoline passing into the circuit.

Carburetors may be equipped with one or the other of these screws. While exceptions exist, on most carburetors the location of the screw will indicate

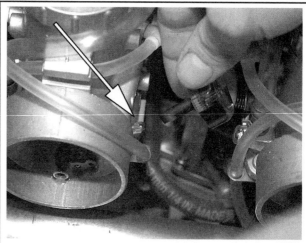

Fig. 100 Pilot air and fuel adjustment screws can look similar to idle speed screws; make sure you are adjusting the right one!

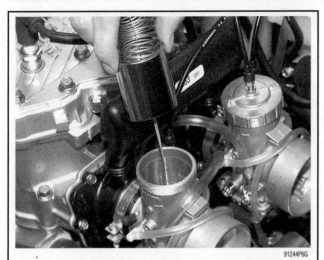

Fig. 101 To adjust the jet needle for mid-range tuning, unscrew the cap from the top of the carburetor . . .

Fig. 104 . . . and carefully remove the jet needle from the throttle slide

Fig. 102 . . . and pull back the spring to release the retainer clip that holds the throttle cable tip

Fig. 105 Move the clip on the needle jet to alter the mid-range tuning as necessary

Fig. 103 Unscrew the jet needle retainer/throttle cable connection . . .

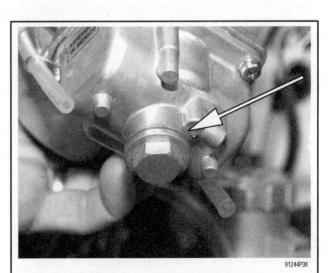

Fig. 106 The main jet can be changed on some carburetors by removing the access plug (arrow) on the carburetor bowl

Fig. 107 Once the access plug is removed, the main jet can be unscrewed

whether it is an air screw or a fuel screw. Generally pilot air screws are located on the intake side of the carburetor, while most pilot fuel screws are located between the throttle slide and the engine manifold.

It is important to know whether you have an "air screw" or a "fuel screw" if you intend to make mixture changes based on spark plug readings or other tests. Turning an air screw in will give a richer mixture, while turning it out will lean the mixture out. For pilot fuel screws, exactly the opposite is true.

Regardless of type pilot screw, settings are given by the manufacturer, and should be adhered to, at least to within certain limits. The pilot screw settings are expressed in turns out from the seated position. The pilot screw's tip is tapered and is mated to an air or fuel passage. To make the adjustment, the screw is turned in gently until you can feel that it is lightly seated, then backed out the given number of turns. For example, if your specification for the pilot screw setting is "2 ½" that is the number of times that the screw is to be turned.

When turning these screws in, it is best to be very careful, as it is possible to ruin the tapered portion of the screw if it is turned down too tightly.

When adjusting the mixture, always turn the pilot screws out to the given specification, then make any necessary adjustments. It should not be necessary to vary the screw setting more than ½ turn from the given setting unless changes have been made to the intake, engine, or exhaust systems. If it is not possible to obtain satisfactory performance with the settings as specified, suspect clogged carburetor passages or air leaks, etc.

Adjusting the pilot screws (air and fuel) usually only affect the mixture within the lower throttle range.

Another adjustment that can be performed to adjust the mixture of fuel and air is changing the position of the jet needle. The jet needle is found inside the carburetor, attached to the sliding throttle valve. In most cases, it is required that the top of the carburetor be removed to access the needle jet. If the mixture needs to be richened, the circlip on the jet needle should be lowered, which would raise its position. For a leaner mixture, raise the circlip on the jet needle, which will lower the position within the needle jet (the needle jet is the stationary part on the carburetor body, and the jet needle is the part which is attached to the throttle valve.) In most cases, adjustment of the jet needle will affect the air/fuel mixture within the mid-to-upper throttle range.

If you have installed a high-performance exhaust on your snowmobile, it may require more than adjustments to the carburetor to obtain a proper air/fuel ratio. Changing the main jet of the carburetor is really the best way to adjust the mixture in this type of situation, as opposed to using the adjustments on the carburetor to an extreme. Due to great amount of testing and adjusting involved in re-jetting a carburetor, we at Chilton recommend having a professional perform this type of procedure. A carburetor that is improperly adjusted and or jetted can quickly ruin an engine quickly; and two-stroke engines can be ruined in a matter of **seconds** if the mixture is too lean. Don't take the chance on frying your motor just to save a couple of dollars; take it to a shop that will set up your snowmobile to run properly.

Fuel Injection Adjustments

▶ **See Figure 108**

One of the great things about modern electronic fuel injection is that your sled comes with a computer to think about things like air/fuel ratios and ignition timing, so you don't have to. But, fuel injection systems vary, there are some systems which do allow for adjustments (but are typically only necessary right after break-in or some major repair). Suffice it to say that these adjustments require, at the least, a gas analyzer and the manufacturer computer system interface tools. In some cases, even seemingly simple adjustments such as throttle position sensor adjustment on some sleds require a very expensive breakout box to perform safely.

Essentially, periodic adjustments are normally necessary or possible on fuel injected sleds. If you have a rideability problem with your engine, and checks of all maintenance items do not uncover a mechanical culprit, then you should seek advice from your dealer. Also, remember that most fuel injection systems utilize self-diagnostic systems which run checks of the electrical components in the system when the engine is first started (that is why they are equipped with ENGINE lights of some sort). If the computer detects a problem, you will be the second one to know when the light comes on.

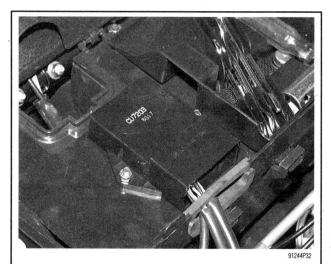

Fig. 108 The computer on fuel injected sleds typically takes care of most adjustments to the fuel system

Oil Injection Pump

▶ **See Figure 109**

In the early days of snowmobiles, oil had to be "pre-mixed" with the fuel to provide lubrication to the internal components of the engine. This entailed pouring a measured amount of two-stroke oil into a measured amount of gasoline to provide the proper ratio of fuel and oil, and pouring it into the gas tank of the snowmobile.

This method is still used today in racing applications, especially with two-stroke motorcycles. The main drawback here is that the ratio of oil and gasoline only suits the engine's lubrication demands at a certain rpm. (usually full throttle) If you've heard the phrase "you have to ride it hard, or it'll foul up," this is in reference to this method of engine lubrication. Since the oil is "pre-mixed" with the fuel, part throttle use of the engine will cause excess oil to build up in the combustion chamber(s), causing the spark plugs to foul. Too little oil in the fuel will starve the engine components of lubrication, possibly causing a piston seizure or other components to fail. (A piston seizure means that the piston actually melts, and bonds to the cylinder from lack of lubrication.) If there is too much oil mixed with the fuel, the spark plugs can become "fouled" with excess oil, and the pistons, cylinders, and expansion chamber(s) become clogged with excess carbon and oil deposits.

To combat this drawback of pre-mixing fuel, the majority of all modern

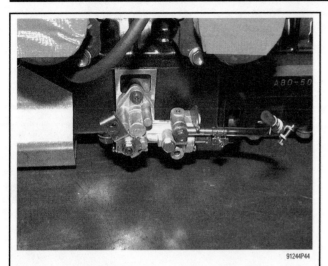

Fig. 109 The oil injection pump is a simple mechanical pump that distributes oil to the engine, based on throttle position

Fig. 111 With the slack taken up in the throttle cable, the first set of marks should align

snowmobiles use oil injection to provide lubrication to the crankshaft, connecting rods, and pistons.

A typical oil injection system consists of an oil tank, injection pump, and lines. The oil injection pump is a simple pump driven from the crankshaft that supplies oil to the engine. The injection pump is proportional to the throttle position, (via cable, or in some cases, linkage) providing a precise delivery of oil in conjunction with engine speed. The metered oil from the injection pump sprays directly into the engine, either through the intake ports, or the crankcase, depending on the manufacturer.

Adjustment

▶ See Figures 110, 111, 112, 113 and 114

Occasional adjustment of the oil injection pump may be required to keep it synchronized with the carburetors/throttle bodies, since the cable which operates the pump can stretch over time. It is important to regularly check the alignment of the marks on the injection pump to verify that the proper amount of oil is injected into the engine.

If your snowmobile engine uses an unconventional oil injection pump, or you cannot find the alignment marks on the pump, contact a dealer regarding any specific procedures or specifications. Although injection pumps are relatively simple, proper synchronization with the carburetors/throttle bodies is absolutely ESSENTIAL for adequate engine lubrication. If you are even remotely

Fig. 112 At full throttle, the second set of marks on the pump lever should align with the pump body

Fig. 110 On some models, the oil injection pump can be hard to access for adjustment; this model requires removal of the carburetors

Fig. 113 If the marks are not aligning properly, use the threaded adjuster to synchronize the carburetors with the oil injection pump

Fig. 114 After any adjustments are made, make sure that the cable is not binding on the lever

Fig. 115 Whether your snowmobile has a single expansion chamber . . .

Fig. 116 . . . or three expansion chambers, they are all secured by springs

in question, do not attempt this procedure; your engine can be **destroyed** if the pump is adjusted incorrectly.

1. Remove the airbox, expansion chamber(s), or any other necessary components to allow viewing of the oil pump lever and synchronization marks.

2. Operate the throttle lever on the handlebars just enough to take up the free-play in the cables. The slides/plates on the carburetors/throttle bodies should not be opening, though.

➡️If you are in doubt of the integrity of the injection pump cable, it should be immediately replaced.

3. Note the relationship of the mark on the pump lever to the mark on the pump itself. The marks should be aligned when the free-play is taken up with the throttle lever.

4. On some models, an additional set of marks on the lever and housing are given for full throttle operation. To check these marks, apply full throttle to the throttle lever, and check the relationship of the marks.

5. If the pump lever is not in alignment with the marks, loosen the locknuts on the injection pump cable and reposition the cable as necessary.

6. After the cable has been adjusted, recheck the relationship of the marks and verify that they are correct. Make sure that the locknuts are secure.

✳️ WARNING

After adjusting the injection pump cable, make absolutely certain that the locknuts are tightened securely. If the cable were to vibrate loose, the incorrect amount of oil will injected into the engine, possibly causing serious engine damage. A light threadlocking compound can be used on the nuts for additional security.

7. Install the airbox, expansion chamber(s) and muffler(s), and any other components that were removed to access the oil pump.

Exhaust System

♦ See Figures 115 and 116

The bulbous, organic shape of a two-stroke engine's exhaust system is space consuming and cumbersome. This can sometimes make access to other components in the engine compartment difficult. Luckily, the manner in which the expansion chamber(s) and muffler(s) are mounted on most sleds makes it easy to remove the system to allow easier access to other components in the engine compartment.

REMOVAL AND INSTALLATION

♦ See Figures 117 thru 124

1. Using a spring removal tool, disconnect the springs that hold the expansion chamber(s) and muffler(s) to the engine and chassis. If a spring removal

tool is not available, locking pliers can be used, but they are not as safe. If the pliers slip from the spring when it is being removed, the spring can become a projectile (and take out an eye), or you might hit yourself with the pliers.

✳️ CAUTION

Use extreme caution when removing the springs that retain the exhaust system; the springs can become high-speed projectiles when they are being removed, causing serious bodily injury.

➡️Make sure to mark the positions of each of the springs; they must be installed in their proper locations since they are of different sizes and strengths.

2. Once all of the springs are removed from the exhaust, remove any additional fasteners that retain the system.

3. Carefully remove the exhaust system from the engine compartment. It may need to be removed in pieces, or as a unit, depending on the manner in which the sled is configured.

4. If necessary, the exhaust manifold can now be unbolted from the cylinders.

To install:

5. If the exhaust manifold was removed, install it using new gaskets. Make sure that the gaskets are installed in the proper direction, and the bolts/studs are properly torqued to the manufacturer's specifications.

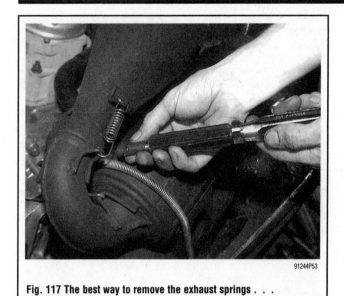

Fig. 117 The best way to remove the exhaust springs . . .

Fig. 118 . . . is with a specialized spring removal tool

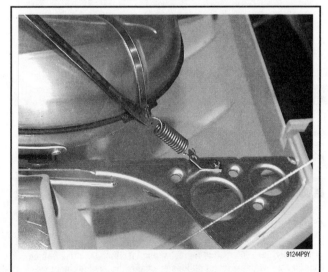

Fig. 119 Here's another example of a spring removal tool

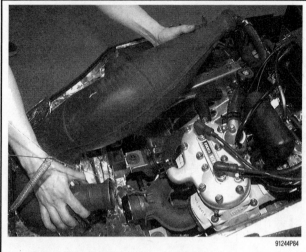

Fig. 120 Once the springs are removed, carefully remove the expansion chamber from the header pipe and muffler

Fig. 121 After the expansion chamber is removed, the muffler can be lifted from the engine compartment

Fig. 122 Whenever the expansion chamber is removed, the gasket should be closely inspected, and replaced if necessary

91244P79

Fig. 123 On most sleds, the expansion chamber-to-muffler gasket is similar to a piston ring

91244P82

Fig. 124 The ring-type gasket allows for a "slip fit" into the muffler flange

6. Replace any damaged gaskets or seals on the exhaust system as necessary.

7. If the exhaust system uses sealants or dressings on the gaskets, apply the appropriate amount to each gasket as necessary. Check with your local dealer about the use of aftermarket sealers and gasket dressings, to make sure that they are compatible with the exhaust system.

8. Install the springs that retain the exhaust system to the engine and engine compartment. Make sure that the springs are installed in their proper locations, since they are of different sizes and strengths.

9. Once the exhaust system is started, start the engine and check for any signs of leakage.

❈❈ CAUTION

REMEMBER that running internal combustion gasoline engines produces CARBON MONOXIDE that can kill you. NEVER, EVER run an engine (even for a short time) in an enclosed area like a shed or a garage. ALWAYS make sure there is plenty of ventilation (meaning that all garage doors and windows are open and, if at all possible, the exhaust pipes are sticking out through them). Better yet, do it on a nice, sunny day, and perform all adjustments outside.

CLEANING

The expansion chambers must be cleaned of carbon build-up periodically to keep engine performance at its peak. The amount of carbon build-up in the expansion chambers depends on several factors, from the type of engine oil used, carburetor adjustment, etc.

A simple but effective expansion chamber cleaning tool can be made from an old throttle cable, or even a speedometer cable. The cable should be around two to three feet long, depending on the size of your particular expansion chamber(s). One side of the cable should be cut clean, with a small piece of tape to hold the cable strands together. Install this end into the drill, and tighten the chuck securely. On the other end of the cable, unravel about eight inches of cable strands. By intentionally fraying the ends of the cable, it can be made to clean the inside of the expansion chamber when mounted in a drill.

❈❈ CAUTION

Use extreme caution when using this method of cleaning the expansion chamber. Do NOT operate the drill with the cable attached if it is not inside the expansion chamber; you can be SEVERELY injured. Wear adequate eye and body protection (like gloves and a face shield) when performing this procedure.

1. Remove the expansion chamber(s) from the snowmobile.

2. Place the expansion chamber in a vise or other means to safely secure it to a stable work surface.

3. Scrape the carbon from the areas around the ends of the pipe with a suitable tool.

4. Once the ends of the expansion chamber are cleaned of carbon, place the cable all the way into the expansion chamber.

5. Carefully run the drill with the cable inside of the expansion chamber, letting it "beat" around inside the chamber. The beating action of the cable inside the expansion chamber will help loosen up the carbon build-up and break it free.

6. Periodically pour out the loose carbon that has broken free from inside the expansion chamber. When loose carbon ceases to come out of the expansion chamber, it can be considered clean.

7. If your snowmobile has multiple expansion chambers, repeat the procedure as necessary.

8. Install the cleaned expansion chamber(s) onto the snowmobile.

DRIVETRAIN MAINTENANCE

The unique drive system of a snowmobile is amazingly simple and efficient. It contains only a fraction of the components used in a typical car's or motorcycle's drive system, making it lighter, and more efficient.

The drive system of a typical snowmobile contains the following components:

- Primary Pulley
- Secondary Pulley
- Drive Belt
- Jackshaft
- Disc Brake
- Chain Case
- Drive Axle

This may look like quite a list on paper, but when you look at the components on a snowmobile, you'll quickly discover its simplicity once you become familiarized with the system.

Although the drive system on a snowmobile is fairly basic, all of the above components need periodic maintenance to keep them operating in top condition. In most cases, the maintenance required in nothing more than simple lubrication or adjustment.

Drive Belt

When it comes to drivetrain maintenance, the drive belt requires the most attention. Because of the design of the drive system, the drive belt takes a lot of abuse.

➡️**Its a good idea to practice removing and installing the drive belt on your sled a few times to get an idea of what is involved in the procedure. Although most snowmobile drive systems are configured in the** same manner, some models may require removal of a panel, or the use of a tool. When you're out on the trail, changing a drive belt can be very frustrating if you are not familiar with the procedure. Practicing at home will make an emergency on the trail much more manageable.

INSPECTION

▶ See Figures 125, 126, 127, 128 and 129

The drive belt should always be checked for wear, fraying and cracks on a regular basis. Keeping a close eye on the condition of the belt will avoid major problems on the trail. If your belt breaks, you're not going to be moving anywhere unless you have a tow rope to attach to a buddy's snowmobile (Unless you actually bought a spare drive belt and keep it stored in the engine compartment—hopefully you have!).

1. To inspect the drive belt, it is best to remove it from the pulleys.
2. Once the belt is removed from the pulleys, look at the sides of the belt. Check for signs of glazing, or torn or shredded cords. Torn or shredded cords typically indicate pulley misalignment, or worn or loose engine mounts.
3. Next, flip the belt inside out and inspect the cogs. If any of the cogs are torn, or worse, missing, the belt is damaged, and should be replaced. If the drive belt is severely damaged, the pulleys may be misaligned, or may be functioning improperly.

Fig. 127 The cracks on this drive belt mean that it is time for replacement

Fig. 125 The drive belt should be removed from the pulleys to allow for closer inspection of its condition

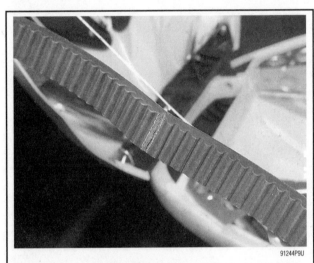

Fig. 128 Here's an example of a severely dry-rotted belt. This kind of deterioration typically comes with age

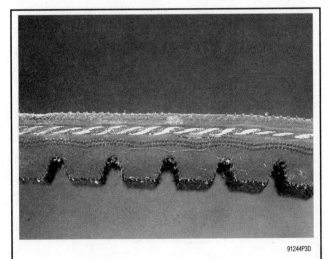

Fig. 126 An example of a healthy drive belt

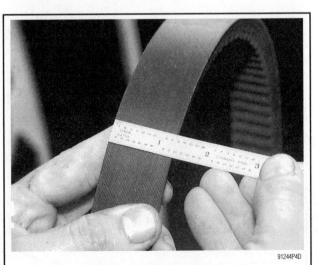

Fig. 129 The belt should be measured in several locations to check for narrow spots, or excessive wear

4. Using a caliper or a drafting ruler, measure the width of the belt in different places around its length. For maximum accuracy, a caliper can be used. The belt should be the same width at every measurement point. If there are any narrow spots (bottle necking) on the belt, it should be replaced. Narrow spots on the belt can be caused by operating the sled with the parking brake on, a frozen track, an excessively high idle, or trying to dig yourself out of deep snow. The actual width of the belt should be compared with the manufacturer specifications; depending on the width of the belt, replacement may be necessary.

5. If you are in doubt of the condition of the belt, even though it appears to be okay, then by all means, REPLACE IT. If a belt were to break while riding, (especially in deep snow or riding up a hill) the primary pulley can be damaged, as well as possibly causing severe engine damage from the engine over-revving.

REMOVAL AND INSTALLATION

♦ See Figures 130 thru 135

➡Before removing the belt from the pulleys, check for a directional marking. If the belt has no markings, use a marker or paint pen to draw an arrow on the belt so it is installed in the same direction.

1. Remove the drive belt shield or guard to allow access to the belt.
2. Grasp the two halves of the secondary pulley and push them apart, while

Fig. 132 Some models may come with a tool that screws into the secondary pulley . . .

Fig. 130 Most sleds have a shield that covers the pulleys; remove the retaining hardware and flip the shield back to access the belt

Fig. 133 . . . to allow easy drive belt changing

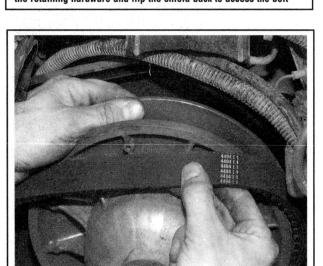

Fig. 131 Expand the pulley by rotating the two halves against each other, then remove the belt

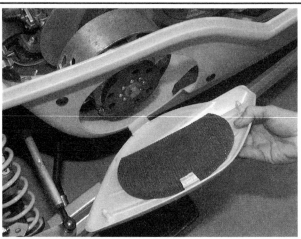

Fig. 134 Some sleds have a removable panel to allow the belt to be removed from the front pulley

Fig. 135 Once the panel is removed, the belt can be slipped off the primary pulley

simultaneously lifting up on the belt to roll it over the outer half of the pulley. This may take some strength, (and patience) to perfect. You might want to have someone with experience demonstrate the technique to you if you are having difficulty removing the belt on your particular sled.

➡Some models use a small tool that screws into the secondary pulley that holds the halves apart, making belt changing a breeze. Check with your owner's manual or dealer to find if there are any special tools or techniques for removing the belt on your sled.

3. Once the drive belt is free of the secondary pulley, slip it underneath the primary pulley so it can be removed from the engine compartment. Some models have an access cover on the left side of the cowl to make it easier to remove the drive belt from the primary pulley.

To install:

4. Compare the new belt with the old unit to confirm the belt is the correct width and length. Keep in mind that a new belt will be slightly wider and shorter than the old unit.

➡If a new drive belt is being installed, it should be noted that a short break-in period (around 30 miles) is required. When riding with a new belt, avoid strong acceleration and deceleration, or high-speed cruising.

5. A new belt typically has mold-releasing agents on its surface as a result of the manufacturing process. To keep the "slime" build-up from forming on the pulleys, use a wire brush to scrub the **sides** of the belt. Then, wipe the sides of the belt clean with acetone.

6. Before installing a new belt, look for an arrow to indicate the direction of rotation; an arrow cannot be found, install the belt so the part number or other script can be read while standing in front of the pulleys.

7. Slip the drive belt onto the primary pulley.

8. Position the drive belt onto the bottom half of the secondary pulley, then slip the remainder of the belt over the top of the pulley while separating the pulley halves.

9. Rotate the secondary pulley a few times to allow the belt to fall into position. In most cases, the top of the belt should be flush with the top of the pulley. Place a straightedge over the two halves of the pulley and check the belt position. If the belt is too high or too low, adjustment will be required. Check with your owner's manual for more information on adjustment, since there may be a particular method for adjusting the tension.

10. Secure the drive belt shield.

➡In some cases, alignment of the primary and secondary pulleys may need to be adjusted when installing a new drive belt. If the sled has been in an accident, or if the engine was removed, the center-to-center distance between the pulleys may need to be checked, and adjusted if necessary. Even installing an exact replacement of the old belt (same part number, same manufacturer) may require slight center-to-center pulley alignment on some models.

The pulleys (also commonly referred to as "clutches" or "sheaves") are the heart of the snowmobile drivetrain. The unique design of the pulleys allows a constantly variable drive rate, when combined with the drive belt.

For a more in-depth description of the function of the drive system can be found in section 9 of this book.

INSPECTION

▶ **See Figures 136 and 137**

The pulleys should be inspected periodically for rubber build-up, or signs of excessive wear. The best time to inspect the pulleys is when the drive belt is removed for inspection or replacement. When inspecting the pulleys, focus on the pulley halves where the drive belt rides.

1. To thoroughly inspect the pulleys, remove the drive belt as described in this section.

2. Any rubber build-up or "slime" found on the pulley halves should be removed to ensure the operation of the pulleys and belt. If the build-up is minimal, a light grade Scotch-Brite® pad or light grade steel wool can be used to clean the pulley halves. Heavier build-up may require **light** scraping with a

Fig. 136 Example of rubber build-up on pulley halves

Fig. 137 A light grade abrasive pad can be used to clean rubber build-up from the pulleys

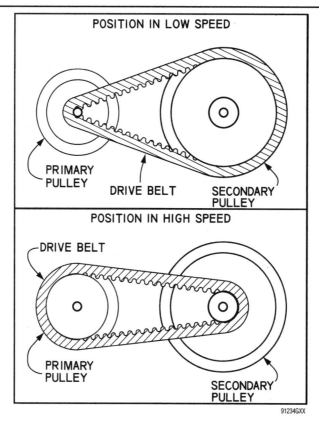

POSITION IN LOW SPEED

PRIMARY PULLEY

DRIVE BELT

SECONDARY PULLEY

POSITION IN HIGH SPEED

DRIVE BELT

PRIMARY PULLEY

SECONDARY PULLEY

91234GXX

Typical snowmobile transmission detail

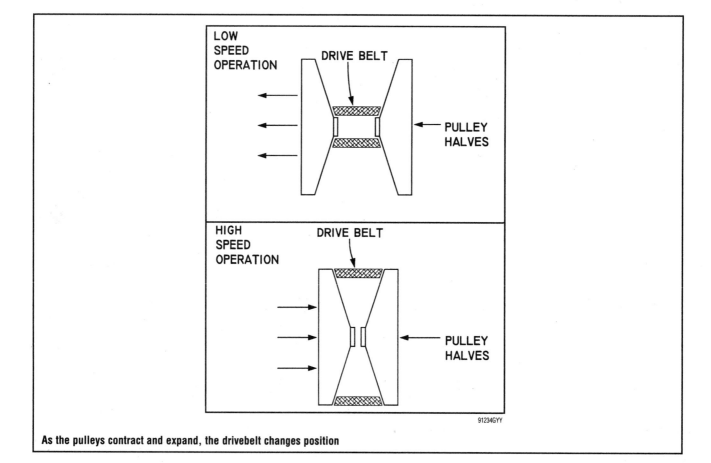

LOW SPEED OPERATION

DRIVE BELT

PULLEY HALVES

HIGH SPEED OPERATION

DRIVE BELT

PULLEY HALVES

91234GYY

As the pulleys contract and expand, the drivebelt changes position

suitable tool (don't gouge the metal). When you're done cleaning the build-up from the pulley, spray a clean rag with brake cleaner, and wipe the surface clean. Do NOT use any silicone-based products, spray oils, etc. on or near the pulleys, as they will cause belt slippage.

3. In addition to looking for rubber build-up, look for any damage to the surface. If there are any knicks or heavy scratches, they should be carefully filed flat with a file to prevent damage to the drive belt. Be VERY careful when filing the surface; remove only the raised portion of the damaged area. Filing the entire scratch or knick out of the pulley will cause problems with balance, and cause problems with the belt.

ALIGNMENT

See Figures 138, 139, 140, 141, and 142

The alignment of the primary and secondary pulleys may need to be checked and adjusted if the drive belts wear excessively, or if engine performance seems sluggish. If the sled has been in an accident, or if the engine was removed, the alignment of the pulleys may need to be checked, and adjusted if necessary.

Also, installing a new drive belt may require slight center-to-center pulley alignment, even if an exact replacement of the old belt (same part number, same manufacturer) is used. Usually, the distance between the two pulleys requires adjustment.

Fig. 140 To accurately align the pulleys on most snowmobiles, a special alignment tool is usually required

Fig. 138 This motor mount has a large slotted hole for adjustment of the primary pulley

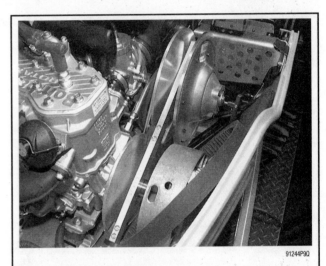

Fig. 141 Since all snowmobiles are made differently, pulley alignment tools are made specifically for each model

Fig. 139 This engine has an adjustable torque link that keeps the pulleys in alignment under acceleration

Fig. 142 Some pulleys use shims (arrow) for alignment

Because of the special tools typically required for pulley alignment, no accurate procedures can be given here. However, pulley alignment is usually achieved by repositioning the engine on its mounts and/or adjusting the position of the secondary pulley on the jackshaft with the use of shims. In any case, a qualified service facility can supply you with the special tools and specifications necessary to align the pulleys on your particular sled.

ADJUSTMENT

Pulley adjustment is one of the most common ways to increase the performance of a snowmobile. Most modern sleds have some means of adjusting the pulleys (also known as "clutches") to compensate for varying conditions. Different altitudes and different types of snow can sometimes require adjustment of the primary and secondary pulleys to keep the engine operating in its peak power range.

Primary Pulley

▶ See Figures 143, 144, 145 and 146

The primary pulley, also known as the drive clutch, or drive sheave, is attached directly to the crankshaft of the engine. The rate at which the pulley halves expand and contract coincides directly with the engine speed. At idle, the pulley halves are at their furthest distance apart, which is just slightly wider than

Fig. 143 The spring controls the engagement speed in the primary pulley

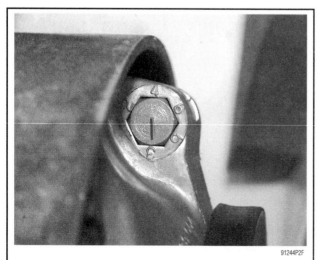

Fig. 144 Some primary pulleys have external adjustment of the cam arms. The numbers allow equal adjustment of each cam arm

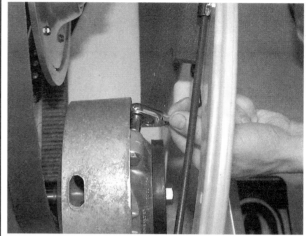

Fig. 145 To adjust the cam arms on this primary pulley, the nuts are loosened just enough to allow the bolt to turn . . .

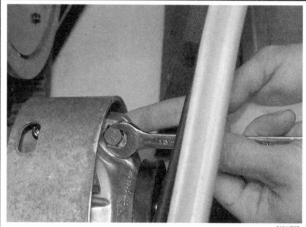

Fig. 146 . . . and then adjusted to a lower or higher number. Each cam arm pivot bolt must be aligned with the same number for balance

the drive belt. As soon as the rpm increases, and the belt engages with the pulley.

There are two components in a primary pulley assembly that can be adjusted (or in some cases, changed) to alter its engagement characteristics. The first component is the spring. The spring in a primary pulley controls the rpm in which the pulley engages. The stiffer the spring, the higher the rpm will be before the pulley engages.

The second of the two components are the cam arms. The cam arms are essentially centrifugal weights, which control the movement of the pulley halves.

Unfortunately, the methods of adjustment for the primary pulley can greatly differ between manufacturers, so no generic procedures can be given here. Your owner's manual will discuss the manner in which you can adjust the primary pulley on your sled for maximum performance. Some pulleys have eccentric pivots for the cam arms, and some may use shims to tension the spring. An addition, many manufacturers offer different strengths of springs and sizes and shapes of weights to "tune" the primary pulley.

✳✳ WARNING

If you are inexperienced with (or unsure of) the adjustment of the drive pulleys, DO NOT FOOL WITH THEM! Although the drive pulleys are basic in design, they are highly precise. If you want to adjust the drive pulley for performance, and your owner's manual doesn't

cover adjustments, contact a dealer; special tools may be required, since some pulleys require removal for adjustment. He/she may be able to provide accurate information about pulley adjustment for your particular sled.

Secondary Pulley

▶ See Figures 147 and 148

The secondary pulley (also known as the driven pulley, driven sheave, or secondary clutch) is connected to the chaincase, which turns the driveshaft, and rotates the track. Unlike the primary pulley, the secondary pulley is torque-sensitive. The higher the load placed on the pulley, (riding up a hill, accelerating from a stop) the closer together the pulley halves are, which allows the engine to remain in its peak operating range, while providing a higher drive ratio.

The spring is one of the most important components affecting the "shifting" characteristics of the secondary pulley. It should be noted that over time, the tension in the spring weakens from being continuously preloaded (even when the snowmobile is at rest, the spring is preloaded). This will cause the pulley to "open" quicker (changing the drive ratio) and cause sluggish operation. This is especially apparent in deep snow or hilly riding areas. In extreme cases, a weak spring can cause belt slippage, which can cause drive belt failure.

Fig. 147 Changing the spring in the secondary pulley changes the "shifting" characteristics for maximum performance

Fig. 148 The ramps (or helix) on the secondary pulley can also be changed to alter the shifting characteristics (note the different holes for spring adjustment)

Because the spring becomes fatigued from constant use, replacement of the spring every 2000 miles (or every other season) is recommended.

Along with the spring, the ramps, or helix, work to provide the proper drive ratio regardless of load. The angle of the ramps dictates the manner in which the pulley halves contract and expand, which controls the drive ratio.

As with the primary pulley, the methods of adjustment for the secondary pulley can greatly differ between manufacturers. Detailed procedures for pulley adjustments would be a book in itself, so no procedures are given here. Your owner's manual should discuss the manner in which you can adjust the secondary pulley on your sled for maximum performance. If not, contact a dealer who can discuss the "tuning" options for your secondary pulley.

Jackshaft

▶ See Figure 149

The jackshaft, also known as the countershaft, is an axle that transmits power from the secondary pulley to the chaincase. The jackshaft is supported by a bearing inside the chaincase, and an external bearing on the opposite side, behind the secondary pulley. The bearing inside the chaincase is lubricated by the chaincase oil, making lubrication unnecessary. The external bearing, however, (behind the secondary pulley) is mounted inside of its own housing. Because of the location of the external bearing though, it is frequently overlooked when performing maintenance.

Fig. 149 The jackshaft bearing is located directly behind the secondary pulley (note carburetor inlet, sometimes the carburetors must be removed to allow access to the bearing)

BEARING LUBRICATION

Some jackshaft bearings are sealed, and lubrication is not necessary, or possible. On most models though, a grease fitting is mounted on the bearing housing. To lubricate the jackshaft bearing, attach a grease gun to the fitting and inject grease into the bearing until it pushes out from the seal(s). Make sure to wipe away any excess grease, since it can be spun off the bearing onto the secondary pulley, causing belt slippage.

BEARING INSPECTION AND REPLACEMENT

The easiest way to inspect the jackshaft bearing is to remove the drive belt from the secondary pulley, and check for play. If a "clunking" is felt when moving the pulley up and down, it may be in need of replacement.

In most cases, the bearing can be replaced by removing the secondary pulley from the jackshaft, and unbolting the bearing and housing from the bracket. In some circumstances, though, the use of a bearing puller may be necessary to remove the bearing from the jackshaft. After the new bearing is installed, the secondary pulley will have to be aligned, requiring special alignment tools. If you do not have access to these tools, replacement of the jackshaft bearing should be left to a qualified service facility.

Chaincase/Gearcase

♦ **See Figures 150 thru 155**

The majority of all snowmobiles use a chaincase (or in some situations, a gearcase) to transmit power from the jackshaft to the drive axle, which rotates the track. In its most basic form, the chaincase contains a chain, sprockets, bearings, and a tensioning mechanism. The drive sprocket is typically smaller than the driven unit, providing a slight reduction in gear ratio. The tensioning mechanism is provided to keep the chain tight, and to compensate for wear.

The chaincase contains oil to provide lubrication to the bearings, chain and sprockets and/or gears. To keep the chaincase and its components in top condition, the oil should be changed regularly, and the chain tension should be adjusted. If your snowmobile's chaincase is actually a gearcase, then adjustment of the chain is not necessary, since gears are used to transmit power to the drive axle.

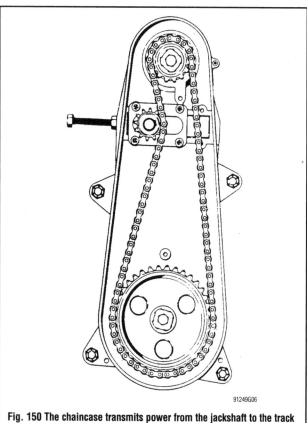

Fig. 150 The chaincase transmits power from the jackshaft to the track

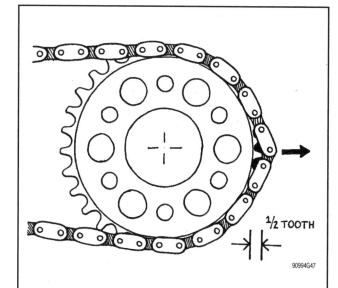

Fig. 151 A quick way to check chain stretch (after the slack is adjusted) is by pulling the chain off the rear sprocket. If you can see more than ½ tooth, then the chain is stretched and should be retensioned

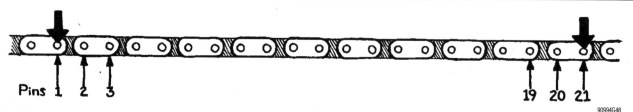

Fig. 152 A more precise method of checking chain stretch is to measure the distance of a set number of links (in this example, 20 links which means the distance between 21 pins) and compare it to specification

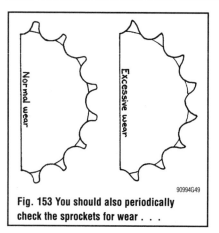

Fig. 153 You should also periodically check the sprockets for wear . . .

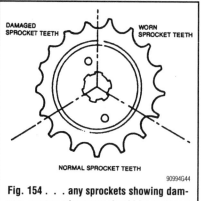

Fig. 154 . . . any sprockets showing damage, or excessive wear should be replaced

Fig. 155 An example of a severely worn countershaft sprocket

Fig. 156 It's important to select the proper viscosity and type of chaincase oil for your particular sled

SELECTING THE PROPER OIL

♦ **See Figure 156**

Snowmobile chaincases and gearcases, whether they are chain-driven or gear driven, can sometimes require special oil. If you are not sure whether your sled uses gear drive or chain drive, ask your local dealer or look in your owner's manual, since this may have an affect on the type of oil required.

Also, talk to other snowmobile riders (preferably those who ride the same model) and see what they use. Choose a name brand oil which meets the requirements set by your snowmobile's manufacturer. Of course, probably more important than anything else, use the correct viscosity for the ambient temperature range, and change your oil often.

Viscosity

According to the Society of Automotive Engineers' (SAE) viscosity classification system, an oil with a high viscosity number (such as SAE 75 or SAE 90) will be thicker than one with a lower number. (SAE 10W). The "W" in 10W indicates that the oil is desirable for use in winter riding, and not stand for "weight". Through the use of special additives, multiple-viscosity oils are available to compensate for differences in temperature.

The gearcase oil for your snowmobile should be of a viscosity suitable for the outside temperature in which you'll be riding (cold, really cold, frozen, or insane). Oil must be thin enough to get between the close-tolerance moving parts it must lubricate. Once there, it must be thick enough to separate them with a slippery oil film. If the oil is too thin, it won't separate the parts; if it's too thick, it can't squeeze between them in the first place—either way, excess friction and wear takes place.

Additives

Another thing to consider when selecting chaincase oil is additives. friction modifiers and Extreme Pressure (EP) additives are valuable in so-called boundary lubrication, where there is metal-to-metal contact due to the absence or breaking down of the oil film between moving parts. Friction modifiers, or anti-wear agents, deposit protective surface films which reduce the friction and heat of metal-to-metal contact. Extreme pressure additives work by reacting chemically with metal surfaces involved in high-pressure contact.

Synthetic Oil

Just like synthetic engine oil, synthetic chaincase oils are another of those touchy topics among the sled-riding public. Years ago, when synthetics were first introduced to the market, people balked about the lubrication characteristics, claiming it was all hype.

Today, manufacturers supply their snowmobiles with synthetic lubricants straight from the factory. In all forms of motorsports, many racing teams rely upon synthetic oils to protect their high dollar, high rpm and high visibility investments.

It's obvious that synthetic lubricants have been proven effective in today's engines.

Synthetic oils are assembled from different compounds into specifically sized and shaped hydrocarbons. On the other hand, conventional oils are based on hydrocarbons, but because they are refined, the sizes and shapes of these molecules are highly irregular. This is what makes petroleum-based oil inferior to synthetics.

One drawback though. Synthetic oils are often more expensive than conventional oils. BUT, if the extra protection they offer is worth it to you, then you may want to give synthetics a try.

LEVEL CHECK

The fluid level of your chaincase (or gearcase) is usually checked in one of two ways; using a dipstick, or a check plug. Regardless of the manner in which the chaincase oil level is checked, the snowmobile should usually be on a perfectly level surface to assure a proper reading. Make sure that it is sitting level (side-to-side **and** front-to-back) when you check the oil level.

The oil in the chaincase should be checked regularly, to be certain that the oil level has not decreased (indicating leakage) or increased (indicating water contamination).

If you have to keep adding oil to the chaincase, the seal on the drive axle may be leaking, or the side cover may have a faulty gasket. In any case, excessive oil consumption indicates leakage, which should be promptly repaired.

Water contamination is caused from moisture condensation inside the crankcase, humidity, or faulty seals. If water is found in the chaincase, it should be drained immediately, and refilled with clean oil.

With A Dipstick

♦ **See Figures 157 thru 163**

1. Place the snowmobile on a level surface (side-to-side **and** front-to-back).
2. Remove the dipstick from the engine case. Most dipsticks simply pull out of the chain case, but some use a threaded dipstick; gently turn the tab counterclockwise until it is free. Then remove it by pulling straight upward.
3. Wipe the dipstick clean using a rag or paper towel (making sure that no debris or lint is left on the dipstick when it is inserted back into the oil).
4. Insert the dipstick back into the crankcase or oil tank. If the dipstick is threaded, do NOT thread it back into the chaincase. On most threaded dipsticks the level is marked so that the dipstick is inserted into the hole, BUT is not threaded in place.
5. Remove the dipstick and hold it vertically with the end of the dipstick facing the ground. We know this is contrary to what you have seen every television gas station attendant do, but if you try to hold it horizontally there is a good chance that the oil will flow up the dipstick and give a false high reading (or worse, a false acceptable reading when the level is really low). If however, you follow our advice and hold it vertically the oil will NOT flow up the dipstick (unless it is anti-gravity oil, in which case you should call Mulder and Scully) and you will never be left with too little oil in your snowmobile.

Fig. 157 Most chaincases have a dipstick to check the oil level . . .

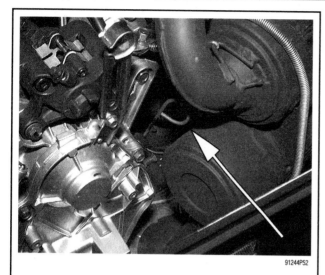

Fig. 158 . . . but some are not easily accessed

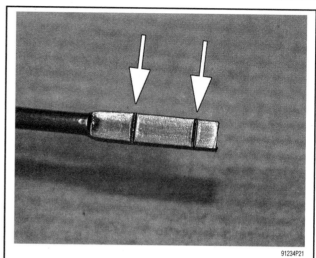

Fig. 161 The oil level should always be between the two marks on the dipstick

Fig. 159 This dipstick simply pulls straight out of the chaincase

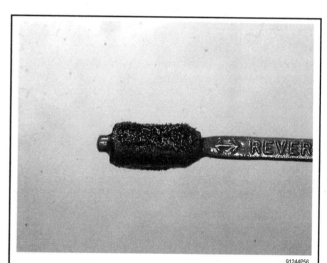

Fig. 162 Some dipsticks have a magnet to collect particles; small, fuzzy particles are a product of normal wear

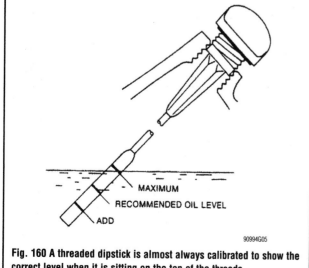

Fig. 160 A threaded dipstick is almost always calibrated to show the correct level when it is sitting on the top of the threads

Fig. 163 Add oil to the chaincase if the level is low

➡️Some dipsticks have a magnet on the tip to collect fine metal particles in the crankcase. Small, fine particles can usually be considered normal (a product of normal wear), but larger bits of metal might indicate problems in the chaincase. Make sure to wipe the magnet clean before inserting the dipstick.

6. If necessary, add oil (of the proper type and viscosity) to keep the level between the markings. If the oil level has risen, there is a good chance that water has made its way into the chaincase. The oil should be changed immediately to prevent any damage to the bearings, gears, and/or chain.

With a Check Plug

♦ See Figure 164

1. Place the snowmobile on a level surface (side-to-side **and** front-to-back).
2. Locate the check plug on the side of the chaincase (the check plug is usually noted with an arrow or other identification).
3. With a rag handy, remove the check plug from the side of the engine. With the snowmobile on a fully level surface, a small amount of oil should dribble from the hole. If a large amount of oil comes out of the check hole, water my be present in the chaincase.
4. If oil does not come out of the hole, the oil level is low, and oil should be added.

➡️Some check plugs have a magnet on the tip to collect fine metal particles in the crankcase. Small, fine particles are no cause for concern (a product of normal wear), but larger bits of metal might indicate problems in the chaincase. Make sure to wipe the magnet clean before inserting the check plug into the chaincase.

5. Leave the check plug out, and add oil through the fill hole, located on the upper half of the chaincase. Add oil (of the proper type and viscosity) slowly; when oil starts to dribble out of the check hole, the oil level is correct.

➡️When adding oil, be careful not to add too much too quickly. If oil begins to pour out of the check hole, do not add any more oil. Wait until the oil slows to a small drip; this indicates a proper oil level.

6. Install the check plug and tighten it securely. In most cases, you can get away without having to replace the washer on the check plug; however, keep a new one handy should the old washer start to leak.
7. Wipe off the excess oil from the check plug area with a rag or paper towel.
8. Don't forget to install the fill hole cap!

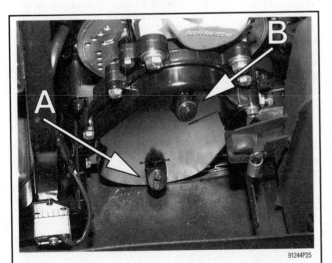

Fig. 164 This chaincase uses a check plug (A) to automatically adjust the level when oil is added through the filler plug (B)

DRAIN AND REFILL

In order to monitor the health of your chaincase, the fluid should be changed on a regular basis. In most situations, the chaincase oil should be changed once a season, or every 1000 miles. However, if your manufacturer's recommen-

dations suggest a longer interval, keep in mind that you can never go wrong by changing the chaincase oil sooner than the manufacturer recommends.

Quite frankly, you can **never** change oil too often. If you can afford to change all of your fluids in your sled after every ride, then hey, have at it. You might spend a lot of money, but your snowmobile will be in top shape internally. Understand that doing this is rather extreme, but changing the fluids in your sled before the recommended service intervals cannot cause any harm in most cases. So, the more you change your oil, the better off your sled will be.

Basically, there are two methods to changing the chaincase oil. The most convenient way, which is unfortunately not the most common, is with a drain plug. A small access hole in the lower cowl allows oil to be drained out of the bottom of the chaincase, just like an automobile. The second method, which is more common, is somewhat messy, and not as simple.

With A Drain Plug

♦ See Figures 165, 166, 167 and 168

➡️The warmer the ambient temperature, the easier the fluid will drain from the chaincase. If the ambient temperature is on the cold side, use a blow dryer to warm up the chaincase, which should speed things up a bit.

1. Place the snowmobile on a level surface (side-to-side **and** front-to-back).
2. Position a drain pan underneath the chaincase drain plug.
3. Remove the dipstick or fill plug from the upper portion of the chaincase.

Fig. 165 Some chaincases are equipped with a drain plug (arrow) to make changing the oil easier

Fig. 166 Before loosening the drain plug, position a drain pan to catch the oil in the chaincase

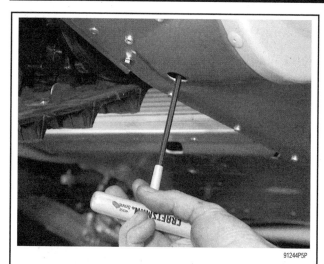

Fig. 167 Once the drain pan is in position, remove the drain plug and drain the chaincase oil

Fig. 168 Make sure to use a funnel when filling the chaincase with fresh oil

4. Using the appropriately sized wrench, loosen the drain plug.
5. Once the drain plug is loosened, unscrew it by hand while pushing upwards on the threads. Once the drain plug is free of the threads, quickly pull it away, and allow the chaincase oil to drain into the pan.

➡If the drain plug is equipped with a magnet, inspect the metal shavings; fine particles can be considered normal, but large chunks of metal might indicate problems with the bearings, sprockets or chain. If you do find any questionable debris attached to the drain plug, place it into a plastic bag for safe keeping, and show it to a reputable mechanic for closer inspection.

6. Once the oil has thoroughly drained from the chaincase, install the drain plug. If equipped, install a new copper washer on the drain plug to prevent leakage. When tightening the drain plug, DON'T overtighten it! The chaincases and covers are made of aluminum alloy, and the threads can strip easily.
7. Using a funnel, add the proper amount (and type/viscosity) of oil to the chaincase. Be careful not to overfill the chaincase when adding oil; too much oil will cause the oil to cavitate excessively, reducing the lubrication properties of the oil.
8. Once the oil level is correct, install the dipstick (or check plug and fill plug) to the chaincase.

➡After you change your oil, you'll have to get rid of the old oil. Whatever you do, DON'T dump it into the ground, into the gutter, into the sewer, or your neighbor's yard, no matter now much you hate him. Used oil contains acids and heavy metals, which can contaminate a water supply and cause health problems. Find a local gas station or auto parts store that will let you dispose of used oil properly. This is the only way of legally disposing of used oil. Any other method of disposing of used oil (like pouring the used oil back into the new oil containers and throwing them in the trash) is considered criminal, and could land you some time in court and a heavy fine if you get caught. But hey, why take the risk? Proper oil disposal helps to clean up the environment.

Without A Drain Plug

1. Place the snowmobile on a level surface (side-to-side **and** front-to-back).
2. In most cases, it will be necessary to remove the exhaust system to gain access to the side of the chaincase. Remove the springs and other hardware, and set the exhaust system aside.
3. Place an old towel or a few rags between the bottom of chaincase and the cowl. This will help soak up the majority of the oil in the chaincase when the cover is removed.
4. Working around the perimeter of the chaincase cover, loosen the bolts in a criss-cross pattern until all of the bolts are loosened enough to be removed by hand.

✳✳ WARNING

ALWAYS loosen the chaincase cover bolts gradually in one or two passes of a cross-wise pattern. Remember that these covers are aluminum and are prone to warping if exposed to uneven clamp loads. Install and tighten the bolts to specification using a torque wrench.

5. While holding the cover in place, unthread the bolts. When all of the bolts are free, let the cover break free and release the oil from the chaincase. This part can get a little messy, so be prepared to clean up any excess oil that does not get soaked up by the towel or rags underneath the cover. If the cover does not separate right away, lightly tap the cover (be hold your hand on the cover to control the oil as much as possible) with a soft mallet to break the gasket free.

✳✳ WARNING

If locking compound residue is found on the chaincase cover bolts when they are removed, the bolts should be cleaned thoroughly, and installed using fresh compound. The cover bolts on some models may be prone to vibrating loose; the chain and sprockets can be destroyed if the cover vibrates loose and loses all of the chaincase oil. Check with a dealer or reputable service facility to find out if the use of locking compound on the chaincase cover bolts is necessary.

6. Once all of the oil is drained, clean the bottom of the chaincase and the cowl, the chaincase cover, and the gasket mating surfaces.
7. Install a new O-ring or gasket to the chaincase cover.

➡It may be necessary to use a gasket adhesive to keep the O-ring or gasket in place when the cover is installed.

8. Install the cover to the chaincase, threading the bolts and lockwashers hand-tight. Make sure that the gasket or O-ring stays in place when the cover is mounted.
9. Working in a criss-cross pattern, tighten the chaincase cover bolts to the proper torque (specified by the manufacturer) to prevent warpage of the cover.
10. Using a funnel, add a small amount of oil to the chaincase.
11. Check for any signs of leakage around the perimeter of the chaincase. If any leakage is detected, the gasket or O-ring is most likely incorrectly seated.
12. If the chaincase is properly sealed, add the proper amount (and type/viscosity) of oil to the chaincase. Be careful not to overfill the chaincase when adding oil; too much oil will cause cavitation, reducing the oil's lubrication properties, and shortening the lifespan of the parts.
13. Once the oil level is correct, install the dipstick (or check plug and fill plug) to the chaincase.
14. Install the exhaust system as necessary.

ADJUSTMENT

▶ See Figures 169, 170, 171 and 172

On most snowmobiles, the drive chain tension should be checked (and adjusted if necessary) AT LEAST every 500 miles, but it is a good idea to do so more often if your sled is ridden hard.

A means of adjustment is usually provided for the drive chain to compensate for wear of the chain and sprockets. As the chain wears, it "stretches" and requires adjustment to keep it tensioned properly on the sprockets. If the chain is not kept in adjustment, the excess slack will cause the sprockets to wear even faster, which consequently causes the chain to stretch further. In an extreme case, the chain could break (leaving you stranded on the trail) if it is not kept in proper adjustment.

➡ If your snowmobile's chaincase is actually a gearcase, then adjustment of the chain is not necessary, since gears are used to transmit power to the drive axle.

The majority of all chaincases use a roller tensioner that is adjusted with a bolt or screw. Some models may use a spring that tensions the roller, making adjustment unnecessary (and impossible). Other models may require a procedure that involves turning the secondary pulley a few times to take up the slack

Fig. 171 . . . and align the hole in the bolt to reinstall the pin. In most cases, the bolt should be turned counterclockwise just enough to allow the pin to be installed

Fig. 169 A hitch pin retains this adjustment bolt. To adjust the tension on the chain, remove the pin . . .

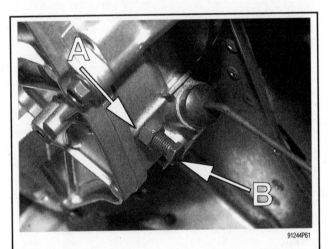

Fig. 172 Here's another method of chaincase adjustment. The locknut (A) should be loosened to allow movement of the adjustment bolt (B)

on the chain, (as if the sled was moving) removing the hitch pin on the adjuster bolt, and tightening the bolt by hand. Some manufacturers also may require the chaincase cover to be removed when performing this procedure to actually measure the slack on the chain as it is being adjusted. This can be done when the chaincase oil is changed.

Because of the many different types and configurations of chaincases, it is virtually impossible to list every procedure for adjusting the drive chain tension in this book. However, your owner's manual should discuss the specific procedure for adjusting the drive chain on your particular sled. If you are unsure about the procedure, or have questions, don't hesitate to call a dealer or qualified mechanic. If the drive chain is incorrectly tensioned, (too loose or too tight) the chain may break, leaving you stranded.

Driveshaft & Sprockets

DRIVESHAFT

The driveshaft is the axle that transmits power from the chaincase to the track. Sprockets are mounted to the driveshaft, and mesh with the track, which drives the sled.

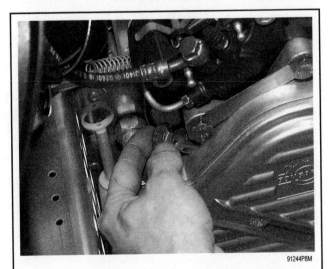

Fig. 170 . . . and turn the screw clockwise by hand . . .

The driveshaft on the majority of modern snowmobiles is supported by a bearing inside the chaincase, and an external bearing on the opposite side (similar to the jackshaft). The bearing inside the chaincase is lubricated by the chaincase oil, making lubrication unnecessary. The external bearing, however, is mounted inside of its own housing (which is usually the speedometer drive gear case). Because of the location of the external bearing though, it is frequently overlooked when performing maintenance.

Bearing Lubrication

If your snowmobile is equipped with a grease fitting on the bearing housing, or speedometer drive gear, it should be lubricated according to the manufacturer's specifications.

➡**Make sure to use the proper grease when lubricating the bearings; mixing two different types of grease can cause lubrication problems.**

To lubricate the driveshaft bearing, attach a grease gun (with the appropriate grease) to the fitting and inject grease into the bearing until it pushes out from the seal(s). Make sure to wipe away any excess grease, since it can be spun off the bearing onto the track.

Bearing Inspection And Replacement

To inspect the driveshaft bearings, the sled should be safely elevated, with the track clear of the ground. Grab the driveshaft and rock it back and forth. If a "clunking" is felt when moving the driveshaft, it may be in need of replacement. In some cases, it may be necessary to loosen the tension on the track to "feel" for any looseness in the driveshaft.

In most cases, driveshaft bearing replacement is a major repair, involving removal of the chaincase. Also, special tools may be necessary on some models. If you do not have access to these tools, replacement of the driveshaft bearings should be left to a qualified service facility.

SPROCKETS

Inspection

▶ **See Figures 173 and 174**

To inspect the driveshaft sprockets, the sled should be safely elevated, with the track clear of the ground. While rotating the track by hand, look for chips, missing teeth, or cracks in the sprockets. If the sprockets are damaged, the driveshaft will have to be removed so the sprockets can be pressed off and replaced.

Fig. 173 The condition of the drive sprockets (arrow) should be checked for damage

Fig. 174 Look for signs of excessive wear, cracking, or missing teeth on each sprocket

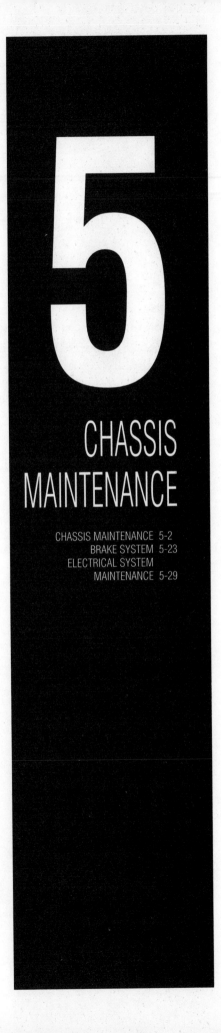

5

CHASSIS MAINTENANCE

CHASSIS MAINTENANCE

Control Cables

INSPECTION

▶ See Figure 1

Inspecting the cables for kinks, fraying and contamination is important for proper operation, as well as safety. If a cable were to break on the trail, you could be left without brakes, or worse, no throttle. By inspecting your snowmobile's operating cables on a regular basis, problems of this nature can be avoided.

LUBRICATION

▶ See Figures 2, 3 and 4

➡Do not lubricate Teflon lined cables as the cable is designed to be self-lubricating. Adding lubricant will only cause problems. Check your owner's manual or with your snowmobile's manufacturer (or even the cable manufacturer, if you can find them) to see what type you have.

1. Disconnect the cable and drip cable lubricant down the housing. There are special cable lubricating fittings that make this easier and neater. Add lubricant until it runs out of the other end of the cable.
2. Lubricate the ends of the cable with grease where they connect to the controls and levers. A dab of grease at the cable openings will help prevent the entry of dirt and moisture into the cable.

ADJUSTMENT

▶ See Figures 5 and 6

The majority of control cables all have some form of adjustment to compensate for the natural stretching of the cable and wear of parts, like brake pads. In most cases, a threaded adjuster on the lever perch is used for cable adjustment. Most are the "thumbwheel" type, meaning that they can be operated by hand. Other adjusters are usually hex-shaped, and require a wrench for adjustment. In addition to the adjuster on the lever, an adjuster is usually found on the other end of the cable where it activates the brake lever (or carburetor).

➡When making cable adjustments at the perch, always position the threaded adjuster with the slot facing downward. If the slot is facing upward, dirt and water can accumulate and enter the cable.

The threaded adjusters on a lever perch (or lever, in the case of a thumb throttle) can be used for keeping cables adjusted properly in most cases. However, if the adjuster is at the end of its threading, screw the perch adjuster all the way in, then adjust the cable at the other end. By doing this, the perch adjuster can be used for more convenient adjustments. If a cable is reaching the end of the threads on both adjusters, it's likely that the cable is stretched beyond its useable limits, and should be replaced.

➡For adjustment of the throttle cable(s), refer to section four of this book; the carburetor(s) may require synchronization when the cables are adjusted.

Fig. 1 Cables should be inspected frequently for signs of contamination. Rust has set in on this cable from water inside the sheath

91235P48

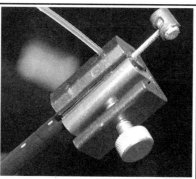

Fig. 2 An example of a cable lubrication tool

91230P14

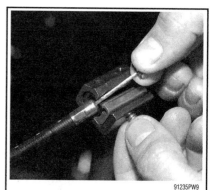

Fig. 3 Once the cable is removed from the lever, position the tool onto the cable . . .

91235PW9

Fig. 4 . . . then place the lubricant spray tube into the tool and spray lubricant into the cable

91235PW8

Fig. 5 Most cables have a means of adjustment to compensate for wear. Some adjusters are built into the cable . . .

91230P06

Fig. 6 . . . while others are located at the cable ends

91245P33

REPLACEMENT

♦ **See Figures 7 thru 12**

Cable replacement usually involves disconnecting the ends, and removing any necessary clamps, straps, or anything else that retains the cable. Some cables can be simple to replace, while others, like some carburetor cables, may require removal of components (such as the airbox).

When replacing a cable, always make sure that is routed properly. Before removing the old cable, note the routing. Be sure to route the new cable in the same manner to avoid any problems with chafing or kinking. Once the cable is replaced, turn the handlebars from side-to-side, and check for any problems. There should not be any binding when the lever (or throttle) is operated.

Fig. 7 To replace a throttle cable, remove the throttle lever pivot . . .

Steering Linkage

A typical steering linkage setup on a snowmobile consists of a steering shaft, (on which the handlebars are attached) and tie rods, which attach to the suspension linkage. Every time you turn the handlebars, these parts work together to turn your skis so your snowmobile goes in the direction that you want it to.

Inspection of the steering linkage should be performed on a regular basis. Along with the brakes, steering input is essential for safety.

INSPECTION

The front of the snowmobile should be lifted from the ground to inspect the steering linkage. While turning the handlebars from side-to-side, there should not be any binding or resistance. If everything is moving smoothly, check for wear of the bearings and bushings. Clunking or excessive play generally means that something is worn out. Having another person turn the handlebars while you look for play in the bushings or bearings can speed up the process, since worn bushings and other components can be hard to locate at times.

The tie rod ends can be checked by rocking the ski from side-to-side. If there is any clunking or play, they are worn out and should be replaced.

LUBRICATION

♦ **See Figures 13, 14, 15 and 16**

Lubricating the steering linkage can be as simple as applying a grease gun to a zerk fitting or be as tedious as disassembling the whole unit. If your snowmobile doesn't have grease fittings, the steering shaft will have to be removed to be able to apply new grease. As previously stated, always replace any fasteners removed for lubrication with new ones.

Tie rod ends may or may not have fittings. If not, they are maintenance free and do not require lubrication. If the rubber boot is torn, the tie rod end life span will be seriously shortened. Dirt and mud will cling to the exposed grease and grind away at the metal. Usually a torn boot on a tie rod end cannot be replaced separately; the tie rod end must be replaced as a unit.

Fig. 8 . . . and any bushings or spacers

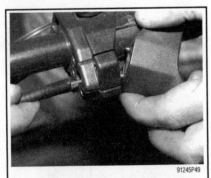

Fig. 9 Once the lever is disconnected, pull the cable end from its recess, and slide it through the slot in the perch

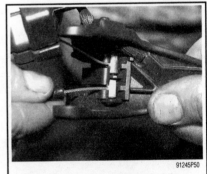

Fig. 10 The barrel tip on the end of the cable can now be disengaged from the lever

Fig. 11 Then remove the throttle slide from the carburetor . . .

Fig. 12 . . . and disconnect the cable. Finally, the cable end can be unscrewed from the throttle slide cap

Fig. 13 Most tie rod ends do not require lubrication, and are maintenance-free

Fig. 14 Most snowmobiles have grease fittings (arrow) on the front spindle housings for quick lubrication

Fig. 15 Before connecting a grease gun to the fitting, wipe it clean with a rag

Fig. 16 Make sure the grease in the gun is compatible with the existing grease in the spindle housing

ALIGNMENT

▶ See Figures 17, 18, 19, 20 and 21

If your snowmobile is pulling to one side, or "darting", chances are the alignment is incorrect. A small amount of toe can drastically affect the steering characteristics of the snowmobile.

For maximum maneuverability, the skis should be kept in proper alignment. Unless you have hit something (like a rock or tree stump) or replaced worn components, the alignment does not need regular adjustment. But, occasionally, mishaps occur, and it may be necessary to make some adjustments to keep your sled tracking in a straight line.

The easiest way to measure the alignment is to center the handlebars, and then measure the distance between the ski mounts on both sides of the spindle. It is important to measure at a reference point that is equal on both sides of the spindles; usually, the shape of the skis themselves will not allow this, since they are bowed slightly. If the distance of the front measurement is *less*

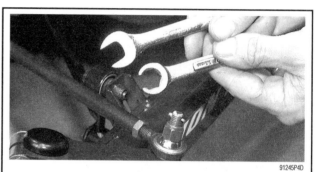

Fig. 19 If the alignment is incorrect, the tie rods can be adjusted by loosening the locknuts on each tie rod end. If possible, use a line wrench on the locknut to prevent stripping

Fig. 17 With the handlebars centered, measure the distance between the ski mounts in front of the spindles . . .

Fig. 20 Loosen the outer tie rod end locknut . . .

Fig. 18 . . . and to the rear. The distance should be equal (zero toe)

Fig. 21 . . . and the inner locknut. When loosening the locknuts, keep in mind that one tie rod end will have left-hand threads

than the rear measurement, the skis have toe-in; if the opposite is true, the skis have toe-out.

➡ **For most snowmobiles, it is desirable not to have any toe, but have the skis perfectly parallel with each other. Check with your dealer about the correct alignment settings for your particular sled.**

If the toe is not within factory specifications, the tie rods will need to be loosened and rotated to point the skis in the proper direction. When loosening the tie rod locknuts, keep in mind that one nut on each tie rod will have left-hand threads. This is so the tie rods can be twisted to adjust the alignment without removing them from the steering arms. Make sure to tighten the nuts securely when the alignment is correct.

If you have set the alignment on your sled, and are still experiencing steering problems, it might be better to have a dealer perform a full alignment check. In some cases, special alignment tools are necessary to perform an accurate alignment.

COMPONENT REPLACEMENT

▶ **See Figures 22, 23, 24 and 25**

If you find that parts of your steering linkage are worn, and you want to replace them yourself, there are some important guidelines to follow:

• When disassembling steering linkage (and other suspension parts), replacement of all fasteners is recommended. Suspension and steering fasteners are critical components. If a fastener were to fail, you could be seriously injured, or even killed. Don't take the chance—spend a few extra dollars and buy new nuts, bolts, and cotter pins.

Fig. 22 After the locknut has been loosened, mark its position with a paint marker . . .

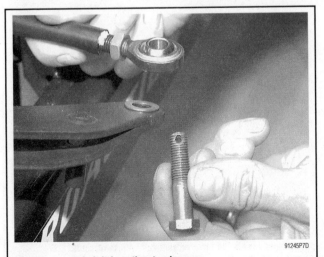

Fig. 23 . . . unbolt it from the steering arm . . .

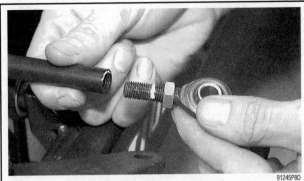

Fig. 24 . . . and unscrew it from the tie rod. Keep in mind that most tie rod ends have left-handed threads on one side

Fig. 25 When the new tie rod end is installed, be sure to use a new cotter pin (if applicable)

• It's a good idea to use liquid locking compound on suspension fasteners as a safety measure. Although most suspension fasteners use locking washers and nuts, a dab of thread lock on standard nuts and bolts will help to keep things secure, and give you peace of mind.

• Keep track of the order of washers and spacers. When it comes time for reassembly, chances are you'll forget the order in which they need to be installed. Don't be afraid to draw diagrams or take notes—it's worth the extra effort to ensure that everything gets installed properly.

If you have inspected the steering linkage, and found that the bushings and/or tie rod ends are worn, they can usually be replaced with simple hand tools. In most cases, disassembling the linkage at the pivot points and fitting new bushings is all that is required.

Tie rod ends are one of the most common components of the steering linkage that "wears out" over time. A generic procedure is given here for removal and replacement of tie rod ends.

1. First, remove the locknut on the threaded portion of the tie rod.
2. Next, mark the position of the relationship of the tie rod end and the threaded portion of the tie rod with a paint marker or other suitable means. By doing this, you'll avoid any major deviations from the original alignment settings.
3. Now the nut that secures the tie rod end to the spindle can be removed. Some snowmobiles might use a cotter pin with a castellated nut, and others might use a self-locking nut. Remove the cotter pin, if equipped.
4. After the nut is removed, gently tap on the area of the spindle where the stud of the tie rod protrudes (NOT on the stud!). If the tie rod does not break free, a tie rod puller tool may be necessary for removal. Also, liberal use of penetrating oil will help the removal process.
5. Once the tie rod end is free from the spindle, it can be unscrewed from the tie rod.
6. Count the number of threads up to the reference mark on the old tie rod end. With the new tie rod end, count the same number of threads, and make a reference mark with a paint marker or other means.
7. Thread the tie rod end onto the tie rod until it reaches the markings placed on the threads.
8. Install the stud into the spindle, and torque the nut to the specification required by the snowmobile manufacturer.

➡If the tie-rod end stud spins when the nut is tightened, use a pair of adjustable pliers to hold the stud inside the tapered housing (like you're forcing the stud through the steering arm); this usually prevents the stud from turning.

9. If a cotter pin is used, replace it with a new one. When installing a new cotter pin, push the pin through the hole in the stud and through the castellated nut, then bend the ears to hold the pin securely. It is most common for mechanics to bend one of the ears back over the nut, parallel to the direction the pin was inserted. The other ear is usually bent slightly around the circumference of the nut and cut short (leaving just enough of the bend to hold it in position).

10. When you are satisfied that the rod is properly installed and adjusted, tighten the locknut on the threaded portion of the tie rod.

Front Suspension & Skis

SUSPENSION LINKAGE

▶ **See Figures 26 thru 41**

Although the suspension designs change from one model to another, one thing remains consistent: they all use pivot points. Manufacturers have used many different methods of providing a pivot point for each component, which can be broken down into four basic types; Bonded Rubber, Plastic or Urethane Bushing, Roller Bearing, and Heim-type.

As with most automotive applications, bonded rubber suspension bushings consist of a metal shell, a rubber bushing, and an inner metal sleeve. The rubber is bonded to the metal, so the rubber actually flexes around the inner and outer sleeves. This design allows for some cushioning of the suspension, and also eliminates the need for maintenance. However, the constant flexing of the rubber can cause it to tear, or lose its bond to the metal sleeve.

Urethane or plastic bushings don't provide as much flex as rubber bushings do, but provide more precise and crisp handling characteristics. The main reason for this is because they actually rotate around the pivot, instead of flex, as rubber bushings do.

Some snowmobiles are equipped with exposed metal joints, commonly called "Heim" joints. These joints are usually self-lubricating, and do not require maintenance of any kind. If you have found excessively loose Heim joints, they will have to be replaced.

Roller bearing pivot points are not very common on snowmobiles, especially front suspensions. Roller bearings are usually found on pivot points of the rear suspension, where any kind of flexion is not allowed.

➡**Manufacturers usually use more than one type of pivot point in a front suspension system.**

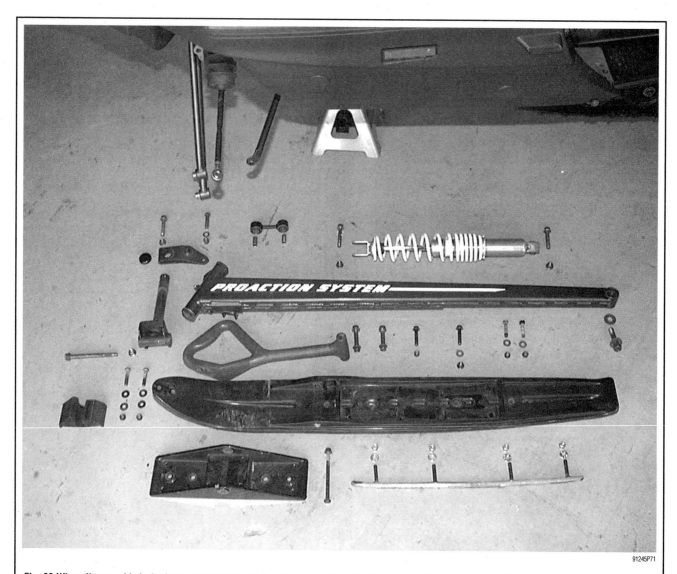

Fig. 26 When disassembled, the front suspension looks complicated, but is actually quite simple, and can be serviced with basic tools

91245P71

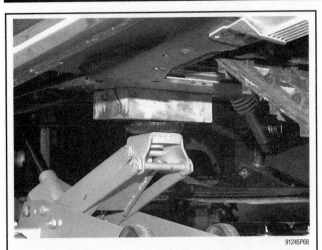

Fig. 27 When jacking the front of the sled to place it on jack stands for suspension inspection, it's a good idea to use a wood block to avoid damage

Fig. 28 Sometimes disassembly of the suspension bushings is the best method of inspection

Fig. 29 Example of a rubber bushing; these kind of bushings do not require any maintenance

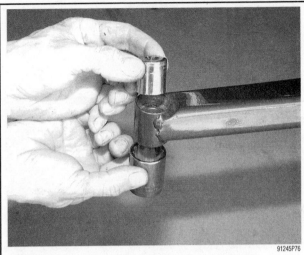

Fig. 30 Rubber bushings can be pressed out by using large sockets . . .

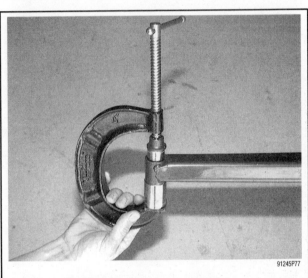

Fig. 31 . . . and a large C-clamp

Fig. 32 Make sure to keep track of the order of washers and spacers for proper assembly

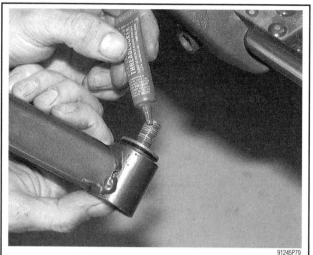

Fig. 33 It's a good idea to use locking compound on suspension fasteners for safety

Fig. 36 When installing new bushings, use a wooden block to tap them into position

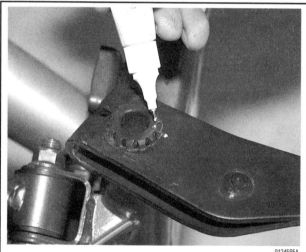

Fig. 34 Items like steering arms should be matchmarked to avoid problems with assembly

Fig. 37 Heim joints typically do not require lubrication

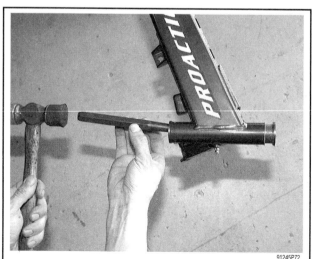

Fig. 35 Sometimes, plastic bushings might require the use of a punch and hammer for removal

Fig. 38 Keeping the suspension and steering components lubricated properly will prevent premature wear of the bushings

Fig. 39 On most sleds, the front suspension bushings can be lubricated and/or replaced by simply removing the pivot bolt

Fig. 40 Sometimes items like spindles . . .

Fig. 41 . . . and suspension bushings require disassembly for lubrication

Inspection

Regardless of the type of pivot point, the inspection of the suspension is universal. Any looseness or play in the suspension usually means worn out pivots. The only exception to this rule is bonded rubber bushings; a small amount of flexion is desired to compensate for chassis flex and smooth out the ride.

When inspecting suspension components with bonded rubber bushings, look for torn or bulged rubber from the side of the bushing where it attaches to the frame. With the front of the snowmobile raised from the ground, grab the ski mount and rock it in a front-to-back and up-and-down motion. (Be careful not to knock the snowmobile from the stands). Look for excessive movement from the pivot points of the suspension. If movement seems to be excessive, the bushings will have to be replaced. Unfortunately, bushings of this design usually require them to be pressed out of the suspension arm.

If your urethane or plastic bushings are worn and require replacement, they can be replaced by tapping the old ones out with a blunt-tipped punch, and pushing in new ones once the necessary components are disassembled. Don't forget to grease the inner sleeve before assembly.

Heim joints are usually replaced in the same manner as a tie-rod; unscrewing the end from the suspension arm. Make sure to mark the position of each joint before removal, since the suspension geometry can be adversely affected if the joint is installed incorrectly.

Lubrication

➡Check with your dealer about the use of grease on plastic or urethane bushings; some manufacturers may recommend using the bushings "dry" without lubrication of any kind. Each manufacturer has different recommendations, and it is advisable to adhere to them in most situations.

If your snowmobile has urethane or plastic bushings, then chances are that it contains fittings on the pivot points to lubricate the bushings. Simply attach the grease gun to the fitting, and pump in fresh grease (make sure the grease in the gun is compatible with the existing grease) until the old grease begins to seep from the bushing pivot. If there aren't any fittings for greasing the bushings, they will have to be disassembled periodically for lubrication. As with the steering linkage, it's not a bad idea that the suspension pivot bolts be replaced when the suspension is disassembled.

✷✷ CAUTION

Suspension bolts are usually of high grade (tensile strength); using hardware store bolts of a low grade rating can cause SEVERE damage to your sled (and yourself) if a pivot bolt were to break while riding. NEVER, EVER use fasteners of unknown grade on suspension system components.

SHOCK ABSORBERS

Adjustments

◆ See Figure 42

Most snowmobiles have some basic form of adjusting the shocks for a softer or stiffer ride. For improved ride characteristics, the ride height (or preload) should be adjusted for your weight. If the snowmobile sits at the top of its suspension travel, the ride will be harsh, since the suspension can only travel upwards because the shocks are already at the top of their stroke. With you aboard, and the suspension adjusted properly, the snowmobile should sit approximately one third of the total length of the suspension travel. For example, if the total suspension travel of your snowmobile is around nine inches, the shocks should be compressed around three inches with you aboard. This will allow your suspension to operate in **both** directions, smoothing out the terrain as you ride.

Avoid that urge to grab that tool and crank those springs as tight as they'll go! With some testing, you'll find that the suspension doesn't need to be nearly as stiff as you might think. The notion that "the higher it sits, the better" is far from reality. A supple and compliant suspension will not only make the snowmobile handle better, but will keep you from being pounded by every crack and crevice that you ride over.

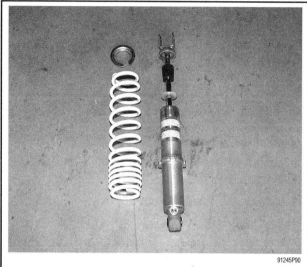

Fig. 42 Typical coil-over shock absorber assembly

ADJUSTING PRELOAD

▶ See Figures 43 and 44

There are two ways of adjusting shocks for preload. The first method uses a notched collar, which rotates around the shock body. The notched collar is part of the lower spring perch. When the tube is rotated, the graduations on the tube increase the amount of tension, or preload, on the spring.

The second type of method uses a threaded adjuster on the shock body. There are usually two threaded rings; one is the spring perch and the other is a locking nut. To adjust the preload, back off the locknut, and twist the spring perch to increase or decrease the preload. After the preload is correct, make sure to tighten the locknut.

In most cases, the spanner required to change the preload is included the tool kit that comes with your snowmobile. Use the wrench to twist the tube in order to change the preload. Don't use a screwdriver or punch to move the adjuster. You can damage the adjuster and the shock body threads by not using the proper tool.

ADJUSTING SHOCK RATES

Some snowmobiles (usually sport or high-performance models) have adjustments for tuning the compression and rebound rates of the shock, as well as a means of adjusting the preload. These adjusters can be found on the shock

Fig. 43 Most front shock absorbers have threaded adjusters to change the spring preload

Fig. 44 This sled allows front preload adjustment by simply turning the spring by hand

Fig. 45 The front skis are attached to the suspension by a single bolt

itself or in some cases, on the fluid reservoir. For optimum performance, the compression and rebound adjustments should be adjusted **after** the preload has been set properly.

Compression adjustment will affect how fast the shock travels upward, or compresses. Rebound adjustment will affect how fast the shock returns from compression (how fast the suspension bounces back). Make adjustments in small increments, to avoid losing track of your previous settings. Most adjusters "click" between adjustments, so it is easier to keep track of things. If there is no clicking mechanism, keep track of the number of turns you make. Most of the time the adjustment to the shock will take a little time to take effect, so fine tuning the compression and rebound should is better performed on the trail.

Inspection

The only periodic MAINTENANCE that should be necessary for your shock absorbers is to perform a visual inspection. Make sure that no fluid is leaking from the shock. A trickle of oil or a thick coating of oily residue (that cannot be traced to another source) is an indication that the shock has lost one or more of its seals. Since the shock depends on fluid under pressure in order to accomplish its job, once a seal is lost, the shock can no longer function properly, and must be replaced.

During a visual inspection you should take time to examine the mounting fasteners, to make sure they are tight and undamaged. Also, take a moment to inspect the spring for damage in the form of cracks along the coils. Damaged components should always be replaced to assure that you have a safe and dependable snowmobile suspension.

SKIS

♦ See Figures 45 thru 55

The front skis are probably subjected to more abuse than any other component on a snowmobile. They are constantly skidding over rocks, tree stumps, logs, and asphalt. Because they are subjected to so much abuse, they should be inspected regularly.

Inspection

To inspect the skis, the front of the snowmobile should be elevated enough to allow a decent view of the entire underside of the skis. Look for excessive wear of the runners also called carbides, or skags) and heavy gouging (plastic skis) or denting (metal skis). If the skis are severely damaged, they will not only affect steering, but they will have a hard time sliding over the snow.

The runners should be replaced whenever they become worn to the point that the steering ability is affected. This usually equates to roughly half the thickness of the runner. Typically, the runners can be replaced by simply unbolting them from the ski and replacing them with new units.

Fig. 46 To detach the ski assembly from the suspension, remove the cotter pin and pivot bolt nut . . .

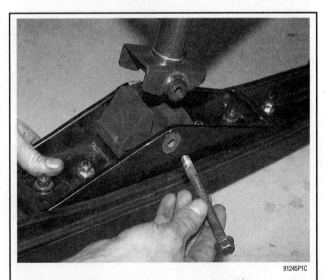

Fig. 47 . . . and remove the pivot bolt from the spindle

Fig. 48 While the ski assembly is removed, grease the pivot bushing

Fig. 51 Replacement runners are available from your local snowmobile dealer

Fig. 49 Make sure the rubber pivot stoppers are installed in the proper direction upon reassembly

Fig. 52 To replace a worn or broken ski, unbolt the metal ski mount . . .

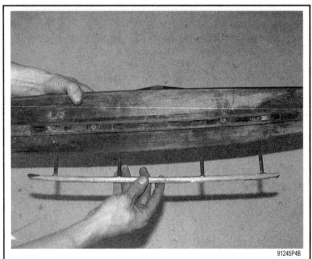

Fig. 50 The metal runners can be replaced by unbolting them from the ski

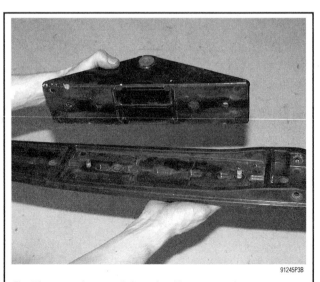

Fig. 53 . . . and remove it from the ski

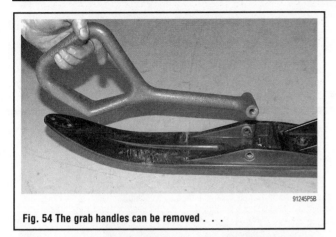
Fig. 54 The grab handles can be removed . . .

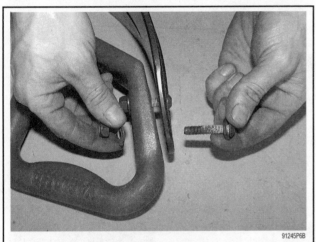
Fig. 55 . . . by simply removing the fasteners

If the skis appear to be in good condition, and the runners are not excessively worn, inspect each ski pivot by holding the steering arm stationary while trying to turn the ski from side-to-side. If there is a "clunking" feeling present, or excessive play, the pivot bushings most likely need replacement.

Replacement

If a ski is damaged and in need of replacement, removal and installation usually requires nothing more than the removal of a single bolt. Some bolts use castellated nuts with cotter pins, and others use locking nuts. In either case, make sure to use a new cotter pin (or locknut) when installing the skis.

When installing the ski, make sure to lubricate the bushing thoroughly to prevent any corrosion build-up, which can cause binding. Check with your local dealer about the type of grease to use, since some plastics may react to different types of grease. In some cases, grease may not be necessary.

✴ CAUTION

Ski pivot bolts are usually of high grade (tensile strength); using hardware store bolts of a low grade rating can cause SEVERE damage to your sled (and yourself) if a pivot bolt were to break while riding. NEVER use fasteners of unknown grade to mount the skis.

Rear Suspension & Track

REAR SUSPENSION

▶ See Figure 56

When it comes to progress, the rear suspension systems on modern snowmobiles have come a LONG way. Some of the suspension systems on modern sleds have as much travel as a motocross bike, turning snowmobiling into a whole new experience.

Along with this complex, long travel design, comes a little more maintenance. Typically, though, the only maintenance involved is lubricating the pivot points, just like the front suspension. The components of the suspension should also be inspected for wear periodically.

Fig. 56 The long-travel suspension systems of modern snowmobiles provide an ultra-plush ride on or off the trail

Inspection

▶ **See Figures 57, 58, 59 and 60**

Occasional inspection of the suspension components will help prevent problems on the trail. Since the rear suspension is underneath the sled, and out of view, it is frequently overlooked for maintenance and inspection.

Fig. 57 A jackstand can be used to elevate the track from the ground for inspection of the rear suspension and track

1. To thoroughly inspect the rear suspension, the rear of the snowmobile should be fully elevated from the ground.

2. Once the sled is safely supported, grab the slide rails and rock them back-and-forth. If a "clunking" feeling is noticed when rocking the slide rails, the pivot bushings/bearings are likely worn. As with the front suspension pivot points, there are usually no provisions for adjustment; if the bushings/bearings are worn, they must be replaced. Replacement of the bushings usually requires removal of the suspension assembly from the tunnel.

3. Next, inspect the wheels; there should not be any chips, cracks, etc. If a wheel is damaged, it can be replaced by simply unbolting it from the slide rail. When installing the wheel mounting bolt(s), it's not a bad idea to use a little bit of locking compound on the threads to keep them from vibrating loose.

4. Check the slide rails for any signs of cracking or bending. The condition of the plastic slide runners (on which the track slides) can be inspected by rotating the track while looking through the openings on the track between the metal track clips. Look for signs of excessive wear, or scratching. If the plastic slide runners are worn, replacement usually requires removal of the suspension assembly from the tunnel. Then, the plastic slide runners are removed from the slide rails with a block of wood and a mallet.

➡**Operating your snowmobile on pack snow or ice can cause overheating of the plastic slide runners. A small amount of loose snow must be present for cooling purposes in order for the plastic slide runners to be lubricated properly.**

5. Next, check the condition of the shock absorber(s), and springs. Leaking shock absorbers indicate a failing unit, and replacement will be required. Broken springs are dangerous, and should be replaced immediately.

6. Once you are finished inspecting the rear suspension, lower the snowmobile to the ground.

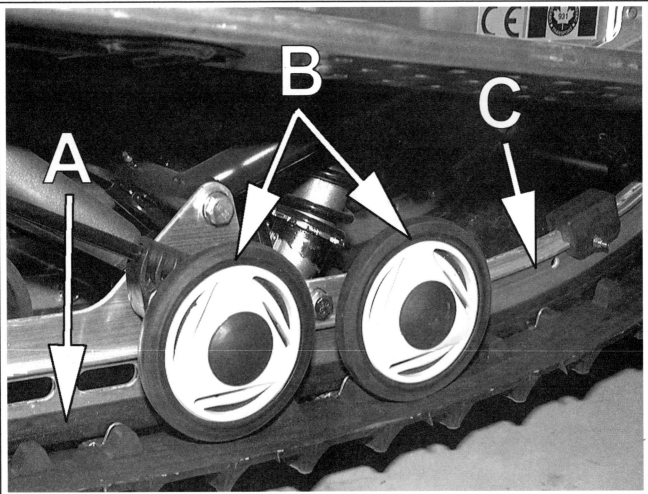

Fig. 58 The plastic slide runners (A) idler wheels (B) and rails (C) should all be closely inspected for damage and/or wear

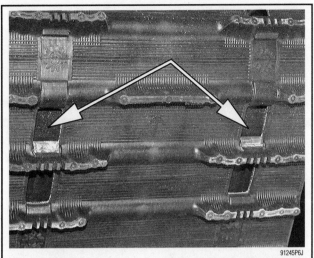

Fig. 59 The slide runners can also be inspected through the openings between the track clips

Fig. 60 Also inspect the suspension bump-stops; they should not be split or torn

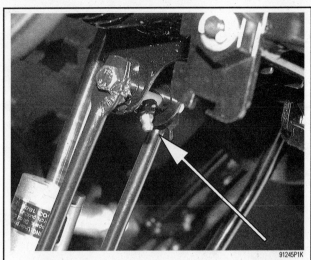

Fig. 61 Grease fittings are usually found on most pivoting points of the rear suspension

Fig. 62 Some grease fittings can be hard to find; make sure that you find all of the fittings when lubricating the suspension

Fig. 63 Most fittings are easily accessed with a grease gun . . .

Lubrication

⬥ **See Figures 61, 62, 63 and 64**

Chances are your snowmobile has fittings on the rear pivot points to lubricate the bushings/bearings. To lubricate the pivot points of the suspension, simply attach the grease gun to the fitting, and pump in fresh grease (make sure the grease in the gun is compatible with the existing grease) until the old grease begins to seep from the bushing/bearing pivot. It may be necessary to use a flexible extension on the end of the grease gun to reach some of the fittings. Wipe the excess grease from the fittings after the joints are lubricated.

If there aren't any fittings for greasing the bushings, they will have to be disassembled periodically for lubrication. This can be quite a daunting task, and might be better left to an experienced service facility.

Adjustments

When it comes to the handling characteristics of a snowmobile, the rear suspension adjustments are critical. One would think that the front suspension would have more of an effect on the handling, but the opposite holds true.

Before you get started on adjusting your suspension, it should be noted that suspension tuning is a matter of trail and error, and can be somewhat time consuming. Oftentimes, one adjustment affects another, which can cause problems. If your

Fig. 64 . . . although some might be a little tricky

Fig. 66 The front limiting straps may have adjustment holes . . .

are unsatisfied with the handling characteristics of your sled, seek advice from an experienced rider who can assist in adjusting the suspension to suit your needs.

SKI PRESSURE

▶ See Figures 65, 66, 67 and 68

The main factor controlling a snowmobile's handling characteristics is ski pressure. Ski pressure is basically the weight ratio between the front skis and

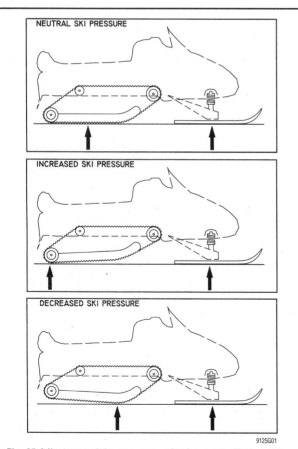

Fig. 65 Adjustment of the rear suspension has great effect on ski pressure

Fig. 67 . . . or threaded adjusters

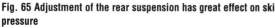

Fig. 68 Adjusting the preload on the rear shock can also change the ski pressure

the track. If too little weight is on the front skis, the snowmobile will not turn well, and will want to travel in a straight line. If there is too much weight on the front skis, the snowmobile will "plow" meaning that the skis will dig into the snow when riding.

It should be noted that the need for ski pressure will vary according to the snow conditions. When riding on hard snow, the ski pressure should be increased to allow the skis to cut into the snow and allow more precise turning. Since the surface of the snow is hard, the skis will stay on top of the snow instead of digging underneath the surface. For soft, fluffy snow, a lighter ski pressure will help to keep the skis floating on the surface, allowing better steering control.

The relationship of the pressure between the front and rear pivot points of the slide rails are what dictates ski pressure. Typically, a limiting strap (or straps) on the front of the suspension can be adjusted to control the ski pressure. Other models may rely on the amount of preload between the front and rear springs of the suspension. Because of the different designs of suspension systems, detailed adjustment procedures cannot be given. Refer to your owner's manual for the specific methods and techniques for adjusting the rear suspension.

PRELOAD

▶ **See Figures 69 thru 75**

Along with the ski pressure, the suspension preload (with the rider aboard) is another important factor in adjusting the suspension properly. Just like the front

Fig. 71 The torsion spring on the rear suspension of this sled has four different adjustment settings for changing the preload

Fig. 69 To measure the preload on the rear suspension, take a measurement of the ride height . . .

Fig. 72 A special wrench (typically included in the tool kit) can be used to change the preload

Fig. 70 . . . and then measure again with a rider aboard

Fig. 73 Coil-over type shocks, whether they have threaded adjusters . . .

Fig. 74 . . . or a notched collar, a special spanner wrench is required to change the preload setting

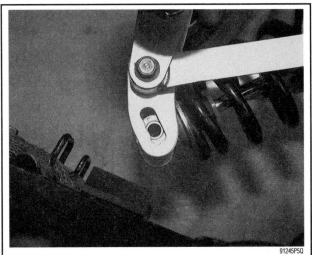

Fig. 75 Some sleds have a sticker on the drive belt guard that suggests different suspension settings for rider weight and snow conditions

skis, the ride height (or preload) should be adjusted for your weight. If the rear suspension sits at the top of its suspension travel, the ride will be harsh, since the suspension can only travel upwards because it is at its maximum height. With you aboard, and the suspension adjusted properly, the snowmobile should sit approximately one third of the total length of the available suspension travel. For example, if the total suspension travel of your snowmobile is around nine inches, the suspension should be compressed around three inches with you aboard. This will allow your suspension to operate in **both** directions, smoothing out the terrain as you ride.

There are several ways of adjusting the suspension for preload. The first method uses a notched collar, which rotates around the shock body (coil-over units). The notched collar is part of the lower spring perch. When the tube is rotated, the graduations on the tube increase the amount of tension, or preload, on the spring.

➥**Adjustment of the preload can affect ski pressure. Keep this in mind when making adjustments.**

The second type of method uses a threaded adjuster on the shock body. There are usually two threaded rings; one is the spring perch and the other is a locking nut. To adjust the preload, back off the locknut, and twist the spring perch to increase or decrease the preload. After the preload is correct, make sure to tighten the locknut.

In most cases, the spanner required to change the preload is included the tool kit that comes with your snowmobile. Use the wrench to twist the tube in

order to change the preload. Don't use a screwdriver or punch to move the adjuster. You can damage the adjuster by not using the proper tool.

Models that use torsion springs typically have two types of adjustment. The first type uses a threaded shaft that is attached to the end of the spring. When the nut is tightened on the shaft, the preload is increased. The second type employs an eccentric-mounted block. Typically, only three or four positions are allowed with this method of adjustment.

Avoid that urge to grab that tool and crank those springs as tight as they'll go! With some testing, you'll find that the suspension doesn't need to be nearly as stiff as you might think. The notion that "the higher it sits, the better" is far from reality. A supple and compliant suspension will not only make the snowmobile handle better, but will keep you from being pounded by every crack and crevice that you ride over.

SHOCK ABSORBER ADJUSTMENTS

▶ **See Figures 76 and 77**

Some snowmobiles (usually sport or high-performance models) have adjustments for tuning the compression and rebound rates of the shock, as well as a means of adjusting the preload. These adjusters can be found on the shock itself or in some cases, on the fluid reservoir. For optimum performance, the compression and rebound adjustments should be adjusted **after** the preload has been set properly.

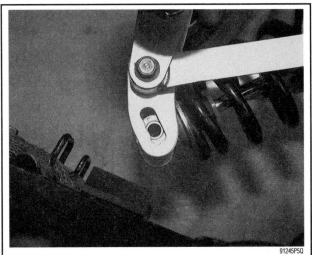

Fig. 76 Sometimes the shock can be repositioned in the suspension linkage for further adjustability

Fig. 77 The suspension on this sled has a different mounting point (arrow) for the shock absorber linkage

Compression adjustment will affect how fast the shock travels upward, or compresses. Rebound adjustment will affect how fast the shock returns from compression (how fast the suspension bounces back). Make adjustments in small increments, to avoid losing track of your previous settings. Most adjusters "click" between adjustments, so it is easier to keep track of things. If there is no clicking mechanism, keep track of the number of turns you make. Most of the time the adjustment to the shock will take a little time to take effect; fine tuning the compression and rebound should be done on the trail.

Additionally, the shock mounting points and linkage may be adjustable on some models. Each model is different, and the adjustment or repositioning of the shocks and linkage can have a drastic affect on the characteristics of the suspension. Your owner's manual should discuss the different adjustments, and the affects they have on the suspension.

TRACK

Inspection

▶ See Figures 78, 79 and 80

Keeping an eye on the condition of the track is important, not only to prevent track damage, but problems on the trail.

1. Raise and safely support the rear of the snowmobile.

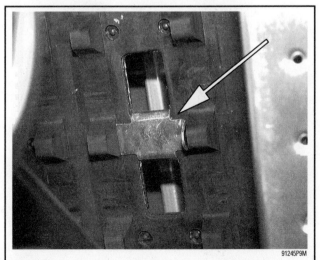

Fig. 78 To inspect and adjust the track, use a jackstand to support the rear of the snowmobile so the track is free to rotate

Fig. 79 Make sure that all of the track clips are securely attached to the track

Fig. 80 Rotate the track and inspect all of the drive lugs (arrows) for any signs of damage

2. While slowly rotating the track by hand, look for cuts, tears, and shredded cords and missing metal clips on both sides of the track. Punctures on the track may be caused by small tree stumps, or sharp rocks. Any shredding, or worn areas on the inside portion of the track indicate improper alignment or tension.

Adjustment & Alignment

▶ See Figures 81 thru 89

Just like the drive chain and cables, the track stretches over time, and requires periodic adjustment to keep it tensioned properly.

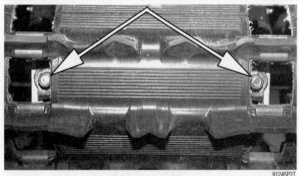

Fig. 81 Depending on the model, some track adjusters are accessed through the openings between the track clips . . .

Fig. 82 . . . and others may be located on the slide rail

Fig. 83 Before the track tension can be adjusted, remove the covers on the rear idler wheels . . .

Fig. 85 Once the rear axle is loosened, turn the adjusters as necessary to tighten (or align) the track

Fig. 84 . . . and loosen the axle

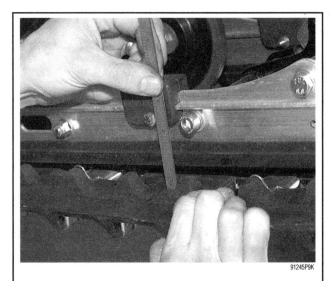

Fig. 86 Measuring track tension with a ruler

Neglecting track adjustment will cause the track to prematurely wear. If the track becomes severely loose, the teeth can "ratchet" or jump teeth on the track, which can cause damage to the track and the sprockets on the driveshaft.

Additionally, if the track is out of alignment, the lugs on the track will prematurely wear, in addition to the rear idler wheels. Also, the increased friction of the wheels rubbing the sides of the lugs on the track will cause sluggish operation.

➡ **For the most accurate track adjustment, the track should be at operating temperature.**

1. Place the snowmobile skis against a wall, and raise the rear of the snowmobile from the ground so the track can freely rotate. This will prevent the snowmobile from traveling on its own if it were to fall from the jackstand.

2. If necessary, clean the suspension and track of any snow or ice, which could affect the adjustment of the track.

3. Measure the tension on the track. The method of measuring tension can vary from one manufacturer to another, but in most cases, a spring scale should be used. The measurement of the scale in relationship to how far the track is pulled from the slide rail varies from one manufacturer to another. Refer to your owner's manual or contact a dealer for the proper measurements for your particular sled.

4. If tension is incorrect, loosen the axle shaft nut (loosen the nut just enough to allow the adjusters to move the axle) for the rear idler wheels, and tighten (or loosen) the adjusters as necessary. Make sure to turn both adjusters the same number of turns, or the track alignment may be affected.

⚙ CAUTION

Adjusting the track too tightly will cause premature wear of the plastic slide runners, idler wheels and bearings. Also, the excessive drag on the drivetrain will severely reduce performance and cause sluggish operation.

5. Once the track tension is correct, the alignment of the track will need to be checked. Make sure the sled is secure on the jackstand(s), and start the engine, and bring up the idle just enough to rotate the track.

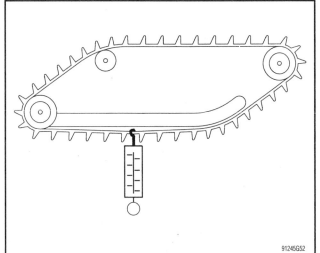

Fig. 87 Some tracks require the use of a pull scale to measure track tension

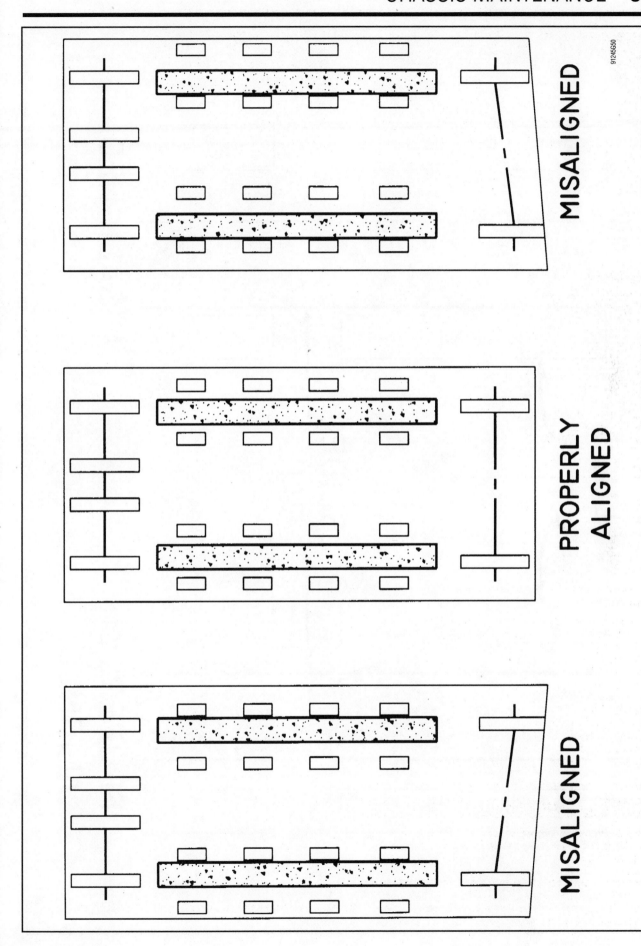

Fig. 88 In order for the track to stay centered, the driveshaft and idler wheel axle must be parallel

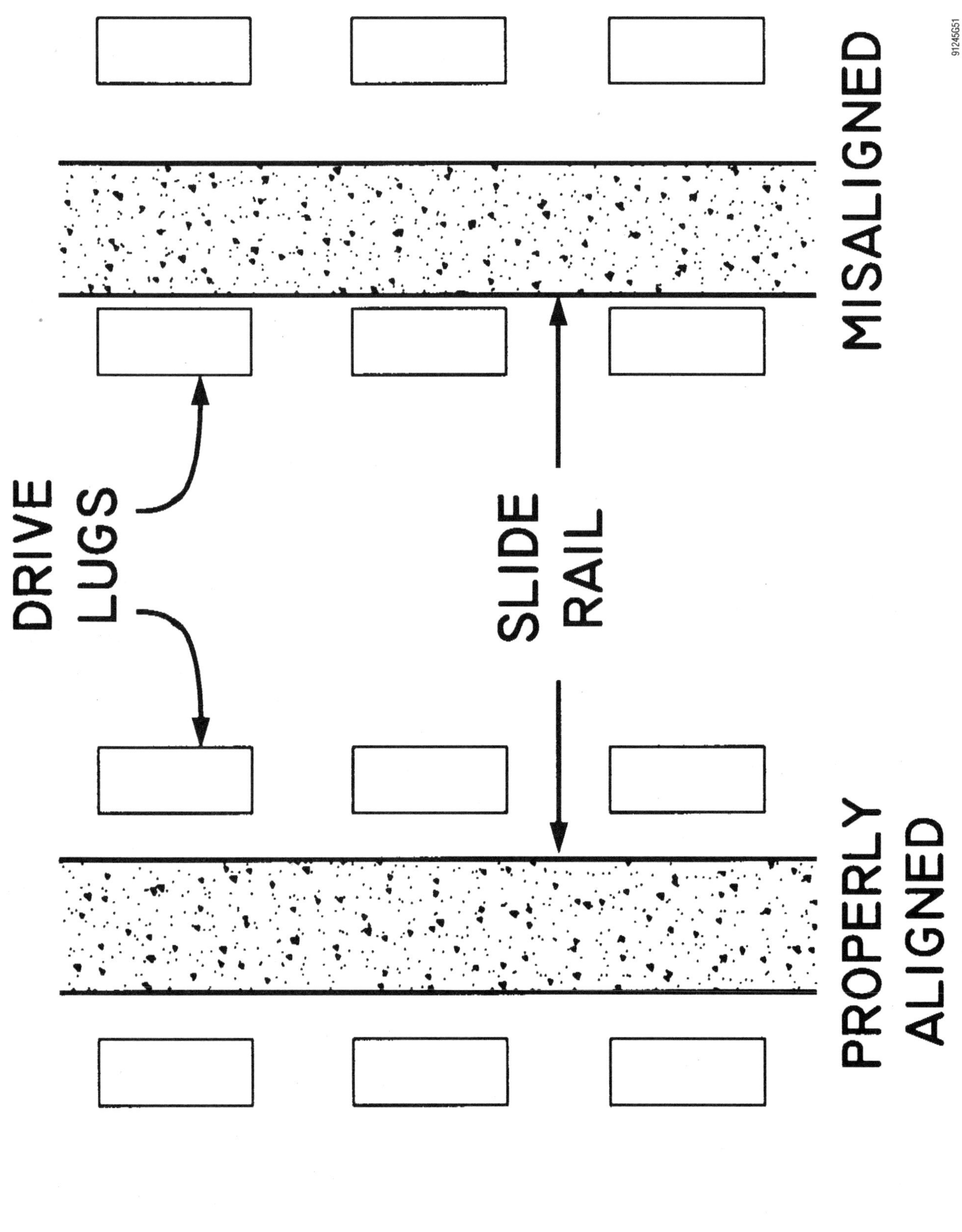

DRIVE LUGS

SLIDE RAIL

MISALIGNED

PROPERLY ALIGNED

91245G51

Fig. 89 Track alignment detail

6. After the track has rotated for a few revolutions, release the throttle and allow the track to come to a stop, **without** using the brake. Turn the engine **off.**

✻ CAUTION

REMEMBER that gasoline-powered internal combustion engines produce CARBON MONOXIDE, which can kill you. NEVER, EVER run an engine (even for a short time) in an enclosed area like a shed or a garage. ALWAYS make sure there is plenty of ventilation (meaning that all garage doors and windows are open and, if at all possible, the exhaust pipes are sticking out through them). Better yet, do it on a nice, sunny day, and perform all adjustments outside.

7. Check the distance of the drive lugs on the track in relationship to the rear idler wheels; they should be equal on both sides. If the track is shifted to one side, the adjusters can be used to center the track. If the track is shifted to the right, tighten the right side adjuster, and loosen the left side adjuster (in equal amounts). If the track is shifted to the left, tighten the left side adjuster, and loosen the right side adjuster (in equal amounts).

✻ CAUTION

NEVER attempt to adjust the alignment of the track with the engine running. Severe bodily injury will occur if body parts (fingers, hands, long hair, etc) are caught in the track. Stay clear of the track when it is rotating.

➡Another way to view the track alignment is by sighting the metal clips attached to the track in relationship to the plastic slide runners. As with the idler wheels, there should be equal spacing on both sides of the track.

8. Repeat steps 5 through 7, and check how the adjustment affected the alignment of the track. Continue to repeat the process until the distance of the drive lugs in relationship to the rear idler wheels is equal on both sides.
9. Once the track has been aligned, recheck the tension, since it might have changed from the alignment of the track.
10. Tighten all fasteners securely. If the axle shaft nut uses a cotter pin, make sure it is replaced with a new one. Cotter pins should never be reused.
11. Once the track tension and alignment is correct, lower the rear of the snowmobile from the jackstand(s).

BRAKE SYSTEM

▶ **See Figures 90 and 91**

The brake system on a snowmobile is similar to a motorcycle or ATV system, with the rotor (or brake disc) attached to the drive axle (via the chaincase), and a caliper (mechanical or hydraulic) with pads provides clamping action to stop the rotating action of the driveshaft. Instead of stopping a wheel, a snowmobile system stops the rotation of the track. Because of the manner in which the track is driven, the rotor is connected to the jackshaft, instead of the driveshaft.

Whether your snowmobile uses a mechanical caliper, or one that is hydraulically actuated, the manner in which it operates is basically the same. Obviously, if your sled has a mechanical brake, you don't need to worry about checking the fluid level in the reservoir. Refer to the sections in this heading that apply to your particular brake system.

Selecting The Proper Fluid

▶ **See Figure 92**

Selecting the proper brake fluid is as easy as looking on the cover of your master cylinder and reading the DOT type that the manufacturer calls for. You will find the cover calls for DOT 3, 4 or 5 brake fluid. In general DOT 4 fluid can be used in place of DOT 3, but NEVER mix DOT 5 fluid with DOT 3 or 4. While

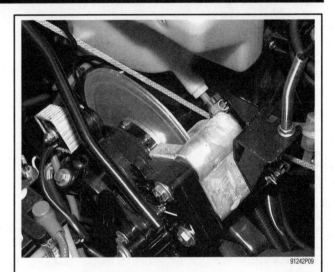

Fig. 91 . . . but some use a mechanical type

Fig. 90 The disc brake system on most snowmobiles uses a hydraulic caliper . . .

Fig. 92 Always use new fluid from an unopened bottle

DOT 3 and 4 fluids have the same general chemical properties, DOT 5 is a whole different ball game.

The difference between DOT 3 and 4 is how well the fluid resists boiling. Temperature ratings for DOT 4 are higher than those of DOT 3. DOT 5 fluids have a temperature rating like the DOT 3 and 4 fluids, but they are silicone based, and unless your brake system is designed for DOT 5, do not use it.

Silicone based DOT 5 fluids do not absorb water in the way that DOT 3 and 4 fluids do. Water contamination is what kills brake fluid and since DOT 5 fluid won't absorb moisture, it would seem that DOT 5 is the way to go. Unfortunately, when water gets into a DOT 5 brake system, it forms droplets. If a droplet gets heated to the point of boiling, it will flash into steam and cause all sorts of nastiness that will result in a loss of braking or possibly locking up the brakes. Although DOT 5 fluid is superior to DOT 3/4 fluid, simply flushing the brake system and installing DOT 5 fluid cannot be done without changing every rubber seal within the hydraulic system.

The DOT 3 and 4 brake fluids are hydroscopic, meaning they absorb fluid. As the moisture content goes up, the resistance to boiling goes down. This is the reason why it is so important to change and flush brake fluid on a regular basis. It is a good idea to change the fluid at least once a year, especially if use your brakes more severely than the average rider.

The brand of brake fluid isn't very critical as long as you choose a high quality name brand or the manufacturers offering. There are "racing" brake fluids out there, but unless they meet a DOT rating, their use is not recommended. The cost of brake fluid is fairly small compared to the job it performs, so don't skimp on quality here!

Checking & Adding Fluid

▶ **See Figures 93 thru 99**

Take a quick glance in your owner's manual. You will find exact instructions on how to check your brake fluid. In general, it is as simple as looking at a translucent reservoir or into a sight glass. The trick is finding out if the handlebars need to be turned one way or the other to make an accurate check. Most likely you will have to turn the handlebars so that the master cylinder is level.

If your snowmobile doesn't have a translucent reservoir or a sight glass, you may have to take the lid off to check the level. Be sure to clean off the fill cover before removing it. You don't want any dirt to fall in and contaminate the system.

➡**If the level is excessively low, you have worn pads, or a leak somewhere in the system. Investigate the cause of the low level before adding fluid.**

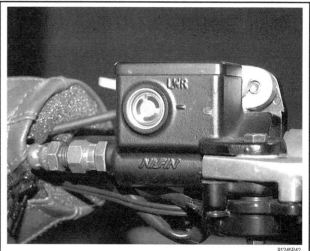

Fig. 94 Most reservoirs have a sight glass for viewing the fluid level in the reservoir

Fig. 95 Pay attention to the warnings and instructions on the reservoir cap

Fig. 93 The fluid reservoir for the disc brake is usually located on the handlebars

Fig. 96 Reservoir caps are held in place by two screws

Fig. 97 Once the screws are removed, carefully remove the cap . . .

Fig. 98 . . . and add fluid as required

Fig. 99 Make sure to push the diaphragm back in before replacing the cap

Bleeding & Flushing

A mushy feeling at the brake lever is most often due to air in the lines. This can happen if the fluid level drops too low, or if a line or hose is disconnected for any reason. This requires brake bleeding to remove the air.

Brake bleeding can be done manually, where the fluid is pumped out using the master cylinder, can be performed using a vacuum pump, or by gravity. A vacuum pump sucks the old fluid out through the bleeder. Gravity bleeding allows the fluid to flow out over a period of time. Manual bleeding is the most common method. Vacuum bleeding is very quick, but requires use of a vacuum pump. One small drawback of vacuum bleeding though, is air sometimes is sucked through the threads of the bleeder, and can obscure the vision of real air bubbles in the fluid. Gravity bleeding is the easiest, but it can take a while and might not dislodge stubborn air bubbles.

Certain precautions should be taken when working with brake fluid:

• Brake fluid absorbs moisture very quickly, and then becomes useless. Therefore, NEVER use fluid from an old or unsealed container.

• Do not mix brake fluids of different types.

• DOT 3 or 4 hydraulic disc brake fluid is recommended for almost all snowmobiles at the time of publication, but you should check your owner's manual to be sure.

• Brake fluid will quickly remove paint Avoid damage to the gas tank and bodywork by placing a protective cover over painted surfaces.

MANUAL BLEEDING

▶ See Figure 100

1. The snowmobile should be on a level surface. If you're using a workstand or lift, make sure the snowmobile is completely level.

2. Obtain a length of transparent plastic hose that will fit tightly over the bleed nipple of the brake caliper. Also, a small cup or plastic bottle will be needed to drain the excess fluid into. Make sure the container will not be attacked by the brake fluid (like a styrofoam cup).

3. Place an appropriately sized box-end wrench over the bleeder valve.

4. Fit the plastic hose to the bleed nipple, and put the other end in the cup, which should have an inch or so of new brake fluid inside. Be sure that the end of the hose is below the surface of the fluid in the cup. This will prevent air from being sucked into the system when the bleeder valve is open.

➡ The hose should not have any sharp bends or kinks; it should loop up from the bleed nipple, and then down towards the cup.

5. Check that the fluid level is topped up to the indicated line.

6. Apply the brake lever slowly several times, then hold it.

7. While holding the brake lever, loosen the caliper bleed nipple. The brake lever will be pulled towards the handgrip and fluid will be forced through the plastic hose. Try to tighten the bleed nipple before the lever bottoms out. Since

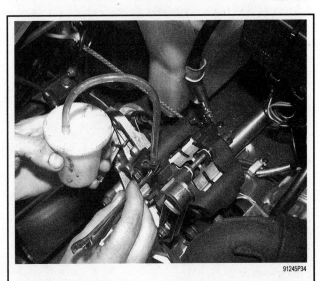

Fig. 100 Manually bleeding the air from the hydraulic brake system

the caliper is on the opposite side of the brake lever on most snowmobiles, this may be easier with an assistant.

8. Note the brake fluid being forced out of the plastic hose. If there was air in the lines, air bubbles will be noted coming out of the hose.

9. Slowly pump up the lever again until resistance is felt, then hold it, and loosen the nipple as before, again checking the fluid being forced out. When air bubbles no longer appear from the plastic hose, the system is bled of air.

➡ **If the fluid level in the reservoir drops too low during the bleeding procedure, air could be drawn into the system, requiring the procedure to be repeated.**

10. Be sure that the master cylinder reservoir is kept full during the bleeding procedure. Top off the fluid level in the reservoir and install the cap when completed.

VACUUM BLEEDING

Vacuum bleeding requires the use of a vacuum pump. The pump can be handheld, or driven from a compressed air source. Basically, a vacuum is applied to the bleeder screw and then the screw is opened. The fluid is sucked from the system along with any trapped air. The bleeder screw is tightened when done and the fluid reservoir topped off. If you choose to use this method, follow the directions provided with the vacuum pump. Be careful not to suck all the fluid from the system!

GRAVITY BLEEDING

To gravity bleed a hydraulic brake system, simply attach a hose to the bleeder nipple and place the open end in a container. Open the bleeder nipple and let the fluid flow out. Keep the reservoir topped off and check the progress from time to time. The longer you let it go, the more bleeding you have done.

FLUSHING THE BRAKE SYSTEM

The procedure for flushing a brake system is identical to that for bleeding, except that the process should be continued until new brake fluid begins to issue from the plastic hose. Remove as much of the old fluid from the reservoir as possible before you start and top off with new. You will begin by pumping out the old fluid with the lever while adding the new fluid in its place. After the new fluid starts coming out, begin checking for air bubbles and continue until you get a solid flow with no bubbles present.

Brake Lines

INSPECTION

Periodically check condition of the hoses and lines. Be sure that all hoses are arranged as the manufacturer intended, and are properly mounted. Check for abrasion damage. Check banjo fittings for signs of seepage.

Over a period of time, brake hoses tend to get hard and lose their flexibility. They can become prone to cracking both internally and externally. Even a hose that looks good on the outside can be breaking down on the inside leading to restricted flow or trapped pressure in the system.

If you have an older snowmobile and you have any doubts to the condition of the brake hoses, replace them. There are many choices available in replacement hose; you can buy original equipment hose, aftermarket hoses or high performance braided steel or Kevlar hoses. The choice is yours.

REPLACEMENT

1. Before attacking your snowmobile's brake hoses or lines, inspect the hoses and compare the replacements with the originals. Make sure they are identical. Hoses that are too short or too long can cause problems with routing or performance.

2. Make a diagram of the brake line and hose routing before you even THINK about digging out your tools. Note the location of every clip, tab, and bracket that the lines go through. If any of them are damaged, get a replacement for it (maybe two). If the line is not correctly routed, you will be replacing it a lot sooner than you think.

3. Protect the paint or bodywork near where you will be working as spilled brake fluid can be harmful to surfaces. This is true for DOT 3 and 4 fluids as DOT 5 silicone fluids aren't as reactive to paint, but you should still be careful.

4. Remove the brake fluid from the master cylinder using a siphon or suction bulb.

5. Clean the connections of dirt and crud. This will prevent dirt from entering the system. In the case of flare nut fittings, clean the area between the nut and the tube. This will make spinning the nut off easier.

6. If the hose connection is a flare nut, use a backup wrench on the female side of the connection and a flare nut wrench on the nut itself.

7. Install the new hose or line and route it in the same manner as the original.

8. Make the connections at either end and tighten them securely. Use new copper washers on the banjo fittings to prevent leaks.

9. Check the lines for interference. Turn the handlebars from side-to-side and make sure nothing binds or kinks.

10. Fill and bleed the system as required.

11. Apply pressure to the system and check the connections for leaks.

Brake Pads

INSPECTION

1. Pads should be replaced when they are worn to the limit lines. These are cut outs or grooves cut into the friction material and indicate the minimum thickness limit. Other types will have tab wear indicators. For others still, the manufacturer will specify minimum pad thickness. In any case, continuing to use a set of brake pads until all of the friction material is gone from the backing plate should be avoided at all costs, since the brake rotor will be destroyed by contact with the backing plate metal.

2. The master cylinder fluid level is usually inscribed on the master cylinder. The fluid level may drop slightly over a period of time as the pads wear, but this drop will be slight. Do not top up a master cylinder reservoir whose level has dropped slightly due to pad wear, since the level will return to the normal level when new pads are fitted. An exception, of course, will be made if braking effectiveness is reduced due to a low level. By then, air may have been introduced to the system, requiring bleeding.

3. Also, check the surface of the brake rotor for scoring, grooves, hot spots, warping, or any other damage. This can be done by sighting the edge of the rotor while spinning the jackshaft. A dial indicator may be used, but a simple visual test is usually sufficient.

REPLACEMENT

Procedures will vary according to the make and model of the snowmobile, but all have basic points in common:

• When new pads are fitted, avoid hard braking if possible for at least the first few rides to give the new pads a chance to seat themselves.

• Brake fluid and solvents must be kept off the brake pads.

• A few older design calipers must be adjusted periodically. This procedure should be outlined in your shop manual or owner's manual.

There are many different styles of brake calipers, each with a different method of removing the pads. In general, disc brake calipers fall into two categories: fixed, and sliding (or floating).

Sliding And Floating Calipers

Sliding and floating calipers have one or more pistons working on one side of the caliper. When the piston presses the pad against the rotor, the caliper slides over and applies the pad on the opposite side as well. Most of the time these calipers will have two rubber bellows on pins from which the caliper body slides; this is the floating type. The sliding type moves on machined areas of the calipers and doesn't use pins.

SLIDING CALIPER

1. Remove the mounting hardware and pull the caliper from the chaincase, or mounting brackets.

2. Remove the pads from the caliper.

3. Clean the body of the caliper and the surface on which the pads move. Lubricate the sliding surfaces.

4. Remove some brake fluid from the reservoir if the level is at or near the full mark.

5. Compress the piston back into the caliper body with either your hands or with a large pair of pliers. If the caliper has a mechanical park brake, make sure to back out the adjusting screw.

> ⁕⁕ **WARNING**
>
> **When compressing the piston back into the caliper body, be very careful not to pinch or damage the dust boot.**

6. Install the new pads and replace the pad retention screw, if equipped. Use non-permanent thread locking compound on the screw.

7. Mount the caliper onto the chaincase or mounting bracket. Use locking compound on the caliper bracket bolts to keep them from vibrating loose.

8. Apply the brakes to seat the pads. Pump the lever until it firms up.

9. Adjust the parking brake as necessary.

10. Check the level of brake fluid, and top off it if necessary.

11. Bleed the brakes as necessary.

FLOATING CALIPER

1. The caliper must be dismounted to change the pads. Loosen any clamps or brackets holding the brake line to the snowmobile. This will keep the metal line from being bent or the hose from twisting severely.

2. Unbolt the caliper from the chaincase and pull it off the mounting. Always support the caliper to keep the brake line from being stressed.

3. If equipped, remove the pad retaining pin(s). The pin(s) may be held by a clip or screwed into the body of the caliper.

4. Remove the pads from the caliper.

5. Clean the body of the caliper and where the pads move. Lubricate the surfaces on which the pads slide.

6. Remove some brake fluid from the reservoir if the level is at or near the full mark.

7. Compress the piston(s) back into the caliper body with either your hands or a large pair of pliers. A C-clamp can also be used. If the caliper is equipped with a mechanical park brake, make sure to back out the adjusting screw.

> ⁕⁕ **WARNING**
>
> **When compressing the piston back into the caliper body, be very careful not to pinch or damage the dust boot.**

8. Install the new pads and replace the pad retention pin with its clip. You may have to slide the caliper to get the holes in the pads to line up with the pins on some designs.

9. Install the caliper and tighten the mounting bolts. Use a threadlocking compound to prevent the caliper bolts from loosening.

10. Install any clips and brackets holding the brake lines or hoses.

11. Apply the brakes to seat the pads. Pump the lever until it becomes firm.

12. Adjust the parking brake mechanism as necessary.

13. Check the level of brake fluid, and top off it if necessary.

14. Bleed the brakes as necessary.

Fixed Calipers

Fixed calipers can be identified by their opposed pistons. A fixed caliper doesn't move during brake application. Fixed calipers are firmly bolted to the suspension and have no moving portion as does a sliding or pivoting caliper.

There are two types of fixed calipers: open back and closed back. Open back calipers have an opening from which the brake pads are removed and installed. Closed back calipers require the removal of the caliper to change the brake pads.

There are many different fixed calipers mounted on snowmobiles, but they all change the pads in a similar fashion.

OPEN BACK

▶ **See Figures 101 thru 108**

1. If equipped, remove the caliper dust cover to expose the tops of the pads and the pad retaining pins.

2. The pad retaining pins will either have to be knocked out with a punch from the back side, unthreaded, or just or simply pulled out by hand after a retaining clip is removed.

3. After removing the pins, remove the spring from the caliper. This spring keeps the pads retracted when the brakes aren't applied, and also keeps the pads from rattling. Make a note of how the spring fits.

4. Remove some brake fluid from the reservoir if the level is at or near the full mark.

5. Remove the pads and carefully press the pistons back into their bores with a C-clamp or pliers. If the opposite piston pushes out while you push in the other one, place a pad or piece of wood between it and the rotor to keep it from moving out. Do not pry on the rotor when pushing in the piston as you can bend or crack it. If the caliper has an integrated mechanical parking brake, back out the adjustment screw.

6. Clean the caliper of brake dust and road grime. Dirt can prevent proper action of the caliper.

7. Drop in the new pads and align the holes for the pad retaining pin(s).

8. Install the spring and the pad retaining pin(s). The spring may be held under the pins in some designs.

9. Pump up the brakes until you see the pads compress against the rotor. Check that both sides apply at the same time.

10. Adjust the mechanical parking brake as necessary.

11. Install the dust shield, if equipped.

12. Check the level of brake fluid and top off. Bleed the brakes as necessary.

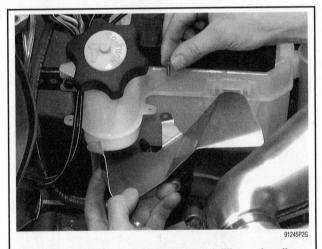

Fig. 101 Some sleds have a shield to prevent spilling engine oil onto the caliper and rotor; it may need to be removed to access the caliper

Fig. 102 The pad retaining pins on this caliper are held in place by small hitch pins, but . . .

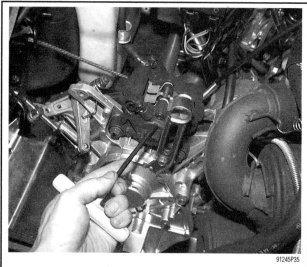

Fig. 103 . . . others might be screwed in place . . .

Fig. 106 . . . be sure to keep track of the manner in which the spring clips are mounted

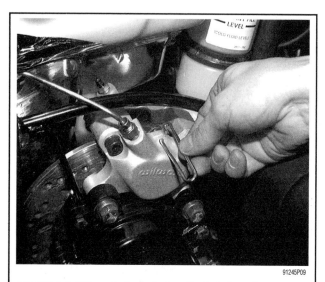

Fig. 104 or held by a single pin that unclips from the caliper

Fig. 107 Once the retaining pins and spring clips are removed, the pads can be pulled out of the caliper

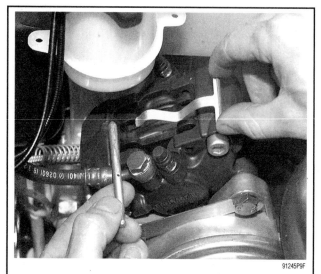

Fig. 105 When removing the retaining pin(s) . . .

Fig. 108 With the pads removed, check for signs of leakage from the caliper pistons

CLOSED BACK

1. The caliper must be dismounted to change the pads. If necessary, loosen the clamps or brackets holding the brake line. This will keep the lines from being bent or the hoses from twisting severely.

2. Unbolt the caliper and pull it away from the mounting. Support the caliper so it doesn't hang on the brake line.

3. Remove the pad retaining pin(s). A pin may be held by a clip or screwed into the body of the caliper.

4. Remove the pads from the caliper.

5. Clean the body of the caliper and the surfaces on which the pads move.

6. Remove some brake fluid from the reservoir if the level is at or near the full mark.

7. Using a C-clamp, carefully compress the pistons back into the caliper body. Don't force the piston; moderate force should be all that is required. If you're working on a caliper with an integrated mechanical parking brake, make sure to back out the adjusting screw.

✴✴ WARNING

When compressing the piston back into the caliper body, be very careful not to pinch or damage the dust boot.

8. Install the new pads.

9. Install the pad retention pin(s) with its clip or by screwing them in place.

10. Install the caliper on the snowmobile and tighten the mounting bolts. Use a threadlocking compound to prevent the caliper bolts from loosening.

11. Install the clips and brackets holding the brake lines or hoses.

12. Apply the brakes to seat the pads. Pump the lever until it gets firm.

13. Check the level of brake fluid, and top it off if necessary.

14. Bleed the brakes as necessary.

ELECTRICAL SYSTEM MAINTENANCE

Battery

▶ **See Figure 109**

Some snowmobiles (typically touring/cross-country models) are equipped with batteries, usually for electric starting. If your sled doesn't use a battery, well quite honestly, you can skip this section. If you do in fact have a battery in your sled, then read on.

The battery is like a pet goldfish; it needs little to keep it alive, but it has a limited life. Feed it properly, and keep its environment clean, and it will live as long as it can. Neglect or abuse it and you will find it belly up at the most inopportune times.

Fig. 109 Snowmobiles equipped with batteries need frequent maintenance to cope with cold weather conditions

CHECKING FLUID LEVEL

Most batteries, up until recently, have been classified as "wet cells" meaning that the electrolyte in the unit has been in liquid form and the level of fluid had to be topped off at times. All snowmobile and motorcycle type batteries uses two dissimilar materials with some type of electrolyte between them. Wet cell batteries that we need to check are what most of us are used to, but recent advances have brought maintenance-free sealed batteries to the snowmobile world. Sealed batteries make routine electrolyte checking unnecessary.

Standard batteries can have some of the electrolytes water portion dissipate with time. Water is needed to bring the level back up to the proper point.

All batteries have some type of electrolyte in them, but sealed batteries recycle the fluid in them and don't lose it to the atmosphere as a standard battery would. As a result, you do not need to check the fluid level in a sealed battery.

Standard batteries will have a level range marked on the case. There will be a high and low level mark. They may have the words "High" and "Low" marked on them or just be a set of parallel lines. If there are no lines, there will be a level tab in the inside of the filler hole.

1. The level of the electrolyte must be maintained between the lines or up to the level tab. Check in all six cells, not just an end one. Some snowmobiles will require that a side panel be removed or the battery removed from the snowmobile completely to see all six cells.

2. If the fluid needs to be topped off, gain clear access to the top of the battery and clean the top with a clean rag to remove any dirt.

3. Remove the cell cap and use a small funnel to add distilled water to the cell. Bring the level up to the mark. Do not use battery acid or the balance of the electrolyte will be effected. Fill only to the mark; do not overfill.

➡**Only pure, distilled water should be used as regular water contains minerals and chemicals that can contaminate the battery.**

4. Do this to all the cells that need it and replace the caps tightly.

TESTING THE BATTERY

1. With the engine not running, the battery voltage should be 12.6 volts minimum (12 volt system) or 6.3 volts (6 volt system). If the voltage is lower than this, charge the battery and let sit off the charger for 3 or 4 hours. Recheck the voltage. If the voltage is still low, the battery is bad. If the battery holds the voltage, look for problems with the charging system.

2. If the battery allows for individual cells to be checked (rare nowadays), each cell should read a minimum of 2.1 volts. If nothing else, all the cells should read about the same. If one is lower than the rest, replace the battery.

3. Remove the caps to the battery and test the electrolyte with a hydrometer. The hydrometer will indicate the state of charge in each cell by measuring the specific gravity of the electrolyte. Read the instructions that came with the hydrometer to learn how to interpret the scale on the tool. Some have floating balls and others have pointers. All the cells should have similar readings otherwise you will need to replace the battery due to a dead cell.

CLEANING THE BATTERY

1. Remove the battery and clean the outer casing with a solution of baking soda and water. Baking soda will neutralize acid. Make sure the caps are on good and tight.

✴✴ WARNING

NEVER let even a small amount of the baking soda solution enter the battery through any means. Baking soda is a "basic" substance (meaning that on the pH scale it is the opposite of an acid). Acids and bases will neutralize each other when combined, that is why you use it to clean the outside of the battery and the area surrounding the battery in the first place. Should some of the solution make it inside the battery, the electrolyte will be ruined.

2. Clean the battery connections and terminals with the same baking soda and water solution. Inspect the cables for frayed ends and corroded wires.

3. Still using the solution, clean the battery tray. Inspect the tray for damage and corrosion. If the tray is rusty (metal trays), consider cleaning it and repainting it. If the corrosion isn't fixed, the battery tray will not live a long life.

4. Install the battery and use some terminal protection gel on the connections. You can buy this at any auto parts supply and it will help keep the white powder from attacking for a while.

SELECTING & PREPPING A REPLACEMENT BATTERY

Since a dead battery can take the fun out of riding, you want to use a good quality battery in your snowmobile at all times. Batteries can get expensive, but if you take good care of your battery, it should last for many seasons.

Use a high quality battery. You can't go wrong with the factory-supplied battery, but they tend to be expensive. You can go with the aftermarket, but find out from your riding pals what brands they have had good luck with. Yuasa® batteries are an excellent replacement for a stock battery, and in some cases, better than what the manufacturer supplies. Yuasa offers batteries for almost every snowmobile and motorcycle application on the planet, so you're bound to find one for your snowmobile.

Find the proper sized battery both physically and in terms of power. The battery needs to fit well in the stock battery tray and to be held by the battery hold-downs, plus the terminals must match. The battery needs to have at least (or more capacity, if your snowmobile has electrical accessories) the electrical capacity of the original. Most snowmobile batteries are rated in amp hours. This number will be printed on the case of the battery or in the literature that came with the battery.

If you are searching for a new battery for your snowmobile, consider replacing a conventional battery with a maintenance-free sealed unit. The price of a sealed battery may be higher than a conventional unit, but the benefits by far outweigh the additional cost.

If you decide to buy a new battery from a mail order warehouse, chances are it will be shipped to you with the electrolyte in a separate container. In most cases, this is true whether you buy a sealed maintenance-free battery, or a conventional battery. Keeping the battery dry indefinitely extends its shelf life, and also ensures that the battery is "new" when it is received. Of course this is requires that you, the consumer, add the electrolyte to the battery. This is a simple procedure, and in the case of the batteries that were supplied to us by Yuasa®, complete instructions were provided to make things easier. We have shown filling both conventional and maintenance-free batteries just to give you an idea of what is involved with setting up a new battery.

➡**After filling a new battery with electrolyte, it should be charged to full capacity before placing the battery back into the snowmobile. Some maintenance-free batteries may not require an initial charge, but in most cases, a new battery must be charged before use. Failure to charge a new battery will permanently decrease the power output, and severely shorten its service life. Always follow the instructions that come with a new battery regarding charging procedures. Improper setup will ruin a new battery.**

Conventional Battery

▶ **See Figures 110 thru 116**

1. Remove the cell caps on the new battery.
2. Cut the tip from the plastic bottle and place the filler tube onto the tip.

✳ CAUTION

When handling electrolyte, always wear eye protection. Electrolyte is a caustic acid, and can cause blindness if it comes in contact with your eyes.

3. Place the filler tube in a cell, and slowly tip the bottle, allowing the electrolyte to fill the cell. Repeat with all of the cells.

4. Let the battery sit for 15-20 minutes, and check the level of each cell. Top off the level of any low cells.

5. Let the battery sit (without the caps installed) for 30 minutes.

6. Attach a battery charger to the new battery, and charge it for the time specified by the manufacturer. This is a very important step; make absolutely certain that the battery has fully charged before use.

Fig. 110 This conventional battery came complete with electrolyte, new terminal bolts, and complete instructions

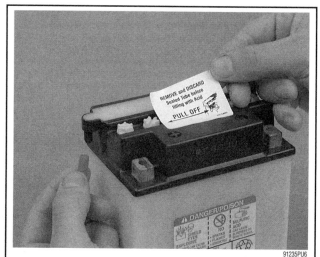

Fig. 111 First, remove the cap on the vent and remove the sticker . . .

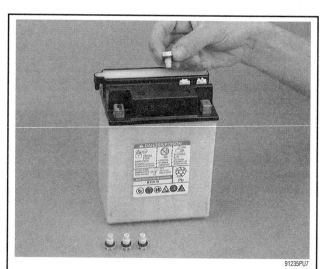

Fig. 112 . . . then remove the caps for the cells. The battery is now ready for electrolyte

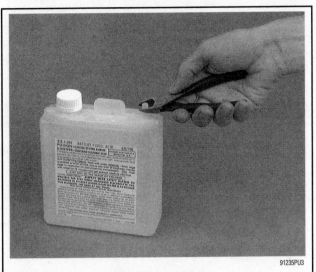

Fig. 113 Cut the cap off the electrolyte container . . .

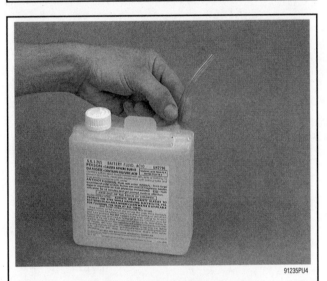

Fig. 114 . . . then place the vent tube on the container . . .

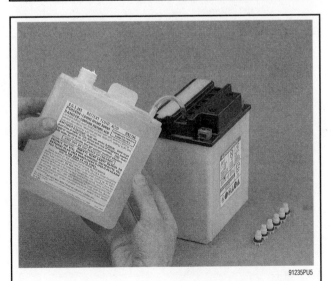

Fig. 115 . . . and use it to carefully fill each cell with electrolyte

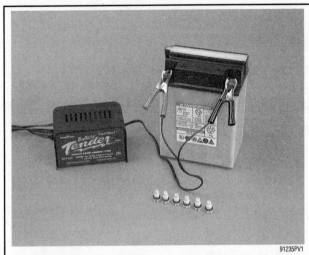

Fig. 116 After sitting for 30 minutes, top off the cells and pre-charge according to the battery manufacturer's instructions

Maintenance-free Battery

▶ **See Figures 117 thru 124**

1. Remove the plastic or metal foil seal that covers the cell caps.
2. Remove the plastic caps on the electrolyte bottle. Do not discard the caps; they are the caps for the cells of the battery.
3. Align the tips of the electrolyte bottle with the cells; then press down on the electrolyte bottle, breaking the foil seals on each of the tips. This should be done in a quick motion to avoid spilling electrolyte from the bottle.

❄❄ CAUTION

When handling electrolyte, always wear eye protection. Electrolyte is a caustic acid, and can cause blindness if it comes in contact with your eyes.

4. Allow the bottle to empty into the cells. Once the cells are full, let the battery sit for 30 minutes.
5. Charge the battery as the manufacturer specifies. As stated earlier, some maintenance-free batteries may not require a charge.
6. Install the caps onto the top of the battery.

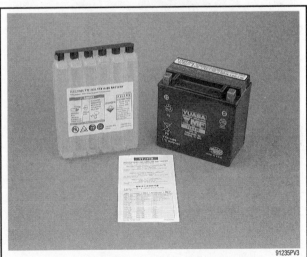

Fig. 117 When it comes time to replace the battery in your snowmobile, sealed batteries make an excellent replacement

Fig. 118 Remove the metal foil seal that covers the cells to prepare the battery for adding electrolyte

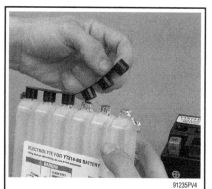

Fig. 119 Next, remove the plastic caps on the electrolyte bottle

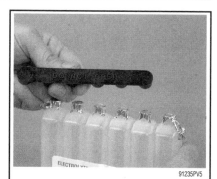

Fig. 120 On this battery, do not discard the caps, for they serve as the sealing caps in service

Fig. 121 Carefully align the tips on the electrolyte bottle with the openings on the battery, then press down on the bottle evenly to break the foil seals on the bottle

Fig. 122 Allow the electrolyte to drain into the cells until the bottle is completely empty

Fig. 123 Next, position the sealing caps . . .

Fig. 124 . . . and firmly press them into place. The battery is now permanently sealed and ready for use

BATTERY CHARGERS

▶ **See Figures 125 and 126**

There will be a time in your snowmobile's life that it will need to have some extra help in the form of a battery charger. When looking for a charger for your car, almost any will do, but a snowmobile is a different animal. A snowmobile battery is quite a bit smaller than a car battery and its needs are different.

If you use a car battery charger on a snowmobile battery, you can boil out all the electrolyte and kill it. The charging requirements for the battery are much lower and are in the range of 2 amps or less. If you have no choice and have to

use a car battery charger, choose the lowest power range (typically 2 amps) and check the battery often during the charge. If it is getting hot or bubbling excessively, remove it from the charger.

The best bet for charging a snowmobile battery is using a specialized snowmobile and motorcycle battery charger. Probably the most convenient is a smart charger such as the Deltran Battery Tender®. This type of charger will provide a low charging rate (say something around 1.25 amps) until the battery is completely charged and then switch to a safe storage rate. This storage rate will keep the battery at peak condition indefinitely and not harm the battery. This is a great feature for seasonal riders, since you can leave the battery plugged into the charger until you are ready to ride.

Fig. 125 The Battery Tender® from Deltran allows for continuous charging without the fear of damaging the battery

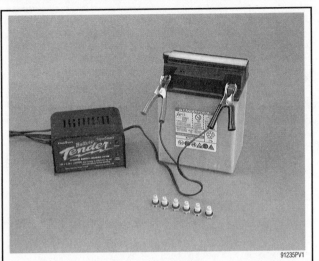

Fig. 126 When charging a conventional battery, be sure to remove the cell caps to allow gasses from the electrolyte to escape

Fig. 127 To replace a headlight, remove the socket . . .

*** CAUTION

USE EXTREME CARE when charging a battery. The process that occurs when charging or discharging a battery allows explosive hydrogen gas to escape from the electrolyte. Any source of ignition (including sparks or open flame) could case a violent explosion of the battery and casing. Besides the normal dangers associated with an explosion, this would also shower the surrounding area with hydrochloric acid. Obviously this could seriously injure or possible even kill anyone within close vicinity of the battery.

Be careful of low priced battery chargers with questionable monitoring circuits. They may not have the smarts to keep your battery from overcharging and boiling off. If you chose a low priced unit, keep an eye on the battery to make sure it is doing OK and not getting hot or off gassing too much.

Some battery chargers come with a harness that you can connect directly to you battery and plug in the charger instead of having to use big clips on the terminals. Some chargers will have a plug that will match the accessory power port on the snowmobile. If your snowmobile doesn't have a power port, it is easy to attach one.

Light Bulbs

Visibility is of paramount importance to a snowmobile rider at night. If you can't see the terrain ahead, then you are in deep trouble. If other riders cannot see you, you can be in even more trouble.

REPLACEMENT

Headlights

▶ See Figures 127, 128, 129 and 130

Headlights come in two general camps: either a sealed beam unit, or a reflector/bulb combination. The latter is the more popular technology as it provides better lighting.

Sealed beam bulbs get replaced as a unit, reflector and all. Reflector/bulb type lamps just need the bulb to be replaced. Most sealed beams can be replaced by an H4 type reflector/bulb lamp unit from the aftermarket. These units will provide superior lighting and replaceable bulbs with a choice of wattage.

The headlight can be held by a retaining ring or in a nacelle or maybe it will be built into the cowl. There are about as many different mounting schemes as there are snowmobiles.

1. If the headlight is held by a retaining ring, remove the ring and pull the lamp forward.

2. If the lamp is held in a nacelle, you may have to remove the nacelle to access the wiring and plug for the lamp.

Fig. 128 . . . then lift off the rubber gasket

Fig. 129 Most headlight bulbs are held in place by a spring clip

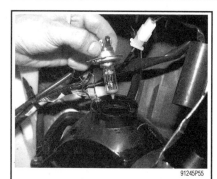

Fig. 130 ALWAYS handle the bulb by the metal base; touching the bulb will severely shorten its life

Fig. 131 To change the tail light bulb, remove the lens . . .

Fig. 132 . . . and twist the bulb from the housing

3. Disconnect the plug from the back of the bulb.

4. If the lamp is a sealed beam unit, remove the lamp. If the lamp is a separate bulb, pull of the rubber cover and unclip the retainer. Pull the bulb out of the housing.

5. Replace the sealed beam with a new bulb and plug in the connector. Install the retaining ring. If you are replacing just a bulb, be sure **not to touch the glass on the new bulb** with your skin or the life of the bulb will be severely reduced. If the bulb was touched, clean it with alcohol and a lint-free wipe. Install the retainer and rubber cover.

6. Install any removed parts and check the aim of the light. Adjust if needed.

Tail lights/Brake lights

▶ See Figures 131 and 132

Most bulbs for running lights (tail lights) are held in the reflectors under the lens, and simply removing the lens allows access to the bulb. The lens may be secured by a couple screws, or in some cases, the lens is snap-fit in place. Sometimes the entire housing will have to be removed from the snowmobile and disassembled to access the bulb.

1. Remove the lens or housing. The mounting screws can be hidden behind a piece of bodywork or buried in a tail housing. Look for screws, bolts or thumbscrews that will need to be removed.

2. Remove the bulb from the socket.

3. Check the socket for corrosion or damage. Light corrosion can be removed by cleaning with a contact cleaner available at auto parts stores or electronics stores. Heavy corrosion may require replacement of the socket or maybe the entire housing if the socket isn't available separately.

4. Clean the interior of the lens, removing any accumulated dust and dirt.

5. Clean the lens with soapy water and dry before installation.

6. Replace the bulb with a proper part. Be careful that you install the proper wattage and size bulb, otherwise the light may not work correctly or could damage the socket and lens. You may want to use a dab of dielectric grease to protect the socket from corrosion.

7. Install the lens and housing. Check the bulb for proper operation.

Dash Panel Lights

▶ See Figures 133, 134 and 135

Dash panel lights, or instrument panel lights can typically be accessed from the rear of the instrument cluster, when the engine cowl is lifted. The rubber sockets typically pull straight out from the rear of the gauge, but some models may use a plastic socket that must be twisted for removal.

1. Open the cowl for the engine compartment.

2. Grasp the bulb socket and pull it out from the rear of the gauge. Some models may have a plastic socket that twists a quarter turn to allow for removal.

3. Remove the bulb from the socket.

4. Check the socket for corrosion or damage. Light corrosion can be removed by cleaning with a contact cleaner available at auto parts stores or electronics stores. Heavy corrosion may require replacement of the socket or maybe the entire housing if the socket isn't available separately.

5. Replace the bulb with a proper part. Be careful that you install the proper wattage and size bulb, otherwise the light may not work correctly or could damage the socket and lens. You may want to use a dab of dielectric grease to protect the socket from corrosion.

6. Install the housing to the rear of the gauge. Check the bulb for proper operation.

Fig. 133 Gauge lights can usually be accessed from the inside of the inside of the cowl

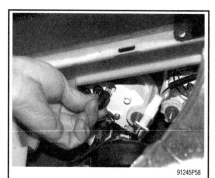

Fig. 134 To remove the rubber socket and light bulb assembly, carefully pull it straight out from the rear of the gauge

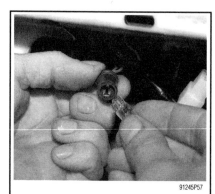

Fig. 135 The bulb usually pulls straight out of the socket

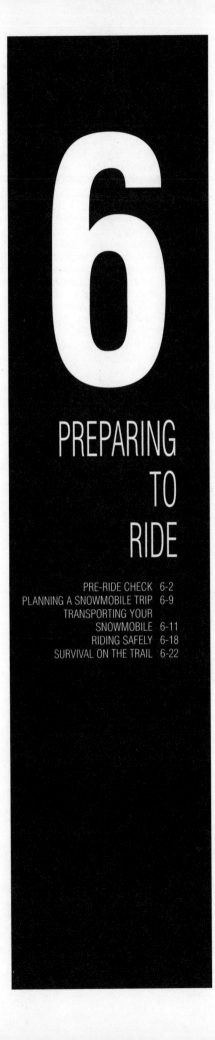

6

PREPARING
TO
RIDE

PRE-RIDE CHECK

▶ See Figures 1 thru 6

Before you go tearing off into the woods, take a little time and inspect your snowmobile. It's easy to get excited when you've pulled into your favorite riding area and see others having fun on their snowmobiles; you probably want to be quick to join in on the fun. But wait!! Did you remember to fuel up? When **was** the last time you checked your oil? It's so easy to forget all of these important things when you've driven for hours to get to your favorite riding area, and all you'd like to do is get your snowmobile off the trailer and get geared up to ride. The LAST thing that you want to be bothered with is inspecting the mechanicals of your snowmobile. You want to RIDE!!

When it comes to riding snowmobiles, one point is always stressed: SAFETY. There are so many different aspects of safety when it comes to riding snowmobiles—safely transporting your snowmobile, courteous riding, crossing adverse terrain, performing maintenance, and the list goes on.

Inspecting your snowmobile before riding it is probably one of the most neglected forms of safety. By inspecting your snowmobile before you ride, you are taking precautions to ensure that your snowmobile is functioning properly, and this affects the safety of both you AND the riders around you. Finding out that your brakes are not properly adjusted **after** you're heading down a steep hill can get pretty scary!

With a little bit of care and time, you can make your riding experience much more fun as well as safe. A few moments before each ride is all that is necessary to help reduce the chance of running into a bad situation. It isn't hard, and with some practice and discipline, it becomes an integral part of the snowmobile riding experience.

Things To Look For

If you keep up on your snowmobile maintenance, the pre-ride check should be short and sweet. In general, the check includes items which effect safety and driveability. You will look at items like your skis, track, oil level, coolant level, brake pads, lights and controls. Depending on the snowmobile, the actual items may change as appropriate (check your owner's manual), but use the following list as a guide:

SKIS

▶ See Figures 7, 8 and 9

Visually inspect your skis prior to any snowmobiling adventure. Check the skis for cracks, bending or other signs of damage. Check the ski movement by pivoting both skis up and down. Skis should pivot smoothly with no signs of binding.

Excessively worn or damaged runners reduce handling performance . If the runners are more than half worn at any point or if they are cracked, do not go riding until they are replaced.

Check the skis for proper alignment. Misaligned skis can result from a hard impact while out riding. Visually inspect the skis and if you notice they are not aligned, measure the distance between the ski brackets at the front and the rear. The front distance should be equal. However, some models may require the distance to be approximately ⅛ in. greater in the front. It is always best to check your owner's manual for the proper specifications.

Fig. 1 Take a couple minutes to inspect your snowmobile's engine . . .

Fig. 2 . . . and suspension for soundness before speeding off to your local riding area

Fig. 3 Frequent inspection of components (like this heat exchanger) will help prevent any unexpected problems from leaving you stranded

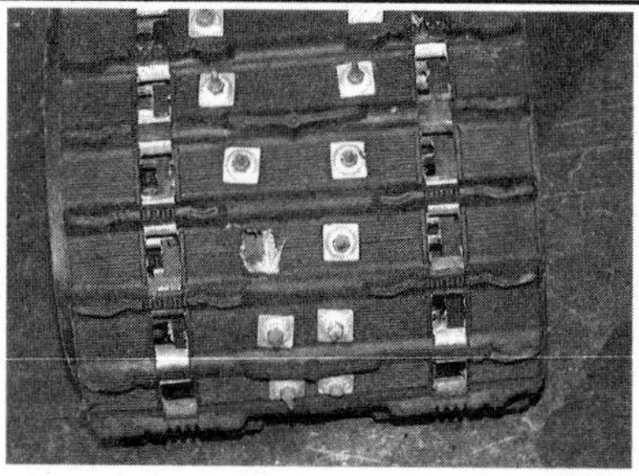

Fig. 4 Trying to ride a snowmobile with this track could be dangerous. The ripped out stud caused a weak spot in the track that could cause it to break

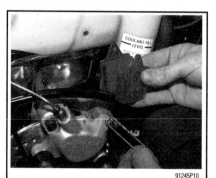
Fig. 5 In addition to keeping the mechanical portions of the brakes properly maintained . . .

Fig. 6 . . . make sure the hydraulic brake reservoir is kept full

Fig. 7 Skis should pivot smoothly with no signs of binding

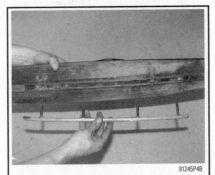

Fig. 8 Excessively worn runners could cause a loss of steering control and handling performance

Fig. 9 Visually inspect the skis and if you notice they are not aligned, measure the distance between the ski brackets at the front and the rear

TRACK

♦ **See Figures 10, 11, 12, 13 and 14**

Your track is the component that puts the power to the snow. Visually inspect the track for signs of broken lugs or other damage prior to each ride. This is especially important if you run studs. A broken stud that is flung off the track at speed can do a lot of damage to your sled, not to mention if it hits someone.

Check the track for proper tension. Correct track tension is important because a loose track will slap the bottom of the tunnel and wear the track, tunnel and heat exchangers. A track that is too tight will wear the slide runners and the rubber on the idler wheels, and reduce performance due to the increased friction.

Fig. 10 The track is the component that puts the power to the snow

Fig. 11 Tracks with studs should be inspected carefully for damage

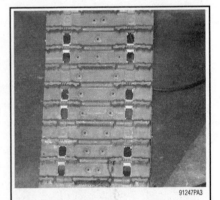

Fig. 12 Inspect the lugs for damage . . .

Fig. 13 . . . and the studs for pull out. This track's strength is compromised by this missing stud

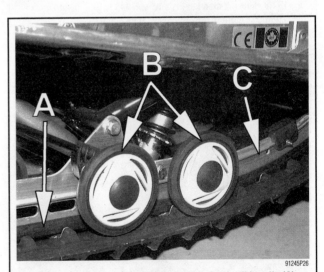

Fig. 14 A track that is too tight will wear the plastic slide rails (A) and the rubber on the idler wheels (B) and may demage the rail (C)

OIL LEVEL

▶ **See Figures 15, 16, 17, 18 and 19**

Engines and chain cases use oil for lubrication and cooling. In the case of most snowmobiles, engine oil is either mixed in with the gasoline or placed in a separate tank to be precisely injected into the engine at the proper time. Snowmobile chain cases usually provide some type way to check of the oil level, such as a dipstick or sight glass. Read your owner's manual or refer to the engine maintenance of this manual to help decide how the level is to be read. To avoid problems, keep both your injection oil and chain case (gear case) oil level topped off at all times.

A low oil level could instantly ruin your engine or chain, while a very low level could lead to a dangerous seizure. At best any type of mechanical seizure would cost you a lot of money for a rebuild or repair, but it could also strand you in the middle of nowhere or cause a serious accident. Bottom line: KEEP AN EYE ON YOUR OIL LEVEL AND CARRY EXTRA OIL WITH YOU.

Fig. 17 The gear case oil level is checked using a dipstick

Fig. 15 By choosing high quality oils, you will help to insure peak protection and performance from your snowmobile

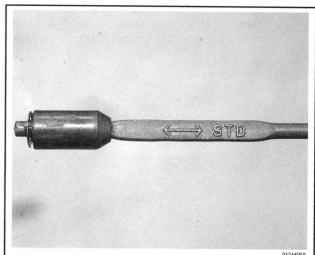

Fig. 18 Gear case oil level should be between the marks on the dipstick

Fig. 16 Keep the injection oil level full to avoid engine damage

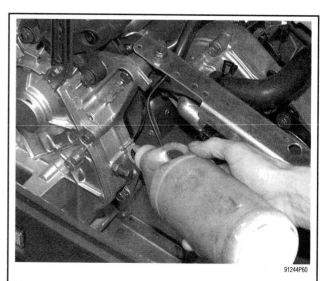

Fig. 19 If the gear case level is low, top off the engine with fresh oil

COOLANT LEVEL

♦ See Figures 20 and 21

❄❄ CAUTION

Never open, service or drain the radiator or cooling system when hot; serious burns can occur from the steam and hot coolant. Also, when draining engine coolant, keep in mind that cats and dogs are attracted to ethylene glycol antifreeze and could drink any that is left in an uncovered container or in puddles on the ground. This will prove fatal in sufficient quantities. Always drain coolant into a sealable container.

Fig. 20 Keep the level of the coolant at level specified on the recovery tank

Fig. 21 Never open the coolant reservoir cap when the engine is hot

If your snowmobile is water-cooled, take a peek at the coolant level in the reservoir. Coolant has a mysterious way of slowly disappearing over a period of time, so even if you don't have any visible leaks, your coolant level may be low. You may spot a slow leak by having to add coolant on a regular basis even if it doesn't leave any drips on the floor.

CABLES AND CONTROLS

♦ See Figures 22, 23 and 24

It is real bummer to have a throttle or brake cable snap during a ride. Look at the cable ends for fraying and damage. If your levers are stiff and sticky feeling, chances are that the cable is in need of lubrication. Also, make sure that the levers aren't bent or binding. It is not uncommon for linkage to rattle apart from time to time. The occasional rock or branch can do damage to the levers and linkage, so beware.

One item that often goes overlooked is the protective rubber boot found at the ends of many cables. This boot is used to keep dirt and moisture from the otherwise unprotected cable end. If the boot becomes damaged with cracks or tears, or if the boot stretches over time, allowing contaminants access to the cable, it is no longer performing its job and should be replaced. If allowed to go unrepaired, it is likely that the cable will suffer a sudden and total loss of operation when it is least expected. This is because of wear and corrosion that will occur on the pivot or sliding point at the cable end. If you don't want to get stranded because of a torn boot, then give a quick visual check before each ride and it won't go unnoticed.

Fig. 22 Keep lever pivots adjusted properly to avoid binding or excessive looseness

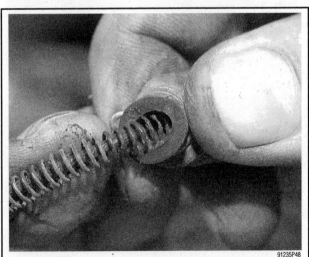

Fig. 23 If cables feel tight or bind, suspect rust inside the cable. Cables in this condition can break at any time on the trail

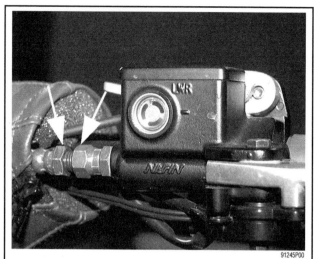

Fig. 24 Some cables are designed for quick adjustment with common hand tools–always keep cables adjusted properly

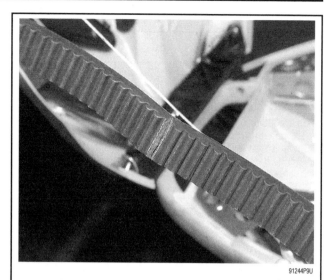

Fig. 26 Visually inspect the drivebelt for defects prior to every ride

BRAKE PADS

▶ See Figure 25

Some snowmobiles have brake pads that are easily seen and can be checked with a glance. Other models require you to remove the pad completely for inspection. Visually inspect the pads for a sufficient amount of material left on the pad. Remember, the longer your ride the more material will be necessary. As you may have guessed, it is a good idea to keep an eye on the condition of the pads.

Fig. 25 The easiest and safest way to check brake pad wear is to remove the pads from the caliper and visually inspect them

DRIVE BELT

▶ See Figures 26 and 27

Open the belt guard and visually inspect the drivebelt. If the belt is worn or damaged, replace it before you go riding. Remember, the drive belt is the link between the engine and your track, so if it fails, you are stuck.

Fig. 27 It is always a good idea to carry a spare drivebelt

LIGHTS

▶ See Figures 28 and 29

If your riding adventures carry you into the evening hours, make sure to check that all your lights work. (Getting caught in the dark a long ways from camp can be a real bummer). This includes the headlamp (high and low beams) and the taillight(s). It is also worth the time to make sure all your warning lights on the instrument pad light up when you turn on the key because you don't want to find out the hard way that your oil warning light is burned out!

BATTERY

▶ See Figure 30

Check the battery for the proper level of electrolyte. Electric start snowmobiles have the battery right underneath the cowling. If you can check it easily, make it a habit to do so. If it isn't easy to see, make it part of your regular main-

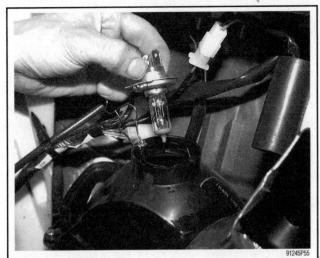

Fig. 28 If a headlight is burned out it can be easily repaired by replacing the bulb

Fig. 29 Taillights are also easily replaced by unscrewing the lens and replacing the bulb

Fig. 30 Keep an eye on the electrolyte level in the battery. Keeping the level correct will ensure proper output

tenance routine. If your battery bails out on you in the middle of nowhere, you might be pulling on that back up starter.

LEAKS

Look over the engine and driveline for obvious leaks. A small leak now may turn into a gusher just as you are entering a turn. It is also a good way to keep a tab on the mechanical condition of your snowmobile. If things have always stayed dry, and now there's a sheen of oil on the crankcase, you have a problem that you need to look into.

AND THE LAST CHECK!

We all know that sometimes it just isn't possible to do all the items in the list. In this (hopefully rare) case, pick the most important items such as oil level and FUEL LEVEL. If you have been looking at all the items in the above list on a continuing basis, you should have a good feel for the overall condition of the snowmobile and skipping an item or two shouldn't hurt once in a while. It still is a good idea to always check these items when you head out for your first ride of the day, and some of the more basic items (oil level, fuel level, etc.) a few more times during a long ride. If you miss one item on that list and it causes you a problem, it is all on you. Snowmobile riding should be fun, but the responsibility of riding is great, and you should respect that, just not for you, but for your fellow riders.

Tools For The Trail

If your snowmobile breaks down in the middle of nowhere, having some basic hand tools to use may be all that is necessary to get you going again. If the spark plug rattles loose when you're miles from camp, a spark plug socket can really come in handy. Carrying tools on your snowmobile (or on your person) can get a little cumbersome, though. By carrying only the tools (and parts) that you need, hauling around a complete 110 piece tool set will be all but eliminated, and you'll still have all of the tools you need to make trailside repairs.

ESSENTIALS

▶ See Figures 31, 32, 33, 34 and 35

There are some tools that are essential to carry with you at ALL times. The first is the tool kit that comes with your snowmobile when it is purchased. If you bought your snowmobile used, and it did not come with a tool kit (usually in the form of a small bag in the compartment in the rear), it would be a good idea to buy a new one from a dealer. Make sure the tool kit is specifically for your snowmobile; other tool kits may not have some special tools that fit the fasteners on your snowmobile.

The original tool kit that was provided with your snowmobile has most of what

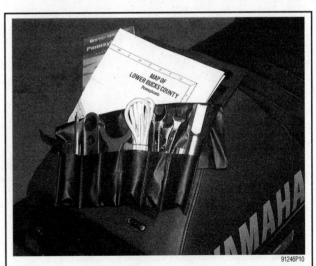

Fig. 31 Make sure the tool kit supplied with your snowmobile is carried with you at all times—it can really help you out in a pinch

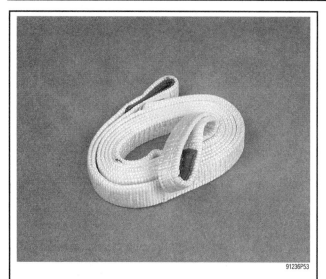

Fig. 32 Every snowmobile rider should carry a tow strap

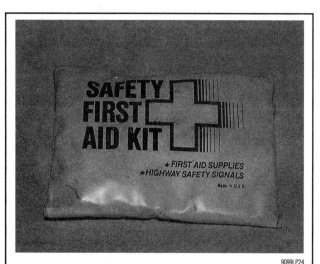

Fig. 33 Be prepared for emergencies—carry a small first aid kit with you

Fig. 34 Most snowmobiles have neat places to carry spare drive-belts and spark plugs

Fig. 35 Make sure that you have extra fuses

you'll need to make repairs in a tight situation. Granted, the tools aren't usually of top notch quality, but they can really help in a pinch. Most factory tool kits come with a spark plug tool, pliers, a screwdriver with changeable tips, and a couple of wrenches, which fit the most common fastener sizes on your snowmobile.

If your snowmobile breaks down and the tools you do have can't be used for repairs, a tow strap can really come in handy. A buddy or good Samaritan can haul you back to camp if you've got a tow strap with you. Make sure the tow strap is of good quality, and it is long enough to provide enough distance between vehicles when towing. Since the tow strap will most likely be stored in the rear compartment, a nylon tow strap would be a better choice, since a canvas strap might get moldy and rot over time.

Another essential tool to carry on every ride is a small first aid kit. If you look around, you can find one that will fit perfectly in the tool compartment of your snowmobile. Make some measurements, and head on down to the local camping supply. First aid kits come in all shapes and sizes, so you should be able to find something that doesn't occupy too much room, and can still be of use in case of an emergency on the trail.

OTHER ITEMS TO CONSIDER

There are so many useful things to carry with you on a ride that can pull you out of trouble. Here is a list of additional items that you should have that can save the weekend. Some of these items may be a bit extreme, but hey, it can't hurt to be a little over-prepared.

- Flash light
- Spare bottle of water
- Locking pliers with cutters
- Bailing wire
- Duct tape
- Nylon tie wraps (wire-ties)
- A few feet of spare fuel line (good for siphoning or repair)
- A knife
- Small flashlight
- Toilet paper (and a magazine)
- Packaged beef jerky (when you get hungry you'll eat anything)
- Matches or a lighter
- Compass
- Flares

This list is generic, and applies to just about anyone who ventures off into the wilderness on (or in) motor vehicles. Over time, you'll probably amass your own custom collection of tools and supplies that apply to your snowmobile.

Here are a few spare items that are snowmobile specific:

- Drivebelt
- Spark plug
- Emergency starter rope
- Throttle and brake cables
- A Chilton's manual for reference

If you pack up everything tight enough, most of these items can fit into the small compartment on the back of your seat. However, a small saddle bag that can be attached to seat might be a better bet.

The benefits of carrying these items far outweighs the extra weight added to your snowmobile. If a buddy breaks down, you might have the extra tools and supplies to help out.

Many cross-country raiders attach tools and supplies over various areas of their snowmobiles. For instance, an extra throttle cable can be stashed in the engine compartment, where it can easily be accessed in an emergency. You can do the same with other tools and supplies. Look for little nooks and crannies to stash parts and supplies, and use appropriate means to secure them. Make sure heat and water aren't going to ruin anything, though. You'll be glad that you went through the extra effort to carry extra tools, parts and supplies; sooner or later you'll be using SOMETHING!!

PLANNING A SNOWMOBILE TRIP

Planning ahead for a day ride, weekend, or camping trip all have one thing in common: BEING PREPARED. After all, it would be safe to say that there won't be an snowmobile shop nearby, or a local camping supply store. Of course this all depends on the location of your riding area. You might be lucky enough to have a convenience store that sells gasoline and soda a few miles down the road. But even then, being prepared will save the inconvenience of having to pick up supplies in the middle of your fun-filled weekend.

Preparing for a weekend ride or snowmobile camping trip can become really hectic and unorganized if you wait until the last minute to round everything up for packing. Its a good idea to make a complete list a few days **before** you get ready to pack everything. Go over the list with your riding buddies; they might think of items that you've overlooked. This way, when it comes time to pack up your truck, trailer and/or snowmobiles, you can check off the list as you pack, and ensure that everything that you had planned to bring along actually gets loaded up.

There's nothing worse than driving for hours to a riding area, and realizing that you forgot your HELMET, or even worse, the KEY to your snowmobile. We've all forgotten to bring things along from time-to-time, but forgetting something really important can absolutely RUIN your weekend. Don't let this happen to you! Having everything that you need for the weekend will make things much more enjoyable.

Here are a few items you may want to consider when planning a trip:
• Obtain a map of the area you wish to explore and determine which areas are open for use.
• Contact the land manager for area restrictions and if crossing private property, be sure to ask permission from the land owner (nobody likes a shotgun pointed at them).
• Check the weather forecast.
• Be sure your sled is properly registered.
• Prepare for the unexpected by packing a small backpack full of emergency items.

What To Bring

♦ See Figures 36, 37 and 38

Discussing in detail what to bring along on an snowmobile camping trip could be a separate book in itself, since the intended plans of your trip can vary

Fig. 37 There are also ultra-compact tents available, like this one that measures only 6x16 inches when broken down

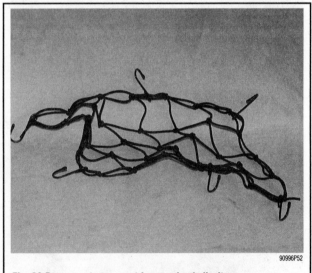

Fig. 38 Bungee nets are great for securing bulky items

so greatly. Just heading out to your favorite riding area for the weekend? Or are you planning a week long excursion in the wilderness and packing all of your camping gear on your snowmobile? Going hunting?

Whatever your plans are, there are some things to bring along that are common to all types of riding. Items like extra fuel, oil, and spare parts are just about essential to bring along for any trip. Earlier in this section, tools and supplies to carry on an snowmobile are discussed in detail. However, extra tools, supplies, and other items that are too big to carry on your snowmobile can be brought along and kept in your tow vehicle in case of an emergency. In addition to these items, there are some basic items listed below that should always be brought along on any trip.

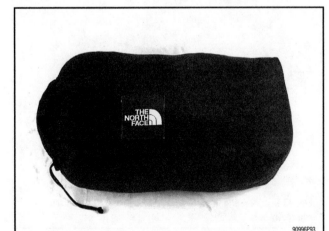

Fig. 36 Rack space is critical when planning an snowmobile camping trip; look for camping items that are compact, like synthetic sleeping bags

ESSENTIAL ITEMS

▶ **See Figures 39 and 40**

One of the most important items is WATER. Sounds obvious, but it requires some forethought if you haven't done any long rides on your snowmobile before. According to the U.S. Army Field Survival Manual FM 21-76, the human body needs at least 2 quarts of water a day in cold climates where your perspiration and loss of body fluids are lower than when in hot climates. The water should be commercially available bottled water or from your home tap. If you run out of water, and have to drink from streams, lakes or ponds, always treat it with water purification tablets, or boil for at least 5 minutes before drinking.

Plenty of food is essential to bring along also. This can be just as critical as water. Dried and canned food is best to bring along, since space and weight requirements are so critical. Of course, if you are setting up camp for the weekend, and regularly returning to camp after a ride, ice chests will be your best bet. Yes we said ice chests. You may be tempted to just stuff your food in the snow, but don't. Just like water, you can never bring enough food along. A riding trip can become a miserable experience if you run out of food, so be sure to bring plenty.

Bringing extra clothing along is a good idea. Even during the warmer months of the season, a cold snap can move in overnight. If you didn't bring along an extra jacket or thermal underwear, things could get really miserable.

ADDITIONAL ITEMS

▶ **See Figures 41 and 42**

As stated earlier, the type of riding you do will dictate exactly what type of gear to bring along. If you haven't gone on long trips with your snowmobile before, check with some local riders to see what extra equipment is required. If you are into long trail expeditions, 4x4 clubs will have tons of information on compact camping gear and accessories, etc. You can also obtain detailed maps of trails and forest areas from local riding clubs, which can be really useful for trail exploration. If play riding at the closest riding area is what you're into, your local snowmobile dealer will be able to tell you which area is closest to you. Most importantly, you can meet other riders and discuss important items to bring along with you to make your weekend fun and carefree.

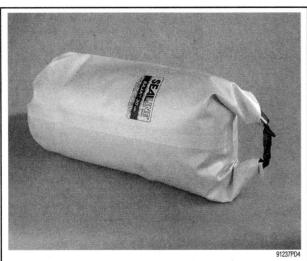

Fig. 39 For weekend camping adventures, dry bags are essential for keeping food and supplies safe from the elements

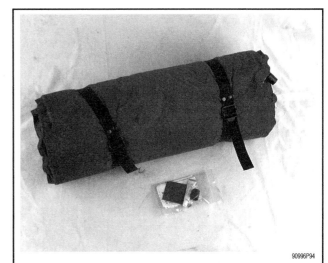

Fig. 41 An inflatable sleeping pad is a nice (but not a necessary) item to bring along on a camping trip

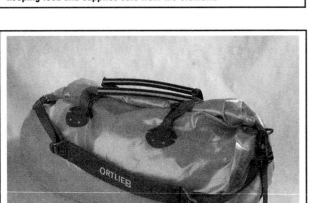

Fig. 40 Whether you're carrying tools, supplies, or food, gear bags are one of the most important items of a well-planned trip

Fig. 42 In addition to gear bags, other cargo-carrying accessories can really help to organize items to bring along for a trip

TRANSPORTING YOUR SNOWMOBILE

Getting your snowmobile to your favorite riding area can become quite a hassle if you don't have a trailer. If you can't make your snowmobile fit into a truck bed (and this is highly unadvisable), a trailer is your only alternative. If you have more than one snowmobile larger trailers that can haul a quantity of snowmobiles are manufactured by several companies.

The majority of snowmobiles will NOT fit into the bed of a pickup truck. Besides, getting your snowmobile up into the bed can be a daunting task. This leaves your truck, SUV or minivan to do the towing chores.

Tow Vehicles

There are a large selection of trailers available that could be used for safely transporting your snowmobile, all different shapes, sizes and price tags. With the exception of a specialized double axle two-level trailer for hauling eight snowmobiles, most trailers can be safely towed by almost any vehicle. For larger trailers such as the one previously mentioned, a truck or van equipped with specialized towing equipment is necessary.

Before you decide to buy a trailer to tow your snowmobile, there are several things to consider.

TOWING CAPACITY

The towing capacity of your vehicle (along with your wallet) will ultimately dictate the type of trailer and quantity of snowmobiles that you can safely tow.

Tow ratings on modern cars and trucks can range from "not recommended for towing" for a small car to 10,000 pounds for a large truck. Information regarding towing capacity can usually be found in the vehicle owner's manual.

If you are able to equip your car for towing, it would be safe to say that one snowmobile and a trailer would be about the most that small cars can handle. As the weight and engine horsepower of your vehicle increase, the ability to tow larger trailers and more snowmobiles increases also.

➡Always check your owners manual for the recommended maximum towing capacity of your vehicle. Do not exceed this capacity.

HITCHES

Once that you have determined your vehicle is suitable for towing snowmobiles on a trailer, a hitch will have to be mounted to your vehicle. Tow hitches are available in different configurations and for a variety of uses. However, we'll look only at those popularly used for towing recreational trailers. We'll also discuss the accessories needed for their safe and proper use.

Hitch Classifications

Automotive manufacturers' tow rating requirements will often list certain types of hitches. Normally, the requirements will be for either "weight distributing," "frame mounted," or "deadweight". Also, manufacturers do not recommend towing with certain hitches. You can tow a lighter load with a heavier hitch, but you can't safely tow a heavier load with a lighter hitch. Before making a hitch selection, however, you need to know your total towed load. This can be calculated by adding the weight of your snowmobile(s), the trailer, and estimating the weight of your accessories and gear.

Four basic classifications are given to conventional hitches: Class I (up to 2000 pounds), Class II (2000 to 3500 pounds), Class III (3500 to 5000 pounds) and Class IV (5000 to 10,000 pounds). Hitch makers have also begun to use the designation of Class V to indicate a heavier duty hitches designed for those who do not want or need to use a weight distributing hitch. Most hitches are considered to be weight carrying (also called "deadweight"), which means they support all of the trailer tongue weight. These are the most popular hitches used to tow light or medium loads (most snowmobiles). Hitches are rated for Gross Trailer Weight (or GTW) and Tongue Weight (or TW). Many Class III and Class IV hitches have weight distributing capabilities, which means they can be used to distribute tongue weight to the front of the tow vehicle to relieve overweight conditions at the rear of the tow vehicle.

CLASS I HITCHES

The smallest hitch is a Class I, and is meant for loads less than 2000 pounds (most snowmobile trailers fall into this category). It comes in three basic types: a bumper mount (not really used these days), a bumper/frame mount (for most modern cars) and as part of a step bumper on a truck. Step bumpers found on trucks don't always have tow ratings, though. Even though a step bumper may have a hole for a hitch ball, the bumper itself may not be strong enough to handle a bouncing tongue load. Before you run off to the auto parts store to buy a hitch ball, be sure the bumper is properly constructed for towing and that it has a tow rating stamped into the metal. Some automotive and aftermarket manufacturers offer replacement step bumpers with high tow ratings.

CLASS II HITCHES

Class II hitches are frame-mounted, which means they connect to the frame or structural crossmembers of the vehicle, not to the bumper. They are rated to tow up to 3500 pounds. Some vehicles may need extra bracing installed to the chassis to help support this type of hitch. On a unibody vehicle, for example, the hitch is bolted to sheetmetal, rather than to a heavy gauge, steel frame. Without extra support, the bolts can pull away from the sheetmetal. Factory installed hitches usually have an extra metal plate for support when the tow package is ordered, as do kits from the better hitch manufacturers.

There are a few variations regarding Class II hitches. One has a ball mount permanently built into the hitch assembly. Some use a receiver, which has a removable ball mount that fits into a square hole. Receiver hitches come in two ball mount sizes. On a receiver hitch, the ball mount is the shank that holds the hitch ball and fits into the receiver. This ball mount shank can be either 1 5/8 or 2 inches square. The smaller shank size is used with a mini hitch, which has a tow rating limited to 3500 pounds. The smaller mini hitch allows better ground clearance and is more easily hidden under the vehicle than a full size hitch.

CLASS III AND IV HITCHES

◆ See Figures 43, 44 and 45

Class III (up to 5000 pounds) and Class IV (up to 10,000 pounds) hitches are necessary for heavy duty towing. This is a weight category for which you will probably need a specially equipped truck and a frame mounted, receiver hitch. Also, in this weight range you'll be getting into very heavy tongue weights, which can drastically affect the way your vehicle handles. A 500 pound tongue weight may not sound like a lot, but that weight takes on a different perspective when it's pushing down on a hitch ball that might be six feet behind the rear axle. This creates a six foot long lever that lifts the front steering wheels of the tow vehicle, drops the front of the trailer and results in sloppy steering, bounce, and sway at the back of the vehicle and at the trailer. Suspension aids may help, but the most successful way to offset this leverage action is with the use of a weight distributing hitch.

9124XP53

Fig. 43 Installing a Class IV hitch is simply a matter of inserting the hitch into the receiver on the tow vehicle . . .

Fig. 44 . . . pushing the hitch pin through the hole in the receiver and the hitch . . .

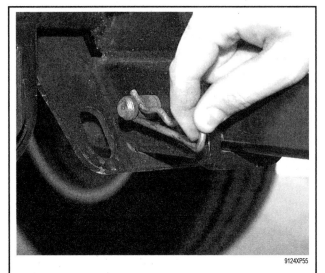

Fig. 45 . . . and fastening the hitch pin with a cotter pin

CLASS V HITCHES

These are large, heavy gauge steel hitches designed for large trucks high tow ratings. Their primary purpose is to allow towing without having to use a weight distributing hitch. Class V hitches are often referred to as "dead weight hitches" or "fifth wheels". A classic example of a fifth wheel type hitch is that used by a tractor-trailer.

Weight Distributing Systems

A weight distributing system spreads tongue weight over the front and rear axles of the tow vehicle and the trailer axle(s). With a 500 pound tongue weight, for example, The weight can be redistributed so that 200 pounds of that weight is on the front axle, 200 on the rear axle and 100 on the trailer axle(s). The result is a stable, controllable tow vehicle and trailer.

The weight distributing system consists of a frame mounted platform and spring bars (also called equalizing bars) that attach to a special ball mount assembly and to the trailer frame. A special ball mount is needed because it mates with the receiver and has sockets into which the spring bars are inserted. The weight distributing ball mount is also adjustable. It is especially important to set the hitch ball angle and to raise or lower the hitch ball to properly set spring bar the height. Two spring bars are usually used on each side of the ball mount. The spring bars have chains connected at the trailer end, which attach to brackets on the trailer tongue. The length of the chains

actually distribute the tongue weight as they are raised or lowered to put tension on the spring bars.

Hooking and unhooking the system only takes a couple of minutes, but some don't like to have to deal with the extra complication of hooking up a weight distributing system. A trailer dealer will be able to discuss with you at length the details of weight distributing systems.

TONGUE WEIGHT

▶ **See Figure 46**

Tongue weight is defined as the weight from the trailer that is applied to the hitch ball. This can vary considerably, depending on the number of snowmobiles and how the trailer is loaded. Excessive tongue weight will cause the rear of the tow vehicle to sag considerably, and handling will be adversely affected. Tongue weight can be too light also, affecting handling.

When you are buying a trailer, discuss with the salesman what you plan to tow, and what you're going to tow it with. This should help to answer most of your questions about the proper tongue weight for your vehicle.

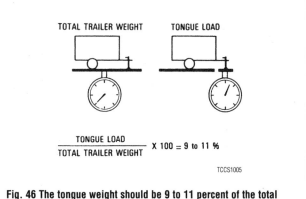

Fig. 46 The tongue weight should be 9 to 11 percent of the total weight of the loaded trailer

HITCH BALLS

▶ **See Figure 47**

Hitch balls comes in three basic sizes: 7/8 inches (up to 2000 pounds; sometimes more), 2 inches (up to 6000 pounds) and 2 5/16 inches (up to 10,000 pounds or more). Most importantly, be sure the ball is the proper size for the trailer. A ball that is too small will cause the coupler to bounce loose.

Fig. 47 To prevent binding and premature wear, always lubricate your hitch ball with a high quality grease

Some hitch balls have extended bases and shanks for special purposes. The base and shank of a hitch ball can have significant effects on weight rating. Also, some shanks may be slightly undersize or oversize. On step bumper hitches especially, be sure the shank (in American measurements) conforms to the hole (which may be in a metric equivalent, especially on some foreign trucks).

A frequently overlooked requirement for hitch balls is the torque recommendation for the mounting nut. The general rule of thumb for proper torque is 85 ft. lbs. (116 Nm) for Class I, 105 ft. lbs. (143 Nm) for Class II, 235 ft. lbs. (320 Nm) for Class III and 300 ft. lbs. (408 Nm) for Class IV.

WIRING A TRAILER TO YOUR VEHICLE

By law, a trailer must have running lights (taillights and/or marker lights), turn signals and brake lights. The electrical system of the tow vehicle must be tapped into to provide power and signals to the trailer lights. But other laws may apply based on where and what you will be towing. Be sure to check with the local authorities for other requirements in your area.

Connectors

▶ See Figure 48

Most small trailers use a four-way connector. One pin in the connector transfers power to the running lights, two others power the turn signals and brake lights. The fourth pin is for ground. The wiring on these flat, four way plugs is usually based on a standard color code. Brown is for taillights and side marker lights. Yellow is for the left turn signal and brake light. Green is for the right turn signal and brake light. White is for ground. Round, four way plugs don't always have a consistent color code, so you may have to figure it out by using a troubleshooting light.

A trailer electrical connector is often included when you buy a new vehicle with a "Towing Package." However, a connector can easily be fitted to most any tow vehicle for operating the trailer lights.

Fig. 48 On vehicles which are pre-wired for trailer towing, connecting a trailer wiring harness is simply a matter of just plugging it into the receptacle

Adapters

▶ See Figures 49 and 50

If your vehicle does not have a towing package, an adapter can be used to tap into the vehicles wiring to provide the necessary signals to a trailer. Most trailer dealers and hitch installation centers will carry a line of easily installed, in-line adapters. These adapters typically consist of a 3 ended wiring harness, two ends of which attach to the male and female sides of your tow vehicle's tail light wiring. The third end of the harness is simply a breakout of those tail light wires and is connected to the trailer. Installation is usually a simply matter of locating the harness under the rear of your tow vehicle, carefully undoing the factory connector, then installing the adapter to either end of the factory harness.

Fig. 49 This 7 pin round to 4 pin flat adapter works well when trying to adapt a small trailer wiring harness to the receptacle usually installed on most trucks

Fig. 50 Once installed, the adapter is held in place by the lid of the receptacle

Just be sure that you use wire ties to safely tuck the adapter out of harm's way, while still leaving a sufficient amount of free wire so that it can connect to the trailer harness. If no adapter kit is available for your tow vehicle, you might have to solder or modify the wiring harness of your vehicle. If you aren't real savvy with electrical items, it may be better to have a dealer or hitch installation center modify your harness for you.

Flashers

The standard flasher that comes with most vehicles is not designed to operate more than the vehicle's lights, so it can overload when a trailer electrical system is connected to the vehicle. This overloading causes the tow vehicle and trailer turn signals to flash rapidly and faintly. Additionally, the dashboard turn signal indicators will also flash quickly and faintly to alert you that a stronger flasher is needed.

Changing to a heavy-duty flasher will usually solve this problem. Be sure you get the right heavy-duty replacement by reading the packaging carefully to make sure it is designed for trailering applications. Many foreign vehicles come with heavy duty flashers.

The flasher is usually located under the dashboard. On most new vehicles, it is connected to the fuse box and simply pulls out. If you have trouble finding it, check your owner's manual or even the cover of the fuse box itself (as most fuse boxes are labeled these days). You might also want to refer to a Chilton Total Car Care manual for your model.

Trailers

♦ **See Figures 51 thru 61**

There are a large selection of trailers available that could be used for safely transporting your snowmobile, all different shapes, sizes and price tags. Anything from a small 4x8 trailer for one snowmobile to a specialized double axle two-level trailer for hauling eight snowmobiles is available. Now of course, the latter would require a truck or van equipped with specialized towing equipment. Load Rite® makes an excellent lightweight aluminum trailer that is well-suited for snowmobiles and snowmobiles, and is light enough to be towed by a car, if equipped with the proper towing equipment.

If your collection of recreational vehicles includes personal watercraft , ATV's or motorcycles, some trailer manufacturers have a trailer which can be converted to haul all three. Special accessories allow each type of vehicle to be safely towed. Motorcycles fit into a special chock at the front of the trailer to keep the bike steady and upright. Snowmobiles have special ski holders to prevent the sled from moving. Personal watercraft rid on special skis that are bolted to the floor of the trailer. When all accessories are removed, an ATV can be driven right up on the trailer.

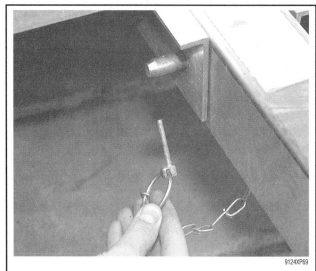

Fig. 53 . . . and remove the lock on the pin . . .

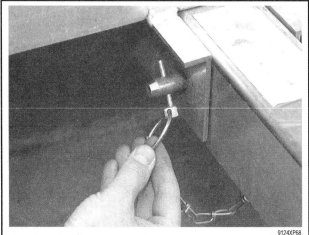

Fig. 51 Lightweight trailers, like those made by Load Rite® are perfect for hauling snowmobiles

Fig. 54 . . . pull out the pin . . .

Fig. 52 A nice feature of Load Rite® trailers are that they pivot on their axles, allowing loading without ramps. To prepare the trailer for loading, unfasten . . .

Fig. 55 . . . and tilt the trailer deck downwards

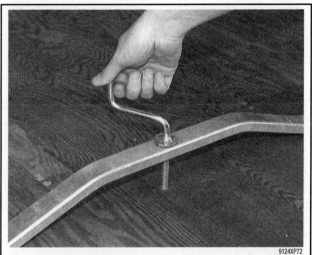

Fig. 56 The snowmobiles are held in place by ski hold-downs which are screwed into the trailer

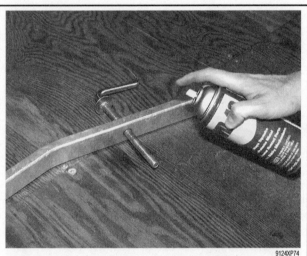

Fig. 57 Lubricate the screws on the ski hold-downs for ease of removal installation

Fig. 58 To load the snowmobile, place the skis at the leading edge of the trailer . . .

Fig. 59 . . . and ride the snowmobile slowly up the trailer . . .

Fig. 60 . . . until the deck starts to level out . . .

Fig. 61 . . . perfect! Install the deck retaining pin, and secure the snowmobile to the trailer

Trailer Hook Up

▶ **See Figures 62 thru 69**

Connecting a trailer properly ensures a safe ride for your favorite play toy. The following sequence of pictures illustrates the proper procedure for connecting a snowmobile trailer.

Fig. 62 Once the hitch is properly installed, place the trailer tongue over the hitch ball

Fig. 63 With the trailer tongue properly located . . .

Fig. 64 . . . secure the tongue lock . . .

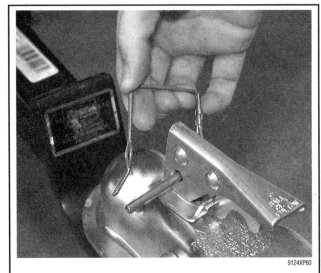

Fig. 65 . . . and install the safety pin . . .

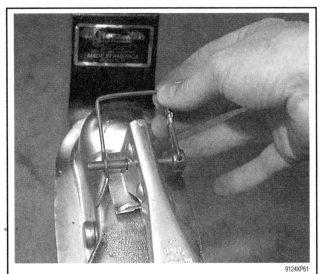

Fig. 66 Make sure to also lock the safety pin

Fig. 67 Connect the trailer wiring harness . . . .

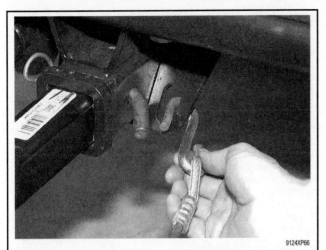

Fig. 68 . . . and the safety chains. Note the direction of the safety chain hook. This position will more positively retain the safety chain on bumpy roads

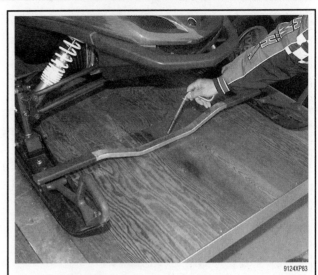

Fig. 70 Use the ski hold-downs in the front . . .

Fig. 69 This is a properly connected trailer

Fig. 71 . . . and a ratchet strap tie-down in the back to secure a snowmobile properly

Securing Your Snowmobile For Transport

♦ See Figures 70, 71, 72 and 73

Whether you are transporting your snowmobile in a truck or on a trailer, it is equally important to secure it properly. The best way to do this is with specialized snowmobile tie-downs. Snowmobile tie-downs are designed to allow the compression of the suspension to prevent the snowmobile from bouncing around on the trailer. Using other means of securing the snowmobile (rope, bungee cords, etc.) is a sure way to get yourself in serious trouble.

To safely secure an snowmobile, a minimum of four tie-downs should be used; one on each corner. If your snowmobile trailer has ski straps built in, you can use two tie-downs at the rear of the trailer.

Make sure the suspension is compressed as far as possible when the tie-downs are tightened. If not, the suspension of the snowmobile could compress when you hit a large bump or dip in the road, and the tie-down may come unhooked. To keep this from happening, you can use duct tape to wrap around the ends of the hooks after they are attached. Or, if your tie-downs are long enough, you can tie the excess of the strap around the hook to prevent it from coming off. It is VERY important to fully compress the suspension to keep slack from developing during towing.

Fig. 72 When loading only one snowmobile, we recommend placing the snowmobile in the center of the trailer for better weight distribution

9124XP87

Fig. 73 Attach the ski hold-downs as illustrated

Trailer Maintenance

As more areas of land are developed, trailering sleds has become almost a necessary means of enjoying snowmobiling. Towing a trailer loaded down with one or more snowmobiles is sometimes a daunting task. There are a lot of things to remember before loading up a trailer and while towing it down the road. As with your tow vehicle, it is vital to remember to maintain your trailer as well. A little maintenance now can save you a lot of aggravation later.

• Inspect the trailer frame—before loading up the trailer and connecting it to your tow vehicle, the structural integrity of the trailer frame should be examined for cracks, bends or breaks. Also, the trailer deck should be inspected for any damage from snowmobiles or rot caused by moisture or aging. The wheels

and bearings should be inspected to ensure they are properly greased and in good condition.

• Inspect the trailer lights—check the wiring harness for loose connections, fraying, cuts or corrosion. If any wiring harness is badly damaged, replace it. It is also a good idea to check the wiring coming from the vehicle. Road salt, dirt and debris can corrode exposed wires. Also make sure the ground wires are not corroded and are properly grounded. Dirt, snow and debris can wreak havoc on your taillights. To avoid this, use a marine-type silicon to seal the taillights.

• Inspect the coupler—make sure the coupler is operable and in good condition. Often times, if a trailer sits outside most of the year, the coupler can corrode and stick. If this happens, spray the coupler's moving parts with a liquid lubricant. Then attach the coupler to the hitch ball on your tow vehicle and see if there is any movement. If there is any appreciable movement, tighten the adjustment bolt to reduce the freeplay.

• Inspect the spare tire—another important aspect that is often overlooked is a spare tire. Unfortunately, most manufacturers don't offer a spare tire with their trailers, and most snowmobilers usually don't think of them until we need one. If you don't have a spare, get one. Either throw it in the back of your vehicle when you're towing your trailer or buy a mounting bracket and attach it to the trailer itself. Although it takes a little extra effort, time and money, it could save a heck of a lot more in the long run.

• Inspect the safety features—another important feature that should be inspected is the safety chains. Check the chain links to make sure they are in good condition and are securely attached to the trailer. If necessary, tighten the safety chain mounting bolts on the trailer. Also check to see if the chains are too long. With a loaded vehicle and trailer, attach the trailer to the tow vehicle. If the chains are touching the ground, they are too long and need to be adjusted. Either adjust them by using the safety chain mounting bolts or couple some of the chain links together until the chain is off of the ground. But remember to make sure the chains are loose enough to allow for turns up to 90 degrees.

A little preseason inspection and maintenance of your trailer will allow you to get to your favorite trail without worrying. By spending part of a weekend inspecting your trailer, you will be sure to get the most out of snowmobiling during the season.

RIDING SAFELY

▶ **See Figures 74, 75, 76, and 77**

Many things make snowmobiling fun: the awe inspiring beauty of a snow filled terrain; the precision performance of a well-designed sled; the satisfaction of traveling the trails with friends and family. Yes, snowmobilers enjoy the wintertime, and that calls for extra responsibility.

In recent years, the popularity of snowmobiles has skyrocketed. Along with the rise in popularity, snowmobile related injuries and deaths have risen substantially. The problem is the perception of snowmobiles as being "easy to ride" and "safe to ride". This false perception of safety lures inexperienced riders into a false sense of security. Most of these naive riders usually hop onto a borrowed snowmobile without any safety equipment or training, and some end up getting seriously injured or even killed. A large portion of snowmobile related injuries and deaths happen to children. Often times young children end up riding full-sized snowmobiles, with absolutely no parental supervision or any safety gear, and are seriously injured. Please, if you have children, **educate** them about riding safely. Make sure they wear appropriate safety gear, and obey the warning labels on snowmobiles regarding age limits. The only way to ensure a future for snowmobile recreation and sports is RESPONSIBILITY. Don't let friends and children become another government statistic.

If you are reading this book, you are probably new to this sport. The best advice we can give you is to take a snowmobile safety course. These courses are designed to give you a very good insight into the operation of your sled, the laws, and the basics.

After the course, the rest is up to you. It will take practice and common sense, but you will find this to be one of the most enjoyable sports there is.

Snowmobiling will take you into some of the most beautiful areas of the wilderness and keep your soul soaring high into the mountains. Ride Safe!

91243P21

Fig. 74 No matter what kind of riding you do proper riding gear is essential for safety

Fig. 75 Certification labels are attached to snowmobiles for a reason—your safety!

Fig. 76 Some snowmobiles are not meant to carry passengers

Fig. 77 In addition to standard warning labels, some snowmobiles have special requirements that should be brought to the operator's attention

Fighting Back Against Land Closure

▶ See Figure 78

Off highway recreation has recently come under attack. The rise in public awareness about pollution and the environment in recent years have caused the off-road community to come under close scrutiny. In a panic-stricken frenzy, environmental extremists are now pushing hard for land closures from the public to "conserve and protect" wilderness areas. With the powerful influence of the media, environmental extremists sometimes misrepresent the off-roading community as careless and destructive to the environment. This slanderous representation of the off-road community is used to gain support from the uninformed public about off-road recreation of all kinds. Such environmental extremists continue to threaten our sports, our recreation, and to some of us, our jobs. It all comes down to this: the off-road community has gained a bad reputation in the eyes of the general population.

There are ways we can fight for our rights to public land as United States citizens. You can help stop closures and unreasonable restrictions on public land. Rights organizations, such as the Blue Ribbon Coalition, fight for our rightful access to public land for off-road recreation of all kinds. The Blue Ribbon Coalition regularly travels to Washington D.C. to speak on behalf of the off-roading community, and uses the judicial system and legislative system to fight for your right to land access.

If you care about keeping your riding area open, join the Blue Ribbon Coalition, and become involved in standing up for your rights as an off-road recreationalist. The Blue Ribbon Coalition will also provide detailed information on how you can make a difference in your local riding area, as well as keep you informed on a national level. Snowmobilers, motorcyclists, ATV riders, four-wheel drive enthusiasts, outdoorsmen, watersport and equestrian recreationalists join the Blue Ribbon Coalition for the common cause of keeping our land from being locked up. These groups all join together and oppose misinformation campaigns and promote reasonable and responsible use of public resources.

There are also many rights groups that also operate on a local level which help fight land closures. By joining these clubs and coalitions, you will not only do your part to keep your riding area open, you may meet new riding partners, and make new friends. The main thing is to get involved. If we don't fight for our rights, they will eventually be taken away and there will soon be nowhere to ride. This is no joke—thousands of acres of public land all over America are **already** closed.

If you're a "regular" at your favorite riding area, Contact the local U.S. Forest Service district, and consider becoming a steward. You'll have to do a little work, (like pruning trees, picking up litter, etc.) but the local rangers will greatly appreciate your efforts, and you will help project a positive image for the snowmobile community. Sacrificing a small amount of your time to maintain your local riding area will ensure a place to ride in the future. Encourage your friends to join, and you'll have so much fun that you'll forget that it's a job.

Fig. 78 Do you know someone who rides like this? Do yourself and them a favor and report them to the local authorities before someone gets hurt

Many of us have witnessed fellow snowmobile riders acting foolishly and carelessly at our favorite riding areas. When an extremist group is working hard to fight for a land closure, a few seconds of video tape or pictures of snowmobilers riding carelessly, littering, or having complete disregard for the environment is all they need to sway a congressman or a news reporter. Unfortunately, the small handful of snowmobile riders who act like idiots are the people who are ruining the reputation of the off-road community. Do everyone a favor and DON'T BE ONE OF THOSE PEOPLE !!!!!

Showing respect for the environment and "treading lightly" are essential to project a positive image for the off-road community. By riding in a responsible and mature manner, we can ensure that the opposition will be unable to slander and misrepresent us all. So get going and **get involved!!**

Safety Tips

Here's a list of tips and pointers for camping and riding your snowmobile. Remember—the rules and etiquette are for consideration and fun for all, not to make things miserable for snowmobile riders. Do your part and be a responsible snowmobile rider; set an example for others. This is the ONLY way that we can keep riding areas open.

ON THE TRAIL

▶ **See Figures 79 and 80**

• Take an snowmobile safety course—they're usually free of charge when you purchase a new snowmobile.
• Don't be fooled into thinking that snowmobiles are "easy to ride". You can be seriously injured or even killed riding an snowmobile.
• Don't drink and ride. In certain areas, you can be convicted of a DUI the same as if you were driving an automobile.
• Always observe and obey the age limit tags and labels placed on snowmobiles. They are placed there for your own safety.
• Use your brain when you ride—always wear a helmet, full eye protection, boots and protective clothing whenever you ride.
• Always offer assistance to somebody in need of it. And always be prepared for medical emergencies with a good first aid kit.
• Regardless of whether you are heading off into the woods for a week on a hunting adventure, or checking out that hill on the other side of your camping area, LET SOMEONE KNOW WHERE YOU ARE GOING. Someone who knows where you're going and when you're planning on returning can suspect trouble if you don't return when planned, and can take action to locate you.

Fig. 79 Always wear a helmet, full eye protection, boots and protective clothing whenever you ride

Fig. 80 It's a smart idea to never ride alone

• Stay on designated road and trails or other areas open for use.
• When approaching a snowmobile that is coming up a hill, they have the right of way. If it's a steep long climb, pull off to the side, and let him pass you before proceeding. Stopping on a long uphill can cause you to lose traction and control.
• If you turn a corner or crest a hill, and there's another snowmobile (or other vehicle) coming straight toward you, turn to the right while slowing down. Your counterpart is supposed to do the same.
• When approaching riders on horseback, pull off to the side of the trail, stop your engine, and take off your helmet. Horses are easily spooked; by taking off your helmet and standing next to your snowmobile, a horse can recognize you as a human.
• Never blaze your own trail. Most off-road riding areas seriously frown on this, and doing so might get you permanently barred from any future visits.
• Always ride with one or more buddies. If an accident were to happen, another can assist or go for help.
• Travel at reasonable speeds to protect you and the environment.
• Be aware of unmarked hazards or obstacles hidden beneath the snow.
• Be considerate of others on the trail and keep to the right.
• Ride only where permitted.
• Yield the right of way to those passing or traveling uphill.

AT THE CAMPSITE

• Use existing campsites whenever possible.
• Only build fires in designated areas using a strong fire ring to contain the coals. Remember that hot coals can easily ignite falling branches and leaves. A fire should never be left unattended and all coals should be thoroughly wetted once you are through with it.
• Pack out what you pack in.
• Let others enjoy the outdoors in peace. Don't play loud music. Maybe you like "Heavy Metal" blasted at top volume, but that's not what others come to nature to experience. Be considerate to others, and be aware of your presence.
• Pick up any litter you find, even if it's not yours!
• Leave gates to trails and roads as you find them.
• Obtain a map of the area you wish to explore and determine which areas are open for use.
• Contact the land manager for area restrictions and if crossing private property, be sure to ask permission from the land owner.
• The TreadLightly! Guide to Responsible Off-Roading contains detailed and informative information when riding into the great outdoors. You can refer to this guide for additional tips and details.

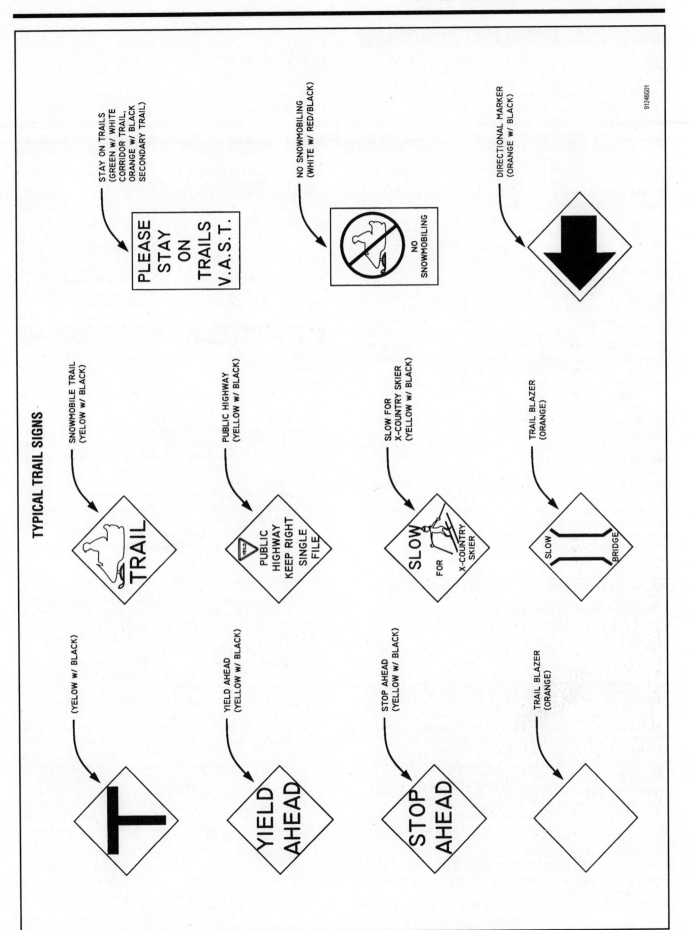

TYPICAL TRAIL SIGNS

STAY ON TRAILS
(GREEN w/ WHITE
CORRIDOR TRAIL,
ORANGE w/ BLACK
SECONDARY TRAIL)

PLEASE STAY ON TRAILS V.A.S.T.

NO SNOWMOBILING
(WHITE w/ RED/BLACK)

NO SNOWMOBILING

DIRECTIONAL MARKER
(ORANGE w/ BLACK)

SNOWMOBILE TRAIL
(YELLOW w/ BLACK)

TRAIL

PUBLIC HIGHWAY
(YELLOW w/ BLACK)

YIELD
PUBLIC HIGHWAY KEEP RIGHT SINGLE FILE

SLOW FOR
X-COUNTRY SKIER
(YELLOW w/ BLACK)

SLOW FOR X-COUNTRY SKIER

TRAIL BLAZER
(ORANGE)

SLOW   BRIDGE

(YELLOW w/ BLACK)

YIELD AHEAD
(YELLOW w/ BLACK)

YIELD AHEAD

STOP AHEAD
(YELLOW w/ BLACK)

STOP AHEAD

TRAIL BLAZER
(ORANGE)

91246G01

Drinking and Riding

Snowmobiling is fun, but it's work, too. It challenges the body and mind, and that's part of the reason you're so relaxed at the end of a day of snowmobiling. Alcohol magnifies and distorts those challenges and can quickly turn an enjoyable outing into a situation that's hazardous for you and others.

Put simply, alcohol and snowmobiling do not mix.

Forget the myth that alcohol warms you up. Yes, it may open the blood vessels and remove the feeling of a chill, but it does nothing to increase body heat. Instead, it can increase the risk of hypothermia. Alcohol also increases fatigue, fogs your ability to make good decisions, and slows your reaction time. It's part of a formula for disaster.

One last point—don't forget that most states and provinces have laws prohibiting the operation of a snowmobile while under the influence of alcohol.

SURVIVAL ON THE TRAIL

Survival on the trail is determined primarily by what your interpretation of survival is, the conditions you will be riding in and the items you carry with you. Different combinations require the rider to have a different base of knowledge and to be able to use different skill sets.

If you primarily ride on groomed trails with plenty of other riders, you most likely won't be carrying survival gear. If you are blazing new trails and will be riding alone, then survival equipment is a must. It is the responsibility of the rider to know the area they will be riding in and to accurately access and account for the conditions they will be riding in.

Another point that should be made is to know about the survival gear your are carrying. All the gear in the world is useless if you don't know how to use it! Carefully read and understand the directions that come with your gear.

In many parts of the country snowmobilers carry with them only the items that originally came with the snowmobile. True, some of them carry a rope tow strap and a few extra tools but for the most part they ride unequipped. This attitude may be a direct result of the popularity of snowmobiling in these areas. If you break down most of time some other snowmobiler will be coming down the trail, and they will most likely stop to see if you need help. But what if they don't?

In some areas of the country it is a totally different scene. You may never see another snowmobiler all day long. Even if there is another snowmobiler out there, they may be over the next ridge and you will never hear them, much less see them. It is in these areas that survival gear and riding with a buddy are most important.

Depending on the area, you may have to worry about someone going to fast around the corner and crossing into your path or someone on the wrong side of the trail. In other areas you worry about avalanches or running out of fuel when you are a long way from anything or anybody. The point is, no matter where you ride, be aware of the conditions.

A common problem no matter where you ride is the ignorant rider who does not understand the hazards of drinking and riding or going to fast for conditions. As I stated, this may just be ignorance, however in some cases it is an "I Don't Care" attitude. The only solution for this situation is to make the proper authorities aware of this rider's ignorance and allow them to properly take care of the situation.

Surviving the trails today is a lot more complex then just jumping on your sled and riding. Now, you need to know the limits of both your sled and yourself. But, when you think about it, it all boils down to good old common sense. Know your experience level, use your knowledge, and understand your sled and it's capabilities.

Survival Skills

Survival is a subject many of us would rather not think too much about, if only because a survival situation on a snowmobiling trip we were involved with would represent a failure of some sort on our part. However, we DO need to think about survival. Why? Well, if the worst happens on one of your trips, the Search and Rescue (SAR) team would much rather find a healthy survivor than someone who perished in the wilderness because they didn't have the skills necessary to survive. More importantly, we would like to keep you happy and healthy enough to buy the next edition of our Snowmobiling Handbook!

When it comes right down to it, how comfortable are you with your training and ability to survive the unexpected wilderness emergency? Does the question give you a moment's discomfort? Even if you are uncertain as to your survival preparedness, do you plan activities that take you into areas where you could conceivably become lost for days? If so, don't you think it's really about time you got some survival training, if only to ensure that everyone in your trip returns happy and healthy.

While there is not enough time or space here to provide you with a complete survival course, our attempt is to point you in the proper direction and encourage you to get some survival training on your own.

Any good survival course will provide you with considerable knowledge in a wide variety of survival techniques for a lot of different climates and topographic regions. However, there is one more important reason for you to attend a survival course; so trained instructors can see you and how you are applying the techniques you are learning. Good survival technique depends on hands-on technique and feedback with a trained survivalist.

➥**It is VERY important to remember that you MUST attend survival training for the areas you will be using as your activity environment. This means the training must include winter survival skills.**

Being Prepared to Survive

The most important part of the survival is being prepared to survive for an extended period of time whenever you leave the comforts of civilization and the nearness of traveled trails. This is not something that is limited to snowmobiling adventures, either. Survival preparation is just as important when you are on a business flight and your flight plan takes you over untracked wilderness.

There are some key areas you need to be aware of in order to survive over the long haul. Sure, most people who survive are rescued within three days of becoming lost while in the wilderness. But, and this is a very big but, there are some people who have to survive for weeks or months before they return to the comforts of home. If you ever have occasion to become one of those people, a strong background in survival knowledge and technique may just save your skin, as surely as ignorance will likely cost you your life. There are significant numbers of wilderness fatalities who would still be alive if only they had learned the skills they needed to survive.

What do you need before you are really prepared for survival? A positive attitude, training and practice, and a few essential pieces of equipment.

ATTITUDE

The proper attitude during a survival situation is all important. Quite simply, you need to WANT to survive and you need to BELIEVE that you can. Otherwise, you become too easily depressed and willing to give up the fight. Most situations are really a fight against the worst that circumstances, climate, weather, terrain, natural enemies and remoteness can throw at you.

As you sit there in your easy chair reading this manual, we have things pretty good. Things can be a whole lot different if you are faced with a snowmobile that will not run, the beginnings of a three-day blizzard, and a hundred miles to the nearest road. The situation gets even more desperate when you have injuries.

Things are also a lot different when you figure out that you are not where you are supposed to be and that you haven't the foggiest idea of just where "here" is!

People who spend a great deal of time in wilderness areas will probably never admit to being truly lost, though they may confess to having been a bit confused for a little while. I guess they had a pretty good idea of where they were within a large area, even if they didn't quite know exactly where they were within a few miles. Most times, they don't allow themselves to become too concerned, because they had enough knowledge to be able to get along quite well, even at the risk of a few days of discomfort.

A positive outlook, no matter how bad the situation, is one of the keys to keeping you alert and aware of what's going on around you. If you become depressed and give up, your chances of long-term survival decrease dramatically.

TRAINING AND PRACTICE

No matter how positive your attitude, you will not do well in a survival situation without the knowledge and skills you need to live off the land with only the barest minimum of equipment and supplies. It takes time to gain these, and you cannot learn everything you need to know from books alone, no matter regardless of how good the text or how reputable its author(s).

Your primary survival tool in any situation is your brain, and it can never be fully effective without the experience of actual survival skills practice. There is absolutely no substitute for starting a fire in the rain without using a lighter or any matches, any more than there is a substitute for preparing food you have obtained by collecting plants. Some of the essential tasks of survival are rather less than pleasant, but you need these skills to keep yourself and your companions alive and healthy enough to continue surviving.

Survival courses are usually a combination of classroom work and hands on experience with the techniques and tools you will need out in the wilderness. Your skills will also improve if you haul them out and use them frequently. Survival skills can be incorporated into many of your weekend activities in the wilderness. You can also challenge yourself from time to time by spending a weekend practicing your survival skills.

BEING PREPARED

There really is not enough space here to tell you how to build survival kits, and doing so would leave you without the training you will need to effectively use the items in the kit. However, there are a few basic principles involved in building a survival kit that we can tell you about to get you thinking.

Before you begin building a survival kit, you need to decide its purpose. Will you need it be small enough to put in your snowmobile's storage pouch, or will you be able to carry it in your saddle bags?

Survival kits should change in content with the season. For instance, you will need more ways of getting fires started really quickly in the winter-time than you will when riding your ATV in the summer, when you will want to trade out some fire-starters for insect repellents.

In addition to whatever else you put in the kit, you should consider getting a miniature survival guide one that has a good plant-identification section. While this may seem to be a trivial recommendation, there are plants that mimic each other in appearance, with one being edible, and the other, well, not . . .

Your best source of information for building an appropriate survival kit will come from a combination of good books and maybe a highly trained wilderness expert (Boy Scout?).

What to Bring on a Trial Ride

It is just Murphy's Law that every time you go out for a trail ride, something can and probably will go wrong. Now I'm not saying that your life will be endangered, but little problems when you are a long way from home tend to grow into big problems if they are not handled quickly. This is why packing some special items on your sled prior to starting your ride will reap big rewards the next time you find yourself in a little bit of a bad situation.

Yes, you could pack many things on your sled but here are a few things we have found to be essential. Of course you would not need all of this equipment each time you go out, but most people go out packed way too light anyway. If you are going on a long ride (especially a planned overnighter) then you probably will have need every item listed here. Like the Boy Scouts motto says, "Be Prepared".

Some Essentials

Here are a list of the most essential items you should carry with you:
- Map and Compass—carrying a map, a compass and a surveying (flagging) tape will help you navigate almost any terrain. Make sure that you remove the surveying tape on your way out
- Flashlight—beyond their use as a light source, flashlights can be used as signaling devices and to scare off any unwanted animal friends who might wander into your camp
- Signaling Devices—in addition to a flashlight and a safety blanket, pack a whistle and signal mirror to attract help if you are stranded
- Extra food—pack high calorie, high energy foods. Power bars are great. Don't forget to include some extra safe (boiled or filtered) drinking water
- Extra clothing—obviously you want to pack warm, dry clothing but here are some other suggestions. A space blanket (the shiny foil type) can be used

as a wind breaker, heat reflector, and as a signaling device to attract rescuers . Wave the red side up when standing on snow; the silver side up when standing on dark grounds. Also, large plastic leaf bags make for quick rain and wind protection. Put one bag over your head, the second around your legs, and the third over your backpack. Make a gap in the first for breathing
- Sunglasses and Sunscreen—even though you will be doing all of your trail riding in winter, the white surface of the snow will reflect a lot of sun. Suprisingly, you can get quite a sunburn. The sunglasses will help shield your eyes from sun glare, give you clearer vision and help to prevent snowblindness
- First aid supplies—beyond the normal bandages and ointments, include a metal cup to melt snow. Snow should always be melted into water. Eating snow will lower your body temperature, something you really don't want to happen. Also, don't forget the toilet paper
- Pocket knife—include the pocket knife is for general cutting duties and the saw is for cutting large pieces of wood for an emergency fire.
- Fire starter—bring two or more fire starting kits, each one different, plus a cigarette lighter. Make sure they all work in wet, cold, and windy conditions
- Snow shovel—always bring a shovel to help you dig your sled out of the snow should you stuff it in a snow bank while trying to hot dog it. Or, to dig a snow shelter or snow pit if you get stranded.
- Low temperature electrician tape—this special tape is handy for general repairs to space blankets, clothing, tents, boots, etc

Minimum First Aid Kit

Here are a list of the minimum items you should carry in your first aid kit:
- 2—Triangular bandages to hold compresses or splints in place.
- 1—"Ace®" bandage to support weakened limb joints or hold compresses or splints in place.
- 8—Sterile pads 4"X 4" to dress large wounds
- 1—4" bandage compress to dresses large wounds
- 6—Band-aids® to treat small wounds
- 1—Roll of adhesive tape to hold compress or splint in place
- 4—Moleskin tape squares to prevent and treat blisters
- 1—Antiseptic soap to clean wounds
- 1—Tube of sunscreen to prevents sunburn
- 1—Tube of Chapstick® to prevents dry lips
- 1—Insect repellent to keep insects away
- 8—Aspirin to relieves aches and pains
- 8—Antacid tablets to relieve nausea
- 1—Pair of small scissors to cut moleskin and tape
- 3—Safety pins to hold compresses or splints in place, open blisters, make arm sling from shirt sleeve.
- 1—TweezersRemove splinters and ticks
- 1—Backpack medical guide
- 1—Bag or box to hold all of the above

THINGS TO REMEMBER

We certainly hope you never become stranded on the trail, but if you do here are some things to remember:
- Seek and create shelter from cold, wind, snow, and rain. If possible, retreat to timbered areas for shelter construction and starting a fire. Use natural shelters like the windless side of ridges, rock croppings, slope depressions, snow blocks, a snow hole at base of standing trees, dense stands of trees, or under downed trees. Improvise a windbreak or shelter from stacked rocks or snow blocks, tree trunks, limbs, bark slabs and evergreen boughs, or dig a snow cave or snow trench with a cover.
- Conserve, share, and create warmth. Conserve body heat by putting on extra clothing. Replace damp clothing or place damp wool clothing over dry wool clothing. Loosen boot laces to increase circulation to the legs and feet. Place feet with boots on in a pack. Use evergreen boughs to insulate your body from ground. Place hands in armpits or crotch. Share body heat. Sit or lie front to back or back to back. Warm hands and feet of an injured person or companions. Create body heat. Nibble high energy goods like candy, nuts or power bars. Sip water kept warm with body heat. Use solid fuel hand warmer, igniting both ends of fuel stick, which is good for approximately four hours of heat. Do isometric exercises to stir up your body's circulation system.
- Prevent heat loss. Remember the body loses heat by respiration, evaporation, conduction, radiation, and convection. To prevent loss by respiration, cover the mouth and nose with loosely woven or knit wool. To reduce evapora-

tion through excessive perspiration, wear clothes that breathe and are in layers. To avoid loss by conduction, use a cover between the body and a cold, wet surface. This insulation is particularly important if you're already wet. To prevent loss by radiation, keep the head, hands, and feet covered. To prevent loss by convection, protect the body from the wind.

• Build a fire. Find dry wood such as dead lower branches and bark from underside of trees. Look under downed trees and inside dead logs for dry kindling. Wet wood will burn as it dries in a strong fire. Select a sheltered area, protected from strong winds, as the site for an emergency campfire. Under snow conditions build a fire base first, with large, four-inch diameter or larger pieces of wood. Put a fire starter on the base, surround the fire starter with branches to hold kindling above the fire starter, then place a crosshatch of kindling and slightly larger wood on the branches. Light fire starter and blow lightly to help its flame ignite kindling. Add progressively larger wood to the flame area.

• Look for hypothermia symptoms. In stage one, the victim begins shivering, has poor coordination, slurs speech, and shows poor judgment. By stage two, when the body temperature is below 95 degrees, muscular rigidity replaces shivering, and the victim becomes more irrational and needs warmth immediately from external sources and protection from further heat loss. Know that the victim is the LAST to realize they are in danger.

• Send for help. If you need to send for help, review the situation and evaluate the facts as you outline information for a rescue group. If possible, send two people who will mark the route on the way out and note the terrain, distance, and time from the accident site to the road. Once the two reach a telephone, they should call either a park ranger, if in a national park, or the local county sheriff, who, in turn, will alert rescue groups. Be sure the rescue group gets the number of the calling telephone and a definite place to meet the callers who will lead them back to the accident site.

• Prepare for the worst and plan for the best. Our hope is that you will never have to use this information, but with this information, the survival training you will be looking into (right?) and the equipment we advise you to bring, you will be prepared to survive.

Medical Emergencies

GENERAL FIRST AID

There are a lot of questions concerning how much first aid training is enough for snowmobilers. It should be noted that, in general, the farther away from civilization you ride, the more competent you ought to be. That makes sense, doesn't it? Yet every day riders head out into the wilderness on long adventures with no more than a passing knowledge of first aid techniques.

When you are in a survival situation, your knowledge of first aid, combined with the knowledge of the others with you, could be your only line of defense between life and death for either yourself or someone in your group. Several types of experiences , where survival techniques are required, begin with an accident of some kind, whether it be a snowmobiling accident or a simple fall while you are off the beaten path. Not only will these situations test your knowledge of first aid, but you will also probably need to be able to apply those skills to someone without anything close to adequate medical equipment or supplies (unless you packed them on your sled like we suggested).

One of the biggest problems when it comes to first aid and emergency training is that current courses generally center on "street" first aid, where there is an assumption that qualified medical help (ambulances and hospitals) are only a phone call away. Now, that's nice when you are actually in that environment, but a lot of the "street" first aid assumptions go straight out the window when you are miles and miles from the nearest phone. Even when you have a cellular telephone, definitive medical care may be several hours—or days—away, depending on the weather conditions.

I am not saying that all snowmobilers should become Emergency Medical Technicians (EMT) prior to going out on their first trail ride. What I am saying is that first aid training should be a part of everyone's life experience. The farther away from civilization you travel, the more training you need.

CARDIO-PULMONARY RESUSCITATION (CPR)

Cardio-Pulmonary Resuscitation (CPR) is one essential emergency medical skill that EVERYONE should know. There is no reason why every snowmobiler should not be capable of saving a friend's life. "Its not necessary" or "We already have enough people who can do CPR" some may say, but what if you are the one who requires CPR and no one around knows it? Can you guarantee that you won't have a heart attack and need CPR yourself on some future trip? Wouldn't you want your trail riding buddies to be able to do something that could save your life? Enough said!

HYPOTHERMIA

Hypothermia is a medical emergency which untreated, results in death. It occurs when the body's temperature falls and the body cannot produce heat as fast as it is being lost. Hypothermia becomes life-threatening when deep-body temperature falls below 95°F.

All winter adventurists and snowmobilers in particular should be aware of this condition and actively observe their riding companions for its symptoms. Hypothermia is the leading killer of people participating in winter recreational activities. It is a silent killer which dulls the brain, the most important tool to winter survival.

• Hypothermia can occur rapidly during cold-water immersion (one hour or less when water temperature is below 45°F). Because water has a tremendous capacity to drain heat from the body, immersion in water considered even slightly cool (e.g., 60°F) can cause hypothermia, if the immersion is prolonged for several hours.

• Generally, deep-body temperature will not fall until after many hours of continuous exposure to the cold, if the individual is healthy, physically active, and reasonably dressed. However, since wet skin and wind accelerate body heat loss, and the body produces less heat during inactive periods, body temperature can fall even when air temperatures are above freezing if conditions are windy, clothing is wet, and/or the individual is inactive.

• Hypothermia may be difficult to recognize in its early stages of development. Things to watch for include unusually withdrawn or bizarre behavior, irritability, confusion, slowed or slurred speech, altered vision, uncoordinated movements, and unconsciousness.

• Even mild hypothermia can cause victims to make poor decisions or act drunk (e.g., removing clothing when it is clearly inappropriate).

• Hypothermia victims may show no heart beat, breathing, or response to touch or pain when in fact they are still alive. Sometimes, the heart beat and breathing of hypothermia victims will be so faint that it can go undetected. If hypothermia has resulted from submersion in cold water, Cardio-Pulmonary Resuscitation (CPR) should be initiated without delay. However, when hypothermia victims are found on land, it is important to take a little extra time searching for vital signs to determine whether CPR is really required. Hypothermia victims should be treated as gently as possible during treatment and evacuation, since the function of the heart can be seriously impaired in hypothermia victims. Rough handling can cause life-threatening disruptions in heart rate.

• All hypothermia victims, even those who do not appear to be alive, must be evaluated by trained medical personnel.

If you should need to treat a hypothermia victim, remember the following points:

• Prevent further exposure to cold
• Remove wet clothing
• As appropriate, initiate CPR
• Rewarm the body by covering with blankets, sleeping bags, and by body-to-body contact
• Handle hypothermia victims gently during treatment and evacuation

FROSTBITE

Frostbite is a thermal injury to the skin which can result from prolonged exposure to moderate cold or brief exposure to extreme cold. When skin is exposed to the cold, blood vessels in the skin clamp down or constrict. As a result of a decreased blood flow to the skin, the fluid in and around skin cells develops ice crystals. This causes frostbite to occur. Areas of the body most prone to frostbite are fingers, toes, hands, feet, nose, ears, and cheeks.

If frostbite is suspected, begin warming the person slowly and seek immediate medical assistance. Warm the person's trunk first. Use your own body heat to help. Arms and legs should be warmed last because stimulation of the limbs can drive cold blood toward the heart and lead to heart failure. Put the affected person in dry clothing and wrap their entire body in a blanket. Never give a frostbite or hypothermia victim something with caffeine in it (like coffee or tea) or alcohol. Caffeine, a stimulant, can cause the heart to beat faster and hasten the effects the cold has on the body. Alcohol, a depressant, can slow the heart and also hasten the ill effects of cold

A loss of feeling and a white or pale appearance in fingers, toes, or nose and ear lobes are usually the first symptoms. However, the signs and symptoms of frostbite vary depending on the severity of the case. A person may experience any of the following:

- Pain in the affected area
- Numbness in the affected area
- Prickly sensations
- Firm, whitened skin areas
- Peeling or blistering
- Itching
- Swelling
- Hard, glossy, grayish, yellow skin

If you think you have frostbite, move indoors to a warm environment as soon as possible. Do not rub the affected area as this can cause further damage due to the presence of ice crystals in the skin cells. Gently re-warm the affected body part by placing it, if possible, against a warm body part (e.g., placing hands under arms), or warming with lukewarm water or warm blankets. Get medical attention as soon as possible.

The treatment of frostbite will depend on the severity of skin damage. Hospitalization may be necessary in some severe cases. Therefore, it's important to seek an evaluation as soon as possible.

SNOWBLINDNESS

Winter fun in the sun may be hazardous to your eyes. Light rays reflect off snow and enter the eye, hitting the cornea and the protective layer. The rays burn the eye, causing temporary blindness. A sunglass lens will reflect light away preventing snow blindness.

Snow blindness may leave eyes red, itchy and sensitive to light. Staying indoors and resting the eyes can help speed recovery.

Food and Water

When it comes to real life survival, food and water become very significant issues. You need both to survive. If you suddenly find yourself in a survival situation, you will need to find both as soon as possible. The longer you are without water, the more dehydrated, weaker, and less able to take care of yourself you will become. Depending on the weather, you will rapidly become more susceptible to hypothermia and frostbite.

Most people can last longer without food than they can without water, so finding water and making it safe to drink will be among your first priorities in a survival situation. This will not be a problem as you can melt the snow you are riding on to create drinking water.

➡**NEVER eat snow to quench your thirst. By eating snow, you lower your body's temperature and put yourself at greater risk for hypothermia. ALWAYS melt snow using a metal cup, then drink the water created by the melted snow. It should also go without saying to never use yellow snow when making water.**

There is a school of thought that results in people taking survival courses without being taught how to identify and use edible plants. The theory is that, since the majority of lost people are found within three days, it is safer not to teach edible plants information because there are harmful plants that closely resemble some of the edible ones. While it is true that most survivors are found

within three days, there are those who are not, either because they did not leave a well designed ride planned, with friends at home who would alert authorities if they became overdue (ride plan), or because the local weather situation was so bad that a search and rescue operation could not be launched immediately.

Yes, you can probably go three full days without food if you really have to. However, you are not going to be very much use to yourself or anyone else at the end of that time.

Feeding yourself in the bush while you are having to survive is not quite the same as getting your food at a market, or pulling leftovers out of the fridge. If you lack expertise in hunting and gathering skills, bring someone on your trip who is a combination of good teacher and an expert in providing for oneself from nature's bounty. This way, the more you learn, the more capable you will become in surviving in the wild.

It does take time to become truly efficient at using the plant, insect, bird, and animal life around you. It takes years to develop true expertise and that expertise cannot always be translated from one region to another. Still, you can learn enough about the edible plants and animals in your area in fairly short order to be able to survive, even if you won't be dining particularly sumptuously.

Avalanches

Avalanche danger is very real for those snowmobilers who travel to the mountains. The following is some basic information on avalanches. Be aware of the snow conditions you are in at all times and sled safe!

- Most avalanches occur on slopes of 30 to 45 degrees, but large ones can occur on slopes as little as 25 degrees
- Snow is most unstable after and during snowfalls or prolonged heating by the sun, especially on steep inclines
- Sunballs and cartwheels on the surface during a warming period could indicate instability in deeper layers
- The most dangerous avalanches usually occur on convex slopes
- Avalanches can take place on short slopes as well as long ones
- Leeward slopes are dangerous because wind blown snow adds depth, creating hard, hollow sounding wind slabs
- South facing slopes are most dangerous in the spring
- Smooth grassy slopes are the most dangerous spots, but avalanches can start among trees under conditions of stress
- Avalanche danger can vary within a slope
- Following an old track does not necessarily mean a slope is safe
- Down-slanting trees and brush indicates previous avalanche launches
- Sun crust on old snow can cause new snow to slide off
- Rough surfaces generally favor stability of new snow cover
- Loose underlying snow layers are more dangerous than compacted ones
- Recent avalanches indicate dangerous conditions
- Snow falling at the rate of an inch or more per hour increases avalanche danger
- Snow crystals in the shape of needles and pellets result in more unstable snow conditions than the typical star-shaped snowflakes
- Snow saturated with water can avalanche, especially on south facing slopes and beneath exposed rock.
- Rapid changes in wind, temperature and snowfall cause changes in the snowpack and may affect stability
- If the snow cracks and the crack runs as you step, the danger of slab avalanche, the most serious type of winter hazard, is high
- Gullies are many times more hazardous than open slopes because they act as natural avalanche chutes.

9124XP1B

Avalanche is a real danger for any rider who rides in the mountains

7

ACCESSORIZING YOUR SNOWMOBILE

ACCESSORIZING YOUR SNOWMOBILE

♦ **See Figures 1 thru 6**

This section is designed to help you choose the proper accessories to help your snowmobile better suit your riding needs. The goal here is to familiarize you with the options that are available when it comes to buying accessories and with the features you should look for to maximize their value.

When looking at modifying your snowmobile with accessories, you have to determine your goals. Are you trying to make your snowmobile a little more versatile? Are you looking into making your snowmobile go faster? Looking for ways to make maintenance easier? Or maybe just a few small accessories to individualize your snowmobile? Whatever your specific goals, this section should help you learn what to look for when choosing accessories.

To really get a good idea of the selection of accessories available for your snowmobile, pick up a some copies of snowmobile magazines or catalogs. Page through them, and you'll be amazed; tons of accessories just waiting to be bolted onto your snowmobile. You will find everything from skid plates to skis and from cargo bags to studded tracks.

So lets get down to business. Make a list of what you want your snowmobile to do. Okay, now that you have that, make a list of possible accessories that will help you achieve your goals. Next, decide if any of the accessories may degrade other aspects of your riding that you aren't willing to sacrifice, and cross them off the list. Now you have your wish list; time to fill it!

The nice thing about snowmobiles and the aftermarket is that you can get almost anything you want. Take your list to your local dealer or snowmobile shop, or call one of the catalog houses. They will help you obtain the stuff you want. Keep in mind that the manufactures often have accessories for your snowmobile that fit and work as the factory intended. You don't have to hit the aftermarket for everything!

What types of accessories do I want on my snowmobile? Let's look at some of the different types of riders and how they may outfit their snowmobiles.

• The hunter/camper might want a cover for the entire snowmobile, specialized racks or a trailer for carrying deer, large gear bags for carrying hunting and camping gear, a rifle/bow rack or scabbard, a winch, and skid plates.

• The sport rider might look for high-performance parts, like exhaust systems, suspension components, pulley (clutch) kits, studded tracks and performance parts kits.

• The touring rider might look for custom seats or back rests, heated grips, a taller windshield, saddle bags and tank bags with map holders.

There are many different needs and even more solutions. Ask the guys at your local snowmobile shop what they think will best suit your needs. They may show you that the manufacturer already makes something that you want. You can also call the catalog houses, as they answer questions all day long and can help point out your choices.

We have chosen examples of accessories from some of the industries known leaders (and in some cases from lesser known but just as high quality manufacturers), and we would like to thank the manufacturers again for their help with the

Fig. 1 From skid plates . . .

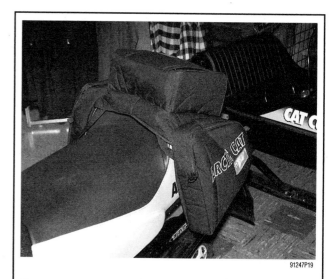

Fig. 3 . . . and from cargo bags . . .

Fig. 2 . . . to skis . . .

Fig. 4 . . . to studded tracks

Fig. 5 Most snowmobile dealers are stocked to the rafters with accessories for your ride. Everything from plastic parts . . .

Fig. 6 . . . to hard core performance items like these studs are available right off the rack

production of this section. That is not to say the brands pictured here are your only options. However it is to say that they are VERY GOOD examples of the high quality accessories that are available, and as such are excellent standards for comparison with the accessories you look at when deciding on a purchase.

Skid Plates

HOW TO SELECT

♦ See Figure 7

Most snowmobiles do not come equipped from the manufacturer with skid plates. If you do a lot of riding in rocky areas or just want the added protection of a skid plate, many fine examples are available from the manufacturers and aftermarket companies alike.

You also have the option of color coordinating your skid plate with your sled, as most come in a rainbow of colors. For our project we chose a black skid plate to contrast our Ski-Doo's screaming yellow color.

If you're in the market for a skid plate, there are some important features to be considered. Things like holes for the drain plugs are nice touches, but most importantly, look for smooth, high quality plastic and factory mounting points. Most skid plates will require you to do at least some drilling on your sled. However, this type of modification should be kept to a minimum with the proper skid plate.

Fig. 7 Skid plates offer substantial protection to the underside of a snowmobile

HOW TO INSTALL

♦ See Figures 8 thru 21

In order to properly install a skid plate, you should have unrestricted access to the under side of your sled, especially the front half near the front suspension. This will require you to use some kind of lifting device. In the accompanying pictures, a strap is wrapped around the front nerf bar of the Ski-Doo and a rope hoist is used to elevate the sled to provide the appropriate access. Conditions at your garage may differ so it will be up to you to devise a proper lifting device. Above all remember to raise and properly support the sled safely.

The whole reason for installing a skid plate is to protect the critical suspension and steering components at the front of the sled. Trial fit your skid plate to determine if it covers the proper area. Note where the attaching points are and if they will interfere with other components on the sled. Is there enough room to fit your hand into the engine compartment to hold the nuts? On most properly designed skid plates, installation should be fairly straight forward. If the skid plate is too difficult to install, either it is of low quality or it is the wrong one for your sled. In either event, don't install it.

Trial fit your new skid plate prior to drilling any holes in either the plate or the sled. Now is the time to discover that the plate does not fit properly or that a critical suspension component does not have its full travel with the plate in place. Have a helper hold the skid plate and look at its position on the sled. Is it

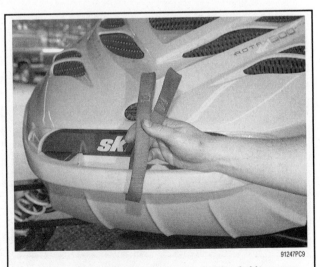

Fig. 8 Using a strap around the front nerf bar of the sled is an easy way to raise it for clearance

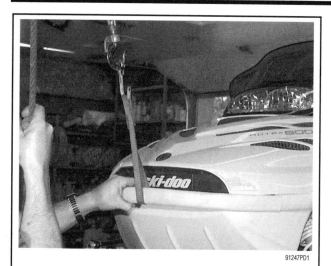

Fig. 9 Lifting and supporting your sled for repair or maintenance can be accomplished with a rope hoist

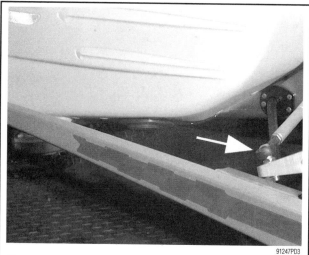

Fig. 12 The skid plate also protects the steering components like this heim joint

Fig. 10 The skid plate is designed to protect the front suspension components

Fig. 13 Position the skid plate under the snowmobile

Fig. 11 Debris can jamb itself up into this area and cause suspension damage

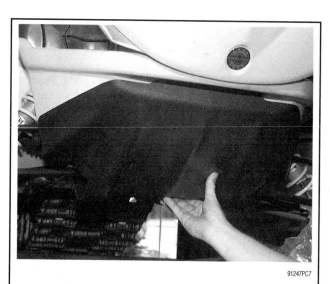

Fig. 14 Lift the skid plate into position and check for proper fit

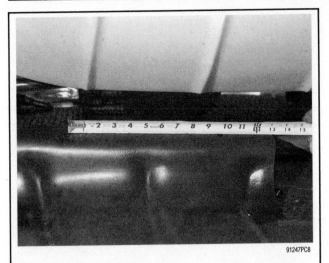

Fig. 15 Carefully measure for proper fastener locations, avoiding any hoses, wiring or other components

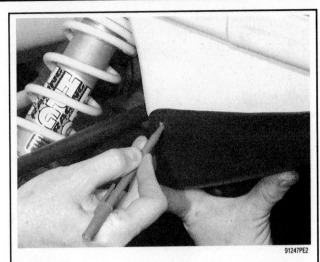

Fig. 18 You can either use the hole in the plate as a template and mark the proper location . . .

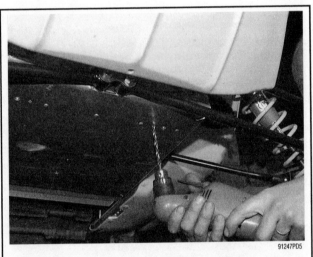

Fig. 16 If drilling into metal portions of the sled, make sure to use a high speed drill bit designed to cut into metal

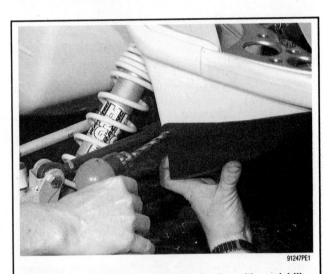

Fig. 19 . . . or continue to hold the skid plate in position and drill right through the plate into the sled

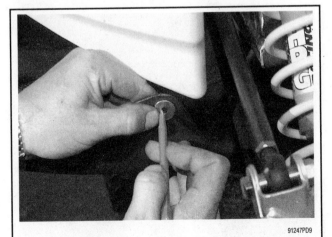

Fig. 17 Start drilling the skid plate by making marks at the proper locations. Use a washer to trace a circle of the proper size to fit the bolt

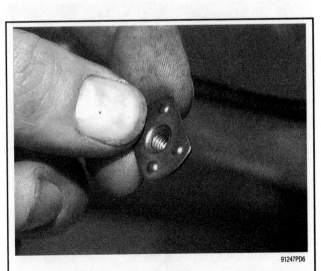

Fig. 20 The skid plate bolts on this Ski-Doo kit are tightened against this specially designed low profile nut

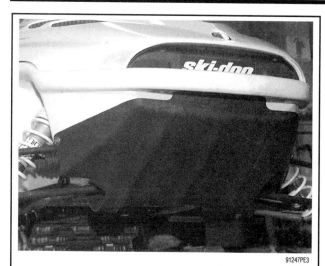

Fig. 21 Here is a properly installed skid plate that is ready for some abuse on the trail

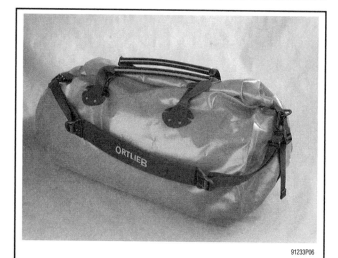

Fig. 22 If you are going on a long trip, a waterproof gear bag like this one will keep clothing and other gear warm and dry

aligned properly? Does it look good? If the answer to these questions is yes, then you are ready to drill.

Drilling into your sled may be a little frightening but it is usually a necessity when installing a skid plate. The old mechanics motto of "measure twice, drill once" is the best advice. Check the back side of any spot you are ready to drill for obstructions. It is so easy to hit a fuel line, coolant line or wiring harness and not even know it until you go out to ride your sled. Take your time and drill slowly. It may come in handy to have a helper hold the skid plate in place while you drill. If your skid plate does not have pre-drilled holes, mark the locations on the skid plate and drill these holes first. Then, transfer the hole locations to your sled and drill the holes on the sled.

Skid plates are fastened to the belly of the sled with nuts and bolts. Lets face it, these plastic plates will take a lot of abuse when you are blasting down the trail. If they are not held on securely, you will probably wind up running over them when they fall off. Or worse, they will get tangled in the steering and cause you to loose control. Use all the fasteners that come with your skid plate and follow the manufacturer's instructions for fastener placement. It is also a good idea to use some type of locking compound, such as Loctite® on the nuts to prevent them from loosening.

After bolting your new skid plate in place, stand back and take a good look at it. Make any necessary adjustments and then head out to the trial to break it in.

Gear Bags

HOW TO SELECT

▶ **See Figures 22 thru 29**

Gear bags aren't really a big priority for a lot of snowmobile riders, but once you've spent a couple weekends riding, you will quickly learn the importance of having gear bags to carry all your stuff. Gear bags are great for organization, protection, and convenience.

The first thing you need to decide is the exact use of your gear bag. Do you just need something to stuff your weekend gear into, or are you looking for heavy duty bags to carry camping gear? You do want waterproof bags, don't you? Do you want to maximize the carrying capacity of your snowmobile? Just looking for something to put all your little things into that fits onto your snowmobile? The choices are endless.

The following pictures show a couple of samples of common gear bags. New gear bags are constantly being introduced for snowmobilers and camper, each with various specialized purposes. What we have shown here is only a small portion of what is available. To get more ideas, go to you local snowmobile or camping dealer, or look in any of the various catalogs which cater to these sports.

Another type of gear bag that should be of major interest to snowmobile rid-

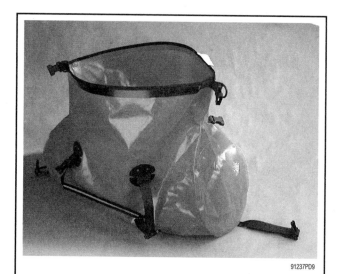

Fig. 23 This bag has a wide opening for easy access

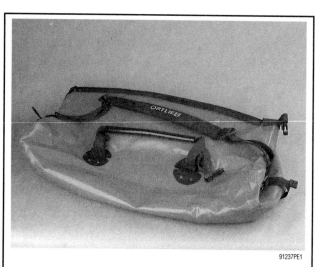

Fig. 24 One of the best features about most gear bags is that they are compactable, and take up little space when not in use

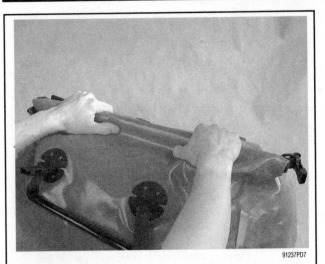

Fig. 25 Instead of using a zipper, this dry bag has extra material that is rolled up . . .

Fig. 28 Like most dry bags, this one rolls up tightly instead of using a zipper to keep the contents dry

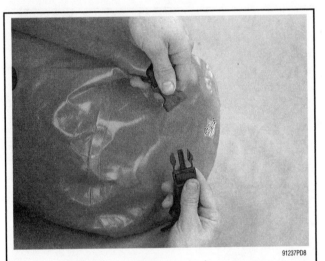

Fig. 26 . . . and held tightly by clips on each side of the bag to seal out water (and keep the contents in)

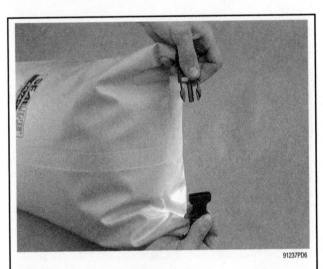

Fig. 29 Once the end of the bag is rolled tightly, the ends fold up and connect together with a plastic clip

Fig. 27 Dry bags are great for snowmobile riders who need to keep gear from getting wet

ers are dry bags. Dry bags were originally developed for whitewater rafters, but work out really well for snowmobile riders who spend any amount of time in wet weather. Dry bags are made from vinyl or rubber coated canvas, and have sealed seams to keep the contents inside the bag dry. Most dry bags are of the "roll closing" type, which eliminate leaky zippers.

Seal Line® and Ortlieb Waterproof Outdoor Gear® are two large manufacturers of dry bags. These fine examples from the catalog of The Rider WearHouse® are just a portion of the large selection of different styles available. The unique way they fold up helps to keep water from entering the bag. Dry bags can easily be strapped onto your sled and then carried around the campsite later. Things that are important to keep dry, such as food, extra clothing, sleeping bags, etc. can be safely stored in a dry bag. If you're into camping trips with your snowmobile, these dry bags are the way to go.

Saddle Bags

HOW TO SELECT

▶ See Figures 30 thru 36

Who needs saddle bags? Well if you have taken our advice and prepared an emergency kit for both mechanical repairs and repairs of the more human kind

Fig. 30 From traditional saddle bags . . .

Fig. 33 . . . and every shape and size in between, you can find exactly what you need to solve any storage solution for your snowmobile

Fig. 31 . . . to seat bags . . .

Fig. 34 Although not a typical saddle bag, this tool caddy helps to keep tools and small parts in neat order

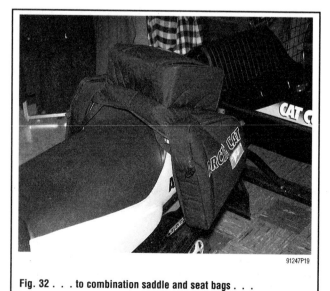

Fig. 32 . . . to combination saddle and seat bags . . .

Fig. 35 The tool caddy's hard sides prevent objects from rolling of the snowmobile seat during service or maintenance. Note the flap pockets which increase storage

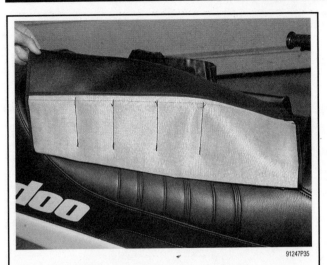

Fig. 36 The smooth under side of the tool caddy prevents damage to the snowmobile seat and plastic

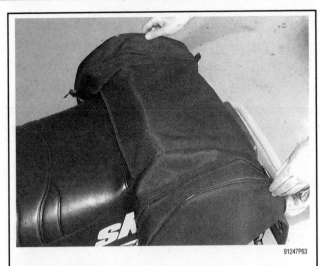

Fig. 37 Most popular styles of saddle bags fit over the rear portion of the snowmobile seat

then you do. Lets face it, storage on snowmobiles is very limited. At best, there is a small storage compartment at the rear of the seat that will hold a few items but in general if you are bringing anything of substance with you then you need a place to put it.

Now some will say they can stuff everything into the pockets of their jacket or bibs. And for a short ride this maybe acceptable. However, if you are planning anything greater than a hour trip, then it would be in your best interest to carry more appropriate gear.

The first thing you need to decide is exactly how much gear you are going to carry and what the exact size of the package is. Do you just need something to throw a few small items in or are you looking to carry half your wardrobe with you? Will you be leaving the items on your sled or carrying them with you to your camp site. Do you need to access them while you are riding (a map) or will you only access them after you have stopped? The choices are endless.

The following pictures show the most common saddle and seat bags. These bags are available from both manufacturers and aftermarket companies alike. What we have shown here is only a small portion of what is available. To get more ideas, go to you local snowmobile dealer, or look in any of the various catalogs or magazines which cater to snowmobilers.

HOW TO INSTALL

▶ See Figures 37 thru 56

Most saddle bags are of a simple strap on design and require little in the way of installation instructions. However, some of the larger bags do have to be securely anchored to prevent them from moving while you are blitzing through the trails.

Saddle bag installation should start with a simple trial fit of the bags on the snowmobile. These particular bags are manufactured for Ski-Doo and designed to fit may of their snowmobiles. By designing a bag for a particular sled or group of sleds, the designers can maximize the amount of storage while minimizing the overall dimensions of the bags.

After reading over the instructions furnished in the kit, it was determined that a drill with the proper size bits and a pop rivet gun were the only tools necessary to install the bags.

We started the installation by attaching the bags at the rear of the snowmobile. These straps simply wrap around the rear bar on the sled and clip back into a latch at the saddle bag. After the bag is positioned properly on the seat, the straps are pulled snug.

The next operation is to install the buckle that attaches the front of the bag to the snowmobile. This requires that a hole be drilled and a pop-rivet be used to secure the buckle to the aluminum. Placement of the buckle is critical. If the buckle is not properly placed, the strap will not reach and the saddle bag will not be properly attached to the sled.

Once the buckle is installed, position the saddle bags on the snowmobile seat and strap them down securely.

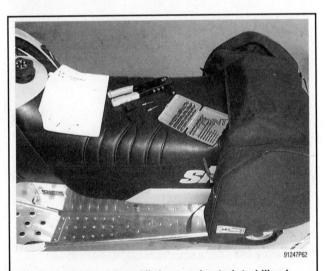

Fig. 38 Installation of the saddle bags requires tools to drill and pop-rivet the buckle to the snowmobile

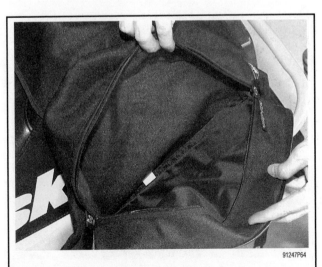

Fig. 39 Properly designed saddle bags will offer spacious storage yet maintain a low profile

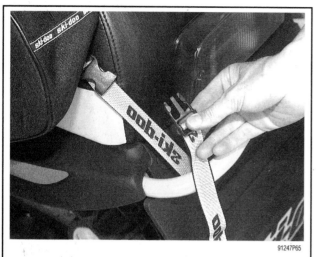

Fig. 40 After positioning the saddle bag on the seat, fasten the rear straps by wrapping them around the rear bar . . .

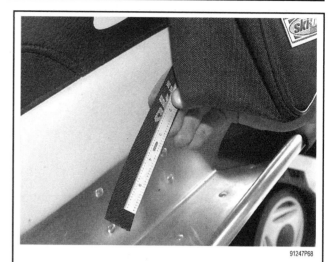

Fig. 43 On these saddle bags, the buckle should be positioned three inches from the end of the strap

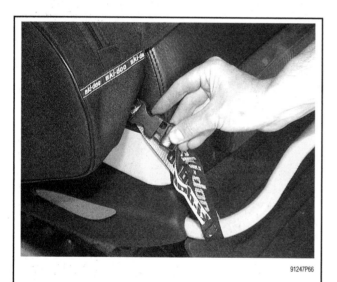

Fig. 41 . . . and clipping the buckle together . . .

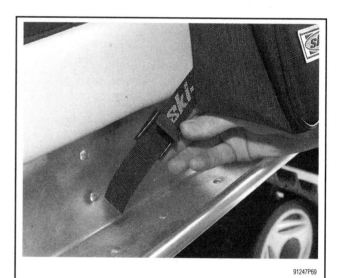

Fig. 44 Position the buckle on the strap . . .

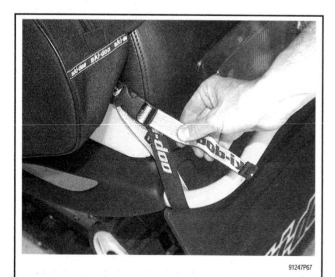

Fig. 42 . . . finally take up the slack by pulling the strap taunt

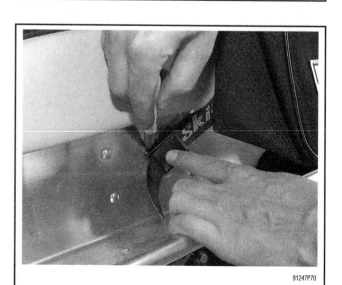

Fig. 45 . . . and mark the correct position on the aluminum

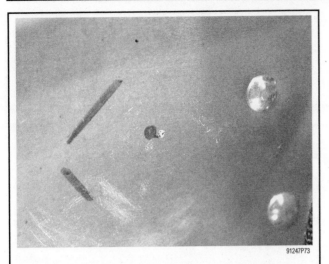

Fig. 46 The rivet hole to secure the buckle can now be properly marked . . .

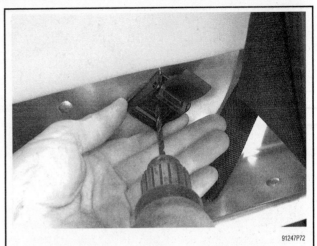

Fig. 49 Trying to drill through the buckle and the aluminum is not a good idea. Chances are the drill bit will bite into the plastic buckle and spin it right out of your hand

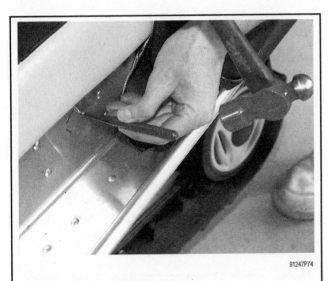

Fig. 47 . . . center punched . . .

Fig. 50 The best way to drill a hole in the buckle is to first center punch the location of the hole . . .

Fig. 48 . . . and drilled

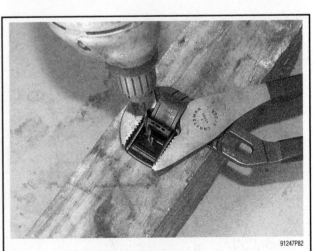

Fig. 51 . . . and then hold the buckle with pliers while drilling. Note the block of wood used to prevent the drill bit from damaging the floor

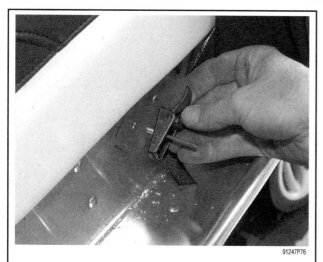

Fig. 52 Once the buckle and snowmobile are drilled, insert a rivet into the buckle and position it correctly

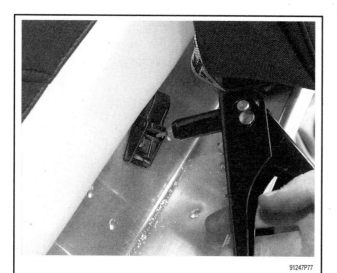

Fig. 53 Use a pop-rivet gun to fasten the buckle to the snowmobile

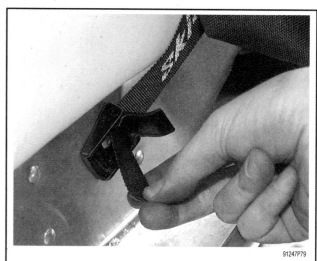

Fig. 55 To finish the installation, thread the front saddle bag strap through the buckle . . .

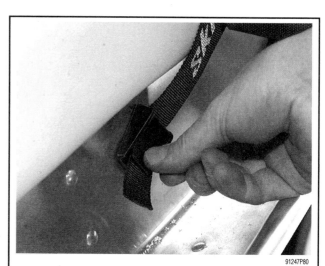

Fig. 56 . . . pull it taunt and then press the buckle cover down to secure the strap in position

Fig. 54 Here is a properly installed buckle

Hoists, Workstands and Rollers

HOW TO SELECT

▶ See Figures 57 thru 62

Simple maintenance like lubrication can be a real pain without some way of lifting your sled. Sure, you can use make shift methods lift the track and skis up off the garage floor, but do you always want to be crawling around to do your maintenance? After performing basic maintenance on your snowmobile on the garage floor a few times, you'll quickly learn the value of a workstand.

There are several types of lifts and workstands available for snowmobiles. Some lift only a portion of the sled off the ground, while others lift the whole snowmobile, but only a foot or two from the ground. These can be convenient and easy to use, but you will still be constantly bending over when working on your snowmobile. The best type of workstand to get is one that will support your snowmobile at a reasonable work height.

Another problem when working with snowmobiles is moving them around. Unless you use some kind of roller to move your sled around your garage, you will be constantly scraping the floor with your expensive carbides and studs. For ease of movement and also to keep your sled up off the concrete, invest in a set of rollers.

Fig. 57 This particular workstand is a professional model used by our friends at Smith Marine for servicing snowmobiles, ATV's and personal watercraft

Fig. 58 Front rollers contain a groove which centers the roller on the ski runner

Fig. 59 Rear rollers are positioned in the center of the track

Fig. 60 A rope hoist attached to the rafters . . .

Fig. 61 . . . works well to lift the rear of a snowmobile for servicing

Fig. 62 Here, an engine hoist, combined with a pole-type jackstand, is used to raise the rear of a snowmobile to perform service on the rear suspension

Getting the front or rear of a snowmobile up off the ground is not as hard as it seems. Any number of lifting devices can be used to quickly raise the snowmobile in the air. During production of this manual, we used just two of the many ways to lift a sled.

The first way was to use an engine hoist attached to the rear bar of the sled. After properly protecting the paint on the bar, the hook from the engine hoist was wrapped around the bar and up the sled went. The second method was to lift the sled using a rope hoist. This assembly was attached to the rafters and is pretty much a stationary piece.

Grips

HOW TO SELECT

▶ **See Figures 63 and 64**

Any part of the snowmobile which your body comes in contact with can be considered a vehicle interface. Changing any of these vehicle interface items, can drastically affect the way your snowmobile "feels" when you ride.

Granted, installing a set of grips on your snowmobile isn't really an accessory, but more of a long-term maintenance item. Depending on how much you ride, your grips will wear out and require replacement at some time in the life of your snowmobile. On the other hand, replacing the stock grips because you don't like their feel could be considered accessorizing.

There are a ton of companies that make aftermarket grips for snowmobiles. They all have unique features, which may or may not appeal to you. Your local snowmobile dealer will most likely have a large inventory of grips for you to select. There is one item of importance that must be noted when looking for a new set of grips; make sure that the grips are both of the same inner diameter. Since motorcycles use twist throttles, the right grip will have a larger inner diameter than the left. Motorcycle grips won't work on your snowmobile unless you buy two of the same pair of grips, and use the two left grips.

HOW TO INSTALL

▶ **See Figures 65 thru 72**

Before you can put on a new pair of grips, you've gotta hack the old ones off. This doesn't mean with an axe, though! A carpet or utility knife should work just fine. Make a slice down the length of the grip, and peel it away from the handlebars. Once the old grips have been cut off, chances are that there will be some rust and scaled paint on the handlebars where the grips were. Be sure to neutralize any rust, and clean the handlebars with some light sandpaper to provide a smooth surface for the new grips.

There are a zillion different methods people have come up with for installing

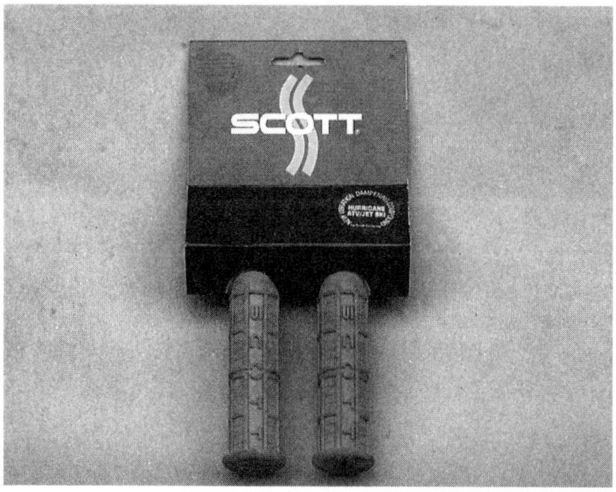

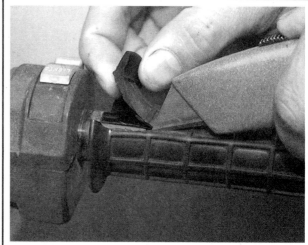

Fig. 63 Grips are probably one of the cheapest accessories you can buy for your snowmobile

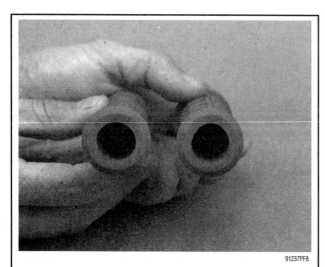

Fig. 64 Make sure that both grips are the same diameter. Motorcycle grips are usually different sizes, since they use twist throttles

Fig. 65 Use a razor blade to slice off those nasty old grips

Fig. 66 Good ol' fashioned dish soap works well for installing new grips. You can mix it with water, or use it full strength

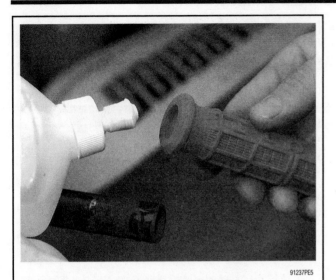

Fig. 67 We chose to use it full strength on our grips

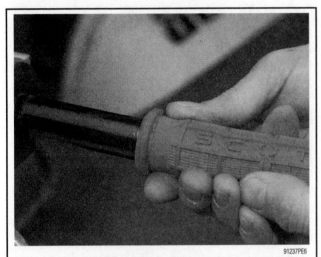

Fig. 68 Once you've lightly coated the handlebar end and the inside of the grip, simply slide it onto the handlebar

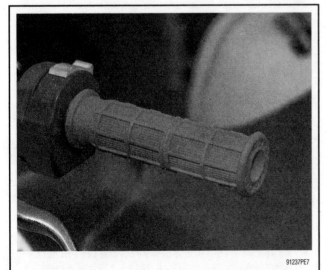

Fig. 69 Once the grip is positioned, simply let the soap dry out

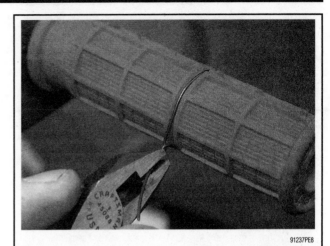

Fig. 70 For additional holding power, the grips can be safety wired in place. The groove on the grip is designed specifically for this purpose

Fig. 71 After the wire has been twisted (not too tightly, or the wire might cut the grip) hook the wire around . . .

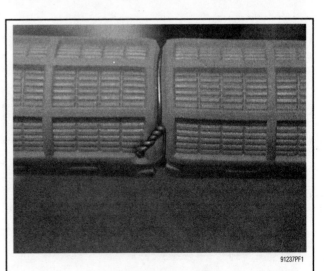

Fig. 72 . . . then push the tip into the grip as shown. The grips are ready to go!

a pair of grips. Everything from carburetor cleaner to trim adhesive. One of the easiest (and safest) ways to install a pair of grips onto your handlebars is with good ol' fashioned dishwashing soap as a lubricant.

Just squirt a little inside the grip, and rub it around with your finger. While you're at it, put a little on the handlebar end too. Don't get too carried away with the soap, because the more that you put on, the longer it will take to dry. (Remember, you only need enough to get the grips in place.) Once everything is lubed up, simply push the grip onto the handlebar end. Position the grips how you want them, and let the soap dry. Be sure to plan ahead here; the soap might take up to 24 hours or more to dry out, depending on the type of soap and how much you used to install the grips.

Once the soap is dry, the friction of the rubber against the handlebars should hold them in place. If you find that the grips move around, you can use safety wire to hold them in place. This is an old trick that motocross racers used to do (and still do) to keep their grips from coming off during a race. Over the years, most aftermarket grip companies adapted this practice, making "safety wire grooves" that are molded into the grips.

To make use of these grooves, grab some safety wire and some pliers, then wrap the wire around the groove in the grip. Using the pliers, twist the wire as shown to provide some tension on the grip. Be careful not to twist the wire too much, otherwise the wire will break or might cut the grip. Once the wire is twisted, cut off the excess, leaving about ⅜ of an inch of twisted wire. Bend the tip of the wire, and push the tip into the grip.

There are two important things to be noted when using safety wire on grips. The first is not to twist the wire too tightly around the grip, since it may pinch the grip and actually cut it. The second, (and most important) is to position the safety wire so the twisted portion is NOT on the portion of the grip where the palm rests.

❋❋ CAUTION

Position the safety wire so the twisted portion is not underneath your hand when resting on the grip.

If you don't like the idea of using wire on your grips to hold them in place, there is "grip glue" which is available from most snowmobile and motorcycle shops. This can make installation a little more difficult (since glue is not always the best lubricant), but the grips will stay on well after the glue dries. Follow the directions on the bottle.

Exhaust Systems

HOW TO SELECT

▶ See Figures 73 and 74

There are many reasons to replace the stock exhaust system on your snowmobile. Maybe yours is rusted out and you wanted something different. Possi-

Fig. 74 Most aftermarket exhaust systems replace the entire set of pipes from the cylinder head back

bly you want a little more rumble to make you grin. Most aftermarket pipes can help you reduce the weight of your snowmobile, sometimes by as much as 10 pounds (44 kilos) or more!

➡ **Keep in mind that some aftermarket exhaust systems are not United States Forestry Service (U.S.F.S.) approved, and may not have a spark arrestor. Most all U.S.F.S. riding areas require an approved spark arrestor.**

There are many different styles of replacement exhaust systems. Most systems replace the entire set of pipes from the cylinder head back. Some of these systems resemble the stock systems, but use bigger pipes or have some other sort of modification that either enhances performance or decreases noise level. Other systems may be completely different from the stock system. You have to be careful with systems like these as you may block easy access to maintenance items.

HOW TO INSTALL

▶ See Figures 75 thru 82

One of the biggest concerns when replacing an exhaust system is how much it is going to effect the tuning of the engine. Simply bolting a new exhaust system to your snowmobile is not the only thing with which you have to concern yourself. Replacement exhaust systems from the aftermarket or performance arm

Fig. 73 If you choose to buy an aftermarket exhaust system for your snowmobile, make sure that it is U.S. Forestry Service approved

Fig. 75 This picture of a burned piston illustrates just how much damage a lean condition can cause. Yes that is a hole burned through the top of the piston

Fig. 76 Be prepared to make adjustments and/or modifications to your snowmobile's carburetor if you buy an aftermarket exhaust system

Fig. 79 The spring removal tool grips the spring tightly so it can be easily expanded for removal

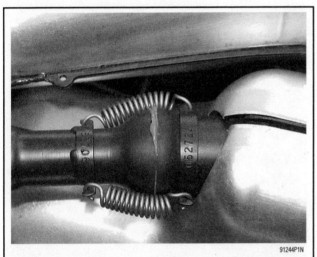

Fig. 77 Most snowmobiles use spring fasteners to hold the pipes together

Fig. 80 Note how this factory system carefully contours around the gear box dipstick. Make sure the new system allows clearance to remove this dipstick after it is installed

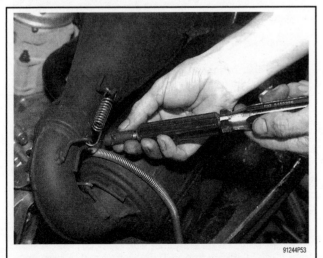

Fig. 78 Always use the proper tool for the job like this spring removal tool

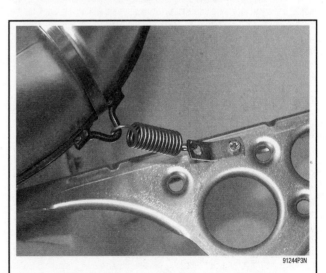

Fig. 81 If there are clearance problems, you might have to bend some mounting tabs

Fig. 82 Pick up some new gaskets when you buy your aftermarket exhaust. Chances are the old gaskets are well worn and would cause an exhaust leak if reused

of the manufacturer will typically have higher rates of flow than the stock systems. This helps performance if your engine is tuned to take advantage of it. If you don't tune the engine and adjust the mixture, chances are that you will cause the engine to run lean. A lean running engine will run hot and eventually damage itself. Low restriction pipes equal higher flow of gases through the engine. Higher flow of gases means you need more air coming into the engine. More air means more fuel that the engine can burn. The end result is that you have to rejet your carburetor to make things right.

Talk to the manufacturer of the system you intend to use. They will be able to give you an idea about what modifications to the carburetion will have to be done. Sometimes they can give you specific changes and might be able to supply a jetting kit matched to the exhaust system. If they don't have that, they can give you some guidance as to typical setting to use as a baseline. If you have done extensive modifications to your engine, the manufacturer may not be able to help you as they can't possibly know every combination of parts that can be bolted to an snowmobile. In this case, a shop familiar with your type of snowmobile may have already done a similar modification and can help you get your snowmobile dialed in.

Once you have figured out your fuel mixture, now you can start thinking about actually installing the exhaust system. Look through the manufacturers instructions. They should give you a list of parts you will need during the job. If they say to reuse any parts, like gaskets, you may want to pick up new ones just in case the old ones are damaged during the removal process.

Before removing any fasteners, hold up the new exhaust system to the snowmobile and try to look for all the places the new system will mount. Look for the way the pipes attach to each other. Check that the pipes and mount will match up. Most quality manufacturers test fit their products so you don't have to do any modifications to the system. Sometimes you will find that the lower priced systems out there require a fair bit of modification to get them to fit. You usually get what you pay for.

If you are sure everything will fit fine and you have all the parts you need, it is time to remove the old system. This can be a real pain, as old exhaust system hardware tends to fuse itself together over a period of time. Liberal doses of rust penetrating lubricant can help break free some of the more stubborn fasteners.

When you have removed the fasteners and disconnected the pipes, be ready to remove the old system. Be careful as the old system may be quite a bit heavier than it may seem, but hey, isn't that one of the reasons you are changing it? Aluminum usually looks cooler than steel, anyway.

With the old system removed, this is a great time to inspect the mounting tabs on the frame and any areas that are normally covered by the exhaust system. Check for rust and corrosion. Clean and paint any areas that may need it. Check the threads on the cylinder head where the pipe base attaches to; often these threads get buggered up due to the high heat encountered at an exhaust port. Check the inside of the exhaust port for excessive carbon. You might catch a problem before an engine teardown is needed. If you are only installing a slip on muffler, check that the end of the pipe is still round and not squashed out of shape. A small pipe expander can help round out a damaged pipe.

Test fit the new exhaust system. Put everything into place, but don't tighten anything or install any springs yet. Check for clearance between all components. If there are clearance problems, you might have to bend some mounting tabs or fabricate spacers.

Once you are convinced that everything is as it should be, you can install the new gaskets and get set to fasten everything down. Check your instructions to see if there are any sequences that you have to follow when tightening the various part of the system. Chance are that you need to start closest to the engine and work your way back. While doing this, keep checking the system alignment as it can change as things snug up.

With the system completely installed, reinstall anything that had to come off in the process. Make sure all the springs are installed in their proper locations.

If your carburetors will need readjustment or rejetting, do this now, before firing up the engine. Once it is complete, check for any fuel leakage before starting the snowmobile.

Ok, now that you have everything done, fire it up! Check for leaking connections, and tighten them up. Run the engine for a while and recheck the connections once they have cooled back down. The next time you go for a ride, keep an eye on the exhaust springs, since things might rattle loose.

Shocks And Springs

▶ **See Figure 83**

Most people who drive cars never think twice about the suspension holding their car up. But since snowmobile riders spend so much time riding on rough surfaces, suspension is always a topic of conversation.

If a single rider is on the snowmobile, it will handle in one fashion, but add a stack of camping gear or start hauling stuff around, and the snowmobile can turn into a completely different animal. Adjustment of the original suspension can only compensate for so much, and in some cases, may not compensate enough. This is where aftermarket shocks and springs can be of great benefit.

Fig. 83 Shocks are an essential part of your snowmobile; changing them can drastically change handling characteristics

HOW TO SELECT

▶ **See Figures 84, 85 and 86**

There are many reasons to change the suspension on an snowmobile. Sometimes the reason is handling and performance; the rider wants to have more control at speed. They may want to stiffen up the chassis so it becomes more reactive and predictable.

Snowmobile manufacturers have to build machines that will meet the needs of most, but can't really make an snowmobile that will meet the desires of all. Certain compromises have to be made so the greatest amount of people will be able to ride the snowmobile. It's great if the stock suspension happens to work for you, but a lot of the time, the snowmobile can be made better with a few tweaks. Sometimes simply replacing worn out stock components can make a

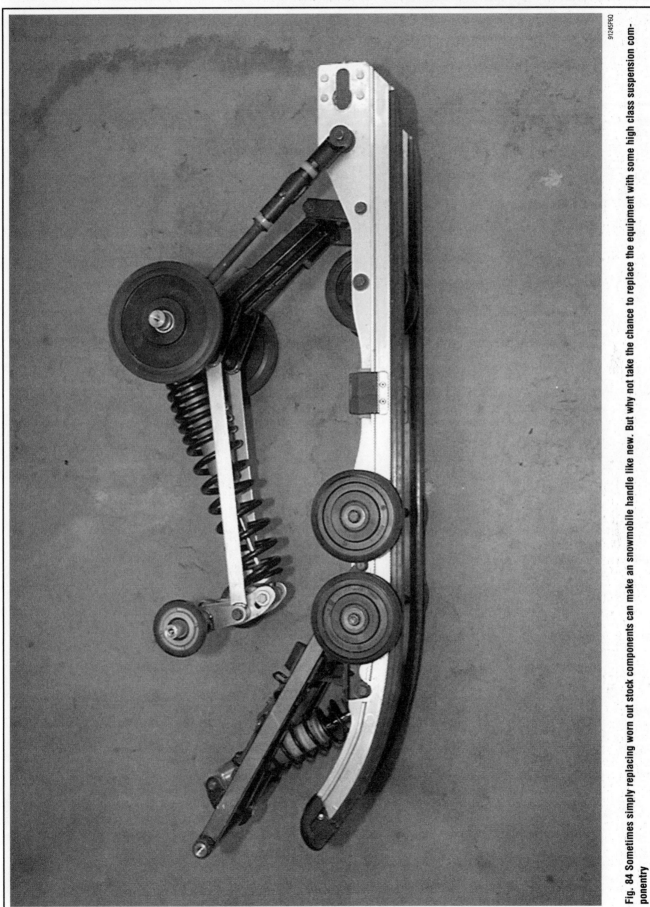

9124SP60

Fig. 84 Sometimes simply replacing worn out stock components can make an snowmobile handle like new. But why not take the chance to replace the equipment with some high class suspension componentry

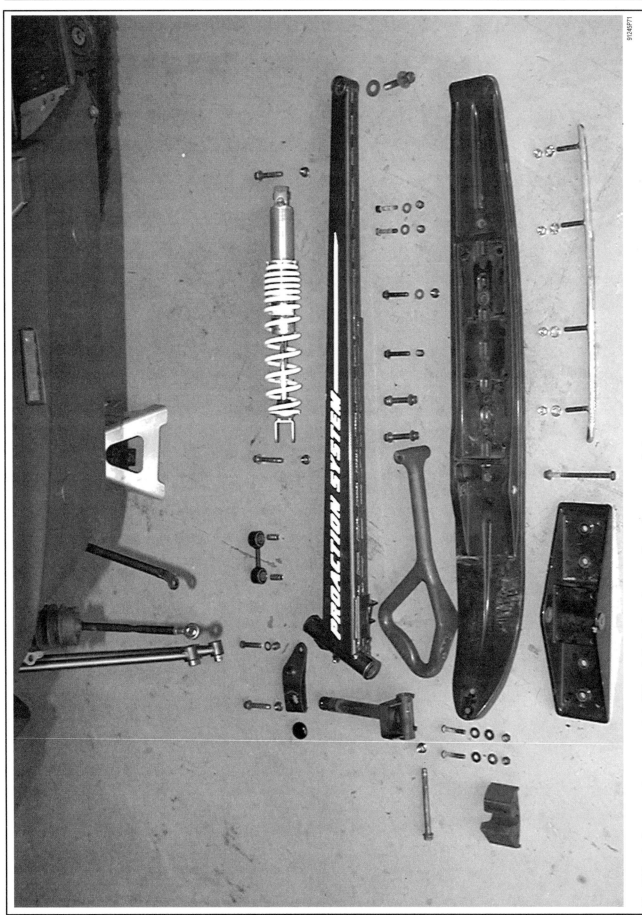

Fig. 85 Purchasing suspension components in kit form is the best way to assure the performance you desire

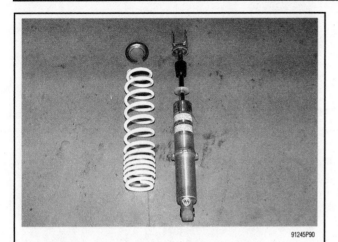

Fig. 86 Shocks and springs can be purchased separately to fine tune the ride of your sled

snowmobile handle like new. But why not take the chance to replace the equipment with some high class suspension componentry?

In general, you can replace either the dampers or the springs in either the front suspension or rear. The front suspension usually has one shock and spring per side, and the rear suspension typically has two shocks.

It is recommended that the front and rear suspensions be modified at the same time with matched components. If you only modify one end of the snowmobile, the suspension can be adversely effected (since the front and rear suspensions interact with each other while the vehicle is moving) and the snowmobile will not handle in a proper manner. Question your local dealer or suspension manufacturer about their recommendations for you particular sled. Also, talk to local riders to get their opinions as to what works best.

Before you start disassembling your sled, you have to decide what your goals are in the suspension modification game. If you are looking for better handling or better control of the snowmobile under extreme loads, you will be aiming for a different set up than the person who wants to make their suspension smoother over the rough stuff. If you are trying to solve a particular suspension problem, check with the suspension manufacturers. They probably have already figured out the solution and have it ready to install.

Most stock suspensions have a minimum of adjustments. They usually come with a preload adjustment and sometimes a damping adjustment. Aftermarket suspensions come with a full range of possibilities. Some aftermarket suspensions resemble the stock pieces, but may have a few little tweaks or maybe better performance.

Other aftermarket suspensions come with enough dials, wheels, adjustments and doodads to keep the most techno-oriented rider happy. There are rear shocks for snowmobiles that have hydraulic (not the typical ramp and peg) preload adjustment, compression damping adjustments, rebound damping adjustment, and remote gas filled reservoirs. All of these adjustments don't usually come cheap, though, and aren't really necessary except for heavy-duty racing applications.

Check with your dealer to find out what they recommend for suspensions. They have a lot of experience with your type of snowmobile. Also check with other people who ride your type of snowmobile and do your type of riding. They can offer some personal insights. Call the manufacturers and find out what they have to offer. They may already offer the suspension you need, and may have it ready to go, packed up in a box.

Snowmobile Cover

HOW TO SELECT

▶ See Figure 87

When selecting a snowmobile you must first determine where the sled is going to be stored. Does the cover need to be waterproof? Is the sled going to

Fig. 87 This cover is manufactured for Yamaha and is custom made for the Yamaha SXR-500

be stored inside or outside? Are you going to trailer the sled with the cover on? Whatever your specific needs, there are covers made to meet your demands.

One feature which you should look for when deciding on a cover are material thickness. The thicker the cover, the more abuse it will take and the better it will stand up to the weather. Also, when the cover is stretched over a sharp corner, it will be less likely to tear.

The pictures show the most common type of snowmobile cover. This cover is manufactured for Yamaha and is custom made for the Yamaha SXR-500 on which it is being installed. Obviously we are only showing you a small portion of what is available. To get more ideas, go to you local snowmobile dealer, or look in any of the various publications that cater to snowmobiles.

HOW TO INSTALL

♦ See Figures 88 thru 95

Installing a snowmobile cover is an easy task as long as you follow a specified order. In the best case it is advisable for two people to install the cover to prevent the snowmobile from being scratched. But in most cases this is not practical so one person must carefully maneuver the cover.

Your first step when installing the cover actually has nothing to do with the cover at all. After you have been hard at it on the trail all day, your sled has picked up quite a bit of dirt. If you immediately install your cover, two things will

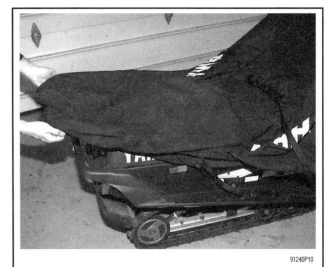

91240P10

Fig. 90 . . . to the rear

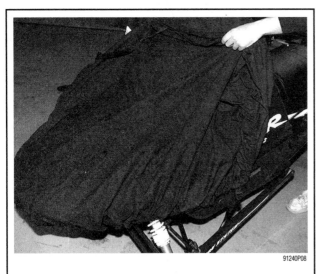

91240P08

Fig. 88 Install the cover from the front of the snowmobile . . .

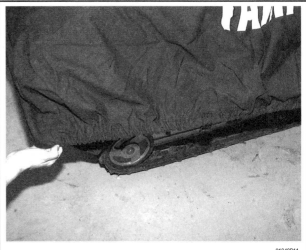

91240P11

Fig. 91 Tuck the cover under the rear of the snowmobile

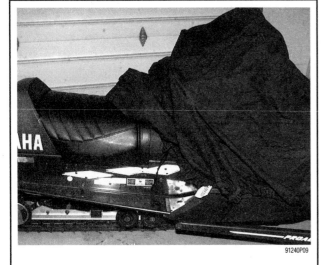

91240P09

Fig. 89 . . . pulling the cover over the snowmobile . . .

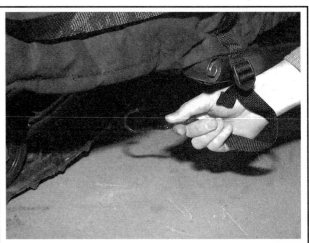

91240P05

Fig. 92 Use the hold down straps on the side of the cover to secure it to the snowmobile

Fig. 93 Once a suitable attaching place is found, pull the cover taut using the straps

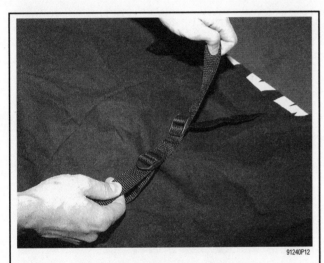

Fig. 94 If equipped, use the straps at the top of the cover to tailor the fit of the cover to the snowmobile

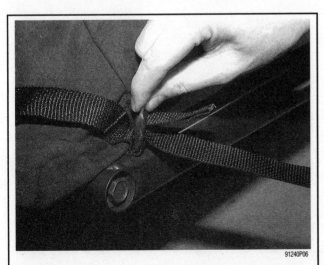

Fig. 95 Cover straps are easily released by lifting the buckle to ease the tension on the strap

happen. First, the under side of your cover will get dirty and then, the dirt on the surface of your sled will be ground into the plastic as you drag the cover over the sled during installation. When you do get around to washing your sled, you will also have to wash the cover to prevent putting a dirty cover on a freshly washed sled. So take the time to at least rinse your sled off prior to installing the cover.

Now that your sled is clean, you can start the cover installation by placing the cover over the nose of the sled and draping it back over the windshield. Take extra care not to drag the cover across the windshield as the plastic is easily scratched. Work your way back slowly, making sure the cover does not get snagged on anything. Finally, tuck the cover in under the rear of the sled.

The next step is to insure the cover stays in place. This is accomplished by the elastic which holds the cover tight to the sled. Also, most covers are equipped with tie-downs to keep the cover in place even through some fierce winds. The tie-downs simply hook to a convenient place on the underside of the sled and are pulled taunt to secure everything in place.

An additional feature of some covers are straps which when pulled tight, allow the cover to be form fitted to the snowmobile. This feature is helpful when transporting your sled with the cover on. It keeps the cover tight and allows very little air to get under the cover to flop it around in the wind.

Studs and Ski Runners (Carbides)

HOW TO SELECT

◢ **See Figures 96, 97 and 98**

Determining the proper traction and control is simple by asking yourself a few questions. What is your riding style? Are you a conservative trail rider, an aggressive rider, or an all out competition racer? How much horsepower does your sled make? (Erase that exaggerated number and put down something more realistic.) Now, go to your local dealer or call a stud manufacturer with this information. Chances are they will use a chart to figure out just the items you will need for balanced handling. Carbides and studs should be selected as a package for properly balanced handling.

Most charts will have your riding type on one axis and the horsepower of your sled on the other axis. Filling in the middle of the chart are all the possible combinations of carbides and studs. You will also get information on just where to put the studs on the track. Studs along the track's center have the greatest control for acceleration. Studs placed along the track edge resist sliding and should be fewer in number to avoid track damage. Stud patterns with the least repetition provide the most traction. Use a stud template for the best results.

➡**To avoid track damage, place no studs within one inch of the track edge.**

While the studs may give you grip, the turning or center carbide has the greatest effect on cornering control. The longer and sharper the carbide, the

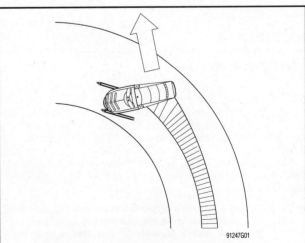

Fig. 96 This is called a loose condition. Note that the back end of the sled is loose or sliding around the turn. This conditions exists because of too much carbide and not enough studding

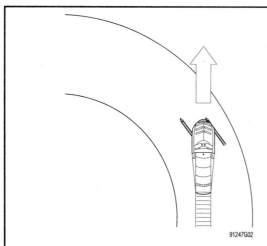

Fig. 97 This is called a tight or push condition. Note that the front of the sled is pushing or plowing straight ahead. This conditions exists because the carbides are too short or the track is overstudded

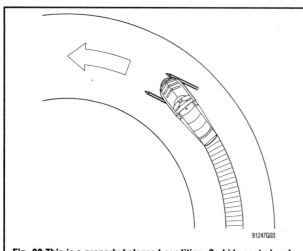

Fig. 98 This is a properly balanced condition. Carbide control and stud quantity are in balance for proper setup and maximum handling control

Fig. 99 Choose quality studs, whether sold by a snowmobile manufacturer . . .

Fig. 100 . . . or an aftermarket company like Woody's . . .

Fig. 101 . . . or Saber

greater the turning effect. Too few studs used with a long turning carbide can result in a loose condition.

HOW TO INSTALL

♦ **See Figures 99 thru 118**

The quantity and type of studs inserted through the track can have several effects on the handling of the sled. If installed improperly, track and/or stud damage can result. If the pushing force from too many studs exceeds the ability of the carbides to steer the sled, a push or tight condition will occur. In this case the sled will continue in a straight ahead motion even though the skis are turned.

In best case scenario is one where a balanced package is purchased from a reputable manufacturer and installed properly. In this way, the sled will handle properly from the first ride.

➥Trail studs should not extend beyond the rubber track lugs more than ⅜ inch. Avoid placing studs inline with heat exchanger and tunnel protector strips to avoid damage. Always factor in suspension travel and track deflection.

Stud holes are drilled in various patterns depending on the desired amount of traction. Stud templates are available from the manufacturers to evenly and

Fig. 102 A special hollow drill bit is used to drill the holes in the track for the studs

Fig. 105 Studs which are placed in a straight line on the track help rapidly propel the snowmobile forward

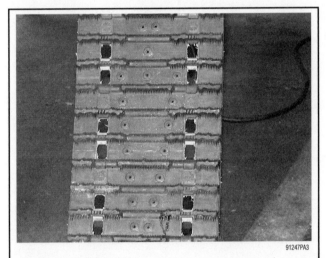

Fig. 103 Stud holes are drilled in various patterns depending on the desired amount of traction

Fig. 106 Stud templates are available from the manufacturers to evenly and accurately space the studs on the track

Fig. 104 This stud was ripped out when the track hit a hard object on the trail. The track strength has been compromised and the track should be replaced

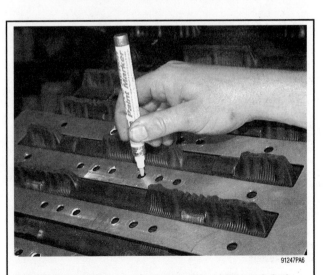

Fig. 107 Using the template, mark the positions of the studs in the recommended pattern

Fig. 108 Using a paint pen makes the marks easier to see

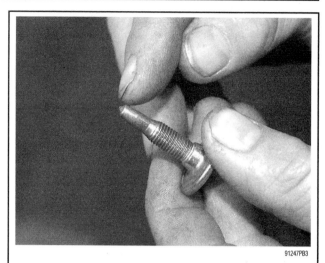

Fig. 111 Stud tips vary greatly and should be customized to your particular riding environment

Fig. 109 Some people like drilling through the holes on the template

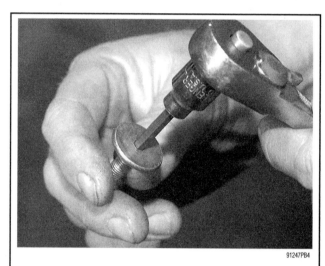

Fig. 112 Most studs are equipped with a hex head for holding the stud in position during tightenting

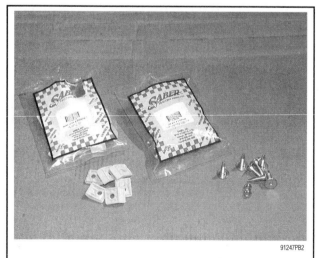

Fig. 110 Quality studs, like those from Saber Traction Products, will come as a complete kit with a template and drill included

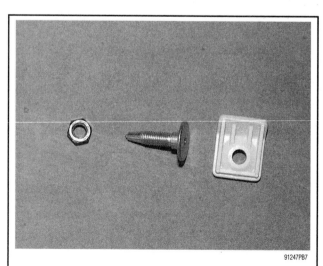

Fig. 113 Studs are made up of three components, the stud, the backer and the nut

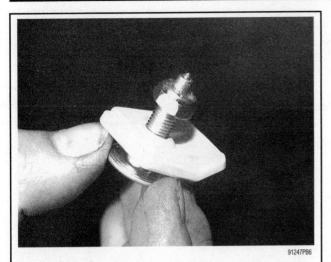
Fig. 114 When installed properly, backers also help to propel the sled

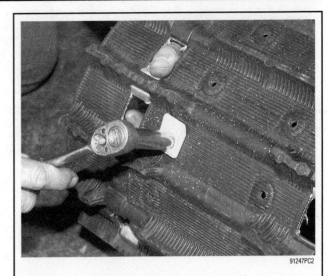
Fig. 117 . . . then tighten the locknut to specification

Fig. 115 After drilling the stud hole, insert the stud through the track . . .

Fig. 118 By properly installing your studs, you lessen the chance of damage to your sled and personal injury

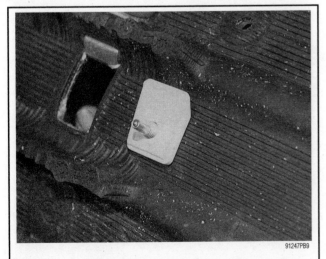
Fig. 116 . . . insert the backer on the stud and position it so that the lip is facing the direction of track rotation . . .

accurately space the studs on the track. Using the template, mark the positions of the studs in the recommended pattern. Mark each location using a paint pen or simply drill through the holes on the template. A special hollow drill bit is used to drill the holes in the track.

After drilling the stud hole, insert the stud through the track. Next insert the backer on the stud and position it so that the lip is facing the direction of track rotation. Tighten the locknut to specification.

And The List Goes On

▶ See Figures 119 thru 128

There are so many available accessories for snowmobiles today that it would be impossible to list them all in one book. What we have tried to represent here are the most common accessories requested by riders.

Looking through some of today's snowmobiling magazines and catalogs, the reader is bombarded with go-fast goodies and color coordinated plastic parts that can virtually transform the performance and looks of a snowmobile . . . but for a price.

Like we have suggested, take a look a what you really want your snowmobile to do and then make a list of components that will satisfy that need. This way you will not spend money on parts and pieces that will not satisfy your objective.

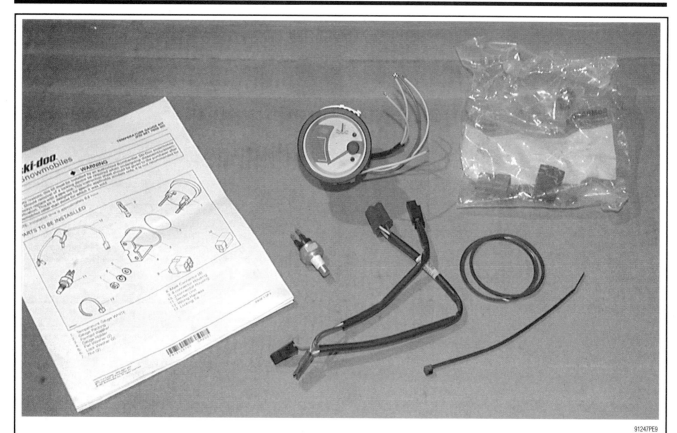

91247PE9

Fig. 119 Coolant temperature gauges are nice addition to a racing sled

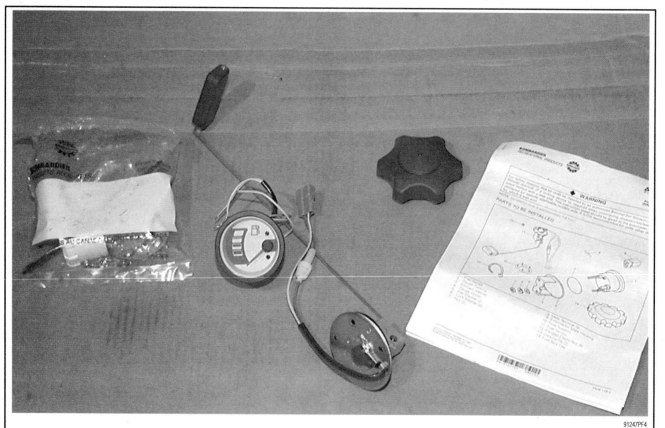

91247PF4

Fig. 120 A fuel level gauge kit is a nice addition to any snowmobile used for touring

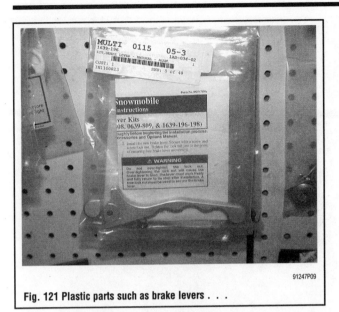

Fig. 121 Plastic parts such as brake levers . . .

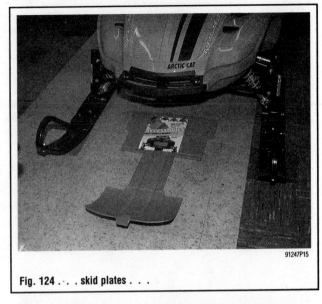

Fig. 124 . . . skid plates . . .

Fig. 122 . . . foot pads . . .

Fig. 125 . . . and bumpers can now all be color coordinated

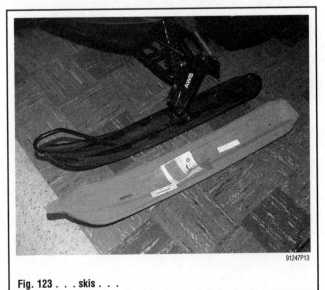

Fig. 123 . . . skis . . .

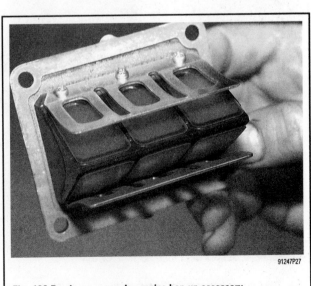

Fig. 126 Reeds are a popular engine hop-up accessory

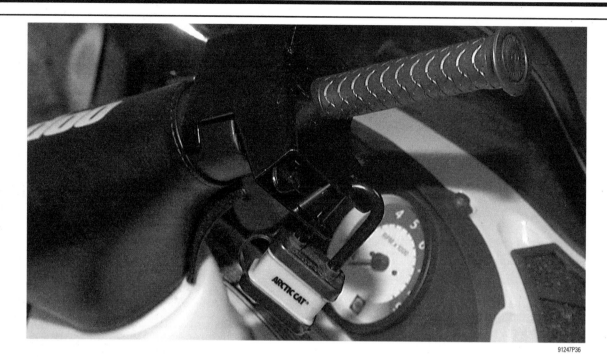

91247P36

Fig. 127 Throttle locks protect your investment

91247PA1

Fig. 128 These special runners keep your feet from slipping off the treads on your sled

8

CLEANING
YOUR
SNOWMOBILE

CLEANING YOUR SNOWMOBILE 8-2

CLEANING YOUR SNOWMOBILE

In order to keep your snowmobile in good mechanical condition, it is important to keep it clean. This way you can find and correct (or prevent) problems that might be unseen beneath the surface of dirt and other various debris that can collect quickly after a couple of rides.

If you ride your snowmobile in mud soaked snow, keeping your snowmobile clean is especially important. Mud and dirt can hide serious problems, such as a cracked tunnel. If left to dry out on the plastic, mud (in certain geographical areas) can permanently stain the plastic. In general, if you ride in a lot of mud, you should thoroughly hose your snowmobile down with fresh water after every ride.

Every time you wash your snowmobile, you'll get a chance to closely inspect it for any problems that may have developed since the last washing. While scrubbing away, it is easy to quickly glance over the mechanicals, looking for kinked cables, loose nuts and bolts, and worn out components. This is a prime example of preventative maintenance which can help to avoid problems on the trail.

In addition to helping you keep your snowmobile in good mechanical order, washing your snowmobile on a regular basis will also help keep it looking good. A snowmobile that is kept clean will hold a higher value than a sloppy one, should you ever decide to part ways with your ride. If a potential buyer sees a clean snowmobile, they will often assume that it was maintained properly too (which will hopefully be true in your case, thanks to this book. You are following our instructions, right?).

Basic Washing

♦ See Figures 1, 2, 3 and 4

Well, washing your snowmobile sounds pretty easy, right? Quite honestly, it is. The same rules apply to washing a snowmobile as with washing an automobile. For those of you who have forgotten (or never learned) we will review.

First some things to NOT do when washing your sled:
• Don't wash your sled in the sun; the drying effects of the sun on the soap will produce streaks on your plastic and paint.
• Don't wash your sled in extremely cold weather. Obviously, the water will turn to ice and may damage components. If you need to wash your sled in extremely cold weather, it is advisable to do so inside. If you are really lucky, you can wash your sled in the comfort of a heated garage.
• Don't wash a sled that has just been running. The heat from the engine will have heated up the plastic on the hood and will cause the soap to dry immediately. Use the back of your hand to test the surface to see if it is too hot (much like the way you test to see if a baby's bottle is too hot).

Now that we have the basics out of the way, let's take a look at some other tips for washing your sled:

• Since the engine and all the related controls are exposed to the elements, we need to keep an eye out for potential problem points. For example: you don't want to spray some heavy duty solvent on the engine to find out later you just doused the electronic control unit for the ignition with water and cleaner! Avoid electronic parts and switches when spraying direct streams of water.
• Don't use a high pressure cleaning wand to spray your snowmobile; water and cleaner can be forced past seals and gaskets into lubricants or other areas not tolerant of water. Use only a low pressure garden hose or equivalent to remove debris.
• If your snowmobile is water-cooled, make sure to thoroughly wash the mud and dirt from the heat exchanger cores. A heat exchanger that is clogged with debris will not be able to cool the engine, since air cannot flow through the cooling fins of the heat exchanger core. Medium water pressure should be able to free most of the dirt and debris from the core of the heat exchanger. Use a toothpick to remove any small pieces of dirt or other debris which might remain lodged in the heat exchanger core.
• If you are using a biodegradable degreaser, let it soak for a couple of minutes before washing it off. Make sure not to let the degreaser dry before you get a chance to rinse it away, since it may leave stains or streaks.

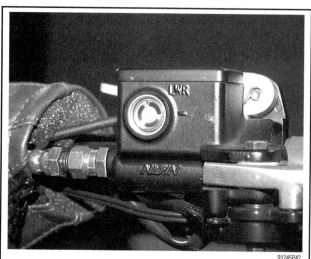
91245P42

Fig. 2 Make sure items like brake cylinders are sealed completely before washing your snowmobile

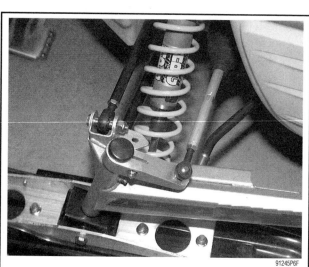
91248P01

Fig. 1 Keeping your snowmobile clean is easy once you have the basics down

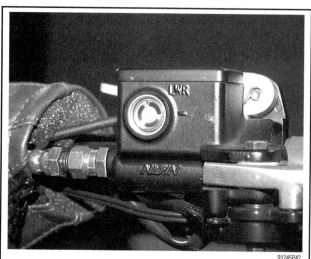
91245P6F

Fig. 3 Pay close attention to areas which are prone to collecting debris, such as the front suspension . . .

Fig. 4 . . . and the rear suspension

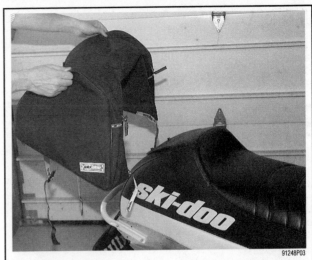

Fig. 5 Start the washing procedure by removing any accessories you do not wish to get wet

Fig. 6 Use compressed air, if available, to blow light debris off the surface of the sled

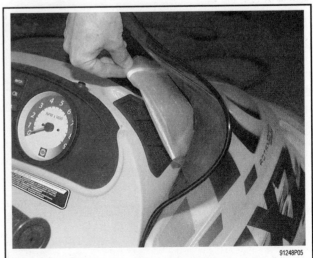

Fig. 7 Use a plastic bag to cover any air inlets to prevent trapping water in the air box

• With your hose's nozzle adjusted to medium spray, thoroughly wet the entire snowmobile, washing off loose grit, dirt, and pollutants.

• Soak towels thoroughly in soapy wash solution. Use minimum application pressure. The soapy solution acts as a lubricant between your wash cloth and the finish. The aim is to loosen dirt and pollutants, float them off the surface, and hold them in suspension within the solution. Floating them off prevents them from scratching the finish. Dunk the cloth frequently in your bucket of wash water to get rid of suspended, potentially abrasive particles. Work with a clean, sopping wet cloth, heavy with solution. While application in a circular motion is easier, and for most detailers more natural, a forward-backward motion is better because it does not leave circular swirl marks in the plastic.

• Rinse well with a medium spray from the hose, flooding areas to float particles off.

• Dry with clean, non abrasive cotton cloths, preferably terry towels, or with a soft chamois.

• As you dry, be sure not to let any water droplets remain, because they'll leave spots behind. Don't neglect to dry your aluminum components. If any dirt comes off on your drying cloth, you didn't wash the finish well enough.

• Do not wash and detail your snowmobile in the sun. Soapy water will dry out faster than you can rinse it off, especially in the summer months.

• As previously mentioned, do your best to keep water away from electrical connections. Even a small amount of water can get into a connector and quickly corrode the terminals.

✳✳ WARNING

Using high water pressure to clean heat exchanger fins and oil cooler fins can cause serious damage. Only use low pressure to safely clean mud and debris from the fins.

THE WASHING PROCEDURE

▶ **See Figures 5 thru 16**

1. Remove any accessories that you don't want to get wet. This may include saddle bags and other items made of fabric.

2. If your sled has collected a lot of dust or other light debris, your first set should be to blow the entire sled off with compressed air. If compressed air is not available, use a feather duster to lightly clean the surface.

3. Cover any exposed areas that should not get wet. This is particularly important when it comes to air inlet ducts and exhaust outlets for the engine.

4. Using a mild detergent, such as car wash soap, fill a bucket with soapy water.

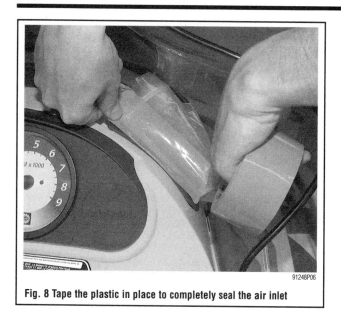

Fig. 8 Tape the plastic in place to completely seal the air inlet

Fig. 11 Adjust your spray nozzle to a medium spray pattern . . .

Fig. 9 Using a mild detergent such as car wash soap . . .

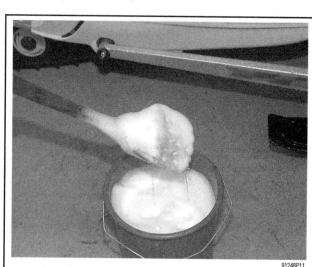

Fig. 12 Using a soft bristled wash brush or a cotton towel, scoop up a bunch of suds . . .

Fig. 10 . . . mix up a bucket of soapy water

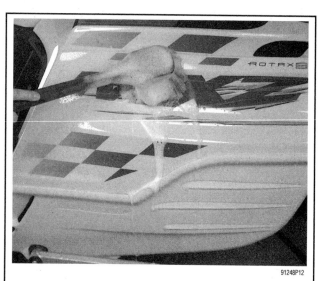

Fig. 13 . . . and apply them to the surface of your sled

Fig. 14 Once you have washed a section, rinse it off using a medium stream of water

Fig. 15 Use a shammy or a soft cotton towel to drag the water off the surface

Fig. 16 Here are the proper tools for washing your sled. A soft bristle brush and terry cloth towel will be hard on dirt but gentile on your sled's finish

5. With a hose adjusted to a medium spray pattern, wet down the entire snowmobile. Start at the top and work your way down. This will wash off any loose dirt.

6. Soak towels or what ever you will be using to clean your sled in wash solution. Use the minimum amount of pressure necessary to clean the sled, since excessive pressure may cause the dirt to scratch the plastic or paint. The aim is to suspend the dirt in your washing tool and soap solution, then float it off the surface of the sled.

7. Dunk the towel in the soap frequently to rid it of suspended dirt. Always try to work with a clean, and fully loaded towel. You can rub in a back-and-forth or circular motion. While a circular motion is more natural, the back-and-forth is actually better because it does not leave circular scratch marks in the plastic or paint.

➡ **You may want to consider washing the dirtiest parts of your sled first. This will allow you the opportunity to change the wash solution and towel once you start to clean the more important painted and plastic surfaces (the ones that show the most). In this case you would ignore our suggestion to work from the top to the bottom.**

8. Pay attention to the hard to reach places. This is where dirt has the best chance of collecting and where it will most probably continue to collect if you don't take the time to clean it properly.

9. After you have finished washing a particular part of your sled, rinse it well with a medium spray of clean, luke warm water. This should completely rinse all soap residue from the sled and float away any dirt that previously took up residence on your paint or plastic.

10. After you have washed the entire sled, dry it with soft towels or a shammy. As you dry, make sure to not let any water droplets remain as they may leave spots after they dry. This is especially important in areas with hard water. The minerals in the water dry to form hard deposits that can damage paint.

11. If during the drying process you discover dirt on your drying towel, stop! Inspect the area and determine where the dirt came from on the sled. Rewash the area and dry.

12. Stand back and admire your sparkling clean sled.

13. You may want to cover the sled at this point to prevent it from getting dirty again while not is use.

TOOLS AND CHEMICALS

Now that we have gone over some washing tips, let's discuss the tools and chemicals that make cleaning your snowmobile easier.

Tools

▶ **See Figures 17, 18, 19 and 20**

A soft wash towel or rag is the best tool for washing dirt off of plastic. A terrycloth towel works well, since it can hold a lot of soapy water. Cotton rags, like the kind that service stations use, might be a little harsh on plastic and in general should not be used. Wash mitts are another option and also hold loads of soapy solution. Wash mitts also have a deep nap that traps dirt and keeps it from returning to the surface of the paint. The important thing here is to look for something that is not going to be abrasive to plastic and paint (like most sponges).

Brushes of all different sizes and types make great tools for hard-to-reach places. Most auto supply stores or hardware stores will have a large selection of brushes. Just like wash rags, it is important to look for brushes with soft bristles that aren't going to scratch paint and plastic. Even brushes that are going to be used for cleaning around axles can't be too stiff, since the seals can be damaged. When choosing a scrub brush, rub the bristles on the back of your hand. If the bristles on a brush feel stiff on the back of your hand, imagine what they can do to the paint and plastic on your snowmobile. A stiff scrub brush will work great for removing dirt on a studded track, but might scratch the paint on the tunnel.

⁂ **CAUTION**

ALWAYS wear adequate eye protection (goggles or safety glasses) when using compressed air to clean your snowmobile.

Fig. 17 Brushes of assorted sizes are really helpful for cleaning dirt out of nooks and crannies

Fig. 18 An adjustable nozzle for a garden hose is excellent for controlling water pressure, making heavy dirt removal easier

Fig. 19 Spray bottles are a good way to apply cleaners and other products

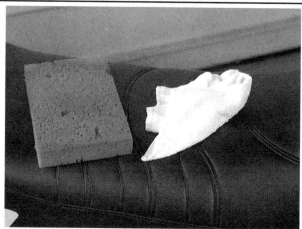

Fig. 20 The important item when washing your sled is a wash cloth (right) that is not going to be abrasive to plastic and paint like a sponge (left)

Compressed air is an excellent tool for cleaning a snowmobile. Before you wet down the snowmobile for washing, use an air nozzle to blow off any loose dirt and debris that has accumulated in the cracks and crevices. Of course you'll need to have a source of compressed air, whether it's a portable air tank or a small compressor. An air nozzle can usually be purchased at an auto supply or hardware store.

❊❊ WARNING

Don't overuse the compressed air as a cleaning tool or you will risk blowing the paint right off the surface of the metal. Keep the air pressure down—it doesn't take much to blow away loose dirt and foliage. Compressed air can also turn a little dirt into a sand blasting material (which will remove or scratch paint).

Other tools for washing can vary according to your particular snowmobile. For instance, if your snowmobile is water-cooled, toothpicks are really useful for dislodging dirt and pebbles from the cooling fins in your heat exchanger. NEVER use a metal pick or screwdriver to clean dirt from your heat exchanger! You could easily slip and puncture the heat exchanger. If you have ever had to replace a radiator on a car or truck, then you already know how expensive they can be. Just imagine the price of a new heat exchanger from the dealer for your snowmobile!

Duct tape is an excellent tool for snowmobile washing, too. "Yeah, right" you're thinking. Seriously, though, duct tape can help you avoid major problems by sealing off your intake snorkel on your air box. Sucking water into your engine can destroy it if enough manages to get into the combustion chamber. Unlike air, water does not compress. Let's say you've just finished washing your snowmobile, and water managed to fill up the air box without you knowing. You hit the start button, and Wham!! A bent connecting rod, cracked piston, head or case. Taking the extra precaution of closing off the intake and exhaust openings can save your engine.

Chemicals

▶ See Figures 21 thru 27

Everybody has their own favorite chemicals for washing their car or truck, and will probably use the same chemicals when they wash their snowmobile. If you have your favorites, by all means use them. However, there are a few considerations that you should keep in mind when selecting cleaning and detailing chemicals.

Dishwashing soap is great for breaking down grease, but can be a little harsh on plastic. Just like dish soap dries out your hands, it also dries out plastic, making it hard and brittle over time. Plastic that is not flexible will crack if bent or flexed. The safe way to go would be to buy "car washing soap" which can be purchased at any auto parts store. Car washing soap is specially formulated to safely remove dirt without damaging paint, or strip-

Fig. 21 Automotive car wash concentrate is not as harsh on plastic as dish soap

Fig. 24 Engine degreasers work great for removing grease and grit, but may attack plastic and aluminum

Fig. 22 Since snowmobiles have so much plastic, it makes sense to use a quality plastic and rubber protectant to keep things looking good

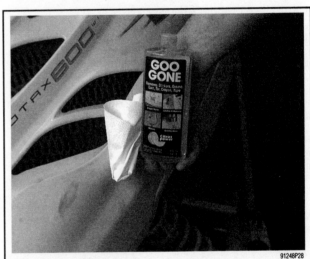

Fig. 25 One of our favorite products for removing grease and other types of oily dirt is Goo Gone®

Fig. 23 If you suspect water has made it's way into an electrical connector and corroded the terminals, spray cleaners are available

Fig. 26 Simply squirt some Goo Gone® on a soft rag . . .

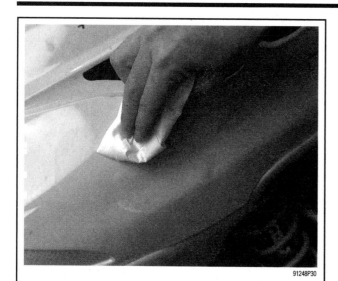

Fig. 27 . . . and apply to the surface. Presto! the goo is gone

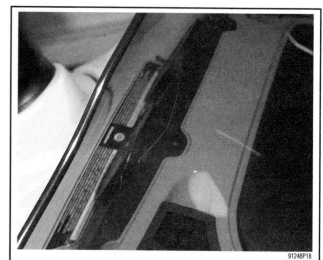

Fig. 28 Sometimes you'll just have to live with scratches like this one on the windshield, since little can be done to remove them

Fig. 29 For lighter scratches, this two step plastic cleaner/polish from Meguiar's will do the trick

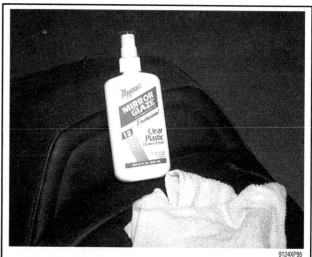

Fig. 30 Quick touch ups can be accomplished with this single step cleaner and polish from Meguiar's

ping away a good wax job. Granted, most of the surface of your snowmobile is plastic, but car washing soap won't dry out your snowmobile's plastic like dish soap can.

Biodegradable degreasers can also be used for washing your snowmobile. Just be careful about diluting it properly, since full strength use can, in some cases, stain plastic (especially white). In general, degreasers should not be used on plastic, though. If you want to use a particular biodegradable degreaser, try it out on the underside of a panel and make sure a stain isn't left behind.

Heavy duty engine degreasers should be used carefully, since most are solvent based, and can ruin and discolor paint and plastic. Just like soap, it is really important not to let the degreaser dry out before you get a chance to hose it off. Also, when applying degreaser to an engine, be careful not to let it splatter onto the plastic. Most heavy duty engine degreasers will stain plastic, especially if the plastic is a light color.

Talk to other riders, and ask them what kind of chemicals they use to help keep their snowmobiles clean. A lot of "home brewed" products can work quite well if used carefully. A word of caution, though. If you are unsure about how a product will affect your snowmobile, test it out on something else that is not of value before using it on your ride. For instance, one rider heard through the grapevine that Raid® bug spray makes a great low-priced engine degreaser. Well, he tried it out on his engine, and some of the paint was eaten away. The point is you have to be careful when using a product for something which it was not meant.

Plastic

♦ **See Figures 28 thru 36**

Overall, the plastic on your snowmobile is incredibly durable. It is safe to say that most snowmobiles would look awful if all of the plastic was made of metal; just imagine how dented and scratched up your snowmobile would look after just a couple of rides! One of the best things about plastic is that the color is molded into the plastic. If you scratch up your plastic on tree branches, at least the scratches are the same color. But even then, your plastic can get downright ugly looking if they are gouged up.

Most plastic has the color molded into it, and simply cleaning with a soapy water solution and a non abrasive cloth will keep it looking good. The trick is not to scratch the surface during cleaning. If the surface does get scratched, a good commercial plastic polish will help get light scratches out and restore the looks of the piece.

Since the plastic on your snowmobile covers most of the vehicle, taking good care of it will help keep your ride looking new. If you are careful when riding and washing your snowmobile, the plastic can maintain its showroom shine for quite a while. Keeping it clean will help it from becoming scratched, but even then, over time the plastic will eventually lose its luster. There are products

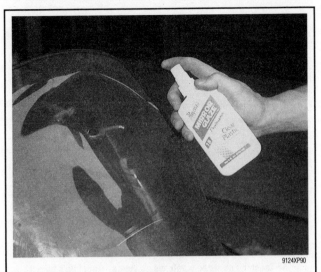

Fig. 31 Simply spray the Meguiar's cleaner/polish on . . .

Fig. 34 Dried out, scratched plastic can be rejuvenated with a good application of plastic protectant

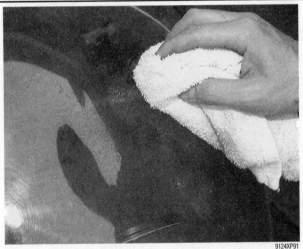

Fig. 32 . . . and spread it around with a soft towel. Then wipe it dry with a clean towel

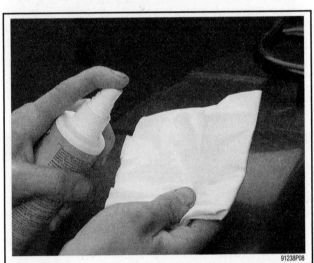

Fig. 35 Using a rag to apply protectant will help to avoid excessive overspray

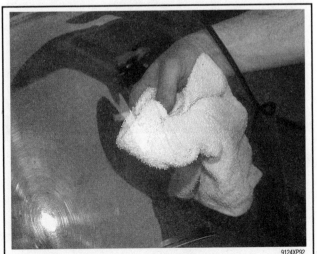

Fig. 33 Plastic cleaner/polishes are especially important to maintain optimum clarity in windsheilds

Fig. 36 Cat Cleaner from Arctic Cat is about the best chemical to remove exhaust stains from the plastic around your exhaust pipe

available to help bring back the shine of your snowmobile's plastic should things start to look hazy.

Plastic can be restored using plastic polishes and scratch removers. Any well stocked auto parts store or your local snowmobile and motorcycle dealer will carry such products. There are different grades of products to match the severity of the damage to the plastic.

Some plastic polish products are designed for maintenance type use, helping to keep the tiny scratches polished out of the plastic. Others are for heavier damage and to reclaim deeply scratched surfaces (which is more for repair than maintenance). Follow the instructions on the bottle exactly. Some manufactures are very specific in the use of their products and recommend that their entire system of products be used since each one is matched to the next.

If you own an older snowmobile, and the plastic is beyond repair, there are some products that can help to improve the luster. Most of these are "home remedies" and aren't products intended for use on plastic. Nevertheless, some of these products can help to spruce up an older snowmobile.

Vinyl floor cleaners, such as Mop n' Glo® can help restore the luster to dingy, dull plastic. Experiment with different ways of applying it to the plastic, such as wiping it on with a rag, or using a spray bottle. Just make sure to do this on an area of the plastic that is not easily seen before applying it all over your snowmobile. Some plastics can react differently, so make sure to test it out before you go too far.

One more thing about plastic. Although this should be considered a last-ditch effort, fine grit scouring pads (like 3M Scotch-Brite®) can be used on old, scratched (we're talkin' really OLD, DRIED OUT, and SCRATCHED) plastic to remove stains and ground-in dirt. Using a scouring pad might scratch the plastic even more, but you'll be able to get those mud stains off of your plastic. Use caution here, since darker plastics might take on a white-colored haze from the abrasiveness of the scouring pad. Once you have the surface clean of stains and marks, applying Armor-All® or other plastic protectant can help to put a little shine into the plastic after it has been scoured down.

Painted Surfaces

♦ See Figure 37

The surfaces of the average snowmobile that are painted are usually the tunnel, suspension, and in some cases, the engine. The primary reason that these surfaces are painted is not for decorative reasons, but for protection against corrosion. Just imagine how fast your frame would rust if it wasn't painted! Of course, there is nothing wrong with putting a little color into that corrosion protector on your sled known as paint.

Depending on where you ride your snowmobile, the tunnel, suspension, and other painted surfaces can quickly become scratched and chipped. Not only does this look bad, but rust or oxidation can quickly set in on those scratches and nicks, since the metal becomes exposed. Once rust sets in, it can creep under the paint, and quickly spread, eventually affecting the structural integrity of the entire component.

To keep rust from setting in, touching up the scratches and chips on your snowmobile's painted components is essential. You can buy touch-up paint from your local snowmobile dealer, or head down to your nearest auto parts store and find a color that best matches the component in need of touch-up.

Here's a basic procedure for touching up scratches and nicks on painted surfaces.

Materials needed:
- All-purpose cleaner or car wash solution
- Color-matched touch-up paint
- Artist's brush
- Extremely fine wet-sanding paper (at least 600 grit)
- Masking tape (optional, depending on scratch size and location)
- Cotton swab
- Glaze
- Wax

90998P08

Fig. 37 Touching up those scratches on your snowmobile's tunnel will help prevent rust from setting in

Steps:
1. Thoroughly clean the nicked or scratched area, using a cotton swab wetted with all-purpose cleaner or car wash solution. If rust has set in, the best thing to do is sand it off with medium grit sandpaper, and treat the bare metal with a rust converter.

2. After the surface is clean and dry, apply a dab of paint to the nick using a modeler's or artist's brush. (Some detailers use the tear-off end of a match from a matchbook.) Apply enough thin layers (coats) of color-matching paint so that the surface of the touch-up is level with, or slightly higher than, the surface of the surrounding finish. If the surface of the touch-up is not even with, or slightly above the surface of the surrounding finish, repeat the dab-and-dry cycle until it is.

3. Wait at least a day or more, (or even a week) to let the touch-up paint thoroughly dry. Actual drying time depends on the ambient temperature and the humidity. Paint takes far longer to dry completely than most people believe, so be patient.

4. When you are sure the touch-up is dry, it can be carefully leveled (if it is not already level) with the surface of the surrounding finish. Rub the spot gently and only enough to bring it level, using a very small piece of 600 grit (or finer) wet-sanding paper.

5. Next, apply glaze to fill in any scratches left by the sandpaper. Then wax and buff the touch-up and a small area surrounding it. If you take your time, the scratch can be blended in so well that it may be hard to detect.

If the scratches and nicks on the painted components don't bother you lookswise, simply spraying the scratched surface with rust converter will help to keep rust from forming. Spray paint can also be used, but if the exposed metal in the scratches is not treated with anti-rust primer or rust converter, rust may make its way back through to the surface.

The important thing is to keep the steel parts of your snowmobile covered with paint of some type to prevent rust from forming. As previously mentioned, if left untouched, rust can really eat into the metal, eventually weakening the component.

Rubber

Rubber items on your snowmobile, such as lever boots, or shaft drive boots, can be spruced up with a light coating of a rubber and vinyl treatment, such as Armor-All®. Rubber and vinyl treatments will keep the rubber moist and supple, which can help to slow cracking and aging. On small areas, spray a rag down, and carefully wipe down the part that you want coated. This way, overspray won't get all over the place and make a mess. Be careful not to get any overspray on your grips! A smooth, glossy grip might look nice, but it can be really hard to hold onto.

If you aren't into Armor-All, there are other products available which can be used to dress rubber and vinyl. Some are formulated differently than others, so you might want to try out a few different brands and find out what works best for you.

Aluminum

♦ See Figure 38

The use of aluminum is becoming more common for components on snowmobiles, mostly to cut down on excess weight. In addition to being lighter than steel, aluminum also is much more resistant to corrosion. Because of aluminum's natural resistance to corrosion, manufacturers sometimes leave components unfinished. Depending on how you look at it, this can be an advantage, or just another thing to tend to when washing and cleaning your snowmobile.

Although bare aluminum does not rust like steel, it can become oxidized over time if neglected. Oxidized aluminum has a gritty whitish dust on the surface. This can be removed with a scouring pad, or if it is really oxidized, sandpaper. Once the surface is smooth, An aluminum polish should be used to remove scratches left behind by the sandpaper or scouring pad. Although the surface oxidation is easily removed, there may be pitting of the surface. Not much can be done to remove heavy pitting, except sanding or grinding it away.

As with steel, the best way to keep aluminum from oxidizing is with paint or anodizing. The aluminum engine cases on most snowmobile engines are painted to prevent corrosion. Other aluminum items, like swing arms, may be "clear coated" with clear paint to prevent premature corrosion.

Distinguishing the difference between bare and clear coated aluminum can be a perplexing task. If the aluminum component is question is colored, chances are that is anodized (a translucent form of clear coating) and is definitely coated. If the aluminum component in question looks rough, but feels smooth, chances are that it also is clear coated. If you look really close, you might be able to see the clear coat on the aluminum. Smooth looking surfaces, though, are the most difficult to identify. Polished bare aluminum can have a chrome-like appearance, but even then, may be clear coated. Sometimes smoothly machined and clear coated components can give the appearance of highly polished bare aluminum. If you just can't tell if the surface is coated or bare, call a dealer and ask if the manufacturer of your snowmobile clear coated

the component in question, or take a look in your owner's manual. Most have warnings about the finish.

✳✳ WARNING

If your tunnel (or any other aluminum component) is clear coated, DO NOT use aluminum polish! This will damage the finish considerably. Aluminum polish is only for bare aluminum. Coated aluminum surfaces (paint, anodized, or powder coat) should be treated just like a painted surface.

By keeping bare aluminum surfaces clean and smooth, oxidation can be avoided. Using aluminum polish is the easiest way to keep unfinished aluminum surfaces smooth and clean. The best part about polishing bare aluminum is that with a little elbow grease, a chrome-like luster can be achieved. Occasional touch-up polishing will be required to keep things looking good, though. But, just like washing your snowmobile, the more you keep up on it, the easier it becomes.

Most aluminum polishes and compounds are not applied like wax—you must keep the polish wet and remove it with a soft rag before it dries to haze, and buff with a clean, soft cloth. But, make sure to read the directions on the can, since there may be specific steps or techniques for a particular product.

Vinyl Seat Covers

♦ See Figure 39

The seat covers on most snowmobiles are made from vinyl. Basic washing will clean vinyl, but just like plastic, constant washing can dry out vinyl. When vinyl dries out, it becomes brittle, and can crack and tear. To compensate for the drying action of washing, a vinyl and plastic treatment should be used.

After your snowmobile has been washed, spraying a rag and using it to wipe your seat is all that is required to keep your seat cover in good condition.

A word of caution though. Don't wipe down your seat right before you plan to ride, since most vinyl treatments will make your seat a little slippery. This can be a little annoying, or even downright dangerous. Wait until your snowmobile is not going to be ridden for a few days before applying vinyl treatment to your seat. This will give the vinyl treatment time to soak into the cover. After it soaks in, buff the surface with a clean towel to remove the excess.

Fig. 38 Most snowmobiles use a lot of aluminum

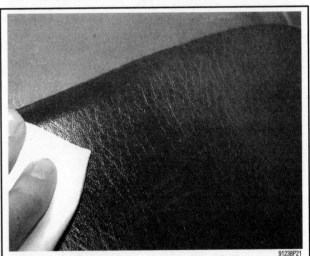

Fig. 39 Seats can also be kept clean and supple with an occasional application of protectant

91240P01

Its going to take more than a little cleanup to restore this ancient sled to its former glory, but you never know what you can do till you try

BASIC
TROUBLESHOOTING
(HOW YOUR
SNOWMOBILE
WORKS)

TROUBLESHOOTING YOUR SNOWMOBILE

Even with the best maintenance, a snowmobile can sometimes fail to perform as hoped. Your snowmobile may refuse to start, or it may stop running properly. You may have a problem with its handling, or maybe one of your accessories stops working. Keep in mind that a snowmobile is a mechanical device subject to wear and failure, just like a car or truck. With proper maintenance and care, most problems can be avoided, but once in a while, a gremlin may sneak up and bite you. In this section, we will look at some of the ways you can troubleshoot problems you may encounter with your snowmobile, and get it back in tip-top shape.

To borrow from The Motorcycle Safety Foundation (MSF) the word "SIPDE" stands for "Scan," "Identify," "Predict," "Decide, " and "Execute." This is the mantra a motorcycle or snowmobile rider should be repeating every second they are riding. By performing "SIPDE" a snowmobile rider can keep a clear view of what is going on around them while riding. This SIPDE concept can be applied to troubleshooting your snowmobile.

Fixing a problem should not be a hit or miss proposition. By charting a plan of action, using as much information available, the process of troubleshooting should be straightforward and easy. When trying to figure out a problem, the biggest mistake one makes is making random guesses, instead of taking an organized, methodical approach.

The Basic Steps Of Troubleshooting

Many hours and dollars were spent designing your snowmobile. Some of the world's best engineers make their livings designing our source of enjoyment. They used standard engineering practices to design them, and by keeping this in mind, we can use the same type of thought patterns to fix them.

1. **Scan:** Look the machine over. Are there any obvious problems? Are there any parts out of place? Are all the connectors fitted tightly? Is there fuel in the tank? Are any wires disconnected? Are there fluids leaking from anyplace

they shouldn't? Is the battery charged? These are all items that can be checked at a glance. The "Scan" portion of troubleshooting should be part of your pre-ride check. By keeping a close eye on your snowmobile, you might catch something that may become a problem later. You would be amazed at how many problems present themselves with just a good looking over. Never skip this step!

2. **Identify:** What may cause this type of problem? For example: If the sled will not start, there is no need to check track alignment. Try to narrow down your search. Was the engine making a noise? Ask yourself what might possibly make that kind of noise and start looking in that area. Did you smell something like burning oil or spilled gasoline? Look for areas that contain those fluids. The idea is to eliminate as many potential areas as possible so your search becomes smaller. Remember that the engineer who designed your snowmobile took it one part at a time; you should also.

3. **Predict**: Now that you have identified the most likely area to explore, it is time to dig a bit deeper. Now it is time to pull out the tools and testers to see if you were right. Pick an area or item that seems to be the most likely culprit. You have been using logic as your detective and now the suspect is in sight. Start testing your assumptions and see if you chose wisely.

4. **Decide:** Did your tests conclude that the item you just tested was the guilty party? Is the problem identified? Can you go onto repairing the problem or is further narrowing required? Will this fix the problem or just cure the symptom? These are things you need to think about. Many times people just fix some symptoms without actually curing the underlying cause.

5. **Execute:** Go ahead! Fix that problem! You may be able to fix the problem right in your own driveway or on the trail, but maybe you can't and will need professional help. Either way, you have figured out what the problem is, you just have to decide how to handle it.

In the rest of this section we will explain how the various systems of a snowmobile work in order to help you troubleshoot your problems.

POWERTRAIN THEORY & DIAGNOSIS

Engine

▶ **See Figure 1**

Snowmobiles are equipped with use two-stroke engines because of their light weight and simplicity. Unlike a four-stroke engine, there is no valve train on a two-stroke engine. Without a valve train, a significant amount of weight is saved, making the engine much lighter than a 4-stroke. Along with the weight savings, the amount of moving parts within the engine are significantly reduced, thereby simplifying the engine.

Another reason why two-stroke engines are used in snowmobiles is their abil-

ity to operate well in cold weather. Because of the design of the two-stroke engine, the crankshaft, pistons, and connecting rods must be lubricated by oil in the fuel/air mixture. On the other hand, a four-stroke engine must draw oil from the crankcase by an oil pump and distributed throughout the internals of the engine. In cold weather, four-stroke engine oil becomes thick, and the oil takes significantly longer to reach the bearings and sliding surfaces of the engine. Two-stroke engines actually have an advantage in cold weather, since lubrication is immediately supplied when the air and fuel mixture is drawn into the cylinders.

OPERATION

▶ **See Figures 2, 3, 4 and 5**

Let's discuss the operation of the two-stroke engine. Basically, this is what happens during a 360° rotation of the crankshaft, beginning with the piston at top dead center (TDC):

Downstroke—the piston descends from the previous cycle and exposes the exhaust port, jetting out the expanding burned gases. Simultaneously, the piston's downward movement compresses the fuel mixture from the previous cycle in the airtight crankcase.

As the piston continues to descend, it also exposes the transfer ports. The compressed mixture waiting in the crankcase now rushes through the ports and fills the combustion chamber, while at the same time sweeping any remaining burned gases out the exhaust port.

Upstroke—after reaching its lowest point of travel, the piston begins to ascend and closes off the transfer ports. At the same time, the piston's upward movement creates a partial vacuum in the crankcase. As the piston continues to ascend, it closes off the exhaust port and begins to compress the mixture in the combustion chamber.

Meanwhile, the bottom of the piston exposes the intake port and a fresh fuel mixture is sucked into the crankcase. When the piston approaches top dead center, ignition occurs and the piston once again descends to begin another cycle. As described, ignition occurs once every 360° or, more appropriately, once every two strokes of the piston (one down and one up). Hence, the term two-stroke engine.

9124XP01

Fig. 1 Snowmobile engines are compact and lightweight, and produce substantial power for their size

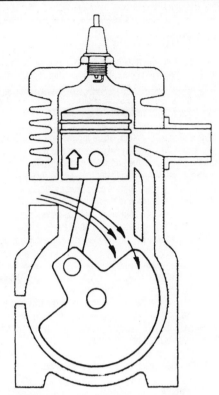

Fuel and air mixture is delivered to crank case below the piston

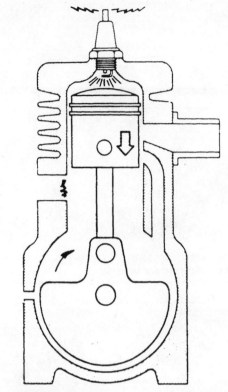

Spark plug ignites the fuel and air mixture from the previous cycle

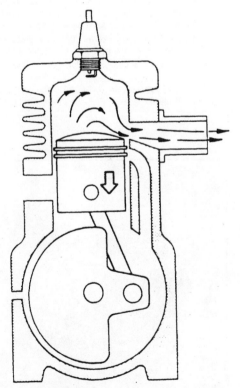

As piston travels down the cylinder bore it opens the exhaust port

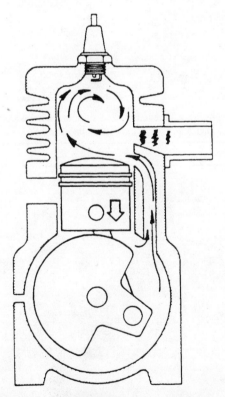

Fuel and air is transferred from the crankcase to the combustion chamber

91249G05

Fig. 2 Two-stroke engine operation

Fig. 3 Two-stroke engines use ports in the cylinder walls to control the entry and exit of the fuel and air mixture

Fig. 4 With the cylinder removed, the transfer ports (arrows) can be seen. They align with the transfer ports in the cylinder

Fig. 5 With the expansion chambers removed from the engine, the exhaust ports are easily viewable

INDUCTION

Piston Port

The piston port system is the most basic method of induction for a two-stroke engine. When the engine is operating, the upward movement of the piston allows the air and fuel mixture (along with oil) to be drawn into the crankcase or lower end of the engine. The vacuum that is created by the piston as it travels up to the top of the cylinder draws in this mixture. Since a vacuum is created within the engine, atmospheric pressure forces air through the carburetor and intake manifold, where it picks up the fuel and oil mixture. This mixture travels through the intake passage and into the crankcase. When the piston travels downwards, the underside of the piston pushes the mixture out of the crankcase and into the cylinder through the intake ports. The "opening and closing" of the intake port is controlled by the lower edge of the piston skirt, along with the position of the port(s) within the cylinder.

Since two-stroke engines do not use valves, the ports in the cylinder walls control the induction and expulsion of the fuel and air mixture in the combustion chamber. The position of the ports has a considerable effect on the performance of the engine.

Piston port engines typically do not produce as much power as reed valve and rotary valve engines, since the relationship of the intake port(s) to the exhaust port(s) cannot vary too greatly.

To achieve maximum performance from a two-stroke engine, manipulation of the intake and exhaust ports provides a substantial increase in performance. However, if there is too much differential between the ports, the air and fuel mixture will be pushed back out of the carburetor.

To allow alterations, a type of one-way valve (or valves) is used to prevent the air and fuel mixture from being "back-fed" through the carburetor(s).

Reed Valves

♦ See Figures 6 and 7

Reed valve systems consist of a reed block, with flexible stainless steel, plastic, or carbon fiber reeds that are opened by vacuum and closed by pressure. The manner in which the reeds are situated on the reed block allows a one-way movement of the air and fuel mixture through the block. The reeds are forced open by when piston is on the upward stroke, and the pressure in the crankcase is below atmospheric pressure. After the piston reaches top dead center and begins its downward stroke, the pressure difference ceases, and the reeds close, keeping the air and fuel mixture within the crankcase.

Over time, the reeds become worn, and require replacement. The material from which the reeds are made from has an effect on their longevity, and engine performance.

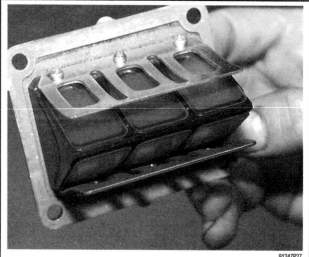

Fig. 6 An example of a reed valve assembly

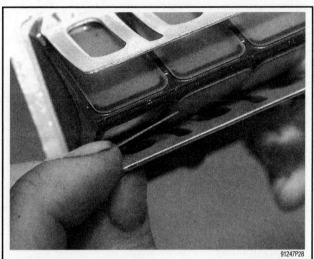

Fig. 7 The thin reeds act as one way valves, preventing the mixture from being forced back out of the carburetor(s)

Rotary Valve

▶ See Figure 8

The rotary-valve operates on the same basic principles as a reed valve, but is constructed differently and offers some distinct advantages.

The valve itself is a resin hardened fiber or metal disc with a cutaway section along its circumference. The disc is mounted either directly to the end of the crankshaft, or driven off a bevel gear, and is enclosed within a narrow sealed chamber located between the crankcase and the carburetor. As the valve rotates, the cutaway section exposes the port and allows the fresh fuel mixture to be drawn into the crankcase. Then, when the cutaway section ends, the port is

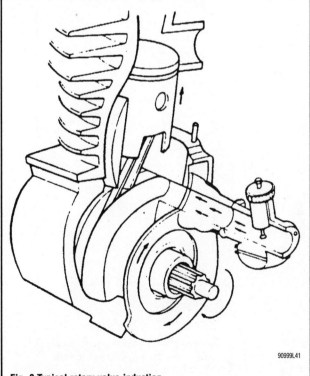

Fig. 8 Typical rotary valve induction

sealed by the disc, preventing any air and fuel from being pushed back through the carburetor(s).

Since the rotary valve does not "flap" like reed valves, the life of the valve is greatly increased. In addition to longer service life, a rotary valve allows for a more precise control of the timing of the intake system, keeping the air and fuel mixture from being pushed back through the carburetor(s).

EXHAUST

▶ See Figures 9 and 10

The exhaust system of a two-stroke engine consists of two primary components; the expansion chamber, and the muffler (also known as a stinger). The expansion chamber consists of a header pipe, diffuser cone, center section, and conical baffle. A typical expansion chamber resembles a swollen hose, only it is constructed of metal. The shape of the expansion chamber helps determine the "power band" characteristics of the engine.

During engine operation, the exhaust port opens, and a positive sonic wave is sent into the expansion chamber. The wave expands inside the chamber, until it reaches the other side of the chamber (known as a conical baffle) which refracts the sonic wave back toward the exhaust port of the cylinder. The return of the sonic wave to the exhaust port creates negative pressure, causing more air and fuel to be taken in and exhaust to be pushed out of the engine. When the piston closes the port in the cylinder, the sonic wave refracts again, still creating negative pressure. When the wave reaches the end of the expansion chamber again, pressure equalization created in the chamber causes the wave to turn and create positive pressure. The wave then travels through the conical baffle to exhaust pipe in time to prevent the exit of a new charge of air/fuel that is being discharged from the exhaust port.

When a two-stroke engine is designed, the expansion chamber is "tuned" to provide a substantial power increase within a specific rpm range. When the engine is operating within this range, it is commonly referred to as "on the pipe" meaning that the sound wave refracting process within the expansion chamber is at its peak. This peak power output is often abrupt and sudden, depending on the shape of the expansion chamber. Other factors such as the intake and exhaust port timing (location), combustion chamber and crankcase compression ratios, and piston displacement are also taken into consideration when matching an expansion chamber to an engine.

➡ For proper two-stroke engine performance, the expansion chamber must be compatible with the engine. Poor engine performance will result from a mismatched expansion chamber, as will large dents in the chamber.

Fig. 9 The expansion chambers, unique to the two-stroke engine, provide substantial power increases, despite their odd shape

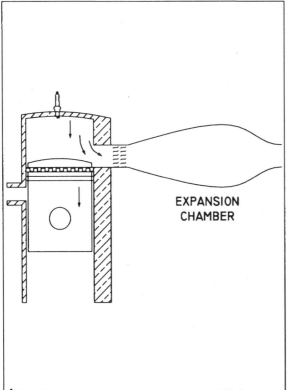

A. When the exhaust port opens, a pressure wave is generated in the expansion chamber by the burned fuel flowing out of the combustion chamber.

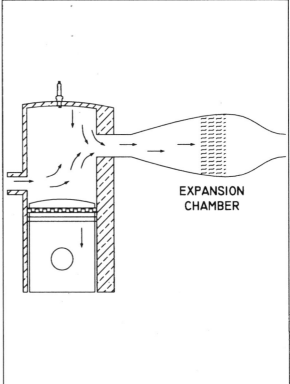

B. The pressure wave travels down the length of the expansion chamber, slowing down as the chamber becomes wider.

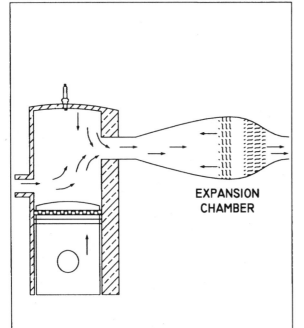

C. The pressure wave increases in speed as it reaches the end of the expansion chamber, where it gradually decreases in diameter. When the wave reaches the end of the chamber, part of the wave is reflected back toward the exhaust port. The rest of the wave exiting the chamber creates low pressure, which travels behind the refracted wave heading back toward the expansion chamber.

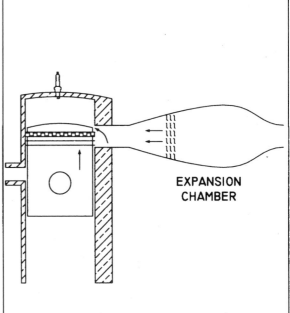

D. The refracted wave continues toward the exhaust port, helping to prevent the new air/fuel mixture from escaping through the exhaust port. This action helps to increase efficiency and power of the engine.

91249G07

Fig. 10 Expansion chamber operation detail

Standard Port

▶ See Figure 11

A standard type exhaust port is basically nothing more than an opening (or openings) within the cylinder to allow the exhaust gas to escape from the combustion chamber. Sometimes aftermarket tuners will modify the port(s) by grinding and polishing the ports for better exhaust flow.

Variable Port

▶ See Figure 12

With a variable port exhaust system, a mechanically (or electronically) controlled "gate" is used to control the size and shape of the exhaust port(s) on the engine. These variable ports are typically referred to as "power valves." The con-

trol of the height and length of exhaust ports and chambers helps to broaden the peak power range of the engine.

Although these power valves provide additional power, they are complex, and require regular cleaning and servicing to keep them functioning properly.

Drive System

OPERATION

▶ See Figures 13, 14 and 15

In comparison with an automobile or a motorcycle, the drive system of a snowmobile is very basic in design. The "transmission" on a snowmobile basi-

Fig. 11 With a standard port exhaust, the pistons can easily be seen through the exhaust ports

Fig. 12 Variable port exhaust systems are typically identified by the actuators above the exhaust ports

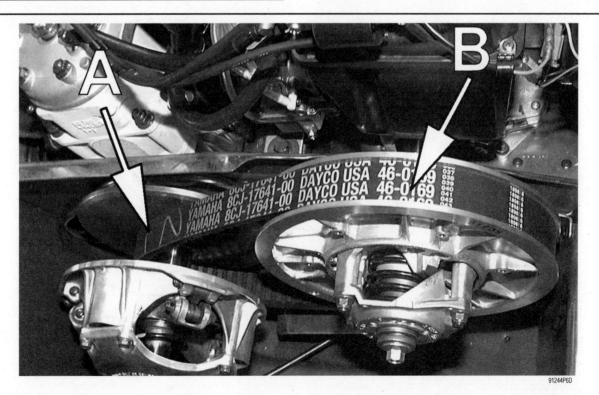

Fig. 13 The primary pulley (A) is mounted to the engine, and the secondary pulley (B) is connected to the chaincase, which drives the track

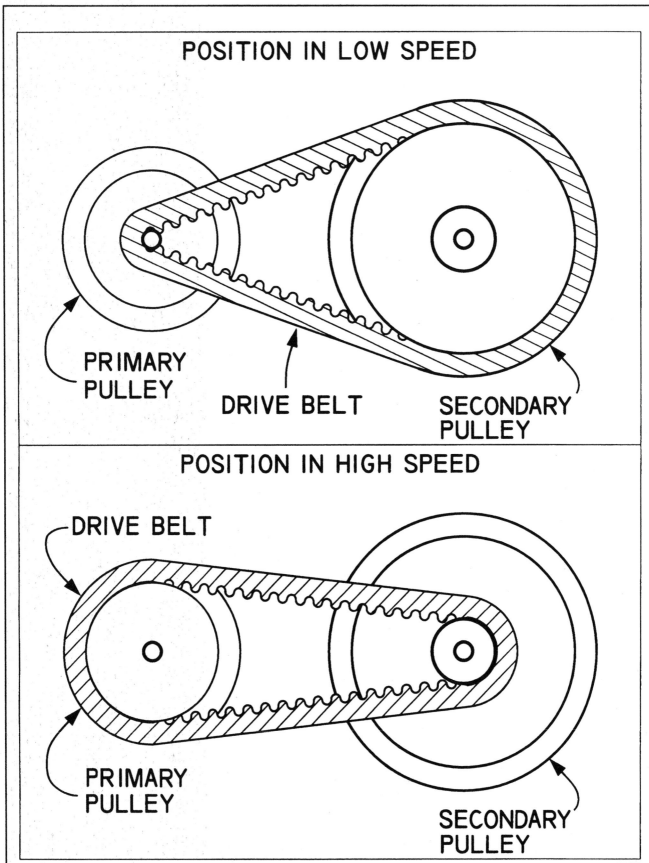

POSITION IN LOW SPEED

PRIMARY
PULLEY

DRIVE BELT

SECONDARY
PULLEY

POSITION IN HIGH SPEED

DRIVE BELT

PRIMARY
PULLEY

SECONDARY
PULLEY

91244GXX

Fig. 14 Typical snowmobile drive pulley detail

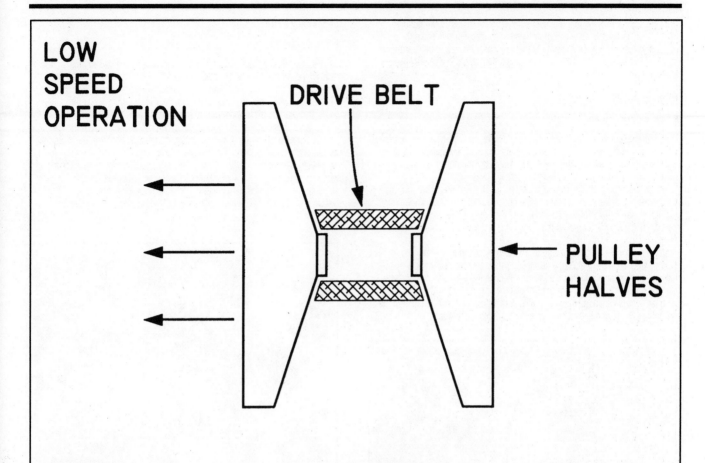

LOW
SPEED
OPERATION

DRIVE BELT

PULLEY
HALVES

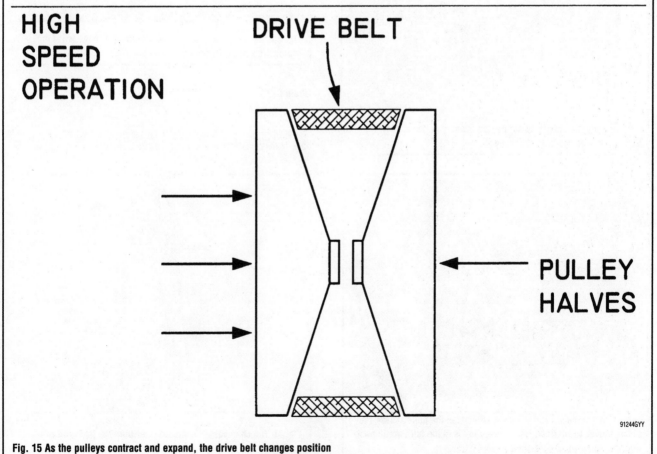

HIGH
SPEED
OPERATION

DRIVE BELT

PULLEY
HALVES

91244GYY

Fig. 15 As the pulleys contract and expand, the drive belt changes position

cally consists of two variable diameter pulleys, and a belt. The two pulleys expand and contract based on engine speed and vehicle speed. From the driven pulley, a chain and sprocket assembly (or chaincase) is used to transfer the power of the engine to the track. Some models may also use a reverse gear in the chain case.

Primary Pulley

▶ See Figures 16 and 17

The primary drive pulley (also referred to as the primary sheave) is mounted on the crankshaft. The pulley movement relies on the centrifugal motion of weights placed on levers within the pulley. The faster the pulley spins, the weights are forced outward, pushing the pulley halves together.

When the engine at idle, the pulley halves are the furthest apart, and the belt cannot be driven by the pulley. When the throttle is applied, engine speed increases, causing the pulley halves to move closer together and contact the belt. This action is what makes the primary pulley act as a "clutch" mechanism.

The Primary pulley can typically be adjusted by changing the weights, or the springs that retain the weights. If stronger springs are installed, the pulley halves will engage at a higher engine rpm. Respectively, heavier weights will cause the pulley to engage with the belt at a lower engine rpm. On most snowmobiles, a means of adjustment is provided to adjust the characteristics of the primary pulley to compensate for operation at different altitudes.

Fig. 16 When the engine is at idle, the primary pulley is "open" with the two halves fully expanded

Fig. 17 As engine speed increases, weights in the pulley cause the pulley halves to contract. Here, the pulley is in the full throttle position

Secondary Pulley

▶ See Figure 18

The secondary pulley (also known as the driven pulley, or secondary sheave) receives power from the primary pulley via drive belt, and transfers it to the track through the chaincase. The secondary pulley expands and contracts like the primary pulley, but also incorporates a helix cam, which keeps the pulley adjusted based on the amount of torque placed on it by the track. The higher the load placed on the pulley, the greater the drive ratio becomes. This design helps keep the engine operating within its peak rpm, regardless of the load from the weight of the snowmobile.

As with the primary pulley, altering the spring tension and helix cam angle will affect the "shifting" of the pulley. Adjusting the pulleys is usually done to compensate for high-altitude operation, or to achieve peak performance from the sled in competition situations. Each snowmobile has specific requirements for adjustment of the pulley.

Fig. 18 The ramps on the secondary pulley (arrow) control the expansion and contraction of the pulley halves

Chain Case

▶ See Figure 19

The chain case is used to transfer the power from the secondary pulley to the track. In most snowmobiles, this is done with a chain and sprockets. A slight

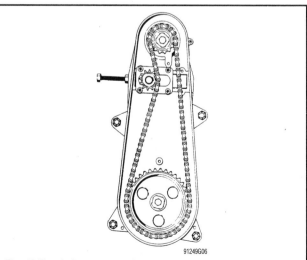

Fig. 19 The chaincase transmits power from the jackshaft to the track

reduction ratio is incorporated into the gears, to provide the proper drive ratio at the track sprockets. The shaft that transfers power from the secondary pulley to the upper chain case sprocket is known as the jackshaft. The jackshaft also is where the disc brake is typically mounted, providing stopping power for the snowmobile. Some models may use gears instead of a chain (and is consequently called a "gear case") and also incorporate a reverse gear.

On most models, occasional adjustment of the chain tensioner is necessary to compensate for the stretch of the chain. Usually a bolt is used to provide tension on the adjuster. Other models may use a hydraulic or spring-loaded tensioner, making adjustment unnecessary.

Powertrain Troubleshooting

Armed with the basic knowledge of how your engine and drive system works, troubleshooting any problems should be fairly straightforward. Refer to the engine and drive system troubleshooting charts for further information.

The fuel system on almost all snowmobiles is made up of a carburetor(s), fuel filter and an oil injection pump (unless the snowmobile requires pre-mixed fuel). The following information encompasses the great majority of components currently in use.

ENGINE TROUBLESHOOTING

Problem	Possible Cause	Inspection/Remedy
Abnormal engine noise	Piston slap; piston-to-cylinder wall clearance too great	Check clearance; replace components as necessary
	Excessive carbon in combustion chamber	Decarbonize
	Knock (especially noticeable at idle): worn connecting rod big end bearing	Replace
	Worn connecting rod or wrist pin bearings	Replace
	Rumble at idle developing into whine at high rpm: crankshaft main bearings worn or damaged	Replace
	Pinging or spark knock: timing too advanced; low quality fuel; excessive carbon buildup in combustion chambers	Adjust ignition timing; use better quality fuel; clean cylinder head chambers
Engine fails to start, but has spark at the plugs	No fuel in the tank; fuel petcock closed or clogged; fuel line clogged	Refuel; turn on or clean petcock; check for fuel at carbs; clean and blow out fuel lines
	Engine flooded	Remove spark plugs and crank engine to blow out
	Crankcase flooded	Remove spark plugs, shut off petcock (if equipped) and crank engine
	Improper fuel/oil ratio	Check injection pump operation
	Low or no compression	Leaking head gasket; warped head; worn or damaged crankshaft seals; poor seal at crankcase mating surface; worn piston rings; worn cylinders
	Carb adjustments wrong	Adjust carb; check float height
Engine fails to start (no spark)	Ignition switched off	Turn on ignition
	Kill switch off	Reset
	Spark plugs worn or fouled	Clean or replace
	Spark plug heat range too cold	Replace with proper spark plug
	Spark plug gap too wide	Reset gap
	Spark plug resistor cap defective	Replace cap
	Plug lead defective or damaged	Replace
	Ignition coil defective	Replace
	Dead battery	Recharge or replace battery
	Blown fuse, circuit breaker or fusible link	Replace or reset
	Loose or corroded battery terminals	Clean and secure the connections
Engine is hard to start	Worn, dirty or improperly gapped plugs	Clean or replace plugs with proper heat range
	Carburetor idle settings wrong; pilot air or fuel	Adjust idle settings or clean carburetors
	Battery low	Recharge or replace battery
	Spark plug leads cracked or dirty	Replace
	Loose or intermittently grounded wires	Check connections and condition of wiring
	Defective coils or condensers	Replace

ENGINE TROUBLESHOOTING

Problem	Possible Cause	Inspection/Remedy
Engine starts but refuses to run	Fuel feed problem	Check fuel supply; check pulse pump, lines, carburetors for blocked passages; fuel tank vent
	Ignition timing incorrect	Adjust (if possible)
	Spark plugs too cold or worn	Replace with proper heat range plugs
Engine idles poorly	Pilot air or fuel passages clogged	Disassemble and clean carburetor(s)
	Idle speed too low	Adjust idle speed as necessary
	Carburetors not properly synchronized	Synchronize and adjust carburetors as necessary
	Spark plugs dirty, worn or incorrect gap	Clean or replace spark plugs
Engine misfire or stumble	Choke(s) out of adjustment	Adjust cable or linkage as necessary
	Dirty carburetor(s)	Disassemble and clean carburetor(s)
	Carburetor(s) misadjusted	Adjust and synchronize carburetors as necessary
	Poor wiring connections in ignition circuit	Check connections at each ignition component
	Defective ignition coils or condensers	Replace
	Air leaks at carburetor manifolds	Fix leaks
	Water in carburetors or tank	Drain carburetor float bowls or drain fuel tank
	Carburetor main jet clogged	Remove and clean
	Fuel tank vent clogged	Clean
	Petcock clogged	Clean
	Dead battery	Recharge or replace battery
	Loose or intermittent connections in ignition circuit	Check connections
	Carburetor float level incorrect	Check float height and needle valve seating
	Float bowl level too low	Adjust float height
Spark plugs foul repeatedly	Plug gap too narrow	Adjust to proper gap
	Plug heat range too low for conditions	Fit a higher heat range plug
	Fuel mixture set too rich	Adjust fuel mixture
	Too much oil in fuel	Check injection pump operation; kinked cable
Loss of compression or power	Holed or damaged piston (severe detonation)	Replace
	Piston partially seizing	Determine cause and replace components as req'd
	Worn piston rings	Replace
	Leaking head gasket	Replace
	Muffler or exhaust port clogged with carbon	Decarbonize
	Clogged air cleaner	Clean or replace
Poor low speed operation	Incorrect ignition timing	Adjust timing
	Defective coil or condenser	Replace
	Carburetor float level incorrect	Adjust
	Pilot screw not adjusted properly	Adjust carburetor
	Spark plug gap too big	Adjust
	Ignition timing incorrect	Adjust

91249C04

ENGINE TROUBLESHOOTING

Problem	Possible Cause	Inspection/Remedy
Poor high speed operation	Spark plug gap too small	Adjust
	Defective ignition coil	Replace
	Carburetor float level incorrect	Adjust float level
	Low compression	Check engine mechanical condition and repair
	Engine carbon fouled	Decarbonize
	Exhaust pipe loose at engine	Tighten connection
	Spark plug too hot	Use colder range plugs
Engine partially seizes or slows after high speed operation	Piston seizure	Determine cause and repair
	Fuel mixture too lean	Adjust carburetors
	Oil injection pump malfunctioning	Check for proper operation; kinked cable, broken belt or drive gear
Engine overheats	Engine is carbon fouled	Decarbonize
	Water pump not working	Repair
	Heat exchanger clogged internally	Replace
	Fan belt slipping or broken	Adjust or replace
	Loss of coolant	Repair leak and fill with proper coolant
	Sticking thermostat	Replace
	Ignition timing too retarded or too advanced	Adjust
	Cooling fins clogged with dirt	Clean
	Air/fuel mixture too lean	Adjust
Engine detonates or preignites	Spark plugs too hot for application	Replace with cooler spark plugs
	Ignition timing too advanced	Adjust
	Insufficient oil in fuel	Check oil injection pump for proper operation
	Air/fuel mixture too lean	Adjust
	Air leaks at carburetor manifolds	Fix
	Engine carbon fouled	Decarbonize
	Fuel octane too low	Use higher octane fuel
Engine backfire	Fuel/Air mixture too lean or too rich	Adjust and synchronize carburetors as necessary
	Carburetor(s) misadjusted	Adjust and synchronize carburetors as necessary
	Sour fuel	Drain or siphon tank and replace with fresh fuel
Excessive exhaust Smoke	Worn rings or bore	Rebuild
	Excessive carbon buildup in engine	Decarbonize
	Overly rich mixture	Adjust carb
	Malfunctioning choke mechanism	Repair the mechanism
Piston seizure	Low oil level	Maintain oil at proper level
	Engine overheating due to too advanced ignition	Check settings
	Insufficient oil	Check oil injection pump
Excessive fuel consumption	Clogged exhaust system	Clean expansion chambers as necessary
	Leaking fuel line connection	Repair connection
	Incorrect carburetor adjustment	Adjust and synchronize carburetors as necessary

91249C05

DRIVE SYSTEM TROUBLESHOOTING

Problem	Possible Cause	Inspection/Remedy
Snowmobile does not move when engine is accelerated	Broken drive belt	Replace drive belt
	Slipping drive belt	Adjust and align pulleys
	Primary pulley not functioning properly	Inspect and repair as necessary
	Heavy snow and ice buildup on track	Clear track of ice and snow
	Parking brake activated	Deactivate parking brake
	Obstruction or foreign matter on skis	Clear skis of obstructions and debris
	Broken drive chain (in chaincase)	Repair as necessary
Clunking or slipping feeling under acceleration	Loose track (drive sprockets slipping on track)	Adjust and align track
	Excessively worn track drive lugs	Replace track
	Broken or worn teeth on drive sprockets	Replace drive sprockets
	Loose drive chain	Adjust drive chain
Sluggish acceleration	Primary pulley engaging too soon	Inspect and repair as necessary
	Slipping drive belt	Adjust and align pulleys
	Worn drive belt	Replace drive belt
	Track adjusted too tightly	Readjust and align track
	Brake dragging	Inspect and repair as system as necessary
	Defective bearings in drive system	Inspect and repair as necessary
Engine speed too high during normal operation	Primary pulley not engaging at proper rpm	Inspect and repair as necessary
	Secondary pulley not functioning properly	Inspect and repair as necessary
	Slipping drive belt	Adjust and align pulleys
Premature drive belt failure	Pulley alignment incorrect	Adjust and align pulleys
	Binding rear track (too tight or ice buildup)	Clear track of ice and snow before operation
	Surface of pulley halves scored or damaged	Repair or replace pulley halves as necessary
	Defective drive belt	Replace
	Pulleys not functioning correctly	Inspect and repair or adjust as necessary
Excessive chaincase noise	Worn drive chain	Replace
	Chain out of adjustment	Adjust drive chain
	Worn or damaged sprockets	Replace sprockets and chain
Erratic operation	Broken spring in pulley	Inspect and repair pulley as necessary
	Binding or broken weights in primary pulley	Inspect and repair pulley as necessary
	Dirt or debris in pulley assemblies	Inspect and repair pulley as necessary

91249C06

FUEL SYSTEM THEORY & DIAGNOSIS

Carburetors

▶ See Figures 20 and 21

Most basically stated, a carburetor mixes air and fuel to form a combustible mixture. Air passes over an opening, drawing gasoline up and into the air stream. The gasoline is atomized as it is sucked from the opening. A throttle plate blocks the airflow to adjust the speed of the engine.

In real life, there must be multiple ways of adjusting the rate of fuel delivery to match the needs of the engine. As a result, the carburetor can have many different circuits and components. If you wish to know more about this subject, brace yourself and read on. Otherwise, skip to the section about accessories and be happy. Carburetors aren't for the faint-at-heart!

A carburetor works due to the "venturi effect." A venturi is a passage with a constricted section through which a fluid moves (in this case the fluid is the air). As the air flows through the constriction, the velocity increases (it speeds up) and the pressure goes down. It is this lower pressure that draws the gasoline through the opening.

Fig. 20 The carburetors are an essential part of the engine—they provide the proper mixture of air and fuel at varying engine speeds

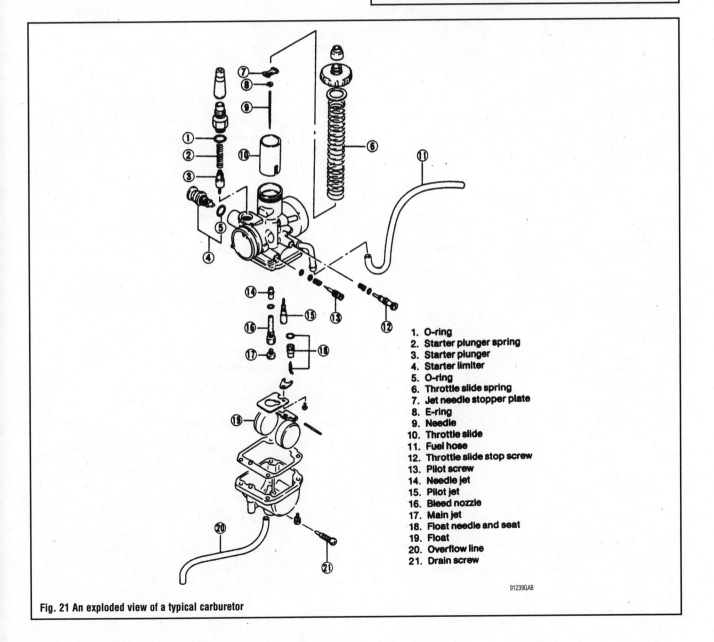

1. O-ring
2. Starter plunger spring
3. Starter plunger
4. Starter limiter
5. O-ring
6. Throttle slide spring
7. Jet needle stopper plate
8. E-ring
9. Needle
10. Throttle slide
11. Fuel hose
12. Throttle slide stop screw
13. Pilot screw
14. Needle jet
15. Pilot jet
16. Bleed nozzle
17. Main jet
18. Float needle and seat
19. Float
20. Overflow line
21. Drain screw

Fig. 21 An exploded view of a typical carburetor

CONSTRUCTION

♦ See Figures 22, 23 and 24

Most carburetors consist of a one-piece body cast from cheap pot metal, although some "racing" units are made from more expensive materials such as magnesium. The body incorporates a bore for the movement of the throttle slide, the venturi, and provides a mounting point for various fuel and air jets.

The body is drilled with a number of fuel and air passages. Among these are the primary air passage, pilot air passage, and pilot outlet or by-pass.

The primary air passage can usually be found just beneath the carburetor intake, and is drilled through to the needle jet. The air taken in through this passage helps to atomize, or mix, the gasoline passing through the needle jet before it enters the venturi. Unless the gasoline is atomized, raw fuel will reach

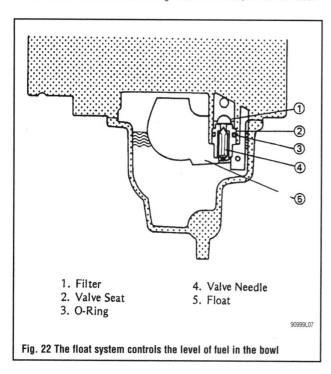

1. Filter
2. Valve Seat
3. O-Ring
4. Valve Needle
5. Float

90999L07

Fig. 22 The float system controls the level of fuel in the bowl

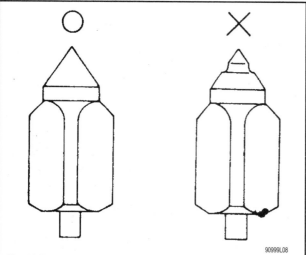

90999L08

Fig. 23 The needle valve on the left is good, but the grooved one of the right needs to be replaced

the combustion chamber, resulting in wet-fouled spark plugs, inefficient combustion, and generally poor operation.

The pilot air passage is located alongside the primary air passage on most carburetors. The air taken in through this drilling is used for idle and low-speed operation.

The pilot outlet is a very small drilling which can be seen on the engine side of the throttle slide bore. The fuel/air mixture for idling passes through here and then to the engine.

The carburetor body also has a place for the attachment of the float bowl. The float bowl houses the float assembly and carries the carburetor's gasoline supply. A part of the float assembly is the float valve which usually consists of a small needle and a needle seat.

The float rises and falls according to the amount of gasoline in the float bowl, alternately pressing the needle against its seat and releasing it, thus controlling the fuel flow. The float bulbs may be made of various materials. Most early carburetors used brass bulbs, but plastic has been used more frequently in recent years. Float needles can be plastic, brass, or neoprene-tipped brass, the last proving most effective. Needle seats are almost always brass, and on most carburetors can be unscrewed for cleaning or replacement.

The great majority of modern carburetors mount the float bowl directly beneath the carburetor body. In this position the fuel supply surrounds the main jet ensuring an accurately metered supply of fuel during acceleration, braking, or banking to either side. This type of carburetor is usually known as "concentric." Not all carburetors were constructed in this manner, and separate float bowl carburetors were the rule for many years.

The throttle slide is the chief metering component of the carburetor. It is controlled directly by the throttle cable, which runs to the lever on the handlebars. When the lever is operated, the throttle cable opens and closes the throttle slide.

The throttle slide determines the size of the carburetor venturi and therefore meters the amount of air in the fuel/air mixture at most of the operating range. Additionally, the needle or jet needle is attached to the slide. This needle works in conjunction with the needle jet and determines the amount of gasoline allowed to pass into the engine primarily in the midrange.

The throttle slide is cylindrical in most carburetors, although there are examples of "square slides" used on some carburetors. The slide has a cutaway at the intake side of the carburetor to allow the entry of air in sufficient quantities to mix with the gasoline when the throttle is closed. The higher the cutaway, the leaner the mixture will be when the slide is just opened. If the size of the cutaway is not matched to the other metering components and the particular needs of the engine, the transition from idle to the main metering system will be greatly impaired.

Formerly, throttle slides were cast from the same material as the carburetor body, but this was found to cause greatly accelerated wear on both slide and body. Today, the slide is commonly steel, often chromed, bringing wear into more acceptable limits.

THROTTLE SLIDE TYPE CARBURETOR OPERATION

♦ See Figures 25, 26 and 27

The operation of a practical carburetor can best be described by dividing it into five circuits, and the components that control each one.

Starting Circuit (0% Throttle Opening)

The engine needs a rich mixture for starting when cold. Since this need is only temporary and the mixture must be balanced when the engine warms up, a manually operated "choke" is incorporated into most carburetors and is controlled by the operator.

There are various ways of creating this rich mixture. The most simple is to reduce the amount of air available to the carburetor by closing off the mouth with a plate.

On some units, a temporary rich mixture is obtained by flooding or overfilling the float bowl. "Ticklers" are provided on the carburetor. When pushed, they depress the float, allowing the float needle to rise from its seat. The fuel level in

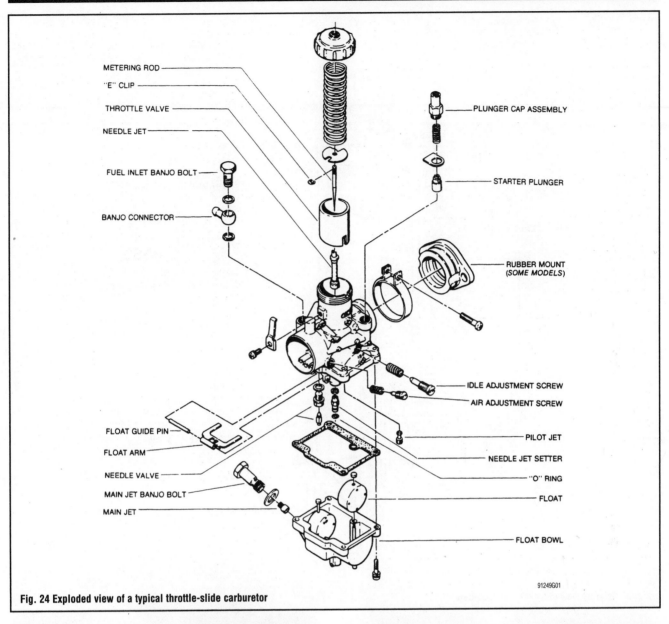

METERING ROD

"E" CLIP

THROTTLE VALVE

NEEDLE JET

FUEL INLET BANJO BOLT

BANJO CONNECTOR

PLUNGER CAP ASSEMBLY

STARTER PLUNGER

RUBBER MOUNT
(*SOME MODELS*)

IDLE ADJUSTMENT SCREW

AIR ADJUSTMENT SCREW

FLOAT GUIDE PIN

FLOAT ARM

NEEDLE VALVE

MAIN JET BANJO BOLT

MAIN JET

PILOT JET

NEEDLE JET SETTER

"O" RING

FLOAT

FLOAT BOWL

91249G01

Fig. 24 Exploded view of a typical throttle-slide carburetor

91244P5G

Fig. 25 Throttle-slide type carburetors use both round slides . . .

A91244P89

Fig. 26 . . . and flat slides, depending on the manufacturer

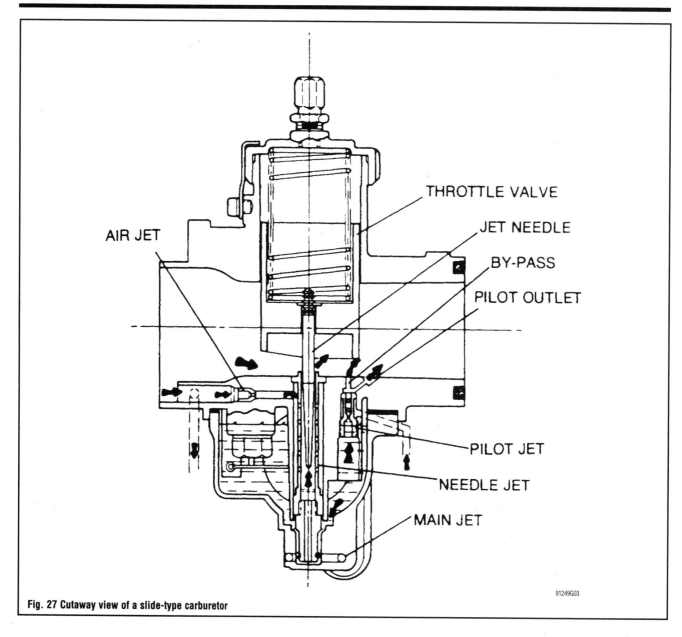

AIR JET

THROTTLE VALVE

JET NEEDLE

BY-PASS

PILOT OUTLET

PILOT JET

NEEDLE JET

MAIN JET

Fig. 27 Cutaway view of a slide-type carburetor

the float bowl then exceeds its normal level and rises through the jets into the venturi where it provides a rich starting mixture.

Other carburetors, such as Mikuni and Dell'Orto use a refined version of the tickler. A starter jet is fitted which a cable or lever activates. When activated, the jet is opened (in most cases a spring-loaded plunger does the opening and closing), and fuel from the float bowl can bypass the normal fuel jets and pass into the carburetor bore. This is also true for some CV type carbs.

Once the engine is started and warmed up, the choke is switched off, and the fuel/air metering is turned over to the idle circuit components.

Idle Circuit (0–10% Throttle Opening)

At idle, under normal operating conditions, the engine requires very little fuel and air. It does, however, require more accurate metering than pure venturi action can provide while the engine is turning relatively slowly and intake air velocity is low.

The idle circuit on most popular carburetors consists of a pilot jet, pilot air passage, and the throttle slide.

The float bowl provides fuel. The amount of fuel is metered by the pilot jet,

while air is taken in through the carburetor venturi and passes under the throttle slide (which is almost, but not quite closed at this point).

Because the idle mixture is so crucial, it is possible to adjust the mixture to compensate for changing conditions so that a good idle is always maintained. For this reason a pilot screw is fitted to most carburetors. The pilot screw is really a tapered needle and is fitted to an air or fuel passage. Turning the screw in or out will change the amount of fuel or air allowed to pass, and hence the mixture. On some carburetors the pilot screw is fitted directly to the pilot air passage and is sometimes called the "pilot air screw." On carburetors of this type, the amount of fuel entering the idling engine is determined by the size of the pilot jet alone, and the amount of air is varied to meet changing conditions.

On other types of carburetors, it is the amount of air which is fixed by the size of the pilot air passage. On these carburetors, the pilot screw changes the amount of fuel passing into the engine.

In operation, piston suction creates a low-pressure area behind the throttle slide. To equalize this low pressure, air rushes through the pilot air passage, mixes with fuel from the pilot jet. This mixture is bled into the carburetor's intake tract through the pilot outlet. The air coming in under the throttle slide is added to this mixture and delivers it to the combustion chamber.

Low-Speed Circuit (10–25% Throttle Opening)

▶ See Figure 28

This circuit uses the same components as the idle circuit. There is, however, an increase in the airflow as the throttle slide rises, and in fuel flow as the needle begins to come out of the needle jet. This effects a transition to the mid-range circuit, since the increased amounts of fuel and air delivered by the needle jet and the venturi overshadow the smaller amounts coming from the pilot outlet, eventually eliminating the idle circuit from the metering system.

Midrange Circuit (25–75% Throttle Opening)

In this circuit, air is supplied by two sources: the venturi and the primary air passage. The more important reason for the air going through the primary air passage, however, is that it mixes with the gasoline in the needle jet (the needle jet has a number of holes drilled in it), and this helps to atomize the fuel before it enters the venturi.

Fuel is supplied by the float bowl and metered by the needle jet and needle. The needle jet on most carburetors is located just above the main jet and works in conjunction with the needle suspended from the throttle slide.

As the slide rises, the air flow through the carburetor is increased, and at the same time the tapered needle allows more and more fuel to pass through the needle jet.

High-Speed Circuit (Full Throttle)

The throttle slide has been lifted clear of the venturi, and no longer controls the amount of air. By the same token, the needle has lifted out of the needle jet, and no longer controls the fuel supply.

Venturi action takes over completely. The amount of air sucked into the engine is determined by the size of the venturi, and the amount of fuel delivered by the size of the main jet. The only other part of the system, which still has a significant effect, is the primary air passage that continues to aid fuel atomization.

It should be understood that the operating ranges of the various metering circuits overlap somewhat, so there is a gradual, rather than an abrupt, transition from one to another as the throttle is operated.

The relative independence of the various circuits, however, should explain why it is fruitless to make random changes in carburetor settings without first determining the nature of the problem, and the range in which it occurs.

THROTTLE-PLATE CARBURETOR OPERATION

▶ See Figure 29

The "throttle-plate" (or butterfly type) carburetor is similar in theory to the throttle-slide types described above except, of course, that there is no moving slide. In its place is a flat plate, which pivots to increase the size of the carburetor throat and allow progressively more of the fuel/air mixture to enter the combustion chamber.

Unlike the throttle-slide carburetors described above, the throttle-plate units do not usually have well defined mid-range circuits, and are best described by breaking the operation down into "low-speed" and "high-speed" circuits.

Starting Circuit

A choke plate on the intake side of the carburetor closes off the mouth to yield a rich mixture needed for starting. A hole in the choke plate allows some air to enter to prevent flooding the engine. In addition, an accelerator pump is fitted which injects a stream of gasoline into the venturi when the throttle is opened.

Low-Speed Circuit

There are three or four idle discharge holes located at the top engine side of the venturi. The main idle discharge hole is variable in size as it works in conjunction with a tapered idle adjusting needle. At idle, the throttle plate stop screw holds the throttle plate open just enough so that this passage is able to discharge its fuel into the engine.

Drawn by piston suction, gasoline rises from the float bowl through the idle tube. As the fuel passes the idle discharge holes, air is drawn in and mixed with it.

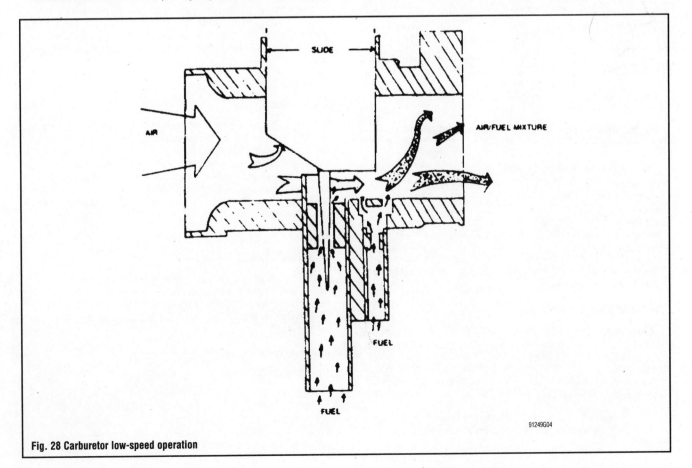

91249G04

Fig. 28 Carburetor low-speed operation

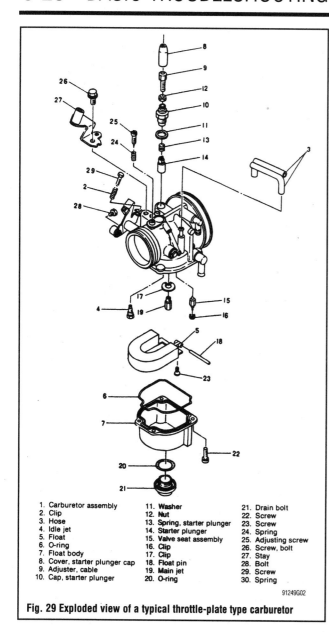

1. Carburetor assembly
2. Clip
3. Hose
4. Idle jet
5. Float
6. O-ring
7. Float body
8. Cover, starter plunger cap
9. Adjuster, cable
10. Cap, starter plunger
11. **Washer**
12. **Nut**
13. **Spring, starter plunger**
14. **Starter plunger**
15. **Valve seat assembly**
16. **Clip**
17. **Clip**
18. Float pin
19. Main jet
20. O-ring
21. Drain bolt
22. Screw
23. Screw
24. Spring
25. Adjusting screw
26. Screw, bolt
27. Stay
28. Bolt
29. Screw
30. Spring

91249G02

Fig. 29 Exploded view of a typical throttle-plate type carburetor

The mixture is then bled into the intake port through the idle hole. The mixture is determined by the idle adjusting needle. If the needle is turned in, the mixture will be leaned, and it will be richened if the needle is turned out.

As the throttle is opened slightly, the other idle discharge holes are exposed in turn, each allowing progressively more fuel and air into the intake port.

Eventually, the throttle plate is opened enough so that engine suction is powerful enough to draw gasoline from the main discharge tube and the transition to the high-speed circuit begins.

High-Speed Circuit

The high-speed circuit begins when all idle discharge holes are exposed, and can no longer supply sufficient gasoline and air for the engine's needs.

As the throttle plate is opened the velocity of the incoming air passing through the venturi is increased, and, as this happens, this air exerts an increasingly powerful suction on the gasoline in the discharge tube just below the venturi. This gasoline is already partially atomized by the air drawn through the well vent.

When the throttle is fully opened, the amount of air in the mixture is determined by the size of the carburetor venturi and the amount of fuel by the size of the main jet.

Fuel Injection System

Ok, now that you have digested all that stuff about carburetors, you have to be thinking, "There has got to be a better way!" In fact, there is, and it is called fuel injection. In its most basic form, fuel injection is defined as injecting fuel into the engine via a pressurized fuel source. Carbs on the other hand, rely on vacuum to draw the air and fuel into the engine.

Fuel injection allows for very precise metering of fuel into the engine. It also allows the mixture to be controlled by a computer that can decide the best course of action for the fuel system in only a few milliseconds. Carbs rely on the shape of needles, the size of orifices and the whims of the person(s) who built or tuned it. Fuel injection is programmed with the purpose of the sled in mind and an attempt is made to optimize the fuel delivery.

Some manufacturers offer fuel injection as an option, allowing the consumer to make the choice between fuel injection and carburetors. Some like carburetors for their ease of tunability, and others might choose fuel injection for the reduction in maintenance. Although let's face it—an engine cowl full of fuel injection components can be quite intimidating!

If fuel injection is so great, why don't all snowmobiles use it? This answer comes down to economics: Carbs are cheaper than fuel injection. Not to mention the fact that the snowmobile manufacturers have done great things with carbs, so why mess with a good thing? But, there are still good reasons for the use of fuel injection.

➡**On some models, servicing of the fuel injection system may void the manufacturer's warranty.**

Let's look into the components of a fuel injection system, and how they all work together to precisely meter the correct amount of air and fuel into your engine.

COMPONENTS AND THEIR OPERATION

▶ See Figure 30

Depending on the manufacturer, the fuel injection system on any one model of snowmobile may be different from another model. Regardless of the manufacturer, a few rules are held to all fuel injection systems. There must be a fuel supply, a fuel injector (or two or three, etc), a method of determining how much air is going into the engine and a central processor (computer) that orchestrates the entire system.

Fuel Pump

▶ See Figure 31

Like any other snowmobile, a fuel injected one will have a fuel tank. The only difference is that the fuel tank may contain a high-pressure fuel pump and a return line for unused fuel. If the fuel pump is not inside the tank, it will be mounted somewhere near. A fuel pump on a fuel injected sled will provide fuel at a high pressure so it can be atomized at the fuel injector nozzle. The entire fuel supply will be routed through a fuel filter that will remove any debris that could clog the injectors. A fuel pressure regulator keeps the injectors fed with a fuel at defined pressures.

Fuel Rail

▶ See Figure 32

After the fuel pump pressurizes the fuel, it is routed to the fuel rail. The fuel rail supplies fuel to each of the injectors. In most cases, the fuel rail is made from extruded aluminum, with a hollow center section. The pressurized fuel is routed inside the hollow area, and regulated by the fuel pressure regulator.

Fuel Pressure Regulator

▶ See Figures 32 and 33

The pressure regulator is a vacuum operated device typically located on the end of the fuel rail. Its function is to maintain a constant pressure across the fuel injector tip. The regulator uses a spring-loaded rubber diaphragm to uncover a fuel return port. When the fuel pump becomes operational, fuel flows past the injector into the regulator, and is restricted from flowing any further by

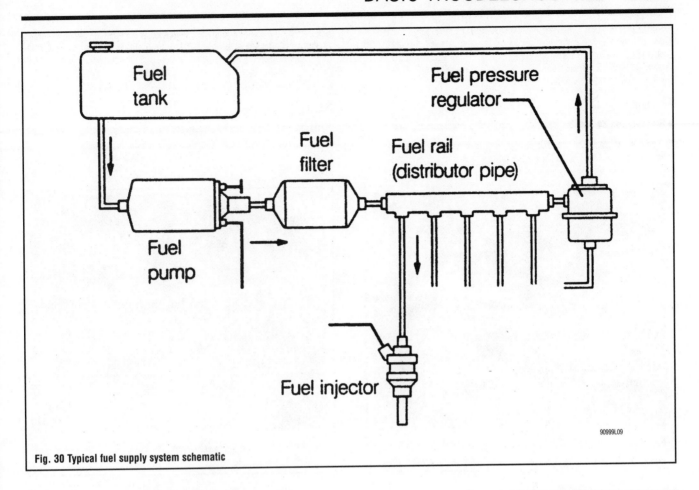

Fig. 30 Typical fuel supply system schematic

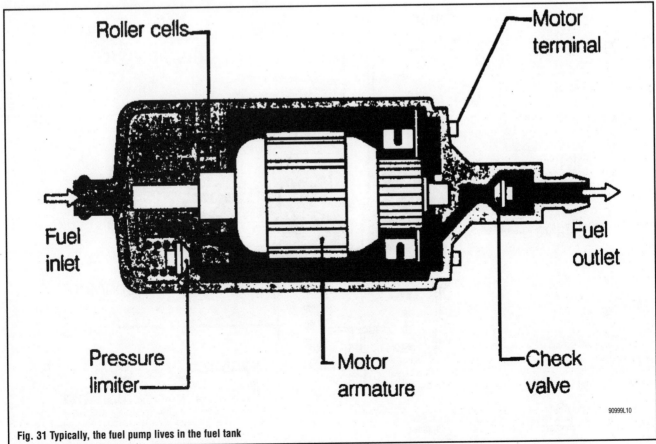

Fig. 31 Typically, the fuel pump lives in the fuel tank

the blocked return port. When fuel pressure reaches the predetermined setting, it pushes on the diaphragm, compressing the spring, and uncovers the fuel return port. The diaphragm and spring will constantly move from an open to closed position to keep the fuel pressure constant. The more constant the fuel pressure, the more precise the injector flow.

Fuel Injectors

▶ **See Figures 34 and 35**

Basically, an electronic fuel injector is an electric solenoid driven by the Electronic Control Unit (ECU). The control module, based on sensor inputs,

determines when and how long the fuel injector should operate. When an electric current is supplied to the injector, a spring-loaded ball is lifted from its seat. This allows fuel to flow through spray orifices and deflect off the sharp edge of the injector nozzle. This action causes the fuel to form an angled, cone shaped spray pattern before entering the air stream in the intake manifold.

Throttle Bodies

The throttle bodies on a fuel-injected snowmobile resemble carburetors. Unlike carburetors though, throttle bodies are nothing more than "air valves" for the engine. The throttle bodies control the amount of air that is allowed into the

Fig. 32 On this engine, the fuel rail is integrated with the fuel injectors (B). The fuel pressure regulator (A) is mounted to the fuel rail

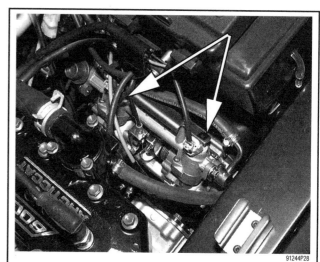

Fig. 34 The injectors (arrows) control the amount of pressurized fuel that enters the engine

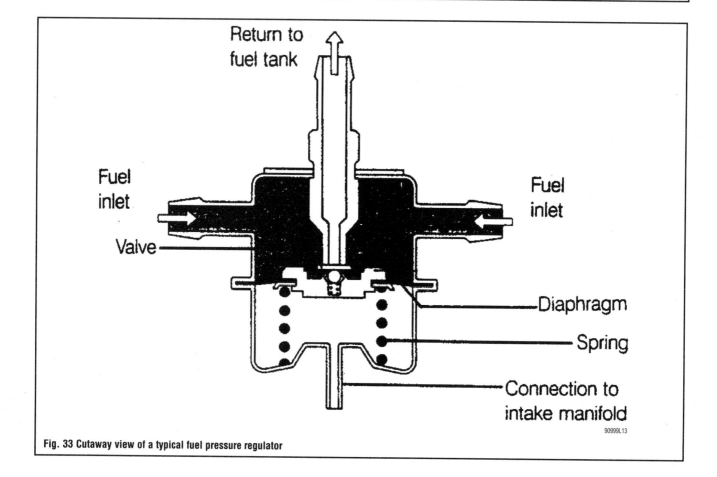

Fig. 33 Cutaway view of a typical fuel pressure regulator

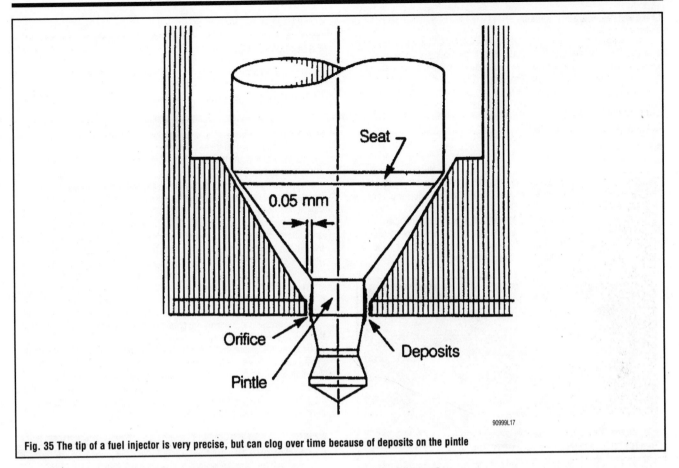

Fig. 35 The tip of a fuel injector is very precise, but can clog over time because of deposits on the pintle

engine. When the throttle lever is operated on the handlebars, the throttle bodies open and close, allowing the speed of the engine to be controlled.

Electronic Control Unit

▶ See Figure 36

The control unit, sometimes referred to as the Electronic Control Unit (ECU), is a digital computer that controls the fuel flow to the engine. The main purpose of the control unit is to receive data from various sensors on the engine, perform computations and comparisons with its internal programs and output signals to various actuators. The control unit can be mounted anywhere on the snowmobile, but usually is located under the cowl in the engine compartment.

Fig. 36 On this fuel-injected snowmobile, the ECU is located in the engine compartment, inside the tool container

Throttle Position Sensor

The Throttle Position Sensor (TPS) may also be called a throttle angle valve, throttle potentiometer or a throttle valve switch. It is connected to the throttle shaft on the throttle bodies, and is controlled by the throttle mechanism. A reference signal is sent to the TPS from the control module. As the throttle valve angle is changed, the resistance of the TPS also changes. At a closed throttle position, the resistance of the TPS is high, so the output voltage to the control module will be low. As the throttle plate opens, the resistance decreases so that, at wide-open throttle, the output voltage should be approximately 5 volts. By monitoring the output voltage from the TPS, the control module can determine fuel delivery based on throttle valve angle.

Problems may occur causing the TPS to become misadjusted, shorted, open or loose. Misadjustment might result in poor idle or poor wide-open throttle performance. An open TPS signals the control module that the throttle is always closed, resulting in poor performance. This usually sets a code. A shorted TPS gives the control module a constant wide-open throttle signal will store a code. A loose TPS indicates to the control module that the throttle is moving. This causes intermittent bursts of fuel from the injector and an unstable idle. Once the fault code is set, the control module will use an artificial default value and some vehicle performance will return.

Intake Air Temperature Sensor

The intake air temperature sensor is usually located within the airbox. This sensor sends a signal to the ECU to determine the temperature of the air that is flowing into the engine. The sensor is typically a variable resistance device, meaning it changes resistance as the temperature of the air changes. The ECU sends a signal to the temperature sensor, and measures the resistance, and calculates the temperature based on the resistance value.

Barometric Pressure Sensor

The barometric pressure sensor is used to compensate for altitude variations. From this signal, the control module modifies the fuel characteristics. The barometric sensor is a design that produces a frequency based on atmospheric pressure (altitude). The sensor is typically located within the ECU, and is not serviceable.

Crankcase Temperature Sensor

The crankcase temperature sensor is typically located on the upper half of the crankcase. Like the intake air temperature sensor, the crankcase temperature sensor is typically a variable resistance device, meaning it changes resistance as the temperature of the crankcase changes. The ECU sends a signal to the temperature sensor, and measures the resistance, and calculates the temperature based on the resistance value.

Coolant Temperature Sensor

▶ See Figure 37

The coolant temperature sensor, also known as a temperature switch, is a thermistor (a resistor which changes value based on temperature) mounted in the engine coolant stream. The sensor provides the control module with engine temperature information.

Two types of sensors are common: the negative temperature coefficient and the positive temperature coefficient. Negative temperature coefficient sensors will show low resistance with high temperature. Positive temperature coefficient sensors will show high resistance with high temperature.

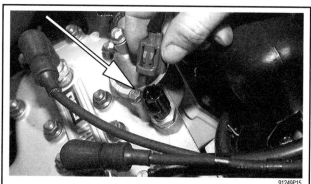

Fig. 37 The coolant temperature sensor (arrow) gives the ECU information about the temperature of the engine

Crankshaft Position Sensor

The engine position sensor is used by the ECU to determine the position of the crankshaft, so the injectors can be operated at the proper time. Some engines may use a sensor with a toothed wheel, and other systems may use a signal from the ignition system to determine crankshaft position and speed.

Engines with a separate sensor typically use a toothed wheel to send a signal to the ECU to determine crankshaft position. Most systems use either a magnetic reluctance type sensor or a Hall effect sensor. These sensors can be differentiated by the number of wires leading to them and the wire function. Normally, magnetic reluctance sensors use two wires. Hall effect sensors use three wires. The first provides power to the sensor. The second is ground. The last wire is the signal back to the control module.

Magnetic reluctance sensors are combined with a reluctor (toothed wheel). As the reluctor turns the high and low parts of the teeth on the reluctor cause the gap between the sensor and reluctor to change. This change in gap causes the magnetic field near the sensor to change. The control module reads this change in voltage to determine engine speed and crankshaft position. It is interesting to note that a magnetic reluctance sensor generates its own voltage during operation.

A Hall effect sensor has a metal pulse ring and a pick-up assembly. The signal is a digital on/off type signal. When the pulse ring travels through the pickup, a permanent magnet inside the pick-up creates a magnetism, which induces voltage. The pulse ring has slots, or one large slot, in the ring, which as they pass, the pick-up loses the magnetism and voltage is lost, thus the on/off signal.

Oil Injection Pump

The majority of all modern snowmobiles use an oil injection pump to provide lubrication to the crankshaft, connecting rods, and pistons. In the early days of snowmobiles, oil had to be "pre-mixed" with the fuel to provide lubrication.

OPERATION

▶ See Figures 38 and 39

First, lets discuss the drawbacks of pre-mixing oil with the fuel. At idle, the need for lubrication is less than at full throttle. When the oil is pre-mixed with the fuel, it only provides proper lubrication within a certain rpm range. Outside of that range, the mixture may be too little, or too heavy. Too little oil in the fuel will starve the engine components of lubrication, possibly causing a piston seizure or other components to fail. (A piston seizure means that the piston actually melts, and bonds to the cylinder from lack of lubrication.) If there is too much oil mixed with the fuel, the spark plugs can become "fouled" with excess oil, and the pistons, cylinders, and expansion chamber(s) become clogged with excess carbon and oil deposits, and the engine will smoke excessively.

Now that the drawbacks of pre-mixing oil and fuel have been discussed, lets look at how an oil injection pump rectifies these drawbacks.

On a typical snowmobile engine, the oil injection pump is a simple pump driven from the crankshaft that supplies oil to the engine based on throttle position. The pump pressurizes the lubricating oil by drawing it between the two gears. A lever connected to the carburetors (throttle bodies) controls the amount of oil that is sprayed into each intake port. Since the oil injection pump is synchronized with the throttle, oil is sprayed into the cylinders only as its needed, eliminating excessively rich or lean mixtures of oil and fuel.

Oil injection pumps provide precise dispensing of oil into the engine, eliminating the guesswork of mixing the proper ratio of oil and fuel, and improving the operation of the engine.

Occasional adjustment of the oil injection pump may be required to keep it synchronized with the carburetors/throttle bodies. Other than this adjustment, the oil injection pump is virtually maintenance free. It is important to keep foreign debris from entering the oil tank, and equally important to keep it filled. If the oil injection pump runs out of oil, it may require a special procedure to bleed the air from the system.

Fuel System Troubleshooting

Armed with the basic knowledge of how your fuel system works, troubleshooting any problems should be fairly straightforward. Refer to the fuel system troubleshooting chart for further information.

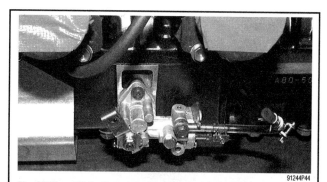

Fig. 38 The oil injection pump is a simple mechanical pump that distributes oil to the engine, based on throttle position

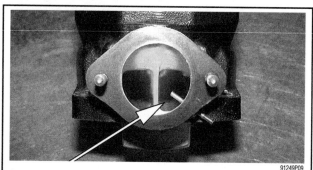

Fig. 39 Oil is pressurized by the injection pump, and distributed through nozzles in the intake ports (arrow) or through the crankcase

CARBURETOR TROUBLESHOOTING

Problem	Possible Cause	Inspection/Remedy
Carburetor floods repeatedly	Float set too high	Adjust
	Float needle sticking	Remove float bowl and clean needle and seat
	Float needle or seat worn or damaged	Replace as necessary
	Float sticking due to misalignment	Correct
	Float punctured	Replace
Idle mixture too lean	Pilot jet too small	Replace with larger jet
	Worn throttle slide	Replace
	Pilot screw out of adjustment	Adjust
Idle mixture too rich	Pilot jet too large	Replace with smaller jet
	Dirt or foreign matter in idle passage	Disassemble and clean carburetor
	Pilot screw out of adjustment	Adjust
Lean mixture at sustained mid-range speeds	Jet needle set too lean	Reset needle clip at lower notch
	Needle or main jet clogged	Remove and clean jets
	Intake manifold air leak	Find leak and rectify
Lean mixture at sustained high-speeds	Main jet too small	Replace with larger jet
	Main jet clogged	Remove and clean
	Float level too low	Remove float and adjust level
Lean mixture during acceleration	Jets clogged	Remove and clean
	Damaged or worn throttle slide	Replace
	Float level too low	Adjust float height
Lean mixture throughout throttle range	Fuel filters clogged or dirty	Remove and clean
	Gas cap vent blocked	Blow clear
	Damaged or worn throttle slide	Replace
	Air leaks at carb manifold	Find leak and rectify
Rich mixture at sustained mid-range speeds	Air cleaner dirty	Clean or replace
	Main jet too large	Replace with smaller jet
	Carburetor flooding	See above
	Needle or needle jet worn	Replace
Rich mixture at sustained high speeds	Main jet too large	Replace with smaller size jet
	Carburetor flooding	See above
	Air cleaner dirty	Replace or clean
Rich mixture throughout range	Carburetor flooding	See above
	Air cleaner dirty	Replace or clean
Erratic idle	Air leaks	Determine source and rectify
	Dirty or blocked idle passages	Clean carburetor
	Idle settings incorrect	Adjust to specifications
	Damage to pilot screw	Replace
	Worn or damaged air seals such as O-rings or	Rebuild carburetor
	Unsynchronized carburetors	Adjust and synchronize as necessary
	Mixture too lean	Adjust carburetor

91249C10

SUSPENSION THEORY & DIAGNOSIS

In the early days of the snowmobile, suspension was not of great concern, since the sleds were not capable of major speeds. As snowmobiles developed over the years, greater speeds could be achieved from sleds as more advanced and powerful engines were being used. In order to make use of the higher speeds available, primitive suspension systems were used on the front skis to help make the handling of the sled easier and more comfortable for the operator. As development continued, suspension designs were adapted to the rear track, as well as improvements to the front skis.

Fortunately, suspension systems on modern snowmobiles have evolved dramatically, providing razor-sharp handling and a plush, comfortable ride. The improved handling and ride of the modern sled has made snowmobiling a much more exciting and accommodating experience.

Front Suspension

The different types of front suspension designs on modern snowmobiles are actually quite similar to the suspension systems used on cars and some trucks. Parallel arm, strut-type, and leaf spring suspensions are all derivatives of suspensions found on automobiles. All of these types of suspensions are intended to provide a smooth, plush ride and improved handling, regardless of the design. All manufacturers use different designs for a variety of reasons, including cost, intended purpose, simplicity, and performance.

PARALLEL ARM

♦ **See Figures 40, 41 and 42**

The majority of modern snowmobiles use the parallel arm type of suspension. This suspension design is essentially the same type that is used on an Indy-type racecar. It is of no consequence that snowmobiles use this design; it ensures that the front skis always remain at horizontal with the snow surface, regardless of suspension movement. Although the angle of the skis in relation-

ship to the snow surface is consistent, the distance between the skis can vary slightly as the suspension operates. This variance is caused by the arc of the parallel arms as they pivot around the mounting points on the front of the snowmobile. The longer the length of the arms, and the less the arm movement, the less the distance between the skis will change. This is the only negative attribute to the parallel arm design. Most manufacturers design the front suspension with this minor flaw in mind, compensating with the use of longer arms in relationship to the overall suspension travel.

Within this parallel arm design, there are two variations; a double "A" arm type, and a radius rod type, used with a trailing arm. Both types function in virtually the same manner. The A-arm type does not need to use a trailing arm, because the triangular shape of each of the arms stabilizes the fore-and-aft movement. With radius rods, a trailing arm is used to control fore-and-aft movement.

Maximum control is of utmost importance on a modern snowmobile, especially when some are capable of triple-digit speeds. Of all suspension designs, the parallel arm design continues to prevail as the suspension of choice for snowmobiles as well as high-performance automobiles.

STRUT-TYPE

The strut-type front suspension system found on some snowmobiles is similar to the MacPherson strut suspension found on most modern automobiles. A telescopic strut (similar to a motorcycle fork) is used to suspend each ski, and a pair of links are used on each strut to provide a means of steering. With this design, the strut stays horizontal to the snow surface as with parallel link suspension. An additional advantage, however, is the distance between the skis stays consistent as the struts move up and down.

Although the strut type suspension seems like it would be more beneficial on a snowmobile, the weight of each strut and strut housing make it less than desirable for performance. In addition to this weight penalty, a strut type suspension cannot provide the amount of travel a parallel arm type can provide.

LEAF SPRING

♦ **See Figures 43 and 44**

The leaf spring suspension system has been employed practically since the inception of the snowmobile. Throughout the 60's and 70's, a large majority of snowmobiles were equipped with leaf spring type front suspension systems.

The typical leaf spring suspension on a snowmobile consists of leaf springs with bushings at each end that attach the springs to the skis. Some models may use a multiple-layer leaf spring, and others a single spring. Shock absorbers mounted between the ski and spring perch are also used on some models to provide dampening action.

From a technological standpoint, leaf spring suspension is considered rudimentary, and outdated. Although leaf springs are one of the most basic forms of suspension, it is however, simple and lightweight. It does not provide long length travel like a parallel arm, or the consistency of a strut. It does, however, provide a simple and effective means of suspension for the front of the sled with a minimum of moving parts.

Fig. 40 An example of a typical parallel arm front suspension

Fig. 41 Another example of a parallel arm suspension (note the long trailing arm)

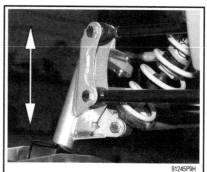

Fig. 42 As the ski moves up and down, the parallel arms keep the ski in full contact with the snow surface

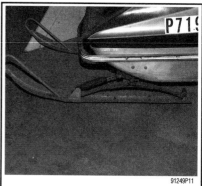

Fig. 43 An example of a leaf spring suspension on an older snowmobile

On modern snowmobiles, leaf spring suspension is usually found on entry-level sleds, as well as utility models. Utility models use leaf spring suspension because of its simplicity and light weight, and ease of maintenance.

Rear Suspension

▶ See Figures 45, 46, 47, 48 and 49

The rear suspension system on the modern snowmobile may look incredibly complex and confusing to the untrained eye. Basically, though, the linkage of the suspension allows the slide-rails (the bottom half of the suspension on which the track slides) to move up and down at each end, as well as both ends. This action allows the track to conform to the snow surface, which aids in traction, as well as a smooth ride for the snowmobile operator.

Although every manufacturer has its own method of suspending the track; most are equally effective, just different in design. Even different models from the same manufacturer may employ different methods of linkage to provide suspension.

Depending on the design of the suspension, some might use coil-over springs and shocks, and others may use torsion-type springs (which resemble springs found on a mousetrap). In some cases, both types of springs are used.

Typically, torsion springs are found on older models, but some later model snowmobiles still use them on the rear suspension. One of the drawbacks of a torsion spring is frequent breakage. On some models, the track may suffer extensive damage if a torsion spring were to break.

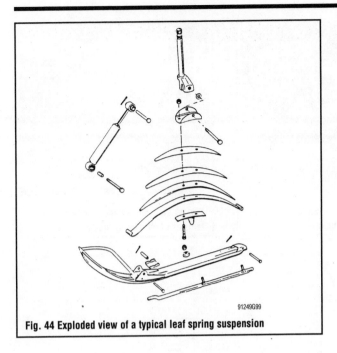

91249G99

Fig. 44 Exploded view of a typical leaf spring suspension

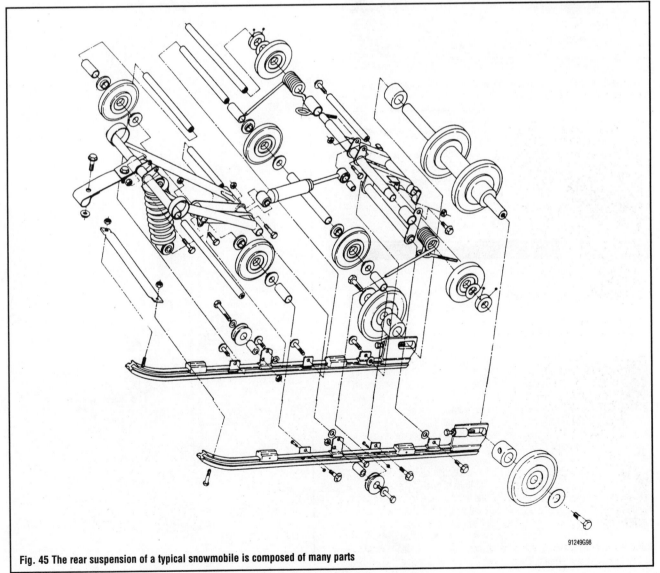

91249G98

Fig. 45 The rear suspension of a typical snowmobile is composed of many parts

Fig. 46 The suspension systems on modern snowmobiles provide several inches of travel

Fig. 47 Rear suspension assembly removed from a snowmobile

Fig. 48 Snowmobile rear suspension systems use both coil springs . . .

Fig. 49 . . . and torsion springs to support the weight of the snowmobile

Coil springs, on the other hand, rarely break, and offer easier adjustment, provided the shock body is threaded.

The entire suspension can be repositioned in the tunnel on some models for increased adjustability. This ability to reposition the entire suspension is very useful for snowmobile riders who might ride on groomed trails one weekend, and change tracks to ride in the deep powder snow of mountain riding. The reasons for this need in repositioning the track include keeping the track from hitting the tunnel when running a deeper lug track, and handling.

Shock Absorbers

▶ See Figures 50 thru 55

Whether a snowmobile is equipped with coil-over shock absorbers, struts, or leaf springs, the shock absorber itself performs the same function—control the rate of spring oscillation.

Let's discuss the operation of a shock absorber. The compression stroke of the shock absorber begins when it receives a load compressing both the outer spring and the shock hydraulic unit itself. The cylinder, which contains fluid, rises along the piston rod, causing pressure on the oil beneath the piston. This slows or "damps" the rate of compression. The oil flows through the piston orifice and enters the space above the piston after pushing up the non-return valve held down by a valve spring. At the same time, a small amount of the oil is forced through a base valve, and then another base valve, and enters the chamber between the cylinder and the shock outer shell. When the cylinder, rising along the piston rod, meets the rubber bumper at the top of the rod, the compression ends.

The tension of the spring (mounted on the shock absorber or otherwise) eventually forces the shock absorber to extend to its normal or static length. The cylinder moves down along the piston rod; the oil which had been forced above the piston returns through the piston orifice and through the piston valve to the space beneath the piston. The oil which had been forced between the cylinder and the outer shell also returns to the reservoir beneath the piston after passing through a base valve. The oil resists the attempt of the outer spring to return suddenly to its normal length. This is known as rebound damping.

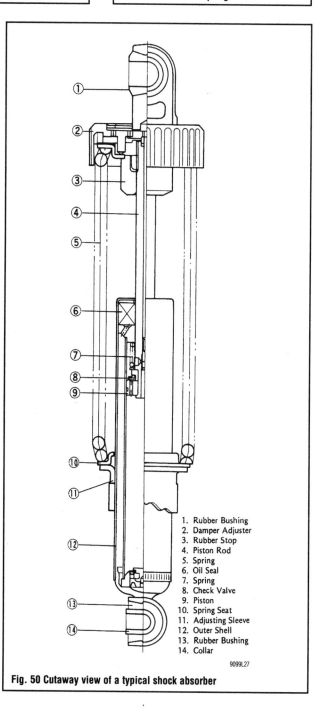

1. Rubber Bushing
2. Damper Adjuster
3. Rubber Stop
4. Piston Rod
5. Spring
6. Oil Seal
7. Spring
8. Check Valve
9. Piston
10. Spring Seat
11. Adjusting Sleeve
12. Outer Shell
13. Rubber Bushing
14. Collar

Fig. 50 Cutaway view of a typical shock absorber

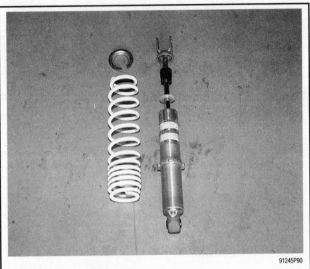

Fig. 51 Typical coil-over shock with spring removed

Fig. 52 Most coil-over shock absorbers have threaded bodies for adjustment of the spring

Fig. 53 Coil-over assemblies usually require a special spanner wrench for adjustment of the spring

Fig. 54 Some shock absorbers have remote reservoirs with adjustability for the ultimate in performance

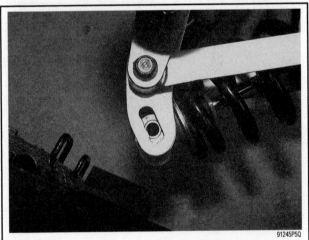

Fig. 55 This coil-over shock mount is slotted for additional adjustability

Some snowmobiles use a combination gas/oil shock instead of the oil type just described. They function similarly, except pressurized nitrogen helps prevent the oil from cavitating (foaming) during periods high shock movements. In some cases, these types of shocks have a separate reservoir that is separate from the shock. High-performance snowmobiles usually come equipped with this type of shock absorber.

Almost all production snowmobile shock absorbers are sealed, and cannot be disassembled. In fact, on some models, it is dangerous to attempt to do so, since they contain high-pressure gas.

If the shock leaks oil, looses its damping ability, is damaged through collision or extreme use, both units should be replaced. The springs, however, should have a longer life, and in most cases last the life of the sled.

Suspension Troubleshooting

In most cases, any problems that arise with suspension systems can be traced to worn parts. Pivot bearings or bushings, ball joints, and shock absorbers all wear out over time, and should be inspected frequently to avoid problems. In some cases, squeaking or binding suspensions may just be in need of lubrication.

Shock absorbers that lose their dampening function may be broken internally, or may be leaking. Of course any problems like this can only be repaired by replacement, since shock absorbers cannot (in most cases) be disassembled.

Use the Suspension Troubleshooting chart to help narrow down the possible cause of any suspension problem on your snowmobile.

SUSPENSION TROUBLESHOOTING

Problem	Possible Cause	Inspection/Remedy
Front suspension seems too stiff	Excessive spring preload	Adjust spring preload to rider weight
	Bent or binding suspension pivots	Inspect and replace components as necessary
	Shock absorber dampening settings too stiff	Adjust shock absorbers as necessary
Rear suspension seems too stiff	Excessive spring preload	Adjust spring preload to rider weight
	Bent or binding suspension pivots	Inspect and replace components as necessary
	Shock absorber dampening settings too stiff	Adjust shock absorbers as necessary
Rear suspension bottoms frequently	Spring preload too light	Adjust spring preload to rider weight
	Excessive weight load on suspension	Remove extra weight (cargo or passenger)
	Too light of spring rate used for rider	Replace spring with heavier rate
Unusual handling	Loose or worn suspension components	Inspect and replace components as necessary
	Ski runners worn	Replace ski runners
	Broken spring or other suspension component	Inspect and replace components as necessary
	Loose or missing suspension fasteners	Replace or tighten fasteners
Wandering or darting steering	Ski alignment incorrect	Align skis (toe and camber)
	Worn suspension or steering components	Inspect and replace components as necessary
	Ski pressure incorrect	Adjust rear suspension as necessary
	Excessively stiff front suspension	Reset front preload
	Ski runners worn	Replace ski runners
	Bent suspension or steering components	Inspect and replace components as necessary
Hard to turn	Excessive ski pressure	Adjust rear suspension as necessary
	Worn ski runners	Replace
	Incorrectly adjusted rear suspension	Adjust rear suspension as necessary
	Binding steering linkage	Inspect and lubricate steering as necessary
Pulls to one side	Faulty right or left shock	Replace shocks as a set
	Skis out of alignment	Align skis (toe and camber)
	Bent suspension or steering components	Inspect and replace components as necessary
Clunking or loose feeling steering	Loose steering linkage fasteners	Tighten fasteners as required
	Worn suspension components	Inspect and replace components
	Loose suspension pivot fasteners	Tighten fasteners as required
	Worn steering components	Replace components as necessary
Skis lift from snow surface upon acceleration	Excessive weight transfer	Adjust rear suspension as necessary
	Suspension incorrectly adjusted	Adjust rear suspension as necessary
	Front limiter strap improperly adjusted	Adjust front limiter strap
	Improper rider position	Sit further forward on seat
Suspension bounces continuously	Worn shock absorbers	Replace as necessary
	Incorrectly adjusted shock absorber settings	Adjust shock absorbers as necessary
	Leaking shock absorber	Rebuild or replace as necessary

91249C11

BRAKE SYSTEM THEORY & DIAGNOSIS

Unlike a car or motorcycle, the brake system of a typical snowmobile is quite basic, and usually employs few components. Cars and motorcycles usually have a brake disc or drum to stop each wheel. A snowmobile, on the other hand, uses a singular disc to stop the track from rotating. Since the track is the only component that "rotates" over the on the snow surface, this is the only practical method of providing stopping power on a snowmobile.

Operation

The brake disc (or rotor) on most sleds is located on the jackshaft, opposite the secondary pulley. A caliper, which houses the brake pads, is mounted in line with the disc. When the brake lever on the handlebars is operated, the pads in the caliper are forced against the disc under pressure. Since the jackshaft is connected to the track sprockets with a drive chain, (or in some cases, gears) the track rotation will be slowed.

The heart of the brake system is the caliper. Although the brake rotors (or discs) may have slight variations in design, (vented, drilled, or slotted) they are basically the same. Calipers, on the other hand, employ different methods to provide the clamping action necessary to stop a disc from turning.

There are several types of calipers. One kind consists of a rigidly mounted (commonly referred to as fixed) caliper with two (or multiples of 2) moveable pistons, one on each side of the disc. These types of calipers are most always hydraulically operated.

Another type of caliper is the "sliding caliper" type. As opposed to the fixed caliper described above, this assembly mounts the caliper to a bracket by means of sliding shafts. There is typically only one piston, and when pressure is applied to this piston, it presses its pad against the disc, and the caliper shifts slightly in the opposite direction bringing the opposing pad into contact as well. The "floating caliper type" is very similar to the "sliding" type and can use the same description. The majority of brake disc calipers found on modern snowmobiles fall under this category, whether they are mechanically or hydraulically operated.

Whether the brake system is hydraulic or mechanically actuated, the basic operation is the same. A more detailed operation of each system is described below.

HYDRAULIC BRAKE SYSTEM

▶ See Figures 56, 57, 58, 59 and 60

With a hydraulically operated brake system, fluid is used to operate the caliper instead of mechanical linkage.

The master cylinder, usually located on the handlebars, contains a fluid reservoir, a piston assembly for applying hydraulic pressure to the system, and a lever for moving the piston assembly. When the lever is operated, the piston pushes brake fluid through the hose under pressure. When the pressurized fluid reaches the caliper, the pistons (or piston, depending on the design) are forced outward. The pressurized fluid from the master cylinder forces the brake pads, which are mounted directly in front of the caliper pistons, against the brake disc (or rotor).

Fig. 56 A typical hydraulic disc brake assembly, mounted on the chaincase

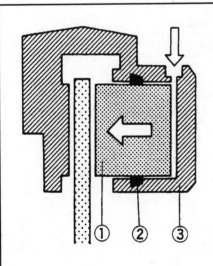 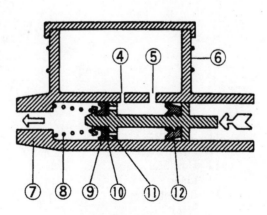

1. Piston
2. Fluid Seal
3. Caliper
4. Relief Port
5. Supply Port
6. Reservoir
7. Master Cylinder
8. Spring
9. Primary Cup
10. Non-return Valve
11. Piston
12. Secondary Cup

Fig. 57 When brakes are applied, fluid is forced from the master cylinder to the caliper

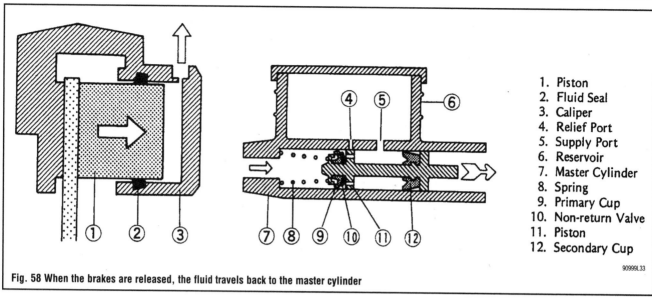

1. Piston
2. Fluid Seal
3. Caliper
4. Relief Port
5. Supply Port
6. Reservoir
7. Master Cylinder
8. Spring
9. Primary Cup
10. Non-return Valve
11. Piston
12. Secondary Cup

Fig. 58 When the brakes are released, the fluid travels back to the master cylinder

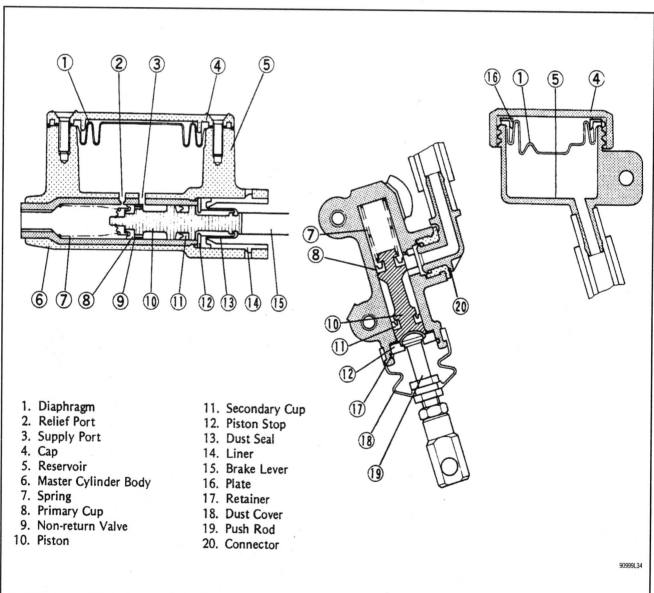

1. Diaphragm
2. Relief Port
3. Supply Port
4. Cap
5. Reservoir
6. Master Cylinder Body
7. Spring
8. Primary Cup
9. Non-return Valve
10. Piston
11. Secondary Cup
12. Piston Stop
13. Dust Seal
14. Liner
15. Brake Lever
16. Plate
17. Retainer
18. Dust Cover
19. Push Rod
20. Connector

Fig. 59 Cutaways of the brake system hydraulic components

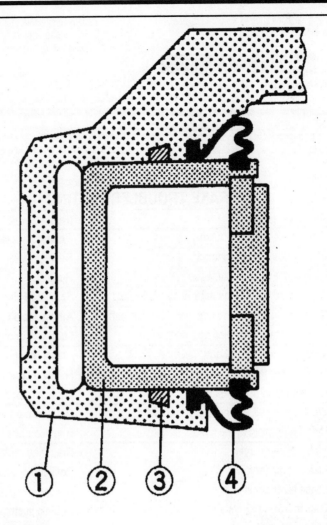

1. Caliper
2. Piston
3. Fluid Seal
4. Dust Seal

90999L35

Fig. 60 A typical rebuild kit will contain the fluid seal and the dust seal. Sometimes they will even include a new piston

Because of the characteristics of hydraulic pressure, a substantial amount of force is applied to the pistons in the caliper when the lever on the handlebars is operated. This results in less force being needed to operate the brake lever on the handlebars. This is the primary reason why hydraulic brake systems are used on high-performance snowmobiles.

MECHANICAL BRAKE SYSTEM

▶ See Figure 61

Mechanical brake systems usually use a cable to actuate the caliper to provide stopping power. When the lever on the handlebars is operated, the cable is pulled inside the cable housing, and the caliper is operated. The typical mechanical brake caliper uses a cam-type mechanism inside the caliper to provide clamping power. Others may use a "worm" gear, and some might be a simple cantilever-type, similar to a bicycle.

Typically, mechanical brake systems are found on older snowmobiles, and entry-level models. Equipping an entry-level sled with a mechanical brake helps keep the price as low as possible.

Some snowmobiles also may use a mechanical brake system in addition to a hydraulic system. In this type of application, the mechanical brake is used as a parking and/or emergency brake. This can be of great benefit if the hydraulic

91245P21

Fig. 61 Mechanical brake systems use a cable-actuated caliper, which uses an eccentric cam mechanism to force the pads against the rotor

unit were to fail while out on the trail. The mechanical brake caliper in this type of application is of the same design as previously described.

Brake System Troubleshooting

Using the wrong friction material can lead to improper braking. The brakes may react too strongly or require too much pressure to activate them. If the fluid seal on the caliper is leaking, the friction material can get soaked and lose effectiveness.

Refer to the brake system troubleshooting chart for information on how to diagnose disc brake problems.

1. Typically, ineffective brakes can be the result of oil on the pads. It is almost impossible to remove lubricants of any kind, since the pad material is very porous. The only means of repair in this situation is pad replacement.

2. Glazing of the pads and rotor can also cause poor braking. This can be fixed by removing the pads and inspecting the pads and rotor. Use light grade sandpaper to remove the glaze from the rotor, as well as the pads (don't breathe the dust!). Sandpaper can also he used to clean up rust or corrosion on the brake rotor.

Other common problems with disc brakes include bad fluid seals, damaged or corroded caliper pistons and seized caliper slides.

BRAKE TROUBLESHOOTING

Problem	Possible Cause	Inspection/Remedy
Brake does not hold	Brake pads glazed or worn	Repair or replace pads
	Brake pads oil impregnated	Replace pads
	Brake rotor worn or damaged	Replace
	Air in brake lines or insufficient hydraulic fluid	Flush and bleed system
	Brake cable improperly adjusted (mechanical)	Adjust cable as necessary
	Brake control cable binding (mechanical)	Lubricate or replace cable as necessary
Brake drags	Lack of play in the linkage	Adjust linkage as necessary
	Weak or damaged return spring (mechanical)	Replace spring
	Cable binding (mechanical)	Lubricate, or replace as necessary
Scraping noise	Worn brake caliper cam (mechanical)	Replace cam as necessary
	Pads worn down to the rivets	Replace pads (and rotor as necessary)
Excessive lever travel with loss of braking power	Air in hydraulic system	Drain and replace fluid, then bleed system
	Master cylinder low on fluid	Refill the cylinder and bleed system
	Loose lever adjuster bolt	Secure and adjust lever and bolt
	Leak in hydraulic system as evidenced by fluid loss	Rebuild system as necessary
	Worn pads	Replace pads as necessary
Brake squeal	Glazed pads	Deglaze or replace pads
	Improperly adjusted caliper	Adjust caliper
	Extremely dusty brake assembly	Thoroughly clean out assembly
Brake shudder	Distorted pads	Replace pads
	Oil or brake fluid impregnated pads	Replace pads
	Loose mounting bolts	Secure assembly
	Warped rotor	Replace rotor
Pads dragging on rotor	Loose adjusting ring	Secure adjusting ring
	Piston binding in bore	Rebuild caliper assembly
	Relief port blocked by piston in master cylinder	Rebuild caliper assembly
	Cable adjusted too tightly (mechanical)	Adjust cable as necessary
	Caliper out of adjustment	Adjust
	Caliper pivot frozen	Clean and lubricate pivot

91249C13

ELECTRICAL THEORY & DIAGNOSIS

Basic Electrical Theory

♦ See Figure 62

For any 12 volt, negative ground, electrical system to operate, the electricity must travel in a complete circuit. This simply means that current (power) from the positive terminal (+) of the battery must eventually return to the negative terminal (-) of the battery. Along the way, this current will travel through wires, fuses, switches and components. If, for any reason, the flow of current through the circuit is interrupted, the component fed by that circuit would cease to function properly.

Perhaps the easiest way to visualize a circuit is to think of connecting a light bulb (with two wires attached to it) to the battery—one wire attached to the negative (-) terminal of the battery and the other wire to the positive (+) terminal. With the two wires touching the battery terminals, the circuit would be complete and the light bulb would illuminate. Electricity would follow a path from the battery to the bulb and back to the battery. It's easy to see that with longer wires on our light bulb, it could be mounted anywhere. Further, one wire could be fitted with a switch so that the light could be turned on and off.

The wiring circuit on a snowmobile differs from this simple example in two ways. First, instead of having a return wire from the bulb to the battery, the current travels through the frame of the snowmobile. Since the negative (-) battery cable is attached to the frame (made of electrically conductive metal), the frame of the vehicle can serve as a ground wire to complete the circuit. Secondly, most snowmobile circuits contain multiple components which receive power from a single circuit. This lessens the amount of wire needed to power components on the snowmobile.

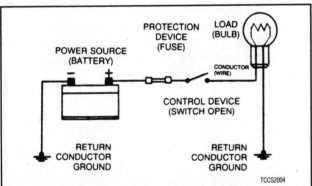

TCCS2004

Fig. 62 This example illustrates a simple circuit. When the switch is closed, power from the positive (+) battery terminal flows through the fuse and the switch, and then to the light bulb. The light illuminates and the circuit is completed through the ground wire back to the negative (-) battery terminal. In reality, the two ground points shown in the illustration are attached to the metal frame of the vehicle, which completes the circuit back to the battery

HOW DOES ELECTRICITY WORK: THE WATER ANALOGY

Electricity is the flow of electrons—the subatomic particles that constitute the outer shell of an atom. Electrons spin in an orbit around the center core of an atom. The center core is comprised of protons (positive charge) and neutrons (neutral charge). Electrons have a negative charge and balance out the positive charge of the protons. When an outside force causes the number of electrons to unbalance the charge of the protons, the electrons will split off the atom and look for another atom to balance out. If this imbalance is kept up, electrons will continue to move and an electrical flow will exist.

Many people have been taught electrical theory using an analogy with water. In a comparison with water flowing through a pipe, the electrons would be the water and the wire is the pipe.

The flow of electricity can be measured much like the flow of water through a pipe. The unit of measurement used is amperes, frequently abbreviated as amps (**a**). You can compare amperage to the volume of water flowing through a pipe.

When connected to a circuit, an ammeter will measure the actual amount of current flowing through the circuit. When relatively few electrons flow through a circuit, the amperage is low. When many electrons flow, the amperage is high.

Water pressure is measured in units such as pounds per square inch (psi); The electrical pressure is measured in units called volts (**v**). When a voltmeter is connected to a circuit, it is measuring the electrical pressure.

The actual flow of electricity depends not only on voltage and amperage, but also on the resistance of the circuit. The higher the resistance, the higher the force necessary to push the current through the circuit. The standard unit for measuring resistance is an ohm (). Resistance in a circuit varies depending on the amount and type of components used in the circuit. The main factors which determine resistance are:

• Material—some materials have more resistance than others. Those with high resistance are said to be insulators. Rubber materials (or rubber-like plastics) are some of the most common insulators used in vehicles as they have a very high resistance to electricity. Very low resistance materials are said to be conductors. Copper wire is among the best conductors. Silver is actually a superior conductor to copper and is used in some relay contacts, but its high cost prohibits its use as common wiring. The wiring on most all snowmobiles is made of copper.

• Size—the larger the wire size being used, the less resistance the wire will have. This is why components which use large amounts of electricity usually have large wires supplying current to them.

• Length—for a given thickness of wire, the longer the wire, the greater the resistance. The shorter the wire, the less the resistance. When determining the proper wire for a circuit, both size and length must be considered to design a circuit that can handle the current needs of the component.

• Temperature—with many materials, the higher the temperature, the greater the resistance (positive temperature coefficient). Some materials exhibit the opposite trait of lower resistance with higher temperatures (negative temperature coefficient). These principles are used in many of the sensors on the engine.

OHM'S LAW

There is a direct relationship between current, voltage and resistance. A statement known as Ohm's law can sum up the relationship between current, voltage and resistance.

Voltage (E) is equal to amperage (I) times resistance (R): E=I x R
Other forms of the formula are R=E/I and I=E/R

In each of these formulas, E is the voltage in volts, I is the current in amps and R is the resistance in ohms. The basic point to remember is that as the resistance of a circuit goes up, the amount of current that flows in the circuit will go down, if voltage remains the same.

The amount of work that the electricity can perform is expressed as power. The unit of power is the watt (w). The relationship between power, voltage and current is expressed as:

Power (w) is equal to amperage (I) times voltage (E): W=I x E

This is only true for direct current (DC) circuits; The alternating current formula is a tad different, but since the electrical circuits in most snowmobiles (and cars, for that matter) are DC type, we need not get into AC circuit theory.

Electrical Components

POWER SOURCE

Power is supplied to a snowmobile by two devices: The battery, and the alternator. The battery supplies electrical power during starting or during periods when the current demand of the snowmobile's electrical system exceeds the alternator output capacity . The alternator supplies electrical current when the engine is running. Just not does the alternator supply the current needs of the snowmobile, but it recharges the battery.

The Battery

In most modern vehicles, the battery is a lead/acid electrochemical device consisting of three or six 2 volt subsections (cells) connected in series, so that the unit is capable of producing approximately 6 or 12 volts (respectively) of electrical pressure. Each subsection consists of a series of positive and negative plates held a short distance apart in a solution of sulfuric acid and water.

The two types of plates are of dissimilar metals. This sets up a chemical reaction, and it is this reaction which produces current flow from the battery when its positive and negative terminals are connected to an electrical load. The power removed from the battery is replaced by the alternator, restoring the battery to its original chemical state.

The Alternator

◆ See Figure 63

On some snowmobiles there isn't an alternator, but a generator. The difference is that an alternator supplies alternating current, which is then changed to direct current for use on the snowmobile, while a generator produces direct current. Alternators tend to be more efficient and that is why they are used.

Alternators and generators are devices that consist of coils of wires wound together making big electromagnets. One group of coils spins within another set and the interaction of the magnetic fields causes a current to flow. This current is then drawn off the coils and fed into the snowmobile's electrical system.

GROUND

Two types of grounds are used in snowmobile electric circuits. Direct ground components are grounded to the frame through their mounting points. All other components use some sort of ground wire, which is attached to the frame, or chassis of the vehicle. The electrical current runs through the chassis of the vehicle and returns to the battery through the ground (-) cable. If you look, you'll see that the battery ground cable connects between the battery and the frame or chassis of the vehicle.

➡**It should be noted that a good percentage of electrical problems can be traced to faulty grounds.**

PROTECTIVE DEVICES

It is possible for large surges of current to pass through the electrical system of your snowmobile. If this surge of current were to reach the load in the circuit, it could burn it out or severely damage it. It can also overload the wiring, causing the harness to get hot and melt the insulation. To prevent this, fuses, circuit breakers and/or fusible links are connected into the supply wires of the electrical system. These items are nothing more than a built-in weak spot in the system. When an abnormal amount of current flows through the system, these protective devices work as follows to protect the circuit:

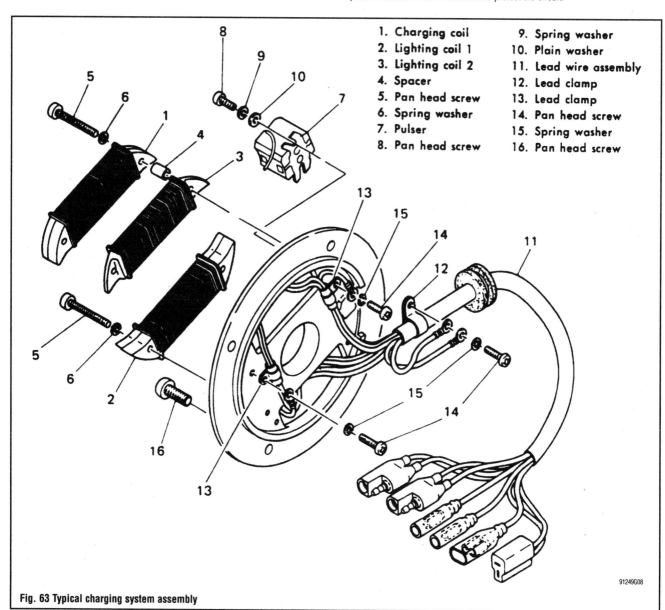

1. Charging coil
2. Lighting coil 1
3. Lighting coil 2
4. Spacer
5. Pan head screw
6. Spring washer
7. Pulser
8. Pan head screw
9. Spring washer
10. Plain washer
11. Lead wire assembly
12. Lead clamp
13. Lead clamp
14. Pan head screw
15. Spring washer
16. Pan head screw

Fig. 63 Typical charging system assembly

91249G08

• Fuse—when an excessive electrical current passes through a fuse, it "blows" (the conductor melts) and opens the circuit, preventing the passage of current.

• Circuit Breaker—a circuit breaker is basically a self-repairing fuse. It will open the circuit in the same fashion as a fuse, but when the surge subsides, the circuit breaker can be reset and does not need replacement.

• Fusible Link—a fusible link (fuse link or main link) is a short length of special, high temperature insulated wire that acts as a fuse. When an excessive electrical current passes through a fusible link, the thin gauge wire inside the link melts, creating an intentional open to protect the circuit. To repair the circuit, the link must be replaced. Some newer type fusible links are housed in plug-in modules, which are simply replaced like a fuse, while older type fusible links must be cut and spliced if they melt. Since this link is very early in the electrical path, it's the first place to look if nothing on the vehicle works, but the battery seems to be charged and is properly connected.

✳ CAUTION

Always replace fuses, circuit breakers and fusible links with identically rated components. Under no circumstances should a component of higher or lower amperage rating be substituted.

SWITCHES & RELAYS

▶ **See Figures 64, 65 and 66**

Switches are used in electrical circuits to control the passage of current. The most common use is to open and close circuits between the battery and the various electric devices in the system. Switches are rated according to the amount of amperage they can handle. If a sufficient amperage rated switch is not used in a circuit, the switch could overload and cause damage.

Some electrical components which require a large amount of current to operate use a special switch called a relay. Since these circuits carry a large amount

Fig. 64 The control switches on the handlebars can usually be accessed by unscrewing the two halves

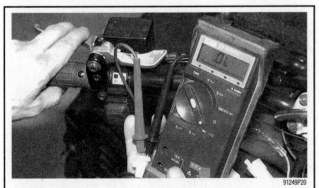
Fig. 65 A multimeter can be used to test for a properly functioning switch

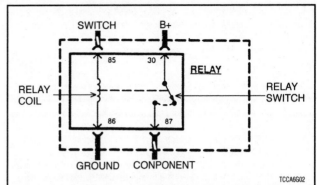
Fig. 66 Relays are composed of a coil and a switch. These two components are linked together so that when one operates, the other operates at the same time. The large wires in the circuit are connected from the battery to one side of the relay switch (B+) and from the opposite side of the relay switch to the load (component). Smaller wires are connected from the relay coil to the control switch for the circuit and from the opposite side of the relay coil to ground

of current, the thickness of the wire in the circuit is also greater. If this large wire were connected from the load to the control switch, the switch would have to carry the high amperage load and there would be an increased size of the wiring harness. To prevent these problems, a relay is used.

Relays are composed of a coil and a set of contacts. When the coil has a current passed though it, a magnetic field is formed and this field causes the contacts to move together, completing the circuit. Most relays are normally open, preventing current from passing through the circuit, but they can take any electrical form depending on the job they are intended to do. Relays can be considered "remote control switches." They allow a smaller current to operate devices that require higher amperages. When a small current operates the coil, a larger current is allowed to pass by the contacts. Some common circuits which may use relays are the horn, headlights, starter, electric fuel pump and other high draw circuits.

LOAD

Every electrical circuit must include a "load" (something to use the electricity coming from the source). Without this load, the battery would attempt to deliver its entire power supply from one pole to another instantly. This is called a "short circuit." All this electricity would take a short cut to ground and cause a great amount of damage to other components in the circuit by developing a tremendous amount of heat. This condition could develop sufficient heat to melt the insulation on all the surrounding wires and reduce a multiple wire cable to a lump of plastic and copper.

WIRING & HARNESSES

The average snowmobile contains yards of wiring, with hundreds of individual connections. To protect the many wires from damage and to keep them from becoming a confusing tangle, they are organized into bundles, enclosed in plastic or taped together and called wiring harnesses. Different harnesses serve different parts of the vehicle. Individual wires are color coded to help trace them through a harness where sections are hidden from view.

Snowmobile wiring or circuit conductors can be either single strand wire, multi-strand wire or printed circuitry. Single strand wire has a solid metal core and is usually used inside such components as alternators, motors, relays and other devices. Multi-strand wire has a core made of many small strands of wire twisted together into a single conductor. Most of the wiring in a snowmobile electrical system is made up of multi-strand wire, either as a single conductor or grouped together in a harness. All wiring is color coded on the insulator, either as a solid color or as a colored wire with an identification stripe. A printed circuit is a thin film of copper or other conductor that is printed on an insulator backing. Occasionally, a printed circuit is sandwiched between two sheets of plastic for more protection and flexibility. A complete printed circuit, consisting of conductors, insulating material and connectors for lamps or other components is called a printed circuit board. Printed circuitry is used in place of individual wires or harnesses in places where space is limited, such as in instruments.

Since electrical systems can very sensitive to changes in resistance, the selection of properly sized wires is critical when systems are repaired. A loose or corroded connection or a replacement wire that is too small for the circuit will add extra resistance and an additional voltage drop to the circuit.

The wire gauge number is an expression of the cross-section area of the conductor. snowmobile from countries that use the metric system will typically describe the wire size as its cross-sectional area in square millimeters. In this method, the larger the wire, the greater the number. Another common system for expressing wire size is the American Wire Gauge (AWG) system. As gauge number increases, area decreases and the wire becomes smaller. An 18 gauge wire is smaller than a 4 gauge wire. A wire with a higher gauge number will carry less current than a wire with a lower gauge number. Gauge wire size refers to the size of the strands of the conductor, not the size of the complete wire with insulator. It is possible, therefore, to have two wires of the same gauge with different diameters because one may have thicker insulation than the other.

It is essential to understand how a circuit works before trying to figure out why it doesn't. An electrical schematic shows the electrical current paths when a circuit is operating properly. Schematics break the entire electrical system down into individual circuits. In a schematic, usually no attempt is made to represent wiring and components as they physically appear on the vehicle; switches and other components are shown as simply as possible. Face views of harness connectors show the cavity or terminal locations in all multi-pin connectors to help locate test points.

CONNECTORS

♦ **See Figures 67, 68 and 69**

Three types of connectors are commonly used in snowmobile applications—weatherproof, molded and hard shell.

• Weatherproof—these connectors are most commonly used where the connector is exposed to the elements. Terminals are protected against moisture and dirt by sealing rings, which provide a weathertight seal. All repairs require the use of a special terminal and the tool required to service it. Unlike standard blade type terminals, these weatherproof terminals cannot be straightened once they are bent. Make certain that the connectors are properly seated and all of the sealing rings are in place when connecting leads.

• Molded—these connectors require complete replacement of the connector if found to be defective. This means splicing a new connector assembly into the harness. All splices should be soldered to insure proper contact. Use care when probing the connections or replacing terminals in them, as it is possible to create a short circuit between opposite terminals. If this happens to the wrong terminal pair, it is possible to damage certain components. Always use jumper wires between connectors for checking circuits.

• Hard Shell—unlike molded connectors, the terminal contacts in hard-shell connectors can be replaced. Replacement usually involves the use of a special terminal removal tool that depresses the locking tangs (barbs) on the connector terminal and allows the connector to be removed from the rear of the shell. The connector shell should be replaced if it shows any evidence of burn-

ing, melting, cracks, or breaks. Replace individual terminals that are burnt, corroded, distorted or loose.

Test Equipment

Pinpointing the exact cause of trouble in an electrical circuit is most times accomplished by the use of special test equipment. The following describes different types of commonly used test equipment and briefly explains how to use them in diagnosis. In addition to the information covered below, the tool manufacturer's instructions booklet (provided with the tester) should be read and clearly understood before attempting any test procedures.

JUMPER WIRES

✸✸ CAUTION

Never use jumper wires made from a thinner gauge wire than the circuit being tested. If the jumper wire is of too small a gauge, it may overheat and possibly melt. Never use jumpers to bypass high resistance loads in a circuit. Bypassing resistance, in effect, creates a short circuit. This may, in turn, cause damage and fire. Jumper wires should only be used to bypass lengths of wire or to simulate switches.

Jumper wires are simple, yet extremely valuable, pieces of test equipment. They are basically test wires which are used to bypass sections of a circuit. Although jumper wires can be purchased, they are usually fabricated from lengths of standard automotive wire and whatever type of connector (alligator clip, spade connector or pin connector) that is required for the particular application being tested. In cramped, hard-to-reach areas, it is advisable to have insulated boots over the jumper wire terminals in order to prevent accidental grounding. It is also advisable to include a standard automotive fuse in any jumper wire. This is commonly referred to as a "fused jumper." By inserting an in-line fuse holder between a set of test leads, a fused jumper wire can be used for bypassing open circuits while still protecting the circuit. Use a 5 amp fuse to provide protection against voltage spikes.

Jumper wires are used primarily to locate open electrical circuits, on either the ground (-) side of the circuit or on the power (+) side. If an electrical component fails to operate, connect the jumper wire between the component and a good ground. If the component operates only with the jumper installed, the ground circuit is open. If the ground circuit is good, but the component does not operate, the circuit between the power feed and component may be open. By moving the jumper wire successively back from the component toward the power source, you can isolate the area of the circuit where the open is located. When the component stops functioning, or the power is cut off, the open is in the segment of wire between the jumper and the point previously tested.

You can sometimes connect the jumper wire directly from the battery to the "hot" terminal of the component, but first make sure the component uses 12 volts in operation. Some electrical components, such as fuel injectors or sensors, may be designed to operate on about 4 to 5 volts, and running 12 volts directly to these components will cause damage.

TCCA6P03

Fig. 67 Hard shell (left) and weatherproof (right) connectors have replaceable terminals

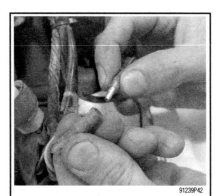

91239P42

Fig. 68 An example of a weatherproof bullet connector

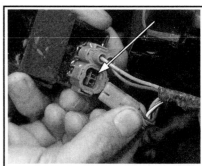

91239P53

Fig. 69 If you look closely, you can see the rubber gasket on the inside of the female connector

TEST LIGHTS

♦ **See Figure 70**

The test light is used to check circuits and components while electrical current is flowing through them. It is used for voltage and ground tests. To use a 12 volt test light, connect the ground clip to a good ground and probe wherever necessary with the pick. The test light will illuminate when voltage is detected. This does not necessarily mean that 12 volts (or any particular amount of voltage) is present; it only means that some voltage is present. It is advisable before using the test light to touch its ground clip and probe across the battery posts or terminals to make sure the light is operating properly.

✳ WARNING

Do not use a test light to probe electronic ignition, spark plug or coil wires. Never use a pick-type test light to probe wiring on computer controlled systems unless specifically instructed to do so. Any wire insulation that is pierced by the test light probe should be taped and sealed with silicone after testing.

Like the jumper wire, the 12 volt test light is used to isolate opens in circuits. But, whereas the jumper wire is used to bypass the open to operate the load, the 12 volt test light is used to locate the presence of voltage in a circuit. If the test light illuminates, there is power up to that point in the circuit; if the test light does not illuminate, there is an open circuit (no power). Move the test light in successive steps back toward the power source until the light in the handle illuminates. The open is between the probe and a point which was previously probed.

The self-powered test light is similar in design to the 12 volt test light, but contains a 1.5 volt penlight battery in the handle. It is most often used in place of a multimeter to check for open or short circuits when power is isolated from the circuit (continuity test).

The battery in a self-powered test light does not provide much current. A weak battery may not provide enough power to illuminate the test light even when a complete circuit is made (especially if there is high resistance in the circuit). Always make sure that the test battery is strong. To check the battery, briefly touch the ground clip to the probe; if the light glows brightly, the battery is strong enough for testing.

➡**A self-powered test light should not be used on any computer controlled system or component. The small amount of electricity transmitted by the test light is enough to damage some electronic components.**

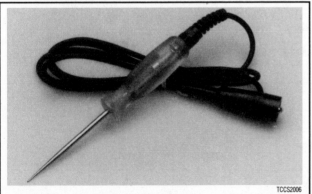

Fig. 70 A 12 volt test light is used to detect the presence of voltage in a circuit

TCCS2006

MULTIMETERS

♦ **See Figure 71**

Multimeters are an extremely useful tool for troubleshooting electrical problems. They can be purchased in either analog or digital form and have a price range to suit any budget. A multimeter is a voltmeter, ammeter and ohmmeter (along with other features) combined into one instrument. It is often used when testing solid state circuits because of its high input impedance (usually 10 megaohms or more). A brief description of the multimeter main test functions follows:

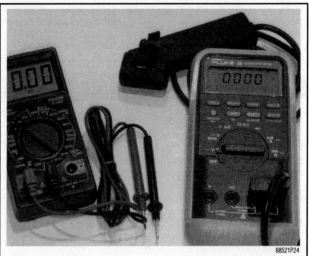

Fig. 71 Digital multimeters are great for diagnosing problems with electrical circuits

88521P24

• Voltmeter—the voltmeter is used to measure voltage at any point in a circuit, or to measure the voltage drop across any part of a circuit. Voltmeters usually have various scales and a selector switch to allow the reading of different voltage ranges. The voltmeter has a positive and a negative lead. To avoid damage to the meter, always connect the negative lead to the negative (-) side of the circuit (to ground or nearest the ground side of the circuit) and connect the positive lead to the positive (+) side of the circuit (to the power source or the nearest power source). Note that the negative voltmeter lead will always be black and that the positive voltmeter will always be some color other than black (usually red).

• Ohmmeter—the ohmmeter is designed to read resistance (measured in ohms) in a circuit or component. Most ohmmeters will have a selector switch which permits the measurement of different ranges of resistance (usually the selector switch allows the multiplication of the meter reading by 10, 100, 1,000 and 10,000). Some ohmmeters are "auto-ranging" which means the meter itself will determine which scale to use. Since the meters are powered by an internal battery, the ohmmeter can be used like a self-powered test light. When the ohmmeter is connected, current from the ohmmeter flows through the circuit or component being tested. Since the ohmmeter's internal resistance and voltage are known values, the amount of current flow through the meter depends on the resistance of the circuit or component being tested. The ohmmeter can also be used to perform a continuity test for suspected open circuits. In using the meter for making continuity checks, do not be concerned with the actual resistance readings. Zero resistance, or any ohm reading, indicates continuity in the circuit. Infinite resistance indicates an opening in the circuit. A high resistance reading where there should be none indicates a problem in the circuit. Checks for short circuits are made in the same manner as checks for open circuits, except that the circuit must be isolated from both power and normal ground. Infinite resistance indicates no continuity, while zero resistance indicates a dead short.

✳ WARNING

Never use an ohmmeter to check the resistance of a component or wire while there is voltage applied to the circuit.

• Ammeter—an ammeter measures the amount of current flowing through a circuit in units called amperes or amps. At normal operating voltage, most circuits have a characteristic amount of amperes, called "current draw" which can be measured using an ammeter. By referring to a specified current draw rating, then measuring the amperes and comparing the two values, one can determine what is happening within the circuit to aid in diagnosis. An open circuit, for example, will not allow any current to flow, so the ammeter reading will be zero. A damaged component or circuit will have an increased current draw, so the reading will be high. The ammeter is always connected in series with the circuit being tested. All of the current that normally flows through the circuit must also flow through the ammeter; if there is any other path for the current to follow, the ammeter reading will not be accurate. The ammeter itself has very little resistance to current flow and, therefore, will not affect the circuit, but it will measure current draw only when the circuit is closed and electricity is flowing. Excessive current draw can blow fuses and drain the battery, while a reduced current draw can cause motors to run slowly, lights to dim and other components to not operate properly.

Electrical Systems Troubleshooting

♦ See Figure 72

When diagnosing a specific problem, organized troubleshooting is a must. The complexity of a modern snowmobile demands that you approach any problem in a logical, organized manner. There are certain troubleshooting techniques that are standard:

• Establish when the problem occurs. Does the problem appear only under certain conditions? Were there any noises, odors or other unusual symptoms?

• Isolate the problem area. To do this, make some simple tests and observations, then eliminate the systems that are working properly. Check for obvious problems, such as broken wires and loose or dirty connections. Always check the obvious before assuming something complicated is the cause.

• Test for problems systematically to determine the cause once the problem area is isolated. Are all the components functioning properly? Is there power going to electrical switches and motors. Performing careful, systematic checks will often turn up most causes on the first inspection, without wasting time checking components that have little or no relationship to the problem.

• Test all repairs after the work is done to make sure that the problem is fixed. Some causes can be traced to more than one component, so a careful verification of repair work is important in order to pick up additional malfunctions that may cause a problem to reappear or a different problem to arise. A blown fuse, for example, is a simple problem that may require more than another fuse to repair. If you don't look for a problem that caused a fuse to blow, a shorted wire (for example) may go undetected.

Experience has shown that most problems tend to be the result of a fairly simple and obvious, such as loose or corroded connectors, bad grounds or damaged wire insulation, which causes a short. This makes careful visual inspection of components during testing essential to quick and accurate troubleshooting.

Testing

OPEN CIRCUITS

♦ See Figure 73

This test already assumes the existence of an open in the circuit and it is used to help locate the open portion.
1. Isolate the circuit from power and ground.

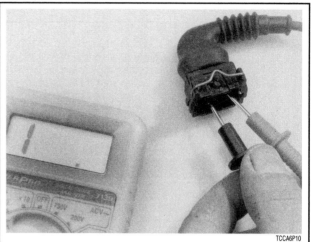
TCCA6P10

Fig. 73 The infinite reading on this multimeter (1 .) indicates that the circuit is open

2. Connect the self-powered test light or ohmmeter ground clip to the ground side of the circuit and probe sections of the circuit sequentially.
3. If the light is out or there is infinite resistance, the open is between the probe and the circuit ground.
4. If the light is on or the meter shows continuity, the open is between the probe and the end of the circuit toward the power source.

SHORT CIRCUITS

➥**Never use a self-powered test light to perform checks for opens or shorts when power is applied to the circuit under test. The test light can be damaged by outside power.**

1. Isolate the circuit from power and ground.
2. Connect the self-powered test light or ohmmeter ground clip to a good ground and probe any easy-to-reach point in the circuit.
3. If the light comes on or there is continuity, there is a short somewhere in the circuit.
4. To isolate the short, probe a test point at either end of the isolated circuit (the light should be on or the meter should indicate continuity).
5. Leave the test light probe engaged and sequentially open connectors or switches, remove parts, etc. until the light goes out or continuity is broken.
6. When the light goes out, the short is between the last two circuit components which were opened.

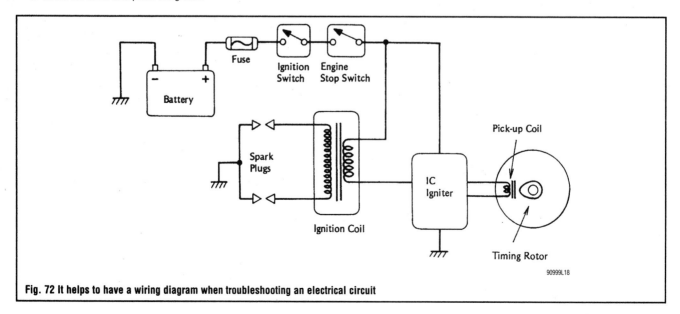
90999L18

Fig. 72 It helps to have a wiring diagram when troubleshooting an electrical circuit

VOLTAGE

This test determines voltage available from the battery and should be the first step in any electrical troubleshooting procedure after visual inspection. Many electrical problems, especially on computer controlled systems, can be caused by a low state of charge in the battery. Excessive corrosion at the battery cable terminals can cause poor contact that will prevent proper charging and full battery current flow.

1. Set the voltmeter selector switch to the 20V position.
2. Connect the multimeter negative lead to the battery's negative (-) post or terminal and the positive lead to the battery's positive (+) post or terminal.
3. Turn the ignition switch **ON** to provide a load.
4. A well charged battery should register over 12 volts. If the meter reads below 11.5 volts, the battery power may be insufficient to operate the electrical system properly.

VOLTAGE DROP

When current flows through a load, the voltage beyond the load drops. This voltage drop is due to the resistance created by the load and also by small resistance's created by corrosion at the connectors and damaged insulation on the wires. The maximum allowable voltage drop under load is critical, especially if there is more than one load in the circuit, since all voltage drops are cumulative.

1. Set the voltmeter selector switch to the 20 volt position.
2. Connect the multimeter negative lead to a good ground.
3. Operate the circuit and check the voltage prior to the first component (load).
4. There should be little or no voltage drop in the circuit prior to the first component. If a voltage drop exists, the wire or connectors in the circuit are suspect.
5. While operating the first component in the circuit, probe the ground side of the component with the positive meter lead and observe the voltage readings. A small voltage drop should be noticed. The resistance of the component causes this voltage drop.
6. Repeat the test for each component (load) down the circuit.
7. If a large voltage drop is noticed, the preceding component, wire or connector is suspect.

RESISTANCE

♦ See Figure 74

1. Isolate the circuit from the vehicle's power source.
2. Ensure that the ignition key is **OFF** when disconnecting any components or the battery.
3. Where necessary, also isolate at least one side of the circuit to be checked, in order to avoid reading parallel resistances. Parallel circuit resistances will always give a lower reading than the actual resistance of either of the branches.
4. Connect the meter leads to both sides of the circuit (wire or component) and read the actual measured ohms on the meter scale. Make sure the selector switch is set to the proper ohm scale for the circuit being tested, to avoid misreading the ohmmeter test value.

Wire and Connector Repair

Almost anyone can replace damaged wires, as long as the proper tools and parts are available. Wire and terminals are available to fit almost any need. Even

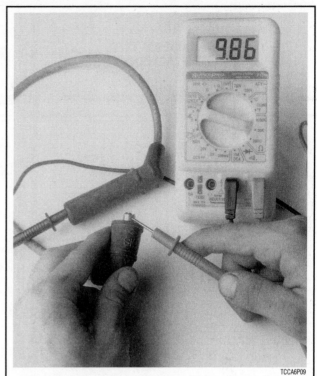

Fig. 74 Spark plug wires can be checked for excessive resistance using an ohmmeter

TCCA6P09

the specialized weatherproof, molded and hard shell connectors are now available from aftermarket suppliers.

Be sure the ends of all the wires are fitted with the proper terminal hardware and connectors. Wrapping a wire around a stud is never a permanent solution and will only cause trouble later. Replace wires one at a time to avoid confusion. Always route wires exactly the same as the factory.

➡If connector repair is necessary, only attempt it if you have the proper tools. Weatherproof and hard shell connectors require special tools to release the pins inside the connector. Attempting to repair these connectors with conventional hand tools will damage them.

Reading Wiring Diagrams

♦ See Figures 75 thru 80

For many people, reading wiring diagrams, or schematics, is a black art. It isn't as bad as it seems, since wiring diagrams are really nothing more than connect-the-dots with wires!

If you look at the sample diagrams, you will see that they contain information such as wire colors, terminal connections and components. The boxes may contain information such as internal configurations as would be handy to figure out what is going on inside a relay or switch.

There is a standard set of symbols used in wiring diagrams to denote various components. If the wiring diagram doesn't provide a reference for the symbols, you should be able to pick out their meanings from other information given.

The wiring diagram will use abbreviations for wire colors. There will be a chart somewhere in the wiring diagram or in the manual you are using to decode them.

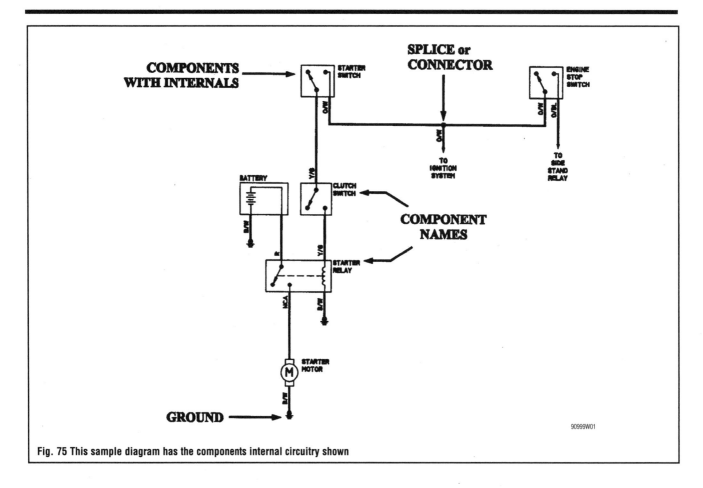

Fig. 75 This sample diagram has the components internal circuitry shown

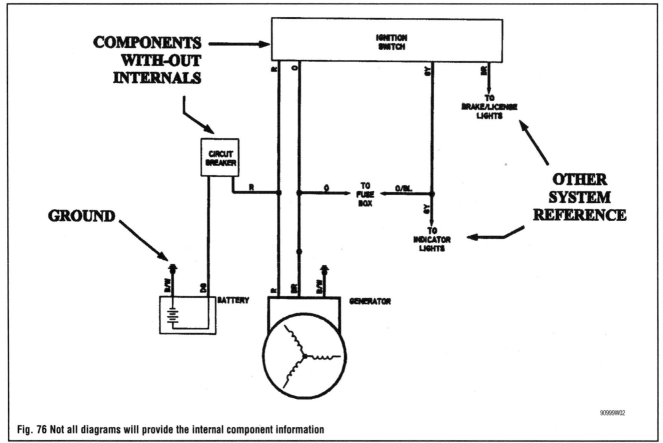

Fig. 76 Not all diagrams will provide the internal component information

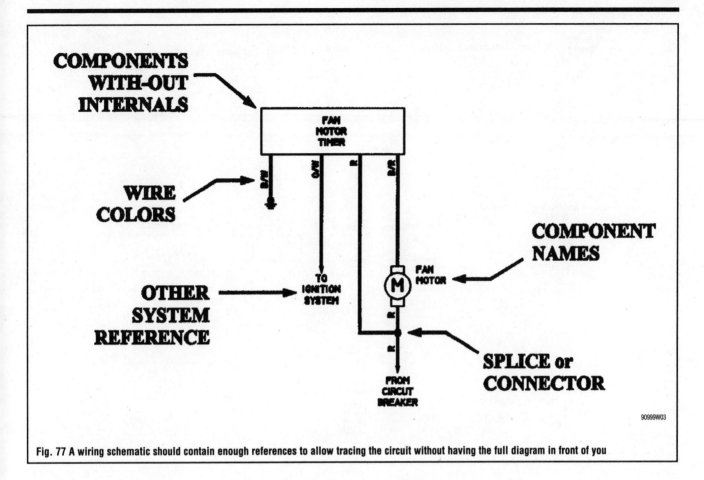

COMPONENTS WITH-OUT INTERNALS

WIRE COLORS

OTHER SYSTEM REFERENCE

COMPONENT NAMES

SPLICE or CONNECTOR

FAN MOTOR TIMER

TO IGNITION SYSTEM

FAN MOTOR

FROM CIRCUT BREAKER

90999W03

Fig. 77 A wiring schematic should contain enough references to allow tracing the circuit without having the full diagram in front of you

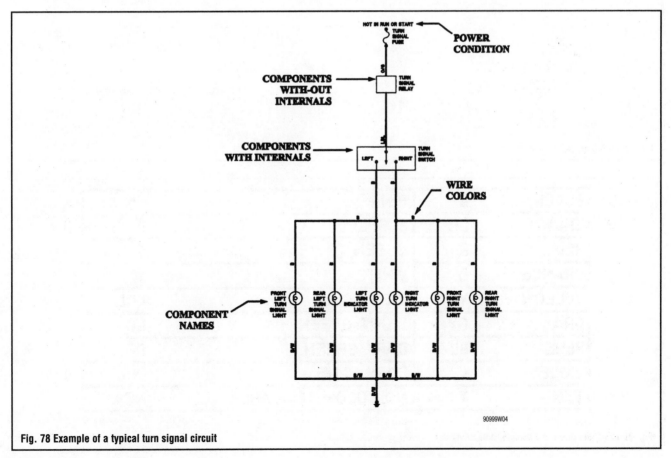

POWER CONDITION

COMPONENTS WITH-OUT INTERNALS

COMPONENTS WITH INTERNALS

WIRE COLORS

COMPONENT NAMES

HOT IN RUN OR START

TURN SIGNAL FUSE

TURN SIGNAL RELAY

TURN SIGNAL SWITCH

LEFT   RIGHT

FRONT LEFT TURN SIGNAL LIGHT

REAR LEFT TURN SIGNAL LIGHT

LEFT TURN INDICATOR LIGHT

RIGHT TURN INDICATOR LIGHT

FRONT RIGHT TURN SIGNAL LIGHT

REAR RIGHT TURN SIGNAL LIGHT

90999W04

Fig. 78 Example of a typical turn signal circuit

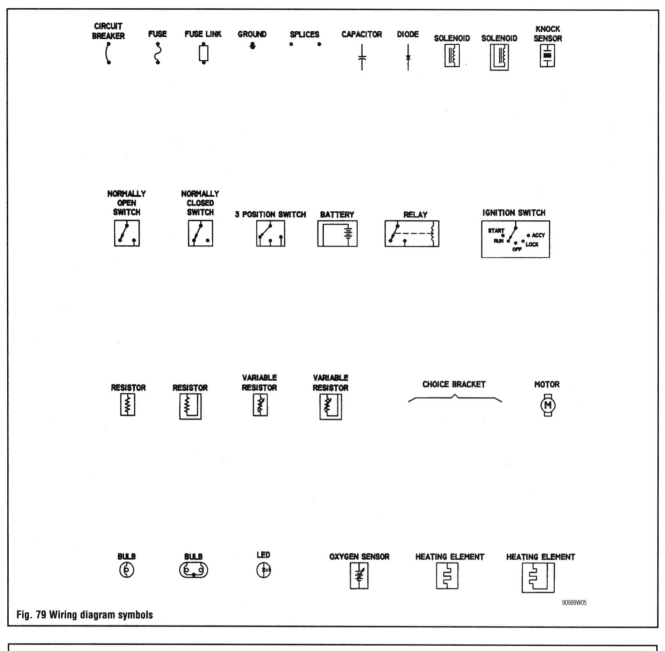

Fig. 79 Wiring diagram symbols

BLACK	B	PINK	PK
BROWN	BR	PURPLE	P
RED	R	GREEN	G
ORANGE	O	WHITE	W
YELLOW	Y	LIGHT BLUE	LBL
GRAY	GY	LIGHT GREEN	LG
BLUE	BL	DARK GREEN	DG
VIOLET	V	DARK BLUE	DBL
TAN	T	NO COLOR AVAILABLE	NCA

Fig. 80 Examples of some wire color abbreviations

ELECTRICAL TROUBLESHOOTING

Problem	Possible Cause	Inspection/Remedy
Battery does not charge	Defective battery	Test each cell; replace if shorted cell(s) are evident
	Battery electrolyte level low	Top up
	Broken or shorting wires in charging circuit	Check continuity and condition of wire insulation
	Loose or dirty battery terminals	Clean terminals and secure connections
	Defective voltage regulator	Test and replace if necessary
	Defective alternator	Replace
	Defective silicon diode	Replace
Excessive battery charging	Defective battery (shorted plates)	Replace battery
	Voltage regulator not properly grounded	Secure
	Regulator defective	Replace
Unstable charging voltage	Intermittent short	Check wiring for frayed insulation
	Defective key switch	Replace
	Intermittent coil in alternator	Replace
Electric starter spins, but engine does not	Broken starter clutch	Replace
	Solenoid not functioning properly	Test and replace if necessary
	Starter clutch arm broken	Inspect or replace
Starter does not turn over but warning lights dim when starter button is pushed, or engine turns over slowly	Low battery	Charge or replace battery
	Battery terminals loose or corroded	Clean terminals and secure connections
	Drive belt dragging on primary pulley	Inspect
	Partial engine siezure	Inspect engine for damage
	Starter armature bushings worn	Replace starter
	Starter defective	Replace starter
Clicking sound when starter button is pushed; engine does not turn over	Low battery	Charge or replace battery
	Battery terminals loose or corroded	Clean terminals and secure connections
	Defective starter solenoid	Replace
	Engine seized or hydrolocked	Inspect engine for damage
Nothing happens when the starter button is pushed	Loose or broken connections in starter switch or battery leads	Check switch connections; check battery terminals; clean and tighten battery leads
	Low or dead battery	Recharge or replace battery
	Fusible link severed	Replace fusible link

91249C01

ELECTRICAL TROUBLESHOOTING

Problem	Possible Cause	Inspection/Remedy
Brake light does not illuminate when lever is pulled	Burned out bulb	Replace
	Defective lever switch	Replace
	Broken or severely corroded wiring	Repair or replace
	Switch out of adjustment	Adjust switch
No spark or weak spark	Defective ignition coil(s)	Replace
	Defective spark plug(s)	Replace
	Plug lead(s) or wires damaged or disconnected	Check condition of wires and connections
Carbon-fouled spark plugs	Mixture too rich	Adjust carburetors; check air cleaner
	Plugs too cold for conditions	Use hotter plugs
	Idle speed set too high	Adjust carburetors
Oil-fouled spark plugs	Improperly adjusted oil injection pump cable	Adjust
	Kinked or binding cable	Adjust
	Malfunctioning oil injection pump	Inspect and replace if necessary
Spark plug electrodes burned or overheated	Spark plugs too hot for conditions	Use colder plugs
	Engine overheating	See above
	Ignition timing incorrect	Adjust
	Mixture too lean	See above

91249C02

10

LONG-TERM
STORAGE

STORING YOUR SNOWMOBILE

▶ See Figures 1 and 2

Not all of us are lucky enough to live in an area where you can ride your snowmobile twelve months out of the year. Depending on the conditions where you live and depending upon your own desire to ride, you should take steps to preserve your precious machine(s) during the off-season.

Leaving a snowmobile sit without proper preparation for an extended period of time allows oxidation, corrosion and deterioration to set in. If you know (or even suspect) that you will not be using your snowmobile for a month or longer, follow these storage procedures to assure proper care and readiness of your snowmobile when you return to riding.

A little bit of effort at the end of the riding season can make a world of difference on how well your machine runs over time, how easy it is to get started, and how long it will give you faithful service. Some items we will mention here are a must do and others are a good idea, which if you are very picky about your machine, you will want to do. Note that these suggestions are a general guideline, you should check your owner's manual for specific things related to your machine.

If your machine has a battery/fuel injection then there is a specific method of taking care of that which will be detailed in your owners manual.

Preparation For Storage Checklist

▶ See Figures 3 thru 4

• Clean the machine both on the outside and under the hood. Make sure there is no dirt or grime anywhere including grease or oil on the motor. Paint the pipes with a heat resistant paint to keep them from rusting up. Treat the seat and other vinyl with a protectant.

• Either drain the fuel tank or add some fuel stabilizer to it. If you drain the tank, make sure that
you also drain the carburetors (a good idea no matter what). If you use fuel stabilizer, add it to the tank and then run the machine for a few minutes to make sure that the fuel with the stabilizer gets circulated into the carburetors.

• Change all of your fluids before storage. During the off-season, when the snowmobile is idle, your fluids are there simply to fight corrosion. Once the snowmobile is removed from storage, those fluids will be called upon to lubricate, cool and/or transmit power, but for now, you want them to inhibit corrosion and nothing more.

Fig. 1 Leaving a snowmobile sit in conditions like this allows oxidation, corrosion and deterioration to set in

Fig. 3 Make sure to thoroughly clean and lubricate your sled prior to placing it into storage

Fig. 2 If you live in an area where this sort of scene is common, you might want to consider storing your snowmobile inside even during the riding season (just so you can find it when you want to go riding). Note the Geo Tracker under the snow pile

Fig. 4 Changing all the vital fluids on your sled keeps the internal components from corroding during the off-season and provides fresh lubrication for the initial startup

- Poor a little bit of sled oil into each cylinder and with the kill switch or ignition turned off rotate the motor around a couple of times. You can also use a fogging oil for this purpose. This will keep the internals of the motor lubed so they don't rust during the off-season.

- Before placing the snowmobile into storage, be sure to remove the cell cap(s) and check the fluid level. If necessary, top-off any cells using distilled water. Either remove the battery or place it on a automatic charger which will maintain a proper charge, without overcharging it.

- Remove the belt from the clutches, wipe clutches off with a solvent (lacquer thinner works well) and spray all clutch surfaces with a silicone spray of some sort. This will keep them from corroding or rusting

- Grease all grease points on the machine. This will force any moisture out of the joints and keep them from rusting solid over the summer

- Store the machine inside a dry place (shed or covered trailer) and cover it to keep the dust off it. Block it up in the air so that the suspension (front and rear) hang free. Blocks under the belly pan/bulkhead and under the rear bumper work well for this. Once its in the air loosen the tension on the track so that it hangs loose so that the track won't stretch over the summer if your machine has an older track on it. If it has a newer track with Kevlar belts then don't loosen the track. Kevlar tracks will shrink over the summer and will require a break-in period again in the fall when you tighten them back up. You can also back off all shock/spring adjustments so that the springs are as loose as possible.

Cleaning your Snowmobile

◆ See Figures 5 thru 11

Hopefully, you already understand the benefits of washing your snowmobile. Besides giving you a chance to inspect all the various components of your snowmobile (while you clean them), you have the opportunity to protect these parts from moisture and corrosive agents in the atmosphere. Everything from painted parts to powdercoat to plastic should be cleaned and given a coating of some protectant to reduce the possibility of damage or corrosion during storage.

Refer to the "Cleaning Your Snowmobile" for recommendations regarding the care and treatment of the different materials on your snowmobile. Obviously plastic is not protected in the same fashion as rubber or paint. The key is to completely clean the snowmobile (with a proper wash) and THEN protect the various surfaces of the snowmobile before placing it in storage.

➡ Regular washing and cleaning of your snowmobile should be part of your routine whether or not you are planning on putting your snowmobile in storage.

While washing your snowmobile, you have a perfect opportunity to look out for potential problems. Keep your eyes open for loose or missing fasteners, cracked or damaged components and weeping or leaking seals. A loose or missing fastener may be a wake-up call to pay closer attention to basic mainte-

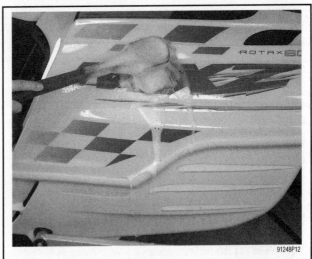

Fig. 6 . . . and cleaning should be part of your routine whether or not you are planning on putting your snowmobile in storage

Fig. 7 Drying your sled thoroughly prior to storage is important to preventing the sled from freezing in extreme weather and also to prevent bare metal from rusting

Fig. 5 Regular rinsing. . .

Fig. 8 Thoroughly cleaning a sled will reveal items such as this skid plate that is in bad need of repair

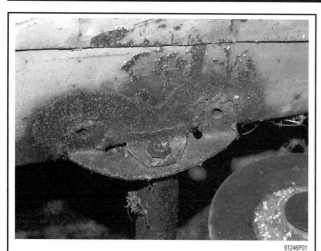

Fig. 9 Items like this rusty suspension bracket can also be noticed during routine cleaning. Once dry, sanding and painting this area should be your first priority

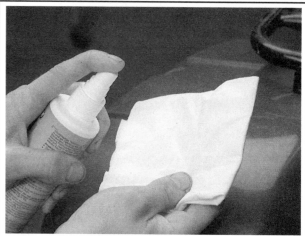

Fig. 11 Using a rag to apply the protectant will help to avoid excessive overspray

nance and your pre-ride checks, or it could be a warning sign that some other problem is developing. A good cleaning, followed by observation after operation of the snowmobile will help determine if a seal is leaking badly (and should be replaced) or if a slight amount of seepage is responsible for accumulated fluids, dirt or grime on a part of the snowmobile.

The longer you plan on keeping your snowmobile in storage, the more important your cleaning and protecting ritual will become. If an snowmobile is only going to be in storage for a few months, chances are that few components are going to wear out just because of time and exposure (unless of course they were just about gone to begin with, but your inspection should have revealed that). If however, the snowmobile may be stored for a longer period of time (measured in years instead of months) then your chance of items like seals drying, cracking or melting their way onto shafts becomes greater. One of the biggest advantages of cleaning your snowmobile before placing it into storage is if a seal were to fail during storage, you will more quickly identify it when removing the snowmobile from storage later, since you knew it wasn't leaking before.

➡ **Cleaning and protecting your snowmobile before storage is definitely a case of an ounce of prevention being worth a pound of cure. But if your sled requires a pound of cure when it is removed from storage, it will simply require that much LESS than it would if it hadn't been properly detailed.**

There are a lot of products available to beautify rubber, vinyl and plastic. Keep in mind, the truth is that rubber and vinyl will eventually dry out and crack,

no matter how much you use protective treatments. Exposure to ultraviolet radiation, the evaporation of component oils and oxidation will take their toll on everything from skis to seats. Most products on the market cannot prevent the natural aging of these components, but you should be able to at least lengthen their usable life while making them better looking in the process.

Draining the Fuel System

▶ **See Figures 12, 13, 14 and 15**

Over time the most volatile compounds found in a sample of gasoline will evaporate, leaving the remaining fluid less combustible. This will lead to difficult starting and rough running for your engine. BUT, this is the least of your worries when it comes to gasoline and any form of long term storage.

As gasoline evaporates it can leave behind a varnish which will coat and possibly clog critical fuel delivery systems. Needle jets, floats and valves in carburetors can be rendered useless by enough of this varnish. All of this adds up to a poor running snowmobile (if it runs at all) and lengthy or costly repairs as parts must be removed and cleaned, or in some cases, replaced.

You basically have two options when it comes to preventing fuel system damage during months when your snowmobile is being stored. Either you can completely drain the fuel system or you can add a fuel stabilizer to the system and make sure it is completely mixed with the gasoline.

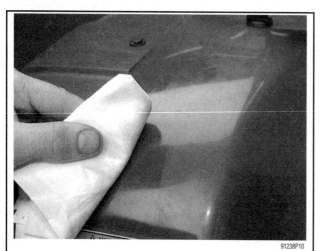

Fig. 10 Dried out, scratched plastic an be rejuvenated with a good application of plastic protectant

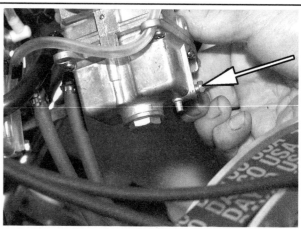

Fig. 12 Some models have a carburetor drain designed right into the carburetor bowl. Just loosen the screw to drain the carburetor of all fuel

Fig. 13 The water and sediment in the bowl of this carburetor has accumulated during storage—draining the carburetor before placing your snowmobile in storage will help prevent these kind of problems

Fig. 14 Without fuel in the carburetor, the chance of corrosion inside the carburetor may be increased—use a light spray oil to coat the inside of the carburetor to prevent corrosion from forming

Fig. 15 Its not a bad idea to replace the fuel filter with a fresh one before storage

Add Stabilizer Or Drain?

Your decision on whether to add fuel stabilizer or to completely drain the system should really depend on how long the snowmobile is going to be stored and how much aggravation you are willing to go through. Frankly, adding stabilizer is the easier of the 2 solutions, but for long term storage (again, speaking more in terms of years than months) draining is the better solution. Since most snowmobiles are two-strokes, there is not much of a choice. Two-strokes which have to pre-mix the oil and fuel before it goes in the tank should be drained completely. The lubricating properties of the oil in the fuel will be long gone when the riding season comes around. In general, you should wait until your going to ride before mixing fuel and oil for a two-stroke engine.

➡**On newer EFI models some manufacturers are recommending the addition of fuel stabilizer. After the stabilizer is added the engine should be allowed to idle 3-4 minutes to ensure the stabilizer is flushed through the system. Check your owner's manual for the proper procedure for your sled.**

ADDING FUEL STABILIZER

♦ See Figure 16

This is the solution most people prefer because it is a lot easier than draining the system. But, remember that, using fuel stabilizer is more suited to a storage time that is measured in months and NOT years. This makes it sufficient for most off-season storage needs. If you decide to use this method, be sure to follow the stabilizer manufacturer's instructions, but keep the following points in mind:

• It is best to add most stabilizers right before filling the tank, as this gives the stabilizer the best chance to fully mix with the gasoline as the tank is filled.

• After adding stabilizer, be sure to operate the engine for a few minutes to give the fuel/stabilizer mixture an opportunity to reach all parts of the system, like the internals of the carburetor.

• Gas from your last fuel fill-up will be in the system for a long time, so if possible, avoid oxygenated fuels which use alcohol, since alcohol absorbs water and may promote corrosion in the fuel system. If you can't avoid fuel with alcohol in it, then pay extra-close attention to the next point.

• Be sure to TOP-OFF the fuel tank to minimize the amount of air (and therefore moisture) that is present in the tank. If you store a metal fuel tank with air in it, the moisture will cause rusting on the inside of an uncoated tank and that rust can play havoc with your fuel system come riding season. Most snowmobiles have plastic fuel tanks these days, so rust may not be a problem, but water in the fuel can still cause problems.

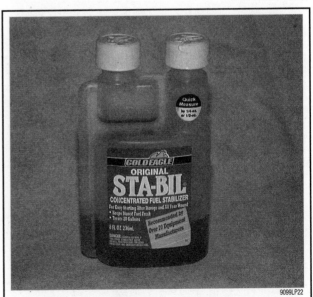

Fig. 16 This bottle of fuel stabilizer comes with a handy feature, a built-in measuring and dispensing cup

DRAINING THE SYSTEM

▶ **See Figure 17**

If you are really serious about storing your snowmobile (and you should be if it is going to be stored for time periods measured in years instead of just months), then you should completely drain the fuel system. But remember that if you do remove all of the fuel (and therefore remove the danger of varnish build-up), you have another concern, in the form of corrosion. Air contains a certain amount of moisture, so if you drain the fuel system completely, leaving only air behind, then there will be moisture to help corrode metal surfaces in the system(s).

To prevent your carburetors from becoming corroded, apply a light spray oil to the bowl and float, and the venturi. After everything is oiled down, install the float bowl and install the carburetors to the snowmobile.

Fig. 18 Always maintain the engine coolant at the proper level as specified on the coolant reservoir

Fig. 17 Without fuel in the carburetor, the chance of corrosion may be increased. Use a light spray oil to coat the inside of the carburetor to prevent corrosion from forming during storage

Fig. 19 On most engines it is a messy task to drain the engine coolant. Large drain pans are a must here

Changing Fluids

It doesn't matter what the fluid's job is normally, when it comes to storage, ALL FLUIDS have one major job. During the off-season, when the snowmobile is idle, all of your fluids are there simply to fight corrosion. Once the snowmobile is removed from storage, those fluids will be called upon to lubricate, cool and/or transmit power, but for now, you want them to inhibit corrosion and nothing more.

There is a lot of debate between "experts" who will advise you to change all fluids before storage or only after storage. Some people advise that you only change some fluids. Many will draw upon years of experience, saying that they never changed this or that fluid and have never had a problem (and they may be right). But it is hard to make generalizations. What works for one make or model (or in one part of the country) may not work for another.

With that said, we are going to make a generalization here. You NEVER lose by changing all of your fluids before storage. Add up all the fluids your snowmobile needs, and compare the dollar amount to the value of the snowmobile. If the value of the snowmobile is greater (and it should be significantly so in most cases), then your motivation is simple. Changing all fluids is CHEAP INSURANCE.

Engine Coolant

▶ **See Figures 18, 19 and 20**

Engine coolant has 2 purposes. The primary purpose is temperature control of the engine (to cool it during operation and protect it from freezing when not running). But it also contains rust inhibitors to prevent corrosion as well as lubricants for the water pump and seals. If your coolant is close to the replacement interval in your snowmobile's owners manual, then you should replace it now, before putting it in storage. Like engine oil, it is best to put nothing but fresh fluids in the system.

Fig. 20 Some home made draining tools also help make the job a little easier and less messy

Replacing the coolant before storage is especially important if the snowmobile is to be stored outside or in an unheated garage/shed where it may be subjected to sub-freezing temperatures. As coolant ages, it not only loses its ability to inhibit corrosion and cool the motor, but it also will lose its ability to resist freezing. As the freezing point of your coolant is raised by age, the possibility of severe engine damage caused by the coolant freezing and expanding increases. It would be a shame to loose an engine all because you wouldn't spring for a gallon of coolant.

Chain Case Oil

▶ See Figures 21 thru 26

The chain case on many snowmobiles is vented to the atmosphere. It will acquire moisture through condensation as the snowmobile is used. Hopefully during use, the oil heats up sufficiently so that moisture will evaporate. To be sure you have removed as much moisture as possible, take this opportunity to change the chain case oil (if you have enough drain pans, do it as the engine oil drains).

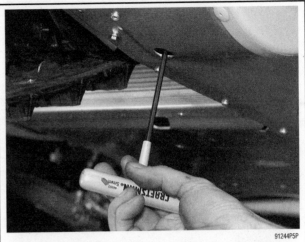
Fig. 23 On some sleds, the chain case lube can be drained using a built in drain plug. However, on most, the chain case cover must be removed to allow the lube to drain

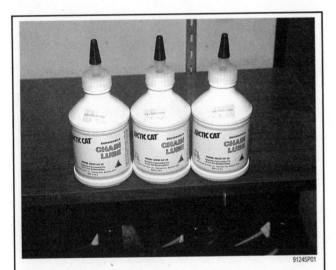
Fig. 21 Either chain case lube . . .

Fig. 24 On most sleds, a long funnel is required to reach the chain case without spilling lube all over the floor

Fig. 22 . . . or transmission lube can be used to refill your sleds chain case reservoir. Check your owner's manual for the type recommended by your manufacturer

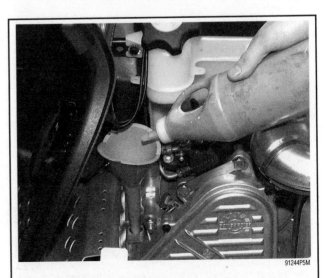
Fig. 25 Pour the lube in slowly to prevent overfilling the system

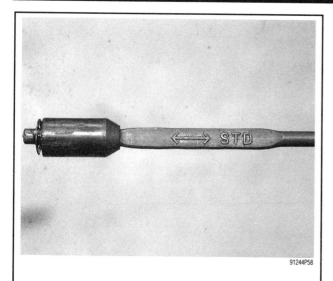

Fig. 26 Check the chain case for proper oil level using the dipstick

Once again, by changing this oil you will help to reduce the amount of corrosion which will take place during the time the snowmobile is left in storage.

Brake Fluid

▶ See Figures 27, 28, 29 and 30

One of the most ignored parts of maintenance tends to be the replacement of hydraulic brake fluids. Remember that DOT 3 & 4 fluids are highly hydroscopic, meaning that they will readily absorb moisture from the atmosphere. Even if you never remove the master cylinder cover, it is likely that some moisture will get into the system over time and this can cause corrosion. If the reservoir is cloudy, or the fluid is more than 2 years old, its time for a brake fluid change.

Lubricate The Engine

▶ See Figures 31

If the engine was run (in order to change the oil) then the cylinder should not require any special attention for normal storage (consisting of a few months). But, if the storage is going to be any longer OR if you want the extra level of protection, you can coat the cylinder with some additional engine oil.

Remove and inspect the spark plug (if it needs to be replaced, you might as

Fig. 28 Use only fresh, clean brake fluid when refilling the system to avoid contamination problems

Fig. 29 Remove the reservoir cap and inspect the rubber gasket for damage. Replace as necessary

Fig. 27 Brake fluid level can be easily inspected by viewing the fluid level through the sight glass

Fig. 30 Refill the system to the proper level and then bleed the brake lines of all trapped air

Fig. 31 Most snowmobile manufacturers recommend some type of storage oil be used in the engine to prevent corrosion. Arctic Cat's 'Engine Storage Preserver' is a fine example of this type of oil

Fig. 32 Unless you have a sealed, maintenance-free battery, you should remove the caps and check the battery fluid level and condition before storage

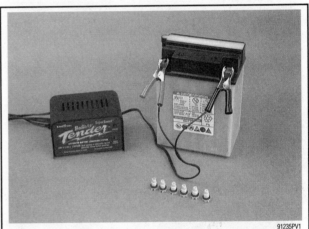

Fig. 33 After adding any water to the battery, be sure that it gets a chance to mix with the electrolyte. Attaching a trickle charger like the Battery Tender® for a few hours, should do the trick. (Uh . . . pun intended.)

Fig. 34 With a sealed battery, you obviously won't be opening any cell caps to add distilled water, but there is still a way to check the electrolyte the battery removed. Just remove the battery and view the level through the plastic case

well do it since you're going through the trouble to remove it anyway). Next, pour 1–2 tablespoons of fresh, clean engine oil through the spark plug hole. Rotate the engine to spread the oil around the cylinder, then install the spark plug.

➡Rotating the engine should be done slowly to prevent the addition of gasoline to the cylinders.

To rotate the engine, keep the spark plug out to relieve engine compression, and use the pull starter. Remember, don't rotate the engine too fast, or gasoline might be sucked into the cylinder and wash away all of the oil.

An alternative to pouring oil into the engine is to use a fogging oil. With the engine at an idle pull back air intake boot and inject fogging oil onto the intake for about 10-20 seconds. Quickly turn the engine OFF. The fogging oil will lubricate the cylinders and prevent corrosion.

Maintain The Battery

CHECKING THE FLUID

◆ See Figures 32, 33 and 34

One of the most important parts of battery care is to maintain the fluid level. If the electrolyte level is allowed to drop beyond a certain point the plates will corrode and the battery will not be able to receive or hold a charge. Before placing the snowmobile into storage, be sure to remove the cell cap(s) and check the fluid level. If necessary, top-off any cells using DISTILLED water. Only fill the battery to the fill lines on the case or to the bottom of the cell opening in the top of the battery case if no fill line is present (or as directed by the battery manufacturer).

➡After adding any water to the battery, be sure that it gets a chance to mix with the electrolyte. The best way to do this is to operate the snowmobile (but since you just went through a lot of trouble to NOT OPERATE IT, we recommend attaching a TRICKLE charger for a few hours, this should do the trick. (Uh . . . pun intended.)

If you are using a sealed battery, you obviously won't be opening any cell caps to add distilled water, but there is still a way to check the electrolyte the battery removed. Just remove the battery and view the level through the plastic case.

Also, some automotive batteries use sight glasses in the top of the battery case, so check with the battery manufacturer to see if they have provided a similar method of checking your battery.

REMOVE IT OR TEND IT?

▶ **See Figures 35, 36 and 37**

The second most important part of battery maintenance is making sure that it is properly charged. If you have just checked the fluid level, then you are in the perfect position to check the charge using a hydrometer designed just for that purpose. Because the specific gravity of electrolyte will change with the amount of charge present, you will be able to check the exact condition of each battery cell by using a hydrometer (that is, unless it is a sealed battery).

But even if the charge is fine now, there is no telling how it is going to be in a few months. Chances are, it is NOT going to be fully charged after a couple months, and may be dead. Batteries will self discharge over time (which will allow for changes to the chemical composition of the plates inside the battery). If allowed to discharge often enough or long enough, the battery will become permanently discharged and useless.

For this reason you are going to want to make sure that the battery is fully charged when you put the snowmobile into storage and then hook it up to an automatic charger (such as the Battery Tender®) which will maintain a proper charge, without overcharging it. Or, if you do not have an automatic battery charger, use a trickle charger for a few hours at least once every month.

If you are lucky enough to be storing the snowmobile in an attached garage, then you will be fine leaving the battery in place. You will be fine, that

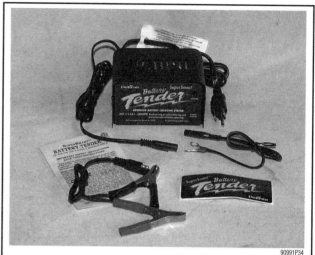

Fig. 37 The Battery Tender® from Deltran allows for continuous charging without the fear of damaging the battery

is, as long as an extension cord or outlet is handy to make sure the battery can be kept fully charged. But, if the snowmobile is to be stored outside, in a detached garage or shed, you really should remove the battery and store it elsewhere.

Inspect the Drive Belt

▶ **See Figures 38, 39, 40, 41 and 42**

Inspect the drive belt for signs of glazing or cracking. A glazed belt will be perfectly smooth from slippage, while a good belt will have a slight texture of fabric visible. Cracks will usually start at the inner edge of the belt and run outward.

Remove the belt from the pulleys, wipe pulleys off with a solvent (lacquer thinner works well) and spray all pulley surfaces with a silicone spray of some sort. This will keep them from corroding or rusting.

Lubricate The Chassis

▶ **See Figures 43, 44, 45 and 46**

Now is a good time to lube and grease any pivot points, such as suspension bushings, steering gear, cables and levers. The depth to which you pursue lubing will have something to do with your normal maintenance routine.

Fig. 35 If your snowmobile is to be stored outside, it is best to disconnect the battery . . .

Fig. 36 . . . remove it from the snowmobile, and store it indoors

Fig. 38 Always remove the drivebelt for storage . . .

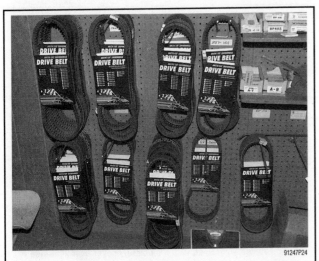

Fig. 39 . . . and replace it with a new one when the riding season comes again next year

Fig. 42 Wipe pulleys off with a solvent (lacquer thinner works well) and an abrasive pad to clean the pulley sprocket surfaces of all residue. Then, spray all pulley surfaces with silicone spray

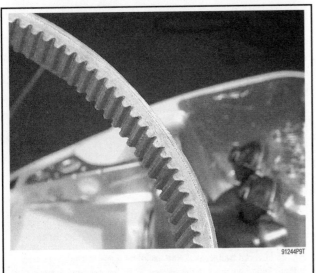

Fig. 40 Inspect the belt for signs of wear . . .

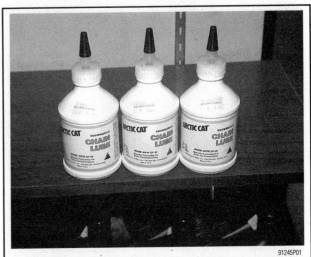

Fig. 43 A large selection of lubricants can be found at your local parts store or dealership

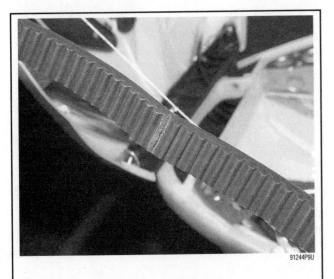

Fig. 41 . . . or cracking that may indicate problems

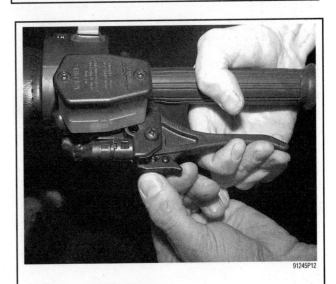

Fig. 44 By lubricating controls . . .

Fig. 45 . . . suspension components . . .

Fig. 47 You will want to place a high quality cover over your sled to keep it away from prying eyes, ultraviolet radiation, and whatever else might come its way while in storage

Fig. 46 . . . and track assemblies you can insure your sled will be ready to ride come winter

Fig. 48 Covered trailers make an excellent place to store your sled without taking up room in the garage. This fine example is from Load-Rite®

If lubing items such as the steering shaft only involves a grease gun and a zerk fitting you will be much more likely to do that now (regardless of when it is next due), then you would be if it involved removing the steering shaft by hand.

Cover and Protect The Sled

◆ See Figures 47 and 48

Ideally, you will want to place a high quality cover over your sled to keep it away from prying eyes, ultraviolet radiation, and whatever else might come its way. BUT, there are a few things to be careful of with covers. If you are going to buy one, make sure it has a soft inner lining to prevent scratching of the plastic. Also, make sure it is not made of a plastic material, but instead choose one that breathes. A non-breathable, plastic material will trap condensation, promoting corrosion and mold, while a breathing cover will allow moisture to evaporate, further protecting your snowmobile.

Unfortunately, snowmobiles have lots of neat, tight, little nooks and crannies (like Thomas' English Muffins®). This is not only a problem when it comes to cleaning, but when it comes to RODENTS. Many small, furry animals are attracted to these nooks and may think it is nest building time. They also have the unfortunate habit of shredding things like seats, wiring harnesses and air filters. If possible, check the snowmobile every week or so to discourage nesting. Hey, you can always get a cat and allow them access to the storage area (as long as they don't like to stretch their claws on your seat).

Store the sled in a dry place (shed or covered trailer) with the previously mentioned cover over it to keep the dust off it. Block it up in the air so that the suspension (front and rear) hang free. Blocks under the belly pan/bulk head and under the rear work well for this. Once its in the air loosen the tension on the track so that it hangs loose so that the track won't stretch over the summer if your machine has an older track on it. If it has a newer track with Kevlar belts then don't loosen the track. Kevlar tracks will shrink over the summer and will require a break-in period again in the fall when you tighten them back up. You can also back off all shock/spring adjustments so that the springs are as loose as possible.

Fig. 49 Typical example of the "Off-season Blues". These guys just can't wait to get back on their sleds and go riding. Vroom . . . vroom!

Leave It In Storage

▶ See Figure 49

Once you have put your snowmobile into storage mode, LEAVE IT ALONE. You can drool on it (as long as you dry it afterwards). You can rub body parts against it (as long as you don't scratch it up). You can get dressed up in your gear, sit on it and go "Vroom . . .Vroom." while spitting on yourself. But don't start it just to listen to or "warm the motor." Idling it won't warm the motor very much, probably will not charge the battery, definitely won't do anything for the drivetrain and will most likely leave some condensation in the exhaust to help rust get started. LEAVE IT ALONE UNTIL IT IS PROPERLY REMOVED FROM STORAGE.

REMOVING YOUR SNOWMOBILE FROM STORAGE

▶ See Figure 50

If you followed our instructions last spring, then you should be in GREAT SHAPE and we will have you riding in a few hours (barring any unexpected problems).

Also, if you come across an abandoned baby (the proverbial snowmobile that has been forgotten about in the shed or barn for the past decade or so) then you should follow these steps towards reawakening it gently. Of course, the longer the snowmobile has been in storage, the more items you are going to need to check. If the snowmobile was stored for more than one season you should start to suspect ANY RUBBER item (hoses, seals) and any wear items (cables, fluids, lights). Don't assume that anything is in good shape until you have checked and proven it to be serviceable.

Removal From Storage Checklist

• Add fresh fuel and check all the fluids like chain case oil, anti-freeze (if your sled is water cooled) and brake fluid. Check the chain tension.
• Using a clean rag and a good solvent, wipe down the pulley surfaces.

Fig. 50 These are just some of the abandon snowmobiles in the back room at M&S Sales and Service. Sleds that have been stored this long should be thoroughly inspected prior to riding

• Check the exhaust pipe to make sure a rodent hasn't made it his home for the year. If said rodent has set up house, issue an eviction order.
• Make sure all controls work freely.
• Lube any appropriate chassis points. Make sure everything that has a grease Zerk fitting or lube point is lubed well.
• Remove the cell cap(s) and check the fluid level in the battery. If necessary, top-off any cells using distilled water. Place the battery on an automatic charger which will bring it up to a full charge slowly, without overcharging it.
• Check the plastic side rails.
• Install a new set of spark plugs properly gapped. You might want to wait until after the first start to install your new plugs. This way the oil that you put in the cylinders for storage will coat your old plugs and not the new ones.
• Start the machine and let it idle to warm up. DON'T start it and wack the throttle open. Give the engine a chance to circulate oil/fuel mixture over all the internals. After it is warmed up, block the rear of the machine up and spin the track easily. Checking for loose track clips, proper track tension and proper track alignment.
• Check the front skis for proper alignment and adjustment.

Fill the Fuel Tank

If you drained the fuel system before storage then it is time to refill the gas tank and prime the system using fresh gasoline. As usual, be very careful when working around gasoline.

❊❊❊ CAUTION

Gasoline is VERY DANGEROUS STUFF. It is HIGHLY flammable and it is very easy to get yourself killed. Don't work around open flames or things that might cause a spark.

If you used fuel stabilizer, than you've got another choice to make here. The longer the snowmobile has been in storage, the less volatile the fuel will be, even if you used stabilizer. If you just stored it for the off-season, then you are likely to be in good shape.

If you didn't add stabilizer or if you are resurrecting a long forgotten beast, then chances are that your fuel system is clogged with varnish, and the carburetor bowl is corroded. Both of these potential nightmares must be remedied before the engine can come to life.

If your carburetor contains varnish, then it may require a rebuild before it will perform properly. To help determine if this is going to be a problem, remove the float bowl (assuming that you have drained any fuel that was left, or that it was in storage so long that no fuel is present). Once the float bowl has been removed from the carburetor, examine the float and chamber for varnish and corrosion. If either is evident, you are probably going to have to disassemble and clean or completely rebuild the carburetor.

Once you are ready to go you will want to prime the fuel system before attempting to start the engine (this helps to prevent unwanted excessive drain on your new or freshly charged battery). Usually, priming is as easy as turning on the petcock. BUT, you may have a vacuum actuated petcock which prevent fuel from flowing to the carburetor unless engine vacuum is applied to one side of a pressure valve. Most vacuum actuated petcocks have a prime setting which allows fuel to flow without vacuum, but if yours does not then you will either need a hand held vacuum pump, or you are simply going to have to crank for a little while.

Check the Fluids

ENGINE COOLANT

▶ **See Figure 51**

If the snowmobile was properly prepped and the coolant was changed before storage, just make a quick level check.

If the snowmobile is being resurrected or if you didn't change the coolant before storage, you should at least check the level and check the specific gravity. Specialized hydrometers (available in most auto parts stores) are available to give you an indication of the coolants ability to resist freezing and boiling. If the level is OK and the coolant is still giving adequate protection, then you are free to leave it in the system.

Of course, if you don't know how long the coolant has been in the system, you should change it. Remember that the other job coolant performs is to prevent corrosion while lubricating the water pump seal(s). Coolant usually looses its ability to do these jobs properly LONG BEFORE a hydrometer will tell you that it is bad. If the coolant is more than a year old, then you probably want to save yourself the hassle down the road and replace it now.

Fig. 51 Check the level and specific gravity of the engine coolant prior to starting the engine for the first time

CHAIN CASE OIL

▶ **See Figures 52 and 53**

Check the fluid level. If the level has gone down, look for a leak. If the level has gone up, then you have a significant amount of condensation (water) mixed in with the oil and it should be replaced to prevent damage to the snowmobile's components.

➡ **Keep in mind that although these fluids will not contain the corrosive byproducts of combustion, they are JUST as likely to contain condensation. If you want to be certain that your gears and shafts are protected from moisture, then you should replace the oil before running the snowmobile.**

Fig. 52 The chain case oil is checked by simply removing the dipstick . . .

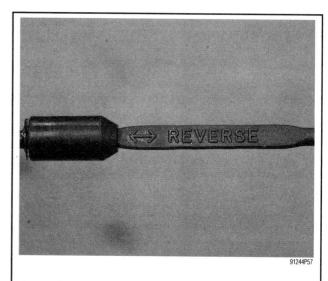

Fig. 53 . . . and reading the lubricant level on the end

As usual, if you are resurrecting a beast which has been in storage for some years, then do yourself a favor, just drain and replace all gear oils now.

BRAKE FLUID

▶ **See Figures 54, 55 and 56**

Check the fluid level in the brake master cylinder. If the snowmobile has mechanical brakes, double check that the linkage moves freely.

Recently, manufacturers have been recommending annual or bi-annual brake or clutch hydraulic fluid changing. Obviously this is an area that a lot of people ignore with seemingly little trouble (until their machines start to age and a caliper piston freezes or seals are torn by corrosion and begin to leak). If your fluid is due for a change, then well, there is really no better time than the present. But, even if it is not due for one, consider performing one now anyway. We aren't talking about a lot of fluid in most cases. The smartest course of action is to flush and refill these systems EVERY YEAR. It is the best way you can assure yourself that the system components will continue to operate properly and remain corrosion free for many years.

Of course, if you don't know when any of the hydraulic fluids were changed last, DO IT NOW!!!

Fig. 54 Check the brake fluid level by simply noting the level on the reservoir sight glass

Fig. 55 For brake reservoirs without a sight glass, remove the reservoir cap and note the fluid level

Fig. 56 If the fluid level needs to be adjusted, always use new fluid from an unopened container

2–STROKE OIL

▶ See Figures 57, 58 and 59

DON'T forget to fill the injection oil tank! When the level in the oil tank becomes low, air can be drawn into the oil pump, (even if your warning light is not illuminated) and the engine will be starved of oil. By the time you have figured out that there is something wrong with your oil pump, the motor will most likely be seriously damaged.

If the "low oil" light on your sled is illuminated just after startup, stop the engine IMMEDIATELY and investigate the problem.

➡Using the manufacturer recommended two-stroke oil while the snowmobile is under warranty is advisable, just in case problems arise. If engine damage occurs, having proof that factory lubricants were used (and properly mixed into the fuel) will help to avoid any battles with the manufacturer, should you make a warranty claim. Once your snowmobile is "out of warranty" you can use whatever oil you choose.

❈❈ WARNING

If air is drawn into the oil injection pump, there will be no indication from the engine that this has occurred. Your engine will be seriously damaged due to lack of lubrication.

Fig. 57 Fill the reservoir with a fresh supply of high quality 2-stroke injection oil prior to starting the engine

Fig. 58 The use of a high quality injection oil will keep your engine in peak condition and prevent driveability problems

Fig. 59 This destroyed piston is from a two-stroke engine that did not have the proper ratio of oil mixed into the fuel

Service the Drive Pulleys

♦ See Figures 60, 61, 62, 63 and 64

Using a clean rag, wipe the pulley halves clean with a solvent (lacquer thinner works well). Install a fresh drive belt.

Perform A Mickey Mouse Check

♦ See Figures 65, 66, 67, 68 and 69

Before attempting to fire up your snowmobile, check for evidence of visiting or nesting rodents. Look for signs that your snowmobile has not been alone during storage, such as small animal turds, gnawed wiring, shredded hide of the naugha (that strange, elusive animal with a fake leather skin), etc.

Make sure there are no rodents sleeping in the machine (and that no nesting rodents have left anything behind that could really stink when heated). The only way to be sure of this is to disassemble the air intake tract (air cleaner and any ducting) as well as any plastic which could hide a sleeping rodent. This is an excellent time to check the condition of the air filter and clean or replace it, as necessary and as applicable to your model. Use a flashlight to inspect the opening in the muffler to make sure no one is residing in there either. You WON'T BELIEVE THE SMELL if you miss a nest in the muffler and start the engine.

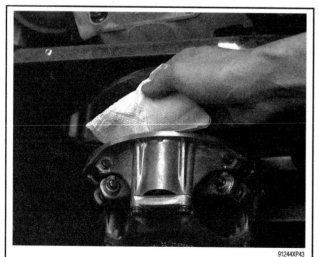

Fig. 60 Using a clean towel soaked in paint thinner, wipe the pulleys clean of any oil residue

Fig. 61 When choosing a new drivebelt, make sure the belt width matches the old belt

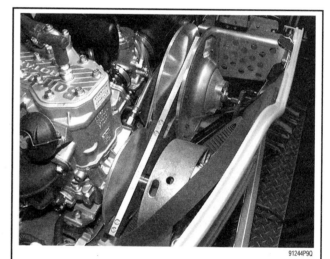

Fig. 62 It is a good idea to check pulley alignment prior to installing a new drivebelt

Fig. 63 Installing a fresh drive belt at the beginning of the season will assure satisfactory performance

Fig. 64 Adjusting the pulleys to specification will prevent premature drivebelt failure

Fig. 67 Since most snowmobile exhausts exit on the bottom of the chassis . . .

Fig. 65 Rodents just love foam filters, inspect the filter carefully for signs being eaten away

Fig. 68 . . . it is wise to remove the exhaust to check for nesting rodents prior to starting the engine for the first time

Fig. 66 As necessary, remove the air box to inspect for evidence of "extra-rodential" activity

Fig. 69 Make sure there are no rodents sleeping in the machine and that if they have been there at one time they left nothing behind that could really stink when heated

✳✳ WARNING

If any evidence of extra-rodential activity is found, be sure to check the snowmobile's electrical, air intake and exhaust systems VERY CAREFULLY to avoid causing unexpected damage when attempting to start the motor.

Inspect and Adjust Controls

▶ See Figures 70, 71 and 72

You should have checked the cables and levers for freedom of movement while you were checking the sled during the end of season chores. Perform this ritual again as the season approaches to ensure corrosion hasn't set in during your sled's time in storage. Also, this is the time to make sure the cables and levers are all properly adjusted. Refer to the maintenance sections of this book and check your snowmobile owner's manual to make sure that all controls working properly. Improperly adjusted controls can lead to VERY SHORT and VERY DANGEROUS rides.

Fig. 70 A sticky throttle cable can result in a VERY SHORT and VERY DANGEROUS ride

Fig. 71 Check the opposite end of the cable at the engine to ensure it is free from damage

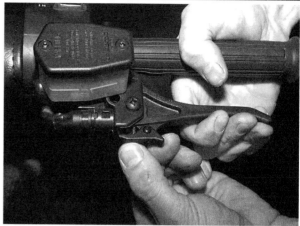

Fig. 72 Most snowmobiles are equipped with hydraulic brakes, however you must not forget to inspect the brake lever for proper operation

Lubricate the Chassis

▶ See Figures 73, 74 and 75

Make sure that all levers, pivot points and cables move freely without binding or excessive resistance. Check the suspension for smooth, proper travel.

It is never a bad idea to lube all chassis points when you are removing the snowmobile from storage. If it has been more than one season, then you should lube all points to prevent sudden and troubling binding.

✳✳ CAUTION

Any source of binding or excessive resistance on levers or pivot points MUST be found and repaired before any attempt is made to ride the snowmobile. Chassis or control instability could easily lead to a very serious accident. Improperly operating components may be signs of an impending equipment failure.

Check The Battery

▶ See Figures 76 and 77

Once again, if you have had the battery on a Battery Tender® or other automatic charger, then you are probably in good shape, but, just to be sure, make

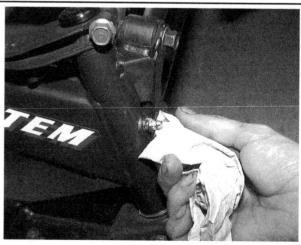

Fig. 73 Prior to lubricating, wipe the fitting clean to prevent dirt from entering and clogging the fitting

Fig. 74 Lubricate all components with Zerk fittings using a cartridge type grease gun

Fig. 75 Here is a Zerk fitting location on the rear suspension

Fig. 76 Checking the electrolyte level is easy in a sealed battery. Simply view the level through the plastic case

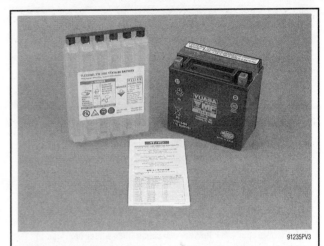

Fig. 77 When it comes to replacing the battery in your snowmobile, you can't go wrong with a maintenance free, sealed battery like this one from Yuasa/Exide

an electrolyte level and charge check. Remove the vent caps (unless it is a sealed battery) or peer through the transparent casing and make sure the fluid is at the proper level. Use a hydrometer to check for proper charge.

➡While you are checking the fluid level, use a flashlight to take a look at the tops of the battery plates. If there is a significant amount of white corrosion, then your battery is either toast, or almost toast and you really should replace it, even if it does seem to take a charge. You don't want it to strand you next week, do you? Having to use the manual pull starter on your 500cc snowmobile can be a real pain (in the back).

If the battery is not fully charged, place it on a charger to make sure it is ready to go when you are finished prepping the snowmobile.

If the battery is completely discharged, you are going to want to consider replacing it. Even though you may be able to get it to hold a charge, a battery which has sat discharged for any length of time will never hold a full charge again. And the longer it sat discharged, the worse off it will be. It may very well bail at an inconvenient time, making you get acquainted with that back up pull starter.

Inspect the Rear Suspension

▶ See Figures 78, 79 and 80

Check the plastic side rails and other rear suspension components for damage and correct as necessary.

Fig. 78 Place a close eye on your suspension system prior to the riding season. Any breakage here can cause your sled to sit idle for a while

Fig. 79 Improper track tension can cause idler wheel bearings to become damaged

Fig. 81 Place a few tablespoons of fresh oil into the spark plug hole to help lubricate the piston and rings on initial startup

Fig. 80 Inspect and adjust the shock/spring settings for your particular type of riding style

Remove & Inspect The Spark Plugs

ENGINE IN GOOD CONDITION

If you checked the spark plugs and coated the cylinders with fresh oil before storing the snowmobile, then the plug will be in good shape, but you will still want to pull it out so you can recoat the cylinder wall with oil before attempting to start the engine.

• Install a new set of spark plugs properly gapped. You might want to wait until after the first start to install your new plugs. This way the oil that you put in the cylinders for storage will coat your old plugs and not the new ones.

ENGINE FROZEN

▶ See Figure 81

If you didn't properly prep the snowmobile or if you are resurrecting a sled after a lengthy storage, you are definitely going to want to check the plugs and prime the cylinder with oil. This can be done easily enough:

1. Remove the spark plugs and check the gap. Replace the plug and/or adjust the gap, as necessary.

➥Remember that a sleeping snowmobile may be difficult enough to awaken without adding poor spark to the equation.

2. Pour 1–2 tablespoons of fresh, clean engine oil through each spark plug hole.

3. Rotate the engine to spread the oil around the cylinder. You have a few choices on how to rotate the engine. You can rotate it by hand, which is slower and more gentle (lowering the chance of gouging a cylinder wall if a ring is

reluctant at first) or you can use the electric starter (if you are more sure that the rings won't be reluctant). To rotate the engine by hand, keep the spark plug out to relieve engine compression.

➥If, even after adding oil, the engine is difficult or impossible to turn, DO NOT FORCE IT. First, add a few tablespoons of kerosene to the cylinder through the spark plug hole and give it some time to work on the rust. Then after allowing it to sit (for as long as overnight if necessary) add some more oil to lubricate the surfaces (should be piston and rings break free). Just remember, that if rust has frozen the seized the motor, there is a good chance the rings are already ruined. But, if you force the motor and break the rings, chances are even better that the cylinder and piston could be further damaged by the pieces.

4. Install the spark plugs.

Start the Engine

Once you are certain everything is working, hop on and give the starter rope a good tug. If the engine is reluctant to start, remember that the engine has been sitting for a while and may need a few pulls more. Don't immediately think something is wrong.

If you are lucky enough to have an electric starter, remember it needs time to cool down between starting attempts. DON'T hold the starter button for more than a few seconds, and try to wait a minute between tries. It can be frustrating, but there is no reason to burn out a perfectly good starter motor with excessive cranking, especially when your snowmobile is just waking up for the first time this season.

If the engine does not seem to catch after a few tries, double check the basics:
• Is the FUEL on?
• Is the IGNITION on?
• Is the ENGINE kill tether in place?

If the engine will still not start, refer to the troubleshooting section to see what you've forgotten.

When the engine fires, give it a few seconds to warm up and for the oil to circulate before revving the motor. Follow your usual warm-up routine, which probably means riding slowly and moderately until the engine has fully warmed.

Performing The Pre-Ride Check

Before attempting to start and ride the snowmobile, you should now take an opportunity to perform a COMPLETE pre-ride check as detailed in "Preparing to Ride". Obviously you have already addressed some of the items, but you don't want to leave anything out.

After it is warmed up, block the rear of the machine up and spin the track easily. Checking for loose track clips, proper track tension and proper track alignment.

During that first ride of the season, take special care to listen and feel for potential problems you may have missed.

After all has been checked and the engine is running smooth, there is just one more thing to do—Have fun !!!!

GLOSSARY

Understanding your snowmobile mechanic is as important as understanding your sled. Many rider have difficulty understanding snowmobile terminology. Talking the language of snowmobiles makes it easier to effectively communicate with professional mechanics. It isn't necessary (or recommended) that you diagnose the problem for them, but it will save them time, and you money, if you can accurately describe what is happening. It will also help you to know why your sled does what it is doing, and what repairs were made.

ACCELERATOR PUMP: A small pump located in the carburetor that feeds fuel into the air/fuel mixture during acceleration.

ADVANCE: Setting the ignition timing so that spark occurs earlier before the piston reaches top dead center (TDC).

AFTER TOP DEAD CENTER (ATDC): The point after the piston reaches the top of its travel on the compression stroke.

AIR CLEANER: An assembly consisting of a housing, filter and any connecting ductwork. The filter element is made up of a porous paper, sometimes with a wire mesh screening, and is designed to prevent airborne particles from entering the engine through the carburetor or throttle body.

AIR/FUEL RATIO: The ratio of air-to-gasoline by weight in the fuel mixture drawn into the engine.

ALTERNATING CURRENT (AC): Electric current that flows first in one direction, then in the opposite direction, continually reversing flow.

ALTERNATOR: A device which produces AC (alternating current) which is converted to DC (direct current) to charge the battery.

AMMETER: An instrument, calibrated in amperes, used to measure the flow of an electrical current in a circuit. Ammeters are always connected in series with the circuit being tested.

AMP/HR. RATING (BATTERY): Measurement of the ability of a battery to deliver a stated amount of current for a stated period of time. The higher the amp/hr. rating, the better the battery.

AMPERE: The rate of flow of electrical current present when one volt of electrical pressure is applied against one ohm of electrical resistance.

ANALOG COMPUTER: Any microprocessor that uses similar (analogous) electrical signals to make its calculations.

ANTIFREEZE: A substance (ethylene or propylene glycol) added to the coolant to prevent freezing in cold weather.

ARMATURE: A laminated, soft iron core wrapped by a wire that converts electrical energy to mechanical energy as in a motor or relay. When rotated in a magnetic field, it changes mechanical energy into electrical energy as in a generator.

ATDC: After Top Dead Center.

ATMOSPHERIC PRESSURE: The pressure on the Earth's surface caused by the weight of the air in the atmosphere. At sea level, this pressure is 14.7 psi at 32°F (101 kPa at 0°C).

ATOMIZATION: The breaking down of a liquid into a fine mist that can be suspended in air.

AXIAL PLAY: Movement parallel to a shaft or bearing bore.

BACKFIRE: The sudden combustion of gases in the intake or exhaust system that results in a loud explosion.

BACKLASH: The clearance or play between two parts, such as meshed gears.

BACKPRESSURE: Restrictions in the exhaust system that slow the exit of exhaust gases from the combustion chamber.

BALL BEARING: A bearing made up of hardened inner and outer races between which hardened steel balls roll.

BALL JOINT: A ball and matching socket connecting suspension components (steering knuckle to lower control arms). It permits rotating movement in any direction between the components that are joined.

BALLAST RESISTOR: A resistor in the primary ignition circuit that lowers voltage after the engine is started to reduce wear on ignition components.

BATTERY: A direct current electrical storage unit, consisting of the basic active materials of lead and sulphuric acid, which converts chemical energy into electrical energy. Used to provide current for the operation of the starter as well as other equipment, such as lighting.

BEARING: A friction reducing, supportive device usually located between a stationary part and a moving part.

BEFORE TOP DEAD CENTER (BTDC): The point just before the piston reaches the top of its travel on the compression stroke.

BEZEL: Piece of metal surrounding headlights, gauges or similar components; sometimes used to hold the glass face of a gauge in the dash.

BI-METAL TEMPERATURE SENSOR: Any sensor or switch made of two dissimilar types of metal that bend when heated or cooled due to the different expansion rates of the alloys. These types of sensors usually function as an on/off switch.

BLOCK: See Engine Block.

BLOW-BY: Combustion gases, composed of water vapor and unburned fuel, that leak past the piston rings into the crankcase during normal engine operation.

BOOK VALUE: The average value of sled, widely used to determine trade-in and resale value.

BORE: Diameter of a cylinder.

BRAKE CALIPER: The housing that fits over the brake disc. The caliper holds the brake pads, which are pressed against the discs by the caliper pistons when the brake pedal is depressed.

BRAKE FADE: Loss of braking power, usually caused by excessive heat after repeated brake applications.

BRAKE HORSEPOWER: Usable horsepower of an engine measured at the crankshaft.

BRAKE PAD: A brake shoe and lining assembly used with disc brakes.

BRAKE SHOE: The backing for the brake lining. The term is, however, usually applied to the assembly of the brake backing and lining.

BTDC: Before Top Dead Center.

BUSHING: A liner, usually removable, for a bearing; an anti-friction liner used in place of a bearing.

CALIPER: A hydraulically activated device in a disc brake system, which is mounted straddling the brake rotor (disc). The caliper contains at least one piston and two brake pads. Hydraulic pressure on the piston(s) forces the pads against the rotor.

CAMSHAFT: A shaft in the engine on which are the lobes (cams) which operate the valves. The camshaft is driven by the crankshaft, via a belt, chain or gears, at one half the crankshaft speed.

CAPACITOR: A device which stores an electrical charge.

CARBON MONOXIDE (CO): A colorless, odorless gas given off as a normal byproduct of combustion. It is poisonous and extremely dangerous in confined areas, building up slowly to toxic levels without warning if adequate ventilation is not available.

CARBURETOR: A device, usually mounted on the intake manifold of an engine, which mixes the air and fuel in the proper proportion to allow even combustion.

CENTRIFUGAL ADVANCE: A mechanical method used by clutch systems on snowmobiles.

CETANE RATING: A measure of the ignition value of diesel fuel. The higher the cetane rating, the better the fuel. Diesel fuel cetane rating is roughly comparable to gasoline octane rating.

CHECK VALVE: Any one-way valve installed to permit the flow of air, fuel or vacuum in one direction only.

CHOKE: The valve/plate that restricts the amount of air entering an engine on the induction stroke, thereby enriching the air:fuel ratio.

CIRCLIP: A split steel snapring that fits into a groove to hold various parts in place.

CIRCUIT BREAKER: A switch which protects an electrical circuit from overload by opening the circuit when the current flow exceeds a pre-determined level. Some circuit breakers must be reset manually, while most reset automatically.

CIRCUIT: Any unbroken path through which an electrical current can flow. Also used to describe fuel flow in some instances.

CLEARCOAT: A transparent layer which, when sprayed over a paint job, adds gloss and depth as well as an additional protective coating to the finish.

CLUTCH: Part of the power train used to connect/disconnect power to the drive track.

COIL: Part of the ignition system that boosts the relatively low voltage supplied by the electrical system to the high voltage required to fire the spark plugs.

COMBUSTION CHAMBER: The part of the engine in the cylinder head where combustion takes place.

COMPRESSION CHECK: A test involving removing each spark plug and inserting a gauge. When the engine is cranked, the gauge will record a pressure reading in the individual cylinder. General operating condition can be determined from a compression check.

COMPRESSION RATIO: The ratio of the volume between the piston and cylinder head when the piston is at the bottom of its stroke (bottom dead center) and when the piston is at the top of its stroke (top dead center).

CONDENSER: An electrical device which acts to store an electrical charge, preventing voltage surges.

CONDUCTOR: Any material through which an electrical current can be transmitted easily.

CONNECTING ROD: The connecting link between the crankshaft and piston.

CONTINUITY: Continuous or complete circuit. Can be checked with an ohmmeter.

COOLANT: Mixture of water and anti-freeze circulated through the engine to carry off heat produced by the engine.

CRANKCASE: The lower part of an engine in which the crankshaft and related parts operate.

CRANKSHAFT: Engine component (connected to pistons by connecting rods) which converts the reciprocating (up and down) motion of pistons to rotary motion used to turn the driveshaft.

CURB WEIGHT: The weight of a snowmobile without passengers or payload, but including all fluids (oil, gas, coolant, etc.) and other equipment specified as standard.

CYLINDER BLOCK: See engine block.

CYLINDER HEAD: The detachable portion of the engine, usually fastened to the top of the cylinder block and containing all or most of the combustion chambers. On overhead valve engines, it contains the valves and their operating parts. On overhead cam engines, it contains the camshaft as well.

CYLINDER: In an engine, the round hole in the engine block in which the piston(s) ride.

DEAD CENTER: The extreme top or bottom of the piston stroke.

DETERGENT: An additive in engine oil to improve its operating characteristics.

DETONATION: An unwanted explosion of the air/fuel mixture in the combustion chamber caused by excess heat and compression, advanced timing, or an overly lean mixture. Also referred to as "ping".

DIAPHRAGM: A thin, flexible wall separating two cavities, such as in a fuel pump.

DIGITAL VOLT OHMMETER: An electronic diagnostic tool used to measure voltage, ohms and amps as well as several other functions, with the readings displayed on a digital screen in tenths, hundredths and thousandths.

DIODE: An electrical device that will allow current to flow in one direction only.

DIRECT CURRENT (DC): Electrical current that flows in one direction only.

DISC BRAKE: A hydraulic braking assembly consisting of a brake disc, or rotor, mounted on an axleshaft, and a caliper assembly containing, usually two brake pads which are activated by hydraulic pressure. The pads are forced against the sides of the disc, creating friction which slows the snowmobile.

DISPLACEMENT: The total volume of air that is displaced by all pistons as the engine turns through one complete revolution.

DOWEL PIN: A pin, inserted in mating holes in two different parts allowing those parts to maintain a fixed relationship.

DRIVE TRAIN: The components that transmit the flow of power from the engine to the track. The components include the clutch, transmission and drivebelt.

DRY CHARGED BATTERY: Battery to which electrolyte is added when the battery is placed in service.

DVOM: Digital volt ohmmeter

ECM: See Electronic Control Unit (ECU).

ECU: Electronic control unit.

ELECTRODE: Conductor (positive or negative) of electric current.

ELECTROLYTE: A solution of water and sulfuric acid used to activate the battery. Electrolyte is extremely corrosive.

ELECTRONIC CONTROL UNIT: A digital computer that controls engine functions based on data received from various sensors.

ENAMEL: Type of paint that dries to a smooth, glossy finish.

END-PLAY: The measured amount of axial movement in a shaft.

ENGINE: The primary motor or power apparatus of a snowmobile, which converts liquid or gas fuel into mechanical energy.

ENGINE BLOCK: The basic engine casting containing the cylinders, the crankshaft main bearings, as well as machined surfaces for the mounting of other components such as the cylinder head, oil pan, transmission, etc.

EP LUBRICANT: EP (extreme pressure) lubricants are specially formulated for use with gears involving heavy loads.

ETHYL: A substance added to gasoline to improve its resistance to knock, by slowing down the rate of combustion.

ETHYLENE GLYCOL: The base substance of antifreeze.

EXHAUST MANIFOLD: A set of cast passages or pipes which conduct exhaust gases from the engine.

FEELER GAUGE: A blade, usually metal, of precisely predetermined thickness, used to measure the clearance between two parts.

FILAMENT: The part of a bulb that glows; the filament creates high resistance to current flow and actually glows from the resulting heat.

FIRING ORDER: The order in which combustion occurs in the cylinders of an engine. Also the order in which spark is distributed to the plugs by the distributor.

FLAME FRONT: The term used to describe certain aspects of the fuel explosion in the cylinders. The flame front should move in a controlled pattern across the cylinder, rather than simply exploding immediately.

FLAT SPOT: A point during acceleration when the engine seems to lose power for an instant.

FLOODING: The presence of too much fuel in the intake manifold and combustion chamber which prevents the air/fuel mixture from firing, thereby causing a no-start situation.

FLYWHEEL: A heavy disc of metal attached to the rear of the crankshaft. It smoothes the firing impulses of the engine and keeps the crankshaft turning during periods when no firing takes place. The starter also engages the flywheel to start the engine.

FOOT POUND (ft. lbs. or sometimes, ft. lb.): The amount of energy or work needed to raise an item weighing one pound, a distance of one foot.

FRONTAL AREA: The total frontal area of a snowmobile exposed to air flow.

FUEL FILTER: A component of the fuel system containing a porous paper element used to prevent any impurities from entering the engine through the fuel system. It usually takes the form of a canister-like housing, mounted in-line with the fuel hose, located anywhere on a snowmobile between the fuel tank and engine.

FUEL INJECTION: A system replacing the carburetor that sprays fuel into the cylinder through nozzles. The amount of fuel can be more precisely controlled with fuel injection.

FUSE: A protective device in a circuit which prevents circuit overload by breaking the circuit when a specific amperage is present. The device is constructed around a strip or wire of a lower amperage rating than the circuit it is designed to protect. When an amperage higher than that stamped on the fuse is present in the circuit, the strip or wire melts, opening the circuit.

FUSIBLE LINK: A piece of wire in a wiring harness that performs the same job as a fuse. If overloaded, the fusible link will melt and interrupt the circuit.

HALOGEN: A special type of lamp known for its quality of brilliant white light.

HEAT RANGE: A term used to describe the ability of a spark plug to carry away heat. Plugs with longer nosed insulators take longer to carry heat off effectively.

HEAT EXCHANGER: Part of the cooling system for a water-cooled engine and connected to the engine with rubber hoses. Through the radiator, excess combustion heat is dissipated into the atmosphere through forced convection using a water and glycol based mixture that circulates through, and cools, the engine.

HORSEPOWER: A measurement of the amount of work; one horsepower is the amount of work necessary to lift 33,000 lbs. one foot in one minute. Brake horsepower (bhp) is the horsepower delivered by an engine on a dynamometer. Net horsepower is the power remaining (measured at the flywheel of the engine) that can be used to turn the track after power is consumed through friction and running the engine accessories.

HYDROCARBON (HC): Any chemical compound made up of hydrogen and carbon. A major pollutant formed by the engine as a by-product of combustion.

HYDROMETER: An instrument used to measure the specific gravity of a solution.

IDLE MIXTURE: The mixture of air and fuel (usually about 14:1) being fed to the cylinders. The idle mixture screw(s) are sometimes adjusted as part of a tune-up.

INCH POUND (inch lbs.; sometimes in. lb. or in. lbs.): One twelfth of a foot pound.

INDUCTION: A means of transferring electrical energy in the form of a magnetic field. Principle used in the ignition coil to increase voltage.

INJECTOR: A device which receives metered fuel under relatively low pressure and is activated to inject the fuel into the engine under relatively high pressure at a predetermined time.

INPUT SHAFT: The shaft to which torque is applied, usually carrying the driving gear or gears.

INTAKE MANIFOLD: A casting of passages or pipes used to conduct air or a fuel/air mixture to the cylinders.

JOURNAL: The bearing surface within which a shaft operates.

JUMPER CABLES: Two heavy duty wires with large alligator clips used to provide power from a charged battery to a discharged battery.

JUMPSTART: Utilizing a sufficiently charged battery to start the engine of another snowmobile with a discharged battery by the use of jumper cables.

KEY: A small block usually fitted in a notch between a shaft and a hub to prevent slippage of the two parts.

KNOCK: Noise which results from the spontaneous ignition of a portion of the air-fuel mixture in the engine cylinder caused by overly advanced ignition timing or use of incorrectly low octane fuel for that engine.

LACQUER: A quick-drying automotive paint.

LITHIUM-BASE GREASE: Chassis grease using lithium as a base. Not compatible with sodium-base grease.

LOCK RING: See Circlip or Snapring

MANIFOLD VACUUM: Low pressure in an engine intake manifold formed just below the throttle plates. Manifold vacuum is highest at idle and drops under acceleration.

MANIFOLD: A casting of passages or set of pipes which connect the cylinders to an inlet or outlet source.

MASTER CYLINDER: The primary fluid pressurizing device in a hydraulic system. In automotive use, it is found in brake and hydraulic clutch systems and is pedal activated, either directly or, in a power brake system, through the power booster.

MISFIRE: Condition occurring when the fuel mixture in a cylinder fails to ignite, causing the engine to run roughly.

MODULE: Electronic control unit, amplifier or igniter of solid state or integrated design which controls the current flow in the ignition primary circuit based on input from the pick-up coil. When the module opens the primary circuit, high secondary voltage is induced in the coil.

MULTI-WEIGHT: Type of oil that provides adequate lubrication at both high and low temperatures.

NEEDLE BEARING: A bearing which consists of a number (usually a large number) of long, thin rollers.

NITROGEN OXIDE (NOx): One of the three basic pollutants found in the exhaust emission of an internal combustion engine. The amount of NOx usually varies in an inverse proportion to the amount of HC and CO.

OCTANE RATING: A number, indicating the quality of gasoline based on its ability to resist knock. The higher the number, the better the quality. Higher compression engines require higher octane gas.

OEM: Original Equipment Manufactured. OEM equipment is that furnished standard by the manufacturer.

OHM: The unit used to measure the resistance of conductor-to-electrical flow. One ohm is the amount of resistance that limits current flow to one ampere in a circuit with one volt of pressure.

OHMMETER: An instrument used for measuring the resistance, in ohms, in an electrical circuit.

OSCILLOSCOPE: A piece of test equipment that shows electric impulses as a pattern on a screen. Engine performance can be analyzed by interpreting these patterns.

O2 SENSOR: See oxygen sensor.

OUTPUT SHAFT: The shaft which transmits torque from a device, such as a transmission.

OVERHEAD CAMSHAFT (OHC): An engine configuration in which the camshaft is mounted on top of the cylinder head and operates the valve either directly or by means of rocker arms.

OVERHEAD VALVE (OHV): An engine configuration in which all of the valves are located in the cylinder head and the camshaft is located in the cylinder block. The camshaft operates the valves via lifters and pushrods.

OVERSTEER: The tendency of some snowmobiles, when steering into a turn, to over-respond or steer more than required, which could result in excessive slip of the rear. Opposite of understeer.

OXIDES OF NITROGEN: See nitrogen oxide (NOx).

OXYGEN SENSOR: Used with a feedback system to sense the presence of oxygen in the exhaust gas and signal the computer which can use the voltage signal to determine engine operating efficiency and adjust the air/fuel ratio.

PARTS WASHER: A basin or tub, usually with a built-in pump mechanism and hose used for circulating chemical solvent for the purpose of cleaning greasy, oily and dirty components.

PAYLOAD: The weight the snowmobile is capable of carrying in addition to its own weight. Payload includes weight of the driver, passengers and cargo, but not coolant, fuel or lubricant, etc.

PCM: Powertrain control module.

PERCOLATION: A condition in which the fuel actually "boils," due to excessive heat. Percolation prevents proper atomization of the fuel causing rough running.

PICK-UP COIL: The coil in which voltage is induced in an electronic ignition.

PISTON RING: An open-ended ring which fits into a groove on the outer diameter of the piston. Its chief function is to form a seal between the piston and cylinder wall. Most automotive pistons have three rings: two for compression sealing; one for oil sealing.

POLARITY: Indication (positive or negative) of the two poles of a battery.

POWER-TO-WEIGHT RATIO: Ratio of horsepower to weight.

POWERTRAIN: See Drivetrain.

PCM: See Electronic Control Unit (ECU).

Ppm: Parts per million; unit used to measure exhaust emissions.

PREIGNITION: Early ignition of fuel in the cylinder, sometimes due to glowing carbon deposits in the combustion chamber. Preignition can be damaging since combustion takes place prematurely.

PRELOAD: A predetermined load placed on a bearing during assembly or by adjustment.

PRESS FIT: The mating of two parts under pressure, due to the inner diameter of one being smaller than the outer diameter of the other, or vice versa; an interference fit.

PRIMARY CIRCUIT: The low voltage side of the ignition system which consists of the ignition switch, ballast resistor or resistance wire, bypass, coil, electronic control unit and pick-up coil as well as the connecting wires and harnesses.

Psi: Pounds per square inch; a measurement of pressure.

PUSHROD: A steel rod between the hydraulic valve lifter and the valve rocker arm in overhead valve (OHV) engines.

RACE: The surface on the inner or outer ring of a bearing on which the balls, needles or rollers move.

RADIATOR: See heat exchanger.

REAR MAIN OIL SEAL: A synthetic or rope-type seal that prevents oil from leaking out of the engine past the rear main crankshaft bearing.

RECTIFIER: A device (used primarily in alternators) that permits electrical current to flow in one direction only.

REGULATOR: A device which maintains the amperage and/or voltage levels of a circuit at predetermined values.

RELAY: A switch which automatically opens and/or closes a circuit.

RESIN: A liquid plastic used in body work.

RESISTANCE: The opposition to the flow of current through a circuit or electrical device, and is measured in ohms. Resistance is equal to the voltage divided by the amperage.

RESISTOR SPARK PLUG: A spark plug using a resistor to shorten the spark duration. This suppresses radio interference and lengthens plug life.

RESISTOR: A device, usually made of wire, which offers a preset amount of resistance in an electrical circuit.

RETARD: Set the ignition timing so that spark occurs later (fewer degrees before TDC).

RING GEAR: The name given to a ring-shaped gear attached to a differential case, or affixed to a flywheel or as part of a planetary gear set.

ROCKER ARM: A lever which rotates around a shaft pushing down (opening) the valve with an end when the other end is pushed up by the pushrod. Spring pressure will later close the valve.

ROLLER BEARING: A bearing made up of hardened inner and outer races between which hardened steel rollers move.

ROTOR: The disc-shaped part of a disc brake assembly, upon which the brake pads bear; also called, brake disc.

RPM: Revolutions per minute (usually indicates engine speed).

SEALED BEAM: A automotive headlight. The lens, reflector and filament from a single unit.

SECONDARY CIRCUIT: The high voltage side of the ignition system, usually above 20,000 volts. The secondary includes the ignition coil, coil wire, distributor cap and rotor, spark plug wires and spark plugs.

SENDING UNIT: A mechanical, electrical, hydraulic or electromagnetic device which transmits information to a gauge.

SENSOR: Any device designed to measure engine operating conditions or ambient pressures and temperatures. Usually electronic in nature and designed to send a voltage signal to an on-board computer, some sensors may operate as a simple on/off switch or they may provide a variable voltage signal (like a potentiometer) as conditions or measured parameters change.

SHIM: Spacers of precise, predetermined thickness used between parts to establish a proper working relationship.

SHIMMY: Vibration (sometimes violent) in the front end caused by misaligned front end or worn suspension components.

SHORT CIRCUIT: An electrical malfunction where current takes the path of least resistance to ground (usually through damaged insulation). Current flow is excessive from low resistance resulting in a blown fuse.

SINGLE OVERHEAD CAMSHAFT: See overhead camshaft.

SKIDPLATE: A metal plate attached to the underside of the body to protect vulnerable parts from damage.

SNAP RING: A circular retaining clip used inside or outside a shaft or part to secure a shaft, such as a floating wrist pin.

SOHC: Single overhead camshaft.

SOLENOID: An electrically operated, magnetic switching device.

SPARK PLUG: A device screwed into the combustion chamber of a spark ignition engine. The basic construction is a conductive core inside of a ceramic insulator, mounted in an outer conductive base. An electrical charge from the spark plug wire travels along the conductive core and jumps a preset air gap to a grounding point or points at the end of the conductive base. The resultant spark ignites the fuel/air mixture in the combustion chamber.

SPECIFIC GRAVITY (BATTERY): The relative weight of liquid (battery electrolyte) as compared to the weight of an equal volume of water.

SPLINES: Ridges machined or cast onto the outer diameter of a shaft or inner diameter of a bore to enable parts to mate without rotation.

STARTER: A high-torque electric motor used for the purpose of starting the engine, typically through a high ratio geared drive connected to the flywheel ring gear.

STRAIGHT WEIGHT: Term designating motor oil as suitable for use within a narrow range of temperatures. Outside the narrow temperature range its flow characteristics will not adequately lubricate.

STROKE: The distance the piston travels from bottom dead center to top dead center.

SYNTHETIC OIL: Non-petroleum based oil.

TACHOMETER: A device used to measure the rotary speed of an engine, shaft, gear, etc., usually in rotations per minute.

TDC: Top dead center. The exact top of the piston's stroke.

THERMOSTAT: A valve, located in the cooling system of an engine, which is closed when cold and opens gradually in response to engine heating, controlling the temperature of the coolant and rate of coolant flow.

TIE ROD: A rod connecting the steering arms. Tie rods have threaded ends that are used to adjust toe-in.

TOE-IN (OUT): A term comparing the extreme front and rear of the skis. Closer together at the front is toe-in; farther apart at the front is toe-out.

TOP DEAD CENTER (TDC): The point at which the piston reaches the top of its travel on the compression stroke.

TORQUE: Measurement of turning or twisting force, expressed as foot-pounds or inch-pounds.

TRANSDUCER: A device used to change a force into an electrical signal.

TRANSISTOR: A semi-conductor component which can be actuated by a small voltage to perform an electrical switching function.

TUNE-UP: A regular maintenance function, usually associated with the replacement and adjustment of parts and components in the electrical and fuel systems of a snowmobile for the purpose of attaining optimum performance.

UNDERSTEER: The tendency of a sled to continue straight ahead while negotiating a turn.

UNLEADED FUEL: Fuel which contains no lead (a common gasoline additive). The presence of lead in fuel will destroy the functioning elements of a catalytic converter, making it useless.

VACUUM GAUGE: An instrument used to measure the presence of vacuum in a chamber.

VALVE CLEARANCE: The measured gap between the end of the valve stem and the rocker arm, cam lobe or follower that activates the valve.

VALVE GUIDES: The guide through which the stem of the valve passes. The guide is designed to keep the valve in proper alignment.

VALVE LASH (clearance): The operating clearance in the valve train.

VALVE TRAIN: The system that operates intake and exhaust valves, consisting of camshaft, valves and springs, lifters, pushrods and rocker arms.

VALVE: A device which control the pressure, direction of flow or rate of flow of a liquid or gas.

VARNISH: Term applied to the residue formed when gasoline gets old and stale.

VISCOSITY: The ability of a fluid to flow. The lower the viscosity rating, the easier the fluid will flow. 10 weight motor oil will flow much easier than 40 weight motor oil.

VOLT: Unit used to measure the force or pressure of electricity. It is defined as the pressure

VOLTAGE REGULATOR: A device that controls the current output of the alternator or generator.

VOLTMETER: An instrument used for measuring electrical force in units called volts. Voltmeters are always connected parallel with the circuit being tested.

WATER PUMP: A belt driven component of the cooling system that mounts on the engine, circulating the coolant under pressure.

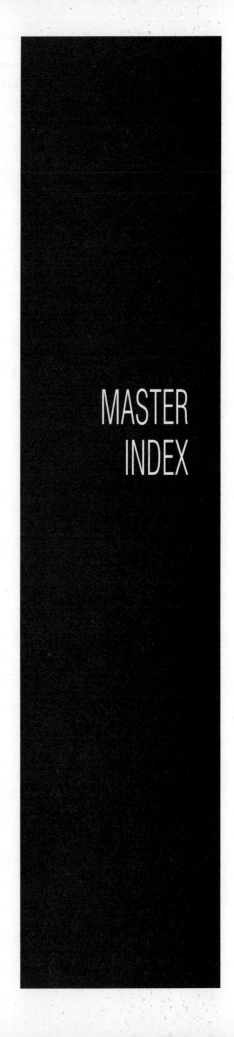

MASTER
INDEX